Vital Records of Wakefield New Hampshire 1887–1998

Richard P. Roberts

HERITAGE BOOKS
2012

HERITAGE BOOKS
AN IMPRINT OF HERITAGE BOOKS, INC.

Books, CDs, and more—Worldwide

For our listing of thousands of titles see our website
at
www.HeritageBooks.com

Published 2012 by
HERITAGE BOOKS, INC.
Publishing Division
100 Railroad Ave. #104
Westminster, Maryland 21157

Copyright © 1999 Richard P. Roberts

All rights reserved. No part of this book may be reproduced or transmitted in any form or by any means, electronic or mechanical, including photocopying, recording or by any information storage and retrieval system without written permission from the author, except for the inclusion of brief quotations in a review.

International Standard Book Numbers
Paperbound: 978-0-7884-1411-4
Clothbound: 978-0-7884-9292-1

TABLE OF CONTENTS

Introduction   1

Births   4

Marriages   205

Deaths   404

INTRODUCTION

Early vital records of many New Hampshire towns can be located either through the State's Vital Records Department or on microfilms made available through LDS Family History Centers. Some, however, have been lost or are inaccessible for various reasons. A valuable, but time-consuming, source of information for events occurring after 1886 is the vital statistics which are provided in a section of the Annual Town Reports of many New Hampshire towns. Many of these town reports have been collected at the New Hampshire State Library in Concord, as well as more local repositories.

The amount of information published in these Annual Town Reports varies tremendously over time. Early records are far more detailed and comprehensive. Recent records are rather cursory, but issues of confidentiality and sensitivity to the privacy of those residents still living offsets the lack of information of genealogical value.

While the information provided is often very helpful, one must remember that it is not fool-proof or universally accurate, nor is it the primary source or the actual vital record itself. The fact that much of the data is self-reported suggests that it is reliable. However, errors in transcription, spelling, and printing often are obvious. Foreign names often have been hopelessly abbreviated or misspelled. There are several variations of some French and Eastern European surnames which are listed separately but are undoubtedly the same families. In addition, there may be two children listed as the third child of a particular couple, or the mother's maiden name, age or place of birth differs or is inconsistent from one entry to another. It is also important to note that a birth, marriage or death may have been reported in another town although the subject resided in Wakefield, or the entry may not have been made in the first place.

Despite these shortcomings, the information contained in the Annual Town Reports can be a valuable tool for the genealogist.

Marriage and death records from the late 1800's often identify parents who were married nearly a century before. Many immigrants from Canada and Eastern Europe, or their children, have lived in Wakefield during the time period covered by these records. Finally, those families that have remained in Wakefield for several generations can be traced and connected to the present.

Births - To the extent the information is available, the entries in the list of births are given as follows: child's name; date of birth; place of birth (Wakefield, unless otherwise indicated); the number of children in the family; father's name, place of birth, age and occupation; and the mother's maiden name, age and place of birth. The residence of the parents is sometimes given when it is other than Wakefield. As noted above, the amount of information in earlier records is substantially greater.

At times, the given names of many children are missing from the early reports. In this case, the sex of the child is given and they are listed chronologically at the beginning of the surname heading. On occasion, the child's name can be determined from marriage or death records, as well as secondary sources. These names are shown in brackets where available.

Several birth records were submitted and published long after the event occurred. Often entire families were listed and other times only individuals were submitted. When these entries have been made, the year in which they were published is included in parentheses at the end of the entry.

Marriages - To the extent the information is available, the entries in the list of marriages follow this format: groom's name; groom's residence; bride's name; brides residence; date of marriage; place of marriage (Wakefield, unless otherwise indicated); H, signifying husband's information, and W, signifying wife's information, each in the following order - age, occupation, number of the marriage (if other than first), father's name, father's place of birth, father's occupation, mother's name, mother's place of birth, and mother's occupation. The name of the official conducting the marriage has been omitted but is generally provided in the original document.

Deaths - To the extent available, the entries in the list of deaths contain the following information: name of decedent; place of death; date of death; age at death; cause of death; marital status; birthplace; father's name; father's place of birth; mother's name; and mother's place of birth. Later entries give the residence of the individual.

Most of the entries listing a cause of death are self-explanatory. In older entries, the phrase "senectus" is sometimes used and is essentially equivalent to "old age", and "phthisis" is similar to "consumption" and "tuberculosis". As one would expect, the death records often contain somber entries for young mothers and small children, as well as tragic instances of individuals passing before their time due to accidents or suicide.

BIRTHS

ABBOTT,
Brian Gould, b. 5/31/1950; second; Ralph E. Abbott (W. Lebanon, ME) and Helen L. Grace (West Milton)
Erville William, b. 10/1/1918; fifth; Ralph E. Abbott (engineer, 33, Wolfeboro) and Blanche E. Brown (29, Eastport, ME)
John Emerson, b. 7/10/1948; first; Ralph E. Abbott (W. Lebanon, ME) and Helen L. Grace (West Milton)
John Emerson, b. 12/14/1970 in Rochester; John E. Abbott and Mona M. Bouchard
Linda Marie, b. 6/2/1955 in Rochester; second; Harry Arthur Abbott, Jr. (Center Harbor) and Louise Lillian Hall (Newburg, ME)
Rosalie Ellen, b. 7/12/1959 in Rochester; fifth; Francis N. Abbott (Meredith) and Florence M. Jones (Porter, ME)
Stacey Lee, b. 3/28/1968 in Rochester; John E. Abbott and Mona J. Bouchard
Susan Elizabeth, b. 7/7/1959 in Rochester; third; Ralph E. Abbott (W. Lebanon, ME) and Helen L. Grace (W. Milton)

ACKLEY,
Ian Lang, b. 2/9/1987 in Wolfeboro; Allen L. Ackley and Catherine A. Agosta

ADAMS,
Breyana Marie, b. 4/22/1994 in Wolfeboro; Edward Paul Adams and Tammy Lynn McCarthy
Meagan Kelly, b. 6/2/1985 in Portsmouth; Jeffrey G. Adams and Eileen F. Streeter

ADJUTANT,
Celia, b. 5/16/1904; fifth; Charles Leonard Adjutant (laborer, 42, Tuftonboro) and Lena Eaton (23, Brookfield)
Christopher Arnold, b. 9/15/1932 in Rochester; Joseph Adjutant and Evelyn Hill
Deborah Ann, b. 4/20/1952 in Rochester; second; Joseph W. Adjutant (Rochester) and Palma L. Whitnall (Rochester)
Glenn Michael, b. 7/20/1997 in Dover; Russell Thomas Adjutant and Roxanne Lee Racicot
Jacob Leon, b. 6/11/1993 in Rochester; Gary Leon Adjutant and Naomi Leah Whiting

Kelly Ann, b. 8/2/1967 in Wolfeboro; third; Ronald H. Adjutant
  (Wolfeboro) and Susan E. Kelly (Jersey City, NJ)
Melissa Margaret, b. 1/12/1974 in Wolfeboro; Ronald H. Adjutant and
  Susan E. Kelly
Robert Arnold, b. 7/20/1956 in Rochester; second; Christopher A. Adjutant
  (Union) and Betty Lou Pillsbury (Farmington)
Roland, b. 9/27/1905 in Sanbornville; sixth; Leonard C. Adjutant
  (carpenter, 43, Ossipee) and Lena E. Eaton (27, Brookfield);
  residence - Sanbornville
Royal, b. 9/27/1905 in Sanbornville; seventh; Leonard C. Adjutant
  (carpenter, 43, Ossipee) and Lena E. Eaton (27, Brookfield);
  residence - Sanbornville
Russell Dennis, b. 4/15/1908; sixth; Charles L. Adjutant (carpenter, 45,
  Wolfeboro) and Leila E. Eaton (30, Brookfield)
Warren Alan, b. 7/23/1958 in Wolfeboro; third; Joseph W. Adjutant
  (Rochester) and Palma L. Whetnall (Rochester)

AINSWORTH,
Charles W., b. 2/22/1901; seventh; William W. Ainsworth (laborer, Calais,
  VT) and Nellie J. Alexander (Canada)

AKERS,
James Warren, b. 5/5/1986 in Portsmouth; Melvin E. Akers and Cynthia L.
  White

ALBEE,
Hans Olaf, b. 6/28/1981 in Rochester; Mark W. Albee and Ingrid K.
  Johannessen

ALLARD,
Gertrude, b. 4/10/1898; second; C. E. Allard (mill hand, Conway) and
  Vesta M. Lord (Cornish, ME)

ALLEN,
Alice, b. 12/15/1867; fourth; Mark I. Allen (Brookfield) and Melissa M.
  Hawkins (Center Ossipee) (1940)
Alice Genevieve, b. 2/27/1906; second; William M. Allen (farmer, 35,
  Philadelphia, PA) and Zaidee Neal (23, Waite, ME)
Charles Albert, b. 8/29/1873; second; William Henry Allen (Wakefield)
  and Elizabeth Betsey Nichols (Wakefield) (1938)

Charles Melvin, b. 4/5/1871; fifth; Mark Iretus Allen (Brookfield) and Mellissa W. Hawkins (Ossipee) (1941)
George William, b. 9/3/1877; third; William H. Allen (Wakefield) and Lizzie B. Nichols (Wakefield) (1936)
Joshua Daniel, b. 12/7/1987 in Portsmouth; Daniel J. Allen and Cheryl L. Dufault
Lenora Jane, b. 10/26/1864; second; Mark Iretus Allen (Brookfield) and Mellissa W. Hawkins (Ossipee) (1941)
Mark O., b. 9/14/1974 in Wolfeboro; Douglas M. Allen and Ann M. Milligrock
Marshall Tuktock, b. 11/4/1972 in Wolfeboro; Douglas M. Allen and Hannah M. Millegrock
Melvin Neal, b. 8/28/1908; third; William M. Allen (farmer, 38, Philadelphia, PA) and Zaidie Neal (25, Waite, ME)
Philip, b. 8/30/1904; first; William M. Allen (nurse, 34, Philadelphia, PA) and Zaidee Neal (22, Waite, ME)
Samuel, b. 11/26/1860; William Y. Allen and Mary W. Merserve (1933)

ANDERSON,
Christine, b. 7/10/1967 in Wolfeboro; second; Robert J. Anderson (Jersey City, NJ) and Margaret A. Dee (Englewood, NJ)
Deborah Lyn, b. 7/20/1966 in Wolfeboro; first; Robert J. Anderson (Jersey City, NJ) and Margaret A. Dee (Englewood, NJ)
Gary Joseph, b. 6/29/1959 in Wolfeboro; first; Richard W. Anderson (Somerville, MA) and Beatrice A. Duchano (Wolfeboro)
Patricia Iris, b. 2/24/1983 in Wolfeboro; John A. Anderson and Melody A. Karrh
Robert Gates, b. 5/8/1970 in Lynn, MA; Robert G. Anderson and Mildred F. Zalenski

ANTHONY,
Garrett Andrew, b. 8/5/1992 in Rochester; Andrew Herbert Anthony and Cathleen Mary DiPrizio
Harry Edward, II, b. 8/24/1972 in Rochester; Harry E. Anthony and Joyce C. Bradley
Lacey Jill, b. 11/28/1987 in Wolfeboro; William J. Anthony, Jr. and Sheila Jones

ARCHIBALD,
daughter, b. 4/12/1902; first; Reuben Archibald (laborer, 48, Wakefield) and Rosie Sawyer (16, Standish, ME)
Charles Everett, b. 6/21/1870; first; Josiah Archibald (South Wakefield) and Charlotte Butler (Wakefield) (1938)

ASKINS,
Matthew Paul, b. 3/15/1983 in Rochester; Paul R. Askins and Anne R. Guldbrandsen

ASPINALL,
daughter, b. 6/7/1892; first; Charles Aspinall (laborer) and Mary A. Copp (Wakefield)

ATHERTON,
Lillian May, b. 4/16/1922; first; Howard Atherton (garage owner, Houlton, ME) and Elizabeth Runnels (Union); residence - Union

AUBERT,
Donald Lionel, b. 2/19/1953 in Rochester; third; Lionel Albert Aubert (Somersworth) and Annetta C. Viel (Rollinsford)
Roger Gerald, b. 9/7/1949; second; Lionel A. Aubert (NH) and Annette C. Viel (NH)

AULD,
daughter, b. 2/5/1912; second; Louis Auld (laborer, 28, PEI) and Addie McLane (27, PEI)

BABB,
Phillip Johnothan, b. 4/2/1993 in Rochester; Johnothan Lee Babb and Kristan Elizabeth Loncaric

BAIN,
Amanda Beth, b. 5/7/1981 in Dover; Kevin Bain and Janet L. Doyle

BAKER,
son, b. 5/21/1905 in Sanbornville; first; Joseph Baker (laborer, 22, New York, NY) and Delia Dupres (16, Biddeford, ME); residence - Sanbornville

BALDWIN,
Annalise Roslyn, b. 9/18/1987 in Rochester; Russell I. Baldwin and Sharon L. Vanderhoof
Carlene Georgenia, b. 5/10/1924; first; Henry A. Baldwin (laborer, Chelsea, MA) and Alice L. Grassie (Rochester); residence - Union
Robert Scott, b. 7/7/1989 in Rochester; Russell Thomas Baldwin and Sharon Lee Vanderhoof

BALL,
James Charles, Jr., b. 9/23/1987 in Rochester; James C. Ball and Colleen M. Patterson
Justin Lee, b. 4/15/1986 in Rochester; James C. Ball and Colleen M. Patterson

BANCROFT,
Christopher Neil, b. 6/29/1984 in Norwalk, CT; Christopher M. Bancroft and Nancy E. O'Neil
Monica Jeanne, b. 7/25/1989 in Melrose, MA; Christopher Marler Bancroft and Nancy Elizabeth O'Neil

BARBER,
Melody June, b. 5/14/1946; second; Charles R. Barber (Franklin) and June C. Wentworth (Union)
Tami April, b. 4/21/1959 in Rochester; fourth; Charles R. Barber (Franklin) and June C. Wentworth (Union)

BARDSLEY,
Johnathan Clifford, b. 9/14/1989 in Dover; Clifford Wright Bardsley and Michele Denise Bernier

BARIBEAU,
Lillian Rachel, b. 6/21/1992 in Rochester; Gary Joseph Baribeau and Maura Elizabeth McHugh

BARKER,
Jane Margaret, b. 2/11/1967 in Wolfeboro; first; Gary Lee Barker (Columbus, KS) and Roberta F. Ridlon (Bridgton, ME)

BATEMAN,
Joseph Everett, b. 11/2/1995 in Rochester; Michael Joseph Bateman and Stephanie P. Nichols
Samantha Alysse, b. 8/4/1992 in Rochester; Michael Joseph Bateman and Stephanie Patricia Nichols
Thomas Alfred, b. 12/9/1997 in Wolfeboro; Michael Joseph Bateman and Stephanie Patricia Nichols

BATES,
Katelyn Talia, b. 6/23/1991 in Wolfeboro; Robert Andrew Bates and Jo-Ann Arlene Shackford
Lauren Ann, b. 3/11/1990 in Wolfeboro; Robert Andrew Bates and Jo-Ann Arlene Shackford

BAUD,
Joshua Oscar, b. 11/17/1982 in Wolfeboro; Richard P. Baud and Lenora M. Sykie

BAXTER,
Shelby Alexis, b. 7/18/1994 in Wolfeboro; Brian Alan Baxter, Sr. and Patricia Lorraine Franklin

BAYER,
Christine Marie, b. 8/29/1987 in Rochester; David E. Bayer and Anne Marie McNally

BEAL,
Jaqueline Lois, b. 4/7/1925; second; Roscoe E. Beal (Biddeford, ME) and Rosie A. Hill (W. Newfield, ME)

BEAN,
Harold Norman, b. 9/25/1932 in Sanbornville; Harold Bean and Cora York
Helen May, b. 8/2/1930; second; Harold Bean (Ossipee) and Cora York (Meadersboro)

BEAUDETTE,
Cyrile Antoine, b. 1/28/1903 in Sanbornville; second; Henry Blaudette (sic) (laborer, 30, Newport) and Marie Pourtrie (38, Canada); residence - Sanbornville

Henry J.S., b. 2/29/1904; fifth; Henry Beaudette (laborer, 31, Groton, VT) and Marie Pourtrie (39, Canada)

Joseph A.U., b. 5/13/1900; first; Henry J. Beaudette (laborer, Groton Pond, VT) and Marie Partrie (Canada); residence - Sanbornville

Mary Alice, b. 6/18/1906; sixth; Henry Beaudette (laborer, 34, Groton, VT) and Mary Pourtrie (41, Canada)

BEAUPRE,

Joanne Elizabeth, b. 6/6/1967 in Wolfeboro; third; Kenneth J. Beaupre (Franklin) and Priscilla A. Copp (Wolfeboro)

Matthew Kenneth, b. 9/9/1974 in Wolfeboro; Kenneth J. Beaupre and Priscilla A. Copp

Stephen Peter, b. 2/1/1965 in Wolfeboro; second; Kenneth J. Beaupre (Franklin) and Priscilla A. Copp (Wolfeboro)

BEAUREGARD,

Olivia Rose, b. 7/4/1997 in Wolfeboro; David Robert Beauregard and Lisa Beth Tenk

BECKWITH,

Jeremy Matthew, b. 9/23/1989 in Wolfeboro; John Edward Beckwith, Jr. and Jennifer Rose Putney

Jessica Rose, b. 11/26/1990 in Wolfeboro; John Edward Beckwith and Jennifer Rose Putney

John Edward, Jr., b. 12/2/1960 in Wolfeboro; sixth; John E. Beckwith, Sr. (St. Mary, PA) and Barbara L. Chick (Wakefield)

BEDARD,

Cassandra Ashley, b. 6/22/1991 in Wolfeboro; Brian Henry Bedard and Pamela Jean Fulton

BEELER,

Brian Allen, II, b. 10/26/1974 in Rochester; Brian A. Beeler and Janice E. Kasakowski

BEFERA,

Dolores Marie, b. 2/12/1938; second; Nicholas Befera (Winslow, PA) and Marie Irene Belfort (New Haven, CT)

BELLEMUR,
son, b. 6/20/1887; fourth; Charles Bellemur (laborer, Canada) and Cilina Giline (Canada)

BELLEVEAU,
son [Fred], b. 7/3/1888; third; Lewis Belleveau (barber, Canada) and Eliza Morrow (Canada)
daughter, b. 11/9/1891; fourth; Louis Belleveau (barber, Canada) and Lizzie Morrow (Canada)

BENCE,
Robert Ryan, b. 10/2/1974 in Wolfeboro; Joseph C. Bence and Deborah R. Hollis

BENNETT,
Ashley Barnard, b. 4/3/1984 in Dover; James W. Bennett, Jr. and Susan B. Clement
James William, Jr., b. 4/15/1949; first; James W. Bennett, Sr. (Tuftonboro) and Hazel B. Perry (Wolfeboro)
Ryan Douglas, b. 3/17/1980 in Dover; James W. Bennett, Jr. and Susan B. Clement
Susan Lee, b. 5/22/1952 in Wolfeboro; second; James W. Bennett (NH) and Hazel B. Perry (NH)

BENTZLER,
Keith Allen, b. 4/12/1968 in Rochester; Edward W. Bentzler and Gloria M. Fifield
Raymond Richard, b. 10/9/1961 in Rochester; second; Edward W. Bentzler (Loyal, WI) and Gloria M. Fifield (Rochester)

BERRY,
Leonard F., b. 12/10/1924 in Sanbornville; first; Leonard W. Berry (lineman, Moultonboro) and Marion A. Ingalls (Arlington Heights, MA); residence - Sanbornville

BETTENCOURT,
Jamie, b. 6/24/1977 in Rochester; Joseph M. Bettencourt and Judith A. Blecher

BICKFORD,
Arthur Frank, b. 5/30/1918; first; Arthur B. Bickford (farmer, 25, Wakefield, MA) and Vivian G. Weeks (20, Tuftonboro)
Carroll Freeman, b. 4/26/1936; second; Carroll Bickford (Wolfeboro) and Blanche Jenness (Wakefield)
Dorothy May, b. 5/26/1935; first; Carroll Bickford (Wolfeboro) and Blanche Jenness (Wakefield)
Evelyn, b. 3/22/1909; first; Albion M. Bickford (farmer, 37, Farmington) and Bertha E. Rines (28, Wakefield)
Joshua VanPatrick, b. 1/8/1989 in Wolfeboro; Carl Patrick Bickford and Melissa Jean Williams
Kenneth Stewart, b. 10/10/1937; first; Frank L. Bickford (Boston, MA) and Eleanor Kenney (Sanbornville)
Marcia Louise, b. 3/14/1941; second; Frank Lovewell Bickford (Boston, MA) and Eleanor Helen Kenney (Wakefield)

BIEMER,
daughter, b. 6/24/1889; fifth; Charles Biemer (laborer, Canada) and Cieleno ----- (Canada)

BIERWEILER,
Robert Alan, b. 8/17/1935; first; Frederick Bierweiler (Somerville, MA) and Ferne L. Harrison (Rowley, MA)

BILLADEAU,
son, b. 7/5/1892; fourth; Felix Billadeau (laborer, Canada) and Phoebe Vailicourt (Canada)

BILLEVEAU,
Eddie, b. 7/25/1896; fifth; Leon Billeveau (barber, Canada) and Eliza Morrow (Canada)

BIRD,
Brendan Christopher, b. 4/2/1993 in Dover; Christopher Scott Bird and Tracy Leigh Hovey

BLACKINGTON,
daughter, b. 11/26/1897; third; F. Blackington (mill hand, Union, ME) and Emma J. Brown (Somerville, ME)

BLACKWOOD,
Carrie Jo, b. 8/22/1985 in Rochester; John J. Blackwood and Linda J. Flaherty
John James, b. 3/14/1944; first; James Blackwood (Scotland) and Leola Deschesne (Fort Fairfield, ME)
William Olsen, b. 6/14/1946; second; James Blackwood (Dunfrie, Scotland) and Leola P. DesCheane (Fort Fairfield, ME)

BLADES,
Jennifer Jeanne, b. 7/28/1964 in Wolfeboro; second; James M. Blades (Summit, NJ) and Pamela J. Pray (Boston, MA)

BLAIR,
Alfred Clifford, Jr., b. 7/10/1944; first; Alfred Clifford Blair (Laconia) and Elaine A. Anderson (W. Milton)
David Paul, b. 8/15/1954 in Wolfeboro; third; Alfred Clifford Blair, Jr. (Laconia) and Elaine A. Anderson (West Milton)
Gene Anderson, b. 8/9/1966 in Rochester; fourth; Alfred C. Blair, Sr. (Laconia) and Elaine A. Anderson (West Milton)
Leon Walter, b. 11/12/1948; second; Alfred C. Blair (Laconia) and Elaine A. Anderson (Milton)
Marleen Ann, b. 3/12/1968 in Rochester; Alfred C. Blair and Brenda D. Dodier
Melinda Adrienne, b. 8/3/1971 in Rochester; Alfred C. Blair, Jr. and Brenda J. Dodier

BLAKE,
daughter, b. 12/6/1890; second; Simon Blake (farmer, Brookfield) and Georgie Palmer (Roxbury, MA)

BLANCHETT,
son, b. 8/6/1887; fifth; Napoleon Blanchett (carpenter, Canada) and Lucy --- (Bartlett)

BLANCHETTE,
Jennie Fleurida, b. 6/2/1910; fifth; Albert Blanchette (laborer, 45, Canada) and Arlene Seamer (42, Canada)

BLAND,
Matthew Everett, b. 1/13/1984 in Rochester; Raymond F. Bland and Maria E. Gouvalavis

BLAY,
Katelyn Michelle, b. 5/13/1993 in Wolfeboro; Phillip Charles Blay and Catherine Ann Fenderson
Kyle Charles, b. 6/23/1989 in Wolfeboro; Phillip Charles Blay and Catherine Ann Fenderson

BODAH,
Jacob Chandler, b. 11/9/1992 in Rochester; Gary Lee Bodah and Antoinette Alison Sparhawk

BODWELL,
Charles Henry, b. 4/3/1957 in Wolfeboro; first; John E. Bodwell (Acton, ME) and Jean A. Miliner (Wakefield, MA)
Deborah Lee, b. 12/30/1959 in Wolfeboro; second; John E. Bodwell (Acton, ME) and Jean Audrey Miliner (Wakefield, MA)
Lance Gregory, b. 2/13/1963 in Wolfeboro; third; John E. Bodwell (Sanford, ME) and Jean A. Miliner (Wakefield, MA)

BOGGS,
Cheyanne Ashley Mae, b. 2/25/1992 in Rochester; Eric Montgomery Boggs and Amanda Lee Huggard

BOISVERT,
Sera Rae, b. 3/19/1998 in Rochester; Troy Adam Boisvert and Mindy Jeanne Stark

BONSER,
Jeanne Elizabeth, b. 4/14/1923; first; Harold E. Bonser (printer, Woodland, WA) and Marian D. Brown (Wakefield); residence - Sanbornville
William Edward, b. 1/1/1927; second; Harold E. Bonser (Woodland, WA) and Marion D. Brown (Wakefield)

BOOTHBY,
Barbara Lucinda, b. 2/22/1924; fourth; Jesse E. Boothby (lumberman, Parsonsfield, ME) and Christine I. Hill (Balmoral, NS)

BOSTON,
Bonnie Jo, b. 11/28/1970 in Rochester; Randolph D. Boston and Joyce M. Goodrow

BOUCHARD,
Alexander Roland, b. 3/19/1989 in Rochester; Ernest Roland Bouchard, Jr. and Elizabeth H. Black

BOURDMAN,
Frank, b. 4/21/1900; fourth; Frank Bourdman (laborer, Canada) and Marie Doeye (Canada); residence - North Wakefield

BOWDEN,
Robin Roberta, b. 7/26/1957 in Rochester; fourth; Robert L. Bowden (Seal Harbor, ME) and Roberta E. Cate (Brookfield)
Roger Dale, b. 6/27/1953 in Rochester; second; Robert Lawrence Bowden (Seal Harbor, ME) and Roberta E. Cate (Brookfield)
Roxanne Lynn, b. 6/1/1954 in Rochester; third; Robert Lawrence Bowden (Seal Harbor, ME) and Roberta Evelyn Cate (Brookfield)

BOWLES,
Richard James, b. 1/15/1942; fourth; Charles Myron Bowles (Boscawen) and Gladys Bundy (Montpelier, VT)

BOYCE,
son, b. 10/27/1902; second; Orrin E. Boyce (railroading, 21, Eliot, ME) and Annie Evans (18, Nottingham); residence - Dover

BOYD,
Alice Gertrude, b. 3/15/1899; first; William T. Boyd (laborer, Biddeford, ME) and Mary W. Maleham (Wakefield); residence - Sanbornville
Jonathan Barrett, b. 9/25/1990 in Dover; Stephen Tracey Boyd and Brenda Lee Stewart
Traci Lynn, b. 3/14/1986 in Rochester; William J. Boyd and Judith L. Whitehouse

BOZUWA,
Gijsbert Paul, b. 5/8/1960 in Hanover; second; Gerard Gijsbert Bozuwa (Indonesia) and Titial J. Wetseiaar (Netherlands)

BRACKETT,
son [Arthur W.], b. 1/25/1887; first; Cecil A. Brackett (RR brakeman, Wakefield) and Annie M. Wiggin (Wakefield)
daughter, b. 2/12/1888; first; Asa M. Brackett (bookkeeper, Wakefield) and Alma E. Kenerson (Albany)
daughter, b. 1/29/1889; first; Daniel Brackett (conductor, Wakefield) and Ida F. Rice (Porter, ME)
Ada, b. 3/27/1869; first; Jane Brackett (Wakefield) (1937)
Bethany Ann, b. 10/6/1951; third; Ralph E. Brackett (NH) and Pauline F. McCrillis (NH)
Candace Rae, b. 10/7/1948; second; Ralph E. Brackett (Needham, MA) and Pauline F. McCrillis (No. Conway)
Doris M., b. 4/1/1900; third; John E. Brackett (fireman, Wakefield) and Mary E. Kenney (Salem, MA)
Estella F., b. 5/3/1897; second; John E. Brackett (engineer, Wakefield) and Mary E. Kenney (Salem, MA)
Evelyn Emmeline, b. 6/16/1906; third; Nelson Brackett (clerk, 27, Charlestown, MA) and Blanche Ayers (24, New Durham)
Helen, b. 4/3/1895; first; John E. Brackett (fireman, Wakefield) and Mary E. Kenney (Salem, MA)
John Edward, b. 6/7/1871; fifth; Charles E. Brackett (Acton, ME) and Elizabeth R. Wiggin (Wakefield) (1938)
Peggy Ann, b. 9/9/1936; first; Ralph E. Brackett (Sanbornville) and Pauline F. McCrillis (North Conway)
Ralph Edward, b. 8/13/1906; fourth; John E. Brackett (engineer, 35, Wakefield) and Mary E. Kenney (34, Salem, MA)
Stephen Edward, b. 8/24/1997; Timothy Edward Brackett and Jeneen Meleda Thompson
Theodore Nelson, b. 4/16/1904; second; Horatio Nelson Brackett (sail maker, 25, Charlestown, MA) and Blanche Ayers (22, New Durham)
William Freeman, b. 3/1/1869; fourth; Charles E. Brackett (Acton, ME) and Elizabeth R. Wiggin (Wakefield) (1937)

BRADBURY,
Nathan Kyle, b. 11/15/1976; David Lee Bradbury and Margaret J. Horne

BRAGG,
George Lloyd, b. 8/9/1941; first; Earl Bragg (Acton, ME) and Claire Webber (Lyman, ME)

BRECKLAND,
Gwenith Jean, b. 4/19/1957 in Rochester; first; Arthur G. Breckland (Middleton, MA) and Peggy J. Grigsby (Boise, ID)

BREWER,
George Raymond, b. 11/4/1949; third; Aaron W. Brewer (Royalston, MA) and Lillian A. Bosworth (Athol, MA)

BREWIER,
stillborn son, b. 10/1/1894; first; Isadore Brewier (laborer, Canada) and Mary Umboir (Canada)

BRIGGS,
Wayne Otis, b. 3/11/1940; first; Wilbert Otis Briggs (Marblehead, MA) and Edna Louise Grace (Milton)

BRISARD,
Brian Todd, b. 12/6/1991 in Rochester; Todd Edward Brisard and Gina Marie Countryman

BRITTON,
daughter, b. 4/22/1951; third; Paul J. Britton (Wolfeboro) and Emma Lagace (No. Conway)

BROCHU,
Nicholas Lee, b. 3/28/1986 in Wolfeboro; Larry Brochu and Denise D. Boshears
Paula Marie, b. 2/24/1952 in Wolfeboro; sixth; Leo Paul Brochu (ME) and June D. Durgin (ME)
Sara Rose, b. 11/15/1998 in Rochester; Allen Joseph Brochu, Jr. and Kimberly Jo Gagnon

BROOKES,
Thomas Michael, b. 2/25/1986 in Wolfeboro; Donald O. Brookes and Linda J. Moyse

BROOKS,
Carl Lawrence, b. 10/1/1967 in Rochester; second; Samuel C. Brooks (Rochester) and Kathleen J. Hill (Manchester)

Emilee Ann, b. 9/24/1991 in Wolfeboro; William Edward Brooks and Theresanne Ames
Louis Gerard, b. 7/11/1969 in Wolfeboro; Louis W. Brooks and Justine E. Cameron
Rheba Elizabeth, b. 6/24/1911; fourth; Walter E. Brooks (clergyman, 30, England) and Alice E. Harling (27, England)

BROUILLARD,
Constance Elizabeth, b. 4/17/1937; second; Henry J. Brouillard (Sanbornville) and Grace M. King (East Weymouth, MA)
Isadore Henry, b. 6/6/1914; first; Simon Brouillard (laborer, 40, Canada) and Ida Martin (40, Canada)
Patricia A., b. 10/28/1935; first; Henry Brouillard (Sanbornville) and Grace King (East Weymouth, MA)

BROWN,
daughter [Audrey R.], b. 8/20/1887; first; Plummer A. Brown (blacksmith, Ossipee) and Laura V. Rice (Freedom)
daughter, b. 6/11/1905; second; Joseph Brown (laborer, 32, Poland) and Mary Smith (30, Poland)
son, b. 6/28/1916; second; William E. Brown (chauffeur, 22, So. Berwick, ME) and Laura E. Gowen (18, Milton); residence - Dover
Adam Addison, b. 8/3/1898; fifth; Plummer A. Brown (RR foreman, Ossipee) and Laura V. Rice (Freedom)
Amy Louise, b. 7/1/1986 in Wolfeboro; James W. Brown and Robin M. Kilmer
Angela Rose, b. 3/6/1993 in Wolfeboro; Patrick Brian Brown and Valerie Jean Bartlett
Basil Irving, b. 1/30/1891; second; Plummer A. Brown (conductor, Ossipee) and Laura V. Rice (Freedom)
Charlotte L., b. 5/3/1897; fourth; P. A. Brown (conductor, Ossipee) and Laura V. Rice (Freedom)
Chauncy Ellsworth, b. 9/7/1891; first; Edward E. Brown (merchant, Somersworth) and Mabel G. Dore (Wakefield)
Erin Elizabeth, b. 5/11/1981 in Wolfeboro; Walter R. Brown, Jr. and Janet L. Herbert
Ernest, b. 12/15/1870; fourth; George Brown (Ossipee) and Sarah Gowdy (Lowell, MA) (1937)
Fred, b. 8/6/1877; first; John Brown (Union) and Louise Brown (Wakefield) (1936)

Gordon James, b. 4/2/1974 in Rochester; Dana E. Brown and Charlotte D. Hicks

Hazel, b. 6/22/1897; first; Charles B. Brown (farmer, Wolfeboro) and Mabel F. Trott (Portland, ME)

Jessica Ann, b. 2/16/1997 in Rochester; Patrick Brian Brown and Valerie Jean Bartlett

Lee Ann, b. 2/8/1963 in Wolfeboro; first; Ronald R. Brown (Portland, OR) and Irene L. Pippin (Alfred, ME)

Mara Irene, b. 10/9/1984 in Wolfeboro; Walter R. Brown, Jr. and Janet L. Herbert

Marion, b. 3/25/1897; second; Edward E. Brown (merchant, Somersworth) and Mabel G. Dore (Wakefield)

Mason Wentworth, b. 2/26/1894; third; Plummer A. Brown (conductor, Ossipee) and Laura V. Rice (Freedom)

Matthew Terrence, b. 3/3/1968 in Wolfeboro; Walter E. Brown and Ann L. Smith

Nancy Louise, b. 10/17/1969 in Wolfeboro; Walter E. Brown and Ann L. Smith

Nathan Aaron, b. 9/10/1983 in Wolfeboro; James W. Brown and Robin M. Kilmer

Olive, b. 5/9/1895; third; Daniel B. Brown (physician, Wakefield) and Mary A. Paul (Wakefield)

Rebecca Lyn, b. 5/2/1990 in Rochester; Thomas Joseph Brown and Victoria Lee Fogg

Richard Eugene, b. 9/16/1923; first; Clyde H. Brown (baggage master, Ossipee) and Lucinda E. Nason (Brookfield); residence - Ossipee

Ronald Stephen, b. 1/29/1974 in Wolfeboro; Walter E. Brown and Ann L. Smith

Shaina Marie, b. 7/6/1986 in Rochester; Thomas J. Brown and Victoria L. Fogg

Susan Mary, b. 12/29/1974 in Wolfeboro; Walter E. Brown and Ann Louise Smith

Thomas Joseph, II, b. 3/7/1988 in Rochester; Thomas J. Brown and Victoria L. Fogg

Wlordystorf, b. 4/10/1907; third; Antonia Brown (laborer, 43, Russia) and Francisca Mingen (32, Russia)

BROWNELL,

Francis Stanley, b. 4/3/1921; first; Willard Brownell (chauffeur, 24, Albany, NY) and Ida Evans (20, Wakefield); residence - Albany, NY

BRUCE,
Paul Alden, b. 7/25/1974 in Rochester; Douglas P. Bruce and Marjorie B. Hayward

BRYANT,
Bruce Shepardson, b. 4/20/1935; first; Merton E. Bryant (Snowville) and Velma C. Shepardson (Phillipston, MA)
Douglas Edward, b. 10/6/1938; second; Merton Ellis Bryant (Snowville) and Velma Clara Shepardson (Athol, MA)

BRYD,
Branden Zak, b. 9/28/1992 in Rochester; Wayne Edward Bryd and Wendy Ann Hubbard

BUBAR,
Nancy Maria-Ann, b. 8/11/1984 in Hanover; George L. Bubar, Jr. and Karen Jo Lavertue

BUMFORD,
Arlene Frances, b. 1/11/1919; first; Scott H. Bumford (machinist, 21, Lebanon, ME) and Flora A. Hobbs (18, Lebanon, ME)

BURLEIGH,
son [Harry W.], b. 2/21/1889; George W. Burleigh (merchant, Wakefield) and Alice L. Powell (England)
Casandra Lynn, b. 5/1/1968 in Rochester; Charles P. Burleigh and Elizabeth F. Perkins
Frank Alexander, Jr., b. 1/21/1935; third; Frank A. Burleigh (Rochester) and Corinne M. McHugh (Wolfeboro)
Lorraine Mae, b. 5/13/1933 in Rochester; Frank A. Burleigh and Corrinne McHugh

BURR,
Alissa Jill, b. 5/1/1980 in Rochester; Gary A. Burr and Sally Ann Shea

BURRILL,
son, b. 12/20/1902; third; Israel L. Burrill (broker, 57, Yarmouth, NS) and Pauline Miett (27, Plymouth, MA); residence - Union

BURROUGHS,
Luella Louise, b. 11/13/1924; third; Ralph John Burroughs (electrician, Wakefield) and Luella Sanborn (Wakefield); residence - Sanbornville

BURROWS,
son [Ralph John], b. 11/18/1890; fourth; Edgar H. Burrows (engineer, Brookfield) and Grace Ricker (Biddeford, ME)
Julia M., b. 1/19/1899; first; Isaiah H. Burrows (farmer, Middleton) and Mary A. Battersby (New York, NY); residence - Union

BUSWELL,
Elinor Lorraine, b. 6/8/1951; fourth; Ellis W. Buswell (NH) and Frances L. Meserve (NH)
Jessica Lee, b. 12/10/1977 in Wolfeboro; Roland R. Buswell and Gloria J. Varney

BUZZELL,
Virgil R., b. 4/13/1919; third; Richard Buzzell (farmer, 29, Pittsfield, ME) and Carrie Raymond (16, Palmyra, ME); residence - Pittsfield, ME

CADDELL,
Earl Franklin, III, b. 8/13/1949; first; Earl F. Caddell II (Buckeye, AZ) and Joanne M. Fauci (Belmont, MA)

CAIN,
Spenser Catherine, b. 8/10/1991 in No. Conway; James David Cain and Theresa Margaret Holmes

CALBERT,
Phillis Odrey, b. 8/25/1914; fifth; James Calbert (sawyer, Halifax, NS) and Bessie Tuttle (Raymond)

CALLAGHAN,
Deanna Lee, b. 12/7/1977 in Rochester; David W. Callaghan and Diane M. LaFleur

CAMPBELL,
daughter, b. 7/24/1890; second; Elbert R. Campbell (carpenter, Barnard, VT) and Ella M. Davis (Lyman, ME)

daughter [Mildred E.], b. 12/10/1905; third; Ernest C. Campbell
(brakeman, 37, Barnstead, VT) and Mary E. Perkins (36, So. Acton,
ME); residence - Sanbornville
daughter [Madeline], b. 12/10/1905; fourth; Ernest C. Campbell
(brakeman, 37, Barnstead, VT) and Mary E. Perkins (36, So. Acton,
ME); residence - Sanbornville
Catherine Anne, b. 9/15/1988 in Hanover; Douglas G. Campbell and
Cynthia A. Lupien
Edwin Elbert, b. 3/30/1897; fourth; E. R. Campbell (carpenter, Barnard,
VT) and Mary L. Davis (ME)
Eleanor P., b. 3/30/1909; fifth; Ernest C. Campbell (woodsman, 40,
Barnard, VT) and May E. Perkins (40, Acton, ME)
Emma Phoeby, b. 9/17/1893; third; Elbert R. Campbell (carpenter,
Barnard, VT) and Stella M. Davis (Lyman, ME)
Kenneth Roof, b. 2/1/1964 in Wolfeboro; second; Kenneth B. Campbell
(Greely, CO) and Martha A. Roof (Columbus, OH)
Thelma May, b. 7/4/1903; second; Ernest C. Campbell (brakeman, 35,
Barnard, VT) and May E. Perkins (34, Acton, ME)

CANNEY,

Haleigh Anne, b. 6/23/1997 in Wolfeboro; Kevin Scott Canney and Alice
Marie Morrill
Jordan Philip, b. 10/26/1994 in Wolfeboro; Kevin Scott Canney and Alice
Marie Morrill
Sienna Orlene, b. 6/6/1996 in Rochester; Alfred B. Canney, Jr. and Tammy
Jo Eaton

CAPACH,

Nicole Bert, b. 10/19/1985 in Wolfeboro; James F. Capach and Melody L.
Smith

CARBERRY,

Samantha Jade, b. 10/27/1991 in Rochester; Andrew James Carberry and
Allyne Deidre Morrill
Tiffany Lee, b. 3/22/1982 in Rochester; John H. Carberry and Donna L.
Richardson

CARPENTER,

Nichelle Marie, b. 10/5/1990 in Wolfeboro; Howard James Carpenter and
Donna Marie Lamy

CARRUTHERS-BETHELL,
Amy Juliette, b. 12/11/1993 in Wolfeboro; Russel Edward Bethell and Jennifer Lee Carruthers

CARTER,
son [Charles William], b. 2/12/1889; first; William Carter (woodcutter, Newport, ME) and C. Etta Drew (New Durham)
Mary Etta, b. 8/11/1890; second; William Carter (wood cutter, Montpelier, VT) and C. Etta Vallie (New Durham)

CASPERONIS,
Kasey Lynn, b. 12/10/1990 in Portsmouth; Scott Allen Casperonis and Angela Monique Charest
Kelsey Ann, b. 4/19/1995 in Wolfeboro; Scott Allen Casperonis and Angela Monique Charest

CASS,
Eleanor May, b. 4/3/1917; first; Elmer K. Cass (laborer, 15, Parsonsfield, ME) and Alta M. Londo (16, Newfield, ME)
Frances Iva, b. 1/17/1920; second; Elmer Kincaid Cass (surveyor, 27, Parsonsfield, ME) and Alta Mabel Louds (20, West Newfield, ME); residence - Madison

CATES,
Pearl Francis, b. 3/20/1905 in Union; fourth; Alfred A. Cates (farmer, 33, Harrison, ME) and Florie Richardson (27, Megalloway, ME); residence - Union

CAVERLY,
Laure Jane, b. 9/28/1949; first; Albert Dean Caverly (MA) and Elizabeth G. Naylor (NH)

CHADBOURNE,
Robert Daniel, b. 2/28/1961 in Wolfeboro; third; Robert L. Chadbourne (Amesbury, MA) and Maxine F. Mills (Lovell, ME)
Valerie Jean, b. 9/30/1965 in Wolfeboro; fourth; Robert L. Chadbourne (Amesbury, MA) and Maxine F. Mills (Lovell, ME)

CHAMBERLAIN,
Joseph, b. 5/28/1895; second; T. Chamberlin (sic) (laborer, Canada) and Eugenie Marshall (Canada)
Joseph A., b. 3/3/1899; fourth; T. Chamberlain (section hand, PQ) and Eugenie Marshall (PQ)
Joseph Romeo, b. 4/8/1897; third; T. Chamberlain (laborer, Canada) and Eugenia Marshall (Canada)

CHAPMAN,
Charles Robinson, b. 7/10/1871; second; Charles Chapman and Mary F. Cummings (Wakefield) (1934)
George Arthur, b. 9/15/1925; third; Homer L. Chapman (Canada) and Eleanor A. Wyman (Waltham, MA)
George W., b. 10/10/1869; first; Charles Chapman and Mary F. Cummings (Wakefield) (1935)
Harris Wyman, b. 12/1/1913; first; Homer Chapman (foreman, 25, Coaticook, PQ) and Elinore Wyman (21, Waltham, MA)
John Homer, b. 2/17/1917; second; Homer L. Chapman (sup. ice co., 28, Quebec) and Elinore A. Wyman (24, Waltham, MA)

CHAREST,
Abby, b. 6/23/1981 in Concord; Peter I. Charest and Nancy L. McKenna

CHASE,
Elmer Lorenzo, b. 1/3/1914; second; George W. Chase (laborer, 34, Madison) and Ruth W. Drowns (24, Bridgton, ME)
Gilbert Leonard, Jr., b. 9/10/1950; first; Gilbert L. Chase (Derry) and Helen L. Stewart (Rumford, ME)

CHENEY,
Charles Franklin, b. 1/27/1875; fourth; Charles Henry Cheney (So. Berwick, ME) and Sarah Nancy Burke (Wolfeboro) (1939)

CHEPOKISTH,
Powell, b. 9/19/1916; fourth; George Chepokisth (laborer, 33, Poland) and Nellie Mingin (30, Poland)

CHESLOCK,
Joseph Michael, b. 10/21/1987 in Dover; Michael W. Cheslock and Vickie L. Joyal

CHIARADONNA,
Stefanie Linda, b. 4/1/1982 in Rochester; Vincent A. Chiaradonna and Diane L. Illingworth

CHICK,
son, b. 9/29/1892; first; Charles Chick (blacksmith, Milton) and Vesta Randall (Great Falls); residence - Berwick, ME
Barbara Lillian, b. 3/17/1926; second; Ralph H. Chick (Wakefield) and Lillian M. Look (Boston, MA)
Brian Scott, b. 5/14/1956 in Wolfeboro; fourth; George E. Chick (ME) and Vivian M. Shaw (NH)
David Michael, b. 11/18/1952 in Wolfeboro; third; George E. Chick (Newfield, ME) and Vivian Mae Shaw (Dover)
Doris Madeleine, b. 1/19/1904; sixth; George H. Chick (carpenter, 42, Waterboro, ME) and Jennie S. Waldron (40, Wakefield)
Esther Lilly, b. 2/3/1907; first; Harry W. Chick (surveyor, 20, Wakefield) and Helen A. Blake (20, Woburn, MA)
George Earle, b. 5/6/1906; seventh; George H. Chick (millman, 45, Waterboro, ME) and Jennie S. Waldron (43, Wakefield)
Jerre Steven, b. 9/22/1951; second; George E. Chick (NH) and Vivian M. Shaw (Dover)
Lewis Sumner, b. 2/4/1891; third; George Hanson Chick (Waterboro, ME) and Jennie S. Waldron (Wakefield) (1942)
Marjorie Florence, b. 8/9/1928; third; George E. Chick (Wakefield) and Isabel Ringer (Allston, MA)
Ralph Hansen, b. 7/15/1884; first; George Hansen Chick (Waterboro, ME) and Jennie Waldron (Wakefield) (1940)
Ralph Hanson, b. 5/20/1923; first; Ralph Chick (carpenter, Wakefield) and Lillian Look (Boston, MA)
Sumner Lewis, b. 4/5/1939; first; George Chick (Newfield, ME) and Edith Corliss (Northwood)
Willard Clayton, b. 10/3/1896; fourth; George Chick (carpenter, Waterboro, ME) and Jane Waldron (Newfield, ME)

CHIPOKAS,
Peter, b. 1/29/1921; sixth; J. Chipokas (laborer, 37, Russia) and Nellie Murgin (33, Russia); residence - Sanbornville

CHIPOKOS,
Mary, b. 4/16/1919; sixth; Jurgis Chipokos (laborer, 36, Russia) and Nellie Mingin (31, Russia)

CHIRADONNA,
Suzanne Louise, b. 10/15/1985 in Rochester; Vincent A. Chiradonna, Jr. and Diane L. Illingworth
Vanessa Lynne, b. 10/15/1985 in Rochester; Vincent A. Chiradonna, Jr. and Diane L. Illingworth

CHURCHILL,
Marjorie, b. 8/18/1896; third; C. I. Churchill (merchant, Brookfield) and Amanda E. Place (Middleton)

CIAMPA,
Jonathan Andrew, b. 6/13/1987 in Wolfeboro; Anthony Ciampa, Jr. and Sharyn R. Singelais

CLARK,
son [Edwin L.], b. 5/19/1887; second; Mayhew C. Clark (farmer, Wakefield) and Eliza R. Furber (Wolfeboro)
Barbara E., b. 7/4/1917; third; J. Frank Clark (clerk, 26, Dover) and Gladys M. Pickering (24, Rochester)
Cheryl Ann, b. 12/20/1946; first; Kenneth F. Clark (Sanbornville) and Mildred M. Williams (Ft. H.C. Wright, NY)
Dorothy Madeline, b. 10/8/1913; first; John Frank Clark (laborer, 22, Dover) and Gladys M. Pickering (20, Rochester)
John Edwin, b. 9/9/1922; second; Edwin L. Clark (lumber dealer, Wakefield) and Edith Loring (Milford)
Kenneth Frank, b. 5/16/1915; second; John F. Clark (clerk, 24, Dover) and Gladys M. Pickering (22, Rochester)
Loring Townsend, b. 5/19/1915; first; Edwin L. Clark (farmer, 28, Wakefield) and Edith C. Loring (30, Milford)
Ruth E., b. 9/7/1919; fourth; J. Frank Clark (Wakefield) and Gladys Pickering (Wolfeboro) (1937)
Samantha Elizabeth, b. 4/12/1989 in Rochester; George Henry Clark, III and Anna Elizabeth Lund

CLEALE,
Catherine, b. 5/8/1963 in Rochester; third; Ralph M. Cleale, 3d (Boston, MA) and Carol L. Potter (Houlton, ME)

CLEMENTS,
daughter, b. 6/7/1917; second; Ralph W. Clements (lumberman, 31, Laconia) and Catherine Hanagan (22, Lawrence, MA)

CLIFFORD,
daughter, b. 11/26/1893; sixth; Charles H. Clifford (engineer, Denmark, ME) and Eliza E. Buzzell (Bridgton, ME)
Ralph L., b. 7/15/1895; seventh; Charles A. Clifford (engineer, Denmark, ME) and Eliza Buswell (Bridgton, ME)

CLOUGH,
David Jerome, Jr., b. 5/18/1974 in Wolfeboro; David J. Clough and Terri L. Goodwin
David Joseph, b. 2/19/1951; first; Herbert E. Clough (Milton Mills) and Colleen J. Morrill (Brookfield)

COBURN,
Elaine Gertrude, b. 8/10/1944; first; Ernest A. Coburn and Evelyn M. Leighton (Milton)

COLBATH,
son, b. 4/23/1921; second; Robert N. Colbath (laborer, 21, Wakefield) and Emily A. Cook (21, Wakefield); residence - Sanbornville
Bethany Virginia, b. 5/12/1957 in Rochester; fourth; Richard P. Colbath (Wolfeboro) and Virginia A. Stevens (Sandown)
Blanche Mabel, b. 6/9/1878; third; Walter George Colbath (Boston, MA) and Emma Belle Knox (West Ossipee) (1941)
Dale Robert, b. 3/5/1961 in Rochester; seventh; Richard P. Colbath (Wolfeboro) and Virginia A. Stevens (Sandown)
Isabelle Myra, b. 1/17/1877; second; Walter George Colbath (Boston, MA) and Emma Belle Knox (West Ossipee) (1941)
John E., b. 4/20/1894; eighth; Charles W. Colbath (laborer, Boston, MA) and Emily S. Bickford (Wolfeboro)
Jonathan Dale, b. 8/13/1982 in Rochester; Dale R. Colbath and Deborah Murphy

Laura Lynn, b. 6/30/1985 in Wolfeboro; Randy P. Colbath and Joyce L. Lavertue

Lee Ann Louise, b. 6/2/1958 in Rochester; fifth; Richard P. Colbath (Wolfeboro) and Virginia A. Stevens (Sandown)

Lindsey Marie, b. 12/17/1988 in Wolfeboro; Randy P. Colbath and Joyce L. Lavertue

Rainsford Elwood, b. 3/28/1919; first; Robert N. Colbath (laborer, 19, Wakefield) and Emily A. Cook (19, Wakefield)

Randy Philip, b. 6/8/1959 in Rochester; sixth; Richard P. Colbath (Wolfeboro) and Virginia A. Stevens (Sandown)

Richard Paul, b. 5/17/1935; third; Robert N. Colbath (Sanbornville) and Emily A. Cook (North Wakefield)

Robert Norman, b. 6/9/1899; seventh; Walter G. Colbath (Boston, MA) and Emma Knox (West Ossipee) (1942)

COLBURN,

Leroy Walter, b. 4/24/1923; seventh; Archie W. Colburn (farmer, No. Windham, CT) and Grace M. Barrington (So. Framingham, MA)

Marion H., b. 6/13/1924; eighth; Archie W. Colburn (farmer, No. Windham, CT) and Grace M. Barrington (So. Framingham, MA)

COLBY,

Richard George, Jr., b. 6/18/1943; first; Richard George Colby (Newton) and Ruth Ellen Wilkins (Tyngsboro, MA)

Zackery Douglas Richard, b. 9/20/1989 in Dover; John Wallace Colby and Dianne Patricia Betts

COLCORD,

daughter, b. 1/29/1890; first; Harvey Colcord (farmer, Tuftonboro) and Dell L. Seward (Wakefield)

COLE,

Stacey Lynn, b. 10/27/1977 in Rochester; Stanley R. Cole and Sally A. Gray

COLLYNS,

Lydia Kaye, b. 3/10/1998 in Lebanon; Donald Collyns and Sandra K. Brooks

COLUMBUS,
daughter, b. 2/24/1893; fourth; Odilon Columbus (laborer, Canada) and Malvina V. Hall (Milton)

COMEAU,
Jodi Michelle, b. 9/13/1977 in Rochester; John R. Comeau and Vickie L. Trask

CONNELL,
Meaghan Alicia, b. 9/10/1984 in Concord; Kevin P. Connell and Kimberly A. Cornell
Peter Thomas McMahon, b. 2/12/1987 in Concord; Kevin P. Connell and Kimberly A. Cornell
Sarah Elizabeth, b. 5/3/1982 in Wolfeboro; Kevin P. Connell and Kimberly A. Cornell

CONSTANT,
daughter, b. 9/20/1910; eighth; Elmer Constant (laborer, 33, Canada) and Marie Splane (32, Canada)

COOK,
son [Wilfred J.], b. 5/25/1902; sixth; Elmer Cook (laborer, 34, Wenham, MA) and Lillian Clow (32, Wolfeboro)
son [Harold M.], b. 10/24/1905 in North Wakefield; seventh; Elmer M. Cook (farmer, 39, Wenham, MA) and Lillian B. Clow (36, Wolfeboro); residence - N. Wakefield
Caroline Pauline, b. 3/18/1928; second; Clarence C. Cook (Middleton) and Pauline Tufts (Middleton)
Emily A., b. 9/25/1899; fifth; Elmer M. Cook (farmer, Wenham, MA) and Lillian B. Clow (Wolfeboro)
Hazel May, b. 8/29/1894; first; Elmer M. Cook (farmer, Wenham, MA) and Lillian Clow (Wolfeboro)
Lucy, b. 10/15/1867; first; Samuel J. Cook (Middleton) and Rebecca H. Downs (East Rochester) (1936)
Mamie, b. 12/2/1896; third; Elmer M. Cook (farmer, MA) and Lillian Libby (NH)

COPLEY,
John Henry, b. 8/9/1943; first; William Henry Copley (Lynn, MA) and Nancy Emma Ferguson (Georgetown, MA)

CORMIER,
Bernard Ronald, Jr., b. 12/7/1968 in Rochester; Bernard R. Cormier and Marlene E. Wilson
Chris Ann, b. 9/18/1980 in Rochester; Daniel S. Cormier and Maryellen Cressey
Joseph O.A., b. 7/5/1897; fourth; Frank Cormier (laborer, Canada) and Marie Perron (Canada)
Michelle Marie, b. 10/8/1971 in Rochester; Bernard R. Cormier and Marlene E. Wilson
Steven Daniel, b. 1/23/1983 in Rochester; Daniel S. Cormier and Maryellen Cressey

CORNWELL,
Amy Kathleen, b. 11/22/1989 in Dover; Dean Whitney Cornwell and June Alice Genna

CORSON,
Elizabeth Mae, b. 10/13/1920; first; Raymond S. Corson (laborer, 26, Newfield, ME) and Beatrice M. Whitlock (19, Portland, ME); residence - Newfield, ME
Florence M., b. 11/29/1901; first; John E. Corson (farmer, Wakefield) and Idella L. Wiggin (Wakefield)
Frances Marjorie, b. 11/22/1921; second; Raymond S. Corson (laborer, 27, Newfield, ME) and Beatrice Whitlock (20, Portland, ME); residence - Newfield, ME
Gladys Karen, b. 12/12/1936; fifth; Raymond Corson (Newfield, ME) and Beatrice Whitlock (Portland, ME)
Raymond William, b. 10/19/1924; third; Raymond S. Corson (surveyor, Newfield, ME) and Beatrice M. Whitlock (Portland, ME)

COSLETT,
John Scott, Jr., b. 12/23/1976 in Rochester; John Scott Coslett and Leeann L. Colbath

COTE,
Marie Grace, b. 7/16/1903 in Sanbornville; first; Moses Cote (laborer, 24, Canada) and Rosie Moore (22, Canada); residence - Sanbornville
Maurice Wilfred, b. 8/24/1926; second; Robert C. Cote (Canada) and Sadie A. Deroche (Wakefield)

COTTON,
Brenna Elizabeth, b. 5/9/1997 in Wolfeboro; Mark Allen Cotton and Erin Colleen O'Meara
Casey Michael, b. 1/19/1990 in Dover; Michael Henry Cotton and Bonnie Lee Foster
Charlene Ann, b. 4/6/1955 in Wolfeboro; fourth; Charles Almond Cotton (NH) and Mary Agnes Borsey (Stamford, CT)
Charles John, Jr., b. 6/12/1964 in Wolfeboro; first; Charles J. Cotton, Sr. (Stamford, CT) and Judith M. Manka (Rochester, NY)
Jason Alan, b. 9/22/1971 in Wolfeboro; James A. Cotton and Beverly A. Williams
John Michael, b. 8/4/1966 in Rochester; second; Charles J. Cotton (Stamford, CT) and Judith M. Manka (Port Chester, NY)
Mark Allen, b. 10/26/1966 in Rochester; fifth; Charles A. Cotton (Brookfield) and Mary A. Borsey (Stamford, CT)
Meara Jo, b. 4/1/1994 in Wolfeboro; Mark Allen Cotton and Erin Colleen O'Meara
Michael Henry, b. 11/3/1971 in Rochester; Michael H. Cotton and Theresa E. Shea
Tina Marie, b. 3/7/1973 in Rochester; Michael H. Cotton and Theresa E. Shea

COUCH,
Cindi Irene, b. 5/24/1971 in Wolfeboro; John A. Couch and Emilia J. Dion
Shaun Raymond, b. 10/5/1983 in Wolfeboro; John A. Couch and Emelia J. Dion

COURTNEY,
Daniel Terrance, Jr., b. 6/16/1987 in Rochester; Daniel T. Courtney and Hope F. Keaton

COUTRE,
Ida Mary, b. 8/9/1915; first; Aime Coutre (factory em., 20, Somersworth) and Leda Drapeau (19, Wakefield)

COWAN,
Erford Oswold, b. 10/28/1914; second; Lester Cowan (laborer, 27, Bangor, ME) and Bertha Cook (26, Detroit, ME)
Wayne, b. 6/1/1946; third; Erford O. Cowan (Sanbornville) and Marcella M. Goupil (Lampdon, Canada)

COX,
Alan Richard, b. 8/28/1938; third; Henry Eugene Cox (East Wakefield) and Octavia Agnes Lofquist (Brainerd, MN)
Hugo Lofquist, b. 2/7/1940; fourth; Henry Eugene Cox (East Wakefield) and Octavia Lofquist (Brainerd, MN)

CRAFT,
Clayton Chester, b. 11/27/1914; third; Harry L. Craft (physician, 36, NB) and Bessie Darby (35, Alburg, VT)
Donald Darby, b. 12/25/1912; second; Harry L. Craft (physician, 32, NB) and Bessie A. Darby (31, Alburg, VT)

CRATEAU,
son, b. 2/29/1892; second; Pierre Creteau (laborer, Canada) and Clara McNies (Canada)
daughter, b. 2/17/1893; second; Charles Crateau (laborer, Canada) and Mary Dronin (Canada)
daughter, b. 3/17/1893; fourth; Edward Crateau (laborer, Canada) and Emelie ----- (Canada)
stillborn daughter, b. 3/9/1912; fourteenth; Edward Crateau (laborer, 49, Canada) and Emily Rhobinhymer (42, Canada)
Albert Willie, b. 10/30/1897; fifth; Charles Crateau (laborer, Canada) and Mary Drouin (Canada)
Arthur, b. 6/14/1895; third; Ernest Cretteau (sic) (laborer, Canada) and Josie Abaer (Canada)
Arthur, b. 8/17/1909; thirteenth; Edward Crateau (laborer, 44, Canada) and Emilly Hymer (38, Canada)
Dilvina, b. 2/17/1901; sixth; Ernest Crateau (laborer, Canada) and Josephine Heber (Canada); residence - Sanbornville
Edward, b. 8/24/1896; sixth; Edward Crateau (laborer, Canada) and Emily Robenhymer (Canada); residence - Sanbornville
Eva M.J., b. 1/18/1898; fifth; Ernest Cratteau (sic) (laborer, Canada) and Josephine Herbert (Canada)
Frank, b. 7/5/1894; third; Charles Crateau (laborer, Canada) and Mary Drown (Canada)
Fred J., b. 5/1/1905; ninth; Charles Crateau (carpenter, 38, Canada) and Mary Drouin (35, Canada)
George A., b. 5/18/1900; sixth; Charles Crateau (laborer, Canada) and Mary Drouin (Canada)

Grace Mary, b. 6/12/1905 in Sanbornville; twelfth; Edward F. Cretteau (sic) (laborer, 40, Canada) and Emily Robinhymer (35, Canada); residence - Sanbornville

Joseph, b. 7/21/1896; fourth; Charles Cretteau (sic) (laborer, Canada) and Marie Drouin (Canada); residence - Sanbornville

Joseph Telesphore, b. 12/4/1896; fourth; Ernest Cretteau (sic) (laborer, Canada) and Josephine Albert (Canada); residence - Sanbornville

Laura Marie, b. 4/21/1894; second; Ernest Crateau (laborer, Canada) and Josie Abbott (Canada)

Lydia O., b. 6/28/1903; eighth; Charles Crateau (laborer, 38, Canada) and Mary Drouin (33, Canada)

Marie Lillian Alma, b. 5/25/1912; first; James Crateau (laborer, 22, Canada) and Delvina Drouin (23, Canada)

Marie M., b. 1/21/1909; tenth; Charles Crateau (carpenter, 42, Quebec) and Marie Drouin (38, Quebec)

Mary, b. 2/26/1900; sixth; Edward Crateau (laborer, Canada) and Emily Robinhomer (Canada)

Mary A., b. 1/6/1895; fifth; Edward Cretteau (sic) (laborer, Canada) and Emily Robenhymer (Canada)

Mary Regina, b. 5/9/1898; sixth; Edward Cratteau (sic) (laborer, Canada) and Emily Robinhomer (Canada)

Mary Vildea Odeanna, b. 8/22/1902; ninth; Edward Crateau (laborer, 36, Canada) and Emile Robinheimer (32, Canada); residence - Sanbornville

Remond, b. 8/31/1901; seventh; Charles Crateau (laborer, Canada) and Mary Drouin (Canada)

Viola, b. 6/20/1904; tenth; Edward Crateau (laborer, 40, Canada) and Emilie Robenhimer (36, Canada)

Wilfred William, b. 9/26/1911; eleventh; Charles Crateau (bridge builder, 44, Canada) and Mary Drouin (41, Canada)

William, b. 6/22/1907; twelfth; Edward Crateau (laborer, 41, Canada) and Emily Robenhymer (36, Canada)

CRAWFORD,
Amy Elizabeth, b. 10/11/1983 in Wolfeboro; David E. Crawford and Cindy G. Luscomb

Codie Dale, b. 11/17/1994 in Rochester; Dale Erving Crawford and Carrie Ann Gibbons

Corey Daryl, b. 6/13/1996 in Wolfeboro; Dale E. Crawford and Carrie Ann Gibbons

Dale Erving, b. 6/25/1973 in Wolfeboro; Daryl E. Crawford and Lucille C. Worster
Dara Elyse, b. 10/18/1985 in Wolfeboro; Daryl E. Crawford and Lucille C. Worster
Darcy Elaina, b. 11/12/1981 in Wolfeboro; Daryl E. Crawford and Lucille Worster
Daryl Ellsworth, II, b. 9/17/1971 in Wolfeboro; Daryl E. Crawford and Lucille C. Worster
David Erving, Jr., b. 5/26/1980 in Wolfeboro; David E. Crawford and Cindy G. Luscomb
Derek Elton, b. 1/23/1979 in Wolfeboro; Daryl E. Crawford and Lucile C. Worster
Kathryn Marie, b. 10/9/1967 in Nashua; second; William B. Crawford (Rochester) and Roberta J. Choate (Pittsburgh, PA)

CREW,
Amanda Ann, b. 8/15/1995 in Wolfeboro; Kenneth Allan Crew and Michelle An Baillargeon
Emily Elizabeth, b. 1/24/1998 in Wolfeboro; Kenneth A. Crew and Michelle Ann Baillargeon

CROWLEY,
Daniel Francis, b. 2/19/1997 in Rochester; Christopher Joseph Crowley and Julie Ann Storey
Edward Francis, b. 5/13/1944; second; Frank L. Crowley (Ridgeboro, VT) and Ruth M. Jewell (Lincoln, NE)

CUMMINGS,
stillborn son, b. 12/12/1888; third; Joseph Cummings (laborer, Manchester) and Mary Cummings (Canada)
stillborn son, b. 12/12/1888; fourth; Joseph Cummings (laborer, Manchester) and Mary Cummings (Canada)
son, b. 11/27/1889; fifth; Joseph Cummings (laborer, Manchester) and Mary Chitty (Canada)
son, b. 11/23/1893; first; Hary Cummings (shoe cutter, Haverhill, MA) and Lulu Drury (Wakefield)
Lizzie Louise, b. 9/12/1857; sixth; Samuel Cummings (ME) and Nancy B. Neal (Brookfield)

CUNNINGHAM,
Dylan Michael, b. 11/9/1997 in Rochester; Shawn Michael Cunningham and Jodi Marie Dubois

CURLEY,
Robert Walter, b. 11/19/1954 in Wolfeboro; second; Reuben Milton Curley (PA) and Florence Elizabeth Harsh (PA)

CURRIER,
Alfred A., b. 9/23/1892; second; Fred Currier (laborer, Canada) and Virginia Duval (Milton Mills)

CURTIS,
daughter [Eva M.], b. 7/12/1892; third; Joseph S. Curtis (merchant, Brookfield) and Fannie E. Butler (Lebanon, ME)

CUTTER,
Arthur Earl, Jr., b. 3/13/1965 in Exeter; fourth; Arthur E. Cutter, Sr. (Keene) and Patricia H. Tuttle (Farmington)

CYR,
Clayton Douglas, b. 4/26/1998 in Wolfeboro; Jonathan Michael Cyr and Bonnie Christine Martell
Hayden Henry, b. 3/24/1996 in Wolfeboro; Jonathan Michael Cyr and Bonnie Christine Martell

DADMUN,
Karl Lee, b. 8/28/1941; first; Carl Francis Dadmun (Allston, MA) and Luella Constance Seltsam (E. Foxboro, MA)

DALPHOND,
son, b. 3/15/1910; second; George Dalphond (laborer, 36, Canada) and Odeine Couture (29, Canada)

DAME,
Corrinne Eleanor, b. 8/25/1939; first; Howard Emerson Dame (Wakefield) and Virginia Arvida Littlefield (Wakefield)
Delina Etta, b. 5/30/1903; second; Daniel E. Dame (hostler, 30, Portsmouth) and Minnie Meathable (24, Farmington); residence - Union

Howard Emerson, b. 6/6/1915; first; Emerson Dame (clerk, 41, Portsmouth) and Josephine Pinkham (24, Middleton)
Howard Payson, b. 12/1/1942; second; Howard Emerson Dame (Union) and Virginia A. Littlefield (Union)
Laura Lee, b. 3/16/1961 in Rochester; first; Howard P. Dame (Rochester) and Elinore F. Kraus (Brooklyn, NY)

DAMON,
Tara Amy, b. 10/9/1984 in Wolfeboro; James R. Damon and Kathie E. Nason

DANAIS,
Emma Anderson, b. 7/15/1997 in Wolfeboro; Michael Edward Danais and Karla Amy Anderson

DANIELL,
Elise Nicole, b. 9/18/1992 in Dover; John Joseph Daniell and Jane Ellen Mee
Kayla Marie, b. 2/18/1995 in Dover; John Joseph Daniell and Jane Ellen Mee

DANONCOURT,
Ryan James, b. 4/18/1997 in Wolfeboro; Steven Danonocourt and Darcie Ann Nason

DAVENPORT,
son, b. 9/22/1922; second; George Davenport (care taker, Tonawanda, NY) and Wilda Whitten (So. Berwick, ME)
daughter, b. 2/12/1925; third; George Davenport (Tonawanda, NY) and Wilda Whitten (So. Berwick, ME)
Dora May, b. 4/13/1927; fourth; George H. Davenport (Tonawanda, NY) and Wilda E. Whitten (So. Berwick, ME)
George Henry, Jr., b. 10/8/1920; first; George H. Davenport (carpenter, 42, Tonawanda, NY) and Wilda E. Whitten (22, S. Berwick, ME); residence - Sanbornville

DAVID,
Alyssa Marie, b. 4/24/1990 in Rochester; Jerome Jude David and Sheryl Ann Rapisardi

DAVIS,
son, b. 3/4/1887; first; Fred H. Davis (Jackson) and Nellie E. (Bangor, ME)
daughter, b. 3/9/1889; first; Charles M. Davis (laborer, Jackson) and Julia A. Williams (Effingham)
son, b. 3/12/1890; second; Charles M. Davis (laborer, Effingham) and Julia A. Williams (Effingham)
son, b. 6/4/1890; first; Justin E. Davis (brakeman, Wakefield) and H. Imogene Lang (Brookfield)
son, b. 10/14/1890; second; Fred H. Davis (railroading, Jackson) and Nellie E. Emerson (Bangor, ME)
son, b. 3/28/1892; second; Justin E. Davis (brakeman, Wakefield) and Imogene H. Lang (Brookfield)
stillborn son, b. 2/16/1895; first; Edwin M. Davis (farmer, Springvale, ME) and Alice Burke (Boston, MA)
son, b. 5/17/1900; second; Curtis A. Davis (merchant, Bradford) and Grace Howland (Lyme); residence - Sanbornville
son, b. 3/13/1905 in Sanbornville; fourth; Edwin M. Davis (painter, 33, Springvale, ME) and Alice Burke (31, Boston, MA); residence - Sanbornville
Casey Colby, b. 5/21/1977 in Wolfeboro; Daniel R. Davis and Jacqueline Keating
Cecil F., b. 7/17/1902; fifth; George T.G. Davis (laborer, 29, Wakefield) and Fannie Reed (24, Newfield, ME)
Charles Foss, b. 3/6/1898; second; Edwin M. Davis (farmer, Sanford, ME) and Alice Burke (Boston, MA)
Dorothy Isabel, b. 3/17/1897; second; George Davis (laborer, Wakefield) and Fanny Reed (Wakefield)
Forest Ellsworth, b. 2/20/1896; first; Fred H. Davis (section hand, Jackson) and Bertha McDonald (Wakefield)
Frances L., b. 11/22/1907; first; George T. Davis (fireman, 26, Ossipee) and Edna A. Curtis (18, Brookfield)
Frank B., b. 7/5/1900; third; Edwin M. Davis (laborer, Sanford, ME) and Alice Burke (Boston, MA); residence - Sanbornville
George T. Grafton, b. 11/2/1873; fourth; Mayhew Davis (Wakefield) and Lydia Abbott (Water Village) (1940)
Jayme Lyn, b. 9/27/1974 in Wolfeboro; Daniel R. Davis and Jacqueline A. Keating
Justin Eddie, b. 10/31/1869; third; Mayhew C. Davis (Wakefield) and Lydia F. Abbott (Tuftonboro) (1937)

Marion Lucille, b. 9/19/1904; fourth; Ernest W. Davis (blacksmith, 28, Buxton, ME) and Lillian Merrow (26, Newfield, ME)

Marjorie May, b. 12/24/1915; first; Forrest E. Davis (laborer, 19, Wakefield) and Bertha M. Brown (18, Dover)

Mildred Marjory, b. 2/28/1908; sixth; George T.G. Davis (sawyer, 34, Wakefield) and Fannie I. Reed (29, Newfield, ME)

Tammy Lynn, b. 2/1/1964 in Rochester; third; Reginald A. Davis (Bristol, England) and Rita J. Cate (Rochester)

William Sidney, b. 10/7/1950; third; Sidney Davis (Tamworth) and Ruth E. Tyler (Alton)

Zoe Inez Mae, b. 10/11/1937; first; Clayton Davis (New Hampton) and Katherine Maleham (Wakefield)

DEBLASI,

Linda Elizabeth, b. 4/25/1973 in Wolfeboro; Anthony J. DeBlasi and Janet R. Gibson

DEE,

Frederick John, b. 9/2/1982 in Dover; Raymond H. Dee and Nancy L. Dean

DEHARNAIR,

Joseph Willie, b. 5/14/1897; first; Alfred Deharnair (laborer, Canada) and Amanda Ouelette (Canada)

DEITRICK,

Alexis Jordin, b. 8/18/1996 in Rochester; Todd Eugene Deitrick and Traci Lyn Knox

DELAN,

Olga Belle, b. 6/19/1908; first; Alfred DeLan (laborer, 28, Boston, MA) and Dora Fellows (29, Wakefield)

DELISLE,

Haley Dawn, b. 10/25/1991 in Portsmouth; Richard David Delisle and Lisa Marie Greene

DELOLLIS,

David Arthur, b. 11/13/1964 in Wolfeboro; second; Joseph B. DeLollis (Boston, MA) and Barbara King (Winchester, MA)

DEMARAIS,
Atonia, b. 11/1/1905 in Sanbornville; third; Valmore Demarais (laborer, 28, Canada) and Emma Lamie (28, Somersworth); residence - Sanbornville

DEMERETT,
daughter, b. 5/27/1929; fifth; William Demerett (Wakefield) and Eva Landry (W. Newfield, ME)

DEMERRITT,
Harold Harvey, b. 1/18/1895; second; Myen Demerritt (shoemaker, Newfield, ME) and Maud I. Drury (Wolfeboro)

DEMING,
Troy Allen, b. 3/23/1970 in Rochester; John B. Deming and Barbara J. Moors

DEMOTT,
Natalie Hope, b. 5/13/1993 in Wolfeboro; Brian Keith Demott and Tami Lyn Kelley

DENLEY,
Andrew Palmer, b. 12/27/1984 in Wolfeboro; William P. Denley and Susan E. Gamble
William Bradford, b. 4/28/1991 in Wolfeboro; William Palmer Denley and Susan Elizabeth Gamble

DEROCHERS,
Alfonso Henry, b. 6/1/1907; fourth; Philbert Derochers (laborer, 35, Canada) and Mary L. Marcoux (25, Wakefield)

DEROUCHE,
Mary Alice, b. 6/1/1902 in Sanbornville; first; Philbert Derouche (laborer, 28, Canada) and Mary Marcoux (21, Wakefield); residence - Sanbornville

DERROCHERS,
Mary, stillborn, b. 4/17/1904; second; Philbert Derrochers (laborer, 28, Canada) and Mary Marcou (22, Wakefield)

DESROCHERS,
Henry, stillborn, b. 6/18/1905 in Sanbornville; third; Philibert Desrochers (laborer, 31, Canada) and Marie Marcoux (23, Sanbornville)

DEWOLF,
Carla Madeleine, b. 6/16/1961 in Wolfeboro; second; Donald J. DeWolf (Lincoln, NE) and Davena Rogers (Manchester)
Mark David, b. 5/14/1959 in Wolfeboro; second; Donald J. DeWolf (Lincoln, NE) and Davena Rogers (Manchester)

DEXTER,
Sheri Ann, b. 11/14/1977 in Rochester; Ernest C. Dexter and Patricia L. Taylor

DEZAN,
Tyler Lee, b. 8/19/1988 in Rochester; Douglas F. Dezan, Jr. and Lisa A. Braden

DICEY,
Natalie A., b. 6/13/1883; tenth; George Dicey (Jackson) and Susan Durrell (Union) (1940)
Stella E., b. 4/25/1871; sixth; George W. Dicey (Jackson) and Susan Durrell (Union) (1938)

DICKAU,
Marc Gabriel, b. 10/28/1979 in Rochester; Richard A. Dickau and Lucy Walkewicz

DILLION,
Victoria Kaytlyn, b. 3/7/1993 in Rochester; Jeffrey Wayne Dillion and Kelly Jo Glidden

DION,
Eric Jason, b. 7/5/1974 in Wolfeboro; Albert J. Dion and Barbara M. Krohn

DIPRIZIO,
Cathleen Mary, b. 12/29/1968 in Rochester; Charles C. DiPrizio and Earleen S. Dodier

Charles Constandino, b. 9/11/1943; second; Constandino DiPrizio (Everett, MA) and Marie Evelyn DiPrizio (Italy)

Christine Marine, b. 7/6/1967 in Rochester; first; Charles C. DiPrizio (Wolfeboro) and Earleen S. Dodier (Wolfeboro)

Dianne Marolyn, b. 8/28/1951; second; John N. DiPrizio (Middleton) and Enid M. Lowe (Acton, ME)

Joseph Charles, Jr., b. 8/1/1978 in Rochester; Joseph C. Diprizio and Kimberly A. Lefavour

Mary Francina, b. 9/22/1978 in Rochester; Carmen J. DiPrizio and Joyce A. Wentworth

Prisco Charles, b. 5/2/1941; first; Constantino DiPrizio (Boston, MA) and Marie Evelyn DiPrizio (Italy)

DOBLE,

Ellen Margaret, b. 2/9/1917; first; Henry L. Doble (teamster, 25, So. Weymouth, MA) and Celia M. Loughlin (34, No. Cambridge, MA)

DODGE,

Frances Icona, b. 7/8/1909; fifth; John W. Dodge (shoe mfg., 37, So. Berwick, ME) and Antoinette P. Healey (32, Raymond); residence - Marblehead, MA

DODIER,

son, b. 7/2/1904; eighth; Joseph Dodier (laborer, 33, Canada) and Edith Perron (30, Canada)

Bessie Eva, b. 1/18/1894; second; Frank Dodier (brakeman, Canada) and Georgia Canston (Newburyport, MA)

Beverly Ann, b. 6/14/1935; second; Archie Dodier (Sanbornville) and Ada McLachlan (Providence, RI)

Bryan Lee, b. 10/28/1955 in Rochester; sixth; Donald Raymond Dodier (Somerville, MA) and Ruth Emma Valley (Milton Mills)

Bryan Lee, b. 6/4/1983 in Wolfeboro; Bryan L. Dodier and Nancy Clark

Claire Jean, b. 5/8/1937; third; Archie J. Dodier (Sanbornville) and Ada L. McLachlan (Providence, RI)

Daniel Christopher, b. 12/4/1976 in Rochester; Leslie Dodier and Kathleen G. Cunniff

Dora Phoebe Mary, b. 12/1/1912; fourteenth; Joseph Dodier (laborer, 42, Canada) and Edith Perron (37, Canada)

Edward, b. 4/15/1896; Frank Dodier (laborer, Canada) and Georgia Custo (Canada); residence - Sanbornville

Frank, b. 8/31/1895; third; Joseph Dodier (laborer, Canada) and Edith
    Perron (Canada)
Frank, b. 2/2/1897; fourth; Joseph Dodier (laborer, Canada) and Edith
    Perron (Canada)
Gail Lynn, b. 8/7/1959 in Rochester; eighth; Donald R. Dodier
    (Somerville, MA) and Ruth E. Valley (Milton Mills)
Gregory Barry, b. 9/20/1978 in Wolfeboro; Barry C. Dodier and Bonnie L.
    Brenton
Jacob Lawrence, b. 8/15/1975 in Rochester; Stanley L. Dodier and
    Deborah A. Inman
Joseph, b. 4/30/1900; sixth; Joseph Dodier (laborer, Canada) and Edith
    Perron (Canada); residence - Sanbornville
Joseph Archie, b. 4/4/1908; eleventh; Joseph Dodier (laborer, 38, Canada)
    and Edith Perron (35, Canada)
Larry Calvin, b. 10/21/1957 in Rochester; seventh; Donald R. Dodier
    (Somerville, MA) and Ruth E. Valley (Milton Mills)
Leonard Paul, b. 1/15/1933 in Wolfeboro; Archie J. Dodier and Ada L.
    McLachlan
Leslie Wayne, b. 1/22/1974 in Rochester; Leslie Dodier and Kathleen G.
    Cunniff
Mary R. Angelina, b. 3/20/1911; thirteenth; Joseph Dodier (laborer, 40,
    Canada) and Edith Perron (37, Canada)
Mary Rosie Perron, b. 8/16/1909; twelfth; Joseph Dodier (laborer, 39,
    Canada) and Edith Perron (36, Canada)
Matthew Carl, b. 2/22/1983 in Wolfeboro; Barry C. Dodier and Bonnie L.
    Brenton
Olida, b. 5/12/1902 in Sanbornville; seventh; Joseph Dodier (laborer, 31,
    Canada) and Edith Perron (28, Canada); residence - Sanbornville
Phebe M., b. 9/26/1898; fifth; Joseph Dodier (laborer, Canada) and Edith
    Perron (Canada)
Raymond R., Jr., b. 12/23/1968 in Wolfeboro; Raymond R. Dodier and
    Lorraine B. Worster
Raymond Ralph, b. 4/16/1947; second; Ralph W. Dodier (Dorchester, MA)
    and Barbara W. Miliner (Wakefield, MA)
Rhonda Rae, b. 12/6/1971 in Wolfeboro; Raymond R. Dodier and Lorraine
    E. Worster
Roland Robert, b. 12/5/1970 in Wolfeboro; Raymond R. Dodier and
    Lorraine B. Worster
Thomas Allan, b. 6/19/1947; second; Carl A. Dodier (Somerville, MA) and
    Janet M. Nelson (Peabody, MA)

Wayne Donald, b. 2/22/1951; third; Donald R. Dodier (MA) and Ruth E. Valley (NH)

DOE,
Andrew Philip, b. 4/1/1966 in Wolfeboro; sixth; Robert T. Doe (Cambridge, MA) and Marian L. Hutchins (Wolfeboro)
Laurie Lynn, b. 10/19/1956 in Wolfeboro; fourth; Robert T. Doe (Cambridge, MA) and Marian L. Hutchins (Wolfeboro)
Linda Lee, b. 10/19/1956 in Wolfeboro; fifth; Robert T. Doe (Cambridge, MA) and Marian L. Hutchins (Wolfeboro)
Robert Tristram, Jr., b. 11/26/1949; first; Robert T. Doe, Sr. (Cambridge, MA) and Marion L. Hutchins (Wolfeboro)
Steven Edwin, b. 9/21/1955 in Wolfeboro; third; Robert Tristram Doe (MA) and Marian L. Hutchins (NH)
Thomas Paul, b. 3/12/1952 in Wolfeboro; second; Robert T. Doe (MA) and Marion L. Hutchins (NH)

DOMPIER,
Jennifer Lynn, b. 7/28/1976 in Wolfeboro; Gary L. Dompier and Nancy E. Mills

DONNELLY,
Michael Bruce, b. 3/18/1961 in Wolfeboro; fifth; Robert B. Donnelly (Beverly, MA) and Barbara A. Chick (Somerville, MA)
Patricia Ellen, b. 6/13/1959 in Wolfeboro; fourth; Robert B. Donnelly (Beverly, MA) and Barbara A. Chick (Somerville, MA)

DORE,
Louis G., b. 5/9/1871; second; Gilman P. Dore (Wakefield) and Katie Donovan (Boston, MA) (1936)

DOUGLAS,
daughter, b. 9/9/1911; fourth; Frank Douglas (laborer, 27, Albany) and Jennie Harmon (21, Brookfield)
son, b. 7/3/1915; second; Charles W. Douglas (laborer, 22, Bridgton, ME) and Anna M. Libby (18, So. Windham, ME)
Florence May, b. 9/10/1907; second; Frank Douglas (laborer, 33, Albany) and Jennie M. Harmon (16, Brookfield)
Richard Edwin, b. 1/5/1949; third; Richard E. Douglas (Wolfeboro) and Dona Miliner (Sanbornville)

DOUGLASS,
Charles Franklin, b. 4/14/1906; first; Frank Douglass (laborer, 22, Albany) and Jennie M. Harmon (15, Brookfield)
Priscilla Ann, b. 12/21/1942; first; Richard Erwin Douglass (Wolfeboro) and Dona Miliner (Sanbornville)
Sheila Elizabeth, b. 5/16/1947; second; Richard E. Douglass (Wolfeboro) and Donna Miliner (Sanbornville)

DOVE,
Benjamin Earhart, b. 3/13/1981 in Rochester; William F. Dove and Catherine A. Sargent

DOWER,
Michael Dennis, b. 4/1/1966 in Wolfeboro; first; William A. Dower, Jr. (Honolulu, HI) and Elizabeth A. Hyde (Riverdale, MD)

DOWNS,
daughter, b. 3/9/1889; second; Charles S. Downs (brakeman, Wakefield) and Isa B. ----- (Alton)
stillborn son, b. 1/9/1925; third; Winfred E. Downs (Wolfeboro) and Carrie S. Wentworth (Acton, ME)
son, b. 2/26/1926; first; Frank Downs and Gertrude Johnson (Lebanon, ME)
Cora Rachel, b. 4/25/1920; first; Winfred E. Downs (farmer, 32, Wolfeboro) and Carrie Wentworth (27, Acton, ME)
Fred Wentworth, b. 2/11/1926; fourth; Winfred Downs (Wolfeboro) and Carrie Wentworth (Acton, ME)
Hazel Agnes, b. 10/29/1906; second; Harry A. Downs (laborer, 24, Wakefield) and Agnes Sawyer (23, Limestone, ME)
James Mason, b. 3/29/1956 in Rochester; first; Fred W. Downs (Union) and Hilda E. Joy (Rochester)
Jeffrey Malcolm, b. 10/9/1957 in Rochester; second; Fred W. Downs (Union) and Hilda E. Joy (Rochester)
Jennifer Marie, b. 7/3/1964 in Rochester; third; Fred W. Downs (Union) and Hilda E. Joy (Rochester)
Joshua Nicholas, b. 5/17/1986 in Wolfeboro; Jeffrey M. Downs and Janette H. Morrill
Lucy Caroline, b. 8/4/1927; fifth; Winfred E. Downs (Wolfeboro) and Carrie Wentworth (Acton, ME)

Matthew James, b. 10/23/1983 in Hanover; Jeffrey M. Downs and Janette Morrill

Melissa Jean, b. 8/19/1979 in Rochester; James M. Downs and Therese C.E. Soucy

Nancy Lee, b. 1/28/1951; second; Fred W. Downs (Wakefield) and Virginia A. Stevens (Sandown)

Nellie May, b. 5/25/1903; first; Harry Downs (laborer, 20, Wakefield) and Agnes Shaw (20, Caribou, ME)

Ruth Virginia, b. 9/27/1925; sixth; Edgar Ira Downs (Ossipee) and Edith Newcomb (Westerly, RI)

Winifred, b. 8/5/1921; second; Winfred E. Downs (farmer, 33, Wolfeboro) and Carrie Wentworth (28, Acton, ME)

DOYLE,

son [Clayton Cecil], b. 10/8/1916; first; Smith Pike (putative father, RR conductor, Middleton) and Mabel E. Doyle (25, Wakefield)

Mabel Eva, b. 3/15/1891; eighth; John Doyle (laborer, New York, NY) and Amanda Wentworth (Milton)

DRAPEAU,

daughter, b. 9/15/1887; first; Eusebe Draheau (sic) (laborer, Canada) and Aurelie Carrier (Canada)

son [George], b. 10/15/1889; second; Eusebe Drapeau (laborer, Canada) and Aurelie ----- (Canada)

daughter [Eva], b. 8/23/1891; third; Eusebe Drapeau (carpenter, Canada) and Amelie Drapeau (Canada)

son, b. 9/7/1893; fourth; Eusebe Drapeau (laborer, Canada) and Orelle Carrier (Canada)

Dunat, b. 7/31/1903 in Sanbornville; ninth; Eusebe Drapeau (laborer, 41, Canada) and Orille Corrier (42, Canada); residence - Sanbornville

Emilienne, b. 7/17/1899; seventh; Eusebe Drapeau (laborer, Canada) and Orrille Corrier (Canada); residence - Sanbornville

George Alfred, b. 8/3/1914; fifth; George Drapeau (laborer, 24, Wakefield) and Lucy Houde (30, Wakefield)

Joseph Armand, b. 3/17/1898; sixth; Eusebe Drapeau (laborer, Canada) and Orrille Carrier (Canada)

Joseph Arthur, b. 4/16/1912; third; George Drapeau (laborer, 22, Wakefield) and Lucy M. Houde (28, Wakefield)

Joseph Dona, b. 3/5/1910; first; George Drapeau (laborer, 30, Wakefield) and Lucy Houde (26, Wakefield)

Joseph Eddie, b. 2/10/1911; second; George Drapeau (laborer, 21, Wakefield) and Lucy M. Houde (27, Wakefield)
Leda M., b. 1/1/1896; fifth; Eusebe Drapeau (laborer, Canada) and Orrilla Carrier (Canada); residence - Sanbornville
Leon J., b. 7/16/1901; eighth; Eusebe Drapeau (laborer, Canada) and Orille Corrier (Canada); residence - Sanbornville
Marie, b. 4/10/1913; fourth; George Drapeau (laborer, 24, Wakefield) and Lucy Houde (29, Wakefield)
Mary Elaine, b. 10/16/1906; tenth; Eusebe Drapeau (carpenter, 44, Canada) and Aurillie Courier (45, Canada)
Roger William, b. 4/14/1934; first; Edward G. Drapeau (Sanbornville) and Dorothy K. Sibley (Sanbornville)
Victor Lawrence, b. 1/31/1919; eighth; George Drapeau (laborer, 29, Wakefield) and Lucy Houde (33, Wakefield); residence - Sanbornville

DREW,
stillborn son, b. 6/3/1906; seventh; John W. Drew (lumber dealer, 37, Cambridge, ME) and Mary A. Farrell (35, Ireland)
stillborn son, b. 10/15/1919; fourth; Charles A. Drew (mill hand, 33, Sanbornville) and Iva M. Reed (23, Union); residence - Union
daughter, b. 12/1/1922; second; Harold S. Drew (carpenter, Wakefield) and Charlotte L. Brown (Wakefield); residence - Union
stillborn daughter, b. 5/8/1926; third; Harold S. Drew (Wakefield) and Charlotte Brown (Wakefield)
Audrey Elizabeth, b. 4/14/1920; first; Harold S. Drew (carpenter, 24, Wakefield) and Charlotte L. Brown (22, Wakefield); residence - Union
Austin F., Jr., b. 6/13/1930; second; Austin F. Drew (Wakefield) and Arlene R. Whitten (So. Berwick, ME)
Bessie Jane, b. 9/11/1934; fifth; Frank P. Drew (Ossipee) and Bessie E. Morrison (Stow, ME)
Brenda Lee, b. 5/31/1960 in Rochester; seventh; Donald K. Drew (Madison) and Viola B. Sprague (Newfield, ME)
Caroline Mary, b. 1/23/1928; fourth; Harold Drew (Union) and Charlotte Brown (Sanbornville)
Charles Maurice, b. 3/19/1912; first; Charles A. Drew (mill operative, 25, Wakefield) and Iva May Reed (15, Wakefield)
Clyde Arthur, b. 9/25/1916; third; Charles A. Drew (mill operative, 29, Wakefield) and Iva May Reed (20, Wakefield)

Daisy Bertha, b. 11/24/1929; fourth; Charles A. Drew (Wakefield) and Cora May Dunn (Quincy, MA) (1930)

Donald Kenneth, Jr., b. 9/29/1956 in Rochester; sixth; Donald K. Drew (Madison) and Viola B. Sprague (Newfield, ME)

Edward Francis, b. 9/18/1928; third; Charles A. Drew (Sanbornville) and Cora M. Dunn (Dorchester, MA)

Enoch Franklin, Jr., b. 7/30/1946; second; Enoch F. Drew (Madison) and Lillian G. Wentworth (Wolfeboro)

Esther Stevens, b. 1/30/1923; second; Lyle S. Drew (manufacturer, Wakefield) and Harriet E. Locke (No. Adams, MA); residence - Union

Fannie, b. 3/8/1892; seventh; James A. Drew (laborer, Brookfield) and Clara A. Glidden (Alton)

Fanny, b. 5/18/1896; eighth; James A. Drew (day laborer, Brookfield) and Clara A. Glidden (Alton)

Frederic James, b. 7/2/1927; second; Charles A. Drew (Wakefield) and Cora M. Dunn (Dorchester, MA)

Frederick Eugene, b. 5/25/1924; first; Herbert Drew (laborer, Bow) and Laura Cashin (Pembroke)

Harold Sinclair, b. 5/7/1895; second; George W. Drew (carpenter, Exeter) and Maley E. Stevens (Middleton)

Hazel May, b. 4/13/1913; second; Charles A. Drew (laborer, 26, Wakefield) and Iva M. Reed (16, Wakefield)

Lyle S., b. 2/13/1891; first; George W. Drew (carpenter, Exeter) and Malie E. Stevens (Middleton)

Marilyn J., b. 8/11/1930; fifth; Harold S. Drew (Wakefield) and Charlotte Brown (Wakefield)

Marjorie Jeannette, b. 6/20/1940; first; Donald Kenneth Drew (Madison) and Viola Belle Sprague (Newfield, ME)

Mary Ellen, b. 4/6/1926; first; Charles Drew (Wakefield) and Carrie Dunn (Dorchester, MA)

Nancy Caroline, b. 4/9/1940; second; Leon Robert Drew (Madison) and Martha Iva Grosmith (London, England)

Priscilla Pauline, b. 3/26/1933 in Sanbornville; Harold Drew and Charlotte Brown

Robert Franklin, b. 12/26/1936; first; Leon Robert Drew (Madison) and Martha Grosmith (London, England)

Sandra May, b. 10/29/1938; first; Enoch Franklin Drew (Madison) and Lillian Greta Wentworth (Wolfeboro)

Shirley Demerise, b. 6/28/1948; first; Richard Drew, Jr. (Turners Falls, MA) and Doris L. Vachon (Wolfeboro)
Wanda Jean, b. 9/30/1949; fourth; Donald K. Drew (NH) and Viola B. Sprague (ME)

DROWN,

Debra Kay, b. 10/21/1955; first; William Franklin Drown (Ossipee) and Lois Elaine Wilkinson (E. Lebanon, ME)
Edgar Ira, b. 8/24/1917; first; Edgar I. Drown (farmer, 24, Moultonville) and Irene Newcomb (20, Westerly, RI)
Margaret Louise, b. 2/2/1924; fifth; Edgar L. Drown (laborer, Ossipee) and Edith I. Newcomb (Westerly, RI)
Marjorie Irene, b. 8/5/1920; third; Edgar L. Drown (farmer, 27, Ossipee) and Edith I. Newcomb (24, Westerly, RI)
Mary Evelyn, b. 12/14/1918; second; Edgar I. Drown (teamster, 25, Ossipee) and Edith I. Newcomb (22, Westerly, RI)
Marylin Leona, b. 3/1/1933; first; Herbert L. Drown (Sanbornville) and Myra F. Rourke (Manchester) (1934)
Mildred Elizabeth, b. 3/2/1927; seventh; Edgar Drown (Ossipee) and Edith J. Newcomb (Westerly, RI)
Patricia Evelyn, b. 8/16/1963 in Rochester; third; Paul A. Drown (Wolfeboro) and Patricia A. Walsh (Cambridge, MA)
Patrick Allen, b. 5/27/1961 in Wolfeboro; second; Paul A. Drown (Wolfeboro) and Patricia A. Walsh (Cambridge, MA)
Paul Wayne, b. 11/19/1956 in Rochester; first; Paul A. Drown (Wolfeboro) and Quava P. Walsh (Cambridge, MA)
Philis Eleanor, b. 1/26/1922; fourth; Edgar J. Drown (laborer, Ossipee) and Edith Irene Newcomb (Westerly, RI)
Rebecca Lynn, b. 9/14/1953 in Rochester; first; Stephen Carroll Drown (Wolfeboro) and Mary H. Dodge (Chelsea, MA)
Stephen Carroll, b. 2/6/1931 in Wolfeboro; Edgar I. Drown and Edith I. Newcomb (1932)

DROWNS,

Franklin W., b. 2/4/1902 in Sanbornville; fifth; Stephen D. Drowns (laborer, 30, Eaton) and Clara C. Peavey (30, Farmington); residence - Sanbornville
Gene F. Victoria, b. 3/26/1928; eighth; Edgar Drowns (Ossipee) and Edith Newcomb (Westerly, RI)

Leon H., b. 1/21/1900; fourth; Stephen Drowns (laborer, Eaton) and Carrie C. Peavey (Farmington)

Paul Arnold, b. 2/24/1935; eleventh; Edgar I. Drowns (Ossipee) and Edith S. Newcomb (Westerly, RI)

DRUGG,

Charles Scott, b. 3/6/1964 in Wolfeboro; second; Charles J. Drugg (Greenfield, MA) and Mary E. Garvin (Wakefield)

James Howard, b. 6/4/1959 in Wolfeboro; first; Charles J. Drugg, Jr. (Greenfield, MA) and Mary E. Garvin (Wakefield)

Ryan Charles, b. 8/24/1989 in Rochester; Charles Scott Drugg and Patricia Ann Hogan

DUBOIS,

stillborn son, b. 3/17/1903 in Sanbornville; sixth; Sostheme Dubois (laborer, 30, Canada) and Olivene Patrie (33, Canada); residence - Sanbornville

Annie M., b. 11/16/1901; fourth; Sostheme Dubois (laborer, Canada) and Olivia Patria (Canada)

Joseph, b. 7/3/1899; second; Sosthemi Dubois (Canada) and Olevin Poutrie (Canada); residence - Sanbornville

Joseph Arthur, b. 3/17/1903 in Sanbornville; seventh; Sostheme Dubois (laborer, 30, Canada) and Olivene Patrie (33, Canada); residence - Sanbornville

Mary, b. 10/30/1904; seventh; Sostheme Dubois (laborer, 31, Canada) and Olesina Patry (34, Canada)

Sothem, b. 6/15/1900; third; Sostheme Dubois (laborer, Canada) and Olive Patrie (Canada); residence - Sanbornville

DUCHANO,

daughter, b. 10/14/1926; first; Oscar Duchano (Wakefield) and Doris Pratt (Wolfeboro)

child, b. 12/30/1945; second; Oma Arthur Duchano (Sanbornville) and Muriel T. Wiggin (Ossipee)

child, b. 12/4/1953 in Wolfeboro; first; Donald Duchano (Wolfeboro) and Rosalyn Ring (Medford, MA)

Carole Joyce, b. 7/24/1947; first; Omer A.J. Duchano (Sanbornville) and Marjorie W. Williams (Malden, MA)

Cathy Elda, b. 1/22/1953 in Wolfeboro; second; Robert Joseph Duchano (NH) and Gloria M. Paolucci (NH)

Donald Rae, b. 9/25/1933 in Wolfeboro; Oscar J. Duchano and Doris E. Pratt

Helen Elizabeth, b. 1/31/1958 in Wolfeboro; second; Donald R. Duchano (Wolfeboro) and Rosalyn R. Ring (Medford, MA)

Joseph A.O., b. 2/3/1919; seventh; Mose Duchano (mason, 45, Canada) and Mary Welch (33, Salmon Falls); residence - Sanbornville

Joseph Oscar, b. 3/13/1907; fifth; Moses Duchina (sic) (laborer, 31, Canada) and Mary Welch (21, Salmon Falls)

Joseph Raymond, b. 6/3/1914; fifth; Moses Duchano (laborer, 39, Canada) and Marie Welch (29, Salmon Falls)

Karen Judith, b. 10/31/1963 in Wolfeboro; fifth; Donald R. Duchano (Wolfeboro) and Rosalyn R. Ring (Medford, MA)

Marie Alice, b. 1/17/1904; second; Moses Duchanno (sic) (laborer, 28, Canada) and Marie Welch (18, Salmon Falls)

Mary Irene, b. 2/27/1921; eighth; Mose Duchano (laborer, 46, Canada) and Mary Welch (36, Salmon Falls); residence - Sanbornville

Norman Peter, b. 11/8/1942; fifth; Oscar Joseph Duchano (Sanbornville) and Doris Evelyn Pratt (Ossipee)

Raymond Leo, b. 3/2/1917; sixth; Moses Duchano (RR employee, 41, Canada) and Mary Welch (32, Salmon Falls)

Richard Lewis, b. 4/4/1939; first; Omer A.J. Duchano (Wakefield) and Muriel Thelma Wiggin (Center Ossipee)

William Mose, b. 2/11/1952 in Rochester; second; Omer A.J. Duchano (Sanbornville) and Marjorie W. Williams (Malden, MA)

William Robert, b. 9/26/1959 in Wolfeboro; fourth; Donald R. Duchano (Wolfeboro) and Rosalyn R. Ring (Medford, MA)

DUCHESNEAU,

Laura Marie, b. 7/6/1911; fourth; Moses Duchesneau (laborer, 37, Quebec) and Marie Welch (26, Salmon Falls)

DUDLEY,

Candice Lynn, b. 8/17/1985 in Rochester; Kenneth A. Dudley and Lisa M. Glennon

Jason Alan, b. 11/27/1989 in Wolfeboro; Kenneth Alan Dudley and Lisa Mary Glennon

Jessica Theresa, b. 6/27/1977 in Dover; Richard L. Dudley and Constance M. Turgeon

Joseph Winburn, b. 3/8/1979 in Dover; Richard L. Dudley and Constance M. Turgeon

Michael Allen, b. 7/16/1995 in Wolfeboro; Kenneth Allen Dudley and Lisa Mary Glennon
Richard Lee, b. 1/18/1947; first; Fred W. Dudley (Rochester) and Frances C. Holmes (Dover)
Sandra Louise, b. 5/5/1948; second; Fred W. Dudley II (Rochester) and Frances C. Holmes (Dover)

DUFFANY,
Scott Alexis, b. 10/30/1958 in Wolfeboro; fifth; Thomas A. Duffany (Ctr. Ossipee) and Irene R. Ives (Willimantic, CT)

DUFFY,
Peter Joseph, b. 7/31/1992 in Rochester; Mark Peter Duffy and Linda Marie Jones

DUNN,
Frederick Demarest, b. 3/1/1932 in Wolfeboro; Robert H. Dunn and Sally Henning

DUPREY,
Edwin Tilden, b. 2/26/1924; third; Edwin T. Duprey (painter, Peabody, MA) and Minnie Bell (Canada)

DUQUETT,
daughter [Victoria M.], b. 4/4/1893; second; Leon Duquett (laborer, Canada) and Emma Hall (Canada)

DUTTON,
Dean Curtis, b. 10/30/1974 in Wolfeboro; Mark E. Dutton and Betty Ann Turner

DYER,
daughter [Lucie M.], b. 9/7/1905 in Sanbornville; ninth; Joseph Dyer (section hand, 36, Canada) and Edith Parent (33, Sainie, PQ); residence - Sanbornville
Fred Joseph, b. 2/9/1907; tenth; Joseph Dyer (laborer, 36, Quebec) and Edith Parent (33, Quebec)

DYMOND,
Cheri Jean, b. 6/11/1981 in Rochester; Charles A. Dymond and Christine J. Smith

EASTMAN,
Duane Michael, b. 8/11/1972 in Rochester; Harry H. Eastman, Jr. and Karen E. Karcher
Harold Alton, b. 9/1/1909; fifth; Arthur J. Eastman (teamster, 32, Bartlett) and Marion Swett (25, Fryeburg, ME)
Lori Anne, b. 1/23/1967 in Rochester; first; Harry Hanson Eastman (Rochester) and Karen E. Karcher (Rochester)
Madaline Grace, b. 9/9/1907; fourth; Arthur Eastman (laborer, 30, Bartlett) and Marion Swett (23, Fryeburg, ME)
Sherry Lynne, b. 1/17/1970 in Rochester; Harry H. Eastman, Jr. and Karen E. Karcher

EATON,
Ethel Ann, b. 2/13/1938; first; George William Eaton (Dorchester, MA) and Ethel Brenn (Hingham, MA)
John Irving, b. 11/10/1939; sixth; Gertrude Russell Eaton (Danvers, MA)

ECKHARDT,
John Carl, Jr., b. 5/9/1916; first; J. Carl Eckhardt (physician, 27, Washington, DC) and Ruth Tappan (25, Washington, DC)

EDGERLY,
Lloyd Arnez, b. 4/4/1953 in Rochester; fourth; Chester Guy Edgerly (Craftsbury, VT) and Ethel E. Hale (Stowe, VT)

ELDRIDGE,
Cheryl Marie, b. 9/18/1978 in Wolfeboro; Rodney W. Eldridge and Dorothy E. Dufault
Tanya Elaine, b. 10/27/1980 in Wolfeboro; Rodney W. Eldridge and Dorothy E. DuFault
Trista May, b. 4/25/1986 in Wolfeboro; Rodney W. Eldridge and Dorothy E. Dufault

ELLIOTT,
Christopher Michael, b. 2/2/1995 in Wolfeboro; Mark Allen Elliott, Sr. and Laura Jean Nason

Michael Almon, b. 6/13/1959 in Wolfeboro; first; Henry A. Elliott
(Wolfeboro) and Donna B. Drew (Acton, ME)
Milford Lauren, b. 10/3/1918; first; Herbert Kimball (putative father) and
Cora M. Elliott (18, Manchester)
Stanley Frank, b. 4/5/1919; sixteenth; Frank Elliott (teamster, 43,
Stoneham, MA) and Minnie Graton (44, Manchester)

ELLIS,

stillborn son, b. 9/14/1922; fourteenth; Henry P. Ellis (laborer, Gilmanton)
and Leila I. Patch (Newfield, ME)
Charles Patch, stillborn, b. 12/1/1921; fourteenth; Henry P. Ellis (laborer,
38, Gilmanton) and Lelia I. Patch (39, W. Newfield, ME)
Henry Page, Jr., b. 9/22/1923; fifth; Henry P. Ellis (laborer, Gilmanton
I.W.) and Lela I. Patch (W. Newfield, ME)
Horace Dana, b. 11/5/1918; first; Henry P. Ellis (carpenter, 35, Gilmanton)
and Lelia I. Patch (35, Newfield, ME)
John Henry, b. 9/1/1920; thirteenth; Henry P. Ellis (laborer, 36) and Lelia
Patch (38, W. Newfield, ME)

EMERSON,

son, b. 4/13/1901; third; Berton E. Emerson (lumberman, Raymond) and
Mary E. Kenney (Canada); residence - Middleton
Clara E., b. 1/19/1900; second; Herbert E. Emerson (saywer, Raymond)
and Mary E. Kennie (NB); residence - Union

EMERY,

Grace Campbell, b. 1/26/1891; third; W. Stanley Emery (clergyman,
Providence, RI) and Ethel N. Julian (St. Andrews, NB)
Margaret Therese, b. 4/27/1888; first; W. Stanley Emery (clergyman,
Providence, RI) and Ethel N. Julian (St. Andrews, NB)
Violet Catherine, b. 6/13/1889; second; William Stanley Emery
(clergyman, Portsmouth, RI) and Ethel Nauton (St. Andrews, NB)

EVANS,

Abbie Josephine, b. 11/7/1871; first; Albert Levi Evans (Wakefield) and
Hattie Goodale (Peabody, MA) (1939)
Clarence David, b. 1/17/1879; third; John William Evans (Wakefield) and
Nellie M. Farnham (Reading, MA) (1938)
Ida May, b. 4/8/1900; first; George Evans (printer) and Emma Watson
(Boston, MA)

Laura Abbie, b. 10/1/1869; first; John W. Evans (Wakefield) and Melvina Farnham (Salem, MA) (1940)
Leah Marie, b. 8/25/1993 in Rochester; Michael Travis Evans and Donna Marie Trainor
Richard, b. 10/29/1908; first; Victor C. Evans (farmer, 24, Wakefield) and Mattie Weeks (21, Wakefield)

EVELETH,
Brooke Miranda, b. 8/19/1980 in Wolfeboro; William A. Eveleth and Rebecca G. Sykie
Darren Eugene, b. 2/24/1979 in Rochester; William A. Eveleth and Brenda L. Runnells
Samantha Shine, b. 6/2/1982 in Sanbornville; William A. Eveleth and Rebecca G. Sykie
Samuel Crowell, b. 6/2/1982 in Sanbornville; William A. Eveleth and Rebecca G. Sykie

FALL,
Marguerite, b. 11/18/1912; first; Arthur S. Fall (clerk, 34, Ossipee) and Mary A. Carruthes (27, England)

FANTASIA,
Sandra Victoria, b. 3/29/1997 in Wolfeboro; Daniel Joseph Fantasia and Stacey Linda Muise

FARLEY,
Ayla Eva, b. 6/26/1996 in No. Conway; Michael Philip Farley and Ariane Sprengling

FARNHAM,
son, b. 10/25/1915; third; Albert J. Farnham (merchant, 43, Wakefield) and Lena Lowd (36, Acton, ME)
Annie Marjorie, b. 9/21/1875; Edward B. Farnham and Jennie Watts (1932)
Harry Manson, b. 9/18/1936; first; Harry Farnham (Acton, ME) and Pauline Horne (Acton, ME)
Hazel A., b. 12/1/1897; second; J. Frank Farnham (manufacturer, Acton, ME) and Ora Cutts (Milton)
Katie May, b. 7/31/1874; second; Edward B. Farnham (Wakefield) and Jennie H. Watt (North Hatley, Canada) (1938)

Norris A., b. 2/11/1907; second; Albert J. Farnham (carpenter, 35, Wakefield) and Lena M. Lowd (27, Acton, ME)

Ruby F., b. 7/25/1904; first; Albert J. Farnham (carpenter, 32, Wakefield) and Lena M. Lowd (24, Acton, ME)

Sarah Jean, b. 1/28/1991 in Dover; Robert Morrissey Farnham and Shirley Jean Huey

FARON,

David Loring, b. 1/26/1974 in Wolfeboro; Waldomar F. Faron and Sarah S. Reed

FELLOWS,

daughter [Ethel], b. 11/6/1890; sixth; Horatio B. Fellows (farmer, Wakefield) and Belle P. Tibbetts (Newfield, ME)

Celia Maria, b. 11/25/1875; second; Horatio Bartlett Fellows (Wakefield) and Belle Frances Tibbetts (Newfield, ME) (1941)

George, b. 7/29/1890; sixth; J. Porter Fellows (farmer, Wakefield) and Mary Abbie Pike (Wakefield)

Katherine K., b. 9/2/1915; fourth; John K. Fellows (freightman, 32, Peabody, MA) and Kate Tennelly (28, Peabody, MA)

Mildred Hazel, b. 12/29/1910; third; John K. Fellows (brakeman, 27, Peabody, MA) and Catherine Fennelly (24, Peabody, MA)

Oscar J., b. 11/9/1908; second; John K. Fellows (RR brakeman, 25, Peabody, MA) and Catherine Fennelly (21, Peabody, MA)

Sarah Minnie, b. 9/10/1875; first; James Porter Fellows (Wakefield) and Mary Abbie Pike (Middleton) (1940)

FERNALD,

Arthur Norman, b. 12/13/1893; second; William E. Fernald (merchant, Boston, MA) and Augusta M. Horn (Boston, MA)

Marjorie Claire, b. 4/29/1896; third; William E. Fernald (retail merchant, Boston, MA) and Augusta M. Hurn (Boston, MA)

FETH,

Bethani Marie, b. 1/9/1989 in Portsmouth; John Hartley Feth and Deborah Anne Duff

Chelsea Lynn, b. 10/20/1987 in Portsmouth; John Feth and Deborah A. Duff

FIELD[S],
Gordon Henry, b. 11/29/1915; fourth; Rene E. Field (shipping clerk, 23, Boston, MA) and Elsie H. Zimmer (23, Boston, MA)
Hazel Elizabeth, b. 8/22/1913; second; Rene Fields (laborer, 21, Boston, MA) and Elsie Zimmer (21, Boston, MA)
Rene Eugene, b. 11/29/1915; third; Rene E. Field (shipping clerk, 23, Boston, MA) and Elsie H. Zimmer (23, Boston, MA)

FIFIELD,
Barbara Ann, b. 4/20/1945; fifth; Charles R. Fifield (Wakefield) and Louise Drapeau (Cedar Grove, ME)
Bryan Leslie, b. 7/13/1982 in Rochester; Leslie H. Fifield and Cynthia G. Thomas
Charles Russell, b. 6/7/1914; first; George Fifield (laborer, 29, Conway) and Blanche Penney (22, Porter, ME)
Charles Russell, b. 5/22/1942; third; Charles Russell Fifield (Wakefield) and Louise Drapeau (Cedar Grove, ME)
Francis Henry, b. 11/1/1917; third; George R. Fifield (farmer, 32, Conway) and Blanche E. Penney (25, Porter, ME)
Frank Herbert, b. 9/13/1952 in Wolfeboro; first; George R. Fifield, Jr. (Wakefield) and Lavina Brewer (Winchendon, MA)
George Russell, b. 4/25/1925; sixth; George R. Fifield (Conway) and Blanche Penney (Porter, ME)
Harriet Lavina, b. 10/25/1953 in Wolfeboro; second; George Russell Fifield, Jr. (NH) and Lavina Brewer (MA)
Herman James, b. 12/28/1915; second; George R. Fifield (farmer, 31, Conway) and Blanche Penney (23, Porter, ME)
Leslie Herman, b. 7/19/1956 in Rochester; fourth; George R. Fifield (Wakefield) and Lavina Brewer (Winchendon, MA)
Louise May, b. 6/27/1928; seventh; George R. Fifield (Conway) and Blanche Penney (Porter, ME)
Mary Louise, b. 12/13/1946; sixth; Charles R. Fifield (Wakefield) and Louise Drapeau (Cedar Grove, ME)
Mildred Roberta, b. 2/19/1920; fourth; George R. Fifield (farmer, 35, Conway) and Blanche E. Penney (27, Porter, ME)
Mildred Rosetta, b. 12/2/1954 in Rochester; third; George Russell Fifield, Jr. (Wakefield) and Lavina Brewer (Winchendon, MA)
Robert Alfred, b. 4/5/1944; fourth; Charles R. Fifield (Wakefield) and Louise Drapeau (Cedar Grove, ME)

Sarah Jane, b. 11/26/1922; fifth; George R. Fifield (farmer, Conway) and Blanch Penney (Porter, ME)

Tammi Leigh, b. 5/3/1970 in Rochester; Charles R. Fifield and Judith L. Turbide

Tina Louise, b. 5/22/1968 in Wolfeboro; Charles R. Fifield and Judith L. Turbide

FIORE,

Cody James, b. 7/5/1994 in Rochester; Steven James Fiore and Patricia Elaine Pike

FISHER,

Andrew John Frederick, b. 11/21/1983 in Wolfeboro; John F. Fisher and Mary L. Welch

Bonnie Mae, b. 4/3/1955 in Wolfeboro; fourth; Frederick Fisher (MA) and Helen Inez Meserve (NH)

Brittany Erin, b. 7/8/1985 in Wolfeboro; John F. Fisher and Mary L. Welch

Bruce Meserve, b. 9/1/1953 in Wolfeboro; third; Frederick Fisher (MA) and Helen I. Meserve (NH)

Harold Joseph, b. 10/24/1960 in Wolfeboro; seventh; Frederick Fisher (Needham, MA) and Helen I. Meserve (Wakefield)

Jason Hal, b. 7/16/1984 in Rochester; Harold J. Fisher and Cheri A. Yeaton

John Frederick, b. 10/19/1948; first; Frederick Fisher (Needham, MA) and Helen I. Meserve (Wakefield)

Mary Lee, b. 9/5/1956 in Wolfeboro; fifth; Frederick Fisher (Needham, MA) and Helen G. Meserve (Wakefield)

Michael Joseph, b. 1/19/1982 in Rochester; Harold J. Fisher and Cheri A. Yeaton

Paulette, b. 11/10/1951; second; Frederick Fisher (MA) and Helen G. Meserve (NH)

Sarah Eileen, b. 12/22/1988 in Portland, ME; Bruce Meserve Fisher and Susan Eileen Stewart

Tiffani Ann, b. 6/1/1988 in Rochester; Harold J. Fisher and Cheri A. Yeaton

Wendy Lucille, b. 2/22/1958 in Wolfeboro; sixth; Frederick Fisher (Needham, MA) and Helen I. Meserve (Wakefield)

FITZ,
Carl Westley, b. 4/27/1891; first; Mark S. Fitz (engineer, Salisbury, MA) and Augusta S. Rines (Wakefield)
Frank, b. 10/22/1906; first; Frank Fitz (mine supt., 37, Woodland, CA) and Helena Richardson (35, Boston, MA); residence - Cienequita, Mexico
Harry Mark, b. 9/13/1899; third; Mark S. Fitz (RR engineer, Amesbury, MA) and Augusta S. Rines (Wakefield); residence - Sanbornville
Maurice Gale, b. 5/17/1901; fourth; Mark S. Fitz (engineer, Amesbury, MA) and Augusta S. Rines (Wakefield); residence - Sanbornville
Rolond Bartlett, b. 7/13/1893; second; Mark S. Fitz (engineer, Salisbury, MA) and Augusta S. Rines (Wakefield)
Russell Norman, b. 5/16/1903; fifth; Mark S. Fitz (engineer, 38, Amesbury, MA) and Augusta S. Rines (36, Wakefield); residence - Sanbornville

FLETCHER,
Richelle Ruth, b. 7/27/1970 in Rochester; Richard I. Fletcher and Diane R. Dodier

FLOOD,
Benjamin Seymour, b. 2/11/1996 in Wolfeboro; David Arthur Flood and Louise Anne Seymour
Sebastian Seymour, b. 2/13/1998 in Wolfeboro; David Arthur Flood and Louise Anne Seymour

FLOYD,
Helen Elizabeth, b. 2/28/1932 in Sanbornville; John D. Floyd, Jr. and Edith M. Nason

FLYNN,
Kathleen Elizabeth, b. 7/21/1947; second; Stanley A. Flynn (Naples, ME) and Reta E. Bean (No. Conway)

FOGG,
Daniel Edwin, b. 11/5/1939; third; Raymond Daniel Fogg (Ossipee) and Lois Chipman (Milton)
Kaylee Ann, b. 6/25/1998 in Dover; Nathan Robert Fogg and Deborah Ann Otto

Kendra Rennee, b. 6/8/1991 in Rochester; Kenneth Robert Fogg and
    Michelle Diane Mooney
Kody Robert, b. 7/26/1998 in Wolfeboro; Kenneth Robert Fogg, II and
    Dolores Veronica Hodge
Relf Gregory, b. 5/8/1961 in Wolfeboro; third; Neil S. Fogg (Haverhill,
    MA) and Ruth E. LeGeyt (Hartford, CT)
Sara Rae, b. 3/9/1984 in Wolfeboro; Relf G. Fogg and Annette Rae Propp
Seth Otto, b. 6/30/1995 in Dover; Nathan Robert Fogg and Deborah Ann
    Otto
Victoria Lee, b. 10/12/1965 in Wolfeboro; first; Kenneth R. Fogg
    (Wolfeboro) and Sandra A. Nason (Wolfeboro)

FOLLMER,
Gayle Marie, b. 11/8/1963 in Wolfeboro; second; Samuel F. Follmer
    (Bloomsburg, PA) and Margaret H. Holman (Arlington, MA)

FOOTE,
Lowell Sanborn, b. 6/2/1891; first; Arthur L. Foote (lawyer, Lewiston,
    ME) and Carrie B. Sanborn (Somersworth)

FORD,
Gordon Mark, b. 1/3/1955 in Wolfeboro; second; Donald Edward Ford
    (MA) and Patricia L. Buckland (MA)
Kimberly Barbara, b. 1/7/1987 in Rochester; Paul R. Ford and Kelly J.
    Bickford
Susanne, b. 6/13/1953 in Rochester; first; Donald Edward Ford
    (Bryantville, MA) and Patricia L. Buckland (Plymouth, MA)

FOSTER,
son, b. 7/6/1889; fifth; Collie Foster (laborer, Canada) and Louisa G. -----
    (Canada)

FOX,
Cynthia Belle, b. 2/28/1957 in Rochester; first; Marshall H. Fox (Sanford,
    ME) and Priscilla P. Drew (Union)
Harvey Dunham, b. 9/21/1933 in Sanford, ME; Arthur Fox and Isabelle
    Fox
Kerry Marshall, b. 2/25/1960 in Rochester; second; Marshall H. Fox
    (Sanford, ME) and Priscilla P. Drew (Union)

Sarah Anne, b. 4/27/1990 in Rochester; Kerry Marshall Fox and Annette Louise Gagnon

William Arthur, b. 1/21/1993 in Rochester; Kerry Marshall Fox and Annette Louise Gagnon

FREEMAN,

son, b. 9/14/1894; fourth; William C. Freeman (salesman, Cambridge, MA) and Elizabeth Morrison (Roxbury, MA); residence - Brooklyn, NY

Everett Orvis, b. 8/18/1898; second; Everett K. Freeman (clerk, NS) and Helen S. Fursden (NB)

Mary Mildred, b. 9/1/1896; first; E. K. Freeman (clerk, Kempt, NS) and Helen M. Fursden (Frederickton, NB)

FUEHRER,

Robert George, b. 9/12/1961 in Rochester; first; Robert C. Fuehrer (New York, NY) and Dorothy S. Ward (Caribou, ME)

FURBISH,

Hollie Noel, b. 12/26/1974 in Rochester; Michael Furbish and Deborah Diane Day

FYFFE,

Richard Norman, b. 5/30/1972 in Wolfeboro; Richard Fyffe and Norma G. Samuelson

GAGE,

Edith Helen, b. 9/27/1891; first; James Lester Gage (expressman, Wakefield) and Hannah Demeritt (Durham)

Elizabeth, b. 3/17/1877; fourth; George Gage (Dover) and Lydia J. Bennett (Wolfeboro) (1935)

Eric Alexander, b. 7/24/1971 in Rochester; Raymond A. Gage and Darlene J. Leigh

GAGNE,

Fred, b. 11/20/1903; third; Joseph Gagne (laborer, 32, Canada) and Josephine LaClare (35, Canada); residence - Sanbornville

Heidi Lynn, b. 12/9/1980 in Rochester; Alan J. Gagne and Karen S. Lodge

Joseph, b. 4/6/1902 in Sanbornville; third; Joseph Gagne (laborer, 32, Canada) and Josephine LaClair (34, Canada); residence - Sanbornville

Richard Allan, b. 2/21/1943; twelfth; Harold Prentice Gagne (E. Orford, ME) and Fayelyn Mae Cousens (Lewiston, ME)

GAGNON,
son, b. 1/4/1893; fourth; Ernest Gagnon (laborer, Canada) and Georgiana Legary (Wakefield)
son [Arthur, Jr.], b. 12/1/1893; first; Arthur Gagnon (laborer, Canada) and Adaline Patrie (Canada)
son, b. 10/11/1917; fifth; Joseph Gagnon (laborer, 34, Lewiston, ME) and Fidelia Lefay (27, Canada)
son, b. 12/8/1926; fourth; Arthur Gagnon (Wakefield) and Grace Laverture (Lewiston, ME)
Albert Arthur, b. 6/21/1922; second; Arthur Gagnon (trainman, Wakefield) and Grace Lavertu (Wakefield)
Anna, b. 7/23/1890; first; Ernest Gagneon (sic) (laborer, Canada) and Georgiana Legary (Wakefield)
Anna Elizabeth, b. 5/27/1921; first; Arthur E. Gagnon (brakeman, 28, Wakefield) and Grace E. Lavertee (21, Wakefield); residence - Sanbornville
Arthur Aristide, b. 11/30/1908; first; Ameda Gagnon (carpenter, 30, Canada) and Demerise M. Lamie (21, Wakefield)
Constance Marie, b. 10/26/1942; second; Alfred Joseph Gagnon (Sanbornville) and Marie Rose Buchette (Lynn, MA)
David Lee, b. 12/11/1939; second; Oscar Ernest Gagnon (Wakefield) and Viola Ruth Downs (Portsmouth)
Donald, b. 12/11/1939; third; Oscar Ernest Gagnon (Wakefield) and Viola Ruth Downs (Portsmouth)
Emily M., b. 11/25/1895; second; Eugene Gagnon (laborer, Canada) and Amanda Butler (Canada)
Jacqueline May, b. 3/29/1941; second; Alfred Joseph Gagnon (Wakefield) and Marie Rose Buchette (Lynn, MA)
Joseph E.O., b. 5/12/1900; eighth; Ernest Gagnon (laborer, Canada) and Georgia LeGerry (Union); residence - Sanbornville
Joseph E.O., b. 7/27/1901; fourth; Eugene Gagnon (laborer, Canada) and Amanda Butler (Canada); residence - Sanbornville
Joseph Eugene, b. 3/4/1898; seventh; Ernest Gagnon (laborer, Canada) and Georgina Legare (Canada)
Joseph Lorenzo, b. 4/29/1908; thirteenth; Ernest Gagnon (laborer, 40, Canada) and Georgia LeGerry (35, Wakefield)

Leo Ernest, b. 9/13/1923; third; Arthur L. Gagnon (brakeman, Wakefield) and Grace Lavertu (Wakefield)

Marie Alice, b. 8/29/1906; twelfth; Ernest Gagnon (laborer, 38, Canada) and Georgia LeGarry (34, Union)

Mary, b. 6/6/1897; Arthur Gagnon (laborer, Canada) and Adeline Partrie (Canada)

Mary A., b. 11/30/1894; fifth; Ernest Gagnon (laborer, Canada) and Georgia LeGary (Canada)

Mary Amanda, b. 12/17/1897; third; Eugene Gagnon (laborer, Canada) and Amanda Butler (Canada)

Mary Eczelia, b. 8/4/1906; seventh; Eugene Gagnon (laborer, 41, Canada) and Amanda Butler (32, Canada)

Mary Eva, b. 6/8/1904; tenth; Ernest Gagnon (laborer, 42, Canada) and Georgia Legary (35, Wakefield)

Mary Lucia, b. 3/22/1905 in Sanbornville; sixth; Ludger Gagnon (laborer, 40, Canada) and Mandy Butler (31, Canada); residence - Sanbornville

Meeddie Joseph, b. 6/6/1905 in Sanbornville; eleventh; Ernest Gagnon (laborer, 37, Canada) and Georgia Legerry (33, Wakefield); residence - Sanbornville

Orril, b. 5/12/1902 in Sanbornville; ninth; Ernest Gagnon (laborer, 34, Canada) and Georgia Legary (30, Sanbornville); residence - Sanbornville

Roger Bruce, b. 8/1/1941; fourth; Oscar Ernest Gagnon (Wakefield) and Viola Ruth Downs (Portsmouth)

Ronald Alfred, b. 5/25/1935; first; Alfred J. Gagnon (Sanbornville) and Marie R. Buchette (Lynn, MA)

Victor LeGarey, b. 11/25/1896; sixth; Ernest Gagnon (laborer, Canada) and Georgia LeGarey (Canada)

Virginia Rose, b. 6/10/1946; fifth; Oscar E. Gagnon (Sanbornville) and Viola R. Downs (Portsmouth)

Wilfred, b. 4/18/1903 in Sanbornville; fifth; Eugene Gagnon (laborer, 38, Canada) and Manda Butler (29, Canada); residence - Sanbornville

GALABRUN,
Kristin Mae, b. 4/10/1981 in Wolfeboro; Jean Galabrun and Margaret Lamke

GARJAIL,
Richard A., b. 5/30/1929; first; Arthur Garjail (E. Lebanon, ME) and Charlotte R. Wiggin (Wakefield)

GARLAND,
son, b. 9/24/1921; second; Arthur Garland (shoe dealer, 39, Sanbornville) and Mary Drew (22, Wolfeboro); residence - Sanbornville

Agatha, b. 10/19/1896; first; Wilbur Garland (laborer, Brookfield) and Hattie M. Avery (Wolfeboro)

Amey Lynn, b. 10/15/1971 in Wolfeboro; Corliss F. Garland and Gail Wiedeman

Andrew Roland, b. 11/3/1995 in Rochester; Brian Andrew Garland and Janice Louise Golden

Arthur Albert, b. 5/24/1951; first; Willis F. Garland (NH) and Marjory A. Williston (ME)

Babetta Rose, b. 1/4/1948; first; Forrest A. Garland (Sanbornville) and Patricia A. Witham (Dover)

Bessie Ethel, b. 6/10/1907; seventh; Fred Garland (laborer, 28, Brookfield) and Hattie M. West (29, Brookfield)

Brian Andrew, b. 3/29/1968 in Wolfeboro; Roland E. Garland and Alice L. Creamer

Bruce Clyde, b. 4/20/1952 in Wolfeboro; first; Earl F. Garland (NH) and Gloria G. McNally (MA)

Catherine Louise, b. 8/23/1955 in Rochester; first; Paul David Garland (Wolfeboro) and Shirley L. Adjutant (Wolfeboro)

Cindy Lee, b. 5/18/1961 in Rochester; third; Paul D. Garland (Wolfeboro) and Shirley L. Adjutant (Wolfeboro)

Corliss Frank, b. 12/12/1943; seventh; Fred E. Garland (Sanbornville) and Verlie E. Tufts (Sanbornville)

Dawn Robin, b. 6/5/1963 in Wolfeboro; second; Robert G. Garland (Sanbornville) and Judith M. Robinson (Freedom)

Deborah Lynne, b. 11/11/1964 in Wolfeboro; first; Terry R. Garland (Rochester) and Suzanne B. French (Milton Mills)

Denise Linette, b. 5/8/1971 in Wolfeboro; Terry R. Garland and Suzanne B. French

Doreen Leigh, b. 7/26/1968 in Wolfeboro; Terry R. Garland and Suzanne French

Doris Marion, b. 1/29/1906; sixth; Fred Garland (section hand, 27, Brookfield) and Harrie M. West (28, Brookfield)

Dorothy M., b. 9/26/1915; eleventh; Fred Garland (laborer, 37, Brookfield) and Hattie M. West (37, Brookfield)

Earl Francis, b. 3/14/1925; second; Fred E. Garland (Wakefield) and Verlie Tufts (Wakefield)

Earle Norman, b. 7/21/1947; fourth; Russell W. Garland (Sanbornville) and Rita A. Chantany (East Barnet, VT)

Ernest E., b. 12/6/1899; second; Fred Garland (laborer, Brookfield) and Hattie M. West (Brookfield)

Florence Mildred, b. 6/21/1913; first; Olive A. Garland (17, Wolfeboro)

Forrest Arthur, b. 10/28/1920; first; Arthur A. Garland (shoe dealer, 38, Sanbornville) and Mary Drew (21, Wolfeboro); residence - Sanbornville

Forrest Arthur, Jr., b. 9/29/1950; second; Forrest A. Garland (Sanbornville) and Patricia A. Witham (Dover)

Fred L., b. 6/25/1901; third; Fred L. Garland (laborer, Brookfield) and Hattie West (Brookfield)

George F., b. 10/9/1867; John F. Garland (Wakefield) and Ellen B. Garland (Durham, PQ)

Gloria Jean, b. 8/26/1946; first; Willis F. Garland (Sanbornville) and Virginia R. Wilson (Malden, MA)

Guy West, b. 12/10/1897; first; Fred Garland (laborer, Brookfield) and Hattie M. West (Brookfield)

Harold Edwin, b. 1/24/1910; eighth; Fred Garland (laborer, 31, Brookfield) and Hattie M. West (32, Brookfield)

Helen M., b. 4/21/1930; fourth; Fred E. Garland (Sanbornville) and Verlie E. Tufts (Wakefield)

Herbert C., stillborn, b. 5/9/1905 in Sanbornville; first; Chester A. Garland (RR employee, 24, Brookfield) and Vera M. Colbath (20, Conway); residence - Sanbornville

James Francis, b. 5/4/1955 in Rochester; third; Forrest Arthur Garland (Sanbornville) and Patricia Ann Witham (Dover)

Kenneth Warren, b. 11/26/1935; fifth; Fred Garland (Sanbornville) and Verlie Tufts (Sanbornville)

Michelle Lee, b. 3/24/1980 in Wolfeboro; Robert W. Garland and Kathryn A. Donnelly

Mildred Elizabeth, b. 11/20/1921; first; Fred E. Garland (track man, 20, Sanbornville) and Verlie E. Tufts (17, Sanbornville); residence - Sanbornville

Morey Scott, b. 1/6/1945; second; Howard A. Garland (Sanbornville) and Ruth F. Hutchinson (Athol, MA)

Paul David, b. 2/26/1937; first; Arthur A. Garland (Sanbornville) and Marion Davis (Sanbornville)

Paul David, Jr., b. 7/11/1958 in Rochester; second; Paul D. Garland (Wolfeboro) and Shirley L. Adjutant (Wolfeboro)

Robert Irving, b. 11/8/1938; sixth; Fred Earl Garland (Sanbornville) and
   Verlie E. Tufts (Sanbornville)
Robert Warren, b. 1/27/1961 in Wolfeboro; first; Robert I. Garland
   (Sanbornville) and Judith M. Robinson (Freedom)
Roland Everett, b. 11/7/1927; third; Fred E. Garland (Wakefield) and
   Verlie Tufts (Wakefield)
Roy Lloyd, b. 9/18/1911; ninth; Fred Garland (laborer, 33, Brookfield) and
   Hattie West (33, Brookfield)
Russell W., b. 10/29/1912; tenth; Fred Garland (laborer, 34, Brookfield)
   and Hattie M. West (34, Brookfield)
Ruth Willett, b. 3/13/1916; first; Bernice M. Garland (18, Wolfeboro)
Sandra Louise, b. 10/30/1943; third; Russell William Garland
   (Sanbornville) and Rita Arlene Champany (E. Barnet, VT)
Sharron Ann, b. 9/19/1949; fifth; Russell W. Garland (Sanbornville) and
   Rita A. Champney (East Barnet, VT)
Stanley Lloyd, b. 10/1/1917; twelfth; Fred Garland (laborer, 39,
   Brookfield) and Hattie West (39, Brookfield)
Terry Raymond, b. 10/25/1942; first; Forrest Arthur Garland
   (Sanbornville) and Rita Elizabeth Bean (North Conway)
Terry Raymond, Jr., b. 2/7/1978 in Wolfeboro; Terry R. Garland and
   Suzanne French
Timothy Robin, b. 6/28/1963 in Wolfeboro; first; Roland E. Garland
   (Sanbornville) and Alice L. Creamer (Gore, GA)
Tina Louise, b. 8/12/1973 in Wolfeboro; Corliss F. Garland and Gail
   Wiedeman
Wayne Alan, b. 5/16/1965 in Wolfeboro; third; Robert I. Garland
   (Sanbornville) and Judith M. Robinson (Freedom)
Willis Frank, b. 9/2/1922; third; Arthur Garland (shoe dealer, Wakefield)
   and Mary Drew (Wolfeboro); residence - Sanbornville

GARVIN,
stillborn daughter, b. 1/18/1888; fifth; James W. Garvin (merchant,
   Wakefield) and Charlotte Maleham (Wakefield)
son [Richard], b. 11/14/1927; third; James P. Garvin (Wakefield) and
   Rosanna Hill (Newfield, ME)
Charlotte Rosana, b. 12/6/1891; seventh; James W. Garvin (merchant,
   Wakefield) and Charlotte J. Maleham (Wakefield)
Joan, b. 8/3/1926; second; Josiah D. Garvin (Wakefield) and Annie J.
   Perkins (New Durham)

John H., Jr., b. 11/26/1897; first; John H. Garvin (merchant, Wakefield) and Kate P. Dow (Salem, MA)

Josiah Dow, b. 4/16/1899; second; John H. Garvin (merchant, Wakefield) and Kate P. Dow (Salem, MA); residence - Sanbornville

Josiah Dow, b. 12/10/1924 in Sanbornville; first; Josiah Dow Garvin (teamster, Sanbornville) and Annie J. Perkins (New Durham); residence - Sanbornville

Mary Almira, b. 3/9/1890; sixth; James W. Garvin (merchant, Wakefield) and Charlotte J. Malham (Wakefield)

Mary Elizabeth, b. 1/10/1925; first; John H. Garvin, Jr. (Wakefield) and Grace E. Dowd (Holyoke, MA)

GAUTHIER,

Diane Faye, b. 12/5/1953 in Wolfeboro; second; Armand Joseph Gauthier (NH) and Pauline S. Welch (Ctr. Ossipee)

Homer Arthur, b. 10/25/1919; second; Rosaire C. Gauthire (sic) (laborer, 28, Canada) and Jennie Welch (22, Salmon Falls); residence - Sanbornville

Joseph Armand, b. 10/30/1926; fourth; Rosaire Gauthier (Canada) and Jennie Welch (So. Berwick, ME)

Leo, b. 7/2/1917; first; Rosaire Gauthier (RR employee, 27, Canada) and Jennie Welch (20, So. Berwick, ME)

Mary Alice Jennie, b. 11/24/1923; third; Rosaire Gauthier (trackman, Canada) and Jennie Welch (Salmon Falls)

Sherry-lee Mary, b. 11/19/1950; first; Armand J. Gauthier (Sanbornville) and Pauline S. Welch (Ctr. Ossipee)

GAYAUD,

Adrien Andre Joseph, b. 6/10/1982 in Rochester; Sylvestre A.B. Gayaud and Chantal D.M. Louesdon

GEARY,

Philip Edward, Jr., b. 10/26/1963 in Wolfeboro; second; Philip Edward Geary (Wolfeboro) and Selma Jane Emerson (Pittsfield)

GEHRING,

Austin Richard, b. 1/4/1995 in Wolfeboro; Robert Dana Gehring and Ann Louise Weismann

Robert Henry, b. 12/3/1984 in Wolfeboro; Robert D. Gehring and Ann L. Weismann

GELINAS,
Mark Eugene, b. 12/12/1953 in Rochester; first; Albert Louis Gelinas (Farmington) and Mildred Elizabeth Drown (Wakefield)

GENTILE,
Raina Emerentiana, b. 11/10/1998 in Wolfeboro; Phil A. Gentile and Nicole Emerentiana Giacalone

GEOTIS,
Taylor James, b. 11/25/1990 in Rochester; Philip Geotis and Barbara Ellen Wallace

GERARD,
Angela Marie, b. 6/1/1974 in Wolfeboro; William P. Gerard and Katherine A. Elwell
Cheryl Lynn, b. 9/6/1968 in Wolfeboro; Randolph J. Gerard, Jr. and Linda A. Mooney
Erik Jonathon, b. 7/24/1975 in Wolfeboro; Randolph J. Gerard and Linda A. Mooney
Harry Arnold, b. 4/29/1948; first; Randolph J. Gerard (Boston, MA) and Phyllis E.C. Drown (Wakefield)
Scott Anthony, b. 11/23/1970 in Wolfeboro; Randolph J. Gerard, Jr. and Linda A. Mooney
Sharon Alyce, b. 11/23/1970 in Wolfeboro; Randolph J. Gerard, Jr. and Linda A. Mooney
William Paul, b. 10/12/1951; third; Randolph Gerard (Boston, MA) and Phyllis E.C. Drown (Wakefield)
William Paul, Jr., b. 8/7/1977 in Rochester; William P. Gerard and Katherine A. Elwell

GERRISH,
Thad David, b. 5/2/1977 in Sanford, ME; David P. Gerrish and Doris E. Bragg

GILBERT,
daughter, b. 2/11/1892; third; Napoleon Gilbert (laborer, Canada) and Mary Couture (Canada)
Eunice May, b. 5/8/1914; second; Herbert W. Gilbert (painter, 35, Lynn, MA) and Gretchen Ware (21, Lynn, MA)

GILLEY,
Chynna Brie, b. 1/29/1990 in Concord; Calvert Baline Gilley and Donnal Angelique Marie Rattee

GILLIS,
David Michael, b. 2/13/1984 in Wolfeboro; Ronald B. Gillis and Wanda L. Dansereau

GILMAN,
daughter, b. 11/22/1892; second; John B. Gilman (brakeman, Ossipee) and Ethel M. Lane (Wakefield)
Annie May, b. 8/23/1891; first; John B. Gilman (brakeman, Tamworth) and Ethel M. Lane (Wakefield)
Cody Lloyd, b. 10/16/1994 in Rochester; Jeffrey Carl Gilman and Kellie Ann Carpenter

GINTER,
Kate Allison, b. 11/14/1986 in Rochester; Charles A. Ginter, III and Pamela H. Jones

GLENNON,
Chad William, b. 10/31/1978 in Rochester; Patrick W. Glennon and Valerie J. Hall
Janice Maria, b. 3/18/1957 in Rochester; fifth; Wesley J. Glennon (Malden, MA) and Harriette L. Karcher (Wolfeboro)
Jennifer Ann, b. 10/12/1967 in Rochester; first; Wesley J. Glennon, Jr. (Rochester) and Helen M. Luscomb (Wolfeboro)
Joseph Michael Edward, b. 9/21/1980 in Rochester; Patrick W. Glennon and Valerie J. Hall
Kristopher Patrick James, b. 5/5/1977 in Rochester; Patrick W. Glennon and Valerie J. Hall
Lauretta Pamela, b. 7/24/1953 in Rochester; fourth; Wesley Joseph Glennon (Malden, MA) and Harriette L. Karcher (East Wolfeboro)
Liza Mary, b. 1/8/1964 in Rochester; eighth; Wesley J. Glennon (Malden, MA) and Harriette L. Karcher (East Wolfeboro)
Patricia Joan Marie, b. 2/27/1985 in Rochester; Patrick W. Glennon and Valerie J. Hall
Patrick William, b. 3/26/1951 in Sanbornville; third; Wesley Joseph Glennon (Malden, MA) and Harriett L. Karcher (East Wolfeboro)

Richard M., Jr., b. 10/5/1973 in Dover; Richard M. Glennon and Patricia
J. Brochu
Richard Michael, b. 2/22/1950; second; Wesley J. Glennon (MA) and
Harriette L. Karcher (NH)
Thomas Anthony, b. 2/15/1958 in Rochester; seventh; Wesley J. Glennon,
Sr. (Melrose, MA) and Harriette L. Karcher (Wolfeboro)
Timothy Allen, b. 2/15/1958 in Rochester; sixth; Wesley J. Glennon, Sr.
(Melrose, MA) and Harriette L. Karcher (Wolfeboro)
Wesley Joseph, Jr., b. 3/31/1948; first; Wesley J. Glennon (Malden, MA)
and Harriette L. Karcher (East Wolfeboro)

GLIDDEN,
David Neal, b. 10/12/1983 in Rochester; Danny K. Glidden and Jean M.
Stanley
Eugene E., b. 8/25/1869; twelfth; John H. Glidden (Effingham) and Abbie
Young (Wakefield) (1937)
Inez Lilla, b. 7/17/1892; first; Eugene E. Glidden (blacksmith, Wakefield)
and Tillie A. Libby (Brookfield)
Josie B., b. 6/2/1879; first; Jerome A. Glidden (teamster, 23, Wakefield)
and Dora G. Wentworth (18, Cranston, RI) (1919)
Sydney A., b. 5/13/1888; fourth; Jerome A. Glidden (teamster, 32,
Wakefield) and Dora G. Wentworth (27, Cranston, RI) (1919)
Victoria Rose, b. 10/25/1990 in Wolfeboro; Michael Paul Glidden and
Brooke Willett

GOGGIN,
Brittney Nila, b. 5/17/1989 in Portsmouth; Daniel James Goggin and
Michele Nila Lavanway
Ryan Patrick, b. 10/26/1986 in Portsmouth; Daniel J. Goggin and Michele
N. LaVanway
Shawn Michael, b. 5/21/1995 in Dover; Daniel James Goggin and Michele
Nila Lavanway

GOODWIN,
son [Harry S.], b. 1/20/1887; second; Hilton S. Goodwin (laborer, Acton,
ME) and Estella L. Campbell (Wakefield)
son [Ray T.], b. 9/16/1888; third; Hilton S. Goodwin (laborer, Acton, ME)
and Estella L. Campbell (Wakefield)
Mattie Hazel, b. 12/16/1891; first; Charles F. Goodwin (fireman,
Bucksport, ME) and Bertha H. Andrews (Great Falls)

Pauline M., b. 3/24/1905 in Union; fourth; Hilton S. Goodwin (railroad hand, Acton, ME) and Estella L. Campbell (Wakefield); residence - Union

GOSLIN,
Kacey Rae, b. 8/23/1983 in Rochester; Garry M. Goslin and Janice A. Arsenault

GOULD,
Jonathan James, b. 1/13/1989 in Rochester; James Joseph Gould, III and Donna Marie Hoffman

GOYETTE,
stillborn daughter, b. 6/4/1897; fourth; George Goyette (laborer, Canada) and Arthemise Gauthier (Canada)

GRAFF,
daughter, b. 5/8/1910; fifth; Joe Graffe (sic) (laborer, 45, Russia) and J. Marunkunzer (29, Russia)
Broneslow, b. 5/28/1907; third; Joseph Graft (sic) (laborer, 42, Russia) and Tad'gs Marcindwich (25, Russia)
Jennie Nellie, b. 7/12/1904; second; Joseph E. Graff (teamster, 39, Russia) and Jennie L. Graff (23, Russia) (1918)

GRAHAM,
Kyle Otto, b. 4/3/1983 in Cleveland, OH; David M. Graham and Mary M. Ratliff

GRAY,
Donald Francis, b. 1/20/1960 in Rochester; third; Frank N. Gray (Rochester) and Jean C. Chretien (Rochester)
Dorothy Marion, b. 7/15/1916; first; Robert Gray (painter, 20, Gonic) and Marion Morrison (18, Somerville, MA)
Jaimy Adam, b. 9/24/1988 in Wolfeboro; John F. Gray, III and Jutta R. Keller
John Frank, III, b. 4/23/1958 in Rochester; second; Frank N. Gray (Rochester) and Jean C. Chretien (Rochester)
John Robert, b. 3/2/1992 in Rochester; Craig Robert Gray and Kirsten Elizabeth Lygren

Nicholas John, b. 12/2/1983 in Wolfeboro; Donald F. Gray and Charlene B. Hall

GREGOIRE,
Anthony Gerard, b. 8/29/1975 in Rochester; Gerard J. Gregoire and Donna L. Scala
Eric Patrick, b. 3/16/1997 in Rochester; Eric Scot Gregoire and Sarah Anne Wilkinson

GRENIER,
Taylor Christian, b. 1/23/1993 in Dover; Marshall G. Grenier and Stacey L. Husson

GRIFFIN,
Emily Ann, b. 6/1/1984 in Rochester; Michael E. Griffin and Robin M. Borner

GRIFFITH,
Heather Lee, b. 8/18/1966 in Dover; first; Weston H. Griffith (Newburg, OR) and Nancy L. Wiggin (Rochester)
Weston Harris, Jr., b. 9/21/1967 in Dover; second; Weston H. Griffith (Newberg, OR) and Nancy Lee Wiggin (Rochester)

GUILMETTE,
David Jonathan Patrick, b. 7/24/1989 in Dover; Richard David Guilmette and Eleanor Dennis

GUTH,
Kristin Elizabeth, b. 1/23/1989 in Rochester; Mark Lincoln Guth and Sandra Ann Lasseter

HACKETT,
Thomas Philip Robert, b. 2/8/1993 in No. Conway; Thomas James Hackett and Susan Eliza Morrill

HADDOCK,
Charles William, b. 10/26/1890; third; George C. Haddock (laborer, Lebanon, ME) and Etta J. Hill (Bartlett)

HAINES,
son, b. 12/26/1888; first; Hattie Haines (Wakefield)

HALDERMAN,
Nathaniel James, b. 1/9/1984 in Portsmouth; Richard D. Halderman and Brenda G. Jones

HALEY,
Roy Curtis, Jr., b. 7/26/1973 in Rochester; Roy Curtis Haley and Carlene Evelyn Gould

HALL,
daughter, b. 8/6/1888; first; Fred Hall (laborer, Canada) and Mary Dugat (Canada)
Alyssa Paige, b. 4/9/1991 in Rochester; Gregory Wayne Hall and Denise Elizabeth Joy
Ashley Annette, b. 1/11/1985 in Rochester; Gregory W. Hall and Denise E. Joy
Frank Wiggin, b. 4/9/1877; second; Charles H. Hall (Wakefield) and Maria Chapman (Acton, ME) (1942)
Fred Kendall, b. 12/4/1913; fourth; Perley Hall (laborer, 31, Sawyer River, VT) and Myrtle Sprague (25, Springvale, ME)
Harold Ellsworth, b. 8/28/1915; fifth; Perley Hall (farmer, 25, Sawyers River, VT) and Myrtle Sprague (27, Springvale, ME)
Hazen Jay, b. 2/18/1903; first; Frank W. Hall (farmer, 25, Wakefield) and Mary A.S. Wilson (26, Moncton, NB); residence - Union
Heidi Ann, b. 10/25/1977 in Rochester; Kenneth A. Hall, Jr. and Carrie Taylor
Julia Marie, b. 7/4/1989 in Wolfeboro; James Henry Hall, III and Virginia Ruth Morrill
Kyle Gregory, b. 5/4/1995 in Wolfeboro; Gregory Wayne Hall and Denise Elizabeth Joy
Nathan Timothy, b. 2/15/1997 in Rochester; Timothy Hall and Nicola Jutta Elliott

HALLAM,
Jeremy Nichole, b. 1/16/1980 in Wolfeboro; Timothy D. Hallam and Janice S. Sciarpelletti

HALLORAN,
Kailan Tracey, b. 9/29/1986 in Wolfeboro; Robert H. Halloran and Carol L. Hayworth

HALLOWELL,
Jennifer, b. 3/14/1974 in Wolfeboro; Bruce J. Hallowell and Mary Merritt

HAMILTON,
stillborn son, b. 3/31/1894; second; John S. Hamilton (section man, Conway) and Sadie M. Doyle (Wakefield)
stillborn daughter, b. 12/14/1898; fourth; John E. Hamilton (laborer, Eaton) and Sadie M. Doyle (Wakefield)
stillborn daughter, b. 7/22/1903 in Sanbornville; fifth; John E. Hamilton (RR employee, 37, Conway) and Sadie M. Doyle (29, Wakefield); residence - Sanbornville
Elizabeth, b. 12/16/1929; first; Harry Hamilton (Dover) and Mary E. Calhoun (Boiestown, NB)
Ernest Erville, b. 4/26/1891; first; John E. Hamilton (laborer, Conway) and Sarah M. Doyle (Wakefield)
Raymond E., b. 3/3/1897; third; John E. Hamilton (laborer, Conway) and Sadie M. Doyle (Wakefield)

HAMLIN,
stillborn daughter, b. 2/26/1892; second; Edwin F. Hamlin (manufacturer, Boston, MA) and Josephine Littlefield (Portsmouth)

HAMMOND,
Carl, b. 12/20/1901; first; George L. Hammond (merchant, Tamworth) and Lena A. Hill (Parsonsfield, ME)
John Wayne, Jr., b. 8/7/1965 in Rochester; first; John W. Hammond (Sanbornville) and Roberta A. Leighton (Union)
John William, b. 12/1/1946; first; Robert T. Hammond (Acton, ME) and Lillian M. Hammond (Brookfield)
Kenneth Lloyd, b. 4/24/1904; second; George L. Hammond (merchant, 28, Tamworth) and Lena A. Hill (24, Parsonsfield, ME)
Robert Edwin, b. 9/3/1966 in Rochester; second; John W. Hammond (Wolfeboro) and Roberta A. Leighton (Rochester)

HANEY,
son, b. 5/11/1894; William A. Haney (laborer, Plymouth) and Addie A. Avery (Wolfeboro)

HANIS,
Lisa Marie, b. 12/26/1967 in Rochester; Kenneth W. Hanis and Emelia J. Dion

HANSCOM[B],
Gladys, b. 3/11/1896; third; Frank Hanscom (mill hand, Middleton) and Julia Reed (Wakefield)
Minerva, b. 1/24/1892; first; John H. Hanscom (operative, Middleton) and Julia O. Reed (Wakefield)
Rose Elizabeth, b. 1/15/1875; second; Reuben Hanscom (No. Berwick, ME) and Elizabeth M. Earl (Acton, ME) (1943)
Waverly, b. 3/17/1895; second; Frank Hanscomb (moulder, Middleton) and Julia Reed (East Wakefield)

HANSEN,
Dirck, b. 1/8/1945; first; William Hansen (Boston, MA) and Fanny E. Fletcher (Acton, ME)
Lisa Louise, b. 11/7/1950; fourth; William Hansen (Boston, MA) and Fanny E. Fletcher (Acton, ME)
Marna, b. 5/30/1946; second; William Hansen (Boston, MA) and Fanny E. Fletcher (Acton, ME)
Mary Ellen, b. 11/4/1947; third; William Hansen (Boston, MA) and Fannie E. Fletcher (Acton, ME)
William, Jr., b. 9/28/1951; fifth; William Hansen (MA) and Fanny E. Fletcher (ME)

HANSON,
daughter, b. 4/11/1890; first; Joseph H. Hanson (brakeman, Brookfield) and Lucretia Weeks (Brookfield)
son, b. 5/29/1892; third; Sidney I. Hanson (brakeman, Wakefield) and Mary T. Johnson (Wakefield)
daughter, b. 3/3/1894; second; William F. Hanson (laborer, Middleton) and Maud Johnson (New Durham)
Barbara Belle, b. 3/16/1920; third; Ralph W. Hanson (B&M watchman, 27, Wakefield) and Lois Mary Knight (20, Wakefield)

Donald Karl, b. 11/11/1924; fifth; Ralph W. Hanson (foreman ice co.,
    Wakefield) and Marjory Knight (Wakefield); residence - Sanbornville
Edward Marshall, b. 9/15/1946; third; Ralph W. Hanson, Jr. (Sanbornville)
    and Arlene F. Day (Berlin)
Eileen Mary, b. 7/29/1948; fourth; Ralph W. Hanson, Jr. (Sanbornville)
    and Arline F. Day (Berlin)
Mabel M., b. 10/17/1900; second; L. Hanson (mill hand, Ossipee) and
    Addie Shackford (Porter, ME)
Marion A., b. 9/3/1916; second; Ralph Hanson (store keeper, 24,
    Wakefield) and Marion McCrillis (23, Wakefield)
Mary Elizabeth, b. 3/12/1932 in Rochester; Ralph W. Hanson and L.
    Marjorie Knight
Philip Sidney, b. 4/12/1914; first; Ralph W. Hanson (clerk, 21, Wakefield)
    and Marion A. McCrillis (20, Wakefield)
Ralph Waldo, b. 6/20/1922; fourth; Ralph W. Hanson (clerk, Wakefield)
    and Lois Marjory Knight (Wakefield)
Robert Sidney, b. 10/16/1936; first; Philip S. Hanson (Sanbornville) and
    Ruth E. Horne (No. Shapleigh, ME)
Scott Mitchell, b. 12/30/1988 in Dover; Mitchell L. Hanson and Marie Ann
    Dupuis

HARDEN,
daughter, b. 1/25/1890; first; Charles Harden (laborer, Burlington, VT) and
    Mary A. Copp (Wakefield)

HARDING,
Melvin, b. 3/27/1895; first; Charles Harding (laborer, Denmark, ME) and
    Nellie M. Dyer (Brownfield, ME)

HARRIS,
Lana Elaine, b. 4/4/1941; first; Russell Lionel Harris (Mexico, ME) and
    Gladys May Reed (Wakefield)
Lance Wayne, b. 6/3/1943; second; Lionel Russell Harris (Canton, ME)
    and Gladys Mary Reed (Union)
Michael Scott, b. 1/30/1992 in Dover; Scott Daniel Harris and Stephanie
    Anne Schwarz
Thelma Pearl, b. 9/17/1939; second; Rex Wendal Harris (So. Rumford,
    ME) and Jennie Mae Reel (Acton, ME)

HART,
daughter [Bertha E.], b. 10/5/1887; third; Loammi Hart (farmer, Eaton) and Hannah W. Harmon (Freedom)
daughter [Lula P.], b. 1/28/1889; fourth; Loami Hart (farmer, Eaton) and Hannah W. Harmon (Freedom)
son [Walter H.], b. 12/19/1891; sixth; Loammi Hart (farmer, Eaton) and Hannah H. Harmon (Freedom)
daughter, b. 5/25/1900; eighth; Loammi Hart (teamster, Eaton) and Hannah U. Hammond (Freedom)
child, b. 4/8/1913; third; Lulu Hart (23, Wakefield)
Blanche Isabel, b. 9/9/1890; fifth; Loanni Hart (farmer, Eaton) and Hannah H. Harmon (Freedom)
Mary Olive, b. 7/3/1896; seventh; Loammi Hart (farmer, Eaton) and Hannah Harmon (Freedom)
Walter Hubbard, Jr., b. 1/28/1922; first; Walter H. Hart (RR brakeman, Wakefield) and Hazel Hamm (Farmington); residence - East Wakefield

HARTFORD,
daughter, b. 1/29/1908; first; Levi Hartford (laborer, 26, Deerfield) and Annie M. McConnell (17, Manchester)
daughter, b. 2/1/1908; fifth; Perley W. Hartford (laborer, 34, Deerfield) and Sadie J. Thompson (25, Haverhill, MA)

HARVEY,
Kenneth S., b. 3/18/1894; first; William S. Harvey (telegrapher, Newfoundland) and Maud Chamberlin (Newfoundland)
LeRoy Southerland, b. 10/12/1897; fourth; W. S. Harvey (telegrapher, Newfoundland) and Maud S. Cambers (Newfoundland)
Steward L., b. 9/26/1895; second; William L. Harvey (telegrapher, Newfoundland) and Maud L. Chambers (Newfoundland)

HASKELL,
Christian James, b. 3/30/1996 in Wolfeboro; Rhodes Clifford Haskell, Jr. and Kimberley Sue Philbrook
Devon Joseph, b. 9/28/1994 in Wolfeboro; Rhodes Clifford Haskell and Kimberly Sue Philbrook

HASTINGS,
Burleigh Taylor, b. 3/4/1992 in Rochester; Gerald Paul Hastings and Stephanie Marie Dostie

HATCH,
Norman Leslie, stillborn, b. 4/15/1912; fourth; Herbert O. Hatch (brakeman, 31, Wolfeboro) and Ethel G. Nute (30, Milton)
Walter Waldo, b. 12/11/1918; fourth; Herbert O. Hatch (brakeman, 37, Wolfeboro) and Ethel Nute (36, Milton)

HAYDEN,
Lillian Ethellinda, b. 2/17/1906; second; William Hayden (teamster, 32, Boston, MA) and Etta P. Burnham (22, Saco, ME)
William Clarence, b. 1/1/1908; third; William F. Hayden (laborer, 34, Boston, MA) and Etta P. Burnham (24, Saco, ME)

HAYES,
daughter, b. 8/15/1887; first; Joseph E. Hayes (job teamster, Wolfeboro) and Grace L. Haines (Wakefield)
Bert Alexander K., b. 12/30/1916; second; Arthur Hayes (laborer, 29, Suncook) and Josephine Field (17, Avon, CT)
Dorris Abbie, b. 6/28/1898; fourth; Joseph E. Hayes (hotel keeper, Wolfeboro) and Grace L. Haines (Wakefield)
Eva Clara, b. 12/6/1892; second; Joseph E. Hayes (truckman, Wolfeboro) and Grace L. Haines (Wakefield)
Francis Richard, Jr., b. 7/9/1960 in Melrose, MA; first; Francis R. Hayes (Lynn, MA) and Rose C.D. Piano (Malden, MA)
Joseph E., b. 6/21/1897; third; Joseph E. Hayes (hotel keeper, Wolfeboro) and Grace L. Haines (Wakefield)

HAYNES,
Iris Fay, b. 8/4/1909; first; Charles L. Haynes (clerk, 25, Wakefield) and Verna E. Merrow (22, Bridgton, ME)
Ruby Louise, b. 8/1/1909; second; Edwin M. Haynes (tinsmith, 28, Laconia) and Mary E. Fields (20, Conway)
Shirley May, b. 9/2/1906; first; Edward Haynes (tinsmith, 25, Laconia) and Mary E. Fields (17, Conway)

HAYWARD,
Alden Eric, b. 12/11/1990 in Rochester; Alden Frederick Hayward and Janna Marie Jerome
Jacob Alan, b. 10/9/1987 in Rochester; Donald H. Hayward and Jennifer M. Downs
Jonathan Donald, b. 4/12/1982 in Rochester; Donald H. Hayward and Jennifer M. Downs

HEALY,
Cody James, b. 6/1/1993 in Wolfeboro; Timothy Edward Healy and Candace Lenore Loring
Timothy Russell, b. 5/14/1989 in Rochester; Timothy Edward Healy and Candace Renore Loring

HEATH,
daughter, b. 6/29/1891; first; Talmon S. Heath (Newfield, ME) and Caddie M. Stevens (Parsonsfield, ME)
daughter, b. 3/6/1893; first; Charles D. Heath (brass finisher, Parsonsfield, ME) and Maud G. Sanborn (Wakefield)
son, b. 3/12/1924 in Union; fifth; Charles E. Heath (brass finisher, Parsonsfield, ME) and Marion L. Harnden (Denmark, ME); residence - Union
Cecil Newton, b. 2/26/1906; second; Charles E. Heath (blacksmith, 37, Parsonsfield, ME) and Maude G. Sanborn (30, Union)
Erwin Leslie, b. 6/9/1911; first; Charles E. Heath (blacksmith, 42, Parsonsfield, ME) and Marion L. Harnden (23, Denmark, ME)
Leona Virginia, b. 4/3/1925; sixth; Charles E. Heath (Parsonsfield, ME) and Marion L. Harden (Denmark, ME)
Lucian, b. 10/11/896; fourth; Talman Heath (laborer, Newfield, ME) and Caddie M. Stevens (Parsonsfield, ME)
Mattie Maria, b. 12/10/1894; third; Talmon S. Heath (mill hand, Newfield, ME) and Caddie M. Stevens (Parsonsfield, ME)
Myrtle Marion, b. 10/30/1917; fourth; Charles E. Heath (blacksmith, 49, Parsonsfield, ME) and Marion L. Harnden (29, Denmark, ME)
Ruby Emma, b. 5/29/1893; second; Talmon S. Heath (brass finisher, Newfield, ME) and Caddie M. Stevens (Parsonsfield, ME)
Sidney J., b. 8/18/1916; third; Charles E. Heath (blacksmith, 47, Parsonsfield, ME) and Marion L. Harnden (28, Denmark, ME)
Thelma Pearl, b. 1/24/1913; second; Charles E. Heath (blacksmith, 44, Parsonsfield, ME) and Marion L. Harnden (25, Denmark, ME)

HEBERT,
Kari Beth, b. 3/24/1980; Alfred A. Hebert, Jr. and Anita M. Gaugher
Thomas Alan, b. 12/5/1990 in Dover; Roger Martin Hebert and Susan
    Marie Turner

HELANDER,
Dawn Marie, b. 3/16/1967 in Brockton, MA; second; Carl F. Helander, Jr.
    (Brockton, MA) and Nancy E. Willis (Beverly, MA)

HEMARD,
Rebecca Louise, b. 1/18/1972 in Wolfeboro; Lawrence F. Hemard and
    Suzy Lee Snoddy

HENDERSON,
Fay Ann, b. 10/9/1959 in Rochester; second; Ronald E. Henderson
    (Rochester) and Mary R. Head (Warm Springs, GA)
Michael Earl, b. 11/25/1956 in Rochester; first; Ronald E. Henderson
    (Rochester) and Mary R. Head (Warm Springs, GA)
Timothy James, b. 12/1/1983 in Rochester; Timothy Henderson and
    Christine M. Bonoyer

HERMONAT,
Connor Sullivan, b. 5/23/1998 in Dover; William Andrew Hermonat and
    Kimberly Sue Ross
Spencer Travis, b. 1/6/1997 in Dover; William Andrew Hermonat and
    Kimberly Sue Ross
William Andrew, IV, b. 11/7/1995 in Dover; William Andrew Hermonat,
    III and Kimberly Sue Ross

HERRICK,
George, b. 10/12/1933 in Rochester; George Herrick and Edith Nason

HERVIEUX,
Gregory Raymond, b. 2/8/1984 in Nashua; Gerard R. Hervieux and Judith
    A. Blease

HICKEY,
Adam Jacob, b. 10/20/1977 in Dover; Daniel J. Hickey and Constance A.
    Kastberg

HIGH,
Rebecca Lynn, b. 7/22/1977 in Rochester; John G. High and Cheryl L. Wilkins

HILL,
daughter, b. 4/12/1914; second; Claudian F. Hill (clerk, 25, Boston, MA) and Ella M. Hart (17, Wakefield)
daughter, b. 12/13/1919; first; John K. Hill (hotel clerk, 31, Lynn, MA) and Dorothy L. Tibbetts (18, Brookfield); residence - North Wakefield
son, b. 7/4/1924 in Union; second; Waldo L. Hill (brass foundry, Wakefield) and Viola Kimball (Middleton)
daughter, b. 10/24/1925; third; Waldo Hill (Wakefield) and Vila Kimball (Middleton)
Almon Douglas, b. 1/5/1871; third; Asa Washington Hill (Wakefield) and Matilda Frances Jones (Wakefield) (1941)
Bessie Luciana, b. 4/22/1920; first; Peter Hill (laborer, 21, West Newfield, ME) and Verlie E. Tufts (25, Wakefield); residence - Sanbornville
Craig Matthew, b. 10/4/1988 in Rochester; Craig Hill and Lorna L. Smith
Greta Evelyn, b. 6/20/1911; third; Leslie Hill (brass finisher, 27, Parsonsfield, ME) and Ellen Willey (22, Wakefield)
Harry Morton, b. 12/11/1912; first; Claudian F. Hill (clerk, 24, Boston, MA) and Ella M. Hart (16, Wakefield)
Helen Silvia, b. 9/18/1916; fourth; Leslie Hill (brass finisher, 33, Parsonsfield, ME) and Ellen E. Willey (27, Wakefield)
Herbert Donald, b. 5/21/1920; thirteenth; Lewis Hill (farmer, 55, W. Newfield, ME) and Rose Patch (41, W. Newfield, ME); residence - W. Newfield, ME
Justin Thomas, b. 4/10/1990 in Dover; Alfred James Hill and Marybeth Towle
Laura Jean, b. 10/28/1972 in Rochester; Roland G. Hill and Joyce L. Hayward
Leon Waldo, b. 11/13/1904; first; Leon Hill (mill operative, 21, Effingham) and Ellen E. Willey (15, Wakefield)
Lottie May, b. 11/15/1897; third; Carlton M. Hill (laborer, Tamworth) and Laura J. Tibbetts (Wolfeboro)
Margaret Isabel, b. 7/7/1890; seventh; David D. Hill (carpenter, Canada) and Margaret T. Adams (Scotland)
Megan Elise, b. 11/25/1987 in Dover; Alfred James Hill, Jr. and Marybeth Towle

Ormand Adam Dekoto, b. 12/13/1891; second; David D. Hill (carpenter, Canada) and Margaret F. Adams (Scotland)

Owen Reginald, b. 9/15/1909; second; Leslie Hill (brass finisher, 25, Parsonsfield, ME) and Ellen E. Willey (21, Wakefield)

Pammie Lou, b. 6/15/1961 in Rochester; fourth; Wallace F. Hill (Wakefield) and Pauline A. Dodier (Biddeford, ME)

Patricia Mae, b. 12/14/1946; first; Wallace F. Hill (Wakefield) and Pauline A. Dodier (Biddeford, ME)

Pearl Frances, b. 10/28/1906; first; Leon Hill (brass finisher, 22, Parsonsfield, ME) and Florence E. Lord (16, Shapleigh, ME)

Penny Lee, b. 9/23/1957 in Rochester; third; Wallace F. Hill (Wakefield) and Pauline A. Dodier (Biddeford, ME)

Phyllis Fannie, b. 7/13/1916; third; Claudian F. Hill (manufacturer, 28, Boston, MA) and Ella May Hart (20, Wakefield)

Scott Alan, b. 1/11/1970 in Rochester; Alfred J. Hill and Dorothy A. Smith

Teresia Louise, b. 12/30/1912; second; Carroll C. Hill (teamster, Rockland, ME) and Ruth E. Libby (Newfield, ME)

Virginia May, b. 5/12/1922; second; John K. Hill (hotel manager, Lynn, MA) and Dorothy J. Tibbetts (Brookfield); residence - North Wakefield

Wayne Edward, b. 5/25/1949; second; Wallace F. Hill (NH) and Pauline A. Dodier (ME)

HILMAN,

Ashlee Nacole, b. 7/10/1997 in Wolfeboro; John M. Hilman and Judith A. Miller

HINKLEY,

Justin Everett, b. 5/4/1979 in Portsmouth; Bruce E. Hinkley and Virginia A. Brennan

HINDS,

son, b. 4/23/1921; sixth; David C. Hinds (laborer, 35, NS) and Flora L. Steele (36, PEI); residence - Sanbornville

HOBBS,

Harley Russell, b. 11/4/1961 in Wolfeboro; third; Howard G. Hobbs (Hampton) and Violet H. Kimball (Sanbornville)

Holly Lou, b. 8/16/1957 in Rochester; first; Howard G. Hobbs (Hampton) and Violet H. Kimball (Sanbornville)

Howard Theodore, b. 9/19/1959 in Wolfeboro; second; Howard G. Hobbs (Hampton) and Violet H. Kimball (Sanbornville)

HODGDON,
Dorris Estelle, b. 9/2/1899; third; George H. Hodgdon (carpenter, Parsonsfield, ME) and Sarah Y. Glidden (Wakefield)
Sumner Myron, b. 2/12/1898; fourth; Horace S. Hodgdon (fireman, No. Auburn, ME) and Therese Harmon (Hollis, ME)
William Francis, b. 9/27/1891; second; Horace S. Hodgdon (laborer) and Theresa Harmon (Hollis, ME)

HODGKINS,
Ruth Maude, b. 7/5/1903; fourth; Charles F. Hodgkins (laborer, 36, Gorham, ME) and Minnie J. Hersom (35, Lebanon, ME)

HODSDON,
son, b. 6/20/1888; third; Charles T. Hodsdon (laborer, So. Berwick, ME) and Emma L. Swasey (Ossipee)
Eliot Edson, b. 9/27/1894; third; Horace S. Hodsdon (fireman, Parsonsfield, ME) and Theresa Harmon (Hollis, ME)
Harold Edward, b. 7/1/1893; second; George H. Hodsdon (carpenter, Parsonsfield, ME) and Sarah Glidden (Wakefield)
Jimmie O., b. 6/13/1898; first; Jesse F. Hodsdon (laborer, No. Berwick, ME) and Mary L. Drew (Brookfield)
Martha E., b. 12/5/1901; fifth; Horace S. Hodsdon (RR fireman, Parsonsfield, ME) and Terese Harmon (Hollis, ME)

HOISINGTON,
Jennifer Anne, b. 4/5/1974 in Rochester; Edmond S. Hoisington and Nancy I. Leske

HOOPER,
Carrol, b. 8/10/1915; third; John E. Hooper (RR engineer, 36, Boxford, MA) and Alice E. Wilkins (26, Acton, ME)
Christina, b. 8/17/1912; second; John E. Hooper (engineer, 33, Boxford, MA) and Edna A. Wilkins (23, Acton, ME)
Hattie May, b. 9/1/1893; ninth; Charles E. Hooper (farmer, Somersworth) and Nellie J. Downs (Milton)
Jesse, b. 7/3/1895; eighth; Everett C. Hooper (farmer, Somersworth) and Nellie J. Downs (Wakefield); residence - South Wakefield

Jessica Ann, b. 5/7/1985 in No. Conway; Randy P. Hooper and Karen S. Nason

John Homer, b. 3/1/1921; fourth; John E. Hooper (42, Boston, MA) and Edna A. Wilkins (32, Acton, ME); residence - Sanbornville

Kathleen Louise, b. 3/6/1984 in Wolfeboro; Randy P. Hooper and Karen S. Nason

Randy Paul, Jr., b. 1/17/1988 in Rochester; Randy Paul Hooper and Karen Sally Nason

Robert Wilkins, b. 12/9/1909; first; John E. Hooper (fireman, 30, Boxford, MA) and Edna Wilkins (20, Acton, ME)

Stephen John, b. 3/4/1989 in Wolfeboro; Randy Paul Hooper and Karen Sally Nason

HOPPLE,
Cassandra Lee, b. 8/31/1982 in Wolfeboro; Thomas E. Hopple and Julie E. Morgan

HORN,
Amanda Lee, b. 9/3/1988 in Rochester; Vaun E. Horn and Deborah L. Cheney

Carroll Ann, b. 12/17/1957 in Rochester; fifth; Clyde H. Horn (Acton, ME) and June E. Runnels (Union)

Jessica Storm Smith, b. 2/8/1993 in Rochester; Vaun Eugene Horn and Deborah Lee Cheney

Richard Arnold, b. 8/8/1949; second; Arnold L. Horn (ME) and Catherine M. French (NH)

Rodney Allan, b. 1/5/1951; third; Clyde H. Horn (Acton, ME) and June E. Runnells (NH)

Sheri Lynn, b. 10/6/1956 in Rochester; fourth; Clyde H. Horn (Acton, ME) and June E. Runnels (Union)

Wendy Lorraine, b. 8/6/1949; second; Clyde H. Horn (ME) and June E. Runnells (NH)

Wilbur Henry, b. 4/14/1863; John Jackson Horn and Edith Helen Deshown (1933)

HORNE,
son, b. 5/29/1889; first; Edwin H. Horne (RR fireman, Wakefield) and Hannah Runnels (Acton, ME)

Bertha Louise, b. 4/10/1865; first; Horace Horne (NH) and Susan Kimball (Portsmouth) (1937)

Charles Edwin, b. 3/14/1941; second; Charles Edwin Horne (Marblehead, MA) and Elizabeth H. Wentworth (W. Newfield, ME)
Sharon Lee, b. 9/15/1944; first; Archie A. Horne (Wolfeboro) and Mary Erna Hansen (Boston, MA)

HOUDE,
Ellen Aurellia, b. 3/28/1910; first; Edward J. Houde (laborer, 27, Wakefield) and Mary A. Drapeau (22, Wakefield)
Francis Albert, b. 7/22/1927; eighth; Edward J. Houde (Wakefield) and Anna M. Drapeau (Wakefield)
Homer Louis, b. 7/20/1913; second; Edward Houde, Jr. (laborer, 31, Wakefield) and Annie Drapeau (27, Wakefield)
Irene Gloria, b. 12/11/1924 in Sanbornville; sixth; Edward J. Houde (pumpman B and M, Sanbornville) and Mary Ann Drapeau (Sanbornville); residence - Sanbornville
Joseph Aimie, b. 10/13/1918; third; Edward J. Houde (pumpman, 36, Wakefield) and Annie Drapeau (31, Wakefield)
Leo Philip, b. 5/19/1926; seventh; Edward J. Houde (Wakefield) and Anna Drapeau (Wakefield)
Marie Regina, b. 5/29/1920; fourth; Edward J. Houde (pumpman B&M, 37, Wakefield) and Anna M. Drapeau (32, Wakefield); residence - Sanbornville
Mary Lucy, b. 5/28/1885; second; Edward Houde (Canada) and Adele Pouliot (Canada) (1937)
Virginia Stella, b. 2/2/1923; fifth; Edward Houde (pumpman B and M, Wakefield) and Anna Drapeau (Wakefield); residence - Sanbornville

HOUGHTON,
Wallace Everett, b. 3/22/1942; second; Virgil Nute Houghton (Littleton) and Mabel Florence Wheeler (Londonderry)

HOUSEL,
Jack Ryan, b. 8/8/1991 in Rochester; William Joseph Housel, III and Deborah Jean Rollins

HOWARD,
Jed Michale, b. 12/24/1980 in Wolfeboro; Michale L. Howard and Cynthia M. Rouleau
Nicholas Edward, b. 5/18/1987 in Dover; William E. Howard and Maureen E. Johnson

Ryan Edward, II, b. 7/12/1987 in Rochester; Ryan E. Howard and Janice M. Radcliffe

HOWE,
son, b. 2/19/1923; third; Scott E. Howe (laborer, Laconia) and Hazel G. Reed (Wakefield); residence - Union

Dennis Allen, b. 6/30/1939; eighth; Edmund Scott Howe (Laconia) and Hazel Gertrude Reed (Wakefield)

Doris Bell, b. 3/13/1922; second; Scott Howe (lineman, Laconia) and Hazel Reed (Wakefield); residence - Union

Edwin Eugene, b. 3/16/1921; first; Scott E. Howe (laborer, 31, Laconia) and Hazel Reed (19, Wakefield); residence - Union

Evelyn G., b. 10/29/1930; sixth; Edmund S. Howe (Laconia) and Hazel Reed (Wakefield)

Henry W., b. 3/8/1901; fifth; George W. Howe (laborer, ND) and Hattie L. Ray (Canada)

John Tanner, b. 11/23/1993 in Rochester; Steven Earl Howe and Laurie Ann Mullin

Unice May, b. 1/25/1925; fourth; Scott E. Howe (Laconia) and Hazel G. Reed (Union)

Willis Edmund, b. 9/27/1932 in Wolfeboro; Scott Edmund Howe and Hazel Reed

HOWLAND,
Ernest Melvin, b. 8/14/1920; first; Fred Howland (carpenter, 47) and Edna M. Curry (18, Milton Mills); residence - Crystal

HOYT,
Angela Beth, b. 10/3/1986 in Rochester; Wayne F. Hoyt and Susan A. Dearborn

Benjamin Winfield, b. 7/22/1924; second; Benjamin W. Hoyt (laborer, Dover) and Matilda M. Bell (Lyndonville, VT); residence - Dover

HUCKINS,
Wesley Everett, b. 11/1/1968 in Rochester; Everett E. Huckins and Anita M. Stone

HUDSON,
James G., b. 3/25/1900; first; William Arthur Hudson (clergyman, Chestertown, MD) and Ella Evans (Lempster); residence - North Wakefield

HULL,
Chandler Eagle, b. 7/21/1992 in Wolfeboro; Dana Hull and Lolene Louise Palmer
Christian John, b. 5/29/1994 in Wolfeboro; Dana Eagle Hull and Lolene Louise Palmer
Cyrus Alden, b. 11/9/1998 in Wolfeboro; Dana Eagle Hull and Lolene Louise Palmer
Gloria Dawn, b. 10/16/1995 in Wolfeboro; Dana Eagle Hull and Lolene Louise Palmer

HUNT,
Howard Arthur, b. 7/10/1871; first; Henry K. Hunt (Providence, RI) and Mary F. Canney (Ossipee) (1936)

HUNTRESS,
son, b. 1/22/1892; first; Stillman S. Huntress (sectionman, Harmony, ME) and Emma Richards (Harmony, ME)
Eliza Spring, b. 8/4/1977 in Rochester; Charles H. Huntress and Terri L. Brooks

HURD,
Albertina, b. 12/28/1901; first; Isaac Hurd (laborer, Canada) and Rosa Marcoux (Wakefield)
Arthur Philbert, b. 11/6/1909; sixth; Isaac Hurd (laborer, 32, Quebec) and Rosie Marcoux (26, Wakefield)
Avon Ida, b. 2/25/1903 in Sanbornville; second; Isaac Hurd (laborer, 26, Canada) and Rosa Marcou (20, Sanbornville); residence - Sanbornville
Doris Phoebe, b. 11/15/1906; fifth; Isaac Hurd (laborer, 30, Canada) and Rosa A. Marcoux (23, Sanbornville)
Florence Evelyn, b. 2/9/1913; ninth; Issac Hurd (laborer, 37, Canada) and Rosa Marcoux (30, Wakefield)
Frank, b. 1/24/1908; sixth; Isaac Hurd (laborer, 31, Canada) and Rosie Marcoux (25, Wakefield)
Kristine Anne, b. 12/29/1968 in Wolfeboro; Alton M. Hurd and Gloria J. Potvin

Leo Edward, b. 9/20/1917; tenth; Isaac Hurd (laborer, 41, Canada) and Rose Marcoux (34, Wakefield)

Lillian Arline, b. 3/16/1919; eleventh; Isaac Hurd (laborer, 42, Canada) and Rosa Marcoux (36, Wakefield)

Louis Filbert, b. 11/19/1905 in Sanbornville; fourth; Isaac Hurd (laborer, 29, Canada) and Rosie Marcoux (23, Sanbornville); residence - Sanbornville

Mabel Mary, b. 5/28/1911; eighth; Isaac Huard (laborer, 34, Canada) and Rosie Marcoux (28, Wakefield)

Penny Lou, b. 12/12/1969 in Rochester; Alton M. Hurd and Gloria J. Potvin

Wilfred Oscar, b. 2/1/1904; third; Isaac Hurd (laborer, 29, Canada) and Rosie Marcou (20, Wakefield)

HUSSEY,
Kenneth Russell, IV, b. 4/6/1980 in Rochester; Kenneth R. Hussey, III and Patricia M. Barrett

Matthew David, b. 6/21/1980 in Rochester; David R. Hussey and Beverly M. Cressey

Rhett Butler, b. 4/13/1973 in Rochester; Philip Hussey, Jr. and Donna L. Labrecque

HUSTUS,
Melody Lynn, b. 10/23/1976 in Rochester; Bruce T. Hustus and Sally J. Cunningham

HUTCHINS,
son [Raymond], b. 4/23/1888; first; Samuel L. Hutchins (manufacturer, Wakefield) and Mary A. Corson (Wakefield)

daughter, b. 1/20/1908; third; Roy E. Hutchins (lumber mill, 28, Alexandria) and Jennie J. Moore (22, Candia)

Cynthia Ann, b. 8/6/1957 in Wolfeboro; second; Paul B. Hutchins (Wolfeboro) and Carolyn M. Welch (Pittsfield)

Ellen Mae, b. 6/10/1956 in Wolfeboro; first; Paul B. Hutchins (Wolfeboro) and Carolyn M. Welch (Pittsfield)

Frank Herbert, b. 4/19/1856; second; Hiram W. Hutchins (Wakefield) and Mary F.D. Neal (Brookfield) (1941)

Jamie L., b. 8/16/1959 in Dover; fifth; William E. Hutchins (Grantham) and Mary E. Jackson (Fayetteville, NC)

Joseph Hiram, b. 11/1/1897; second; Edwin H. Hutchins (farmer, Wakefield) and Iva E. Linscott (Newfield, ME)
Marian Louise, b. 8/10/1930; third; Bernard S. Hutchins (Wakefield) and Teresa Hayes (Tuftonboro) (1939)
Mary G., b. 1/8/1888; first; Frank Hutchins (Wakefield) and Mary A. Davis (Wakefield) (1931)
Mary Walker, b. 1/25/1906; second; Maurice B. Hutchins (vet. surgeon, 45, Wakefield) and Alice C. Walker (28, Wakefield)
Mason Edwin, b. 12/30/1883; first; Edwin D. Hutchins (Dover) and Iva E. Linscott (Maplewood, ME) (1938)
Nancy Jane, b. 6/21/1932 in Wolfeboro; Bernard Hutchins and Teresa Hayes
Nancy Lee, b. 7/16/1958 in Wolfeboro; third; Paul B. Hutchins (Wolfeboro) and Carolyn M. Welch (Pittsfield)
Patricia Jane, b. 12/11/1961 in Wolfeboro; fifth; Paul B. Hutchins (Wolfeboro) and Carolyn M. Welch (Pittsfield)
Paul Bernard, Jr., b. 8/30/1960 in Wolfeboro; fourth; Paul B. Hutchins (Wolfeboro) and Carolyn M. Welch (Pittsfield)
Susie Blanche, b. 4/8/1890; second; Samuel L. Hutchins (manufacturer, Wakefield) and Mary A. Corson (Wakefield)

HYNDS,
Daniel Kent, b. 2/22/1920; fifth; David C. Hynds (laborer, 34, NS) and Flora E. Steele (35, PEI)
Elsie Louise, b. 7/11/1924; seventh; David C. Hynds (laborer, NS) and Flora Ella Steele (PEI); residence - Sanbornville

HYNES,
daughter, b. 8/26/1925; eighth; David C. Hynes (NS) and Flora E. Steele (PEI)

INMAN,
Delma Curtis, b. 11/29/1934; fifth; Russell R. Inman (Bangor, ME) and Inzy E. Ferrin (Errol)

JACKSON,
Kati Lynn, b. 5/21/1991 in Rochester; Kevin Jay Jackson and Tami Lynn Lepene
Kristopher Jay, b. 5/19/1988 in Rochester; Kevin J. Jackson and Tami L. Lepene

JENNESS,
Blanche Isabell, b. 9/25/1907; first; Perley A. Jenness (laborer, 31, Wakefield) and Blanche I. Hart (17, Wakefield)
Frank Ellsworth, b. 3/4/1854; fourth; Albert H. Jenness (Union) and Bethia Hathaway (Weymouth, MA) (1936)

JETTE,
Peter David, b. 6/6/1942; first; Romeo Arthur Jette (Sanbornville) and Virginia Ruth Stevens (Sanbornville)
Steven Dodge, b. 12/10/1946; second; Romeo A. Jette (Sanbornville) and Virginia R. Stevens (Sanbornville)

JEWETT,
Richard Irving, b. 8/17/1884; first; Haven R. Jewett (Milton) and Mary N. Sibley (Watertown, MA) (1938)

JOHNSON,
Cassandra Leigh, b. 7/15/1977 in Wolfeboro; Richard G. Johnson and Wanda G. Keller
Chester Raymond, b. 7/23/1892; first; Freeman S. Johnson (Stowe, ME) and Cora L. Mears (Wolfeboro)
Ernest Ellwood, b. 1/29/1873; sixth; Thomas Henry Johnson (New Durham) and Mary Ellen Webster (Orford) (1940)
Ernest Harold, b. 3/26/1899; first; Clarence L. Johnson (mechanic, Stowe, ME) and Angie L. Nutter (Effingham); residence - Union
Hazel M., b. 10/3/1906; second; Freeman L. Johnson (mill operative, 41, Stowe, ME) and Cora L. Mears (38, Wolfeboro)
Herman Earle, b. 8/25/1894; second; Daniel E. Johnson (stable keeper, Jackson) and Ella J. White (Northfield, MA)
Iva May, b. 5/20/1899; second; Myron L. Johnson (mill hand, Stowe, ME) and Ellen F. Durgin (Freedom)
Joseph William, b. 9/6/1919; first; Frederick W. Johnson (laborer, 26, Fulton, NY) and Doris A. Hayes (21, East Wakefield)
Perley Sumner, b. 12/11/1910; first; Albert R. Johnson (brass moulder, 38, Conway) and Hattie M. Evans (30, Stoneham, ME); residence - Merrimac, MA
Rupert Edgar, b. 9/6/1893; first; Daniel E. Johnson (stable keeper, Jackson) and Ellen J. White (Northfield, MA)
Sidney I., b. 1/24/1900; second; Nelson T. Johnson (day laborer, Stowe, ME) and C. Henrietta Tingley (NB); residence - Union

Villa, b. 8/27/1908; second; Ernest B. Johnson (farmer, Fryeburg, ME) and Villa N. Sands (Boston, MA)

JONES,

Gertrude Alice, b. 2/4/1873; Hiram Jones and Elizabeth A. Libbey (1932)

Roland H., b. 7/28/1901; first; Waldo H. Jones (foreman shoe shop, Wakefield) and Edith Hawes (Springfield, MA); residence - Burlington, VT

JOY,

stillborn daughter, b. 7/24/1906; first; Frank D. Joy (mill operative, 24, So. Berwick, ME) and Alice P. Kimball (19, Middleton)

Abbot Leon, b. 9/10/1919; eighth; Frank D. Joy (section man, 37, So. Berwick, ME) and Alice Kimball (32, Wakefield)

Darlene Louise, b. 9/4/1957 in Rochester; sixth; Abbott L. Joy (Union) and Pearl E. Johnson (W. Lebanon, ME)

Darren Mason, b. 12/8/1985 in Rochester; David Joy and Jacqueline L. Putney

David Allan, b. 5/2/1964 in Rochester; third; Richard G. Joy (Union) and Sylvia L. Joy (Milton)

David Allan, Jr., b. 12/13/1984 in Wolfeboro; David A. Joy and Jacqueline L. Putney

Diane Lee, b. 4/28/1946; third; Abbott L. Joy (Union) and Pearl E. Johnson (W. Lebanon, ME)

Donald Albert, b. 1/19/1955 in Rochester; fourth; Abbott Leon Joy (Union) and Pearl Edythe Johnson (W. Lebanon, ME)

Doreen Pearl, b. 7/6/1956 in Rochester; fifth; Abbott L. Joy (Union) and Pearl E. Johnson (W. Lebanon, ME)

Douglas Eugene, b. 7/22/1942; first; Abbott Leon Joy (Union) and Pearl Edythe Johnson (West Lebanon, ME)

Elva Annette, b. 6/13/1910; third; Frank D. Joy (laborer, 28, So. Berwick, ME) and Alice Kimball (23, Middleton)

George Eugene, b. 3/13/1943; second; Lester Eugene Joy (Union) and Gladys Elva Horn (Acton, ME)

Helen Lynn, b. 7/4/1963 in Rochester; third; Douglas E. Joy (Rochester) and Cheryl L. Davis (Milton Mills)

Hilda Elaine, b. 9/28/1936; second; Mason Joy (Union) and Mildred Berry (New Durham)

Ida Elizabeth, b. 5/19/1909; second; Frank D. Joy (laborer, 27, So. Berwick, ME) and Alice P. Kimball (22, Middleton)

Lawrence Ivory, b. 11/19/1911; fourth; Frank D. Joy (laborer, 29, So. Berwick, ME) and Alice Kimball (24, Middleton)

Leah Ann, b. 12/15/1981 in Wolfeboro; Stephen P. Joy and Emmie L. Fulcher

Leslie Earl, b. 6/24/1940; first; Lester Eugene Joy (Union) and Gladys Elva Horn (Acton, ME)

Lester Eugene, b. 3/17/1913; fifth; Frank D. Joy (laborer, 30, So. Berwick, ME) and Alice Kimball (25, Middleton)

Lorraine Ann, b. 8/29/1958 in Rochester; second; Richard I. Joy (Union) and Sylvia L. Smith (Milton)

Malcolm Wentworth, b. 9/13/1936; first; Lester Joy (Wakefield) and Marian Wentworth (Milton)

Mason Irvin, b. 10/8/1916; sixth; Frank D. Joy (fireman, 34, So. Berwick, ME) and Alice P. Kimball (29, Middleton)

Oscar Kimball, b. 2/11/1923; ninth; Frank D. Joy (sectionman, So. Berwick, ME) and Alice P. Kimball (Middleton); residence - Union

Phillip Stephen, b. 8/2/1965 in Rochester; second; Oscar K. Joy (Union) and Jessica-Anne Herbert (Ossipee)

Richard Irving, b. 6/8/1935; first; Mason Joy (Union) and Mildred Berry (New Durham)

Richard Irving, Jr., b. 6/5/1957 in Rochester; first; Richard I. Joy (Union) and Sylvia L. Smith (Milton)

Ronald Stuart, b. 5/18/1944; second; Abbott L. Joy (Union) and Pearl E. Johnson (W. Lebanon, ME)

Stephen Phillip, b. 9/28/1954 in Rochester; first; Oscar Kimball Joy (Union) and Jessie Ann Herbert (Ossipee)

Zachary James, b. 12/5/1987 in Rochester; Richard I. Joy and Robin M. Bernier

JULIAN,

Tabitha Dawn, b. 3/2/1979 in Rochester; Charles P. Julian and Nancy Jean Para

Tammy Nicole, b. 11/15/1976 in Wolfeboro; Charles P. Julian and Nancy J. Para

JUNKINS,

Alice Maude, b. 11/3/1870; fourth; Edwin William Junkins (Wakefield) and Helen P. Dockum (Wolfeboro) (1937)

KAISER,
Molly Anne, b. 2/3/1978 in Wolfeboro; Stuart P. Kaiser and Susan B. Hammond

KALILIKANE,
Sarah Kiyoko, b. 7/17/1985 in Portsmouth; Stephen L. Kalilikane and Ann M. Nelson

KAPLAN,
Jeffrey Finn, b. 6/28/1973 in Wolfeboro; Harold Kaplan and Marie S. Bernhart
Laura Susan, b. 12/2/1971 in Wolfeboro; Harold Kaplan and Marie S. Bernhart

KARCHER,
child, b. 7/25/1931; twelfth; William Karcher (MA) and Martha Woodfert (MA)
Charles Elliott, Jr., b. 12/30/1947; second; Charles E. Karcher (Henniker) and Marion T. Randall (Sanbornville)
Cheryl Diane, b. 1/23/1947; first; Charles E. Karcher (Henniker) and Marion T. Randall (Sanbornville)
Jerry Ann, b. 4/29/1951; third; Charles E. Karcher (Henniker) and Marion T. Randall (Sanbornville)
Karen Elizabeth, b. 3/25/1947; first; William A. Karcher, Jr. (Warner) and Elizabeth Soucy (Brookfield)
Martha Elizabeth, b. 9/1/1935; thirteenth; William A. Karcher (Charlestown, MA) and Martha Wilfert (Roxbury, MA)
Ronald Gerry, b. 1/18/1936; first; Nellie Karcher (Medford, MA)

KASPRZYK,
Graham Louise, b. 5/25/1993 in Rochester; Peter Martin Kasprzyk and Elizabeth Ruth Pretty

KATWICK,
Nina Marie, b. 1/31/1975 in Rochester; Arthur D. Katwick and Catherine M. Martell
Stuart Neal, b. 10/12/1979 in Wolfeboro; Arthur D. Katwick and Catherine M. Martell

KEATING,
Charles Shamus, b. 10/5/1977 in Wolfeboro; James F. Keating, III and Rebecca G. Andrews
Jacqueline Ann, b. 1/2/1950; second; James F. Keating, Jr. (Somerville, MA) and Marilyn J. Drew (Union)
James Francis, 3d, b. 10/28/1947; first; James F. Keating, Jr. (Somerville, MA) and Marilyn J. Drew (Union)
Joanne Lyn, b. 6/8/1952 in Kittery, ME; third; James F. Keating (Somerville, MA) and Marilyn J. Drew (Union)

KELLEY,
Angela Roje, b. 8/15/1970 in Rochester; Michael J. Kelley and Linda L. Littlefield
Cora Josephine, b. 4/16/1917; fourth; Chester Kelley (farmer, 28, Wakefield) and Ada A. Kelley (26, Lynn, MA)
Michael Joe, b. 6/11/1969 in Rochester; Michael J. Kelley and Linda L. Littlefield
Nora Alice, b. 7/11/1955 in Wolfeboro; fourth; Bartholomew P. Kelley (NY) and Elizabeth M. Nicol (NJ)
Rhonda Lee, b. 11/10/1967 in Rochester; second; Michael J. Kelley (Kingman, KS) and Linda L. Littlefield (Rochester)
Tami Lyn, b. 5/9/1966 in Rochester; first; Michael J. Kelley (Kingsman, KS) and Linda L. Littlefield (Rochester)

KELLY,
Catherine Denise, b. 11/10/1987 in Wolfeboro; Dennis B. Kelly and Patricia A. Rouselle
Douglas Paul, b. 11/16/1950; third; Bartholomew P. Kelly (Brooklyn, NY) and Elizabeth M. Nicol (Trenton, NJ)
Glora Beth, b. 9/27/1985 in Wolfeboro; Dennis B. Kelly and Patricia A. Rouselle
Mary Ann, b. 6/10/1994 in Dover; Shawn Patrick Kelly and Diana Lee Hill

KEMP,
Lauren Kathryn, b. 5/9/1991 in Rochester; James Michael Kemp and Debra Ann Ramsey

KENDRICK,
Alyson Nicole, b. 8/23/1989 in Rochester; Michael Edward Kendrick and Susan Elizabeth Zack

Mariah Johanna, b. 11/1/1992 in Rochester; Michael Edward Kendrick and Susan Zack

KENERSON,
Gladis Belle, b. 6/9/1888; second; Ivory Kenerson (manufacturer, Tamworth) and Jennie Wiggin (Wakefield)

KENISTON,
son [Willie], b. 8/18/1913; second; Isaac Keniston (laborer, 43, Effingham) and Rose B. Chase (41, Concord)
Hazel May, b. 4/17/1911; third; Cyrus Keniston (farmer, 33, Effingham) and Martha Dorron (24, St. John, NB)

KENNERSON,
Roger Earl, b. 12/11/1951; second; Robert E. Kennerson (NH) and Anna J. Zubek (PA)
Ronald Robert, b. 10/31/1946; first; Robert E. Kennerson (Rumney) and Anna J. Zubek (Allentown, PA)

KENNETT,
Gloria Frances, b. 6/11/1926; second; Ralph R. Kennett (Madison) and Emma Jewett (Milton)
June Elizabeth, b. 6/24/1920; first; Ralph R. Kennett (RFD carrier, 29, Madison) and Emma S. Jewett (29, Milton); residence - Sanbornville

KENNEY,
Eleanor Horne, b. 6/3/1910; first; Luther Kenney (brakeman, Wolfeboro) and Helen Lucy (North Conway)
John Thomas, III, b. 11/14/1974 in Wolfeboro; John T. Kenney, Jr. and Sandra J. Buswell
Roger Weston, b. 1/4/1937; first; Weston Kenney (Sanbornville) and Beryl Copp (Ossipee)
Wayne Allan, b. 3/23/1938; second; Weston Luther Kenney (Sanbornville) and Beryl Claire Copp (Ossipee)
Weston Luther, b. 8/3/1912; second; Luther Kenney (RR conductor, 29, Wolfeboro) and Helen M. Lucy (28, North Conway)

KENNIE,
Roland, b. 1/16/1900; first; James H. Kennie (teamster, St. Johns) and Annie B. Lombard (Biddeford, ME); residence - Union

Wesley C., b. 3/11/1901; second; James H. Kennie (laborer, St. Johns) and
Annie B. Lombard (Biddeford, ME)

KERDUS,
Zachary Matthew, b. 12/4/1991 in Rochester; Daniel William Kerdus and
Tamara R. Reynolds

KETCHUM,
Suzanna Penn, b. 11/4/1943; third; Bradford Wells Ketchum (West
Roxbury, MA) and Priscilla D. Thompson (Torrington, CT)

KIMBALL,
daughter, b. 1/13/1891; fourth; Frank E. Kimball (laborer, Parsonsfield,
ME) and Annie Patch (Newfield, ME)
daughter, b. 9/15/1901; third; David Kimball (shoe mfr., Middleton) and
Marie J. LaChapelle (Haverhill, MA)
son, b. 1/19/1905; second; Alphonzo Kimball (mill operative, 24,
Middleton) and Myrtie Glidden (20, New Durham); residence - Union
Alfred William, b. 5/28/1910; first; Raymond H. Kimball (shoe maker, 21,
Newfield, ME) and Louise R. Pippin (21, Wakefield); residence -
Farmington
Augusta F., b. 4/5/1897; first; J. W. Kimball (farmer, Wakefield) and Alta
S. Pike (Middleton)
David S., b. 4/3/1906; third; Alphonso E. Kimball (mill operative, 26,
Middleton) and Myrtie E. Glidden (21, New Durham)
David Ward, b. 3/19/1978 in Wolfeboro; John Wayne Kimball and
Catherine L. Garland
Earle Freeman, b. 10/2/1910; third; Oscar Kimball (RR conductor, 28,
Middleton) and Florence Runnels (26, Worcester, MA)
Edna Eliza, b. 3/27/1908; second; Oscar Kimball (conductor, 25,
Middleton) and Florence Runnels (24, Cherry Valley, MA)
Hazel Rose, b. 9/15/1901; third; David Kimball (Middleton) and Marie
LaChappelle (Haverhill, MA) (1940)
Joan Sylvia, b. 12/1/1954 in Rochester; second; John Ward Kimball
(Wakefield) and Sylvia May Hill (Rochester)
John Ward, b. 3/3/1927; first; Cummings Kimball (Presque Isle, ME) and
Marion Evans (Milton)
John Wayne, b. 12/22/1951; second; John W. Kimball (Sanbornville) and
Sylvia M. Hill (Rochester)

John Wayne, b. 12/29/1975 in Wolfeboro; John W. Kimball and Catherine L. Garland
Kimie David, b. 1/14/1973 in Rochester; David L. Kimball and Barbara A. Fifield
Mark Robert, b. 8/29/1961 in Rochester; fifth; John W. Kimball (Wakefield) and Sylvia M. Hill (Rochester)
Mark Ward, b. 10/12/1991 in Rochester; Mark Robert Kimball and Lisa Ann Pouliot
Mikayla Noelle, b. 12/26/1994 in Dover; Mark Robert Kimball and Lisa Ann Pouliot
Roland Calvin, b. 2/24/1929; third; Ward Cummings Kimball (Presque Isle, ME) and Marion Evans (Milton) (1942)
Sonya Ellen, b. 3/21/1980 in Rochester; Mark R. Kimball and Pauline I. Rines
Thomas Calvin, b. 8/9/1959 in Rochester; fourth; John W. Kimball (Wakefield) and Sylvia M. Hill (Rochester)
Violet Hacker, b. 2/22/1928; second; Cummings Kimball (Presque Isle, ME) and Marion Evans (Milton Mills)

KINCEL,
Julie Ann, b. 10/24/1971 in Rochester; Frank J. Kincel and Patricia M. Hill

KING,
Emma, b. 6/19/1892; third; Joseph King (block printer, England) and Emma M. Reed (Wakefield)
Mary Elizabeth, b. 10/2/1889; second; Joseph E. King (block printer, England) and Emma ----- (Wakefield)
Ruth Ellen, b. 2/2/1937; first; Clifford King (Troy, NY) and Hazel I. Grace (Springfield)

KINGSBURY,
Tyler David, b. 2/7/1992 in Rochester; David Wayne Kingsbury and Cynthia Hoage

KINNEY,
Violet C., b. 10/20/1902; third; James Kinney (laborer, 24, St. Johns, NB) and Annie Lombard (42, Biddeford, ME); residence - Union

KINSELLA,
Richard Harold Charles, b. 9/13/1981 in Wolfeboro; Richard C. Kinsella and Shirley M. Ames

KINVILLE,
Christopher Michael, b. 9/28/1971 in Wolfeboro; Robert W. Kinville and Cathy A. Thompson
Maria Michelle, b. 10/4/1975 in Wolfeboro; Richard N. Kinville and Gloria C. Stephens

KIRK,
Jacob Dylan, b. 4/8/1980 in Rochester; Kirk A. Kirk and Lorrie L. Stuart

KITTREDGE,
Aubrey Meghan, b. 1/13/1991 in Dover; James Kevin Kittredge and Cynthia Lee Cummings

KNAPP,
Mabel May, b. 9/28/1927; third; Hiram S. Knapp (KS) and Maggie Alyea (KS)

KNIGHT,
Cecil Everett, b. 7/16/1911; first; Marshall E. Knight (tel. operator, 37, Salmon Falls) and Elizabeth Doyle (29, Wakefield)
Cynthia June, b. 6/10/1940; first; Cecil Everett Knight (Sanbornville) and Dorcas Louise Marsh (Malden, MA)
Florence Evelyn, b. 1/3/1898; first; M. E. Knight (telegrapher, Salmon Falls) and Belle E. Brackett (Wakefield)
John Wallace, b. 7/28/1970 in Sanford, ME; John A. Knight and Nancy L. Fisher
Louiz Marjorie, b. 5/9/1899; second; Marshell E. Knight (telegraph operator, Salmon Falls) and Elizabeth B. Brackett (Wakefield)
Mary Elizabeth, b. 11/6/1947; second; Cecil E. Knight (Sanbornville) and Dorcas L. Marsh (Malden, MA)

KNIGHTS,
Methyl M., b. 6/7/1920; fifth; Frank A. Knights (retailer, 34, N. Waterboro, ME) and Edith E. Kimball (34, Wolfeboro); residence - E. Wakefield

KNOWLES,
Robert Duron, b. 5/14/1945; second; Duron W. Knowles (AL) and Addie M. Hanscome (Standish, ME)

KNOX,
Florence Eloise, b. 6/4/1904; fourth; Manville E. Knox (craneman, 37, Ossipee) and Mabel F. Thompson (25, Salisbury)
Gertrude E., b. 8/2/1887; first; Horatio B. Knox (teacher, Cambria, PA) and Mary E. Roberts (Wakefield); residence - Palmer, MA

KNUDSEN,
Louis William, Jr., b. 10/25/1938; second; Louis William Knudsen (Malden, MA) and Bertha Luella Frazier (Cambridge, MA)

KOUKAL,
Adam Michael, b. 6/15/1988 in Rochester; Larry G. Koukal and Cathy M. Weiner
Aileen Marie, b. 1/25/1985 in Wolfeboro; Larry A. Koukal and Cathy M. Weiner

KRABE[C]K,
Franklin Wendell, b. 3/3/1909; second; Axel Krabeck (farmer, 25, Denmark) and Florence Burleigh (22, Wakefield)
Wilfred, b. 12/28/1907; first; Axel Krabek (pattern maker, 24, Denmark) and Florence I. Burleigh (21, Wakefield)

LABOUITE,
daughter, b. 1/29/1892; first; Cyrille Labouite (laborer, Canada) and Amelia Marcoux (Canada)

LABRE,
Leo Maurice, b. 7/22/1926; second; Luger Labre (Canada) and Clara Wood (Biddeford, ME)

LABRIE,
Darion Alexander, b. 10/21/1997 in Wolfeboro; Gabriel Dominic LaBrie and Angela Jean Horning

LACASSE,
Arthur J., b. 4/1/1895; seventh; Joseph Lacasse (laborer, Canada) and Orille M. Pattrie (Canada)
Lucian, b. 3/12/1918; seventh; Arthur Lacasse (stone mason, 34, Canada) and Anna Goslin (34, Canada)
Mary Regina, b. 11/18/1919; eighth; Arthur Lacasse (laborer, 36, Canada) and Anna Gosslin (37, Canada); residence - Sanbornville

LACOSSE,
daughter, b. 7/15/1893; sixth; Joseph Lacose (sic) (laborer, Canada) and Orelie Patrie (Canada)
Alphonso, b. 1/13/1902 in Sanbornville; eighth; Joseph Lacosse (laborer, 42, Canada) and Olive Patrie (35, Canada); residence - Sanbornville
Gratia Marie Rose, b. 7/7/1912; sixth; Arthur Lacosse (laborer, 28, Canada) and Anna Gosselyn (29, Canada)
Marie Alice, b. 4/9/1910; fifth; Arthur LaCosse (laborer, 26, Canada) and Anna Goslyn (28, Canada)

LAFORTUNE,
Michael James, b. 6/30/1990 in Dover; Daniel Paul Lafortune and Erin Ann McKenney

LAMBERT,
Joseph Charles, b. 9/5/1908; sixth; Albert Lambert (laborer, 42, Canada) and Caroline Beaulieu (33, Canada)

LAMIE,
daughter [Mary E.], b. 11/7/1887; eighth; Moses Lamie (laborer, Canada) and Leah Carrier (Canada)
son, b. 4/13/1890; ninth; Moses Lamie (laborer, Canada) and Leao ---- (Canada)
son, b. 10/14/1891; tenth; Moses Lamie (sectionman, Canada) and Lea Lamie (Canada)
Alexina, b. 12/21/1918; third; Fred L. Lamie (baggagemaster, 41, Somersworth) and Diana Cyr (36, Canada)
Alfred Ardice, b. 5/9/1924 in Sanbornville; fifth; Fred Lamie (flagman B and M, Salmon Falls) and Diana Cyr (Canada); residence - Sanbornville
Annie, b. 2/13/1894; eleventh; Moses Lamie (laborer, Canada) and Lea Collie (Canada)

Joseph Alfred George, b. 4/1/1908; first; Alfred Lamie (RR employee, 30, Somersworth) and Nellie E. Vignault (23, Ossipee)
Marie Annette, b. 3/1/1917; second; Fred L. Lamie (baggage mas., 40, Somersworth) and Diana Cyr (34, Canada)
Mary Diana S., b. 10/13/1915; first; Fred L. Lamie (baggagemaster, 38, Somersworth) and Diana Cyr (33, Canada)
Moses Antonio, b. 5/29/1899; thirteenth; Moses Lamie (laborer, Canada) and Leo Corrier (Canada); residence - Sanbornville
Rita, b. 11/7/1922; fourth; Fred L. Lamie (railroad employee, Somersworth) and Diana Cyr (Canada); residence - Sanbornville

LAMKIN,
Peter, b. 7/4/1936; first; Everett Lamkin (Lynn, MA) and Constance Cook (Hartford, CT)

LAMOINE,
Willis L., b. 4/27/1902; first; John Lamoine (laborer, 23, Nashua) and Nancy Streader (16, Wakefield)

LAMONTAGNE,
Meagen Ruth, b. 8/19/1979 in Wolfeboro; Robert P. Lamontagne and Judith A. Morrill
Rebecca Jane, b. 12/22/1984 in Rochester; Robert P. Lamontagne and Judith Ann Morrill
Thomas James, b. 1/9/1984 in Wolfeboro; Thomas P. Lamontagne and Cynthia L. St. Cyr

LAMSON,
son, b. 8/26/1907; fifth; Daniel L. Lamson (laborer, 45, VT) and Ida M. Wynot (Lunenburg, NS)

LANCTOT,
Ashley April, b. 4/28/1996 in Wolfeboro; Thomas Lanctot, Jr. and Deborah June White

LANDRY,
Dayna Steadman, b. 11/20/1993 in Rochester; Everett James Landry, Jr. and Cheryl Ann Steadman
Louis-James Steadman, b. 11/19/1990 in Rochester; Everett James Landry, Jr. and Cheryl Ann Steadman

Payton Steadman, b. 3/14/1987 in Rochester; Everett J. Landry, Jr. and Cheryl A. Steadman

LANE,
daughter [Ethel May], b. 7/29/1905 in Sanbornville; third; George F. Lane (teamster, 22, Wakefield) and Ida May Davis (24, Tamworth); residence - Sanbornville
Annie May, b. 11/13/1906; fourth; George F. Lane (teamster, 24, Wakefield) and Ida M. Davis (25, Tamworth)
Beatrice Madeline, b. 4/25/1901; first; George Lane (Sanbornville) and Ida Davis (Tamworth) (1944)
Bernice L., b. 2/5/1904; second; George F. Lane (laborer, 21, Wakefield) and Ida M. Davis (23, Tamworth)
Edith May, b. 7/29/1901; third; Charles T. Lane (laborer, Wakefield) and Gertrude M. Sanborn (Acton, ME); residence - Sanbornville
Evelyn Pauline, b. 8/9/1913; fifth; Charles Lane (teamster, 42, Dover) and Gertrude Sanborn (34, Acton, ME)
Gladys Gertrude, b. 4/30/1899; first; Charles T. Lane (laborer, Wakefield) and Gertie M. Sanborn (Acton, ME); residence - Horne's Mills
Harris L., b. 5/23/1904; second; Harry L. Lane (laborer, 27, Dover) and Emma Watson (27, Waltham, MA)
Margaret L., b. 5/9/1903; third; Charles T. Lane (laborer, 30, Dover) and Mary G. Sanborn (24, Acton, ME)
Mary Agnes, b. 9/17/1890; Frank Lane (Wakefield) and Ellen Thurston (Scotland) (1942)
Ruby Winnoa, b. 9/9/1908; fourth; Charles T. Lane (laborer, 38, Dover) and Gertrude Sanborn (29, Acton, ME)

LANG,
daughter, b. 10/28/1887; first; Charles E. Lang (Brookfield) and Mary E. Thurston (Freedom)
Carolyn Palmer, b. 8/2/1923; third; Reuben Lang (janitor, Wakefield) and Bernice Hazel Pike (Wakefield); residence - Sanbornville
Elizabeth Barbara, b. 6/30/1914; first; Reuben P. Lang (merchant, 21, Brookfield) and Bernice H. Pike (25, Wakefield)
Forrest Payson, b. 5/17/1917; second; Reuben P. Lang (teamster, Brookfield) and Bernice Pike (Wakefield)
Gerald Forrest, b. 4/6/1938; first; Forrest Payson Lang (Sanbornville) and Barbara Louise Perry (Wolfeboro)

Hattie Wisdom, b. 9/23/1882; second; Frank Payson Lang (Brookfield) and Ida Rankin (Lewiston, ME) (1941)
Joyce Barbara, b. 10/19/1944; third; Forrest Payson Lang (Sanbornville) and Barbara L. Perry (Wolfeboro)
Philip John, b. 7/8/1940; second; Forrest Payson Lang (Sanbornville) and Barbara Louise Perry (Wolfeboro)
Thomas Alan, b. 10/19/1948; fourth; Forrest P. Lang (Sanbornville) and Barbara L. Perry (Wolfeboro)

LANGDON,
Patricia Anne, b. 3/24/1951; first; William R. Langdon (NH) and Dorothy A. Wentworth (NH)

LANGHILL,
Avis Mildred, b. 9/7/1895; second; Johnson Langhill (laborer) and Mabel Locke (Hampton); residence - Ossipee

LANGLEY,
Lottie, b. 7/4/1902; third; Freeman C. Langley (farmer, 29, Acton, ME) and Kate Davis (31, New York, NY)
Mary K., b. 3/8/1900; first; Freeman C. Langley (farmer, Acton, ME) and Kate Doris (New York)
William D., b. 1/27/1901; second; Freeman C. Langley (farmer, Acton, ME) and Kate Davis (New York, NY)

LANGVILLE,
John Sherburne L., b. 2/4/1894; first; Johnson E. Langville (farmer, NS) and Mabel Y. Lock (Hampton)

LAPOINTE,
Joseph M., b. 4/27/1894; second; John Lapointe (laborer, Canada) and Arvilla Marcoux (Canada)
Richard Gibbs, b. 5/29/1921; first; George J. Lapointe (section man, 19, Wolfeboro) and Pauline A. Gibbs (18, Sagamore, MA); residence - Union

LARSEN,
Jaime Marie, b. 4/16/1998 in Dover; Mark James Larsen and Holly Marie Hudak

LASKEY,
Debra Ann, b. 10/19/1961 in Rochester; second; Kenneth M. Laskey (Milton) and Arline F. Bumford (Sanbornville)

LASSONDE,
Aaron Mathew Richard, b. 3/23/1990 in Rochester; Kenneth Armond Lassonde and Donna Marie Pomerleau

LAUER,
Glenda Gail, b. 3/31/1953 in Rochester; first; William Ward Lauer (Detroit, MI) and Ruth L. Hill (Conway)

LAURION,
Melissa Georgia, b. 9/28/1991 in Rochester; Michael Lucien Laurion and Jane Elizabeth Sinclair

LAVERTUE,
Ann Marie, b. 1/18/1955 in Wolfeboro; first; William John Lavertue (Union) and Cecile Demors (So. Berwick, ME)
Brandon Carl, b. 3/27/1990 in Wolfeboro; Norman Carl Lavertue and Janet Rose Shorey
Cynthia Louise, b. 4/30/1959 in Wolfeboro; third; William J. Lavertue (Union) and Cecile Demers (So. Berwick, ME)
Emily Florence, b. 8/3/1934; second; John Lavertue (Rochester) and Francis Wilson (Union)
Estelle Jean, b. 7/27/1961 in Wolfeboro; fourth; William J. Lavertue (Union) and Cecile Demers (Si. Berwick, ME)
John Francis, b. 6/28/1938; third; John Robinson Lavertue (Rochester) and Frances Lucy Wilson (Union)
Jordan Rose, b. 2/7/1993 in Wolfeboro; Norman Carl Lavertue and Janet Rose Shorey
Joyce Lynn, b. 8/12/1960 in Wolfeboro; first; Norman D. Lavertue (Wolfeboro) and Nancy J. Glidden (Wolfeboro)
Larry Lee, b. 3/2/1966 in Wolfeboro; fourth; Norman D. Lavertue (Wolfeboro) and Nancy J. Glidden (Wolfeboro)
Norman Carl, b. 4/4/1964 in Wolfeboro; third; Norman D. Lavertue (Wolfeboro) and Nancy J. Glidden (Wolfeboro)
Norman Daniel, b. 4/19/1940; fourth; John Robinson Lavertue (Rochester) and Frances Lucy Wilson (Union)

Norman William, b. 4/19/1958 in Wolfeboro; second; William J. Lavertue (Union) and Cecile Demers (So. Berwick, ME)

Randy, b. 12/23/1968 in Wolfeboro; Norman D. Lavertue and Nancy J. Glidden

Sharon Lee, b. 1/10/1959 in Rochester; second; John F. Lavertue (Union) and Phyllis L. Morrill (Wakefield)

Sydney Arlene, b. 3/30/1996 in Wolfeboro; Norman Carl Lavertue and Janet Rose Shorey

Valerie Ann, b. 6/14/1970 in Wolfeboro; Norman D. Lavertue and Nancy J. Glidden

William John, b. 1/15/1933 in Union; John Lavertue and Francis L. Wilson

LEATHERMAN,

Abigail Faith, b. 11/4/1979 in Dover; Wilson K. Leatherman and Ann L. Hartlett

LEEMAN,

Gerald Arnold, b. 7/29/1963 in Wolfeboro; second; Stanwood S. Leeman (Portland, ME) and Marylyn L. Drown (Rochester)

Kevin Herbert, b. 2/1/1954 in Wolfeboro; first; Stanwood Scott Leeman (ME) and Marylin L. Drown (NH)

LEES,

Ernest Mascoe, b. 10/8/1934; tenth; Arthur H. Lees (Providence, RI) and Gladys Hathaway (Exeter, RI)

LEFAY,

Alice Eva, b. 12/24/1920; seventh; Joseph Lefay (teamster, 33, Canada) and Mary L. Lefay (29, Concord); residence - North Wakefield

LEFEBRE,

daughter, b. 7/2/1913; fourth; Joseph Lefebre (laborer, 24, Canada) and Mary L. Seymore (23, Concord)

LEFEVER,

Robert, b. 10/14/1914; fifth; Joseph Lefever (teamster, 25, Rochester) and Mary L. Seymore (26, Concord)

LEFOY,
Irving R., b. 5/16/1911; fourth; Lee Lefoy (teamster, 38, Canada) and Alice Randall (34, Lynn, MA)

LEGARE,
Georgianna, b. 5/28/1878; first; Joseph Legare (Canada) and Adaline Houle (Canada) (1939)

LEGRE,
stillborn son, b. 3/4/1905; third; Angus Legre (laborer, 34, NB) and Magie White (30, Cape Breton)

LEIGHTON,
Apryl Marie, b. 9/9/1975 in Wolfeboro; Robert C. Leighton and Kathy A. Gardner
Ellen Margaret, b. 7/12/1936; eighth; Presco F. Leighton (Middleton) and Gladys Russell (Danvers, MA)
Francis Earl, b. 5/31/1939; ninth; Presco Frank Leighton (Middleton) and Gladys Evelyn Russell (Danvers, MA)
Gary Dennis, b. 5/7/1961 in Rochester; first; Francis E. Leighton (Wolfeboro) and Margaret E. Palmer (Mt. Vernon, NY)
Gregory Donald, b. 9/2/1963 in Rochester; second; Francis E. Leighton (Wolfeboro) and Margaret E. Palmer (Mt. Vernon, NY)
Kathy May, b. 10/21/1955 in Rochester; first; Herbert Frank Leighton (Middleton) and Mildred Addie Ross (W. Lebanon, ME)
Krista Michele, b. 9/17/1974 in Wolfeboro; Robert C. Leighton and Kathy A. Gardner
Michael Jon, b. 7/12/1987 in Wolfeboro; Robert C. Leighton and Kathy A. Gardner
Michelle Marie, b. 6/14/1973 in Wolfeboro; Gary J. Leighton and Linda E. Bollinger
Richard Lloyd, b. 1/11/1957 in Wolfeboro; second; Robert N. Leighton (Wolfeboro) and Ann D. Stevens (Rochester)
Robert Charles, b. 10/6/1948; tenth; Presco F. Leighton (Middleton) and Gladys E. Russell (Danvers, MA)
Robert Charles, b. 10/11/1985 in Wolfeboro; Robert C. Leighton and Kathy A. Gardner

LEMAY,
Brianna Elmedore, b. 12/31/1993 in Wolfeboro; John Maurice Lemay and Florence Frances Flynn

LESPERANCE,
Luke James, b. 8/29/1986 in Rochester; Donald P. Lesperance, Jr. and Lee-Ann Beaupre

LEVESQUE,
Sean Philip, b. 10/10/1987 in Portsmouth; Philip D. Levesque and Kathryn Rushton

LEVIRTU,
Eugene, b. 4/25/1897; sixth; Eugene Levoirtu (sic) (laborer, Canada) and Marguerite Moore (Canada)
Mary Grace Ida, b. 7/7/1899; seventh; Ludger Levirtu (laborer, Canada) and Daisy Moore (Canada); residence - Sanbornville
Rose A., b. 9/9/1900; eighth; Ludger Levirtu (laborer, Canada) and Margurite Moore (Canada); residence - Sanbornville

LIBBEY,
son, b. 2/19/1887; fifth; Washington Libbey (farmer, Wakefield) and Ellen M. Farnham (Wakefield)
Nathan J., b. 10/10/1873; second; Washington Libbey (Wakefield) and Ellen Farnham (Wakefield) (1937)
Scott David, b. 10/9/1882; first; John James Libbey (W. Newfield, ME) and Cora Bell Libbey (So. Effingham) (1943)

LIBBY,
Denise Ann, b. 5/1/1968 in Rochester; Edward E. Libby and Winifred M. Gauthier
Erin Deidre, b. 5/11/1982 in Rochester; Ricky S. Libby and Kathleen D. McGlame
Jason Donald, b. 7/10/1977 in Laconia; Brian K. Libby and Wanda L. Heald
Keith Adam, b. 7/1/1988 in Rochester; Brian K. Libby and Catherine L. Bowden
Lorelei, b. 4/2/1969 in Wolfeboro; Harold W. Libby and Diana M. Bodwell

Marjory, b. 3/15/1903 in Sanbornville; first; Nathan J. Libby (engineer, 29, Wakefield) and Eliza Belle Wilkinson (29, Laconia); residence - Sanbornville

Norma Ernestine, b. 4/4/1912; first; Norman E. Libby (druggist, 35, Tuftonboro) and Katherine Creighton (29, Peterboro)

Raymond Edward, b. 12/4/1925; first; Guy E. Libby (Berwick, ME) and Elizabeth Taylor (Boscawen)

Rosalyn Ann, b. 12/12/1944; first; Arthur L. Libby (Athens, ME) and Jacqueline L. Beals (Sanbornville)

Ryan Stuart, b. 5/11/1982 in Rochester; Ricky S. Libby and Kathleen D. McGlame

Sharon Lee, b. 6/18/1947; third; Arthur L. Libby (Athens, ME) and Jacqueline L. Beal (Sanbornville)

Sharon Michele, b. 4/23/1969 in Rochester; Edward E. Libby and Winnifred M. Gauthier

Stephanie Patricia, b. 7/20/1987 in Concord; Stephen R. Libby and Brenda L. Tuttle

LIGHT,
daughter, b. 2/28/1906; fourth; Angus Light (laborer, 35, Rogersville, NB) and Margaret White (31, Caburt, NB)

Anthony A., b. 8/20/1907; fourth; Henry T. Light (laborer, 42, St. Johns, NB) and Nellie Pelkey (33, St. Johns, NB)

Leslie, b. 1/15/1908; first; Angus Light and Mary A. Lane (17, Wakefield)

LINCOLN,
Sage Elizabeth, b. 9/16/1997 in Wolfeboro; Joseph Bartlett Lincoln and Tricia Lee Segeberg

LINDH,
Rebecca Louise, b. 5/22/1967 in Rochester; first; David C. Lindh (Manchester) and Louise R. Lauze (Dover)

LITCHFIELD,
Norman Gregory, b. 4/16/1906; second; William Franklin Litchfield (Boston, MA) and Bernice Myrtle Hart (Wakefield) (1941)

William H., b. 11/30/1904; first; William F. Litchfield (farmer, Boston, MA) and Bernice Hart (Wakefield)

LITTLE,
Brittany June, b. 7/2/1985 in Dover; Dean M. Little and Kelly J. Colby

LITTLEFIELD,
Betty Elaine, b. 1/1/1947; first; Eugene F. Littlefield (Marlboro, MA) and Louise M. Fifield (Wakefield)
Delbert Wayne, b. 4/28/1953 in Rochester; first; Richard Preble Littlefield (Marlboro, MA) and Lorraine E. Wilson (Brookfield)
Geraldine Marie, b. 9/9/1950; third; Eugene F. Littlefield (MA) and Louise M. Fifield (Wakefield)
Harvey Daniel, b. 7/17/1920; first; Henry H. Littlefield (laborer, 25, Somerville, MA) and Ada V. Lord (19, Acton, ME)
James Eugene, b. 11/28/1948; second; Eugene F. Littlefield (Melboro, MA) and Louise M. Fifield (Wakefield)
Jessica Guild, b. 12/17/1973 in Dover; Nicholas G. Littlefield and Susan G. Williamson
Linda Louise, b. 11/8/1946; first; Robert M. Littlefield (Enfield, ME) and Sylvia M. Hill (Rochester)
Maynard George, b. 1/13/1956 in Rochester; fifth; Eugene G. Littlefield (Marlboro, MA) and Louise May Fifield (Wakefield)
Payson Eastman, b. 6/26/1909; first; Nathan Littlefield (clerk, 24, York, ME) and Grace Eastman (24, Fort Fairfield, ME)
Susan Leslie, b. 7/28/1972 in Rochester; Delbert W. Littlefield and Constance M. Mallica
Virginia Avilda, b. 7/9/1912; second; Nathan L. Littlefield (clerk, 27, York, ME) and Grace F. Eastman (27, Fort Fairfield, ME)
William Earl, b. 9/14/1952 in Rochester; fourth; Eugene F. Littlefield (Marlboro, MA) and Louise M. Fifield (Wakefield)

LIVERMORE,
John Alexander, b. 9/23/1907; third; Edwin Livermore (brakeman, 32, Hudson, MA) and Ellen McDonald (30, No. Sydney, NS)
Lillian Pearl, b. 4/29/1905; second; E. J. Livermore (brakeman, 30, Marlboro, MA) and Ellen McDonald (30, North Sidney, NS); residence - Sanbornville
William Edwin, b. 6/28/1903; first; Edwin J. Livermore (baggagemaster, 29, Fitchburg, MA) and Ellen McDonald (27, N. Sidney, CB); residence - Sanbornville

LOCKE,
John Ellsworth, b. 6/21/1940; third; Ellsworth Stanley Locke (Barrington) and Flora Irene Griffin (Center Ossipee)

LOGAN,
Bethany Anne, b. 2/3/1986 in Wolfeboro; Robert W. Logan and Susan E. Parmenter

LONG,
Mandy Lynn, b. 2/2/1976 in Wolfeboro; Michael T. Long and Kathleen J. Jack

LORD,
daughter, b. 9/14/1890; seventh; Delphis Lord (laborer, Canada) and Delphine ----- (Canada)
son, b. 4/5/1915; fifth; Harvey Lord (sawyer, 35, Acton, ME) and Clara Nichols (34, Ossipee)
Charles Josiah, b. 2/18/1912; third; Elmer Lord (fireman, 27, Somersworth) and Sybil Wiggin (25, Wakefield)
Chester John, b. 3/24/1912; fourth; Harvey Lord (mill man, 31, Acton, ME) and Clara Nichols (30, Ossipee)
Delbert W., b. 2/11/1901; Hiram Lord (Acton, ME) and Lillian May Temple (Waterboro, ME) (1941)
Doris Louise, b. 4/5/1915; sixth; Harvey Lord (sawyer, 35, Acton, ME) and Clara Nichols (34, Ossipee)
Gerald Elmer, b. 5/23/1907; second; Elmer M. Lord (fireman, 25, Somersworth) and Sibyl E. Wiggin (20, Wakefield)
Harold Ansil, b. 4/28/1909; second; Elmer M. Lord (fireman, 23, Somersworth) and Sybil E. Wiggin (22, Wakefield)
Helen Pearl, b. 9/13/1910; third; Harvey Lord (millman, 29, Acton, ME) and Clara A. Nichols (28, Ossipee); residence - Acton, ME
Irene Louise, b. 10/16/1918; eighth; Harvey J. Lord (sawyer, 38, Acton, ME) and Clara A. Nichols (37, Ossipee)

LORING,
Catherine Marie, b. 10/9/1966 in Rochester; first; Russell G. Loring (Laconia) and Nancy J. Doe (Boston, MA)
Lisa April, b. 4/25/1975 in Rochester; Russell G. Loring and Mary L. Fifield

LOUD,
Estelle Myra, b. 10/6/1871; sixth; Ira Stevens Loud (Newfield, ME) and Ella Melvina Davis (Newfield, ME) (1941)

LOUGEE,
Christal Lee, b. 3/12/1971 in Wolfeboro; Philip Lougee and Marjorie F. Labor

LOVER,
daughter, b. 12/5/1888; fourth; Charles Lovie (sic) (laborer, Canada) and Mary J. Raymond (Canada)
daughter, b. 9/9/1905 in Union; first; Peter J. Lover (mill operative, 19, Union) and Alice M. Downs (16, Wakefield); residence - Union
Fred, b. 4/12/1895; fifth; Charles Lover (mill hand, Canada) and Mary J. Raymond (Gorham, ME)

LOW,
Martha Estelle, b. 8/17/1918; first; Edgar Low (merchant, 21, Sanford, ME) and Marjorie Shortridge (20, Brookfield)
Richard Sylvester, b. 7/22/1920; second; Edgar Low (laborer, 23, Sanford, ME) and Marjorie Shortridge (22, Brookfield); residence - Sanbornville

LUKEN,
Ashley Mae, b. 2/6/1987 in Dover; Terry Luken and Donna M. Anderson

LUSCOMB,
Julie Marie, b. 9/10/1982 in Rochester; Kenneth K. Luscomb and Patricia M. Mollica
Karen Krystal, b. 6/23/1951; second; Kenneth K. Luscomb (MA) and Juanita Clough (NH)

LYNCH,
John Patrick, b. 6/13/1974 in Rochester; John R. Lynch and Marie L. McCarthy

LYONS,
Lawrie Rebecca, b. 2/28/1953 in Wolfeboro; second; Donald Henry Lyons (MA) and Helen E. Herrick (NH)

Mark Andrew, b. 10/11/1951; first; Donald H. Lyons (Greenfield, MA) and Helen E. Herrick (Sanbornville)

MACBRIEN,
Theodore, b. 9/9/1940; first; Philip James MacBrien (Lynn, MA) and Mabel Frances Harmon (Ossipee)

MACDONALD,
Gloria Constance, b. 2/9/1927; third; Grover L. MacDonald (Vinalhaven, ME) and Grace R. Jordan (Sturbridge, MA)

MACKIE,
son [Donald], b. 10/7/1912; fourth; George R. Mackie (laborer, 41, Limington, ME) and Olive M. Lavoie (34, Wakefield)
Charlotte Roselma, b. 8/3/1916; fifth; George Mackie (mill hand, 45, Limington, ME) and Olive Lover (38, Wakefield)
Eugene L., b. 3/9/1908; second; George R. Mackie (mill operative, 36, Limington, ME) and Olive M. Lover (29, Wakefield)
George Albert, b. 5/8/1919; first; Clifford P. Mackie (leatherboard mill, 20, Portland, ME) and Elizabeth L. Buzzell (19, Newburyport, MA); residence - Union
Karen Beth, b. 5/24/1947; first; George A. Mackie (Wakefield) and Florence M. Stevens (Wakefield)
Lillian Beatrice, b. 6/3/1896; second; Millard Mackie (weaver, Limington, ME) and Ida Eaton (Brookfield); residence - Union
Madeline F., b. 10/25/1918; sixth; George R. Mackie (mill hand, 47, Limington, ME) and Olive M. Lavoie (40, Wakefield)
Marion A., b. 1/22/1894; first; Millard F. Mackie (mill operative, Limerick, ME) and Ida B. Eaton (Brookfield)
Mary Olive, b. 4/19/1911; third; George R. Mackie (laborer, 39, Limington, ME) and Olive M. Lover (32, Wakefield)
Perley A., b. 9/10/1897; third; Millard Mackie (mill hand, Limington, ME) and Ida Eaton (Brookfield)
Rudolph A., b. 6/14/1906; first; George R. Mackie (spinner, 35, Portland, ME) and Olive M. Lover (28, Union)
Thomas Steven, b. 4/6/1949; second; George A. Mackie (NH) and Florence M. Stevens (NH)

MACLEOD,
Alicia Marie, b. 3/21/1979 in Rochester; Joel H. MacLeod and Mary Ellen T. Stoddard
Joel Hayden, Jr., b. 5/19/1981 in Rochester; Joel H. MacLeod and Maryellen Stoddard
Kelley Marie, b. 3/25/1978 in Rochester; Joel H. MacLeod and Maryellen T. Stoddard

MADDIX,
Alberta A., b. 1/31/1902 in Sanbornville; fourth; W. A. Maddix (ice foreman, 45, Boston, MA) and Alberta Grimes (43, Boston, MA); residence - Sanbornville

MAGEE,
Megan Francine, b. 6/2/1979 in Rochester; Kerry W. Magee and Laura J. Howard

MAGER,
Arthur Fairbanks, b. 5/4/1936; first; Winthrop M. Mager (Taunton, MA) and Louise F. Lapham (Taunton, MA)

MAILLETT,
Ashlee Lorraine, b. 3/14/1991 in Dover; Glen Patrick Maillett and Victoria Lorraine Davis
Kelsey Anne, b. 7/13/1993 in Dover; Glen Patrick Maillett and Victoria Lorraine Davis

MAILLOUX,
Edward Martin, b. 12/27/1946; sixth; Joseph E. Mailloux (Canada) and Blanche I. Elliott (Middleton)
Joseph Frank, b. 4/12/1943; fourth; Joseph Eli Mailloux (Canada) and Blanche Irene Elliott (Middleton)

MALEHAM,
Darlene Althea, b. 4/12/1950; second; Herbert W. Maleham, Jr. (NH) and Marion E. Welch (ME)
Elmer Blakely, b. 12/23/1928; first; Elmer B. Maleham (Wakefield) and Hazel A. Downs (Sanbornville)
Ernest Hazelton, b. 12/21/1907; fourth; Charles H. Maleham (engineer, 33, Wakefield) and Grace Burroughs (29, Wakefield)

Herbert W., b. 9/29/1901; first; Charles Maleham (engineer, Wakefield) and Grace Burroughs (Wakefield)
Katherine Louisa, b. 6/24/1915; fifth; Charles H. Maleham (farmer, 40, Wakefield) and Grace M. Burroughs (35, Wakefield)
Marion Elsie, b. 2/23/1948; first; Herbert W. Maleham (Wolfeboro) and Marion E. Welch (Parsonsfield, ME)
William Hiram, b. 10/12/1960 in Wolfeboro; third; Herbert W. Maleham, Jr. (Wolfeboro) and Marion E. Welch (Parsonsfield, ME)

MALSTON,
Ronald Richard, b. 10/8/1969 in Wolfeboro; Douglas R. Malston and Virginia F. Zalenski

MANCUSO,
Eric William, b. 12/22/1983 in Rochester; Richard W. Mancuso and Dale L. Clark

MANNING,
Bridget Kate, b. 1/20/1987 in Hanover; James B. Manning and Deborah J. Wing

MANSFIELD,
Amanda Lin, b. 2/15/1985 in Rochester; David C. Mansfield and Lorraine A. Stafford
Edith Frances, b. 5/11/1918; first; Burleigh B. Mansfield (physician, 29, Hope, ME) and Florence A. Rand (28, Canada)
Lindsey Erin, b. 2/9/1982 in Rochester; David C. Mansfield and Lorraine M. Stafford

MANSUR,
Ernest William, b. 8/6/1893; third; Hiram W. Mansur (carpenter, Wakefield) and Emma F. Sibley (Medford, MA); residence - Waltham, MA
Eugene Pierce, b. 8/6/1893; second; Hiram W. Mansur (carpenter, Wakefield) and Emma F. Sibley (Medford, MA); residence - Waltham, MA
Maud E., b. 10/18/1875; first; Herbert S. Mansur (Boston, MA) and Lizzie S. Cummings (Wakefield) (1934)

MARCOU[X],
- son [Henry A.], b. 9/22/1887; fifth; Oliver Marcoux (laborer, Canada) and Calacedas ----- (Canada)
- daughter [Phebe S.], b. 6/14/1889; Oliver Marcoux (laborer, Canada) and Sarah Merchant (Canada)
- son [Edward J.], b. 2/1/1892; seventh; Oliver Marcoux (laborer, Canada) and Silada Merchaud (Canada)
- daughter, b. 3/17/1893; first; George A. Marcoux (laborer, Canada) and Rose Brouillard (Canada)
- son, b. 5/8/1893; eighth; Oliver Marcoux (laborer, Canada) and Celas Marshall (Canada)
- Albert J., b. 6/20/1900; seventh; Archie Marcoux (laborer, Canada) and Rose Brouillard (Canada); residence - Sanbornville
- Eugenia, b. 10/3/1896; ninth; Oliver Marcoux (laborer, Canada) and Celas Marshall (Canada); residence - Sanbornville
- George M.A., b. 12/5/1895; third; Archil Marcoux (laborer, Canada) and Rose Broullord (Canada)
- Iesha Brie, b. 4/29/1987 in Rochester; Francis J. Marcoux and Amber Lee Pike
- Joseph N., b. 4/14/1898; fifth; Archil Marcoux (laborer, Canada) and Rose Brouillard (Canada)
- Mary, b. 4/26/1894; second; Archie Marcoux (laborer, Canada) and Rose Brouillard (Canada)
- Mary Alice, b. 6/1/1899; sixth; Archie Marcou (laborer, Canada) and Rose Brouillard (Canada); residence - Sanbornville
- Tabitha Lee, b. 1/22/1992 in Rochester; Francis Joseph Marcoux and Amber Lee Pike

MARSEAR,
- Alfred, b. 9/5/1914; seventh; Fred Marsear (sawyer, 43, Sheffield, VT) and Laura Harnsworth (34, Montpelier, VT)
- Alpha, b. 9/5/1914; eighth; Fred Marsear (sawyer, 43, Sheffield, VT) and Laura Harnsworth (34, Montpelier, VT)

MARSHALL,
- Arthur William, b. 1/15/1907; third; Frank Marshall, Jr. (butcher, 30, Wakefield) and Phoebe J. Littlefield (25, Brookfield)
- Louis Franklin, b. 12/31/1904; second; Frank Marshall (laborer, 27, Wakefield) and Phoebe J. Littlefield (24, Brookfield)

Robert Conrad, b. 4/2/1938; first; Guy Conrad Marshall (York, ME) and
Ruth Eleanor Clark (Wolfeboro)
Samuel Edward, b. 1/30/1904; first; J. Frank Marshall (meat cutter, 27, Wakefield) and Phoebe J. Littlefield (22, Brookfield)

MARSTON,
stillborn son, b. 11/21/1906; first; Wilbur Marston (hostler, 27, Brownfield, ME) and Mary E. Hurd (18, Freedom)
Tammy Jean, b. 12/24/1965 in Wolfeboro; fourth; Freeland S. Marston (Freeport, ME) and Lucille M. Gosselin (Brunswick, ME)

MARTIN,
stillborn daughter, b. 1/25/1899; fourth; Napoleon Martin (laborer, PQ) and Josie Brown (Ossipee)
son, b. 5/7/1915; third; Henry W. Martin (plumber, 32, Galveston, TX) and Alisa M. Mayo (21, Keene); residence - USSS Salem
Adrianna Rose, b. 11/5/1995 in Wolfeboro; William Clyde Martin, III and Cheryl Lynn Brown
Anna Marie, b. 10/12/1982 in Wolfeboro; Alfred G. Martin and Lisa M. Stefanski
Courtney Elizabeth, b. 8/8/1989 in Wolfeboro; William Clyde Martin, III and Cheryl Lynn Brown
David Chris, b. 4/13/1966 in Rochester; tenth; James D. Martin (Revere, MA) and Ruth E. Valley (Milton Mills)
James Daniel, III, b. 4/11/1984 in Wolfeboro; James D. Martin, Jr. and Diana L. Sprague
James David, Jr., b. 4/9/1963 in Rochester; tenth; James D. Martin (Revere, MA) and Ruth E. Valley (Milton Mills)
Kenneth Michael, b. 9/18/1950; second; George R. Martin (Boston, MA) and Margaret L. Drown (Wakefield)
Lafayette, b. 4/30/1896; second; Napoleon Martin (laborer, PQ) and Josie Brown (Ossipee)
Leanne Kristy, b. 7/16/1985 in Wolfeboro; James D. Martin, Jr. and Diana L. Sprague
Louise Ann, b. 7/31/1956 in Wolfeboro; third; George R. Martin (Everett, MA) and Margaret L. Drown (Wakefield)
Wayne Robert, b. 6/18/1948; first; George R. Martin (Boston, MA) and Margaret L. Drown (Wakefield)

MARTINEAU,
stillborn daughter, b. 11/13/1903; sixth; Napoleon Martineau (laborer, 35, Canada) and Josie Brown (31, Ossipee); residence - Union
Chester, b. 5/29/1901; fifth; Napoleon Martineau (laborer, Canada) and Josie Brown (Ossipee); residence - Union
Forest, b. 10/8/1897; third; Napoleon Martineau (laborer, Canada) and Josie Brown (Ossipee)

MASON,
Hannah Joyce, b. 11/11/1992 in Dover; David John Mason and Deborah Jean Brown
Margaret Ruth, b. 6/21/1995 in Dover; David John Mason and Deborah Jean Brown

MASSEY,
Christopher Ryan, b. 2/25/1992 in Dover; William Joseph Massey and Karen Ann Muise

MATHIAS,
Brendon James, b. 12/2/1996 in Rochester; Paul Anthony Mathias and Beverly Lise Gogan

MATTOCKS,
daughter, b. 11/11/1897; first; George Mattocks (farmer, Newfield, ME) and Alice Patch (Newfield, ME); residence - Newfield, ME

MATTRESS,
Stacey Ann, b. 3/18/1977 in Wolfeboro; John E. Mattress and Linda L. Colby

MAXFIELD,
Melissa Lynn, b. 3/29/1981 in Rochester; Danny M. Maxfield and Lori M. Stevens
Travis Danny, b. 3/27/1978 in Rochester; Danny M. Maxfield and Lori M. Stevens

MAY,
Charles Hustin, b. 4/15/1893; first; Hustin May (carpenter, Northfield, VT) and Kittie Durgin (Scotland)

McBRIDE,
Elizabeth Helen, b. 5/11/1974 in Wolfeboro; Wayne F. McBride and Marilyn E. Phillips
John Philip, b. 3/18/1977 in Wolfeboro; Wayne F. McBride and Marilyn E. Phillips

McCARTHY,
Megan Jean, b. 4/29/1988 in Wolfeboro; Francis W. McCarthy and Gloria J. Gray

McCREA,
Lyman Eugene, b. 8/17/1948; first; Frederick G. McCrea (Shannon, NB) and Viola E. Butler (Sherburne, NS)

McCRILLIS,
Bernice Fay, b. 8/23/1912; second; Harry McCrillis (engineer, 36, Rochester) and Ethel May Willey (32, Wakefield)
Ester Louise, b. 2/13/1910; first; Harry H. McCrillis (fireman, 33, Rochester) and Ethel M. Willey (30, Wakefield)
Marion A., b. 5/9/1893; fourth; Frank G. McCrillis (engineer, Lebanon, ME) and Sarah E. McCrillis (Newfield, ME)

McDERMOTT,
Wayne Robert, b. 9/2/1951; second; Paul R. McDermott (MA) and Genevieve M. Bavis (MA)

McDONALD,
daughter, b. 9/30/1888; ninth; Malcolm McDonald (section man, PEI) and Amanda Crockett (Mechanic Falls, ME)
son, b. 12/8/1891; first; Malcolm McDonald (section man, PEI) and Amanda Crockett (Mechanic Falls, ME)
stillborn daughter, b. 9/13/1897; fifth; George A. McDonald (brakeman, Boston, MA) and Louie Parker (Saugus, MA)
Carroll Wesley, b. 1/4/1893; twelfth; Malcolm McDonald (RR section, PEI) and Amanda Crockett (Mechanic Falls, ME)
Edith Shirley, b. 10/24/1909; third; Arthur McDonald (brakeman, 28, Wakefield) and Leona M. Hall (24, Sawyers River, VT)
Ernest E., b. 3/6/1907; second; Alonzo M. McDonald (laborer, 31, Wakefield) and Helen F. Bickford (20, Alton)

Evelyn Ethel, b. 10/10/1908; first; Ronald B. McDonald (blacksmith, 24, Brookfield, PEI) and Susie M. Paine (21, Woodbury, VT)

Evelyn Florence, b. 6/21/1920; first; Carroll W. McDonald (RR section, 27, Wakefield) and Alice J. Livine (26, Canada)

James Joseph, b. 11/27/1935; first; James J. McDonald (Belmont, MA) and Dorothy Clark (Sanbornville)

Janice Lee, b. 8/30/1943; fourth; James J. McDonald, Jr. (Belmont, MA) and Dorothy Madeline Clark (Sanbornville)

John Frank, b. 11/25/1938; third; James J. McDonald, Jr. (Belmont, MA) and Dorothy M. Clark (Sanbornville)

Judith Ann, b. 4/29/1937; second; James McDonald (Belmont, MA) and Dorothy Clark (Sanbornville)

Malcolm, Jr., b. 7/28/1875; second; Malcolm McDonald (PEI) and Amanda Crockett (Mechanics Falls, ME) (1939)

Ralph Harold, b. 11/17/1905; second; Arthur McDonald (woodsman, 24, North Wakefield) and Leona Hall (20, Sawyer's River)

Roy Albert, b. 9/29/1894; fourth; George A. McDonald (farmer, Boston, MA) and Louie G. Parker (Saugus, MA)

Verna Beatrice, b. 2/4/1912; fourth; Arthur McDonald (brakeman, 29, Wakefield) and Leona Hall (27, Sawyer River, VT)

Vincent Sherwood, b. 8/24/1921; sixth; Arthur W. McDonald (brakeman, 37, Wakefield) and Leona M. Hall (35, Sawyers River)

Winfield Scott, b. 6/22/1894; thirteenth; Malcolm McDonald (section man, PEI) and Amanda Crockett (Mechanic Falls, ME)

McDONOUGH,

Ashley Marie, b. 4/28/1991 in Wolfeboro; Steven Paul McDonough and Jill Ellen Barron

Kerin Anne, b. 10/8/1993 in Wolfeboro; Steven Paul McDonough and Jill Ellen Barron

McDOUGAL,

Brody Joseph, b. 3/28/1997 in Portsmouth; Stephen Gerald McDougal and Ruby Ann Rose

Connor Stephen, b. 3/3/1994 in Wolfeboro; Stephen Gerald McDougal and Donna Lee Granigan

McGAW,

Eric Malcolm, b. 10/4/1948; second; David E. McGaw (Winthrop, MA) and Elizabeth M. Tucker (Winthrop, MA)

McINTIRE,
Lynn Marie, b. 4/5/1959 in Rochester; first; Robert E. McIntire (Rochester) and Lena G. Smith (Milton)

McKINNEY,
son, b. 3/14/1980 in Rochester; William J. McKinney and Charlene Bosley
Brian Stewart, b. 6/23/1981 in Wolfeboro; Brian P. McKinney and Lorie A. Wellington
Michael David, b. 2/9/1975 in Wolfeboro; Brian P. McKinney and Diane M. Bouchard
William John, Jr., b. 11/9/1978 in Rochester; William J. McKinney and Charlene E. Bosley

McKUHEN,
Stephanie Ann, b. 1/6/1986 in Rochester; Alan M. McKuhen and Robin A. St. Hilaire

McLELLAN,
Betty Lona, b. 3/17/1934; second; Roderick McLellan (Sydney, NS) and Rose M. Dodier (Sanbornville)
Marilyn Jane, b. 9/22/1935; third; Roderick J. McLellan (Sidney, NS) and Rose Dodier (Sanbornville)

McMANUS,
Caitlyn Elizabeth, b. 2/7/1990 in Rochester; David Michael McManus and Keri Susan Wilfret

McMULLIN,
Leah Elizabeth, b. 4/26/1989 in Rochester; Donald Lee McMullin and Sheila Regina Hurley

McNEIL,
daughter, b. 2/4/1892; third; Phebe McNeil (Canada)

McPHERSON,
Becky Lynn, b. 10/20/1980 in Rochester; Norman L. McPherson and Mildred R. Fifield
Kenneth Earl, Jr., b. 4/27/1966 in Wolfeboro; first; Kenneth E. McPherson (Winchendon, MA) and Carol E. Booth (Manchester)

Kevin Michael, b. 8/11/1970 in Rochester; Russell McPherson and Dianne H. Lowell
Tracie Lee, b. 10/19/1969 in Wolfeboro; Norman L. McPherson and Marie A. Adjutant

McQUIGGAN,
Janice Jeanine, b. 11/18/1976 in Wolfeboro; Richard J. McQuiggan and Janice S. Simons

McWILLIAMS,
Nicholas Francis, b. 1/27/1992 in Dover; Francis Xavier McWilliams and Karen Marie Swanson

MEADER,
Lucy Bell, b. 2/18/1889; first; Ellsworth Meader (laborer, Stoneham, ME) and Annie B. Granner (St. Johns, NB)

MEE,
stillborn daughter, b. 3/8/1889; first; Robert Mee (RR fireman, England) and Ella M. Remick (Brookfield)
daughter, b. 9/28/1891; second; John H. Mee (farmer, Mansfield, England) and Agnes E. Libbey (Wakefield)
Albert, b. 5/29/1875; seventh; John Mee (England) and Ellen Smith (Scotland) (1936)
Jane E., b. 10/7/1877; eighth; John Mee (England) and Ellen Smith (Scotland) (1936)
John, b. 8/2/1889; first; John H. Mee (sectionman, England) and Agnes E. Libbey (Wakefield)
Mary E., b. 10/19/1872; sixth; John Mee (England) and Ellen Smith (Scotland) (1936)
William Nathan, b. 7/17/1894; third; John H. Mee (farmer, England) and Agnes E. Libbey (Wakefield)

MEIKLE,
Helen, b. 8/21/1879; William Alexander Meikle (Scotland) and Catherine Steele (Scotland) (1943)
Jane, b. 8/1/1884; William Alexander Meikle (Scotland) and Catherine Steele (Scotland) (1943)
Mary McArthur, b. 8/16/1877; William Alexander Meikle (Scotland) and Catherine Steele (Scotland) (1943)

MELANSON,
daughter, b. 4/21/1927; second; Osmond J. Melanson (Groveton, MA) and Wilma F. Knox (Seabrook, MA)
Angela Robin, b. 12/6/1989 in Rochester; Ronald Ralph Melanson, Jr. and Lu-Ann Furtado
Lawrence Ernest, b. 5/21/1927; third; Carroll T. Melanson (Canaan) and Hazel Sibley (Lynn, MA) (1940)
Roy Elwin, b. 7/2/1912; second; Fred Melanson (laborer, 26, Canaan) and Carrie Marshall (23, Brighton, MA)

MENARD,
Caswell, b. 8/10/1907; first; Edmund Menard (laborer, 23, Wakefield) and Ethel Fellows (17, Wakefield)

MERCER,
Eric Kenneth, b. 10/13/1997 in Wolfeboro; Scott Eric Mercer and Nicki Lynn Lavanway
Shannon Lynn, b. 12/2/1995 in Wolfeboro; Scott Eric Mercer and Nicki Lynn Lavanway

MERRILL,
Christopher Nathaniel, b. 12/24/1988 in Dover; David E. Merrill and Barbara J. Cormier
Gerald Norman, II, b. 7/4/1973 in Wolfeboro; Gerald N. Merrill and Sherron Murphy

MESERVE,
Clarence Osman, b. 4/4/1884; second; Joseph H. Meserve (Wakefield) and Emma E. Fall (Ossipee) (1944)
David Clarence, b. 9/28/1953 in Wolfeboro; second; Edward Herbert Meserve (NH) and Sarah B. Mackie (MA)
Edward Herbert, b. 11/22/1927; second; Clarence Meserve (Wakefield) and Pauline Carter (Wakefield, MA)
Helen Inez, b. 9/30/1925; first; Clarence O. Meserve (Woodman) and Pauline Carter (Wakefield, MA)
Herbert Everett, b. 8/18/1880; first; Joseph H. Meserve (Wakefield) and Emma E. Fall (Ossipee) (1944)
James Lee, b. 9/25/1940; fourth; Clarence Osmon Meserve (Wakefield) and Pauline Carter (Wakefield, MA) (1941)

John Nathaniel, b. 5/10/1938; third; Clarence O. Meserve (Wakefield) and
Pauline Carter (Wakefield, MA) (1939)
Kathy Sarah, b. 3/27/1959 in Wolfeboro; third; Edward H. Meserve
(Wakefield) and Sarah B. Mackie (Norwood, MA)
Leon Elmer, b. 3/19/1894; third; Joseph H. Meserve (farmer, Wakefield)
and Emily E. Fall (Ossipee)
Paul Chesley, b. 5/22/1935; ninth; Frank C. Meserve (Freedom) and
Marguerite Emerson (Barnstead)
Susan Frances, b. 10/25/1952 in Wolfeboro; first; Edward H. Meserve
(Wakefield) and Sarah B. Mackie (Norwood, MA)

MESREAU,
Eva Alice, b. 11/20/1897; first; Edward Mesreau (mill hand, NB) and Gene
Pudreau (Canada)

METZEN,
Ester Carver, b. 1/11/1921; third; Edward G. Metzen (edge trimmer, 36,
Buffalo, NY) and Hilda Carver (32, Livingston, MT); residence -
Sanbornville
June Anna, b. 5/19/1923; fourth; Edwin Metzen (painter, Buffalo, NY) and
Hilda Carver; residence - Sanbornville

MEYER,
Frederick Augustus, IV, b. 1/4/1981 in Wolfeboro; Frederick A. Meyer, III
and Patricia L. Parker
Trevor Ernest, b. 9/12/1978 in Wolfeboro; Frederick A. Meyer, III and
Patricia L. Parker

MICHALSKY,
Samantha Ann, b. 1/28/1980 in Wolfeboro; Stephen Michalsky, Jr. and
Susan M. Gerak

MIELAUSKAS,
Susan Louise, b. 5/18/1948; second; William F. Mielauskas (No.
Attleboro, MA) and Pauline G. Scheetz (Philadelphia, PA)

MILINER,
Andrew Thomas, b. 6/24/1983 in Rochester; Paul A. Miliner and Lorrie A.
Weeks

Cassandra Gail, b. 10/12/1989 in Wolfeboro; Paul Andrew Miliner and Lorrie Ann Weeks

Catie Marie, b. 9/14/1988 in Wolfeboro; Gary L. Miliner and April J. Welch

Charles Vinton, b. 7/12/1980 in Wolfeboro; Gary L. Miliner and April J. Welch

David Vinton, b. 4/10/1957 in Wolfeboro; fourth; Vinton Miliner (Farmington) and Olida D. Soucy (Salmon Falls)

Dwight Edward, b. 12/8/1948; second; Vinton Miliner (Farmington) and Olida Doris Soucy (Salmon Falls)

Elizabeth Olida, b. 8/22/1987 in Rochester; Paul A. Miliner and Lorrie A. Weeks

Gary Lawrence, b. 12/27/1952 in Rochester; third; Vinton Miliner (Farmington) and Olida D. Soucy (Salmon Falls)

James William, b. 3/16/1947; first; Vinton Miliner (Farmington) and Olida D. Soucy (Salmon Falls)

Kathryn Eileen, b. 4/17/1951; second; Elmor Miliner (Farmington) and Frances M. Corson (Wakefield)

Keith Elmore, b. 2/28/1948; first; Elmore Miliner (Farmington) and Frances M. Corson (Wakefield)

Keith William, b. 4/3/1981 in Rochester; Keith E. Miliner and Sandra J. Taylor

Lori Jean, b. 11/2/1977 in Rochester; Keith E. Miliner and Sandra J. Taylor

Paul Andrew, b. 10/18/1960 in Wolfeboro; fifth; Vinton Miliner (Farmington) and Olida D. Soucy (Salmon Falls)

Ranee Lee, b. 5/27/1969 in Wolfeboro; James W. Miliner and Sandra L. Dudley

Susan Lynn, b. 6/22/1971 in Rochester; Keith E. Milinul (sic) and Sandra J. Taylor

MILLER,

son [Ernest R.], b. 10/11/1896; second; W. R. Miller (mechanic, Brownfield, ME) and Christie G. McDonald (Wakefield)

daughter, b. 2/12/1907; seventh; William H. Miller (laborer, 37, Brownfield, ME) and Christy G. McDonald (29, Wakefield)

Alice Ray, b. 8/7/1905; sixth; William H. Miller (engineer, 32, Brownfield, ME) and Christy McDonald (25, Wakefield)

Audrey A., b. 6/7/1903; fifth; William H. Miller (engineer, 30, Brownfield, ME) and Christie McDonald (22, Wakefield)

Cody Christopher, b. 9/22/1998 in Rochester; Christopher Miller and Jennifer Miller

Frances Ellen, b. 9/24/1908; fifth; Daniel W. Miller (laborer, 38, Jeddo, PA) and Abbie E. Rand (27, Gilford)

Sarah Phyetta, b. 6/23/1911; sixth; Daniel W. Miller (laborer, 42, PA) and Abbie E. Rand (30, Laconia)

William Rodney, b. 11/15/1895; first; William H. Miller (mechanic, Brownfield, ME) and Christy McDonald (Wakefield)

MILLINER,

daughter, b. 8/17/1921; fifth; James W. Milliner (laborer, NB) and Ardena French (New Durham); residence - Farmington

MILLS,

son, b. 12/18/1912; sixth; Fred Mills (sect. foreman, 38, Madbury) and Annie Eaton (38, Brookfield)

Agnes, b. 12/17/1901; second; Fred Mills (mason, Madbury) and Annie Eaton (Brookfield)

Clara May, b. 10/25/1904; third; Fred W. Mills (laborer, 30, Madbury) and Annie L. Eaton (30, Brookfield)

Flora Rebecka, b. 9/28/1910; fifth; Fred Mills (laborer, 35, Madbury) and Annie Eaton (35, Brookfield)

Norman William, b. 3/3/1909; fourth; Fred W. Mills (laborer, 34, Madbury) and Annie L. Eaton (33, Brookfield)

MITCHELL,

Tyler Robert, b. 4/19/1998 in Dover; Robert Lee Mitchell, Jr. and Joyelle Hughson

MOFFETT,

Amber Marie, b. 10/8/1986 in Rochester; David J. Moffett and Rose M. Church

MONAHAN,

son, b. 4/3/1922; ninth; Frank Monohan (sic) (lineman, Cambridge, MA) and Minnie D. Lover (Union); residence - Union

Charles Francis, b. 9/7/1909; second; Francis T. Monahan (brass moulder, 22, Cambridge, MA) and Lumina Lavoie (20, Wakefield)

Francis Melvin, b. 5/19/1919; seventh; Frank T. Monahan (moulder, 32, Cambridge, MA) and Minnie D. Lover (31, Wakefield)

Joseph Paul, b. 3/6/1912; fifth; Frank T. Monahan (brass moulder, 24, Cambridge, MA) and Minnie O. Lavoie (22, Wakefield)
Mary Irene, b. 2/14/1908; first; Francis T. Monahan (core maker, 23, Cambridge, MA) and Lumina Lavoie (19, Wakefield)
Mathew Roy, b. 3/16/1918; sixth; Frank T. Monahan (brass moulder, 31, Cambridge, MA) and Minnie Lavoie (30, Wakefield)
Robert Edward, b. 7/1/1920; eighth; Frank T. Monahan (electrician, 33, Cambridge, MA) and Minnie D. Lover (32, Wakefield)
Wilfred R., b. 4/16/1916; fifth; Frank Monahan (brass moulder, 29, Cambridge, MA) and Minnie Lover (28, Wakefield)

MONROE,
Richie Anne, b. 7/15/1970 in Sanford, ME; Richard S. Monroe and Mary A. Norton

MONSON,
Donald Harris, b. 2/3/1928; third; Hallis Monson (Portland, ME) and Bertha Williams (Ossipee)

MONTGOMERY,
Michael Van, b. 1/29/1971 in Rochester; Richard Montgomery and Su Mai

MOODY,
Jarid Anthony, b. 8/12/1981 in Wolfeboro; Ronald A. Moody and Susan L. Bennett
Keri Sue, b. 1/4/1975 in Wolfeboro; Ronald A. Moody and Susan L. Bennett
Tani Leigh, b. 4/13/1988 in Rochester; Daniel P. Moody and Lois E. Smith

MOOERS,
Christine Elizabeth, b. 7/1/1981 in Rochester; Rodney S. Mooers and Joanne Nicholson
Matthew Scott, b. 8/14/1979 in Rochester; Rodney S. Mooers and Joanne Nicholson
Rebecca Ann, b. 9/26/1985 in Rochester; Rodney S. Mooers and Joanne Nicholson

MOONEY,
James G., b. 4/2/1910; fifth; James S. Mooney (farmer, 41, Tamworth) and Clara Giffin (42, Gillespie, IL)

Scott Everett, b. 2/3/1969 in Wolfeboro; Stanley E. Mooney and Phyllis M. Duplissa

Tammy Lynne, b. 10/5/1971 in Rochester; Stanley A. Mooney and Karen K. Luscomb

MOORE,

Angeline, b. 10/6/1897; ninth; Joseph Moore (laborer, Canada) and Artemise Pourtrie (Canada)

Arthur Romeo, b. 1/31/1914; seventh; Leon Moore (laborer, 41, Canada) and Jennie Bouvin (36, Canada)

Eugene, b. 7/4/1899; first; Malcrom J. Moore (clerk, Effingham) and Lillian M. Harding (Wakefield)

Floyd, b. 6/25/1904; third; Malcom J. Moore (laborer, 29, Effingham) and Lillian Harding (28, Rochester)

George Albert, b. 2/5/1911; fifth; Leon Moore (laborer, 38, Quebec) and Jennie Bourvin (33, Quebec)

Howard P., b. 8/23/1902; second; Malcolm J. Moore (laborer, 27, Effingham) and Lillian Harding (26, Rochester); residence - Union

Joseph Gideon Edward, b. 5/6/1926; third; Andrew Moore (Somersworth) and Juliette Belleau (Canada)

Julia, b. 4/16/1896; eighth; Joseph Moore (laborer, Canada) and Arthemis Pourtrie (Canada); residence - Sanbornville

Marie Laura, b. 1/8/1912; fifth; Leon Moore (laborer, 39, Canada) and Jennie Bernard (34, Canada)

Pamela Jean, b. 7/10/1981 in Salem, MA; Paul A. Moore, Jr. and Susan E. York

MOREAU,

Adam Joseph, b. 3/11/1983 in Exeter; Bruce E. Moreau and Marjorie L. Smart

MOREN,

Barbara Ann, b. 4/19/1931 in Wolfeboro; Joseph Moren and Agnes Hamilton (1932)

MORGAN,

Dorothy A., b. 6/21/1917; first; Russell B. Morgan (clerk, 25, Malden, MA) and Ruth E. Dodge (17, Raymond)

MORIARTY,
Daniel Patrick, b. 6/5/1991 in Rochester; William Edward Moriarty, III and Charlene Anne McGovern
William Edward, IV, b. 3/28/1988 in Dover; William E. Moriarty, III and Charlene A. McGovern

MORIN,
Annette Grace, b. 6/29/1917; first; Samuel Morin (fireman, 23, Ashland) and Ora Dyer (18, Wakefield)
Deborah Jeannette, b. 7/26/1974 in Rochester; Raymond A. Morin and Christine J. Tarlton
Joseph Alfred Richard, b. 6/18/1920; third; Samuel L. Morin (steam engineer, 26, Ashland) and Ora P. Dyer (21, Wakefield)

MORRILL,
Fred Raymond, Jr., b. 2/23/1949; first; Fred R. Morrill, Sr. (Acton, ME) and Eva C. Meyor (Needham, MA)
Howard Earl, b. 4/22/1943; tenth; Harry William Morrill (No. Windham, ME) and Phyllis LaDelle Grant (Acton, ME)
Kenneth Michael, b. 11/8/1996 in Dover; Michael Vernon Morrill and Judith Anne Burker
Leonard Wallace, b. 8/12/1920; sixth; Fred A. Morrill (auto painter, 50, Amesbury, MA) and Bessie E. Tucker (34, Kingston); residence - N. Reading, MA
Phyllis LaDelle, b. 3/28/1941; ninth; Harry William Morrill (No. Windham, ME) and Phyllis LaDelle Grant (Acton, ME)
Robert Lee, Jr., b. 6/16/1987 in No. Conway; Robert L. Morrill and Lisa Ann Weston

MORRISON,
Ruth, b. 2/9/1904; second; George W. Morrison (brass mfr., 35, Moultonboro) and Clara H. Hamlin (29, Newfields)

MORROW,
Nat Lindley, b. 4/18/1897; first; Thomas M. Morrow (machinist, Dover) and Minnie A. Ham (Farmington)

MORSE,
Abbie, b. 10/5/1857; second; Daniel Morse (Morsely, England) and Elizabeth Wiggin (Wakefield) (1936)

MORTON,
Paul Carroll, b. 3/11/1908; first; Charles Morton (clerk, 31, Lynn, MA) and Mabel Richards (26, Wakefield)

MOSCONE,
Adam Scott, b. 6/5/1981 in Dover; John M. Moscone and Jane E. McQuarrie

MUCCI,
Louisa E., b. 10/10/1902 in Sanbornville; Angelo Mucci (merchant, 29, Italy) and Julia Lorenz (24, Italy); residence - Sanbornville
Marion Umile, b. 8/24/1904; third; Angelo Mucci (fruit dealer, 32, Italy) and Julia Lorenz (25, Italy)

MUCHER,
George John, 3d, b. 3/24/1963 in Rochester; first; George J. Mucher, Jr. (Brooklyn, NY) and Dorothy J. Janas (Manchester)
Mary Frances, b. 10/30/1964 in Rochester; second; George J. Mucher (Brooklyn, NY) and Dorothy J. Jonas (Manchester)

MULRAIN,
Eddie, b. 5/28/1892; first; Thomas Mulrain (weaver, Leicester, MA) and Maria McNamara (Ireland)

MURCH,
Dorothy Libbey, b. 7/1/1904; first; Herbert A. Murch (RR mail clerk, 36, Biddeford, ME) and May Hill (30, Fryeburg, ME)

MURPHY,
William Eric, b. 5/28/1979 in Rochester; William J. Murphy, Jr. and Doris E. Nichols

MURRAY,
Jacqueline Elizabeth, b. 9/22/1961 in Wolfeboro; second; Peter J. Murray (Salem, MA) and Nancy C. Drew (Wolfeboro)
Janice Lea, b. 7/17/1963 in Wolfeboro; third; Peter J. Murray (Salem, MA) and Nancy C. Drew (Wolfeboro)
Jennette Marie, b. 2/10/1981 in Rochester; Charles J. Murray and Gloria J. LeBlanc

MYERS,
Jacob Job, b. 9/15/1995 in Dover; Mikel Howard Myers and Sandra Marie Brown

NADEAU,
Anthony Logan, b. 3/23/1977 in Rochester; Robert J. Nadeau and Michelle D. Carvell

NASON,
stillborn daughter, b. 6/6/1915; seventh; Almon L. Nason (laborer, 36, Bridgton, ME) and Nancy J. Streeter (29, Wakefield)
son, b. 4/7/1922; second; Willis L. Nason (laborer, Wakefield) and Maude Reed (Wakefield); residence - Union
son, b. 10/18/1928; second; Fred Nason (Wakefield) and Evelyn Weymouth (So. Boston, MA)
Amy Elizabeth, b. 6/12/1978 in Wolfeboro; Robert A. Nason and Judith A. Patriquin
Beverly Ruth, b. 5/14/1947; second; Glendon R. Nason (Union) and Marion R. Stevens (Union)
Bruce Richard, b. 11/24/1954 in Wolfeboro; second; Lawrence Chesley Nason (Wakefield) and Marilyn Elizabeth French (Milton)
Caitlin Elizabeth, b. 10/29/1989 in Rochester; Todd Cameron Nason and Christine Marie DiPrizio
Carissa Ellen, b. 11/11/1993 in Rochester; Todd Cameron Nason and Christine Marie DiPrizio
Courtney Lyn, b. 2/18/1988 in Rochester; Todd C. Nason and Christine M. DiPrizio
Crystal Marie, b. 6/4/1979 in Rochester; Ernest R. Nason, Jr. and Chris A. Moody
Daniel Gary, b. 5/10/1955 in Rochester; fourth; Glendon Reed Nason (Union) and Marion Ruth Stevens (Union)
Darcie Ann, b. 12/18/1965 in Wolfeboro; second; David H. Nason (Wolfeboro) and Nancy L. Dodier (Cambridge, MA)
David Allen, b. 10/30/1963 in Wolfeboro; first; David H. Nason (Wolfeboro) and Nancy L. Dodier (Cambridge, MA)
David Harry, b. 8/22/1943; fourth; Ernest Everett Nason (Sanbornville) and Dorothy Myrtle Cate (Gray, ME)
Dean Frederick, b. 9/20/1959 in Wolfeboro; first; Fred E. Nason (Wakefield) and Mary J. Bailey (Cambridge, MA)

Dianne Mary, b. 4/12/1952 in Wolfeboro; sixth; Ernest E. Nason (NH) and Dorothy M. Cate (ME)

Donald Robert, b. 8/19/1927; first; Fred H. Nason (Wakefield) and Evelyn Weymouth (Boston, MA)

Dorothy Bianca, b. 1/7/1969 in Wolfeboro; David H. Nason and Nancy Dodier

Dustin Arron, b. 6/15/1985 in Rochester; Clarence C. Nason, Jr. and Noreene L. Provencher

Edith May, b. 4/22/1914; sixth; Almon Nason (laborer, 34, Bridgton, ME) and Nancy Streader (28, Wakefield)

Edward James, b. 1/18/1964 in Wolfeboro; second; Edward B. Nason (Wolfeboro) and Arline M. Zalenski (Boston, MA)

Edward Rodney, b. 3/7/1912; fifth; Almon L. Nason (laborer, 33, Bridgton, ME) and Nancy J. Streader (27, Wakefield)

Eric Lee, b. 2/9/1993 in Wolfeboro; David Allen Nason and Lisa Gail Weeks

Ernest Everett, b. 7/15/1916; eighth; Almon L. Nason (laborer, 37, Bridgton, ME) and Nancy J. Streader (30, Wakefield)

Ernest Raymond, b. 3/27/1938; first; Ernest Everett Nason (Sanbornville) and Dorothy Myrtie Cate (Gray, ME)

Evelyn May, b. 9/12/1940; third; Ernest Scott Nason (Sanbornville) and Dorothy Myrtle Cate (Gray, ME)

Fred Harding, b. 7/22/1907; third; Almon L. Nason (laborer, 28, Bridgton, ME) and Nancy J. Streader (21, Wakefield)

Gerald Almon, b. 8/13/1939; second; Ernest Everett Nason (Wakefield) and Dorothy Myrtle Cate (Gray, ME)

Glendon, b. 12/7/1923; third; Willis Nason (laborer, Wakefield) and Maud Reed (Wakefield); residence - Union

Glenn Arthur, b. 4/10/1964 in Wolfeboro; third; Ernest R. Nason (Wolfeboro) and Meredith J. Cook (Wolfeboro)

Glenn Ray, b. 10/23/1945; first; Glendon Reed Nason (Union) and Marion R. Stevens (Union)

Gregory Alan, b. 2/10/1960 in Rochester; sixth; Glendon R. Nason (Sanbornville) and Marion R. Stevens (Union)

Jacob Elden, b. 9/4/1996 in Wolfeboro; Dean Frederick Nason and Robin Kachoris

James Michael, b. 6/20/1972 in Wolfeboro; Michael W. Nason and Shirley L. Riley

Janet Elizabeth, b. 1/27/1936; second; Edward Nason (Sanbornville) and Ida Drapeau (Brookfield)

Jeremy Michael, b. 5/6/1991 in Wolfeboro; Dean Frederick Nason and Robin Kachoris

Joanne M., b. 10/10/1960 in Wolfeboro; second; Ernest R. Nason (Wolfeboro) and Meredith J. Cook (Wolfeboro)

John Frederick, b. 10/30/1987 in Wolfeboro; Dean F. Nason and Robin Kachoris

Joseph Scott, b. 2/6/1984 in Wolfeboro; Ernest R. Nason, Jr. and Chris A. Moody

Joshua David, b. 6/6/1987 in Rochester; David A. Nason and Lisa G. Weeks

Justin Allen, b. 10/26/1988 in Rochester; David A. Nason and Lisa G. Weeks

Karen Sally, b. 6/28/1965 in Wolfeboro; fourth; Ernest S. Nason (Wolfeboro) and Meredith J. Cook (Wolfeboro)

Kathie Elaine, b. 10/11/1951; third; Glendon R. Nason (Union) and Marion R. Stevens (Union)

Kathleen Faye, b. 10/23/1961 in Wolfeboro; first; Edward B. Nason (Wolfeboro) and Arline M. Zalenski (Boston, MA)

Kayla Ann, b. 7/8/1987 in Wolfeboro; Robert A. Nason and Judith A. Patriquin

Larry Mark, b. 4/27/1957 in Rochester; fifth; Glendon R. Nason (Sanbornville) and Marion R. Stevens (Union)

Lawrence C., b. 1/24/1930; third; Fred H. Nason (Sanbornville) and Evelyn Weymouth (So. Boston, MA)

Marie Elizabeth, b. 5/25/1971 in Wolfeboro; Michael W. Nason and Shirley L. Riley

Maurice E., b. 7/8/1929; fourth; Willis Nason (Sanbornville) and Maude E. Reed (Union)

Michael Wayne, b. 6/19/1949; first; Lawrence C. Nason (Sanbornville) and Marilyn E. French (Milton)

Raymond Libbey, b. 12/7/1908; fourth; Almon L. Nason (laborer, 29, Bridgton, ME) and Nancy J. Streader (23, Wakefield)

Rebecca, b. 1/7/1954 in Wolfeboro; first; Johnnie Willis Nason (Union) and Winifred Downs (Union)

Robert Almond, b. 7/2/1958 in Wolfeboro; third; Lawrence C. Nason (Sanbornville) and Marilyn E. French (Milton)

Rodney Edward, b. 1/6/1937; third; Edward R. Nason (Sanbornville) and Ida M. Drapeau (Sanbornville)

Samantha Marie, b. 1/5/1989 in Dover; Edward James Nason and Tina Maria Sargent

Sandra Ann, b. 8/9/1944; fifth; Ernest Everett Nason (Sanbornville) and Evelyn D. Cate (Gray, ME)

Steven Aron, b. 8/25/1908; second; Joseph F. Nason (Ctr. Sandwich) and Nellie Carlin (New Durham) (1943)

Steven Howard, b. 11/3/1990 in Wolfeboro; David Allen Nason and Lisa Gail Weeks

Travis Tyler, b. 3/20/1997 in Rochester; Clarence Charles Nason, Jr. and Kelly Ann Adjutant

Virginia Inez, b. 1/8/1921; first; Willis Nason (laborer, 18, Sanbornville) and Maud Reed (21, Union); residence - Sanbornville

NEAL,

Elizabeth Edna, b. 12/4/1913; first; Charles H. Neal (shoe turner, 25, Brookfield) and Edna B. Richards (23, Wakefield); residence - Brookfield

June Julie, b. 11/16/1951; first; Ernest C. Neal (NH) and Julia E. Hollenbeck (NH)

Lisa Louise, b. 10/11/1959 in Wolfeboro; first; Ernest C. Neal (Wolfeboro) and Nancy M. Anderson (Braintree, MA)

NEALL[E]Y,

daughter, b. 10/31/1887; seventh; Henry Neally (laborer, Canada) and Flivie Levesque (Canada)

son, b. 4/20/1889; Henry Neally (brakeman, Canada) and Florrie ----- (ME)

Arline, b. 8/20/1881; third; Henry Nealey (Canada) and Flivie Levesque (Canada) (1935)

Buzzell Peter, b. 10/16/1879; second; Henry Nealley (Canada) and Flivie Levesque (Canada) (1939)

Charles, b. 5/11/1894; eighth; Joseph Neally (laborer, Canada) and Nellie Mayew (Canada)

Donald Hiram, b. 12/23/1906; first; Henry L. Nealley (printer, 28, Salmon Falls) and Elsie E. Nichols (26, Wakefield)

Lawrence Rudolph, b. 7/30/1908; second; Henry L. Nealley (printer, 29, Salmon Falls) and Elsie E. Nichols (27, Wakefield)

NEILY,

Andrea Ingrid, b. 2/2/1960 in Wolfeboro; Kennett W. Neily (Rochester) and Judith L. Churchill (Brookfield)

Kenneth Winston, b. 11/3/1932 in Rochester; Guy E. Neily and Jean Murray

NELSON,
child, b. 11/30/1892; first; F. Nelson (teamster, Denmark) and Alice -----
(Wolfeboro)
Christina F., b. 3/25/1890; fourth; Ferdnand F. Nelson (Denmark) and
Caroline Sorenson (Denmark) (1942)

NEUVINE,
Ruth, b. 5/30/1910; second; Alex Neuvine (laborer, 39, St. Lawrence, NY)
and Eva Dumont (23, Salem)

NEVERS,
son [Clarence E.], b. 4/21/1889; second; William H. Nevers (farmer,
Claremont) and Augusta ----- (Wakefield)
Lloyd Edward, b. 1/27/1885; first; William H. Nevers (Newfield, ME) and
Augusta Farnham (Wakefield) (1935)
Walter E., b. 5/22/1891; third; William H. Nevers (mechanic, Claremont)
and Augusta A. Nevers (Wakefield)

NEWBURY,
Alison Priscilla, b. 2/14/1993 in Rochester; Kenneth Charles Newbury and
Dianne Margaret D'Pulos

NEWCOMB,
Kristen Lee, b. 4/16/1989 in Rochester; Glenn Carroll Newcomb and Karen
Lee Pratt
Loretta Lynn, b. 9/3/1966 in Rochester; fourth; Albert L. Newcomb
(Belfast, ME) and Agnes G. Mickelonis (Rochester)
Sherri Ann, b. 11/20/1970 in Rochester; Albert L. Newcomb and Agnes G.
Mickelonis

NEWLING,
Earl H., b. 2/16/1894; second; Charles H. Newling (brakeman, Effingham)
and Etta M. Straw (Barnstead)

NEWTON,
Cali Joan, b. 1/30/1998 in Rochester; Fred Lloyd Newton and Janice Marie
Irving
Madison Jean, b. 2/23/1995 in Rochester; Fred Lloyd Newton and Janice
Marie Irving

NIBLETT,
Edith, b. 12/13/1910; first; Samuel Niblett (farmer, 25, Cheshire, England) and Margaret Glynn (21, Roxbury, MA)

NICHOLL,
Amanda Lauren, b. 8/5/1988 in Portsmouth; Stephen J. Nicholl and Laurie A. LaMonica

NICHOLS,
stillborn son, b. 9/2/1908; first; Lorenzo D. Nichols (section hand, 34, Wakefield) and Anstriss Fellows (34, Wakefield)
James Edward, Jr., b. 3/22/1978 in Rochester; James E. Nichols, Sr. and Maryellen Hassen
Katelyn Alise, b. 6/3/1994 in Dover; Randy Wayne Nichols and Laurie Anne Hersey
Lorenzo Dow, b. 4/26/1874; second; Hiram D. Nichols (Wakefield) and Sarah W. Lane (Wakefield) (1937)
Matthew Gordon, b. 6/11/1991 in Rochester; Donald William Nichols and Susan Patricia Crowley
Phillip Alkeenon, b. 8/6/1991 in Dover; Randy Wayne Nichols and Laurie Anne Hersey
Rupert Lorenzo, b. 9/18/1911; second; Lorenzo Nichols (laborer, 37, Wakefield) and Anstriss Fellows (37, Wakefield)
Sarah Patricia, b. 2/16/1995 in Rochester; Donald William Nichols and Susan Patricia Crowley
Tyler Aaron, b. 10/15/1996 in Wolfeboro; Leigh Allen Nichols and Stephanie Ann Foss

NOLAN,
David John, b. 9/28/1969 in Portsmouth; John F. Nolan and Sally E. Dean
Tahl Joseph, b. 4/23/1974 in Wolfeboro; Stephen J. Nolan and Wanda G. Crawford

NORRISH,
Sean Everett, b. 10/12/1989 in Rochester; Stephen Earl Norrish and Tammy Ann Champy

NOYES,
Nathan Adam, b. 4/11/1978 in Dover; James S. Noyes and Debra L. Faust

NUGENT,
Arline, b. 12/17/1916; fifth; Frank E. Nugent (shoe maker, 44, Lynn, MA) and Blanche Sedgley (27, Bowdoinham, ME)

NUTE,
Charlotte Parker, b. 11/1/1921; second; Harry A. Nute (farmer, 30, Farmington) and Helen E. Wadleigh (26, Union); residence - Union
Myrtle May, b. 3/2/1915; second; Fred S. Nute (mill hand, 47, Milton) and Olive A. Garland (20, Wolfeboro)
Wilfred Stouton, b. 8/21/1916; third; Fred S. Nute (mill hand, 49, Milton) and Olive A. Garland (21, Wolfeboro)

NUTTER,
son, b. 2/1/1889; first; H. N. Nutter (laborer, New Durham) and Dora ----- (Sweden, ME)
Willard N., b. 6/28/1921; second; William H. Nutter (fireman, 29, Fryeburg, ME) and Flora E. Marten (20, Maplewood, ME); residence - Brookfield

O'CONNELL,
Annie Elizabeth, b. 10/3/1898; first; John O'Connell (mill operative, Ireland) and Edith Evans (Boston, MA)
Dennis J., b. 10/15/1908; fourth; John O'Connell (mill overseer, 46, Ireland) and Edith Evans (30, Boston, MA)

O'HANDLEY,
son, b. 6/16/1890; first; Neil O'Handley (carpenter, Scotland) and Catharine ----- (Scotland)

O'NEILL,
Jordan Scott, b. 1/14/1992 in Rochester; Scott Allen O'Neill and Karen Ann Copp

OLBERG,
Kendra Rae, b. 7/25/1986 in Ex; Eric R. Olberg and Donna R. Paige

OLESON,
Abel Richardson, b. 6/18/1985 in Union; William H. Oleson and Michaela I. Brazis

OLKKOLA,
Justin Peter Wiley, b. 5/25/1974 in Wolfeboro; Peter A. Olkkola and Ann S. Wiley

ORVIS,
Bailey Brooks, b. 10/1/1993 in Dover; Stephen Ronald Orvis and Gail Vanessa Cawley

OTIS,
Addie May, b. 10/5/1915; third; Charles Otis (painter, 44, No. Berwick, ME) and Mabel Richards (32, Wakefield)
Walter Raymond, b. 6/25/1911; second; Charles F. Otis (painter, 34, Rochester) and Mabel L. Richards (29, Wakefield)

OUELLETTE,
Adrien Laurent, b. 1/18/1915; fifth; Armand Ouellette (laborer, 38, Canada) and Lydia Lamontagne (38, Canada)
Antoinette F., b. 8/7/1911; fourth; Armond Ouellette (laborer, 33, Canada) and Leda Lamontagne (29, Canada)
David Rolland, Jr., b. 8/7/1979 in Wolfeboro; David R. Ouellette and Donna L. Peterson
Frederick Morile, b. 9/9/1910; third; Armond Ouellette (laborer, 32, Canada) and Lydia Lamontagne (33, Canada)
Tera Lee, b. 12/6/1974 in Wolfeboro; David R. Ouellette and Donna Lee Petersen

PAGEAU,
James William, b. 10/18/1975 in Rochester; James L. Pageau and Joyce L. Hayward
Marc Robert, b. 3/5/1978 in Rochester; James L. Pageau and Joyce L. Hayward

PALMER,
Alesia Marie, b. 9/30/1989 in Dover; Robert Clarence Palmer and Denise Rachel Roy
Jane Marie, b. 5/12/1970 in Dover; John E. Palmer and Louise M. Ouimette
Jason Nathaniel, b. 5/12/1970 in Dover; John E. Palmer and Louise M. Ouimette

Jodene Hollie, b. 6/5/1968 in Dover; John E. Palmer and Louise M.
  Ouimette
Kevin Lloyd, b. 4/6/1971 in Wolfeboro; Fred H. Palmer and Nancy G.
  Mathews
Kimberly Jane, b. 9/15/1969 in Wolfeboro; Fred H. Palmer and Nancy G.
  Mathews

PARENT,
Aaron Paul, b. 8/21/1975 in Wolfeboro; Paul M. Parent and Joanne L.
  Keating
Justin Ryan, b. 7/10/1979 in Wolfeboro; Paul M. Parent and Joanne L.
  Keating

PARIS,
Anne Margaret, b. 11/16/1940; first; Charles Daniel Paris (Wolfeboro) and
  Dorothy Margaret Niblett (Ossipee)

PARISON,
Mikihial Dominic, b. 9/12/1997 in Wolfeboro; Anthony Waldo Parison and
  Randi Jean Romaine

PARKER,
Bonnie Ann, b. 6/10/1982 in Wolfeboro; Mark A. Parker and Gail A.
  Whitaker
Earl Stanley, b. 2/12/1925; third; Lauren E. Parker (Manchester) and
  Evelyn F. Morrill (Rochester)
Elaine Maxine, b. 7/12/1926; fourth; Lauren E. Parker (Manchester) and
  Evelyn Morrill (Rochester)
Irene Evelyn, b. 11/16/1927; fifth; Loren E. Parker (Manchester) and
  Evelyn F. Merrill (Rochester)
Jennifer Lynn, b. 8/13/1979 in Wolfeboro; Mark A. Parker and Gail A.
  Whitaker
Lauren Ellsworth, b. 2/23/1924; second; Lauren E. Parker (mill hand,
  Manchester) and Evelyn F. Morrill (Rochester); residence - Union

PARRON,
Joseph Arthur, b. 1/28/1908; fifth; Joseph M. Parron (laborer, 38, Canada)
  and Delphine Bellanger (31, Canada)

PATCH,
Alice Louise, b. 4/19/1918; second; Mary Eva Patch (Wakefield) (1942)
Amanda Louise, b. 7/18/1992 in Rochester; Glenn Edward Patch and Annette Jean Poulin
Kristina Rae, b. 1/27/1980 in Wolfeboro; Rickey F. Patch and Deborah K. McMahan

PATTERSON,
James Edward, b. 2/9/1964 in Wolfeboro; first; William T. Patterson (Westerly, RI) and Gail L. Adjutant (Wolfeboro)

PAUL,
Ann Carpenter, b. 10/1/1928; first; Samuel H. Paul (Wakefield) and Julia H. Bishop (Gray, ME) (1934)
Arthur Hiram, b. 11/3/1894; fourth; Arthur H. Paul (postal clerk, Wakefield) and Annie H. Nairn (Washington, DC)
Caroline N., b. 9/16/1901; seventh; Arthur H. Paul (railway clerk, Wakefield) and Anna H. Nairn (Washington, DC)
Chesley Arthur, b. 8/28/1892; third; Arthur H. Paul (postal clerk, Wakefield) and Annie H. Nairn (Washington, DC)
Edward Augustus, b. 7/19/1888; first; Arthur H. Paul (postal clerk, Wakefield) and Annie H. Nairn (Washington, DC)
Joseph Nairn, b. 8/18/1890; second; Arthur H. Paul (postal clerk, Wakefield) and Annie H. Nairn (Washington, DC)
Katherine Libby, b. 10/16/1903; third; Henry A. Paul (station agent, 41, Wakefield) and Nancy L. Libby (32, Limerick, ME)
Kenneth Scott, Jr., b. 3/6/1989 in Wolfeboro; Kenneth Scott Paul and Jennifer Ann Glennon
Louis Albert, b. 10/24/1864; fourth; Nathaniel Paul (Sanford, ME) and Elvira Moses (Portsmouth) (1935)
Louise Mary, b. 2/11/1899; sixth; Arthur Paul (postal clerk, Wakefield) and Annie H. Nairer (Washington, DC)
Margaret Palmer, b. 7/5/1902; first; Henry A. Paul (station agent, 43, Wakefield) and Nancy Libby (31, Limerick, ME)
Mary Porter, b. 8/26/1904; eighth; Arthur H. Paul (postal clerk, 45, Wakefield) and Annie H. Nairn (41, Washington, DC)
Samuel Henry, b. 9/28/1896; fifth; Arthur H. Paul (postal clerk, Wakefield) and Annie Nairn (Washington, DC)

PAULANSHATI,
Ana, b. 10/24/1909; first; S. Paulanshati (laborer, 34, Russia) and
Stainislava Mingen (24, Russia)

PAULANSKIS,
Bernice, b. 12/7/1911; second; S. Paulanskis (laborer, 36, Russia) and
Stanasia Mingin (28, Russia)
Joseph, b. 3/16/1913; third; S. Paulanskis (laborer, 37, Russia) and
Stanasia Mingin (29, Russia)
Sophia Paulis, b. 8/18/1914; fourth; Steve Paulanskis (laborer, 38, Russia)
and Stanasia Mingin (30, Russia)

PAULOSKI,
William, b. 10/27/1920; sixth; Stephen Pauloski (laborer, 46, Russia) and
Stanislowa Mingin (35, Russia); residence - Sanbornville

PAWLOSKY,
Johnny Michael, b. 8/28/1988 in No. Conway; Robert E. Pawlosky and
Terry A. Kelly

PAYNE,
Winnifred Muriel, b. 9/29/1913; first; William H. Payne (farmer, 47,
Medura, NY) and Rosalie Rickly (41, Switzerland)

PEARCE,
Devin Michael, b. 3/30/1996 in Wolfeboro; George Michael Pearce and
Cassandra Mara Diprizio
Jennifer Lee, b. 4/7/1980 in Wolfeboro; James C. Pearce and Reita L.
McDonald
Scott James, b. 2/7/1984 in Wolfeboro; Jimmie C. Pearce and Reita L.
McDonald

PEARSON,
Matthew David, b. 5/19/1992 in Lebanon; Jeffrey David Pearson and Joyce
Ellen-Marie Charles

PEAVEY,
daughter, b. 2/10/1887; second; Henry W. Peavey (blacksmith, Strafford)
and Allie F. Prescott (Brookfield)

Allen Wayne, Jr., b. 3/24/1975 in Wolfeboro; Allen W. Peavey, Sr. and Ellen M. Hutchins
Paul Edward, b. 1/26/1980 in Wolfeboro; Paul E. Peavey and Nancy L. Hutchins

PEHOWIC,
Joshua David, b. 12/20/1992 in Wolfeboro; Edward Bernard Pehowic and Robin Lynne Hilman

PELKEY,
stillborn daughter, b. 8/12/1907; first; Benjamin Pelkey (lumberman, 35, Lewiston, ME) and Mary Willard (22, Canada)

PENN,
Susan Renee, b. 3/4/1980 in Wolfeboro; Donald R. Penn and Harriet L. Fifield

PEREWITZ,
Kimberly Marie, b. 8/9/1990 in Dover; Alan Robert Perewitz and Suzanne Theresa Swiechowicz
Stephanie Tayla, b. 1/30/1989 in Dover; Alan Robert Perewitz and Suzanne T. Swiechowicz

PERILLO,
Victoria Ashlynn, b. 5/15/1990 in Hanover; Todd Thomas Perillo and Sara Louise Rawn

PERKINS,
daughter [Eva M.], b. 12/22/1899; third; Samuel Perkins, Jr. (laborer, Middleton) and Bridget McNamara (Ireland)
Christine Marie, b. 9/7/1968 in Rochester; Edward J. Perkins and Joanne D. Pedneault
Edward James, Jr., b. 1/4/1966 in Wolfeboro; first; Edward James Perkins (Farmington) and Joanne D. Pedneault (Portland, ME)
Eric James, b. 9/19/1976 in Wolfeboro; James E. Perkins and Sandra L. Gobillot
Erin Elizabeth, b. 6/14/1978 in Wolfeboro; James E. Perkins and Sandra L. Gobillot
Henry Mose, b. 12/18/1866; third; William H. Perkins (Wakefield) and Susanna G. Moody (Newfield, ME) (1936)

James Andrew, b. 9/4/1895; first; Samuel Perkins (mill hand, Middleton) and Bridget McNamara (Ireland)

Joseph Charles, b. 9/23/1969 in Rochester; Edward J. Perkins and Joanne D. Pedneault

Justin Alexander, b. 6/3/1983 in Rochester; Jeffrey A. Perkins and Janice M. Glennon

Patricia Arlene, b. 3/14/1967 in Rochester; second; Edward J. Perkins (Farmington) and Joanne D. Pedneault (Portland, ME)

Stacia Lee, b. 5/3/1977 in Rochester; Ralph C. Perkins and Pamela L. Maxfield

Stanley A., b. 2/10/1897; second; Samuel Perkins (mill hand, Middleton) and Bridget McNamara (Ireland)

PERRON,

Eva, b. 6/7/1894; first; Joseph Perron (laborer, Canada) and Cecile Cyr (Canada)

Marie Beatrice, b. 4/17/1914; second; Joseph Perron (sole layer, 25, Canada) and Selina LaPointe (22, Wakefield); residence - Springvale, ME

Marie Celedure D., b. 6/3/1916; third; Joseph Perron (shop hand, 27, Canada) and Celinda Lapoint (24, Wakefield); residence - Springvale, ME

PERRY,

daughter, b. 10/30/1932 in Sanbornville; Perley Perry and Inez Garland

Brittany Alyse, b. 4/27/1981 in Wolfeboro; Warren H. Perry and Sherry D. Wilkins

Cora Virginia, b. 8/7/1915 in Wolfeboro; second; Karl G. Perry (farmer, 28, Factoryville, PA) and Cora C. Goddard (30, Cortland, NY)

Eris Mae, b. 11/27/1923; first; Perley D. Perry (laborer, Brookfield) and Inez E. Garland (Brookfield)

Frances Everett, b. 1/16/1926; second; Perley D. Perry (Brookfield) and Inez E. Garland (Brookfield)

James, b. 12/18/1938; second; Silena Perry (1939)

James Everett, b. 6/25/1919; first; James E. Perry (mechanic, 34, Brookfield) and Lilla F. Doyer (24, Lawrence, MA); residence - Sanbornville

John, b. 12/18/1938; first; Silena Perry (1939)

John Charles, b. 9/7/1933 in Wolfeboro; John Perry and Hazel M. Drew

Lewis Alfred, b. 3/27/1928; third; Perley Perry (Brookfield) and Inez Garland (Brookfield)

Paul Joseph Leon, b. 6/22/1935; second; John Perry (PEI) and Hazel M. Drew (Union)

Shardama Ryan, b. 4/8/1980 in Rochester; Warren H. Perry, Jr. and Sherry D. Wilkins

Warren Howard, III, b. 1/6/1979 in Dover; Warren H. Perry, Jr. and Sherry D. Wilkins

William Frances, b. 10/7/1922; third; Perley D. Perry (laborer, Brookfield) and Gladys B. Fogg (Deerfield); residence - Sanbornville

PERSCH,

Christopher Darby, b. 1/14/1970 in Wolfeboro; William J. Persch, Jr. and Jayne-Ann Dombek

Jonathan Michael, b. 7/2/1971 in Wolfeboro; William J. Persch, Jr. and Jayne-Ann Donibek

PHILBRICK,

Mary Frances, b. 3/7/1875; first; John Stinson Philbrick (Wakefield) and Amanda H. Champion (Effingham) (1940)

PHINNEY,

Charles Douglas, Jr., b. 3/7/1990 in Wolfeboro; Charles Douglas Phinney and Tammy Lynn Nason

PICKERING,

daughter [Bertha E.], b. 4/7/1890; first; B. Frank Pickering (farmer, Wakefield) and Nettie S. Sanborn (Kittery, ME)

Frank Myron, b. 1/9/1893; third; Benjamin F. Pickering (carpenter, Wakefield) and Nettie L. Sanborn (Kittery, ME)

John A., b. 5/8/1891; second; B. Frank Pickering (carpenter, Wakefield) and Nettie L. Sanborn (Kittery, ME)

PIGEON,

May Ruth, b. 1/23/1921; second; Moses B. Pigeon (millman, Rackford, PA) and Ruth M. Chick (Woodman); residence - Woodman

PIKE,

son, b. 3/16/1887; fourth; Freeman D. Pike (farmer, Brookfield) and Sophia Ricker (Milton)

daughter, b. 11/9/1888; fifth; W. W. Pike (fireman, Stoneham, MA) and S. A. Tibbetts (Wolfeboro)
daughter [Marion], b. 10/17/1893; third; David C. Pike (farmer, Middleton) and Mary E. Miller (Lawrence, MA)
daughter, b. 8/4/1900; seventh; David C. Pike (farmer, Middleton) and May E. Miller (Lawrence, MA)
daughter, b. 10/22/1902; sixth; Edwin L. Pike (farmer, 27, Rochester) and Mary B. Wentworth (23, Union)
daughter [Mildred C.], b. 6/7/1905 in North Wakefield; seventh; Edwin L. Pike (farmer, 30, Rochester) and Mary B. Wentworth (26, Union); residence - North Wakefield
Agnes E., b. 8/27/1901; fifth; Lincoln A. Pike (laborer, Plymouth) and Mary Wentworth (Parsonsfield, ME)
Beulah, b. 10/15/1902; ninth; David C. Pike (farmer, 37, Middleton) and Mary E. Miller (33, Lawrence, MA); residence - Union
Christopher Gerry, b. 4/7/1989 in Rochester; Lloyd Gerry Pike, Jr. and Carol Anne Randall
Corey Michael, b. 12/7/1987 in Wolfeboro; Kevin L. Pike and Dorothy B. Nason
Dorothy, b. 8/10/1901; eighth; David C. Pike (farmer, Middleton) and Mary Miller (Lawrence, MA)
Edith Maud, b. 8/8/1892; second; David C. Pike (farmer, Middleton) and Mary E. Miller (Lawrence, MA)
Esther, b. 9/4/1899; sixth; David C. Pike (farmer, Middleton) and May E. Miller (Lawrence, MA)
Forrest S., b. 4/17/1897; seventh; Winthrop W. Pike (engineer, Stoneham, MA) and Sarah A. Tebbetts (Wolfeboro)
George H., b. 6/27/1898; fifth; David C. Pike (farmer, Middleton) and May E. Miller (Lawrence, MA)
Grace Elizabeth, b. 5/27/1904; tenth; David C. Pike (farmer, 38, Middleton) and Mary E. Miller (35, Lawrence, MA)
Harold Altar, b. 5/22/1908; ninth; Edwin L. Pike (farmer, 33, Rochester) and Belle M. Wentworth (29, Wakefield)
Helen E., b. 6/18/1895; first; John W. Pike (livery, Middleton) and Eva B. Thurston (Effingham)
Helen S., b. 2/23/1891; first; David C. Pike (farmer, Middleton) and Mary E. Miller (Middleton)
Keigan Scott, b. 12/31/1990 in Wolfeboro; Kevin Loring Pike and Dorothy Bianca Nason

Leslie, b. 2/19/1907; seventh; Edwin L. Pike (farmer, 31, Rochester) and
    Mary P. Wentworth (28, Wakefield)
Lloyd Garey, b. 9/12/1932 in Rochester; Forrest S. Pike and Lois Robinson
Loring Robinson, b. 8/29/1944; third; Forrest S. Pike (Sanbornville) and
    Lois F. Robinson (East Wakefield)
Lyman Willey, b. 9/23/1935; second; Forrest S. Pike (Wakefield) and Lois
    Robinson (East Wakefield)
Meagan Elizabeth, b. 11/20/1991 in Wolfeboro; Kevin Loring Pike and
    Dorothy Bianca Nason
Ralph Leroy, b. 4/21/1905; eleventh; David Pike (farmer, 39, Middleton)
    and May E. Miller (36, Lawrence, MA)
Raymond Earl, b. 4/16/1906; twelfth; David C. Pike (farmer, 40,
    Middleton) and May E. Miller (37, Lawrence, MA)
Roland, b. 8/5/1899; fourth; Lincoln Pike (laborer, Plymouth, VT) and
    Mary Wentworth (Parsonsfield, ME); residence - Union
Susan Helen, b. 3/4/1896; fourth; David C. Pike (farmer, Middleton) and
    May E. Miller (Lawrence, MA)
Timothy John, b. 7/24/1979 in Rochester; Loring R. Pike and Georgia S.
    Promise
Violet May, b. 2/18/1894; seventh; Winthrop J. Pike (engineer, Stoneham,
    MA) and Sarah E. Tibbetts (Wolfeboro)

PIPER,
daughter, b. 10/6/1888; first; James A. Piper (laborer, Newfield, ME) and
    Laura A. Evans (Wakefield)
son, b. 1/9/1890; second; James A. Piper (RR section, Newfield, ME) and
    Laura A. Evans (Wakefield)
daughter, b. 12/31/1890; third; James A. Piper (railroading, Newfield, ME)
    and Laura A. Evans (Wakefield)
David Clare, b. 7/5/1942; first; Lewis Pray Piper (Union) and June Elma
    Ferguson (Georgetown, MA)
Lewis Pray, b. 12/3/1917; second; Charles E. Piper (clerk, Wakefield) and
    Helen Pray (Dover)

PIPPIN,
son [Franklin J.], b. 2/14/1887; sixth; Victor Pippin (laborer, Canada) and
    Susan Thibodou (Canada)
daughter [Louisa R.], b. 11/4/1888; seventh; Victor Pippin (section man,
    Canada) and Susie Thibodo (Canada)

Alfred Victor, b. 5/8/1917; second; Frank Pippin (mill hand, 30, Wakefield) and Jennie Parker (23, Manchester)

Alfred Victor, 2d, b. 6/1/1941; second; Alfred Victor Pippin (Wakefield) and Margaret Evelyn Hill (W. Newfield, ME)

Annie E., b. 7/30/1878; second; Victor Pippin (Quebec) and Susan Thibodeau (NB) (1935)

Florence Sylvia, b. 3/8/1917; second; Charles V. Pippin (laborer, 37, Wakefield) and Florida Currier (22, Ossipee); residence - Milton

Harold Frank, b. 4/23/1911; first; Franklyn Pippin (laborer, 24, Wakefield) and Jennie Parker (17, Manchester)

Raymond, b. 1/19/1920; third; Frank Pippin (mill employee, 33, Union) and Jennie Parker (26, Union); residence - Union

PLACE,
Arleen C., b. 7/20/1906; first; Percy Place (mill operative, 22, Farmington) and Freena Lover (22, Union)

Norman, b. 12/26/1910; second; Percy Place (mill operative, 26, Farmington) and Freena C. Lavoie (27, Wakefield)

PLANT,
stillborn son, b. 10/5/1927; first; Albert Plant and Estelle Maette (Westbrook, ME)

PLANTE,
Edward Ludger, b. 1/14/1914; second; Edward Plante (mill operative, 24, Somersworth) and Eva Lavertu (Canada)

PLOUDE,
Joseph Frank Samuel, b. 10/22/1924; second; Oliver Ploude (laborer, Canada) and Alma Dione (Gonic); residence - Somersworth

PLUMMER,
daughter [Grace A.], b. 5/22/1888; second; Thomas F. Plummer (laborer, Brookfield) and Eliza M. Lang (Brookfield)

Clifton John, b. 9/4/1939; third; Frank H. Plummer (Wakefield) and Ellen Priscilla Pratt (Ossipee)

Earle Wayne, b. 1/20/1945; fourth; Frank H. Plummer (Wolfeboro) and Ellen P. Pratt (Ossipee)

Frank Harrison, b. 11/2/1937; second; F. Harrison Plummer (Wolfeboro) and Ellen Pratt (Ossipee)

James Lawrence, b. 11/2/1937; first; F. Harrison Plummer (Wolfeboro) and Ellen Pratt (Ossipee)
Jean Louise, b. 12/22/1920; first; Eugene O. Plummer (shoe shop foreman, 44, Farmington) and Luella Richardson (35, Boston, MA); residence - Sanbornville
Lana Louise, b. 8/25/1947; fifth; Frank H. Plummer (Wolfeboro) and Ellen P. Pratt (Ossipee)
Vernon Robert, b. 8/8/1949; sixth; Frank H. Plummer (Wolfeboro) and Ellen P. Pratt (Ossipee)

POALOWSKI,
Alena, b. 3/9/1917; fifth; Stanislow Poalowski (laborer, 44, Russia) and S. Mingen (31, Russia)

POELMAN,
Theodore John, b. 7/5/1919; first; Theodore J. Poelman (clergyman, 35, Netherlands) and Helen F. Guptill (25, Berwick, ME)

POISSON,
Dianne Bertha, b. 11/27/1958 in Wolfeboro; first; Norman R. Poisson (Rochester) and Jean C. Dodier (Wolfeboro)

POLIQUIN,
Evan Lee, b. 8/15/1996 in Dover; Raymond Joseph Poliquin and Candace Ellen Lee

POULIOT,
daughter, b. 4/7/1887; fourth; Edward Pouliot (carpenter, Canada) and Selina ---- (Canada)
Edward Joseph, b. 9/23/1878; fourth; Edward Pouliot (Canada) and Celina Birsonneau (Canada) (1940)
Phoebe Mary, b. 10/2/1875; third; Edward Pouliot (Canada) and Celina Birsonneau (Canada) (1937)

POWER,
Emma Louise, b. 7/10/1989 in Portsmouth; Lance Randall Power and Anita Louise Lawrence

PRATT,
Barbara Joan, b. 2/4/1950; second; John C. Pratt (Union) and Martha A. Bailey (Woburn, MA)
David George, b. 2/16/1946; first; John C. Pratt (Union) and Martha A. Bailey (Woburn, MA)
David George, Jr., b. 12/23/1967 in Rochester; David George Pratt and Sandra L. Espie
Jean Elizabeth, b. 10/22/1951; third; John C. Pratt (NH) and Martha A. Bailey (Woburn, MA)
John Charles, b. 2/12/1924; second; George A. Pratt (lineman, Townsend, VT) and Ruth S. Wentworth (Wakefield); residence - Union
John Charles, Jr., b. 5/16/1956 in Rochester; fourth; John C. Pratt (Wakefield) and Martha A. Bailey (Woburn, MA)
Karen Lee, b. 6/25/1965 in Rochester; first; David G. Pratt (Rochester) and Sandra L. Espie (Concord, MA)
Lana, b. 12/10/1943; second; Herman Lester Pratt (Epping) and Hildegard Robertson (Conway)
Laura Ann, b. 1/14/1967 in Rochester; second; David George Pratt (Rochester) and Sandra L. Espie (Concord, MA)
Luann B., b. 11/16/1958 in Rochester; fifth; John C. Pratt (Union) and Martha A. Bailey (Woburn, MA)
Robert Harrison, b. 8/9/1918; first; George H. Pratt (teamster, 24, Townshend, VT) and Ruth L. Wentworth (18, Wakefield)

PRESTON,
Gregory Thomas, b. 11/1/1985 in Rochester; Gerald E.T. Preston and Marybeth I. Maloney

PRIDHAM,
Nathaniel William, b. 9/18/1990 in Sanbornville; Lawrence M. Pridham and Krystle Marie Frybeckwith

PRONOVOST,
Nichole Cathleen, b. 7/9/1984; Alfred Pronovost and Cathleen A. Goodermote
Sarah Elizabeth, b. 2/9/1988 in No. Conway; Alfred J. Pronovost and Cathleen A. Goodermote

PROVENCHER,
Edwald Antonio, b. 8/12/1912; second; Donat Provencher (laborer, 26, Canada) and Melvina Huard (33, Canada)
Henri L. Anthony, b. 7/4/1911; first; Donat Provencher (laborer, 25, Quebec) and Melvina Huard (33, Quebec)

PUTNEY,
Dwayne Edward, b. 2/13/1963 in Rochester; first; Charles W. Putney (Derry) and Rosalyn A. Libby (Wolfeboro)
Jennifer Rose, b. 2/13/1966 in Wolfeboro; third; Charles W. Putney (Derry) and Rosalyn A. Libby (Wolfeboro)

QUIMBY,
stillborn son, b. 2/10/1907; first; Forrest G. Quimby (laborer, 23, Newfield, ME) and Carrie E. Pinkham (32, Middleton)

RAFFERTY,
Rebecca Anne, b. 6/18/1970 in Portsmouth; Dennis F. Rafferty, Jr. and Nancy Young

RAMSEY,
Fred R., Jr., b. 10/17/1930; second; Fred R. Ramsey (NH) and Edna Curry (NH)

RAMY,
Delcy Louise, b. 8/7/1915; seventh; Louis Ramy (carpenter, 34, Quebec) and Mamie Lover (30, Wakefield); residence - Rochester

RAND,
son, b. 6/14/1923; third; Nathan Rand (laborer) and Mabel Bean (Ossipee)
Constance Helen, b. 7/23/1927; first; Lester E. Rand (Wakefield) and Blanche D. Elliott (Middleton)
Dolores Jane, b. 3/18/1929; second; Lester E. Rand (Wakefield) and Blanche I. Elliott (Middleton) (1942)
Earle, b. 3/23/1897; fifth; Oscar Rand (laborer, New Durham) and Eliza McDonald (NS)
Lester E., b. 1/29/1910; first; Frank H. Rand (laborer, 38, Buxton, ME) and Bertha J. Fellows (24, Wakefield)
Priscilla Hazel, b. 1/18/1933 in Wolfeboro; Lester E. Rand and Blanche I. Elliott

RANDALL,
Alan Lee, b. 3/15/1951; second; Frank E. Randall (Sanbornville) and Alberta R. Dunk (Arlington, MA)
Angelica Marie, b. 3/25/1987 in Rochester; Edward A. Randall and Gloria J. Walker
Carol Ann, b. 11/19/1961 in Rochester; fifth; Frank E. Randall (Sanbornville) and Alberta R. Dunk (Arlington, MA)
David Earl, b. 2/1/1948; first; Frank E. Randall (Sanbornville) and Alberta R. Dunk (Arlington, MA)
Earle Frederick, b. 1/24/1895; first; Frank W. Randall (brakeman, Brownfield, ME) and Martha C. Runnels (Wakefield)
Edgar Earl, b. 4/11/1947; first; Fred B. Randall (Sanbornville) and Ruth V. Drown (Wakefield)
Elizabeth Anne, b. 8/1/1971 in Rochester; Edgar E. Randall and Kathy J. Logan
Frank Earl, b. 10/2/1922; second; Earl F. Randall (farmer, Sanbornville) and Mabel A. Weeks (Ossipee)
Frank Gary, b. 4/21/1956 in Rochester; fourth; Frank E. Randall (Sanbornville) and Alberta R. Dunk (Arlington, MA)
Fred Blaisdell, b. 11/13/1924; third; Earl F. Randall (blacksmith, Wakefield) and Mabel Weeks (Ossipee)
Fred Blaisdell, Jr., b. 10/20/1948; second; Fred B. Randall (Sanbornville) and Ruth V. Drown (Wakefield)
Gary Frank, II, b. 4/21/1982 in Dover; Gary F. Randall and Sylvia L. Hopkins
Jennifer Ann, b. 1/4/1968 in Rochester; Edger E. Randall and Kathy J. Logan
Jennifer Sue, b. 5/21/1973 in Rochester; Alan L. Randall and Ruth J. Rouleau
Joyce Elizabeth, b. 5/30/1975 in Rochester; Philip H. Randall and Cheryl A. Fletcher
Kimberly Marie, b. 12/22/1976 in Wolfeboro; Gary F. Randall and Sylvia L. Hopkins
Mabel L., b. 1/28/1896; second; Frank Randall (brakeman, Brownfield, ME) and Mattie Runnells (Wakefield)
Marion Thelma, b. 2/10/1926; fourth; Earl Randall (Wakefield) and Mabel Weeks (Ossipee)
Philip Harry, b. 10/8/1952 in Rochester; third; Frank E. Randall (Ossipee) and Alberta R. Dunk (Arlington, MA)

Ramona Ann, b. 7/22/1964 in Wolfeboro; second; Raymond A. Randall (Sanbornville) and Barbara J. Eldridge (Tuftonboro)
Raymond Ansel, b. 4/10/1928; fifth; Earl Randall (Wakefield) and Mabel Weeks (Ossipee)
Raymond Ansel, Jr., b. 3/9/1951; first; Raymond A. Randall (Sanbornville) and Barbara J. Eldridge (Tuftonboro)
Richard Jay, b. 4/22/1921; first; Earl F. Randall (laborer, 26, Wakefield) and Mabel A. Weeks (19, Ossipee); residence - Sanbornville

RAPOZA,
Gregg Joseph, b. 2/27/1982 in Wolfeboro; Anthony J. Rapoza and Lynn Holland
Neil James, b. 7/20/1980 in Wolfeboro; Anthony J. Rapoza and Lynn Holland

RATLIFF,
Noah Michael, b. 5/27/1998 in Dover; Christopher A. Ratliff and Jennifer Lynn Aimes

REED,
stillborn daughter, b. 7/3/1905 in Union; eighth; Edwin S. Reed (laborer, 40, Wakefield) and Inez M. Dicey (33, Wakefield); residence - Union
son, b. 10/31/1922; second; Austin P. Reed (laborer, Wakefield) and Rosamond Leavitt (Parsonsfield, ME)
child, b. 8/20/1934; first; Arthur W. Reed (Effingham) and Marjorie Davis (Wakefield)
Andrea Nichole, b. 3/5/1988 in No. Conway; Andrew L. Reed and Janis L. Hussey
Anita Jane, b. 3/14/1939; first; Lester Haven Reed, Jr. (Newfield, ME) and Evelyn Florence McDonald (Wakefield)
Earl, b. 3/6/1910; second; Austin P. Reed (laborer, 23, Wakefield) and Gertrude M. Smith (17, Newfield, ME)
Eunice S., b. 9/18/1903; seventh; Edward S. Reed (laborer, 39, Wakefield) and Ines M. Dicey (32, Wakefield); residence - Union
Gladys Mary, b. 5/31/1916; third; James Reed (tel. operator, 28, Lawrence, MA) and Mae McCalleron (25, Nashua)
Hannah, b. 4/14/1905 in East Wakefield; second; Elmer Reed (laborer, 33, Dover) and Cora Martin (21, Acton, ME); residence - East Wakefield
Hazel G., b. 8/12/1901; sixth; Edwin S. Reed (laborer, Wakefield) and Ines M. Dicey (Wakefield); residence - Union

Helen, b. 7/27/1912; second; Arthur G. Reed (clerk, 20, Effingham) and
   Gertrude Carpenter (24, Boston, MA); residence - Lynn, MA
Herbert D., b. 5/25/1878; Ammon Silas Reed (Newfield, ME) and
   Elizabeth Ann Waldron (Acton, ME) (1938)
Iva E., b. 5/5/1896; fourth; Edwin Reid (sic) (Wakefield) and Inez Dicey
   (Wakefield)
James Richard, Jr., b. 12/1/1959 in Rochester; fourth; James R. Reed
   (Biddeford, ME) and Jacqueline L. Beals (Sanbornville)
John, b. 5/18/1894; third; Edward Reed (Wakefield) and Inez May Dicey
   (Wakefield)
Julia Arista, b. 9/15/1872; ninth; Ammon Silas Reed (Newfield, ME) and
   Elizabeth Ann Waldron (Acton, ME) (1938)
Maud Eva, b. 3/16/1899; fifth; Edwin S. Reed (laborer, Wakefield) and
   Ines M. Dicey (Sanbornville); residence - Union
Norman Elsmore, b. 5/18/1920; first; Austin A. Reed (laborer, 33,
   Wakefield) and Rosamond R. Leavitt (20, Parsonsfield, ME)
Sarah Jane, b. 11/5/1870; eighth; Ammon Silas Reed (Newfield, ME) and
   Elizabeth Ann Waldron (Acton, ME) (1938)
Theodore Edwin, b. 7/16/1906; ninth; Edwin S. Reed (mill operative, 41,
   Wakefield) and Inez M. Dicey (34, Wakefield)

REEVES,
Louise, b. 3/24/1910; third; John Reeves (laborer, 36, Salem, MA) and
   Mildred F. Kimball (26, Denmark, ME)

REGENSBURGER,
Jayme Leigh, b. 12/14/1984 in Wolfeboro; Joseph D. Regensburger and
   Laura L. DeForest
Joseph Donald, b. 6/19/1979 in Rochester; Joseph D. Regensburger and
   Laura L. DeForest

REID,
Danielle Teresa, b. 12/7/1984 in Wolfeboro; James R. Reid, Jr. and
   Cynthia A. Hutchins
Jaymee Laree, b. 7/22/1986 in Wolfeboro; James R. Reid, Jr. and Cynthia
   A. Hutchins

REMICK,
daughter [Annie], b. 9/4/1887; first; Alonzo M. Remick (laborer,
   Brookfield) and Hattie Remick (Wakefield)

Helen, b. 1/9/1891; second; Alonzo M. Remick (carpenter, Brookfield) and Hattie M. Maleham (Wakefield)

Mark A., b. 10/24/1898; third; Alonzo M. Remick (carpenter, Brookfield) and Harriet M. Maleham (Wakefield)

William Arthur, b. 1/24/1905; first; Arthur S. Remick (laborer, 22, Brookfield) and Cora Agnes Nason (23, Conway); residence - Sanbornville

REMY,

Clara Teresa, b. 2/13/1908; second; Euclid Remy (woodsman, 26, Canada) and Mary C. Lavoie (23, Wakefield)

Helen Orarilla, b. 5/7/1909; third; Euclid Remy (woodsman, 27, Canada) and Mary S. Lavoie (24, Wakefield)

Rosie E., b. 7/3/1906; first; Euclide Remy (laborer, 25, Canada) and Mary Lavoie (21, Wakefield)

RETTI,

Albert, b. 1/16/1896; first; Jerry Retti (laborer, Canada) and Amanda Drouin (Canada); residence - Sanbornville

REYNALS,

Ruth H., b. 2/18/1897; second; Joseph F. Reynals (mill hand, Daysville, CT) and ----- M. Brown (New Boston, CT)

RHODES,

Alison Hall, b. 4/26/1985 in Dover; Barry C. Rhodes and Lois F. Hall

RICE,

Dorothy F., b. 11/21/1895; third; Irving D. Rice (engineer, Freedom) and Sophronia Tucker (Wakefield)

RICHARDS,

son [Walter W.], b. 12/17/1887; sixth; Charles C. Richards (RR section boss, Milton) and Keziah F. Quimby (Newfield, ME)

daughter [Edna B.], b. 7/28/1890; seventh; Charles C. Richards (farmer, Milton) and Keziah I. Quimby (Newfield, ME)

Allen William, Jr., b. 3/30/1981 in Wolfeboro; Allen W. Richards and Gayle Wareham

Chris Jocelyn, b. 3/15/1973 in Wolfeboro; Douglas C. Richards and Peggy A. Moody

Donald Edward, b. 3/8/1951; fifth; Elden G. Richards (Milton, MA) and Doris E. McKay (MA)

Edith Evelyn, b. 8/9/1918; third; Walter H. Richards (farmer, 30, Wakefield) and Lillian M. Johnson (31, Wakefield)

Eva May, b. 7/1/1914; first; Walter H. Richards (farmer, 26, Wakefield) and Lillian M. Johnson (27, Lowell, MA)

Flora Jane, b. 9/28/1870; first; Edward Richards (Montreal, PQ) and Ellen M. Page (Farmington) (1936)

Josiah Wareham, b. 12/6/1976 in Wolfeboro; Allen W. Richards and Gayle Wareham

RICKER,

Faye Ellen, b. 8/9/1943; first; Robert William Ricker (Lewiston, ME) and Mary Bella Gagne (Welchville, ME)

RIDEOUT,

Dorothy Althea, b. 9/19/1905 in East Wakefield; first; Leon C. Rideout (brakeman, 25, Albany) and Fannie M. Dorr (24, Milton); residence - Conway

Olive Claire, b. 7/30/1909; third; Leon C. Rideout (conductor, 29, Albany) and Janie M. Dorr (28, Milton)

Ruth Edna, b. 7/5/1911; third; Leon Rideout (RR conductor, 31, Albany) and Janie Dorr (30, Milton)

RIDLON,

daughter, b. 5/12/1946; first; Arnold Ridlon (Wolfeboro) and Hazel L. Beal (W. Newfield, ME)

Shirley Faye, b. 4/11/1948; second; Arnold L. Ridlon (Wolfeboro) and Hazel L. Beal (W. Newfield, ME)

RING,

George Daniel, b. 8/5/1990 in Rochester; Kevin Elmer Ring and Patsy Ann Weeks

Zachary Ryan, b. 2/5/1985 in Wolfeboro; Daniel E. Ring and Debra A. Nettelbladt

ROBBINS,

Younger Charles Philip, b. 2/17/1988 in Rochester; Charles P. Robbins and Annie M. Atherton

ROBERGE,
Roger Claude, Jr., b. 4/24/1956 in Kittery, ME; Roger C. Roberge (Troy, VT) and Judith A. McDonald (Rochester)

ROBERTS,
Achsa, b. 1/18/1892; second; Charles F. Roberts (physician, Lebanon, ME) and Eva E. Nute (Farmington)
Rex Nute, b. 1/21/1890; first; Charles F. Roberts (physician, Lebanon, ME) and Eva E. Nute (Farmington, ME)
Samuel Woodbury, b. 8/2/1906; first; John S. Roberts (farmer, 41, Wakefield) and Sarah N. Moulton (40, Wakefield)

ROBIE,
Sarah Elsie, b. 10/19/1913; sixth; Walter D. Robie (mill man, 36, Methuen, MA) and Frances M. Lundberg (34, Salem)

ROBINSON,
Adam Bradford, b. 7/20/1981 in Rochester; Bradford Robinson and Bethany Colbath
Dennis Allen, b. 1/31/1949; fourth; Raymond L. Robinson (NH) and Nellie F. Karcher (MA)
Elaine April, b. 4/7/1942; second; Raymond Leroy Robinson (Dover) and Nellie Frances Karcher (Medford, MA)
Evon Mary, b. 8/23/1910; fourth; David Robinson (teamster, 32, Canada) and Rosie Leviage (28, Canada)
Forest Donald, b. 11/8/1911; second; Frank Robinson (laborer, 27, Wakefield) and Bertha Hart (24, Wakefield)
Forrest Donald, b. 8/11/1960 in Wolfeboro; second; Frank R. Robinson (Wolfeboro) and Anna M. Renfrow (Jackson, MS)
Frank Raymond, b. 2/7/1938; first; Forrest Donald Robinson (Wakefield) and Frances Lillian Meserver (Freedom)
John Joseph, b. 5/27/1908; third; David Robinson (stable keeper, 30, NB) and Rosa LeVeille (26, Rockston, PQ)
Lauryn Katherine, b. 11/25/1988 in Rochester; Wayne A. Robinson, Jr. and Lisa Mae Jerome
Linda Shirley, b. 4/22/1941; second; Donald Forrest Robinson (Wakefield) and Frances Lillian Meserve (Mexico, ME)
Lois Florence, b. 9/23/1909; first; Frank R. Robinson (teamster, 26, Wakefield) and Bertha E. Hart (21, Wakefield)

Lori Beth, b. 7/16/1983 in Rochester; Bradford C. Robinson and Bethany V. Colbath
MacKenzie Layne, b. 9/16/1994 in Wolfeboro; Wayne Albert Robinson, Jr. and Lisa Mae Jerome
Maude Alice, b. 7/11/1876; first; Charles E. Robinson (Brentwood) and Lilla M. Hammond (Brighton, ME) (1937)
Norman Leroy, b. 5/15/1936; first; Burton G. Robinson (Somerville, MA) and Josephine F. Lasky (Milton Mills)
Richard Alan, b. 8/7/1951; second; William A. Robinson (Gloucester, MA) and June Valley (Milton Mills)
Roscoe Chester, b. 1/5/1917; third; Frank Robinson (teamster, 24, Wakefield) and Bertha Hart (29, Wakefield)
Wayne Albert, b. 4/17/1945; third; Raymond L. Robinson (Dover) and Nellie F. Karcker (Medford, MA)
William Austin, Jr., b. 3/26/1949; first; William A. Robinson, Sr. (Gloucester, MA) and June Valley (Milton Mills)
William Austin, III, b. 2/2/1980 in Portsmouth; William A. Robinson, Jr. and Suzanne Peavey

ROGERS,
child, b. 7/4/1981 in Concord; William E. Rogers, Jr. and Diane Gauthier
Elinor Almira, b. 7/19/1894; third; Herbert E. Rogers (farmer, Wolfeboro) and Lillian A. Sanborn (Wakefield)
Gabriel Kriss, b. 8/25/1978; William E. Rogers, Jr. and Diane F. Gauthier
Herbert Sanborn, b. 3/16/1889; first; Herbert E. Rogers (clerk, Wolfeboro) and Lillain Sanborn (Wakefield)
Joshua William, b. 10/30/1973 in Rochester; William E. Rogers and Diane F. Gauthier
Nicholas Barbaro, b. 6/4/1997 in Dover; Norman Foster Rogers and Gina Jo-Anna Barbaro
Una Cleveland, b. 7/29/1915; second; William N. Rogers (student, 23, Wakefield) and Winnie E. Stevens (22, Middleton)
Vincent David, b. 4/30/1898; fifth; Herbert E. Rogers (farmer, Wolfeboro) and Lillian A. Sanborn (Wakefield)
Walter, b. 1/28/1897; fourth; Herbert E. Rogers (farmer, Wolfeboro) and Lillian Sanborn (Wakefield)
Will, b. 6/12/1932 in Concord; William N. Rogers and Margaret Hattie
William Nathaniel, b. 1/8/1892; second; Herbert E. Rogers (farmer, Wolfeboro) and Lillian A. Sanborn (Wakefield)
Zachary, b. 7/19/1984; William E. Rogers, Jr. and Diane F. Gauthier

ROMILLY,
Harold Archibald, b. 12/6/1893; fifth; W.S.L. Romilly (clergyman, England) and Lucy Fowlou (Newfoundland)
John Basil, b. 12/10/1892; fourth; W.S.L. Romilly (clergyman, England) and Lucy F. ----- (Newfoundland)

ROULEAU,
Dack Christopher, b. 2/7/1992 in Wolfeboro; Syd James Rouleau and Rebecca Ann Thompson
Fallon Miranda Mae, b. 8/29/1993 in Wolfeboro; Syd James Rouleau and Rebecca Ann Thompson
Ian George, b. 9/12/1996 in Wolfeboro; Syd J. Rouleau and Rebecca A. Thompson

ROULLARD,
George Homer, b. 3/9/1883; second; Omer A. Roullard (St. George, Canada) and Udoxie Daigneault (Chicopee Falls, MA) (1939)

ROUSSEAU,
Cassandra Marie, b. 11/27/1986 in Rochester; Carlton J. Rousseau and Laura J. Moore

ROUTHIER,
Chloe Ann, b. 2/5/1995 in Dover; Paul Arthur Routhier and Kimberlee Ann Turcotte

ROY,
Georgie Maggie, b. 8/31/1899; fourth; Cyrille Roy (shoemaker, Canada) and Hattie Blowin (Canada)

ROYLE,
Emma Parish, b. 2/28/1992 in Dover; Stephen Royle and Lauree Fletcher
Natalee Mae, b. 4/23/1996 in Dover; Stephen Frederick Royle and Lauree Fletcher

RUFF,
John Charles, b. 9/14/1974 in Wolfeboro; Charles F. Ruff, III and Judith A. Kalled

RUNNALS,
Marshall Winfield, b. 10/23/1910; fifth; Paul M. Runnals (farmer, 35, New Durham) and Blanche B. White (25, New Durham); residence - New Durham

RUNNELLS,
Martha Cora, b. 5/1/1876; Jay Runnells (Acton, ME) and Margaret E. Jack (Burlington, MA) (1941)

RUNNELS,
Elizabeth F., b. 9/30/1903; first; Samuel Runnels (blacksmith, 47, Wakefield) and Mary R. Harriman (40, Madison); residence - Union
Helen M., b. 11/26/1892; first; A. L. Runnels (farmer, Milton) and Carrie E. Chapman (Wakefield)
Martha Palmer, b. 11/13/1906; second; Samuel Runnels (blacksmith, 51, Union) and Mary R. Harriman (43, Madison)
Robert Dean, b. 1/30/1932 in Union; Othello Runnels and Pearl Wilkinson

RUSH,
James Edward, b. 7/13/1918; first; Henry G. Rush (shoe cutter, 24, Derry) and Phoebe E. Crateau (25, Wakefield); residence - Melrose, MA

RUSSELL,
Lelia, b. 6/8/1912; third; Irving Russell (teamster, 37, Athens, ME) and Reina M. Wheeler (29, Harrison, ME)
Ruth R., b. 3/23/1909; second; Irving Russell (woodsman, 33, Athens, ME) and Rowena M. Wheeler (27, Harrison, ME)

RYDL,
Robert Ralph, b. 12/13/1978 in Portsmouth; Ronald R. Rydl and Patricia A. Williams

ST. CYR,
Casey Lynn, b. 1/20/1994 in No. Conway; Leo Albert St. Cyr and Leigh Anne McDormand
Joseph Eugene, b. 8/5/1910; fifth; Alfred St. Cyr (mason, 41, Lancaster) and Melvina Bellecose (36, Canada)
Kaleigh Elizabeth, b. 3/22/1990 in No. Conway; Leo Albert St. Cyr and Leigh Anne McDormand

Shawna Morine, b. 7/22/1987 in No. Conway; Leo St. Cyr and Leigh A. McDormand

ST. PETER,
Marie Rosa A., b. 6/20/1912; sixth; Andrew St. Peter (laborer, 37, Ossipee) and Arre Vignault (30, Ossipee)

ST. PIERRE,
Armand, b. 6/11/1906; second; Andre St. Pierre (section man, 31, Ossipee) and Laura Vigneault (24, Ossipee)
Joseph Arthur, b. 6/5/1907; third; Andrew St. Pierre (laborer, 31, Ossipee) and Laura Vigneault (25, Ossipee)
Joseph George Alfred, b. 10/12/1908; fourth; Andre St. Pierre (laborer, 33, Ossipee) and Leura Vignault (26, Ossipee)
Mary Anne Gracia, b. 9/12/1909; fifth; Andrew St. Pierre (laborer, 34, Ossipee) and Leura Vignault (27, Ossipee)

SAGER,
Weston Robert, b. 11/13/1986 in No. Conway; Richard D. Sager and Lorraine E. Rogus

SAINSBURY,
Ashley Marie, b. 8/4/1996 in Wolfeboro; Scott Alan Sainsbury and Kelly June Thomas

SANBORN,
son, b. 11/11/1889; fourth; J. Irving Sanborn (farmer, Acton, ME) and Ella C. Grant (Acton, ME)
son [Ernest R.], b. 1/12/1890; first; Dyer H. Sanborn (farmer, Wakefield) and Minnie A. Wiggin (Wakefield)
daughter, b. 4/24/1892; fifth; John I. Sanborn (farmer, Acton, ME) and Ella C. Grant (Acton, ME)
Ansel N., b. 1/22/1894; second; Dyer H. Sanborn (carpenter, Wakefield) and Minnie E. Wiggin (Wakefield)
Carroll M., b. 9/13/1893; first; John G. Sanborn (farmer, Acton, ME) and Ida B. Mann (Shapleigh, ME)
Eric Matheu, b. 5/6/1978 in Rochester; Carlton W. Sanborn and Janice M. Glennon
Faye Bettina, b. 4/18/1939; second; Richard Dyer Sanborn (Wakefield) and Bernice Faye McCrillis (Wakefield)

Florence May, b. 9/11/1919; fourth; Ansel N. Sanborn (motion pic. ex., 25, Wakefield) and Maude E. Woodes (27, Haverhill, MA)
Jessie B., b. 1/25/1898; second; John G. Sanborn (farmer, Acton, ME) and Ida B. Mann (Shapleigh, ME)
John Gilman, b. 7/11/1933 in Wolfeboro; Ansel N. Sanborn and Maude E. Woodus
Kayla Maria, b. 4/11/1983 in Rochester; Carlton W. Sanborn, Jr. and Janice M. Glennon
Norris Ray, b. 9/3/1912; second; Ansel Sanborn (news agent, 18, Wakefield) and Maude Woodus (20, Haverhill, MA)
Richard Dyer, b. 5/8/1914; third; Ansel Sanborn (restaurant, 20, Wakefield) and Maude Woodus (21, Haverhill, MA)
Richard Dyer, b. 6/3/1936; first; Richard D. Sanborn (Sanbornville) and Bernice F. McCrillis (Sanbornville)
Sally Ann, b. 12/12/1946; third; Richard D. Sanborn (Sanbornville) and Bernice F. McCrillis (Sanbornville)
Samuel Joseph, b. 11/19/1953 in Ft. Monmouth, ME; first; John Gilman Sanborn (NH) and Nance L. Fay (MA)
Scott Alexander, b. 5/31/1958 in Wolfeboro; fourth; John G. Sanborn (Wolfeboro) and Nance L. Fay (Littleton)
Shaun Michael, b. 1/22/1957 in Wolfeboro; third; John G. Sanborn (Wolfeboro) and Nance L. Fay (Littleton)
Susan Barbara, b. 11/19/1954 in Wolfeboro; John Gilman Sanborn (NH) and Nancy Leona Fay (NH)
Wayne Carlton, b. 4/15/1974 in Wolfeboro; Carlton W. Sanborn and Carol A. Clark
William Edward, Jr., b. 6/19/1989 in Rochester; William Edward Sanborn, Sr. and Tammy Lee Foss

SANTOS,
Alicia Lee, b. 12/13/1973 in Wolfeboro; Stephen A. Santos and Lorraine P. Steadman

SARGENT,
Courtney Lee, b. 2/6/1990 in Wolfeboro; Shaun Desmond Sargent and Margaret Louise Hunter
Jessica Marie, b. 9/3/1991 in No. Conway; Kenneth Alton Sargent and Judith Ann Bellinghiri
John Kenneth, b. 5/7/1985 in Hanover; Kenneth A. Sargent and Judith A. Bellinghiri

SARTWELL,
James Oliver, b. 7/26/1878; first; Warren Sartwell (Essex, NY) and Emma F. Coleman (Portsmouth) (1937)

SAUNDERS,
Auritta Walker, b. 11/24/1896; third; Herbert Saunders (mill hand, Lowell, MA) and Eliza Walker (Boston, MA)

SAWYER,
Luther Eastman, b. 6/2/1928; first; Frank D. Sawyer (Ossipee) and Mary O. Seavey (Limington, ME)

SCALA,
Joseph Daniel, b. 10/24/1997 in Wolfeboro; Dino Anthony Scala and Beth Mary Hayes
Nicholas John, b. 6/24/1980 in Wolfeboro; Michael F. Scala and Marie A. DePalma

SCEGGELL,
Cody Robert, b. 8/26/1995 in Wolfeboro; Stephen Howard Sceggell and Kimberly Ann Mendell
Jeffrey Stephen, b. 10/21/1980 in Rochester; Stephen H. Sceggell and LuAnn B. Pratt
Nicholas Charles, b. 12/11/1983 in Rochester; Stephen H. Sceggell and LuAnn B. Pratt
Stephen Howard, Jr., b. 10/28/1979 in Rochester; Stephen H. Sceggell and LuAnn B. Pratt

SCHWATKA,
Brian Paul, b. 10/9/1974 in Wolfeboro; Paul D. Schwatka and Yvonne T. Dourville

SCOWCROFT,
Shannan Marie, b. 2/13/1973 in Wolfeboro; Thomas W. Scowcroft and Karen E. Steadman

SCUTT,
daughter, b. 7/22/1905 in Sanbornville; first; John Ray Scutt (telephone insp'r, 29, Beatmantown, NY) and Blanche M. Colbath (27, Sanbornville); residence - Barre, VT

SEABOYER,
Evan, b. 12/9/1984 in Wolfeboro; James H. Seaboyer and Lynn A. Colby

SEAMAN,
Sharon Denise, b. 11/18/1972 in Wolfeboro; Thomas B. Seaman and Nancy L. Gates

SEARS,
Philip Joseph, b. 7/15/1941; third; Raymond Leonard Sears (Westmoreland) and Abbie Elizabeth Stewart (ME)
Richard Arthur, b. 3/10/1944; fourth; Raymond L. Sears (Westmoreland) and Abbie E. Stewart (Newry, ME)

SENECAL,
Heather Dawn Kay, b. 7/25/1977 in Sanford, ME; Dana M. Senecal and Janice K. Read

SEVARD,
Flora, b. 2/18/1902 in Sanbornville; tenth; Simeon Sevard (laborer, 42, Canada) and Emily Tromblie (41, Canada); residence - Sanbornville
Joseph A.L., b. 1/10/1898; ninth; Simeon Savard (sic) (laborer, Canada) and Emedie Tremblay (Canada)
Mary Lora, b. 5/18/1899; tenth; Simeon Sevard (laborer, Canada) and Emedie Tremblay (Canada); residence - Sanbornville

SEWALL,
Shandra Elaine, b. 6/18/1974 in Rochester; Jeffrey G. Sewall and Joyce Greene

SEWARD,
Mary F., b. 5/8/1901; first; Byron J. Seward (farmer, Wakefield) and Eliza N. Welch (Ossipee)

SHACKFORD,
daughter, b. 5/7/1896; tenth; S. F. Shackford (farmer, Eaton) and Ada L. Smith (Belfast, ME); residence - East Wakefield
Archie A., b. 1/27/1893; eighth; Stephen F. Shackford (laborer, Eaton) and Ada L. Smith (Belfast, ME)
Emily Rae, b. 4/10/1995 in Wolfeboro; Mark Darin Shackford and Richelle Ruth Zalenski

Lucas Ryan, b. 3/22/1994 in Wolfeboro; Mark Darin Shackford and Richelle Ruth Zalenski

Myrtle Eldora, b. 5/8/1894; ninth; Stephen F. Shackford (farmer, Eaton) and Ada L. Smith (Belfast, ME)

Nellie, b. 9/28/1898; eleventh; S. F. Shackford (farmer, Eaton) and Ada L. Smith (Belfast, ME)

SHARPE,

Eva May, b. 5/31/1909; first; Frank Sharpe (laborer) and Ethel S. Cook (17, Wakefield)

SHEA,

Alfred Henry, b. 4/28/1913; third; Patrick J. Shea (laborer, 32, Boston, MA) and Florence I. Reed (22, Effingham)

Carroll Joseph, b. 8/5/1948; first; Carroll M. Shea (Union) and Janet E. Bailey (Woburn, MA)

Carroll Murl, b. 9/18/1919; sixth; Patrick J. Shea (mill hand, 42, Somerville, MA) and Florence D. Reed (28, Effingham); residence - Union

Evelyn G., b. 10/3/1910; first; Patrick J. Shea (core maker, 27, Boston, MA) and Florence O. Reed (19, Effingham)

Kelly Megan, b. 10/23/1981 in Wolfeboro; Carroll M. Shea and Susan G. Burns

Kyle Tiernan, b. 4/15/1986 in Rochester; Edward D. Shea and Deborah J. Livingston

Michael Patrick, b. 3/25/1978 in Wolfeboro; Carroll J. Shea and Susan G. Burns

Nelson Edward, b. 3/22/1912; second; Patrick J. Shea (mill operative, 28, Boston, MA) and Florence D. Reed (20, Effingham)

Russell Franklin, b. 9/29/1915; fourth; Patrick J. Shea (mill hand, 30, Boston, MA) and Florence Reed (24, Effingham)

Sally Ann, b. 5/26/1958 in Rochester; second; Carroll M. Shea (Union) and Janet E. Bailey (Woburn, MA)

Sheila Catherine, b. 9/10/1946; first; John H. Shea, Jr. (Oak Park, IL) and Nathalie M. Willey (Bangor, ME)

SHEPHERD,

Jordan James Robert, b. 12/7/1992 in Dover; Robert Sueclare Shepherd, Jr. and Karen Anne Cocarus

SHORTRIDGE,
Gladys Frances, b. 7/28/1897; first; Everett Shortridge (farmer, Wolfeboro) and Alice Thompson (Ossipee)

SIBLEY,
Ariel Louise, b. 10/27/1915; sixth; Ernest R. Sibley (laborer, 34, Wakefield) and Ethel M. Richards (32, Wakefield)
Beatrice Emma, b. 2/24/1920; seventh; Ernest Richard Sibley (farmer, 38, Wakefield) and Ethel M. Richards (36, Wakefield)
Dorothy K., b. 5/25/1911; fifth; Ernest R. Sibley (laborer, 30, Wakefield) and Ethel M. Richards (28, Wakefield)
Ernest R., b. 6/23/1909; fourth; Ernest R. Sibley (laborer, 27, Wakefield) and Ethel M. Richards (26, Wakefield)
Lena Marjory, b. 4/29/1908; third; Ernest R. Sibley (laborer, 27, Wakefield) and Ethel M. Richards (25, Wakefield)

SILVESTRO,
Gemma Jean Golden, b. 3/15/1980 in Wolfeboro; Gerard R. Silvestro and Patricia J. Golden
Gina Marie Golden, b. 6/15/1978 in Wolfeboro; Gerald R. Silvestro and Patricia G. Golden

SINCLAIR,
Nicole Ann, b. 8/2/1986 in Rochester; Timothy C. Sinclair and Michelle L. Myers

SMART,
James Woodrow, b. 11/24/1914; third; James E. Smart (laborer, Dexter, ME) and Luella Emerson (Effingham)
Joyce Elaine, b. 3/21/1947; second; James W. Smart (Wakefield) and Etta L. Clark (Sanford, ME)
Leonard, b. 12/3/1912; second; James E. Smart (laborer, 30, Dexter, ME) and Carrie L. Emerson (23, Effingham)
Woodrow, b. 7/22/1941; first; Woodrow Smart (Wakefield) and Etta Clark (Sanford, ME)

SMITH,
son, b. 1/15/1891; second; Charles R. Smith (laborer, Digby, NS) and Ida Foss (Digby, NS)

daughter, b. 4/19/1918; second; Albert Smith (laborer, 25, Dover) and Mary E. Londo (20, Wakefield); residence - W. Newfield, ME
child, b. 1/30/1983 in Rochester; Stephen C. Smith and Pamela Noel
daughter, b. 3/24/1987 in Rochester; Stephen C. Smith and Pamela Noel
Aimee Andrea, b. 2/3/1982 in Wolfeboro; Robert A. Smith and Rita M. Phelan
Albert R., Jr., b. 4/25/1920; third; Albert R. Smith (laborer, 27, Dover) and Mary E. Patch (23, Dover); residence - Sanbornville
Ariel, b. 6/13/1978; Stephen C. Smith and Pamela Noel
Cecil Elmore, b. 8/31/1921; fifth; Guy A. Smith (shoe maker, 40, Franconia) and Clara M. Tufts (37, Middleton); residence - Union
Charles Henry, b. 11/16/1907; first; W. H. Smith (laborer, 39, Newfield, ME) and Mary A. Swett (16, Scarboro, ME)
Christy Marie, b. 4/16/1970 in Rochester; Richard A. Smith and Christine L. Jasztal
David Gene, b. 10/28/1944; fifth; Edmund L. Smith (Farmington) and Hannah E. Demeritt (Milton)
Elizabeth Rose, b. 9/22/1994 in Rochester; Shawn William Smith and Deborah Lee Cheney
Eva May, b. 5/2/1897; first; Charles A. Smith (clerk, Kingston, NY) and Maria J. Hackett (Brookfield)
Florence Mary, b. 11/24/1912; third; William H. Smith (43, Newfield, ME) and Mary G. Smith (21, Wakefield)
George Albert, b. 11/9/1858; Alfred Flavel Smith and Susan E. Mordough (1932)
Guy Raymond, b. 10/23/1915; fourth; Guy A. Smith (mill hand, 33, Franconia) and Clara Tufts (31, Middleton)
Hannah Caitlin, b. 9/6/1984 in Rochester; Stephen C. Smith and Pamela Noel
James Carlton, b. 7/27/1952 in Rochester; eighth; Edmund L. Smith (Farmington) and Hannah T. Demeritt (Milton)
James Lee, b. 1/25/1972 in Rochester; David G. Smith and Renee O. Hill
Jeffrey Wanen, b. 5/24/1968 in Rochester; Wanen H. Smith and Sandra L. Dennison
Jesse Ryan, b. 5/31/1986 in Wolfeboro; William J. Smith and Katherine M. Hall
Kyle Andrew, b. 11/5/1987 in Wolfeboro; William J. Smith and Katherine M. Hall
Marc Henri, b. 5/19/1964 in Rochester; third; Edmund L. Smith, Jr. (Milton) and Monique P. Frerefeau (Chatillon, France)

Mary Cathleen, b. 9/19/1973 in Rochester; Richard A. Smith and Christine J. Jasztal

Michelle Elizabeth, b. 2/17/1970 in Rochester; Edmond L. Smith, Jr. and Monique P. Frerebeau

Mindy Lynn, b. 12/22/1970 in Rochester; Robert R. Smith and Gloria L. Bailey

Percy Miller, b. 2/22/1893; first; Albert G. Smith (clergyman, Pawtucket, RI) and Marion Miller (Glasgow, Scotland)

Robert Andrew, Jr., b. 8/11/1956 in Wolfeboro; first; Robert A. Smith (Melrose, MA) and Beatrice A. Towle (Wakefield)

Shirley Louise, b. 3/29/1946; sixth; Edmond L. Smith (Farmington) and Hannah E. Demeritt (Milton)

Thomas Arthur, b. 5/7/1958 in Wolfeboro; second; Robert A. Smith (Boston, MA) and Beatrice I. Towle (Wakefield)

Thomas Joshua, b. 7/1/1988 in Rochester; Thomas A. Smith and Helen L. Joy

Timothy James, b. 10/2/1970 in Wolfeboro; Robert A. Smith and Beatrice I. Towle

Victoria Nicole, b. 10/16/1998 in Rochester; Chellis William Smith and Cynthis Lynn Bibeault

Walter Joseph, b. 9/21/1912; first; William C. Smith (laborer, 28, Charlestown, MA) and Fannie J. Drew (16, Wakefield)

William Joseph, b. 5/29/1961 in Wolfeboro; third; Robert A. Smith (Wakefield, MA) and Beatrice S. Towle (Wakefield)

William Joseph, b. 7/14/1985 in Wolfeboro; William J. Smith and Katherine M. Hall

SOHN,

Arthur Runnels, b. 9/18/1945; second; Jack Sohn (Bloomfield, NJ) and Lillian M. Atherton (Union)

John Howard, b. 7/20/1943; first; Jack Sohn (Bloomfield, NJ) and Lillian Mae Atherton (Union)

SONGER,

Ellsworth E., b. 11/14/1908; first; John S. Songer (laborer, 27, Howe, PA) and Jessie M. Kimball (17, Wakefield)

SOUCY,

stillborn son, b. 1/4/1927; second; Alphonse Soucy (Salem, MA) and Rose Savertu (Wakefield)

Francis Robert, b. 1/2/1932 in Rochester; Donea F. Soucy and Marion Gagnon

Janie Louise, b. 4/26/1947; second; Armand J. Soucy (Canada) and Laurel M. Bigelow (Somerville, MA)

Jill-Anne, b. 11/2/1950; fourth; Armand J. Soucy (Canada) and Lauriel M. Bigelow (Somerville, MA)

John Jeffrey, b. 6/8/1943; first; Armand Joseph Soucy (Canada) and Laura Mary Bigelow (Somerville, MA)

Joseph Alphonse, b. 5/10/1922; first; Alfonse Soucy (laborer, Salem, MA) and Rosanna Lavertu (Wakefield); residence - Sanbornville

Joseph Roger Alphonse, b. 5/3/1926; tenth; Omer J. Soucy (Canada) and Mary L. Dube (Canada)

Joseph Wilfred Oscar, b. 12/4/1924 in Sanbornville; third; Joseph E. Soucy (iceman, Canada) and Mary Jane Duchano (Sanbornville); residence - Sanbornville

Loretta, b. 11/10/1934; second; Donea F. Soucy (Canada) and Marion Gagnon (Sanbornville)

Mary Ellen, b. 6/17/1957 in Wolfeboro; fourth; Paul D. Soucy (Wolfeboro) and Beverly E. Parker (Lancaster)

Mary Louise, b. 5/14/1951; first; Armond J. Soucy (NH) and Louise L. Swinerton (NH)

Mary Theresa, b. 12/8/1931 in Rochester; Alphonse Soucy and Rose Lavertue (1932)

Meghan Nicole, b. 1/20/1986 in Rochester; Mark F. Soucy and Laurianne Hall

Michael Kenneth, b. 9/9/1993 in Rochester; Mark Francis Soucy and Laurianne Hall

Oscar Joseph, Jr., b. 10/21/1943; first; Oscar Joseph Soucy (Sanbornville) and Dora Mae Davenport (Sanbornville)

Paul Donald, b. 3/1/1933 in Wolfeboro; Albert J. Soucy and Katherine Thompkins

Sally Ann, b. 7/11/1944; second; Armand J. Soucy (Canada) and Lauriel M. Bigelow (Somerville, MA)

Stephen Mark, b. 4/16/1978 in Rochester; Mark F. Soucy and Sally M. Stevens

Wanda Mae, b. 3/16/1953 in Wolfeboro; second; Oscar Joseph Soucy (NH) and Dora Mae Davenport (NH)

SOUZA,
Kathy Ann, b. 8/28/1981 in Wolfeboro; James W. Souza and Dorothy M. Hewitt
Mary Elizabeth, b. 2/13/1983 in Wolfeboro; James W. Souza and Dorothy M. Hewitt

SPARHAWK,
Chandler Ladd, b. 3/7/1952 in Wolfeboro; third; William N. Sparhawk, Jr. (Washington, DC) and Virginia Goodnow (NH)
William Norwood, III, b. 10/12/1949; second; William N. Sparhawk, Jr. (Washington, DC) and Virginia Goodnow (Keene)

SPAULDING,
Carroll Susan, b. 10/19/1946; first; Henry O. Spaulding (Lewiston, ME) and Florence M. Adjutant (Portsmouth)

SPENCER,
Carrie A., b. 3/8/1904; first; Fred Spencer (brass moulder, 42, England) and Sophia Drisco (36, Addison, ME)

SPINNEY,
daughter [Fannie M.], b. 3/7/1900; fifth; Charles N. Spinney (machinist, Eliot, ME) and Clara M. Darling (Malone, NY); residence - Sanbornville
daughter [Leola C.], b. 9/13/1903 in Sanbornville; sixth; Charles H. Spinney (RR mechanic, 45, South Eliot, ME) and Clara M. Darling (37, Malone, NY); residence - Sanbornville
George Marcell, b. 11/19/1869; second; James Twombly Spinney (Wakefield) and Mary Augusta Farnham (Milton) (1942)

SPRAGUE,
Kathleen, b. 4/8/1936; second; Louis E. Sprague (Shapleigh, ME) and Madeline Adjutant (East Wolfeboro)
Louis Ronald, b. 3/16/1935; first; Louis Sprague (Shapleigh, ME) and Madeline Adjutant (East Wolfeboro)

SQUIRE,
Rebecca Gwendelyn, b. 2/6/1966 in Rochester; fourth; Richard T. Squire (Dobbs Ferry, NY) and Helen M. Albee (Charlotte, NC)

SQUIRES,
Geneva Marion, b. 2/11/1928; first; Arthur J. Squires and Hazel M. Johnson (Wakefield)

STALNAKER,
Richard Lee, b. 10/16/1936; second; William Stalnaker (Brooks Co., GA) and Evelyn Shea (Union)
William Roy, b. 8/4/1933 in Rochester; William R. Stalnaker and Evelyn Shea

STAPLES,
Arthur, b. 10/30/1934; second; Christopher Staples (Mirror Lake) and Ada F. Keniston (Webster)

STEADMAN,
Amy Marie, b. 8/3/1982 in Wolfeboro; Charles L. Steadman and Cindy L. Garland

STEPHEN,
Erika Andrea, b. 4/28/1989 in Dover; William David Stephen and Kristin Allen

STEVENS,
son, b. 9/18/1922; second; Walter Ray Stevens (farmer, Middleton) and Mabel A. Swift (Waterford, ME); residence - Union
Alice Ann, b. 4/28/1970 in Rochester; Earl F. Stevens and Janet E. Nason
Brandon Dale, b. 2/19/1987 in Rochester; Kenneth D. Stevens and Lisa L. Bush
Claribell, b. 4/19/1900; fifth; George A. Stevens (laborer, Effingham) and Ida M. Williams (Moultonboro); residence - Sanbornville
Craig Jon, b. 3/3/1960 in Wolfeboro; third; David S. Stevens (Sanbornville) and Beverly A. Dodier (Wolfeboro)
David Ray, b. 9/29/1958 in Rochester; second; Roy A. Stevens (Union) and Barbara A. Hanson (St. Johnsbury, VT)
David S., b. 4/2/1930; sixth; Lloyd Stevens (Sanbornville) and Arlyne D. Dodge (Raymond)
David Spencer, Jr., b. 7/8/1956 in Wolfeboro; first; David S. Stevens (Sanbornville) and Beverly A. Dodier (Wolfeboro)
Donna Marie, b. 9/20/1961 in Rochester; fourth; Roy A. Stevens (Union) and Barbara A. Hanson (St. Johnsbury, VT)

Eleanor J., b. 3/16/1909; third; Frank L. Stevens (clerk, 25, Brookfield) and Myrtle M. Johnson (23, Wakefield)

Florence Gertrude, b. 9/24/1914; third; Ralph W. Stevens (farmer, Newfield, ME) and Helen Weeks (West Ossipee)

Florence May, b. 6/13/1920; first; Walter Ray Stevens (meat dealer, 23, Middleton) and Mabel A. Swift (20, Waterford, ME); residence - Union

Frances Elizabeth, b. 11/9/1937; first; Reginald W. Stevens (Wakefield) and Elizabeth Saunders (Prairie Duchien, WI)

Gary Paul, b. 8/29/1956 in Rochester; first; Roy A. Stevens (Union) and Barbara A. Hanson (St. Johnsbury, VT)

George O., b. 7/7/1862; fourth; George W. Stevens (Newfield, ME) and Eliza Libbey (Barnstead) (1936)

Guy Webster, b. 8/13/1891; first; Everett W. Stevens (sect. foreman, MA) and Lizzie A. Glidden (Wakefield)

Hazel, b. 2/13/1894; third; Everett W. Stevens (sec. foreman, Abington, MA) and Lizzie A. Glidden (Wakefield)

Heather Marie, b. 7/6/1983 in Rochester; Thomas W. Stevens and Priscilla A. Wentworth

Irene Ann, b. 7/31/1984 in Wolfeboro; Richard E. Stevens and Linda A. Horne

Janet Romalda, b. 1/29/1922; third; Lloyd S. Stevens (barber, Wakefield) and Arlyne Dodge (Raymond)

Jeffrey Allan, b. 9/25/1978 in Rochester; Gary P. Stevens and Roberta L. St. Cyr

Lillian C., b. 12/22/1905 in Union; second; John H. Stevens (lumber dealer, 26, Acton, ME) and Lillian B. Brown (27, Wolfeboro); residence - Union

Lloyd E., b. 2/13/1894; second; Everett W. Stevens (sec. foreman, Abington, MA) and Lizzie A. Glidden (Wakefield)

Lois, b. 11/1/1901; first; Roscoe J. Stevens (station agent, Parsonsfield, ME) and Laura Loud (Wakefield); residence - East Wakefield

Lori Marie, b. 3/2/1958 in Rochester; second; William H. Stevens (Middleton) and Kathleen E. Sprague (Union)

Lynn Melody, b. 9/4/1959 in Rochester; third; William H. Stevens (Middleton) and Kathleen E. Sprague (Union)

Marion Ruth, b. 1/20/1925; third; Walter R. Stevens (Middleton) and Mabel Swift (Waterford, ME)

Matthew Thomas, b. 3/18/1978 in Rochester; Thomas W. Stevens and Priscilla A. Wentworth

Michael Kip, b. 1/29/1963 in Rochester; fifth; Earl F. Stevens (Sandown) and Janet E. Nason (No. Wakefield)

Myron, b. 5/15/1910; fifth; Frank L. Stevens (laborer, 26, Brookfield) and Myrtle Johnson (24, Wakefield)

Paula Louise, b. 5/23/1932 in Rochester; Walter Stevens and Mabel Swift

Pearl May, b. 12/7/1927; first; Herbert Stevens (Middleton) and Lillian Campbell (Rowley, MA)

Philip Lawrence, b. 3/16/1906; first; Ralph W. Stevens (laborer, Newfield, ME) and Helen R. Weeks (Ossipee)

Poulla Arlene, b. 6/8/1924 in Sanbornville; fourth; Lloyd E. Stevens (barber, Sanbornville) and Arlyne D. Dodge (Sanbornville); residence - Sanbornville

Ray Albert, b. 1/11/1927; fourth; Walter Stevens (Middleton) and Mabel Swift (Waterford, ME)

Reginald Weeks, b. 5/1/1913; second; Ralph W. Stevens (stable keeper, 29, Newfield, ME) and Helen Weeks (26, Ossipee)

Robert W., b. 9/13/1901; first; Henry D. Stevens (carpenter, Middleton) and Bertha Runnels (Milton)

Roland Ross, b. 8/3/1892; first; Hiram S. Stevens (trader, Freeport, ME) and Hattie B. Ross (Addison, ME)

Samuel R., b. 6/1/1903; second; Henry D. Stevens (carpenter, 30, Middleton) and Bertha R. Runnels (22, Milton Mills); residence - Union

Scott Alan, b. 4/17/1970 in Rochester; Roy A. Stevens and Barbara A. Hanson

Suzan Louise, b. 5/17/1958 in Wolfeboro; second; David S. Stevens (Sanbornville) and Beverly A. Dodier (Wolfeboro)

Tammy Elizabeth, b. 10/30/1964 in Rochester; sixth; Earl F. Stevens (Sandown) and Janet E. Nason (No. Wakefield)

Thomas William, b. 10/16/1953 in Rochester; first; William Huntley Stevens (Middleton) and Kathleen E. Sprague (Union)

Timothy Webber, b. 6/9/1965 in Rochester; fourth; William H. Stevens (Middleton) and Kathleen E. Sprague (Union)

Virginia Ruth, b. 3/31/1917; first; Lloyd E. Stevens (barber, 23, Wakefield) and Dorothy A. Dodge (19, Raymond)

Wayne Albert, b. 7/29/1960 in Rochester; third; Roy A. Stevens (Union) and Barbara A. Hanson (St. Johnsbury, VT)

William Lloyd, b. 7/10/1919; second; Lloyd E. Stevens (barber, 25, Wakefield) and Arlyne Dodge (21, Raymond); residence - Sanbornville

Zachary Jason, b. 12/18/1980 in Rochester; Thomas W. Stevens and Priscilla A. Wentworth

STEVES,
Mary Earnestine, b. 4/28/1911; second; Howard W. Steves (farmer, 40, Elgin, NB) and Lizzie A. Page (Topsham, VT)

STEWART,
Albert Alexander, b. 6/11/1947; first; Albert A. Stewart (Errol) and Ernestine B. Dimond (Gilmanton I.W.)
Ann Elizabeth, b. 12/9/1960 in Wolfeboro; third; Roderick T. Stewart (Chicago, IL) and Dorothy A. Cox (Chicago, IL)
Barbara Ellen, b. 5/20/1958 in Rochester; second; R. Thomas Stewart (Chicago, IL) and Dorothy A. Cox (Chicago, IL)
Daniel Thomas, b. 11/12/1947; third; Leslie D. Stewart (Gorham) and Theresa M. Theoret (So. Berwick, ME)
Joseph Leslie, b. 1/31/1949; fourth; Leslie D. Stewart (Gorham) and Theresa M. Thedret (So. Berwick, ME)
Mary Louisa, b. 1/3/1897; first; Joseph A. Stewart (carpenter, PEI) and Addie M. Shackford (ME)
Patricia Mary, b. 10/23/1946; second; Leslie Daniel Stewart (Gorham) and Theresa M. Thecet (So. Berwick, ME)
Paul Chester, b. 7/5/1948; second; Albert A. Stewart (Errol) and Ernestine B. Dimond (Gilmanton)
Richard Roland, b. 4/11/1947; fifth; Howard C. Stewart (Lemington, VT) and Bernadette L. Morrell (Leominster, MA)
Shelby Kaye, b. 9/11/1990 in Wolfeboro; Carl Eugene Stewart and Joanne M. Nason

STILES,
Earle Gray, b. 3/15/1892; first; Harry G. Stiles (butcher, Ashland, MA) and Christine S. Howard (Bethel, ME)

STIMMEL,
Carol Ann, b. 12/23/1960 in Rochester; fourth; James W. Stimmel (Trexler, PA) and Elsie M. Woodman (Dedham, MA)

STIMSON,
Jessica Sevigny, b. 7/8/1977 in Wolfeboro; Charles T. Stimson and Linda F. Sevigny

STOCKBRIDGE,
Clifford H., b. 3/5/1899; second; H. H. Stockbridge (laborer, Boston, MA) and Melissa Chick (Ossipee)

STONE,
Bruce Edward, b. 7/11/1979 in Rochester; Raymond S. Stone and Patricia A. Morris
Jamie Elizabeth, b. 5/22/1978 in Rochester; Eugene P. Stone and Pamela A. DeRusso

STORM,
Alice Mary Eva, b. 9/28/1899; third; Isaac Storm (laborer, Canada) and Mary Imbo (Canada); residence - Sanbornville
Mary, b. 12/11/1896; second; Isaac Storm (laborer, Canada) and Mary Umbo (Canada); residence - Sanbornville

STORY,
Lena May, b. 1/26/1905; second; William J. Story (clerk, 31, St. Stevens, NB) and Josie Belle Glidden (25, Wakefield)

STREADER,
son, b. 5/22/1888; fourth; Joseph Streader (millman, England) and Valeria I. Dyer (Brownfield, ME)
stillborn son, b. 6/14/1889; sixth; Joseph Streader (laborer, England) and Valeria Dyer (Brownfield, ME)
son, b. 7/8/1890; seventh; Joseph Streader (laborer, England) and Valeria Dyer (Brookfield)
stillborn son, b. 1/23/1892; eighth; Joseph Streader (laborer, England) and Valeria I. Dyer (Brownfield, ME)
stillborn daughter, b. 12/10/1894; seventh; Joseph Streader (laborer, England) and Valeria I. Dyer (Brownfield, ME)
Richard D., b. 7/25/1893; ninth; Joseph Streador (sic) (mill man, England) and Valeria Dyer (Brownfield, ME)

STRONG,
Elizabeth Marie, b. 10/27/1979 in Hanover; Donald J. Strong, Jr. and Joyce E. Barber

STUART,
Dorothy Wilma, b. 1/22/1891; second; Fred R. Stuart (foreman, Bridgton, ME) and Emma L. Boyd (Boothbay, ME)

SULLIVAN,
Abby Kate, b. 9/20/1994 in Rochester; John Sullivan and Jill Richards

SWINERTON,
Alan James, b. 1/25/1958 in Rochester; third; Lawrence A. Swinerton (Milton) and Dorothy O. Gathman (Oak Park, IL)
Beatrice Marie, b. 3/19/1936; third; Richard Swinerton (Milton) and Laura M. Duchano (Sanbornville)
Louise, b. 10/21/1931; first; Richard Swinerton (West Milton) and Laura Duchano (Wakefield)
Richard George, b. 2/15/1941; fourth; Richard G. Swinerton (Milton) and Laura Marie Duchano (Sanbornville)

SYLVIA,
Hester MacAuley, b. 3/1/1980 in Wolfeboro; Robert A. Sylvia and Kathleen MacAuley

SZIRBIK,
Andrea Michelle, b. 7/20/1982; George H. Szirbik and Josephine T. Gallinoto

TAFT,
Isabelle, b. 1/5/1902; third; Arthur L. Taft (manufacturer, 50, Oxford, MA) and Nellie W. Dunham (40, Mansfield, CT); residence - Union

TALBERT,
Tracy Eric, b. 3/18/1960 in Wolfeboro; third; Wilbur R. Talbert (Portsmouth) and Ethel J. Rowe (Pepperell, MA)

TALIAFERRO,
Sarah Rose, b. 5/13/1978 in Wolfeboro; Thomas B. Taliaferro and Sharon L. Libby

TANNER,
son [Patrick J.], b. 7/16/1898; seventh; Hervey E. Tanner (carpenter, Farmington) and Mary O'Hare (Belfast, Ireland)

Audrey Y., b. 4/12/1903; ninth; H. E. Tanner (carpenter, 39, Farmington) and Mary Ann O'Hara (37, Belfast, Ireland)
Betty Jane, b. 1/12/1953 in Rochester; second; Lloyd Cecil Tanner (Wakefield) and Sarah J. Fifield (Wakefield)
Blanche Lenora, b. 9/1/1949; first; Lloyd Cecil Tanner (NH) and Sarah J. Fifield (NH)
Consuelo, b. 1/27/1897; sixth; Hervey E. Tanner (carpenter, Farmington) and Mary A. Chara (Ireland)
Eleanor T., b. 5/29/1900; eighth; Hervey E. Tanner (carpenter, Farmington) and Mary Ann O'Hara (Belfast, Ireland)
Hervey C., b. 3/27/1904; tenth; Hervey Edward Tanner (carpenter, 41, Farmington) and Mary O'Hare (39, Belfast, Ireland)
Lloyd Cecil, b. 5/10/1919; first; Charles E. Tanner (laborer, 25) and Vila L. Kimball (19, Middleton); residence - Milton

TARBOX,
Darren Philip, b. 2/13/1995 in Wolfeboro; Casey Philip Tarbox and Cheryl Lee Massey

TASKER,
Dean Adam, b. 3/9/1968 in Wolfeboro; Bruce D. Tasker and Elinor L. Buswell
Trevor Ellis, b. 10/27/1972 in Wolfeboro; Bruce D. Tasker and Elinor E. Briswell

TERCYAK,
Timothy Michael, b. 12/20/1977 in Rochester; Michael E. Tercyak and Deborah J. Savoie

TESSIER,
stillborn daughter, b. 10/10/1914; fifth; Louis Tessier (mill operative, 28, Suncook) and Lucy Pouliott (27, Wakefield)
Beatrice, b. 4/2/1917; seventh; Louis Tessier (factory hand, 32, Suncook) and Lucy Pouliot (30, Wakefield)
Beatrice Hermine, b. 4/2/1923; eleventh; Louis Tessier (ice man, Suncook) and Lucy Pouliott (Wakefield); residence - Sanbornville
Brenda Jean, b. 1/29/1950; third; George E. Tessier (Gonic) and Marjorie E. Hatch (Wolfeboro)
Charles Louis, b. 2/15/1916; sixth; Louis C. Tesier (sic) (mill hand, 31, Suncook) and Lucy Pouliot (29, Wakefield)

Elizabeth Elsie, b. 5/24/1920; ninth; Louis C. Tessier (laborer, 35, Suncook) and Lucy M. Pouliot (33, Sanbornville); residence - Sanbornville

George Edward, b. 7/2/1933 in Rochester; George E. Tessier and Marjorie E. Hatch

Gerold Wayne, b. 6/2/1936; third; George E. Tessier (Rochester) and Marjorie E. Hatch (Wolfeboro)

Joseph Louis Albert, b. 9/8/1913; fourth; Louis Tessier (laborer, 28, Suncook) and Lucy Pouliot (26, Wakefield)

Kirda Cellia, b. 8/4/1910; second; Louis Tessier (laborer, 25, Suncook) and Lucy Pouliot (23, Wakefield)

Leo Joseph, b. 6/8/1921; tenth; Louis C. Tessier (Suncook) and Lucy M. Pouliot (Wakefield) (1941)

Oliver Leon, b. 9/17/1924; twelfth; Louis Tessier (laborer, Suncook) and Lucy Pouliot (Wakefield); residence - Sanbornville

Raleigh Louis, b. 4/10/1912; third; Louis Tessier (laborer, 26) and Lucy Pouliott (25, Wakefield)

Sandra Mae, b. 6/5/1941; second; George Edward Tessier (Rochester) and Marjorie Emma Hatch (Wolfeboro)

Victoria Phoebe, b. 2/1/1919; eighth; Louis C. Tessier (laborer, 34, Suncook) and Lucia M. Pouliott (31, Sanbornville); residence - Sanbornville

TETU,
Dale Daniel, b. 7/29/1990 in Dover; Tommy Allen Tetu and Doreen Beverly Allyson

TEWKSBURY,
Earl Arthur, b. 3/3/1943; first; Fred Arthur Tewksbury (Sanbornville) and Pearl Nichols (Ossipee)

Fred Arthur, b. 10/16/1897; first; R. S. Tewksbury (fireman, Tamworth) and Martha J. Hill (Bartlett)

Terry Frances, b. 4/16/1944; second; Fred A. Tewksbury (Sanbornville) and Pearle L. Nichols (Center Ossipee)

THOMAS,
Alexander Guilford, b. 1/14/1981 in Rochester; Kenneth G. Thomas and Kathleen J. Towle

Cynthia Lee, b. 11/14/1948; first; Walter C. Thomas, Jr. (Maplewood, MA) and Dorothy G. Colman (Brookfield)

Dorothy L., b. 4/25/1931; first; George Thomas (Middleboro, MA) and Flora Mills (Wakefield)
Kenneth Guilford, b. 11/20/1959 in Rochester; first; James G. Thomas (Boston, MA) and Corinne E. Dame (Rochester)
Lorrie Fuku, b. 12/6/1964 in Wolfeboro; third; Charles L. Thomas (Rochester) and Kazuko Nakahara (Tokyo, Japan)
Roberta Diane, b. 1/4/1950; second; Walter F. Thomas, Jr. (Maplewood, MA) and Dorothy G. Colman (Brookfield)
Rose Marie, b. 11/1/1960 in Rochester; second; James G. Thomas (Boston, MA) and Corinne E. Dame (Rochester)
Wanda Lee, b. 9/7/1961 in Rochester; third; James G. Thomas (Boston, MA) and Corinne E. Dame (Rochester)

THOMPSON,
daughter, b. 2/8/1888; third; Albert H. Thompson (clergyman, Chelsea, MA) and Arvilla Hardy (Ossipee)
daughter, b. 4/22/1929; fifth; George Thompson (Ossipee) and Dorothy M. Hill (W. Newfield, ME)
Arthur S., b. 6/15/1922; second; George Thompson (coal shed B&M, Mountainview) and Dorothy Hill (Newfield, ME)
Barry Jon, b. 1/23/1955 in Wolfeboro; third; Russell Clifton Thompson (NH) and Audrey F. Connaughton (MA)
Benjamin James, b. 7/21/1984 in Rochester; William R. Thompson and Janet L. Peel
Cathy Ann, b. 2/9/1950; second; Russell C. Thompson (Sanbornville) and Audrey F. Connaughton (Lynn, MA)
Christopher Ole Lygren, b. 7/18/1990 in Wolfeboro; Mark Christopher Thompson and Kari Marta Lygren
Ellsworth Raymond, b. 3/11/1933 in Sanbornville; George Thompson and Dorothy Hill
Katherine Mary, b. 9/7/1924; third; George Thompson (laborer, Mountainview) and Dorothy Hill (W. Newfield, ME); residence - Sanbornville
Mark James, b. 2/24/1991 in Dover; Barry Jon Thompson and Pamela Jean Beaudoin
Matthew Alexander, b. 2/25/1980 in Rochester; Barry J. Thompson and Pamela J. Beaudoin
Rebecca Ann, b. 8/29/1964 in Wolfeboro; fourth; Russell C. Thompson (Sanbornville) and Audrey F. Connaughton (Lynn, MA)

Russell Clifton, b. 5/20/1927; fourth; George Thompson (Ossipee) and Dorothy M. Hill (Newfield, ME)

Russell Clifton, Jr., b. 9/21/1947; first; Russell C. Thompson (Sanbornville) and Audrey Connaughton (Lynn, MA)

Sealyn Riley, b. 2/9/1998 in Wolfeboro; Timothy Thompson and Ann Thompson

THORNTON,

Dana Scott, b. 7/9/1965 in Wolfeboro; third; Leif N. Thornton (Quincy, MA) and Judith M. Strachan (Brockton, MA)

THURSTON,

son, b. 5/26/1922; first; Lucellas C. Thurston (wood turner, Stoddard) and Eunice R. Loveren (Hancock); residence - Union

Anthony Clifton, b. 9/16/1956 in Rochester; third; Donald H. Thurston (Rochester) and Geraldine T. Avery (Rumney)

TIBBETTS,

son [Benjamin F.], b. 8/26/1897; second; Fred Tibbetts (engineer, Porter, ME) and Lucy P. Maleham (Wakefield)

Leon Frank, b. 12/21/1898; fourth; Thomas B. Tibbetts (laborer, Wolfeboro) and Etta J. Hamilton (Conway)

Michael Richard, b. 1/18/1947; first; Ernest Tibbetts (Sanford, ME) and Nancy Mills Dawe (Salem, MA)

Ralph Arthur, b. 4/21/1899; first; Arthur D. Tibbetts (laborer, Wolfeboro) and Jerusha J. Spencer (Waterboro, ME)

Timothy Alan, b. 3/8/1957 in Wolfeboro; third; Louis E. Tibbetts (Wakefield) and Arlene R. Laskey (Milton)

Willis Fred, b. 8/4/1893; first; Fred Tibbetts (engineer, Porter, ME) and Lucy P. Maleham (Wakefield)

TIERNEY,

Peter Lyman, b. 4/12/1950; third; John C. Tierney (Indianapolis, IN) and Katherine F. Snow (Winchester, MA)

TILESTON,

Robert Cushing, b. 10/22/1911; first; Alden S. Tileston (civil engineer, 29, Dorchester, MA) and Clara E. Mee (21, Lynn, MA); residence - Arlington, MA

TIMMINS,
Christopher Michael, b. 5/1/1990 in No. Conway; Frank Patrick Timmins and Bernice Mary Allain

TITCOMB,
son [Leon H.], b. 4/4/1889; first; John F. Titcomb (carpenter, Acton, ME) and Abbie ----- (Wakefield)
Eleanor Elizabeth, b. 7/25/1914; first; Leon Titcomb (farmer, Wakefield) and Helen Remick (Wakefield)
Grace Harriett, b. 3/14/1917; second; Leon Henry Titcomb (Wakefield) and Helen Maleham Remick (Wakefield) (1940)

TITUS,
Benjamin Michael, b. 4/18/1998 in Rochester; Todd Titus and Lisa Titus

TODD,
Ryan Durwood, b. 10/10/1993 in Rochester; Robert William Todd, Jr. and Sonia Ann Wilkinson

TOMPSON,
Michelle Elizabeth, b. 11/14/1966 in Rochester; first; Wayne A. Tompson (Rochester) and Martha A. Kinney (Rochester)

TOWLE,
Ann Maria, b. 1/9/1899; first; Charles Towle (laborer, Freedom) and ----- (Charlestown)
Charles E., b. 7/22/1904; third; Charles E. Towle (farmer, 43, Freedom) and Bertha Staples (22, Middleton, MA)
Edith A., b. 6/11/1906; third; Charles E. Towle (farmer, 45, Freedom) and Bertha Staples (27, Middleton, MA)
Grace Ella, b. 2/8/1908; fifth; Charles E. Towle (farmer, 47, Freedom) and Bertha Staples (26, Middleton, MA)
Raymond Eaton, b. 7/25/1907; fifth; Milton Towle (farmer, 38, Eaton) and Mary L. Wentworth (28, Ossipee); residence - Eaton

TRAFTON,
son, b. 4/11/1905 in Union; seventh; Reuben Trafton (barber, 30, Wakefield) and Iva Ham (27, Farmington); residence - Union

daughter [Blanche E.], b. 8/29/1905 in Union; first; Ashton R. Trafton (mill operative, 23, Wakefield) and Bertha M. Lord (16, Ross Corner, ME); residence - Union

Ashton Roscoe, b. 8/9/1885; fourth; Charles Trafton (Acton, ME) and Emily S. Archibald (Wakefield) (1942)

Catherine H., b. 6/22/1907; eighth; Ruben B. Trafton (barber, 32, Wakefield) and Iva M. Ham (29, Farmington)

Donald G., b. 5/11/1909; ninth; Reuben B. Trafton (barber, 34, Wakefield) and Iva M. Ham (31, Farmington)

Dorothy Stevens, b. 8/10/1899; third; Reuben B. Trafton (barber, Acton, ME) and Iva May Horne (Farmington); residence - Union

Esther May, b. 2/28/1904; sixth; Reuben B. Trafton (barber, 28, Wakefield) and Iva M. Ham (25, Farmington)

Helen Madeline, b. 4/28/1913; tenth; Reuben B. Trafton (barber, 38, Wakefield) and Iva M. Ham (35, Farmington)

Julia May, b. 11/1/1912; second; Ashton R. Trafton (laborer, 30, Wakefield) and Bertha M. Lord (28, Shapleigh, ME)

Nat Parker, b. 7/4/1917; eleventh; Reuben B. Trafton (barber, 42, Wakefield) and Iva M. Horn (39, Farmington)

Nellie A., b. 5/26/1901; fourth; Reuben Trafton (heel cutter, Wakefield) and Iva Ham (Farmington); residence - Union

Norman Earl, b. 3/8/1903 in Union; fifth; Reuben B. Trafton (barber, 28, Wakefield) and Iva Ham (25, Farmington); residence - Union

Ralph Bradley, b. 9/1/1941; first; Nat Parker Trafton (Wakefield) and Barbara Belle Hanson (Wakefield)

Robert Parker, b. 1/28/1944; second; N. Parker Trafton (Union) and Barbara B. Hanson (Sanbornville)

Roger Herbert, b. 8/17/1898; second; Reuben B. Trafton (mill hand, Wakefield) and Iva M. Ham (Farmington)

Scott Bradley, b. 4/25/1989 in Dover; R. Bradley Trafton and Elaine Ouellette

Winnifred, b. 8/14/1897; first; Reuben Trafton (mill hand, Wakefield) and Iva Ham (Farmington)

TRAINOR,

Lewis Clarence, b. 9/13/1910; second; James M. Trainor (laborer, 32, Brownfield, ME) and Lulu P. Hart (21, Wakefield)

Marion Edith, b. 3/13/1907; second; James M. Trainor (farmer, 30, Brownfield, ME) and Lulu Hart (18, Wakefield)

Minnie A., b. 5/6/1905; first; James Michael Trainor (farmer, 23, Brownfield, ME) and Lulu Hart (17, East Wakefield); residence - Sanbornville

TROTT,
daughter, b. 7/26/1914; second; Leander Trott (store keeper, 30, Portland, ME) and Hazel Cook (20, Wakefield)
Wesley H., b. 10/14/1894; fourth; Thayer Trott (farmer, Peaks Island, ME) and Emma Mathews (Wakefield)

TRUEDEL,
daughter, b. 4/28/1890; second; Frank Truedel (laborer, Canada)and Amanda ----- (Canada)

TRUMAN,
Jennifer Lynn, b. 3/5/1987 in Rochester; Keith D. Truman and Wendy L. Despard

TUCKER,
son [Willard], b. 5/30/1894; fourth; James F. Tucker (engineer, Somersworth) and Mary F. Brackett (Wakefield)
son [Willis F.], b. 1/14/1901; sixth; James F. Tucker (engineer, Somersworth) and Mary F. Brackett (Wakefield)
son [Harris W.], b. 6/5/1902; seventh; James F. Tucker (engineer, 47, Somersworth) and Mary F. Brackett (40, Wakefield); residence - Sanbornville
James Carroll, b. 4/28/1892; third; James F. Tucker (engineer, Somersworth) and Mary F. Brackett (Wakefield)
Mary Elizabeth, b. 5/21/1906; eighth; James F. Tucker (engineer, 51, Somersworth) and Mary F. Brackett (44, Wakefield)
Morris, b. 6/12/1897; fifth; James F. Tucker (engineer, Somersworth) and Mary F. Brackett (Wakefield)
Pauline Ulrica, b. 9/23/1903; second; Carlton L. Tucker (fireman, 24, Somersworth) and A. Eldena Furbush (24, S. Berwick, ME); residence - Sanbornville
Sophronia, b. 5/25/1857; fifth; James Tucker (Amesbury, MA) and Mary E. Hale (Haverhill, MA) (1936)
Willis Francis, Jr., b. 10/29/1921; first; Willis F. Tucker (laborer, 20, Wakefield) and Helen G. Currell (18, Reading, MA); residence - Sanbornville

TUFTS,
stillborn daughter, b. 9/28/1914; fourth; Frank J. Tufts (painter, 38, Somersworth) and Fannie L. Thompson (29, Andover)
Charles Francis, b. 10/30/1905 in Sanbornville; second; Frank J. Tufts (laborer, 29, Somersworth) and Fannie L. Thompson (21, Andover); residence - Sanbornville
Verlie Elizabeth, b. 7/29/1904; first; Frank J. Tufts (laborer, 28, Somersworth) and Fannie L. Thompson (19, Andover)
Warren Albert, b. 7/21/1908; third; James F. Tufts (laborer, 32, Somersworth) and Francis L. Thompson (23, Andover)

TURBITT,
Damon Pierce, b. 10/22/1993 in Rochester; James William Turbitt, Jr. and Denise Lorraine Read
Holden Read, b. 12/20/1991 in Rochester; James William Turbitt, Jr. and Denise Lorraine Read
Nathaniel James, b. 11/23/1989 in Rochester; James William Turbitt, Jr. and Denise Lorraine Read

TUTTLE,
son [Dana C.], b. 1/17/1889; fifth; Daniel N. Tuttle (farmer, Wakefield) and Ora F. Tibbetts (Wolfeboro)
daughter [Manora], b. 10/3/1890; sixth; Daniel N. Tuttle (farmer, Wakefield) and Ora F. Tibbetts (Wolfeboro)
Abbie F., b. 6/12/1894; seventh; Daniel N. Tuttle (farmer, Wakefield) and Ora F. Tibbetts (Wolfeboro)
Amanda Jean, b. 4/20/1949; second; Irving D. Tuttle, Jr. (Wakefield) and Jean S. Robinson (Melrose, MA)
Carey Lynn, b. 4/28/1978 in Wolfeboro; Irving D. Tuttle, III and Linda L. Laskey
Carrie E. Kelly, b. 9/20/1980 in Dover; Randal C. Tuttle and Pamela J. Hooper
Daniel Douglas, b. 10/1/1976 in Wolfeboro; Irving D. Tuttle, III and Linda L. Laskey
David Carlton, b. 8/11/1956 in Wolfeboro; fifth; Irving D. Tuttle, Jr. (Wakefield) and Jean S. Robertson (Melrose, MA)
Earl Arthur, b. 8/12/1921; second; Arthur L. Tuttle (carpenter, 29, Athens, ME) and Mary Currier (19, York, ME); residence - Sanbornville
Frances Seabury, b. 11/14/1953 in Wolfeboro; fourth; Irving D. Tuttle, Jr. (NH) and Jean S. Robertson (MA)

Gracie May, b. 12/4/1894; first; Horace B. Tuttle (farmer, Wakefield) and Kate V. Weeks (Wakefield)

Irene Isabelle, b. 6/19/1920; first; Arthur L. Tuttle (heel shop foreman, 29, Athens, ME) and Marrie A. Currier (18, York, ME)

Irving D., b. 9/13/1897; eighth; Daniel N. Tuttle (farmer, Wakefield) and Ora F. Tibbetts (Wolfeboro)

Irving Daniel, b. 10/30/1923; third; Irving D. Tuttle (farmer, Wakefield) and Ruth E. Johnson (Waltham, MA)

Irving Daniel, 3d, b. 6/5/1951; third; Irving D. Tuttle, 2d (NH) and Jean S. Robertson (MA)

Jean Louise, b. 3/21/1929; fourth; Irving Tuttle (Wakefield) and Ruth Johnson (Waltham, MA)

Katherine Frances, b. 1/10/1922; second; Irving D. Tuttle (farmer, Wakefield) and Ruth Johnson (Waltham, MA)

TWOMBL[E]Y,

child, b. 8/30/1943; fourth; William H. Twombly (Sanbornville) and Frances Isabelle Derby (Barrington)

child, b. 8/30/1943; fifth; William H. Twombly (Sanbornville) and Frances Isabelle Derby (Barrington)

Hazel, b. 9/15/1930; first; Hattie Twombly (Wolfeboro)

Lawrence C., b. 4/27/1945; fifth; William J. Twombley (Union) and Frances Isabel Derby (Barnstead)

Paul Jefferson, b. 9/13/1935; second; William Twombly (Union) and Frances Deroy (Barnstead)

Philip Douglas, b. 8/2/1942; third; William J. Twombly (Union) and Frances Isabel Derby (Barnstead)

Robert William, b. 3/28/1934; first; William F. Twombly (Union) and Frances Dubee (Barnstead)

Scott Anthony, b. 5/29/1968 in Rochester; Philip D. Twombley and Constance M. Gagnon

Steven Lawrence, b. 9/14/1988 in Rochester; Steven Twombley and Tina L. Pridham

William Jefferson, b. 10/29/1912; second; Clarence H. Twombley (laborer, 27, Conway) and Bertha L. Downs (28, Wakefield)

TYLER,

Devin Charles, b. 6/14/1982 in Rochester; Dennis L. Tyler and Dolores A. Drake

Emily Nicole, b. 9/29/1995 in Wolfeboro; Dennis Linwood Tyler and Marcia Ann Tutein

Haley Ann, b. 6/13/1998 in Wolfeboro; Dennis Linwood Tyler and Marcia Ann Tutein

Leah Nora, b. 4/30/1980; Dennis L. Tyler and Dolores A. Drake

Ryan Joseph, b. 4/14/1992 in Rochester; Dennis Linwood Tyler and Marcia Ann Tutein

UPSON,

Adam Michael, b. 7/9/1993 in Wolfeboro; Peter Allen Upson and Valerie Ann Yuill

Ryan David, b. 1/20/1995 in Wolfeboro; Peter Allen Upson and Valerie Ann Yuill

VACHON,

Leo A., b. 5/2/1931; sixth; Archille Vachon (Broughton, PQ) and Demerise Lamie (Wakefield)

Robert Alan, Jr., b. 7/31/1980 in Rochester; Robert A. Vachon, Sr. and Joan M. Hall

VAIN,

John Henry, b. 7/13/1900; third; Xavier Vain (laborer, Canada) and Marie Dubret (Canada); residence - Union

VALANDRY,

Alice Vena, b. 8/26/1909; seventh; Ovid Valandry (laborer, 34, Biddeford, ME) and Emma Vassell (30, NS)

VALLANDRY,

Henry, b. 7/27/1908; fourth; Ovid Vallandry (laborer, 39, Canada) and Emma Vasselle (29, Canada)

VALLEY,

George W., b. 2/22/1906; sixth; David Valley (laborer, 35, Canada) and Adeline Pourtrie (32, Canada)

Joseph Henry, b. 4/2/1902 in Sanbornville; sixth; David Valley (laborer, 29, Canada) and Adeline Pourtrie (29, Canada)

Lucienne, b. 7/28/1903 in Sanbornville; fourth; David Vallie (sic) (laborer, 30, Canada) and Addeline Patsey (29, Canada); residence - Sanbornville

Marie, b. 3/9/1900; first; David Valley (laborer, Canada) and Adelaide Patrie (Canada); residence - Sanbornville
Mary, b. 8/31/1904; fifth; David Valley (laborer, 32, Canada) and Adelina Patry (31, Canada)
Syriene, b. 3/17/1901; second; David Valley (laborer, Canada) and Adeline Patrie (Canada); residence - Sanbornville

VALLIAE,
Michael Everett, b. 8/13/1966 in Wolfeboro; first; George F. Valliae (Alton, IL) and Mary Elizabeth Knight (Wolfeboro)

VAN DOORN,
Katrina, b. 4/11/1963 in Wolfeboro; first; Roger A. Van Doorn (NY) and Nancy E. Anderson (W. Milton)

VAN DUSEN,
Christopher John, b. 12/23/1973 in Wolfeboro; Charles E. Van Dusen and Helen M. Clinton

VAN DYKE,
William Wilson, b. 2/8/1940; second; Andrew M. Van Dyke (Smithport, PA) and Anne Elizabeth Petty (Washington, DC)

VARNEY,
daughter, b. 8/6/1887; third; John F. Varney (laborer, Milton) and Nancy M. Prescott (Milton)
son [Guy G.], b. 7/16/1889; fourth; John F. Varney (laborer) and Nancy Prescott
daughter [Doris], b. 7/18/1905 in Union; third; Lewis M. Varney (laborer, 28, Farmington) and Grace F. Pinkham (23, Middleton); residence - Union
child, b. 12/8/1941; first; Stanley Maurice Varney (Milton) and Esther Louise Varney (Wakefield)
Bettina Fay, b. 8/12/1928; fifth; Gerald G. Varney (Wakefield) and Eliza J. Jenness (Milton)
Doris Ella, b. 4/20/1925; fourth; Gerald Guy Varney (Wakefield) and Eliza Jane Jenness (Milton)
Gertrude A., b. 7/31/1909; fifth; Lewis N. Varney (sawyer, 33, Farmington) and Grace F. Pinkham (27, Middleton)

Harold Herbert, b. 1/26/1907; fourth; Lewis N. Varney (brass moulder, 29, Farmington) and Grace F. Pinkham (24, Middleton)

Harry, b. 12/2/1891; fifth; John F. Varney (watchman, Milton) and Nancy M. Prescott (Milton)

VASHEY,
Dennis Alan, b. 12/4/1948; first; Henry E. Vashey (Pawtucket, RI) and Mary E. Drown (Wakefield)

VENO,
Grace Rosa Pauline, b. 3/24/1918; sixth; William Veno (mill hand, 28, Ossipee) and Mary A. Lavertu (26, Canada)

Kathryn Estelle, b. 5/18/1926; fifth; Samuel Veno (Brookfield) and Mary G. Burk (Buffalo, NY)

Maryline Louise, b. 9/21/1921; fourth; Samuel A. Veno (laborer, 39, Brookfield) and Mary G. Burke (39, Buffalo, NY); residence - Sanbornville

Richard, b. 11/22/1921; eighth; William Veno (track man, 31, Ossipee) and Mary Lavertee (29, Canada); residence - Sanbornville

Roland Gerard, b. 1/4/1928; ninth; William Veno (Ossipee) and Mary Lavertue (Canada) (1946)

Wilfred Ernest, b. 7/1/1915; fourth; Willie Veno (laborer, 25, Ossipee) and Mary Levirtu (23, Canada)

VIGNEAULT,
Armand Leo, b. 2/16/1913; second; William Vigneault (laborer, 23, Ossipee) and Mary Levertu (21, Canada)

George Arthur, b. 3/18/1914; third; William Vignault (laborer, 24, Ossipee) and Mary Lavertu (21, Canada)

Joseph Alfred, b. 2/15/1912; first; William J. Vigneault (laborer, 21, Ossipee) and Mary A. Levirtu (19, Canada)

Mary Stella Anita, b. 1/7/1920; seventh; William Vigneault (trackman, 30, Ossipee) and Mary Ann Savertu (27, St. Sophie, Canada)

Raymond Alcide, b. 12/18/1916; fifth; William Vigneault (laborer, 27, Ossipee) and Mary Lavertu (24, Canada)

VILLARAS,
Byron Edward, b. 11/22/1994 in No. Conway; Edward Byron Villaras and Diane Michelle Raby

Deanne Dorothy, b. 10/20/1993 in No. Conway; Edward Byron Villaras and Diane Michelle Raby

WADDINGTON,
Dakota A.M., b. 9/13/1995 in Rochester; Robert William Waddington and Theresa Lee Kenney

WADLEIGH,
daughter [Charlotte K.], b. 12/3/1892; third; Frank F. Wadleigh (farmer, Dover) and Mary J. Gilmour (NS)
Agnes F., b. 4/2/1898; fifth; F. F. Wadleigh (farmer, Dover) and Mary J. Gilmore (NS)
Helen, b. 2/1/1895; fourth; F. F. Wadleigh (farmer, Dover) and Mary J. Gilman (NS)

WAGNER,
Meghan Catherine, b. 3/22/1993 in Laconia; George Walter Wagner and Laurie Lynn Doe

WAKEFIELD,
Bessie Ethel, b. 7/26/1919; sixth; Ralph Wakefield (laborer, 34, Moultonboro) and Mary E. Webster (29, Sandwich)

WALDRON,
Carrie Anna, b. 8/4/1895; first; Hiram E. Waldron (farmer, Wakefield) and Sadie M. Fellows (Wakefield)
Clarence, b. 3/28/1901; first; Hiram E. Waldron (laborer, Cambridge, MA) and Rose Billideau (Salem, MA)
Leola I., b. 6/23/1903; second; Hiram E. Waldron (clerk, 30, Wakefield) and Rose Billedeaux (20, Salem, MA)
Louise Narcissa, b. 2/1/1907; third; Charles D. Waldron (merchant, Wakefield) and Mary Philbrick (Wakefield)
Roger Hiram, b. 4/25/1896; first; Charles D. Waldron (Wakefield) and Mary Philbrick (Wakefield) (1937)
Sarah H., b. 5/26/1901; second; Charles D. Waldron (farmer, Wakefield) and Mary Philbrick (Wakefield)

WALLACE,
Angela Lee, b. 8/23/1974 in Rochester; Milton Wallace and Linda L. Dodier

Marion E., b. 9/24/1894; first; Edwin S. Wallace (fireman, Middleton) and Lizzie S. Whitehouse (Middleton)
Melissa Dawn, b. 6/21/1971 in Rochester; Milton Wallace and Linda L. Dodier
Zackery Joel, b. 7/2/1988 in Dover; David L. Wallace and Kimberly J. Waterhouse

WALLINGFORD,
Barbara Lee, b. 12/7/1946; fifth; Collis E. Wallingford (Gonic) and Abbie E. Stewart (Newry, ME)
Scott Allen, b. 2/15/1969 in Rochester; Forrest A. Wallingford and Carolyn N. Dow

WALSH,
Charles Brett, b. 11/12/1901; second; George L. Walsh (farmer, 30, Milton Mills) and Carrie Briggs (28, Paris Hill, ME) (1913)
Ralph W., b. 10/16/1906; third; George L. Walsh (farmer, 35, Milton Mills) and Carrie Briggs (33, Paris Hill, ME) (1913)
Theron Joseph, b. 8/18/1976 in Wolfeboro; Kenneth N. Walsh and Gail K. Miele

WALTON,
Etta Mae, b. 5/3/1988 in Laconia; Fred H. Walton and Denise D. Muise
Teresa Marie, b. 1/9/1986 in Laconia; Fred H. Walton and Denise D. Muise

WALTZ,
Harry Richard, b. 10/7/1933 in Sanbornville; Harry Franklin Waltz and Lena Hodge

WARD,
son, b. 8/26/1891; first; Asa Ward (fireman, Madison) and Annie B. Garland (Brownfield, ME)
daughter, b. 8/2/1892; first; Samuel Ward (section man, Madison) and Mary McDonald
Devon Scott, b. 6/15/1994 in Dover; Jeffrey Allen Ward and Valerie Jean Chadbourne
Lucas James, b. 8/31/1996 in Dover; Jeffrey Allen Ward and Valerie Jean Chadbourne

Mildred Garland, b. 6/2/1893; second; Asa Ward (fireman, Madison) and
Annie B. Garland (Brownfield, ME)
Ralph Nason, b. 1/1/896; third; Asa Ward (laborer, Madison) and Annie B.
Garland (Brownfield, ME); residence - Sanbornville
Raymond Asa, b. 6/21/1899; fourth; Asa Ward (night watchman, Madison)
and Annie B. Garland (Conway)
Robert Joseph, b. 11/26/1990 in Dover; Jeffrey Allen Ward and Valerie
Jean Chadbourne

WARDWELL,
Edwina Marion, b. 9/11/1917; first; Edwin R. Wardwell (farmer, 20,
Melrose, MA) and Marion A. Doherty (18, Boston, MA)

WARNER,
Agnes Isabelle, b. 2/8/1898; fourth; George C. Warner (laborer, Salisbury,
MA) and Lillian E. Davis (New York, NY)
Alice Maud, b. 1/28/1894; second; George C. Warner (laborer, Salisbury,
MA) and Lilla E. Davis (New York, NY)
George L., b. 12/11/1895; third; George C. Warner (laborer, Salisbury,
MA) and Lillian Davis (New York, NY)

WASHBURNE,
Rollin Ervin, Jr., b. 7/28/1979 in Rochester; Rollin Ervin Washburne and
Joyce C. Brown
Tahni Lynn, b. 1/9/1981 in Wolfeboro; Rollin Washburne and Joyce C.
Brown

WATSON,
daughter, b. 9/17/1890; John Watson (laborer, Nottingham, England) and
Ella Thornton (Scotland)
Harry Harvey, Jr., b. 1/4/1968 in Wolfeboro; Harry H. Watson and
Florence E. Hatch
John McClellan, b. 12/16/1864; fifth; Isaac D. Watson (Wolfeboro) and
Esther J. Teere (Isle of Man)

WEBBER,
Todd Otis, b. 2/23/1971 in Wolfeboro; Robert Webber and Sandra Forbes

WEBSTER,
Kristel Anne, b. 9/22/1975 in Wolfeboro; Charles S. Webster and Cynthia A. Hutchins

WEEKS,
daughter, b. 2/20/1887; seventh; Brackett M. Weeks (farmer, Wakefield) and Matilda Allen (Blue Hill, ME)
daughter, b. 6/7/1889; eighth; Brackett M. Weeks (farmer, Wakefield) and Matilda Allen
daughter, b. 6/7/1889; fourth; Nathan O. Weeks (farmer, Wakefield) and Florence E. Shorey (Wolfeboro)
son, b. 4/4/1893; fourth; Nathan O. Weeks (farmer, Wakefield) and Florence E. Shorey (Wolfeboro)
stillborn son, b. 7/15/1916; second; Almon F. Weeks (mechanic, 32, Wakefield) and Gladys H. Bennett (28, Brookline, MA)
Aaron Thomas, b. 9/27/1985 in Wolfeboro; Lisa G. Weeks
Albert Raymond, b. 4/13/1891; third; Nathan O. Weeks (farmer, Wakefield) and Florence E. Shorey (Wolfeboro)
Alice Matilda, b. 12/25/1902; second; William G. Weeks (laborer, 25, Wakefield) and Millie C. Robinson (25, Wolfeboro); residence - Union
Arthur Algernon, b. 6/12/1894; fifth; Nathan O. Weeks (farmer, Wakefield) and Florence E. Shorey (Wakefield)
Arthur Algernon, b. 3/13/1916; first; Arthur A. Weeks (livery stable, 21, Wakefield) and Marion Wallace (20, Boston, MA)
Casey Hackett, b. 6/15/1984 in Rochester; Richard F. Weeks and Martha L. Hackett
Ella May, b. 6/7/1894; seventh; Brackett M. Weeks (farmer, Wakefield) and Matilda Allen (Blue Hill, ME)
Guy B., b. 12/6/1900; first; William G. Weeks (laborer, Wakefield) and Emily C. Robinson (Wolfeboro); residence - East Wakefield
Harry George, b. 6/25/1925; fourth; Guy B. Weeks (Wakefield) and Margaret Stevens (Middleton) (1940)
Henry Allen, b. 3/26/1951; fourth; Guy B. Weeks (NH) and Clara R. Bickford (NH)
Hillary Mary, b. 5/4/1977 in Rochester; Nathan O. Weeks and Sandra L. Jones
Irene Isabella, b. 8/30/1905; fourth; William G. Weeks (farmer, 28, Wakefield) and Mildred Robinson (28, Wolfeboro)

Judy, b. 6/13/1948; third; Guy B. Weeks (Wakefield) and Clara R. Bickford (Wolfeboro)

Kristin Lynn, b. 2/25/1987 in Rochester; Thomas F. Weeks, Jr. and Lynne M. Twombley

Lawrence Paul, b. 8/10/1922; third; Guy B. Weeks (Wakefield) and Margaret Stevens (Middleton) (1940)

Margaret Eva, b. 10/17/1903 in Union; third; Will Weeks (laborer, 25, Wakefield) and Millie Robinson (24, Wolfeboro); residence - Union

Michael Philip, b. 4/11/1984 in Rochester; Thomas F. Weeks, Jr. and Lynne M. Twombley

Nancy Lee, b. 8/6/1945; first; Guy B. Weeks (Wakefield) and Clara M. Bickford (Wolfeboro)

Pamela Lynn, b. 3/14/1959 in Wolfeboro; sixth; Guy B. Weeks (Wakefield) and Clara R. Bickford (Wolfeboro)

Patsy Ann, b. 7/14/1960 in Wolfeboro; seventh; Guy B. Weeks (Wakefield) and Clara R. Bickford (Wolfeboro)

Philip Leslie, b. 9/16/1944; third; Leslie S. Weeks (Center Harbor) and Blanche A. Clapper (Meredith)

Raymond W., b. 9/29/1917; second; Arthur A. Weeks (stable keeper, 23, Wakefield) and Marion Wallace (21, Boston, MA)

Roberta Vera, b. 6/11/1956 in Wolfeboro; fifth; Guy B. Weeks (NH) and Clara R. Bickford (NH)

Sandra Jean, b. 7/16/1946; second; Guy Weeks (Wakefield) and Clara R. Bickford (Wolfeboro)

WEEMAN,

Forrest E., b. 3/17/1931; fourth; Howard Weeman (Bar Mills, ME) and Ella Smith (Acton, ME)

Francis May, b. 3/11/1933 in Union; Howard A. Weeman and Ella F. Smith

Harris E., b. 3/26/1929; third; Howard Weeman (Bars Mills, ME) and Ella F. Smith (Acton, ME)

Howard Arnold, b. 1/6/1927; second; Howard A. Weeman (Bar Mills, ME) and Ella F. Smith (Acton, ME)

Isabel Ella, b. 7/9/1921; second; Howard A. Weeman (brass worker, 26, Bar Mills, ME) and Ella F. Smith (21, Acton, ME); residence - Union

Marion Ruth, b. 9/8/1934; sixth; Howard A. Weeman (Bar Mills, ME) and Ella F. Smith (Acton, ME)

Roger Roy, b. 7/8/1941; seventh; Howard Arnold Weeman (Buxton, ME) and Ella Fairchild Smith (Acton, ME)

WELCH,
Dorothy Marie, b. 12/15/1953 in Wolfeboro; first; Joseph Augustine Welch (ME) and Florence M. Tarr (NH)
Judy Ann, b. 9/19/1945; second; Earlon Frank Welch (Barnstead) and Mildred R. Fifield (Wakefield)
Patsy Jacqueline, b. 1/4/1941; fourth; Robert Edward Welch (Ossipee) and Marion Louise Drew (Brookfield)
Sarah Elizabeth, b. 9/15/1903 in Sanbornville; third; James Welch (laborer, 26, Ossipee) and Mabel Schultz (24, Boston, MA); residence - Ossipee
Warren Walter, b. 4/13/1959 in Rochester; first; Donald E. Welch (Lebanon, ME) and Mariann J. Lougee (Dover)

WELSH,
Kelli Ann, b. 6/14/1991 in Rochester; Keith R. Welsh and Helen M. Goodfield

WENTWORTH,
son [Perley], b. 10/27/1889; second; M. S. Wentworth (farmer, Wakefield) and Alice M. Lunny (Sanford, ME)
son, b. 2/22/1890; third; John A. Wentworth (laborer, Milton) and Annie A. ----- (Milton)
daughter, b. 5/15/1892; eleventh; George E. Wentworth (farmer, Wakefield) and Susan Merrill (Wakefield)
son, b. 4/19/1896; second; Harry Wentworth (day laborer, Milton) and Cora E. Allen (Brookfield)
stillborn daughter, b. 10/12/1904; fifth; Gilbert Wentworth (laborer, 28, Parsonsfield, ME) and Nellie Chadbourne (29, Waterboro, ME)
son [Ernest E.], b. 4/20/1905 in Union; fifth; Fred S. Wentworth (carpenter, 38, Acton, ME) and Delia Barker (37, New Vineyard, ME); residence - Union
stillborn daughter, b. 2/12/1907; sixth; Charles E. Wentworth (shoe worker, 40, Milton) and Carrie L. Place (35, Middleton)
son, b. 4/17/1929; third; Perley Wentworth (Wakefield) and Marguerite Cate (Wakefield) (1930)
son, b. 12/7/1934; second; George Wentworth, Jr. (Newfield, ME) and Mary Jose (Malden, MA)
Alan Earl, b. 8/15/1946; first; Earl R. Wentworth (Wakefield) and Virginia Kimball (Rochester)

Alice, b. 11/11/1893; first; Harry N. Wentworth (farmer, Milton) and Cora E. Allen (Brookfield)
Alice Cora, b. 2/11/1917; second; Austin R. Wentworth (farmer, Wakefield) and Ethel V. Nuttall (Boston, MA)
Austin B., b. 9/20/1888; second; Madison Stacy Wentworth (Wakefield) and Alice M. Lunney (Sanford, ME) (1942)
Carl Homer, b. 12/25/1917; first; Homer R. Wentworth (clerk, 20, Wakefield) and Margie V. Drown (22, Ossipee)
Constance, b. 8/20/1951; second; Earl R. Wentworth (Wakefield) and Virginia Kimball (Rochester)
David Lyon, b. 2/5/1942; first; Arnold Harry Wentworth (Wolfeboro) and Rachel Cora Downs (Union)
Dennis Ladd, b. 1/14/1950; second; Arnold H. Wentworth (Wolfeboro) and Rachel C. Downs (Wakefield)
Dorothy Edna, b. 4/11/1917; second; Roscoe C. Wentworth (mill hand, 27, Milton) and Blanch E. Tufts (19, Middleton)
Earl Roger, b. 6/19/1920; second; Homer R. Wentworth (23, teamster, Wakefield) and Margie V. Drown (24, Ossipee)
Ethel May, b. 6/19/1910; first; Austin Wentworth (farmer, Wakefield) and Ethel Nuttall (Boston, MA)
Eva, b. 10/26/1894; first; Elwin O. Wentworth (jeweler, Wakefield) and Annie M. Clifford (London, England)
Everett Orrin, b. 9/13/1906; first; Harry D. Wentworth (Wakefield) and Lena Avery (Wolfeboro) (1937)
George, b. 7/13/1931; first; George F. Wentworth (Newfield, ME) and Mary E. Jose (Malden, MA)
Gerald Reed, b. 5/29/1933; first; William Wentworth (Union) and Blanche Reed (Canobie Lake) (1934)
Gladys, b. 4/7/1898; fourth; C. E. Wentworth (shoemaker, Milton) and Carrie L. Place (Middleton)
Gladys L., b. 7/24/1893; first; Ham N. Wentworth (clerk, Acton, ME) and Clara A. Penney (Wakefield)
Gloria Losetta, b. 1/6/1928; fourth; Homer Wentworth (Wakefield) and Marjie Drown (Ossipee)
Harold T., b. 7/18/1901; fourth; Fred S. Wentworth (carpenter, Acton, ME) and Delia Barker (New Vineyard, ME)
Homer, b. 3/28/1897; third; C. E. Wentworth (shoemaker, Milton) and Carrie L. Pike (Middleton)
Joan Carol, b. 1/17/1952 in Wolfeboro; first; Roger Place Wentworth (NH) and Celia Frances Cook (Wolfeboro)

Joyce Ann, b. 10/4/1955 in Rochester; fifth; Earl Roger Wentworth (Rochester) and Virginia Kimball (Rochester)

June Parolyn, b. 6/8/1924; third; Homer Wentworth (truckman, Wakefield) and Margie V. Drown (Ossipee); residence - Union

Karen Lynn, b. 6/2/1975 in Rochester; Alan E. Wentworth and Joan M. Comeau

Lloyd Roger, b. 8/28/1919; third; Roscoe C. Wentworth (mill hand, 29, Milton) and Blanche E. Tufts (21, Middleton); residence - Union

Lucille, b. 2/12/1907; seventh; Charles E. Wentworth (shoe worker, 40, Milton) and Carrie L. Place (35, Middleton)

Marion E., b. 7/11/1902; third; Will Wentworth (barber, 23, Brookfield) and Myrtle Nute (20, Salmon Falls)

Mary Althea, b. 5/30/1909; sixth; Fred S. Wentworth (carpenter, 41, Acton, ME) and Delia M. Barker (40, New Vineyard, ME)

Mildred Gladys, b. 6/24/1915; first; Roscoe Wentworth (laborer, 24, Milton) and Blanche Tufts (17, Middleton)

Orville C., b. 1/25/1898; second; E. O. Wentworth (jeweler, Dover, MA) and Annie M. Clifford (London, England)

Oscar H., b. 7/8/1894; first; Henry E. Wentworth (painter, Saco, ME) and Mabel Heath (Newfield, ME)

Phoebe Allison, b. 5/16/1996 in Dover; Michael John Wentworth and Virginia Helen Bean

Reginald Eli, b. 6/5/1901; second; Will R. Wentworth (barber, Brookfield) and Myrtle Nute (Salmon Falls); residence - Sanbornville

Robert J., b. 1/24/1896; second; C. E. Wentworth (shoemaker, Milton) and Carrie L. Place (Middleton)

Richard Allan, b. 11/13/1942; first; Lloyd Roger Wentworth (Union) and Miriam Louise Corson (East Rochester)

Richard Fernald, b. 9/24/1908; second; Harry D. Wentworth (Wakefield) and Lena Avery (Wolfeboro) (1909, 1937)

Roger Place, b. 9/5/1923; first; Robert J. Wentworth (truckman, Wakefield) and Agnes L. Burroughs (Middleton); residence - Union

Ruth, b. 9/17/1899; fifth; Charles E. Wentworth (shoemaker, Milton) and Clara Place Wentworth (Middleton); residence - Union

Sumner D., b. 12/22/1896; third; Fred S. Wentworth (carpenter, Acton, ME) and Delia Barker (New Vineyard, ME)

Viola Meserve, b. 7/28/1899; third; Edwin O. Wentworth (jeweler, Dover, MA) and Annie M. Clifford (London, England); residence - Sanbornville

Walter, b. 6/28/1900; second; Henry Wentworth (Saco, ME) and Mabel Heath (Newfield, ME) (1931)

William Belden, b. 5/29/1922; first; Perley B. Wentworth (farmer, Wakefield) and Marguerite Carter (Wakefield, MA); residence - Woodman

William Clifton, b. 5/27/1910; eighth; Charles E. Wentworth (liveryman, 43, Milton) and Carrie L. Place (39, Middleton)

WEST,

Charles E., b. 1/27/1853; second; Edward West (Lancaster, England) and Sophronia Farnham (Wakefield) (1940)

Kristen Marie, b. 1/15/1989 in Portsmouth; Ernest Dale West and Mary Ellen Grondin

Kristie Marie, b. 10/13/1976 in Wolfeboro; Carl Bruce West and Marie T. Vachon

WESTFALL,

Brandon Michael, b. 4/21/1993 in Rochester; Michael Frederick Westfall and Jean Patricia Stawasz

Nicole Elizabeth, b. 4/24/1997 in Rochester; Michael Frederick Westfall and Jean Patricia Stawasz

WEYMOUTH,

George F., b. 1/26/1890; first; J. Frank Weymouth (brakeman, Parsonsfield, ME) and Sarah Brown (Lewiston, ME)

Helen Janet, b. 10/28/1937; first; Clayton Weymouth (Parsonsfield, ME) and Adeline McLaughlin (Lewiston, ME)

Lena E., b. 8/28/1891; second; James F. Weymouth (laborer, Parsonsfield, ME) and Sarah Brown (Lewiston, ME)

WHEELER,

Erika Catherine Lorraine, b. 6/19/1980 in Rochester; Chester H. Wheeler, Jr. and Karen A. Gautreau

Florence Augusta, b. 8/26/1895; third; Edward J. Wheeler (farmer, NH) and Lillian Pierce (ME)

Virginia Lee, b. 2/4/1978 in Rochester; Alan J. Wheeler and Karen S. Tarlton

WHICHER,
Brenton Elroy, b. 1/27/1989 in Wolfeboro; William Elroy Whicher and Cathleen E. Gordon
Joshua Gordon, b. 4/13/1991 in Wolfeboro; William Elroy Whicher and Cathleen Elizabeth Gordon
William Alexander, b. 11/20/1992 in Rochester; William Elroy Whicher and Cathleen Elizabeth Gordon

WHITCOMB,
Geoffrey Oliver, b. 3/1/1988 in Wolfeboro; James Whitcomb and Elizabeth McCurry

WHITE,
Gail Elizabeth, b. 8/4/1952 in Sanbornville; first; James H. White (MA) and Priscilla Coleman (MA)
Glenn Allen, b. 7/2/1961 in Rochester; third; William E. White (Concord) and Marilyn B. Chick (Natick, MA)
Hannah Rachel, b. 12/5/1983 in Rochester; John F. White and Kathryn J. Taylor
Howard, b. 3/3/1896; second; George H. White and Mary E. Carroll; residence - East Boston, MA
Sandra Jean, b. 3/28/1966 in Wolfeboro; fifth; Charles H. White (Woburn, MA) and Beatrice R. Boyd (Somerville, MA)
Viena Emma, b. 7/7/1899; first; Allen White (section hand, Madison) and Isa M. Colbath (West Ossipee)
Walter L., b. 11/5/1901; second; Allan White (laborer, Madison) and Isa M. Colbath (Wakefield); residence - Sanbornville

WHITEHOUSE,
Herbert Lucien, b. 8/13/1881; fourth; Frank Whitehouse (Paris, ME) and Rhoda McDaniels (Farmington) (1939)
Judith Lynn, b. 8/24/1966 in Rochester; second; Richard A. Whitehouse (Jamaica Plain, MA) and Linda D. Drew (Rochester)
Richard Albert, Jr., b. 12/20/1971 in Rochester; Richard A. Whitehouse and Linda D. Drew

WHITTEMORE,
Aubrey Linda, b. 12/16/1988 in Laconia; Kevin D. Whittemore and Mona J. Chase

Nita Carol, b. 5/4/1957 in Wolfeboro; second; James F. Whittemore (Minden, NY) and Bertha A. Brown (Ashland)

WHITTEN,

Carl Lowell, b. 7/20/1966 in Rochester; third; Joseph D. Whitten (Wolfeboro) and Dorothy J. Dodier (Haverhill, MA)

Joseph Dean, Jr., b. 7/13/1965 in Wolfeboro; second; Joseph D. Whitten (Wolfeboro) and Dorothy J. Dodier (Haverhill, MA)

Leona Dora, b. 7/18/1932 in Wolfeboro; Fredrick Whitten and Laura Labissonere

WIEDEMAN,

Richard Frederick, b. 8/21/1983 in Wolfeboro; Richard C. Wiedeman and Brenda G. Brenton

WIGGIN,

daughter, b. 2/12/1887; eighth; Josiah W. Wiggin (farmer, Wakefield) and Mary W. ----- (Middleton)

daughter, b. 11/27/1887; second; Herbert L. Wiggin (brass finisher, Stratham) and Jennie M. Malonzo (Canada)

son [Ralph Edwin], b. 7/10/1888; second; Edwin O. Wiggin (laborer, Wakefield) and Margaret L. Hulbig (Canada)

son, b. 7/2/1910; fifth; Harry Wiggin (laborer, 27, Wakefield) and Mabel Drown (23, Ossipee)

child, b. 10/26/1945; first; Richard A. Wiggin (Wakefield) and Katherine F. Tuttle (Wakefield)

Albert William, b. 1/13/1925; second; Albert W. Wiggin (Wolfeboro) and Agnes W. Robinson (Boston, MA)

Arthur D., b. 2/4/1890; third; Herbert L. Wiggin (brass finisher, Stratham) and Jennie M. Malonzo

Bruce Robinson, b. 1/15/1930; fourth; Albert Wiggin (Wolfeboro) and Agnes Robinson (Boston, MA) (1936)

Campbell Robinson, b. 4/3/1922; first; Albert W. Wiggin (painter, Wolfeboro) and Agnes W. Robinson (Boston, MA)

Charlotte Elaine, b. 10/18/1908; fifth; Harry L. Wiggin (laborer, 27, Tuftonboro) and Mabelle E. Drown (24, Ossipee)

Ethel M., b. 1/22/1906; first; Harvey F. Wiggin (brakeman, 21, Wakefield) and Myra L. Witham (22, Milton Mills)

Evelyn E., b. 4/24/1916; first; Roscoe Wiggin (mechanic, 28, Acton, ME) and Nellie Drew (18, Tamworth)

Frank A., b. 6/17/1900; second; Alvah A. Wiggin (section hand, Wakefield) and Etta M. Taylor (Porter, ME)

Gordon Elmer, b. 8/14/1933 in Rochester; Albert Wiggin and Agnes Robinson

Gordon Murray, b. 10/14/1936; third; Maurice Wiggin (Tuftonboro) and Mary Cook (Wakefield)

Harry L., Jr., b. 3/13/1903; first; Harry L. Wiggin (laborer, 21, Tuftonboro) and Mabel Drown (19, Moultonville); residence - Union

Judith Lee, b. 2/15/1945; first; Lester A. Wiggin, Jr. (Bridgton, ME) and Audrey E. Drew (Union)

Kathy Jeanne, b. 1/5/1953 in Rochester; fourth; Richard Arthur Wiggin (Wakefield) and Katherine F. Tuttle (Wakefield)

Margaret, b. 3/26/1896; first; Luther E. Wiggin (lumberman, Boston, MA) and Carrie E. Wentworth (Milton); residence - South Wakefield

Marion, b. 5/8/1910; third; L. E. Wiggin (farmer, 44, Boston, MA) and Carrie E. Wentworth (housewife, 35, Milton) (1911)

Mildred E., b. 6/27/1871; second; Frank J. Wiggin (Wakefield) and Augusta Farnham (Wakefield) (1936)

Nancy Lee, b. 7/25/1948; third; Richard A. Wiggin (Wakefield) and Katharine F. Tuttle (Wakefield)

Opal I., b. 5/14/1930; second; Maurice Wiggin (Tuftonboro) and Mamie Cook (North Wakefield)

Pamela Ann, b. 11/14/1946; fourth; Richard A. Wiggin (Wakefield) and Katherine F. Tuttle (Wakefield)

Ralph Edwin, b. 7/10/1888; second; Edwin O. Wiggin (Lebanon, ME) and Margaret L. Hulbig (Montreal, PQ) (1936)

Richard Arthur, b. 5/15/1919; second; Roscoe A. Wiggin (mechanic, 34, Wakefield) and Nellie F. Drew (20, Tamworth)

Richard Irving, b. 8/31/1916; first; Lester A. Wiggin (hotel keeper, 29, Tuftonboro) and Helen M. Jewett (27, Milton)

Stanley Lyman, b. 9/11/1906; first; William E. Wiggin (weaver, 40, Acton, ME) and Laura E. Fox (41, Acton, ME)

Stuart Davis, b. 2/19/1927; third; Alfred W. Wiggin (Wolfeboro) and Agnes Robinson (Boston, MA)

Walter Wentworth, b. 9/19/1899; second; Luther E. Wiggin (lumber dealer, Boston, MA) and Carrie E. Wentworth (Milton)

Wendy Sue, b. 3/18/1965 in Wolfeboro; first; Richard A. Wiggin (Wakefield) and Mary E. Roberts (Haverhill, MA)

Willis Francis, b. 4/28/1908; second; Albert W. Wiggin (laborer, 29, Tuftonboro) and Alice A. McMullen (22, England)

WILDER,
Margaret Jane, b. 8/29/1920; first; Robert F. Wilder (elec. lineman, Dennysville, ME) and Doris M. Page (Milton); residence - Union
Ralph Sidney, b. 8/26/1887; sixth; George S. Wilder (railroading, Conway) and Carrie C. Yeaton (Rollinsford)

WILE,
Donald Alfred, b. 1/20/1920; fifth; Laurie E. Wile (farmer, 34, NS) and Mary E. Linscott (33, Pittsfield)

WILES,
Russell Karl, b. 1/16/1949; first; Russell W. Wiles (MA) and Mary E. Hanson (Sanbornville)

WILKINS,
son [Ernest O.], b. 11/21/1900; fourth; Homer W. Wilkins (farmer, Acton, ME) and Mary B. Hutchins (Wakefield); residence - Sanbornville

WILKINSON,
Beatrice Laura, b. 9/23/1914; fourth; Frank S. Wilkinson (laborer, 32, Freedom) and Lucy Roles (30, Ossipee)
Charles Raymond, b. 9/7/1944; third; Kenneth A. Wilkinson (Reading, MA) and Juanita V. Karcher (Ossipee)
David Richard, b. 3/7/1938; second; Kenneth A. Wilkinson (Reading, MA) and Florence E. Bogart (Lebanon, ME)
George William, b. 9/21/1942; first; Kenneth A. Wilkinson and Juanita Victoria Karcher (Ossipee)
Janus Melvin, b. 11/28/1949; sixth; Kenneth A. Wilkinson (Reading, MA) and Waneta V. Karcher (Ossipee)
Jason Melvin, b. 4/13/1978 in Wolfeboro; James M. Wilkinson and Rose M. Tedford
June Frances, b. 5/13/1947; fifth; Kenneth A. Wilkinson (Reading, MA) and Waneta V. Karcher (Ossipee)
Justen Mark, b. 10/12/1979 in Wolfeboro; James M. Wilkinson and Rose Marie Tedford
Kenneth Albert, 2d, b. 9/2/1943; second; Kenneth Albert Wilkinson (Reading, MA) and Juanita Victoria Karcher (Ossipee)
Kenneth Albert, IV, b. 12/15/1991 in Wolfeboro; Kenneth Albert Wilkinson, III and Joyce Lorraine Moseley

Lorene Victoria, b. 5/19/1946; fourth; Kenneth A. Wilkinson (Reading, MA) and Waneta V. Karcher (Ossipee)

Marjorie Estella, b. 1/24/1919; sixth; Frank S. Wilkinson (36, Freedom) and Lucy M. Roles (35, Ossipee); residence - East Wakefield

Melbourne A., b. 2/17/1916; fifth; Frank S. Wilkinson (laborer, 33, Freedom) and Lucy M. Roles (32, Ossipee)

Sarah Anne, b. 4/4/1971 in Wolfeboro; Durwood F. Wilkinson and Linda M. Worster

Sonia Ann, b. 12/16/1968 in Wolfeboro; Durwood F. Wilkinson and Linda M. Worster

Wilfred Arthur, b. 1/8/1913; third; Frank S. Wilkinson (painter, 30, Freedom) and Lucy Roles (29, Ossipee)

WILKS,
daughter, b. 9/27/1914; second; Albert Wilkins (sailor, 25, Camden, NJ) and Mary B. Willey (18, Wakefield)

Ernest Henry, b. 3/30/1913; first; Albert Wilks (marine, 23, NJ) and Mary Willey (17, Wakefield); residence - NJ

WILLAND,
stillborn son, b. 8/29/1891; fourth; George W. Willand (brakeman, Ossipee) and Grace H. Fay (Southboro, MA)

Grace E., b. 8/16/1902 in Sanbornville; first; George W. Willand (brakeman, 48, Tuftonboro) and Eleanor Edgerly (27, Wolfeboro); residence - Sanbornville

WILLETT,
Joseph Roland, b. 5/18/1908; first; Almond Willett (laborer, 31, Canada) and Leda Lamontagne (32, Canada)

Roch Joseph, b. 7/23/1909; second; Almon Willett (laborer, 32, Canada) and Lida Lamontagne (32, Canada)

WILLEY,
daughter [Ellen E.], b. 9/8/1889; first; Edwin R. Willey (laborer, Wakefield) and Sarah F. Patch (Effingham)

Alice Farnham, b. 6/21/1920; third; Joseph A.C. Willey (farmer, 30, Wakefield) and Althea S. Perkins (29, S. Acton, ME)

Althea Martha, b. 6/28/1918; second; Joseph Willey (farmer, 28, Wakefield) and Althea Perkins (26, Wakefield)

Charles Chandler, b. 3/19/1912; second; Clarence Willey (farmer, 28, Wakefield) and Charlotte Twombley (22, Wolfeboro)
Edwin F., b. 12/6/1887; third; William H. Willey, 2d (farmer, Wakefield) and Maria J. Jones (Randolph, MA)
Frank F., b. 7/31/1878; third; George Henderson Willey (Wakefield) and Harriett McCleary (Berthylmer, IN) (1942)
Gertrude Estelle, b. 2/27/1914; fourth; Clarence D. Willey (Wakefield) and Charlotte Twombly (Wakefield) (1936)
Glendon Burleigh, b. 2/27/1914; third; Clarence D. Willey (Wakefield) and Charlotte Twombly (Wakefield) (1936)
Joseph A.C., b. 5/18/1890; fourth; William H. Willey, 2d (Wakefield) and Maria J. Jones (Randolph, MA) (1938)
Lydia Alice, b. 9/24/1892; fifth; William H. Willey, 2d (farmer, Wakefield) and Maria J. Jones (Randolph, MA)
Martha A., b. 6/28/1896; sixth; John D. Willey (farmer, Wakefield) and Olivia P. Demeritte (Lee)
Nellie Frances, b. 12/26/1911; first; Joseph A.C. Willey (farmer, 21, Wakefield) and Althea S. Perkins (20, Acton, ME)
Nelson Forest, b. 11/6/1909; first; Clarence D. Willey (farmer, 26, Wakefield) and Charlotte G. Twombly (20, Wolfeboro)
William Henderson, b. 12/9/1922; fourth; Joseph Willey (farmer, Wakefield) and Althea Perkins (Acton, ME)

WILLIAMS,
son, b. 3/4/1890; first; Jennie Williams (Effingham)
Aliza Jane, b. 10/25/1967 in Wolfeboro; second; Barney J. Williams, Sr. (Yonkers, NY) and Jame Marie McNelley (Medford, MA)
Barney Joseph, Jr., b. 10/30/1966 in Wolfeboro; fifth; Barney J. Williams (Yonkers, NY) and Jane M. McNelley (Medford, MA)
Blanche Evelyn, b. 10/11/1933 in Union; Jefferson Williams and Cora M. Dunn
Gertrude Martha, b. 9/22/1935; sixth; Jefferson Williams (Ossipee) and Cora Dunn (Dorchester, MA)
Melissa Jean, b. 5/16/1969 in Wolfeboro; Richard J. Williams and Jane M. McNelley
Melvin Frank, b. 11/12/1937; eighth; Jefferson Williams (Ossipee) and Cora Dunn (Dorchester, MA)
Nathaniel Willis, b. 4/4/1985 in Laconia; Barry R. Williams and Patricia L. Vose

Patricia Ann, b. 5/4/1956 in Rochester; second; Reginald P. Williams (Rochester) and Ann V. Maddux (Holland, TX)

Sandra Jean, b. 10/20/1953 in Rochester; first; Reginald Paul Williams (Rochester) and Ann V. Maddux (Holland, TX)

WILSON,

Colby Tanner, b. 5/8/1998 in Wolfeboro; Kenneth Hall Wilson, Jr. and Nicole Michelle Canney

Daniel Edward, b. 9/5/1934; second; Daniel H. Wilson (Union) and Florence Drew (Brookfield)

Daniel Hall, b. 7/30/1914; second; William J. Wilson (farmer, 31, Moncton, NB) and Edith M. Hill (40, Wakefield)

Kenneth Hall, b. 10/16/1938; fourth; Daniel Hall Wilson (Union) and Florence Ellen Drew (Brookfield)

Lester Albert, b. 11/24/1942; fourth; Daniel Hall Wilson (Union) and Florence Ellen Drew (Brookfield)

Lorraine Ellen, b. 10/11/1933 in Brookfield; Daniel H. Wilson and Florence E. Drew

Marlene Elizabeth, b. 7/12/1951; fifth; Daniel H. Wilson (Union) and Florence E. Drew (Brookfield)

Tristan Hunter, b. 9/11/1996 in Wolfeboro; Kenneth H. Wilson, Jr. and Nicole M. Canney

WINSLOW,

Rachel Elizabeth, b. 11/15/1910; third; Howard L. Winslow (supt. of schools, 32, Portland, ME) and Martha E. Shaw (29, Cumberland, ME)

WINTON,

Jeremy David, b. 2/11/1972 in Wolfeboro; Robert D. Winton and Paula Worster

WITHAM,

Lizzie Ann, b. 4/1/1871; third; Josiah Witham (Acton, ME) and Mary E. Willey (Salem, MA) (1937)

WOOD,

Annie Losina, b. 7/10/1895; first; Fred Wood (farmer, Somersworth) and Grace L. Wentworth (Newfield, ME)

WOODARD,
Glenn Andrew, b. 5/20/1967 in Wolfeboro; first; Leonard W. Woodard (Newbury, MA) and Marcia Elaine Bye (Beverly, MA)
John Allen, b. 10/31/1968 in Wolfeboro; John B. Woodard and Carolyn L. Bye

WOODMAN,
son [Harry E.], b. 3/2/1891; third; Frank E. Woodman (stonecutter, Wakefield) and Maud M. Johnson (Biddeford, ME)
son [Kirtland E.], b. 2/26/1901; sixth; Frank Woodman (farmer, Wakefield) and Maud Johnson (Biddeford, ME)
daughter [Bessie], b. 7/31/1906; seventh; Frank Woodman (farmer, Wakefield) and Maude Johnson (Biddeford, ME)
stillborn daughter, b. 6/6/1915; third; Alphonso Woodman (laborer, 33, Middleton) and Mary Willey (19, Wakefield)
Alfred, b. 7/22/1898; fourth; Frank Woodman (farmer, Wakefield) and Maud Johnson (Biddeford, ME)
Clayton, b. 3/5/1894; fourth; Frank Woodman (farmer, Wakefield) and Maud Johnson (Biddeford, ME)
Doris May, b. 6/16/1917; second; Charles Woodman (moulder, 39, Middleton) and Margarette Connors (36, Amesbury, MA)
Florence Maud, b. 8/16/1911; second; Alphonso Woodman (brass worker, 30, Wakefield) and Lillian Roberts (19, Exeter)
Ida Jane, b. 8/31/1856; third; Jonathan Woodman (Wakefield) and Sarah Jane Goudy (Ossipee) (1936)
James Augustus, b. 2/3/1910; first; Alphonso Woodman (laborer, 25, Middleton) and Lillian T. Roberts (18, Exeter)

WOODS,
son, b. 1/20/1905; first; Frank E. Woods (upholsterer, 45, Hebron, WI) and Clara E. Hill (35, Wakefield); residence - East Wakefield

WORSTER,
Lorraine Belle, b. 3/23/1950; second; George O. Worster (NH) and Lucy C. Downs (NH)
Lucille Carrie, b. 5/16/1954 in Rochester; third; George Oliver Worster (Rochester) and Lucy Caroline Downs (Union)
Roslynn Nikole, b. 4/25/1993 in Dover; Don Harland Worster and Sherri Lee Hall

YEATON,
Clarence Palmer, b. 1/3/1892; second; William A. Yeaton (fireman, Seabrook) and Lottie M. Palmer (Ellsworth)
Helen Dorris, b. 2/5/1898; third; William A. Yeaton (engineer, Seabrook) and Lottie M. Palmer (Ellsworth)

YORK,
Fred, Jr., b. 9/4/1899; first; Fred York (laborer, Canada) and Nellie Nealley (Wakefield)
J. Alderic A., b. 5/26/1901; second; Fred York (laborer, Canada) and Nellie Nealley (Sanbornville); residence - Sanbornville

YOUNG,
Alden Norris, b. 12/12/1906; first; James C. Young (blacksmith, 36, Wakefield) and Harriet L. Fellows (32, Wakefield)
Annie Priscilla, b. 7/12/1891; first; Charles B. Young (carpenter, Wolfeboro) and Addie Stevens (Brookfield)
Brett Wallace, b. 5/31/1986 in Exeter; Ian W. Young and Caroline E. Gergler
Edwin Aron, b. 3/13/1925; first; Joseph B. Young (Stoneham, MA) and Lillian Loveimore (Sanbornville)
Roland Wilford, Jr., b. 4/6/1943; second; Roland Wilford Young (Middleton) and Stella Marjorie Budroe (Wolfeboro)
Shirley Ann, b. 10/8/1941; first; Roland Wilford Young (Middleton) and Stella Marjorie Budroe (Wolfeboro)
Stephen Shipman, b. 9/12/1988 in Exeter; Ian W. Young and Caroline E. Gergler

ZAGAR,
Danielle Elizabeth, b. 7/8/1986 in Wolfeboro; Peter J. Zagar and Elizabeth A. Beaumier

ZALENSKI,
Alfred Leonard, Jr., b. 11/23/1972 in Rochester; Alfred L. Zalenski and Diane R. Dodier
Julie Rae, b. 11/14/1979 in Rochester; Alfred L. Zalenski and Diane R. Dodier

ZIMMER,
Edward Frank, b. 11/18/1932 in Rochester; Albert Zimmer and Ruth Copp

ZURHEIDE,
Peter Graham, b. 3/25/1969 in Wolfeboro; Robert G. Zurheide and Joan D. Colquhoun

MARRIAGES

ABERLE,
Jerry D. of Morton, IL m. Nina M. Perry of Morton, IL 9/29/1979; H - 28; W - 27

ABBOTT,
B. F. of Wakefield m. Mary C. Ballard of Wakefield 8/30/1896 in Leighton's Corner; H - 56, mechanic, 2d, widower, b. Ossipee, s/o Nathan Abbott (Ossipee, deceased, farmer) and Betsey Allen (Brookfield, deceased); W - 50, school teacher, b. Wakefield, d/o Jacob Ballard of Wakefield (Wakefield, 79, farmer) and Isabel Dockham (Meredith, 75, housekeeper)

Brian G. of Union m. Cindy L. Priest of Union 8/2/1970 in Union

John E. of Union m. Mona M. Bouchard of Rochester 9/3/1967; H - 19, mill emp.; W - 17, at home

John E. of Union m. Theresa I. Bosquet of Center Barnstead 5/3/1974 in Union

Malcolm J. of Wolfeboro m. Carol A. Adjutant of Union 6/21/1980 in Wolfeboro

Onville L. of Wakefield m. Florence A. Keniston of Center Effingham 10/3/1903; H - 24, brakeman, b. Ossipee, s/o Frank W. Abbott and Mary E. Libbey; W - 24, cook, b. Effingham, d/o Randolph Keniston and Delia N. Canney

Wallace S. of Wakefield m. Dorothy Jackson of Portland, ME 9/2/1921 in Milton Mills; H - 22, rail road, b. Effingham, s/o Onville L. Abbott (Fitchburg, MA, brakeman) and Florence Keniston (Effingham); W - 19, librarian, b. Deering Jct., ME, d/o James Jackson (steam fitter) and Iver Goss (Wayne, ME)

ACKER,
Joseph G., 3d of Wantagh, NY m. Judith Lynn Hoffman of Wakefield 6/18/1966; H - 21, chem. engr.; W - 21, at home

ADJUTANT,
Carl R. of Wolfeboro m. Ellen E. Hill of Wakefield 4/3/1917; H - 22, farmer, b. Wolfeboro, s/o Martin Adjutant and Ella Glidden; W - 26, housekeeper, 2d, b. Wakefield, d/o Edwin R. Willey and Sarah Patch

Christopher A. of Union m. Betty Lou Pillsbury of Union 9/8/1952; H - 20, woodsman; W - 18, shoeworker

Joseph C. m. Evelyn G. Hill 11/23/1929; H - 27, s/o Charles L. Adjutant (Tuftonboro) and Lena Eaton (Brookfield); W - 18, d/o Leslie Hill and Ellen Willey (Union)

Joseph W. of Union m. Palma L. Whetnall of Milton 9/16/1951 in Union; H - 21, laborer; W - 18, at home

Lester Ervin of Sanbornville m. Judy Carrol Kimball of Sanbornville 6/26/1965; H - 26, mill emp.; W - 19, at home

Ronald Harry of Milton m. Susan Elizabeth Kelly of Sanbornville 10/23/1965 in Milton; H - 16, carpenter; W - 17, at home

Samuel D. of Wakefield m. Addie Colbath of Middleton 10/21/1894 in Milton Mills; H - 56, teamster, 2d, b. Tuftonboro, s/o Samuel Adjutant (Ossipee, farmer) and Lucy Dore (Ossipee, housework); W - 23, housework, b. Middleton, d/o Coleman Colbath (West Alton, shoemaker) and Lucinda Hunt (Augusta, ME, housework)

Samuel D. of Wakefield m. Jennie M. French of Wakefield 9/24/1899; H - 60, teamster, 3d, b. Tuftonboro, s/o Samuel Adjutant (Tuftonboro, deceased) and Lucy Dore (Tuftonboro, deceased); W - 45, housekeeper, 3d, b. Middleton, d/o Davis Tufts (Middleton, deceased) and Adaline D. Horne (Middleton, deceased)

Warren A. of Wakefield m. Pamela L. Chesley of Farmington 10/18/1980 in Farmington

ADLINGTON,

Herbert of Kittery, ME m. Ellen I. Clark of Wakefield 2/21/1887; H - 22, RR employee, b. Eliot, ME, s/o Thomas F. Adlington (Wayland, MA, baggagemaster) and Annie E. Lydston (Eliot, ME, housekeeper); W - 28, housework, b. Wakefield, d/o Isaac T. Clark (Wakefield, farmer) and Hannah L. Churchill (Newmarket, housekeeper)

AHERN,

Albert John, Jr. of New Haven, CT m. Nancy Veale Washburn of New Haven, CT 10/5/1975

AKERS,

Lewis Webster of Roxbury, MA m. Ellen Gertrude Akers of Sanbornville 12/12/1949 in Rochester; H - 58, woods clerk; W - 55, teacher

Melvin E. of Wakefield m. Cynthia L. Loncaric of Portsmouth 6/29/1985

ALBEE,
Mark W. of Rockland, MA m. Ingrid K. Johannessen of Wakefield 7/19/1980

ALIBRANDI,
Phillip J. of Wakefield m. Betty C. Jazakawiz of Wakefield 8/12/1978; H - 31; W - 27

ALLAIRE,
Michael F. of Sanford, ME m. Marjorie R. Mercier of Acton, ME 7/9/1970

ALLEGRA,
Joseph Anthony of Wakefield m. Martha Leah Sheran of Wakefield 1/17/1976 in Stratham

ALLEN,
Charles A. of Wakefield m. Hattie L. Thompson of Sanford, ME 12/31/1892 in Rochester; H - 19, laborer, b. Wakefield, s/o William A. Allen (Wakefield, carpenter) and Elizabeth Nichols (Wakefield, dead); W - 19, operative, b. Sanford, ME, d/o George Thompson (Sanford, ME, farmer) and Adeline Allen (Wakefield, housework)

Charles A. of Wakefield m. Harriette M. Martin of Somerville, MA 6/16/1909; H - 35, laborer, 2d, b. Wakefield, s/o William H. Allen and Elizabeth B. Nichols; W - 45, housework, 3d, b. Newfield, ME, d/o Jeremiah Kenerson and Harriette Carlton

Daniel J. of Union m. Cheryl L. DuFault of Rochester 10/25/1986 in Rochester

Robert J. of Burlington, VT m. June F. Wilkinson of Sanbornville 6/25/1966 in Sanbornville; H - 24, mach. opr.; W - 19, at home

ALMEIDA,
Brian L. of Union m. Carrie Jo Garrett of Union 9/21/1996 in Rochester

AMARAL,
Joseph F. of Wakefield m. Grace M. Razeto of Wakefield 12/27/1986

ANDERSON,
James Robert of Epping m. Linda Susan Piatti of Epping 6/4/1977

John A. of Roslindale, MA m. Priscilla Miller of Weymouth, MA 3/17/1944 in Sanbornville; H - 23, US Navy; W - 21, at home

John A. of Walpole, ME m. Elizabeth N. Morrill of Hingham, MA 5/24/1951 in Sanbornville; H - 27, elec. eng.; W - 21, at home

Kenneth of Union m. Gloria L. Wentworth of Union 3/2/1949 in Rochester; H - 24, merchant; W - 21, shoe shop emp.

Kenneth of Union m. Priscilla Katheryn Bailey of Union 8/27/1955; H - 30, yard man; W - 25, secretary

Robert G. of Wakefield m. Mildred F. Zalenski of Wakefield 10/2/1969

ANTHONY,

Andrew H. of Wakefield m. Cathleen M. DiPrizio of Middleton 7/16/1988

ARCHIBALD,

Charles E. of Wakefield m. Bertha J. Duley of Acton, ME 10/8/1893 in Milton Mills; H - 23, clerk, b. Wakefield, s/o Josiah Archibald (Wakefield) and Lottie Butler (Wakefield); W - 17, housework, b. Derry, d/o Frank Duley

James E. of Wakefield m. Emma B. Grace of Guildford 10/3/1901; H - 37, laborer, b. Wakefield, s/o R. B. Archibald (Wakefield, laborer) and Adeline C. Horn (Acton, ME, housewife); W - 25, school teacher, b. Guildford, d/o Moses B. Grace (Guildford, farmer) and Adeline L. Horn (Acton, ME, housewife)

Oscar D. of Wakefield m. Iona L. Ricker of Wakefield 12/21/1895; H - 23, carpenter, b. Wakefield, s/o Josiah E. Archibald (Wakefield, deceased) and Charlotte Butler (Effingham, deceased); W - 21, housework, b. Wakefield, d/o John R. Ricker of Wakefield (Wakefield, 47, farmer) and Emma J.L. Wiggin (Wakefield, 42, housekeeper)

Stewart Gale of Sanbornville m. Evelyn May Dodge of Sanbornville 2/10/1950 in Farmington; H - 51, woodsman; W - 41, at home

ARDREY,

Robert A. of Cambridge, MA m. Lora J. Turner of New Orleans, LA 8/2/1969 in East Wakefield

ARNOTT,
George E. of Wakefield m. Ella T. Hall of Wakefield 8/7/1985 in East Wakefield

ASBY,
Ralph E. of Union m. Dorothy E. Hannemann of Wolfeboro 2/15/1947 in Wolfeboro; H - 45, lumberman; W - 41, domestic

ASHBY,
Edwin Ralph of Sanbornville m. Marilyn P. Robinson of Laconia 12/30/1952 in Laconia; H - 26, US Air Force; W - 21, lab. tech.

ASHWORTH,
John R. of Sanford, ME m. Ethel M. Stiles of Sanford, ME 1/29/1914; H - 31, painter, b. Brooklyn, NY, s/o George Ashworth and Elizabeth A. Clark; W - 24, waitress, b. Sanford, ME, d/o Herbert Stiles and Sarah Bennett

ATHERTON,
I. Howard of Wakefield m. Helen P. Lawrence of Middleton 5/17/1917 in Dover; H - 37, garage owner, 2d, b. Houlton, ME, s/o Howard Atherton and Katherine Rankin; W - 27, teacher, b. Exeter, d/o Samuel A. Lawrence and Augusta Horne
I. Howard of Wakefield m. Elizabeth Runnells of Wakefield 6/16/1921 in Union; H - 40, garage, 2d, b. Houlton, ME, s/o Howard Atherton (ME, blacksmith) and Catherine Rankin (Canada); W - 17, housework, b. Wakefield, d/o Samuel Runnels (Milton, blacksmith) and Mary Harriman (Tamworth)

ATKINSON,
Carl E. of Wakefield m. Pamela K. Osborne of Wakefield 11/5/1988

AVAKIAN,
David M. of Sharon, MA m. Laurie McKinley of Charlestown, MA 10/23/1993

AVERY,
George H. of Rochester m. Mary E. Pike of Sanbornville 4/22/1936 in Rochester; H - 54, saw mill; W - 67, housekeeper

Oscar J. of Wakefield m. Josephine A. Nute of Wakefield 12/12/1914; H - 50, contractor, 3d, b. Lakeport, s/o Stephen Avery and Mary Straw; W - 49, housework, 3d, b. Plymouth, d/o Royal J. Pike and Mary M. Hathorn

Oscar J. m. Flora Colomy 7/18/1926; H - 61, b. Barnstead, s/o Stephen Avery and Mary E. Straw; W - 48, b. Milton, d/o Walter S. Tibbetts and Harriet Downing

AYERS,

Raymond H. of Sanbornville m. Barbara Jones of Tuftonboro 12/22/1991 in Ossipee

BABB,

Charles H. of Wakefield m. Jennie M. Tibbetts of Wakefield 11/18/1902; H - 52, stone mason, 3d, b. Conway, s/o Elibus Babb and Mary Eastman; W - 53, housework, 2d, b. Dover, d/o Daniel R. Gale and Lydia Horn

BAILEY,

Clifton I. of Milton m. Joan Garvin of Sanbornville 5/31/1947 in Sanbornville; H - 22, machine operator; W - 20, clerk

Johnny of Sanbornville m. Bonnie A. Thurston of Strafford 6/2/1973 in Strafford

William Albert of Union m. Elizabeth R. Atherton of Union 7/2/1949 in Union; H - 35, superintendent; W - 45, bookkeeper

BAIN,

Kevin of Sanbornville m. Janet Leslie Doyle of Amherst 5/8/1976 in Amherst

BAKER,

Bert R. of Wakefield m. Mary E. Fogg of Brookfield 11/3/1907 in Eaton; H - 25, mill man, b. Halifax, NS, s/o Reuben Baker and Ada Hobbel; W - 18, housework, b. Ossipee, d/o Daniel Fogg and Julia Collins

James D. of Burlington, MA m. Susan M. Florentino of Saugus, MA 1/5/1985

William Robbins of Brookfield m. Maybell Gertrude Colbath of Wakefield 7/16/1958 in Wolfeboro; H - 76, retired; W - 68, at home

BALDWIN,
Henry A. of Wakefield m. Alice Grassie of Rochester 10/29/1923 in Rochester; H - 21, moulder, b. Chelsea, MA, s/o Robert Baldwin and Georginia Best; W - 19, mill operative, b. Rochester, d/o Louis Grassie and Matilda Cossuier

BALLENTINE,
Jeffrey R. of Wolfeboro m. Lawrice K. Johnson of Wakefield 9/11/1982 in Wolfeboro

BANCROFT,
Charles of Wakefield m. Helen Margaret Jones of York, ME 6/11/1978 in Portsmouth; H - 72; W - 73
Christopher M. of Wakefield m. Martha F. Mara of Lexington, MA 6/30/1973

BANKS,
Donald C. of Sanbornville m. Charlotte J. Morken of Amarillo, TX 9/2/1967 in Sanbornville; H - 35, USAF; W - 37, at home
George W. of Springvale, ME m. Isabel Stiles of Springvale, ME 11/23/1887; H - 21, shoe cutter, b. Lawrence, MA, s/o Thomas H. Banks (England, mechanic) and Sarah Higginbottom (England, housekeeper); W - 18, shoe stitcher, b. Shapleigh, ME, d/o Alfred Stiles (Shapleigh, ME, laster) and Almeda Morrison (Sanford, ME, housekeeper)

BARHAM,
Phillip C. of Rochester m. Leona I. McIntire of Union 5/28/1970 in Union

BARKER,
Gary Lee of Wakefield m. Roberta F. Ridlon of Sanbornville 8/6/1966; H - 23, laborer; W - 18, at home
Robert S. of Weirs m. Elizabeth Belle Knight of Sanbornville 5/28/1938 in Sanbornville; H - 64, clergyman; W - 56, housework
Thomas E. of Wakefield m. Carolyn T. Palmer of Exeter 8/6/1983

BARNETT,
Robert J., Jr. of Laconia m. Sallyann Garland of Sanbornville 5/30/1969

BARRETT,
William Joseph of Boston, MA m. Elizabeth Mary Thorpe of Boston,
    MA 4/18/1942 in Farmington; H - 49, foreman; W - 42, at home

BARROWS,
Ralph James of Standish, ME m. Bonnie Mae Fisher of Wakefield
    7/1/1978; H - 32; W - 23

BARTLETT,
Everett Edmon of Union m. Wanda Jean Drew of Sanbornville
    11/6/1965 in Union; H - 30, mill emp.; W - 16, at home

BARTON,
Ronald E. of Sanbornville m. Karin Goodell of Sanbornville 4/20/1991 in
    Sanbornville
William V. of Roslindale, MA m. Clara E. Shaw of W. Medford, MA
    9/2/1914; H - 45, book keeper, b. London, England, s/o Frederic
    Barton and Anne M. Barton; W - 43, at home, b. W. Medford, MA,
    d/o Ai B. Shaw and Carolyn A. Merrill

BASTABLE,
John Francis of East Wakefield m. Patricia Yvonne Kennedy of
    Bushnell, FL 5/19/1995

BATZER,
Andreas Georg of Boston, MA m. Ulrike Elisabeth Kolbus of Boston,
    MA 3/29/1997

BEACHAM,
Howard of Wakefield m. Hattie F. Haines of Wakefield 6/13/1899 in
    Concord; H - 28, station agent, b. Wakefield, s/o Henry K. Hunt
    (Lakeville, MA, deceased) and Mary F. Canney (Ossipee,
    housekeeper); W - 28, clerk, b. Wakefield, d/o George W. Haines
    (Wakefield, deceased) and Susan A. Nichols (Ossipee, deceased)
Howard A. of Union m. Leah M. Herbert of Wolfeboro 7/22/1947 in
    Wolfeboro; H - 76, retired; W - 39, nurse

BEAIRSTO,
Erling Westley of Stratham m. Barbara Elizabeth Lang of Sanbornville 8/6/1938 in Hampton Falls; H - 28, carpenter; W - 24, stenographer

BEALS,
Ellis of Shapleigh, ME m. Katherine M. Thompson of Wakefield 5/2/1941 in Shapleigh, ME; H - 21, millworker; W - 16, at home

BEAUCHAMP,
Philip J., Jr. of East Wakefield m. Janice A. Burns of East Wakefield 12/31/1990 in East Wakefield

BEAUDETTE,
Henry of Wakefield m. Mary Patry of Wakefield 9/2/1899; H - 26, laborer, b. Groton Pond, VT, s/o Fred Beaudette (Canada, deceased) and Emilies Tracher (Canada, deceased); W - 34, b. Buckland, Canada, d/o Fred Patry (Canada, deceased) and Mary Lachance (Canada, housekeeper)

BEAUDITTE,
Ralph F. of Providence, RI m. Alma F. Brooks of Wakefield 5/1/1922 in Sanbornville; H - 23, engineer, b. No. Troy, VT, s/o Joseph A. Beauditte and Lillian Newerty; W - 23, bookkeeper, b. Lowell, MA, d/o Dennis R. Brooks and Julia Parent

BEAUPRE,
John H. of Wakefield m. Donna L. Richardson of Wakefield 7/21/1979 in Farmington; H - 26; W - 22
Richard Joseph of Sanbornville m. Joyce Lynn Pageau of Sanbornville 6/2/1990 in Sanbornville

BECKLUND,
Richard B. of Waltham, MA m. May E. Lufkin of Chelmsford, MA 8/17/1974

BECKWITH,
William H. of Wakefield m. Dawn M. Fry of Wakefield 6/1/1980

BEGIN,
Raymond J. of Milton m. Joan S. Kimball of Sanbornville 2/30/1974 (sic)

BELANGER,
Albert W. of Dover m. Mary E. Hansen of Sanbornville 10/25/1969 in Sanbornville

BELL,
Louis A. of Bismark, Dak. m. Carrie Rogers of Franklin 11/20/1896; H - 23, showman, "red", b. Bismark, Dak., s/o John Bell of Bismark, Dak. (Dakota, farmer, "red") and Celia ----- (Bismark, Dak., housekeeper, "red"); W - 18, housework, b. Manchester, d/o Oscar Rogers (38, brick mason) and Hattie ----- (37, housework)

BEMIS,
Raymond E. of Portsmouth m. Lillian B. Davis of Wakefield 7/1/1934 in Union; H - 23, draughtsman; W - 19, at home

BENNER,
Richard E. of Farmington m. Sara A. Downs of Sanbornville 2/14/1969 in Sanbornville

BENNETT,
James William of Tuftonboro m. Hazel Bernice Perry of Sanbornville 5/4/1943 in Sanbornville; H - 26, carpenter; W - 22, hair dresser
James William, Jr. of Wakefield m. Susan Barnard Clement of Wakefield 9/25/1977 in Laconia

BENSON,
Barrett Eugene of Watertown, MA m. Pauline Messer Keyes of Woburn, MA 7/31/1954; H - 53, salesman; W - 50, nurse

BENTZLER,
Edward William of Loyal, WI m. Gloria May Fifield of Union 7/18/1959 in Sanbornville; H - 22, USAF; W - 20, shoe worker

BERRY,
Alberton Herman of Union m. Marjorie E. Wilkinson of East Wakefield 7/2/1938 in Alton; H - 22, shoe worker; W - 19, at home

William W. of Wakefield m. Martha M. Wilkins of Wakefield 10/31/1914 in Milton; H - 71, farmer, 2d, b. Wakefield, s/o Francis Berry and Temperance Wiggin; W - 63, housekeeper, 2d, b. Wakefield, d/o Asa M. Farnham and Mary Jones

BERTHIAUME,
R. Peter of Somerset, MA m. Elizabeth A. Giusti of Weymouth, MA 2/21/1970

BEST,
George Cranswyck of Wakefield m. Helen Constance Hobbs of Wakefield 6/26/1938; H - 50, merchant; W - 47, school teacher

BEVARD,
John W. of Wakefield m. Amanda J. Tuttle of Wakefield 10/28/1972 in Milton

BICKFORD,
Albion M. of Wakefield m. Bertha E. Rines of Wakefield 9/17/1904 in Somersworth; H - 35, printer, b. Farmington, s/o Oliver Bickford and Elmina P. Canney; W - 25, housekeeper, b. Wakefield, d/o Charles W. Rines and Mary A. Roberts
Arthur B. of Wakefield m. Vivian G. Weeks of Milton 11/11/1916; H - 23, musician, b. Wakefield, MA, s/o George R. Bickford and Charlotte A. Fonnor; W - 18, weaver, b. Melvin, d/o Frank S. Weeks and Minnie Allie
Carl P. of Wakefield m. Melissa J. Williams of Wakefield 5/24/1987 in Wolfeboro
Carroll F. of Wolfeboro m. Blanche I. Jenness of Wakefield 12/25/1934 in Sanbornville; H - 30, laborer; W - 27, at home
Duane D. of East Wakefield m. Cynthia L. Cunningham of East Rochester 9/11/1993
Everett J. of Sanbornville m. Elsie M. McDonald of Sanbornville 11/15/1946 in Sanbornville; H - 40, painter; W - 52, housework
Maurice R. of Wolfeboro m. Louise E. Paul of Wakefield 9/24/1936 in Sanbornville; H - 21, iceman; W - 19, housework

BLACK,
Philip N. of Dover m. Lana E. Harris of Union 6/20/1969

BLACKADAR,
James A. of Rochester m. Cynthia B. Fox of Union 9/5/1981 in Rochester

BLACKWELL,
Robert Wade of East Wakefield m. Jacqueline Ann Blais of East Wakefield 1/14/1996 in Sanbornville

BLAIR,
Alfred C., Jr. of Sanbornville m. Brenda D. Dodier of Sanbornville 9/30/1967 in Sanbornville; H - 23, mill emp.; W - 19, mill emp.

BLANCHARD,
Elmer S. of Springvale, ME m. Ethel M. Dolan of Springvale, ME 10/23/1948 in Sanbornville; H - 48, farmer; W - 37, at home

BLAND,
Raymond F. of Wakefield m. Maria E. Barrett of Wakefield 8/22/1981 in Manchester

BLANTON,
Henry Mason of Sanbornville m. Nancy Jane Hutchins of Sanbornville 11/11/1955; H - 28, auto mech.; W - 23, at home

BLOUIN,
Joe of Wakefield m. Ethel Colby of Wakefield 12/15/1903 in Union; H - 21, laborer, b. Quebec, s/o O. Blouin and Phoebe Beasant; W - 18, housekeeper, b. Tuftonboro, d/o William Colby and Josephine Brown
Michael A. of Union m. Rosaria Giuist of Union 8/16/1986

BLUMIT,
Arthur P. of Quincy, MA m. Roberta M. Libby of Sanbornville 12/27/1968 in Portsmouth

BOCKMAN,
Joseph Gabriel of Beverly, MA m. Judith Ann Joslin of Beverly, MA 8/29/1998

BODWELL,
John Everett of Acton, ME m. Jean Audrey Miliner of Sanbornville 9/11/1955; H - 22, mill emp.; W - 27, office clerk

BOIS,
Donald G. of Beverly, MA m. Patti Lee Leavitt of Wellesley, MA 7/3/1971

BOND,
Richard M. m. Gladys E. Stevens 11/25/1926; H - 25, b. Newfield, ME, s/o William Bond and Anna M. Guilford; W - 28, b. Newfield, ME, d/o Calvert Stevens and Delia Benson

BONELLI,
Albert A. of Plymouth, MA m. Joy M. Straz of Plymouth, MA 9/8/1984

BOODY,
Charles S. of Wakefield m. Eunice G. Moulton of Wakefield 6/1/1893; H - 38, butter maker, b. Limerick, ME, s/o Joseph B. Boody (Limington, ME, carpenter) and Rebecca Chamberlain (Randolph, VT, housework); W - 40, housework, b. Wakefield, d/o Charles Moulton (Hampton, farmer) and Olive Ayers (Greenland, housework)

BOOTHBY,
Bradford Saunders of Union m. Rose May Johansen of Lincoln, MA 5/4/1957; H - 47, underwriter; W - 43, nurse
Douglas Lloyd of Wakefield m. Christine Louise Dowst of Epsom 2/21/1976 in Epsom

BORELL,
Barry T. of Sanbornville m. Linda L. Bradford of East Hartford, CT 2/24/1968 in Holderness

BOSQUIN,
Edison G. of East Rochester m. Celestia A. Knapp of Sanbornville 5/8/1936 in Sanbornville; H - 21, taxi driver; W - 18, at home

BOSTON,
Henry W. of East Rochester m. Helen L. **Hartford** of East Rochester 2/14/1943 in East Rochester; H - 24, mill emp.; W - 17, at home
Randolph D. of Rochester m. Joyce M. **Goodrow** of Sanbornville 11/22/1969

BOUCHARD,
Ernest R., Jr. of Rochester m. Elizabeth H. **Black** of Wakefield 5/26/1988 in Rochester

BOUDROW,
W. E., Jr. of Lynn, MA m. Diane E. **Languirand** of Salem, MA 6/14/1968

BOULANGER,
Andre A. of Sanbornville m. Helen A. **Greene** of Sanbornville 7/25/1992

BOULE,
William of Wakefield m. Ruth C. **Boyd** of Wakefield 2/23/1980 in Parsonsfield, ME

BOULET,
Alexander m. Harriett **Tibbetts** 10/27/1933 in Danbury

BOURGOIN,
Arthur A. of Lewiston, ME m. Dorothy **Cunningham** of Lewiston, ME 5/29/1936 in Sanbornville; H - 23, clerk; W - 23, nurse

BOURRIE,
Guy A. of Wakefield m. Sandra L. **Hall** of Wakefield 4/24/1983

BOWS,
Clinton J. of North Easton, MA m. Margaret J. **Cunniff** of North Easton, MA 10/7/1984

BOYCE,
Edward O. of Dover m. Annie B. **Prescott** of Wakefield 10/6/1902 in Union; H - 21, night watchman, b. Eliot, ME, s/o Thomas Boyce and Frances Rowe; W - 18, dressmaker, 2d, b. Northwood, d/o Dyer Evans and Hattie -----

BOYD,

William of Wakefield m. Mary Maleham of Wakefield 9/20/1896 in Brookfield; H - 29, engine wiper, 2d, widower, b. Biddeford, ME, s/o James Boyd of Georgetown, ME (Berwick, ME, clergyman) and Mary Cuttings (Waterville, ME, housekeeper); W - 24, waiter, b. Wakefield, d/o W. H. Maleham of Wakefield (Wakefield, 44, carpenter) and Sarah Farnham (So. Boston, MA, 41, housekeeper)

William S. of Milton m. Evelyn M. Nason of Sanbornville 10/15/1960; H - 20, US Navy; W - 20, at home

William T. of Wakefield m. Abbie S. Gage of Wakefield 1/6/1892; H - 24, dentist, b. Biddeford, ME, s/o James Boyd (Berwick, ME, clergyman) and Mary Cuttings (Waterville, ME, housework); W - 19, housework, b. Wakefield, d/o George H. Gage (Wakefield, farmer) and Jennie Cotton (Wolfeboro, housework)

BRACKETT,

Daniel of Wakefield m. Ida F. Rice of Wakefield 12/15/1888; H - 27, conductor, b. Wakefield, s/o Daniel Brackett and Hannah Cook; W - 26, seamstress, b. Freedom, d/o Ivory F. Rice (Freedom, car inspector) and Mary McCartee (Porter, ME, housework)

Daniel of Wakefield m. Annie W. Nowell of Salmon Falls 1/1/1896 in Salmon Falls; H - 34, conductor, 2d, widower, b. Wakefield, s/o Daniel Brackett (Wakefield, deceased) and Hannah Cook (Wakefield, deceased); W - 33, telegrapher, b. Salmon Falls, d/o E. S. Nowell of Salmon Falls (Sanford, ME, 76, RR employee) and A. D. Wentworth (Salmon Falls, deceased)

Forris L. of Sanbornville m. Ada M. Remick of Sanbornville 5/8/1905 in Pittsfield; H - 36, baggage master, b. Wakefield, s/o Asa M. Brackett and Rowena D. Farnham; W - 35, music teacher, b. Sanford, ME, d/o Crosby B. Remick and Jennie B. Goodwin

Harry L. of Wakefield m. Cora May Taft of Wakefield 11/6/1906; H - 28, brakeman, b. Wakefield, s/o Charles E. Brackett and Elizabeth B. Wiggin; W - 25, domestic, b. Douglass, MA, d/o Arthur L. Taft and Nellie Dunham

Herbert C of Wakefield m. Viola E. Stevens of Brookfield 12/25/1901; H - 45, farmer, b. Wakefield, s/o Charles E. Brackett (Acton, ME, farmer) and Elizabeth Wiggin (Wakefield, housewife); W - 21, housework, b. Brookfield, d/o Warren E. Stevens (Bangor, ME, farmer) and Etta Eaton (Brookfield, housewife)

John E. of Wakefield m. Mary E. Kenney of Wakefield 12/5/1893; H - 22, engineer, b. Wakefield, s/o Charles E. Brackett (Acton, ME, farmer) and Lizzie Wiggin (Wakefield, housework); W - 21, housework, b. Salem, MA, d/o Martin Kenney (Boston, MA, mason) and Mary McShane (England, housework)

Ralph E. of Sanbornville m. Pauline F. McCrillis of No. Conway 10/4/1947 in Sanbornville; H - 41, postmaster; W - 32, stenographer

Ralph Edward of Sanbornville m. Pauline F. McCrillis of North Conway 5/9/1936 in Dover; H - 29, post office clerk; W - 21, at home

BRADEEN,

Harry A. of East Waterboro, ME m. Eva L. Woodward of North Waterboro, ME 11/16/1902 in Sanbornville; H - 29, livery business, b. Cleveland, OH, s/o Edward C. Bradeen and Katie Collins; W - 26, housekeeper, b. Waterboro, ME, d/o Timothy Woodward and Almeda Lane

BRANNON,

George P., Jr. of Sanbornville m. Adrienne L. Thomas of Sanbornville 8/22/1992 in Middleton

BRECAUIER,

George J. of White River Jct., VT m. Maude R. McBride of Sanbornville 10/12/1946 in Wolfeboro; H - 40, hospital att.; W - 41, reg. nurse

BREEDLOVE,

Oral E. of Portland, ME m. Judy R. Anderson of Portland, ME 6/22/1980

BRIGHAM,

Chesley H. of Wakefield m. Ethel E. Thurston of Effingham 5/29/1899 in Freedom; H - 25, salesman, b. Boston, MA, s/o George T. Brigham (Southboro, MA, expressman) and Emma J. Hayes (Barrington, housekeeper); W - 23, housekeeper, b. Effingham, d/o Joshua Thurston (Parsonsfield, ME, surveyor) and Arvilla F. Chick (Effingham, housekeeper)

BRISARD,

Robert A. of Somersworth m. Ruth E. Martin of Wakefield 5/17/1986 in Somersworth

BRISSETTE,
Ronald L. of Watertown, MA m. Jean M. Grasso of Newton, MA 9/2/1967; H - 21, USMC; W - 19, clerk typist

BRISSON,
James L. of Sanbornville m. Cinnamon C. Jones of Sanbornville 7/15/1989 in Sanbornville

BRITTO,
Derek John of Plymouth, MA m. Melissa Jeanne Burkhead of Plymouth, MA 11/14/1997 in Sanbornville

BROCHU,
Larry N. of Sanbornville m. Denise D. Boshears of Sanbornville 10/12/1985

BROCK,
Harold Edison of Wolfeboro m. Caroline Nairn Paul of Wakefield 4/26/1943; H - 35, line supt.; W - 41, med. technologist

BRODERICK,
Raymond M. of Wilmette, IL m. Vickie L. Vaughn of Wakefield 9/26/1987

BRODZINSKI,
Paul Joseph, Jr. of Sanbornville m. Karen Elizabeth Eastman of Union 9/19/1975

BRONICKI,
Michael of Summerfield, MA m. Prudence J. Lajoie of Sanbornville 9/28/1996 in Sanbornville

BROOKES,
Donald O. of Wakefield m. Linda J. Colson of Wakefield 6/16/1985 in Ossipee

BROOKS,
George H. of Kennebunkport, ME m. Dorothy Brewster of Kennebunk, ME 9/5/1922 in Sanbornville; H - 25, fisherman, b. Kennebunkport,

ME, s/o Harry H. Brooks and Maude Hutchins; W - 28, at home, b. London, England, d/o John Brewster and Emily Pheby

Louis Waldo of Middleton m. Mary Louise Fifield of Union 12/20/1964 in Sanbornville; H - 17, laborer; W - 18, at home

Samuel Cecil of Middleton m. Kathleen Joy Hill of Union 10/16/1965 in Union; H - 17, laborer; W - 16, at home

Vincent W. of Wakefield m. Gloria L. Smith of Wakefield 4/12/1980 in Middleton

William Edward of Wakefield m. Theresa Anne Ames of Wakefield 8/25/1990 in Tuftonboro

BROUILLARD,

Henry of Sanbornville m. Grace King of Farmington 5/24/1935 in Berwick, ME; H - 21, truck driver; W - 21, shoe worker

Jean of Milton m. Appoline Prince of Wakefield 6/23/1913; H - 65, laborer, 2d, b. Canada, s/o Peter Brouillard and Catherine Desesleurier; W - 62, housework, 2d, b. Canada, d/o Louis Lemirae and Appoline Proulx

BROWN,

Charles B. of Wakefield m. Mabel F. Trott of Ossipee 12/12/1894 in Ossipee; H - 27, laborer, b. Wolfeboro, s/o Moses E. Brown (Wolfeboro, machinist) and Mary A. Bryant (Somersworth); W - 21, housework, b. Portland, ME, d/o Thayer S. Trott (Portland, ME, laborer) and Isie Mathews (Wakefield, housework)

Craig Alan of Farmington m. Janice Faye Hoisington of Union 10/25/1975 in Farmington

Dana E. of Brookfield m. Charlotte D. Hicks of Union 7/5/1971

Fred W. of Wakefield m. Clara A. Perkins of Milton 8/8/1900 in Milton Mills; H - 27, RR brakeman, b. Ossipee, s/o John M. Brown (Wolfeboro, farmer) and A. A. Wentworth (Ossipee, housewife); W - 27, shoe stitcher, b. Acton, ME, d/o George D. Perkins (Acton, ME, millman) and Sarah Bodwell (Acton, ME, housewife)

James W. of Wakefield m. Robin M. Kilmer of Wolfeboro 8/22/1981

Mason W. of Sanbornville m. Ethel L. Lord of So. Berwick, ME 6/5/1921 in So. Berwick, ME; H - 27, RR trainman, b. Sanbornville, s/o Plummer Brown (Ossipee) and Laura V. Rice (Porter, ME); W - 27, bookkeeper, b. Charlestown, MA, d/o Charles T. Lord (So. Berwick, ME, RR engineer) and Lucilla M. Hunter (St. Stephen, NB)

Norman Leavritt, Jr. of West Newbury, MA m. Barbara Anne Crossland of Merrimac, MA 4/14/1964 in Sanbornville; H - 30, plant mec.; W - 25, plastic attndt.

Peter G. of Wakefield m. Lauren A. Cormier of Miami, FL 6/28/1969 in Wethersfield, CT

Rollins G. of Saco, ME m. Eleanor A. Rogers of Wakefield 6/12/1915; H - 24, chemist, b. Brooklyn, NY, s/o Daniel R. Brown and Mary A. Paul; W - 20, at home, b. Wakefield, d/o Herbert E. Rogers and Lillian A. Sanborn

Ronald Stephen of Sanbornville m. Amy Lyn McGuigan of East Wakefield 9/25/1993

Stephen K. of East Wakefield m. Susan L. Albushies of Nashua 8/29/1992 in Laconia

Sumner E. of Rochester m. Janet R. Stevens of Sanbornville 12/14/1947 in Sanbornville; H - 26, telephone emp.; W - 25, nurse

Thomas J. of Wakefield m. Victoria L. Fogg of Wakefield 8/10/1985

Walter E., Jr. of Wakefield m. Sue A. Graves of Hollis, MA 6/20/1981 in Nashua

William E. of Wakefield m. Bernice J. Irwin of Dover 10/5/1915 in Somersworth; H - 22, chauffeur, b. Dover, s/o John Brown and Minnie Duprey; W - 21, at home, b. Dover, d/o Joseph Irwin and Jennie Brownell

William E. of Wakefield m. Audrey A. Miller of Brownfield, ME 9/29/1920 in Ossipee; H - 26, brakeman, 2d, b. So. Berwick, ME, s/o John Brown (Dover, carpenter) and Minnie Duprey (Canada); W - 17, housework, b. Wakefield, d/o Will Miller (Granite, stationary fireman) and Christie McDonald (Wakefield)

William J. of Wakefield m. Celia M. Fellows of Wakefield 11/3/1898; H - 32, RR conductor, b. Ossipee, s/o John F. Brown (Wolfeboro, deceased) and Abbie Wentworth (Ossipee, deceased); W - 23, dressmaker, b. Ossipee, d/o H. B. Fellows of Wakefield (Wakefield, 49, farmer) and Belle Tibbetts (Newfield, ME, 45, housework)

BRUCE,

Douglas P. of Milton m. Marjorie B. Hayward of Union 6/1/1974 in Union

BRYAN,

William F. of Waddell, AR m. Gabriela Grnova of Waddell, AR 6/20/1992

BRYANT,
Merton Ellis m. Velma C. **Shepardson** 6/8/1933 in Rochester

BUBAR,
George L., Jr. of Union m. Karen J. **Lavertue** of Union 9/22/1984

BUMBACA,
Frank J. of East Wakefield m. Jill A. **Stone** of East Wakefield 11/19/1989 in East Wakefield

BUNNELL,
Robert J. of Lawrence, MA m. Shirley A. **Belanger** of Lawrence, MA 7/16/1960 in Sanbornville; H - 36, B.D. opr.; W - 23, wirer

BURDICK,
James J. of Wakefield m. Elaine P. **Souza** of Wakefield 10/6/1972

BURNHAM,
Dean R. of Wakefield m. Lynn M. **Ash** of Wakefield 8/31/1985
John Arthur of Epping m. Loretta **Soucy** of Sanbornville 6/18/1955 in Sanbornville; H - 22, teacher; W - 20, student
Sidney L. of Lawrence, MA m. Neta B. **Wirth** of Lawrence, MA 8/31/1968
Steven of W. Newfield, ME m. Carol A. **Marion** of W. Newfield, ME 12/21/1984

BURR,
Gary A. of Rochester m. Sally A. **Shea** of Wakefield 9/9/1978; H - 20; W - 20

BURROWS,
David I. of Union m. Mildred G. **Wentworth** of Union 8/31/1935 in Union; H - 34, truckman; W - 20, at home

BURTON,
Joseph B. of Sydney, BC m. Mabel G. **Burroughs** of Wakefield 5/29/1920; H - 35, lumber dealer, b. Inverness Co., s/o John F. Burton (Inv's Co., CB) and Mary McDougall (Sydney, CB); W - 36, teacher, b. Biddeford, ME, d/o Edgar H. Burroughs (Brookfield, retired) and Grace Ricker (Biddeford, ME)

BUSWELL,
Roland Roger of Wakefield m. Gloria Jane Seamans of Wakefield 9/4/1976

BUTLER,
David Arthur of Middleton m. Marlene Elizabeth Cormier of Wakefield 12/26/1976 in Rochester
Fred N. of Everett, MA m. Ruth M. Baker of Everett, MA 8/4/1934 in Sanbornville; H - 23, laborer; W - 21, stenographer
Guy Woodman of Boxford, MA m. Alice Agnes Harnois of Newbury, MA 9/19/1962; H - 21, US Navy; W - 18, at home

BUXTON,
William K. of Springfield, MA m. Aila E. Pottala of East Wakefield 7/16/1938 in East Wakefield; H - 33, salesman; W - 32, teacher

BUZZELL,
George A. of Acton, ME m. Catherine Farnham of Wakefield 6/7/1899; H - 22, farmer, b. Acton, ME, s/o Lyman Buzzell (Acton, ME, farmer) and Jane B. Lord (Shapleigh, ME, housekeeper); W - 24, shoe stitcher, b. Wakefield, d/o Edward B. Farnham (Wakefield, farmer) and Jennie H. Watts (Canada, housekeeper)

BYNUM,
Nathaniel Lawson of Union m. Beth Ann Emerson of Milton 7/11/1998 in Milton

BYRD,
James L. of Jennings, FL m. Shirley L. Riley of Sanbornville 5/25/1989 in Sanbornville

CADDEL,
Earl F., Jr. of Wakefield m. Joanne M. Fauci of Wakefield 9/12/1948; H - 18, heavy equip. op.; W - 19, lab. technician

CAIL,
Joseph J. of Wakefield m. Lynda Seaman of Wakefield 8/11/1979 in Wolfeboro; H - 23; W - 18

CALICCHIO,
Michael Louise of Marblehead, MA m. Faith Paula Savickey of Marblehead, MA 2/4/1976

CALL,
Michael R. of Wakefield m. Carol A. Wilshire of Wakefield 8/8/1987 in New Castle

CALLAHAN,
Dennis R. of Sanbornville m. Lenoah Jo May of Sanbornville 2/8/1998 in Wolfeboro

CAMPANO,
Paul F. of Somerville, MA m. Carole M. Giffin of Sanbornville 4/15/1973 in Sanbornville

CAMPBELL,
Jeffrey W. of Dover m. Elizabeth A. Carswell of Wakefield 6/27/1987 in Union
John F. of Wakefield m. Sarah A. Willey of Wakefield 12/7/1887; H - 54, farmer, 2d, b. Shapleigh, ME, s/o John Campbell and Charity Horne; W - 57, housework, b. Shapleigh, ME, d/o Eliphalet Willey and Sally Henderson

CAMPION,
Edwin J. of Wakefield m. Susan L. Cloutman of Wakefield 8/15/1987 in Wolfeboro

CANNEY,
Kevin Scott of East Wakefield m. Alice Marie Morrill of East Wakefield 6/25/1994 in East Wakefield

CAPACH,
James F. of Wakefield m. Melody L. Smith of Wakefield 11/7/1981 in Ossipee

CAPACHETTI,
Carmen L., Jr. of Revere, MA m. Georgiann M. Capachetti of Revere, MA 5/8/1983 in East Wakefield

Carmine L. of Revere, MA m. Lisa R. **Schwager** of Revere, MA 8/10/1985 in East Wakefield

CAPOBIANCO,
Antonio of Framingham, MA m. Annabelle E. **Donnell** of Framingham, MA 3/20/1948 in Union; H - 41, theatre mgr.; W - 27, cashier

CARBERRY,
Andrew J. of Sanbornville m. Allyne D. **Morrill** of Sanbornville 11/25/1989
Harold Herbert of Gorham m. Beatrice Marie **Krohn** of Sanbornville 12/20/1958 in Sanbornville; H - 22, laborer; W - 22, shop emp.

CARBONE,
Joseph of Sanbornville m. Alice Mary **Shea** of Sanbornville 9/22/1962; H - 60, retired; W - 43, housewife

CARLISLE,
Mikel E. of Hamilton, TN m. Cheryl L. **Libby** of Wakefield 9/9/1978; H - 18; W - 16

CARLTON,
David W. of Acton, ME m. Wendy L. **McDormand** of East Wakefield 9/19/1992

CARON,
Randy of Sanbornville m. Kellie A. **Plamondon** of Sanbornville 9/19/1992 in Manchester

CARPENTER,
Richard Edward of East Bridgewater, MA m. Roberta Jane **Buckland** of Sanbornville 4/11/1953; H - 23, US Air Force; W - 20, at home
Stephen E., Jr. of Sanbornville m. Stacy L. **Herbert** of Sanbornville 8/29/1992 in Wolfeboro
Terry N. of Sanford, ME m. Victoria M. **Pendexter** of Sanford, ME 8/28/1982

CARR,
Steven A. of Rochester m. Kim J. **Starrett** of Wakefield 6/21/1980 in Wolfeboro

Thomas A. of Burlington, MA m. Monica-Ingrid Rennesund of Sanbornville 9/29/1991 in Laconia

CARSON,
Henry L. of Chelsea, MA m. Geraldine A. Batstone of Chelsea, MA 10/8/1984

CARSWELL,
Brian L. of Union m. Lori M. Maxfield of Sanbornville 8/9/1986 in Union

CARTER,
William of Wakefield m. Clara E. Valley of Wakefield 7/2/1887; H - 34, laborer, b. Newport, VT, s/o William Carter (England) and Marion Whitcomb (England); W - 18, housework, b. Middleton, d/o Lewis Valley (Canada, shoemaker) and Clara A. Glidden (Alton, housekeeper)

CARUTHERS,
Clifford Mack of Somonauk, IL m. Marydale Stewart of Somonauk, IL 9/28/1991

CASTIGNETTI,
Frank of Malden, MA m. Irene Johnson of So. Pittsburg, TN 9/1/1956 in Sanbornville; H - 40, dog trainer; W - 29, at home

CATE,
Herbert H. of Brookfield m. Mabelle O. Fogg of Sanbornville 4/14/1934 in Rochester; H - 52, painter; W - 25, telephone op.

CAULKINS,
Dale C., Jr. of Sanbornville m. Cynthia Anne Nason of Sanbornville 5/9/1992 in Wolfeboro

CAVERLY,
Albert Dean, Jr. of Union m. Elizabeth G. Naylor of Union 2/5/1949 in Union; H - 19, laborer; W - 16, at home

CEURVELS,
Glenn M. of Franklin, MA m. Linda A. **Lomberto** of Franklin, MA 5/9/1966 in Sanbornville; H - 20, USAF; W - 18, at home

CHADBOURNE,
Robert Gagne of Somersworth m. Ramona Mary **Nason** of Union 6/30/1956 in Sanbornville; H - 22, US Army; W - 21, office work

CHAMBERLAIN,
Ernest G. of Wakefield m. Agnes M. **Craig** of Millinocket, ME 10/7/1913; H - 43, painter, b. Boston, MA, s/o Sylvester Chamberlain and Helen M. Lang; W - 42, housework, 2d, b. Bath, NB, d/o George Craig and Sarah Caughey

Telesphore of Wakefield m. Gracia **Lamontagne** of Wakefield 10/26/1904; H - 37, janitor, 2d, b. Canada, s/o Joseph Chamberlain and Hermine Gregoire; W - 25, housework, b. Canada, d/o Joseph Lamontagne and Annie Joyce

CHANDLER,
C. M. of Wakefield m. I. V. **Cummings** of Boston, MA 12/5/1896 in Belgrade, ME; H - 32, carpenter, b. Fryeburg, ME, s/o S. Chandler (Chatham, deceased, farmer) and A. Brickett (Stowe, ME, deceased); W - 38, nurse, b. Belgrade, ME, d/o J. S. Cummings of Belgrade, ME (OH, 63, clergyman) and A. J. Hersom (Belgrade, ME, 58, housekeeper)

Clarence Ellis of Waltham, MA m. Agnes Rule **Hyde** of Wakefield 12/24/1942 in East Wakefield; H - 54, watchmaker; W - 55, store prop.

Marshall K. of Rochester m. Brinda Ann **Dennehy** of Sanbornville 12/9/1989 in Rochester

CHAPMAN,
Herbert F. of Wakefield m. Alta M. **Grover** of Rochester 11/15/1917; H - 37, tel. lineman, 2d, b. Charlestown, MA, s/o Herbert S. Chapman and Marrietta Swan; W - 38, housework, 2d, b. Rochester, d/o Charles A. Allen and Mary A. Randlett

Homer L. of Wakefield m. Elinore A. **Wyman** of Waltham, MA 11/28/1912; H - 24, ice laborer, b. Coaticook, PQ, s/o John E. Chapman and Ella J. Snow; W - 20, clerk, b. Waltham, MA, d/o George W. Wyman and Mary A. Main

John Homer of Wakefield m. Clara Louise Hayden of Hollis 6/28/1942 in Hollis; H - 25, elec. engineer; W - 22, teacher

CHAREST,
Peter I. of Wakefield m. Nancy L. Roulo of Newmarket 2/2/1979 in Somersworth; H - 33; W - 32
Robert A. of East Wakefield m. Linda M. Wheelock of Leominster, MA 10/13/1984

CHARLES,
Bernard William of Wolfeboro m. Anna Helen Baum of Wakefield 7/3/1940; H - 21, laborer; W - 16, at home

CHASE,
Dean E. of Sanbornville m. Marilyn P. Krause of Hollis, ME 6/14/1969
Earl R. of Marston Mills, MA m. Joan S. Glazebrook of Sandwich, MA 4/15/1972
Frank E. m. Harriet Mildred Howe 9/24/1930; H - 59, s/o James P. Chase (Parsonsfield, ME) and Henrietta Sanborn (Parsonsfield, ME); W - 49, d/o George H. York (Newfield, ME) and Harriet Lord (Limerick, ME)
Otis B., II of Wakefield m. Sandra L. Gallant of Wakefield 7/31/1982
Randall Arthur of Wakefield m. Leslie Moody of Wolfeboro 12/1/1979; H - 26; W - 20
Roger E. of Sanbornville m. Norma J. Jacques of Rochester 7/21/1972 in Strafford

CHASSE,
Robert A. of East Wakefield m. Katherine M. Katwick of East Wakefield 9/20/1986

CHENEY,
Charles F. of Wakefield m. Edwina J. Rice of Wakefield 6/9/1903; H - 28, RR brakeman, 2d, b. Wakefield, s/o Charles H. Cheney and Sarah N. Burke; W - 36, housekeeper, b. Freedom, d/o Ivory F. Rice and Mary McCartre

CHESLEY,
Michael Alan of Middleton m. Tanya Marie Eaton of East Wakefield 4/25/1998

CHESNEY,
David L. of Mission Hill, CA m. Judith A. Brown of Mission Hill, CA 6/20/1970 in Sanbornville

CHIARADONNA,
Vincent A., Jr. of Sanbornville m. Cherrie Greenfield of Sanbornville 7/31/1998

CHICK,
Brian S. of East Wakefield m. Barbara Eugley of Milton 7/16/1974 in Milton Mills
George S. of Wakefield m. Edith M. Corliss of Northwood 6/26/1937 in Northwood; H - 21, laborer; W - 28, at home
Harry W. of Wakefield m. Helen A. Blake of Arlington, MA 9/1/1906 in Rochester; H - 19, surveyor, b. Wakefield, s/o George H. Chick and Jennie S. Waldron; W - 19, teacher, b. Arlington, MA, d/o Chester P. Blake and Ella Louise Eaton
Lewis S. of Wakefield m. Beatrice Hamilton of Waterboro, ME 10/25/1915 in Newfield, ME; H - 24, mill man, b. Wakefield, s/o George H. Chick and Sarah J. Waldron; W - 18, housewife, b. Penacook, d/o Stephen H. Hamilton and Mary Joyal
Ralph H. of Wakefield m. Lillian M. Meserve of Wakefield 6/23/1920 in Rochester; H - 35, carpenter, 2d, b. Wakefield, s/o George H. Chick (Waterboro, ME, mill man) and Jennie L. Waldron (Acton, ME); W - 34, housework, 2d, b. Boston, MA, d/o Hollis Look (Addison, ME, stevedore) and Ellen Avery (Haverhill, MA)
Winfield D. of Wakefield m. Harriette E. Cook of Shapleigh, ME 1/14/1890; H - 32, carpenter, b. Waterboro, ME, s/o Hanson B. Chick (Waterboro, ME) and Mehitable Smith (Waterboro, ME); W - 22, housekeeper, b. Bethlehem, d/o Peltiah Cook (Waterboro, ME) and Dorcas Smith (Waterboro, ME)

CHILLEMI,
John J. of East Boston, MA m. Claire C. Gagne of Lewiston, ME 7/16/1966; H - 31, draft supt.; W - 24, teacher

CHRISTENSON,
Paul A., Jr. of Bourne, FL m. Eugenie H. Fenton of Bourne, FL
12/30/1972

CHRISTIE,
Paul Harold of No. Rochester m. Dorothy May Bickford of Sanbornville 7/2/1955; H - 27, laborer; W - 20, payroll clerk
Paul M., Jr. of Gonic m. Deborah A. Brown of Wakefield 7/10/1982

CIAMPA,
Anthony, Jr. of Burlington, MA m. Sharyn R. Singelais of Wakefield, MA 8/16/1986 in Sanbornville

CINCOTTA,
Phillip G. of New Gloucester, ME m. Mary L. Smith of New Gloucester, ME 1/21/1989 in Sanbornville

CLANCY,
John P. of Woburn, MA m. Phyllis G. Gritano of Medford, MA 9/25/1948 in Sanbornville; H - 22, foundryman; W - 24, salesgirl

CLARK,
Douglas S. of Sanford, ME m. Gina L. Westgate of Sanford, ME 7/29/1984
J. Frank of Wakefield m. Gladys M. Pickering of Wakefield 10/29/1912 in Dover; H - 21, printer, b. Dover, s/o George W. Clark and Elizabeth Tibbetts; W - 19, teacher, b. Rochester, d/o Walter F. Pickering and Lillian Earl
John W. of Wakefield m. Clara B. Weeks of Wakefield 4/1/1984
Raymond Dustin of Union m. Dorothy May Hansen of Union 9/24/1949 in Rochester; H - 28, conv. home att.; W - 32, housework
Raymond Dustin of Wakefield m. Mary Patricia Katwick of Brookfield 7/2/1977 in Sanbornville

CLARKE,
Charles E. of McLean, VA m. Cynthia A. Johnson of Wakefield 8/5/1972 in Sanbornville

CLEARY,
John J. of Boston, MA m. Alice N. Benson of West Roxbury, MA 11/10/1935 in Sanbornville; H - 41, inspector; W - 31, clerk

CLIFFORD,
Stephen Harold of Moultonboro m. Sally Ann Sanborn of Sanbornville 2/27/1965 in Moultonboro; H - 19, S.S. attend.; W - 18, at home

CLOUGH,
Herbert Eugene of Milton m. Colleen Jane Morrill of Wakefield 7/15/1950; H - 20, mill emp.; W - 16, at home

CLOUTIER,
Lucien H. of Union m. Germaine Poirier of Manchester 7/4/1946 in Rochester; H - 38, hotel prop.; W - 37, shop emp.

CLOUTMAN,
James D. of Wakefield m. Edna M. Fellows of Wakefield 4/21/1919 in Sanbornville; H - 62, hostler, 2d, b. Wakefield, s/o Thomas Cloutman (Wakefield, farmer) and Mehitable Watson (Wakefield); W - 33, shoe shop, b. Wakefield, d/o James P. Fellows (Wakefield, farmer) and Mary A. Pike (Middleton)

CLUETT,
Waldron V. of Wolfeboro m. Anita M. Muise of Sanbornville 9/21/1998 in Sanbornville

COBURN,
Stuart R. of Springfield, MA m. Eloise T. Conley of Springfield, MA 7/8/1936 in Sanbornville; H - 21, garage man; W - 18, at home
William F. of Newfield, ME m. Madelon Kenmore of New York, NY 9/16/1907; H - 46, farmer, 2d, b. Montpelier, VT, s/o Clement E. Coburn and Clarissa Plaicy; W - 24, at home, b. Oxford, England, d/o William J. Kenmore and Marie Russell

COFFIN,
Asa K. of Boston, MA m. Edna M. Dennis of Watertown, MA 9/23/1921 in Sanbornville; H - 21, school, b. Watertown, MA, s/o Melvin C. Coffin (Cambridge, MA, accountant) and Josephine Spencer

(Chicago, IL); W - 18, d/o Chester Dennis (Lynn, MA, news paper) and Louretta Davis (Melrose, MA)

COLBATH,
Eugene of Wakefield m. Hattie L. Lewis of Milton 12/6/1894 in Nahant, MA; H - 20, machinist, b. Wakefield, s/o Walter G. Colbath (Brookfield, roadmaster) and Emma B. Knox (Ossipee, housework); W - 18, weaver, b. Milton, d/o James L. Lewis (England, operative) and Ernestine Riconard (France, housework)

Randy P. of Wakefield m. Joyce Lynn Lavertue of Wakefield 12/2/1982

Richard Paul of Sanbornville m. Virginia Anne Downs of Middleton 10/3/1954 in Farmington; H - 19, US Army; W - 23, shoe shop

Robert N. of Wakefield m. Emily A. Cook of Wakefield 10/26/1918; H - 19, laborer, b. Wakefield, s/o Walter G. Colbath and Emma B. Knox; W - 19, housework, b. Wakefield, d/o Elmer M. Cook and Lillian Clow

Robert N., Jr. of Wakefield m. Dorothea Leslie Richards of Portland, ME 8/15/1941 in Wolfeboro; H - 20, soldier; W - 21, at home

Rosemore K. of Wakefield m. Gladys Ford of Sanford, ME 2/1/1909 in Portsmouth; H - 27, laborer, 2d, b. Wakefield, s/o Walter G. Colbath and Emma B. Colbath; W - 20, mill operative, b. Sandwich, d/o Lewis Ford and Orinda Quint

Rossmore K. of Wassaic, NY m. Maybell G. Hall of Wassaic, NY 9/11/1952; H - 70, pump opr.; W - 62, asst. cook

Roswell K. of Wakefield m. Lydia Gay of West Somerville, MA 4/16/1902; H - 21, brakeman, b. Wakefield, s/o Walter G. Colbath and Emma E. Knox; W - 28, housekeeping, 2d, b. Cambridge, MA, d/o Henry E. Fischer and Josephine Folsom

COLBURN,
Phillip E., Jr. of Lowell, MA m. Alice M. Leclair of East Wakefield 9/23/1989

COLBY,
John W. of Wakefield m. Dianne P. Betts of Wakefield 9/2/1988 in Rochester

COLE,
Carleton Woodman of Old Orchard Beach, ME m. Glenora T. G. Boutet of Portland, ME 4/18/1953; H - 38, bookkeeper; W - 25, tel. oper.

Simeon of Wakefield m. Mary J. Locke of Wakefield 1/7/1890; H - 49, farmer, 3d, b. Cornish, ME, s/o Asahel Cole (Cornish, ME) and Desire Brown (Limerick, ME, housekeeper); W - 47, housekeeper, 2d, b. Wolfeboro, d/o James Abbott (Ossipee) and Mary Fall (Ossipee)

Stanley Russell of Union m. SallyAnn Gray of East Rochester 7/24/1976 in East Rochester

COLLARD,
Scott Nelson of Sanbornville m. Ellen Jean Devore of Acton, ME 12/13/1997 in Sanbornville

COLLINS,
Norman A. of Lebanon, ME m. Christina A. Cormier of Kittery, ME 4/8/1989 in Sanbornville

COLLYNS,
Donald of Sanbornville m. Sandra K. Brooks of Derry 8/9/1981 in Londonderry

COLSON,
Howard F. of Tewksbury, MA m. Ruth C. Churchill of Wakefield, MA 8/19/1979; H - 48; W - 22

Joseph B. of Wakefield m. Linda J. Moyse of Wolfeboro 11/8/1980 in Brookfield

COMEAU,
Joseph of Acton, ME m. Elizabeth Gorman of Acton, ME 5/5/1917; H - 23, farmer, b. Newton, MA, s/o Joseph Comeau and Mary Orris; W - 30, clerk, b. Salem, MA, d/o William Gorman and Julia Flynn

COMISKEY,
Hugh T., Jr. of Newtonville, MA m. Beverly M. Brown of Needham, MA 12/9/1961; H - 20, accounting; W - 18, accounting

COMSTOCK,
Theodore R. of Durham m. Nancy Murray of Wakefield 6/19/1971 in Durham

CONNAUGHTON,
John F. of Lynn, MA m. Marguerite Hazel Welch of So. Boston, MA 11/15/1949 in Sanbornville; H - 47, bartender; W - 33, waitress

CONNELLY,
Terrence John of Laconia m. Faye Bettina Sanborn of Sanbornville 2/29/1964 in Sanbornville; H - 22, laborer; W - 24, teacher (but see following entry)
Terrence John of Wakefield m. Francine M. Amgot of St. Adele, Canada 3/16/1964; H - 24, prof. skier; W - 20, teacher (but see preceding entry)

CONNOR,
Jay E. of Union m. Christine E. Hayward of Union 5/3/1971 in Sanbornville

CONRAD,
Walter, Jr. of Marblehead, MA m. Cheryl B. Burt of Marblehead, MA 7/11/1990 in East Wakefield
William G. of Rochester m. Candace R. Brackett of Sanbornville 1/28/1967 in Sanbornville; H - 20, student; W - 18, student

COOK,
Albert of Paterson, NJ m. Anna B. Fellows of Wakefield 6/24/1903 in Sanbornville; H - 35, machinist, b. Stony Creek, CT, s/o Samuel S. Cook and Georgiana Tucker; W - 33, housework, b. Wakefield, d/o Daniel M. Fellows and Sarah Sawyer
George C. of Wakefield m. Annie M. DeCourcy of Wakefield 4/20/1980
William J. of Wakefield m. Elsie E. Craig of Wakefield 12/19/1908; H - 33, millman, 2d, b. Porter, ME, s/o John Cook and Mary J. Cook; W - 25, waitress, b. Malden, MA, d/o David W. Craig and Elsie E. Hoffman

COOPER,
David W. of Marblehead, MA m. Dorothy O. Russell of Marblehead, MA 12/9/1972

CORAZZINI,
Richard M. of Billerica, MA m. Donna L. Saenger of Wakefield 6/23/1984 in Sanbornville

CORL,
Edwin A. of Wappingers Falls, NY m. Ruth C. Redinger of Beverly, MA 9/28/1968

CORMIER,
Bernard R. of Rochester m. Marlene E. Wilson of Union 7/27/1968 in Rochester
Richard Robert of Rochester m. Sandra Elizabeth Walker of Sanbornville 10/18/1975 in Sanbornville

CORNELL,
Stephen T. of W. Greenwich, RI m. Carol J. Curran of W. Greenwich, RI 4/9/1983

CORSON,
Frank W. of Newfield, ME m. Genie A. Trueworthy of Porter, ME 5/16/1887; H - 30, farmer, b. Denmark, ME, s/o Charles H. Corson (Lebanon, ME, shoemaker) and Betsy F. Potter (Denmark, ME, housekeeper); W - 23, housework, 2d, b. Porter, ME, d/o Joseph A. Holmes (Porter, ME, farmer) and Susan A. Clements (Hiram, ME, housekeeper)
John E. of Wakefield m. Idella M. Lang of Wakefield 9/22/1900 in Brookfield; H - 45, laborer, b. Wakefield, s/o Robert Corson (Milton, laborer) and Sarah Nay (Ossipee, housekeeper); W - 35, housework, 2d, b. Wakefield, d/o Josiah W. Wiggin (Wakefield, farmer) and Mary E. Rines (Middleton, housekeeper)
Raymond W. of Wakefield m. Harriet H. Worster of Berwick, ME 7/5/1945 in Somersworth; H - 20, shop foreman; W - 23, secretary

COSLETT,
John Scott of Tamworth m. Leann Louise Colbath of Wakefield 9/25/1976 in Sanbornville

COSTELLO,
John R. of Waltham, MA m. Mary M. Meisner of Chelmsford, MA 7/8/1967; H - 24, nurse; W - 20, attd. nurse

COTE,
Robert C. of Wakefield m. Celedase A. Desroches of Wakefield 6/26/1923 in Sanbornville; H - 22, laborer, b. Isle Verte, Canada, s/o Edouard

P. Cote and Felecite Sirois; W - 21, stenographer, b. Sanbornville, d/o Philibert Desroches and Marie L. Marcoux

COTTON,
Henry John of Brookfield m. Erika K.A. **Garland** of Sanbornville 5/5/1965 in Brookfield; H - 43, carpenter; W - 42, hair dresser

James A. of Sanbornville m. Beverly A. **Getchus** of Rochester 4/20/1968 in Sanbornville

Leslie D. of Malden, MA m. Nina B. **Clark** of Wakefield 5/28/1912; H - 30, merchant, b. Wolfeboro, s/o Daniel J. Cotton and Hattie S. Hurd; W - 29, teacher, b. Wakefield, d/o Mayhew C. Clark and Eliza R. Furber

Mark A. of Sanbornville m. Erin C. **O'Meara** of Sanbornville 8/26/1989 in Sanbornville

Michael H. of Sanbornville m. Theresa E. **Shea** of Sanbornville 8/29/1970 in Sanbornville

Michael H. of Wakefield m. Bonnie L. **Lamper** of Wakefield 1/20/1989

COUCH,
John A. of Lebanon, ME m. Emilia J. **Harris** of Sanbornville 4/25/1970 in Sanbornville

Patrick H. of Wakefield m. Michelle G. **Baxter** of Rochester 8/3/1985 in Rochester

COUGHLIN,
Daniel J., Jr. of Somerville, MA m. Laverne G. **Anderson** of Worcester, MA 6/22/1968

COVEY,
Ernest Frederick of Nashua m. Marylin Leona **Leeman** of Sanbornville 7/25/1964 in Colebrook; H - 40, const. worker; W - 31, housewife

COVIE,
Frank P. of Wakefield m. Gilberte J. **Vanderhaeghe** of Mahwah, NJ 8/8/1984

COWAN,
Erford Oswald of Sanbornville m. Marcelle M. **Trimm** of Sanbornville 6/30/1951 in Wolfeboro; H - 36, mill opr.; W - 28, laundress

COWING,
Leslie B. of Wakefield m. Bertha E. Libbey of Wakefield 11/14/1909;
H - 22, teamster, 2d, b. Bangor, ME, s/o Daniel L. Cowing and
Fannie Pomeroy; W - 21, housework, b. Detroit, ME, d/o Albert
Libbey and Lillian Clow

COX,
Gilbert E. of East Wakefield m. Barbara C. Kidger of Newton, MA
10/22/1947 in Newton, MA; H - 25, linesman; W - 22, draftsman
Gilbert Earl of East Wakefield m. Beatrice Alice Goodale of Farmington
7/8/1955 in Newmarket; H - 33, lineman; W - 31, at home

CRABTREE,
Charlie of Saugus, MA m. Leona Belle Faust of So. Peabody, MA
3/1/1959 in Sanbornville; H - 50, foreman; W - 47, sales lady

CRAM,
John G. of Wakefield m. Mary A. Merrill of Hampton 9/24/1983 in
Hampton Falls
Kenneth Graves of Sanbornville m. Maureen Cheryl Green of Sanbornville
12/31/1997 in Sanbornville

CRATEAU,
James of Wakefield m. Delvina Drouin of Somersworth 4/28/1908 in
Somersworth; H - 18, freight brakeman, b. Canada, s/o Edward
Crateau and Emily Robenhymer; W - 19, mill operative, b. Canada,
d/o Honore Drouin and Delvina Valliere

CRAWFORD,
Dale E. of East Wakefield m. Carrie A. Gibbons of Rochester 9/6/1992 in
Rollinsford
Daryl E. of East Wakefield m. Lucille C. Worster of Union 4/24/1971 in
Union
David Erving of East Wakefield m. Cindy Gayle Luscomb of East
Wakefield 6/28/1975

CREDIFORD,
Maynard of Shapleigh, ME m. Winnifred Newbegin of Shapleigh, ME
6/27/1907; H - 21, farmer, b. Shapleigh, ME, s/o Joseph Crediford

and Sarah Littlefield; W - 25, teacher, b. Rockport, MA, d/o Daniel Newbegin and ---- Wood
Roger H. m. Lila G. Langley 9/4/1932 in Union

CREIGHTON,
Eugene J. of Tilton m. Ethel M. Pike of Wakefield 12/16/1908; H - 27, druggist, b. Peterboro, s/o Julius M. Creighton and Katherine Donald; W - 25, school teacher, b. Rochester, d/o Charles E. Pike and Mary C. Linscott

CREW,
Kenneth A. of East Wakefield m. Michelle A. Legere of East Wakefield 8/28/1994 in East Wakefield

CROCKER,
George H. of Wakefield m. Bertha J. Rand of Wakefield 11/25/1922 in Wolfeboro; H - 47, laborer, 2d, b. Bangor, ME, s/o Henry Crocker and Abbie Willey; W - 38, housekeeper, 2d, b. Wakefield, d/o Horatio B. Fellows and Belle Tibbetts

CROOK,
Douglas V. of Catskill, NY m. Barbara L. Hustedt of Catskill, NY 10/13/1979; H - 34; W - 34

CROTEAU,
Joseph Scott of Wakefield m. Kimberly Dianne Allen of Rochester 6/11/1988 in Barrington

CROWLEY,
Charles H., Jr. of Beverly, MA m. Cathleen A. Lucier of Danvers, MA 5/31/1980

CULVER,
Lewis B. of Stowe, VT m. Mary E. Grace of Sanbornville 7/3/1934 in Rochester; H - 46, blacksmith; W - 40, housework

CUMMINGS,
Harold L. of Stow, MA m. Virginia C. Cribb of Acton, MA 5/18/1979; H - 71; W - 60

Thomas E. of Murphysboro, IL m. Sharyl S. King of Murphysboro, IL 7/14/1984

CUNNINGHAM,
Shawn M. of East Wakefield m. Jody Marie Dubois of East Wakefield 10/19/1996 in Effingham

CURRIER,
Ralph Raymond of Acton, ME m. Irma Jeanne Hutchinson of Wakefield 2/6/1942 in Sanbornville; H - 22, millworker; W - 18, at home
Richard E. of Beverly, MA m. Althea D. Welch of Wakefield 8/19/1961; H - 27, accountant; W - 25, tel. opr.
Sumner S. of Boston, MA m. Ruth D. Ilander of Boston, MA 12/5/1936 in Sanbornville; H - 24, scientist; W - 23, stenographer

CURT,
Arthur Raymond of Somerset, MA m. Barbara Marie Gendreau of Fall River, MA 4/20/1957; H - 41, car dealer; W - 23, at home

CURTIS,
Joseph S. of Wakefield m. Mary M. Taylor of Boston, MA 4/26/1911 in Boston, MA; H - 54, clerk, 2d, b. Brookfield, s/o Tristram B. Curtis and Abigail Sanborn; W - 55, dressmaker, 3d, b. Medford, MA, d/o William G. Weaver and Mary Patterson

CUSHMAN,
Stephen M. m. Caroline Ida Brooks 7/2/1928; H - 24, s/o Michael Cushman (Austria) and Elizabeth Busaa (Austria); W - 22, d/o Dennis Brooks (Montgomery, VT) and Julia Parent (Lowell, MA)

D'ALLESANDRO,
Thomas P. of Reading, MA m. Evelyn J. Sowyrda of Wakefield, MA 11/10/1961; H - 21, trk. driver; W - 18, at home

D'ERCOLE,
Justin Frank of Boston, MA m. Sarah Amy Whitely of Boston, MA 8/29/1998

D'ZURILLA,
Dean E. of Auburn, ME m. Pamela M. Feddern of Wakefield 10/19/1985

DAME,
- Daniel E. of Wakefield m. Josephine L. Pinkham of Middleton 10/7/1908; H - 35, clerk, 2d, b. Portsmouth, s/o John H. Dame and Fidelia A. Philbrook; W - 17, housework, b. Middleton, d/o George E. Pinkham and Laura J. Maine
- Daniel O. of Wakefield m. Gladys E. Wentworth of Wolfeboro 7/28/1918 in Milton Mills; H - 20, mill hand, b. Middleton, s/o Daniel E. Dame and Minnie E. Smith; W - 17, mill hand, b. Acton, ME, d/o John A. Wentworth and Anna A. Laskey
- Harry O. m. Celia C. Dansereau 12/26/1932 in Rochester
- Howard Emerson of Union m. Virginia A. Littlefield of Union 5/14/1938 in Newfields; H - 22, shoe worker; W - 25, at home
- Howard P. of Union m. Elinore F. Kraus of Milton Mills 8/13/1960; H - 17, shoe worker; W - 18, shoe worker

DAMON,
James R. of Milton m. Kathie E. Nason of Wakefield 9/22/1972

DANFORTH,
Bruce E., Jr. of Sanbornville m. Shelley L. Vatcher of Sanbornville 5/19/1990 in Newmarket

DANIELL,
John J. of Wakefield m. Jane E. Mee of W. Newfield, ME 6/27/1986 in Ossipee

DANSEREAU,
Donald O., Jr. of Wakefield m. Lucille A. Danforth of So. Lebanon, ME 6/28/1986 in Rochester

DARLING,
Charles D. of Newburyport, MA m. Lillian E. Nichols of Wakefield 9/20/1919; H - 26, woodworker, b. Tamworth, s/o Henry M. Darling (NB, laborer) and Nellie J. Dow (Tamworth); W - 18, b. Hillsboro, d/o Frank Nichols (Montpelier, VT, stage driver) and Delma St. John (MI)

DAVENPORT,
James D. of Wakefield m. Louise Carter Eatock of Wolfeboro 6/14/1945 in Sanbornville; H - 22, US Army; W - 22, secretary

DAVIDSON,
Daniel S. of Rochester m. Kim Louise McVicar of Wakefield 5/19/1979 in Rochester; H - 20; W - 20
John E., Jr. of Sanbornville m. Robin M. **Brown** of Sanbornville 5/10/1996
John Edward, Jr. of Sanbornville m. Priscilla A. **Grenier** of Sanbornville 10/6/1990 in East Wakefield
William H. of Wakefield m. Vickie S. **Parkhurst** of Allenstown 8/3/1986 in Wolfeboro

DAVIS,
Ansel S. of No. Waterboro, ME m. Maud E. **Littlefield** of No. Waterboro, ME 9/14/1898; H - 21, farmer, b. Somersworth, s/o Samuel Davis of Somersworth (No. Waterboro, ME, 64, overseer) and Melisa ----- (No. Waterboro, ME, 60, housewife); W - 20, teacher, b. Shapleigh, ME, d/o Hallsy Littlefield of No. Waterboro, ME (No. Waterboro, ME, 50, farmer) and Belle Bradeen (No. Waterboro, ME, 45, housekeeper)
Charles E. of Merrimac, MA m. Barbara A. **Greeley** of Merrimac, MA 8/19/1947 in Sanbornville; H - 20, shoeworker; W - 18, at home
Charles M. of Wakefield m. Julia **Williams** of Wakefield 10/12/1888; H - 31, laborer, b. Jackson, s/o Jonathan J. Davis (Northwood, farmer) and Emily S. Brooks (Portland, ME, housework); W - 29, housework, b. Effingham, d/o James Williams (Effingham)
Clayton A. of Wakefield m. Katherine L. **Maleham** of Wakefield 11/21/1935 in Milton Mills; H - 21, farmer; W - 20, at home
Daniel N. m. Helen R. **Colby** 7/1/1933 in Lebanon, ME
Daniel R. of Milton m. Jacqueline A. **Keating** of Wakefield 7/1/1972
Ernest W. of West Newfield, ME m. Lillian A. **Merrow** of Newfield, ME 6/16/1896; H - 21, blacksmith, b. Buxton, ME, s/o C. M. Davis of West Newfield, ME (West Newfield, ME, 45, carpenter) and Marata Libby (Buxton, ME, 46, housekeeper); W - 17, housework, b. Newfield, ME, d/o Melvin Merrow of Newfield, ME (West Newfield, ME, sleigh maker) and Hattie Davis (West Newfield, ME, housekeeper)
Forest E. m. Charlotte **Hoag** 8/24/1928; H - 31, s/o Fred Henry Davis (Jackson) and Bertha MacDonald (Wakefield); W - 22, d/o Albert B. Hoag (Sandwich) and Abbie Peasley (Sandwich)
Forrest E. of Wakefield m. Bertha **Brown** of Wakefield 6/12/1915; H - 19, laborer, b. Wakefield, s/o Fred H. Davis and Bertha H.

McDonald; W - 18, housework, b. Dover, d/o John Brown and Minnie Dupra

Frank E. of Newfield, ME m. Rose M. Comeau of Wakefield 11/24/1907; H - 23, farmer, b. Shapleigh, ME, s/o Charles E. Davis and Ella A. Barker; W - 18, housework, b. Haverhill, MA, d/o Albert Comeau and Mary -----

Fred H. of Wakefield m. Bertha McDonald of Wakefield 3/5/1893; H - 22, RR section, 2d, b. Jackson, s/o Jonathan J. Davis (England, farmer) and Emily S. Brooks (Portland, ME, housework); W - 22, housework, b. Wakefield, d/o Malcolm McDonald (PEI, RR section) and Amanda Crockett (Mechanic Falls, ME, housework)

Gary W. of Wakefield m. Joy A. Tosh of FL 7/9/1988

George E. of Wakefield m. Jessie Chapman of Middleton 10/14/1911 in Farmington; H - 25, laborer, 2d, b. Townsend, MA, s/o Charles Davis and Annie Flagg; W - 20, housework, b. Dover, d/o William Chapman and Amelia Battersby

George T. of Wakefield m. Edna A. Curtis of Wakefield 11/22/1907; H - 26, RR fireman, b. Ossipee, d/o Joseph M. Davis and Louisa M. Hobbs; W - 18, housework, b. Brookfield, d/o Joseph S. Curtis and Fannie E. Butler

George T.G. of Wakefield m. Fannie I. Reed of Newfield, ME 12/18/1892 in Ossipee; H - 19, farmer, b. Wakefield, s/o Mayhew C. Davis (Wakefield, blacksmith) and Lydia F. Abbott (Tuftonboro, housework); W - 15, housework, b. Newfield, ME, d/o Orrin L. Reed (Newfield, ME, farmer) and Alice ----- (Milton Mills, housework)

Harris of Wakefield m. Daisy Thompson of Ossipee 7/2/1898 in Ossipee; H - 20, teamster, b. Wakefield, s/o Mayhew C. Davis (Wakefield, deceased, blacksmith) and Lydia F. Abbott of Wakefield (Tuftonboro, 60, housework); W - 18, housework, b. Ossipee, d/o T. Thompson of Ossipee (Pittsfield, 61, farmer) and Fannie H. Tibbetts (Madison, 51, housework)

Henry of Wakefield m. Pearl A. Hill of Wakefield 10/26/1898 in Dover; H - 24, RR fireman, b. Boston, MA; W - 19, housekeeper, b. Parsonsfield, ME, d/o Leonard Hill of Wakefield (Parsonsfield, ME, 43, farmer) and Ambie G. Varney (Lebanon, ME, 37, housewife)

Joseph W. of Sanbornville m. Joyce R. Taylor of Sanbornville 3/9/1996 in Eaton

Justin E. of Wakefield m. H. Imogene Lang of Brookfield 3/31/1889; H - 20, farmer, b. Wakefield, s/o Mayhew C. Davis (Wakefield, farmer) and Lydia F. Abbott (Ossipee, housework); W - 18, housekeeper, b. Brookfield, d/o Andrew J. Lang (Brookfield, farmer) and Mehitible Sanborn (Wakefield)

Michael John of Kitty Hawk, NC m. Mary L. Fouty of Kitty Hawk, NC 8/5/1998

Ray G. of Newfield, ME m. Lena M. Ham of Newfield, ME 4/6/1914 in Dover; H - 26, farmer, b. Newfield, ME, s/o George W. Davis and Florence G. Goodwyne; W - 28, housekeeper, b. Newfield, ME, d/o Everett E. Ham and Cora B. Coffin

DAVY,

Albert Francis of Sanbornville m. Cynthia Lee Goodwin of Sanbornville 4/14/1978 in Portsmouth; H - 39; W - 32

Norman C. m. Jennie V. Pivoyar 11/24/1932 in Sanbornville

DAY,

Charles Everett, Jr. of Dover m. Goldie Estelle Morrill of Wakefield 1/30/1949 in Concord; H - 20, lumberman; W - 18, at home

DEACON,

Raymond J. of Riverdale, NY m. Margaret M. Wilkinson of Riverdale, NY 8/29/1992

DEARBORN,

Frederick A. of Sanbornville m. Deborah Jo Cole of Sanbornville 8/31/1996

DEBOW,

Ronald D. of Sanbornville m. Tina M. Phillips of Gilmanton I.W. 6/5/1982 in Gilmanton I.W.

Ronald David of Sanbornville m. Paula Sue Helgerson of Woburn, MA 4/28/1997 in Alton Bay

Scott L. of Wakefield m. Patricia L. Phillips of Rochester 11/8/1980 in Gilmanton I.W.

DECOSTE,

Kenneth E. of Chelsea, MA m. Marlene T. Travis of Chelsea, MA 12/28/1984 in East Wakefield

DEFOREST,

Raymond D. of Wakefield m. Lucinda E. Joy of Wakefield 10/23/1982

DEGNON,
Thomas P. of Waynesville, PA m. Jean A. MacCormack of Wakefield 6/24/1972 in East Wakefield

DELAN,
Alfred R. of Wakefield m. Dora White of Wakefield 1/17/1907; H - 26, shoe cutter, b. Boston, MA, s/o Richie Delan and Blanche Quimby; W - 27, housekeepeer, 2d, b. Wakefield, d/o Horatio B. Fellows and Belle F. Tibbetts

Alfred R. of Sanbornville m. Maude L. Doe of Union 7/20/1948; H - 67, ret. RR employee; W - 55, ret. teacher

DELANO,
John P. of Waban, MA m. Lydia L. Frederick of Newtonville, MA 6/22/1946; H - 34, radar prod.; W - 27, publicity work

DELINTSIOTIS,
Vasilos of Sanbornville m. Barbara Karmiris 10/14/1998 in Sanbornville

DELOLLIS,
Joseph Blase of Quincy, MA m. Barbara King of Union 8/10/1962 in Sanbornville; H - 21, mover; W - 19, at home

DEMOTT,
Brian of Sanbornville m. Tami Lyn Kelley of Sanbornville 3/22/1991 in Sanbornville

DENNISON,
Thomas Y. of Rochester m. Lisa M. Stone of Wakefield 6/21/1987 in Rochester

DENNY,
Michael George Stewart of Toronto, Canada m. Judith Katherine Guttadauro of Sanbornville 6/20/1964 in Sanbornville; H - 22, student; W - 22, personnel

DENONCOURT,
Steven R. of Sanbornville m. Darcie Ann Nason of Sanbornville 5/11/1996

DESHARNAIS,
A. of Wakefield m. Amanda Ouellet of Somersworth 6/29/1896 in Somersworth; H - 25, laborer, b. Canada, s/o Louis Desharnais of Canada (Canada, farmer) and Selina Houde (Canada, housekeeper); W - 19, mill operative, b. Canada

DESJARDINS,
David Paul of Sanford, ME m. Ruth Elizabeth Grumann of Sanford, ME 3/25/1995 in Sanbornville

DESMOND,
Gerald Arthur of Peabody, MA m. Rita Marie Pelletier 1/2/1950; H - 24, leather worker; W - 23, at home

DESPARD,
Andrew G. of Sanbornville m. Candice G. Stuart of Rochester 4/3/1993 in Rochester

DESPER,
Donald Edward of Franklin, MA m. Evelyn Ernestine Merrill of Franklin, MA 1/10/1959 in Sanbornville; H - 28, laborer; W - 18, at home

DESROCHERS,
Joseph of Wakefield m. Mary Marcoux of Wakefield 8/28/1900 in Sanbornville; H - 27, laborer, b. Canada, s/o Joseph Desrochers (Canada, farmer) and S. Desrochers (Canada, housewife); W - 18, housework, b. Wakefield, d/o Oliver Marcoux (Canada, laborer) and P. Marshall (Canada, housewife)

DEYAK,
Michael m. Norma Libby 10/27/1929; H - 29, s/o Albert Leyak (sic) (VA); W - 17, d/o Norman Libby (Tuftonboro) and Kathryn Creighton (Peterboro)

DEZAN,
Douglas F., Jr. of Wakefield m. Lisa A. Boyd of Wakefield 7/2/1988
Douglas F., Sr. of Wakefield m. Sharon E. Sullivan of Wakefield 8/9/1986

DICKSON,
William A. of Wakefield m. Gail M. Frost of Wakefield 4/3/1987 in Rochester

DILLINGHAM,
Charles F. of Wakefield m. Alice J. Rand of PEI 10/21/1913 in Groveton; H - 54, RR conductor, 2d, b. Biddeford, ME, s/o L. C. Dillingham and Sarah E. Gilpatrick; W - 52, nurse, 2d, b. PEI, d/o James Robinson and Elizabeth J. Colbath

DION,
Albert J. of Sanbornville m. Barbara M. Krohn of Sanbornville 12/8/1973
Albert John of Wakefield m. Barbara Marie Dion of Wakefield 3/5/1977

DIPRIZIO,
Charles C. m. Earleen S. Dodier 9/24/1966 in Sanbornville; H - 19, mechanic; W - 19, sales clerk

DISTEFANO,
Salvatore of Boston, MA m. Angela Santa Sciucco of Boston, MA 4/18/1964 in Sanbornville; H - 21, auto mec.; W - 18, typist

DIXON,
Eugene F. of Wakefield m. Viola Andrews of Center Ossipee 3/10/1937 in Pembroke; H - 52, salesman; W - 57, at home
George R. of Union m. Annie M. Wiggins of Fort Fairfield, ME 11/4/1960 in Sanbornville; H - 70, retired; W - 66, retired

DODDRELL,
Jeffrey Vincent of Wakefield m. Cheryl Lynn Foss of Milton Mills 10/8/1988 in Milton

DODGE,
Louis A. of Wenham, MA m. Jennie May Moore of Union 10/28/1923 in Union; H - 36, farmer, 2d, b. Wenham, MA, s/o William P. Dodge and Hannah A. Cole; W - 41, nurse, b. Middleton, d/o James D. Moore and Mary F. Kelley

DODIER,
Bryan L. of Sanbornville m. Gloria J. Beckwith of Sanbornville 9/11/1996 in Sanbornville
Bryan Lee of Wakefield m. Gloria Jean Beckwith of Wakefield 9/11/1976 in Sanbornville
Donald R. of Sanbornville m. Ruth E. Valley of Milton Mills 1/14/1948 in Milton Mills; H - 20, woolen mill emp.; W - 18, at home
Donald Raymond of Sanbornville m. Bertha Ann Whittemore of Sanbornville 11/1/1963 in Rochester; H - 36, self emp.; W - 28, at home
Earl S. of Sanbornville m. Mary E. Harrigan of Somerville, MA 4/24/1946 in Berwick, ME; H - 22, truck driver; W - 21, at home
Edward of Sanbornville m. May Brocher of Biddeford, ME 9/1/1924 in Sanbornville; H - 24, cook, b. Sanbornville, s/o Joseph Dodier and Edith Perron; W - 25, spinning, b. St. Juliette Rofton, d/o Theodule Brocher and Camile Belanger
Larry C. of Wakefield m. Tammi J. Moody of Wakefield 4/18/1984
Leslie of Wakefield m. Kathleen G. Cunniff of North Easton, MA 2/17/1973 in Sanbornville
Ralph W. of Wakefield m. Barbara W. Miliner of Wakefield 5/25/1944 in Wolfeboro; H - 22, laborer; W - 18, at home
Raymond R. of Sanbornville m. Lorraine B. Worster of Union 7/12/1968 in Sanbornville
Roland Robert of Union m. April Kathleen Wilson of Union 9/19/1998 in Union
Stanley L. of Sanbornville m. Deborah A. Inman of Milton 8/17/1974 in Milton
Stanley L. of Wakefield m. Susan A. Hurlbutt of Wakefield 2/25/1984

DOE,
George Arthur of Wakefield m. Margaret Palmer Paul of Wakefield 8/23/1950; H - 67, farmer; W - 49, teacher
Robert T. of Wakefield m. Marian L. Hutchins of Sanbornville 10/3/1948 in Sanbornville; H - 21, auto mechanic; W - 18, waitress
Stephen E. of Wakefield m. Cindy L. Bacon of Wakefield 9/6/1986 in So. Wakefield
Walter E. of Center Ossipee m. Evelyn M. Wasson of Wakefield 5/5/1934 in Freedom; H - 23, laborer; W - 19, housework

DOEN,
Loram of Wakefield m. Ruth M. Chick of Wakefield 11/9/1914; H - 27, farmer, b. NS, s/o Nathan M. Doen and Annie A. Fuller; W - 20, housework, b. Wakefield, d/o George H. Chick and Jane Waldron

DONAHUE,
Patrick J., Jr. of Sanbornville m. Cheryl S. Rolfe of Nashua 11/3/1973 in Nashua

DONATI,
Edward Louis of Needham, MA m. Catherine Florence Martin of Walpole, MA 9/5/1964; H - 63, const. engr.; W - 47, nurse

DONEGAN,
Bruce W. of Breckenridge, CO m. Nancy C. Tucker of Breckenridge, CO 8/11/1979; H - 28; W - 28

DORING,
Stanley M. of Quincy, MA m. Stella M. McKinnon of Acton, ME 8/30/1947 in New Durham; H - 53, steamfitter; W - 46, dressmaker

DOUGHERTY,
Timothy C. of Wakefield m. Sandra J. Dodge of Wakefield 5/12/1984

DOUGLAS,
Richard Erwin of Wakefield m. Dona Miliner of Wakefield 12/28/1941 in Wolfeboro; H - 21, RR emp.; W - 20, housework

DOUGLASS,
Daniel H. of Wakefield m. Mary A. Pitton of Wakefield 10/7/1904; H - 70, farmer, 2d, b. Bridgton, ME, s/o Daniel Douglass and Mary Ann Sawyer; W - 54, housework, 2d, b. Boston, MA, d/o Willard F. Sisson and Elizabeth Jane

Frank of Wakefield m. Jennie M. Harmon of Wakefield 9/12/1905; H - 21, laborer, b. Albany, s/o Charles Douglass and Matilda Douglass; W - 15, housework, d/o John Harmon and Sarah Eaton

Richard E. of Sanbornville m. Geraldine M. Littlefield of Union 6/22/1969

DOW,
Curtis M. of Ossipee m. Deborah L. Garland of Wakefield 11/13/1981

DOWNS,
Arthur E. of Sanford, ME m. Althea J. Downs of Wells, ME 10/12/1983

Fred W. of Union m. Virginia A. Stevens of Middleton 11/3/1948 in Milton; H - 22, mill emp.; W - 18, waitress

Harry A. of Wakefield m. Agnes Sawyer of Limington, ME 10/10/1902; H - 20, farmer, b. Wakefield, s/o Thomas J. Downs and Cora L. Hamilton; W - 19, housework, 2d, b. Limington, ME, d/o Osgrove Sawyer and ----- Butler

J. Frank of Wakefield m. Mary J. Swan of Boston, MA 9/11/1893; H - 34, farmer, b. Milton, s/o John R. Downs (Rochester, farmer) and Mary Shorey (Rochester, housework); W - 32, cook, b. Boston, MA, d/o John Swan (Boston, MA) and Mary Nuna (Boston, MA)

James M. of Wakefield m. Theresa C. Soucy of Brookfield 3/3/1979; H - 23; W - 19

Jeffrey M. of Wakefield m. Deborah A. Vachon of Milton 7/23/1978: H - 21; W - 21

Jeffrey M. of Wakefield m. Janette H. Smith of Wakefield 4/8/1983

Winfred E. of Wakefield m. Floy L. Everingham of Warren, ME 8/16/1916 in Wolfeboro; H - 28, laborer, b. Wolfeboro, s/o Thomas J. Downs and Cora L. Hamilton; W - 23, nurse, b. Somerset, MA, d/o Rev. J. E. Everingham and Florence M. Coleman

Winfred E. of Wakefield m. Carrie Wentworth of Wakefield 7/16/1919 in Union; H - 31, laborer, 2d, b. Wolfeboro, s/o Thomas J. Downs (Milton, farmer) and Cora L. Hamilton (Fryeburg, ME); W - 36, 2d, b. Acton, ME, d/o Fred S. Wentworth (Acton, ME, carpenter) and Mary Barker (New Vineyard, ME)

DOYLE,
Fred of Wakefield m. Emma M. Pippin of Wakefield 5/15/1907 in Rochester; H - 21, mill operative, b. Wakefield, s/o John Doyle and Amanda E. Wentworth; W - 21, mill operative, b. Wakefield, d/o Victor Pippin and Susan Thibedeau

George H. of Wakefield m. Hannah Brown of Rochester 1/29/1911 in Rochester; H - 32, counter moulder, b. Wakefield, s/o John Doyle and Amanda Wentworth; W - 25, machine operator, b. Eastport, ME, d/o William Brown and Mary McCutcheon

DRAGO,
Paul Joseph of Wakefield m. Ann Marie Dupre of Wakefield 6/7/1997 in Kingston

DRAPEAU,
Edward m. Dorothy Sibley 10/7/1933 in Wolfeboro
Euclide of Wakefield m. Grace E. Libbey of Springvale, ME 6/27/1921; H - 19, mechanic, b. Wakefield, s/o Eusebe Drapeau (Canada, carpenter) and Aurelie Currier (Canada); W - 18, shoe shop, b. W. Newfield, ME, d/o John Libby (Woodman, blacksmith) and Cora Glidden (Effingham)
Frank m. Guineve Demarest 10/19/1931; H - 76, s/o Noel Drapeau (Canada) and Mary Oeur (Canada); W - 75, d/o M. Demarest (Canada) and Mary Burton (Canada)
George of Wakefield m. Lucie Houde of Wakefield 4/12/1909; H - 19, laborer, b. Wakefield, s/o Eusebe Drapeau and Aurelie Carrier; W - 25, clerk, b. Wakefield, d/o Edward Houde and Adele Pouliot
Paul D. of Sanbornville m. Thalia R. Clark of Sanbornville 1/18/1970
Victor L. of Sanbornville m. Anita T. Blanchette of Berlin 6/15/1948 in Berlin; H - 29, cook; W - 21, at home
Victor Lawrence of Wakefield m. Shirley Inez Thompson of Rochester 12/28/1942 in Rochester; H - 23, US Army; W - 19, shoe shop emp.

DREGER,
Gary Rhinehart of Milford, MA m. Barbara Frances McIntire of Milford, MA 12/20/1975

DRENA,
Mark D. of East Wakefield m. Deborah A. Green of East Wakefield 12/25/1983

DREW,
Charles A. of Wakefield m. Iva M. Reed of Wakefield 1/8/1911 in Brookfield; H - 24, laborer, b. Wakefield, s/o James A. Drew and Clara A. Glidden; W - 15, domestic, b. Wakefield, d/o Edward S. Reed and Inez M. Dicey
Charles A. of Wakefield m. Iva May Reed of Wakefield 3/4/1918 in Rochester; H - 30, mill operative, 2d, b. Wakefield, s/o James A. Drew and Clara Glidden; W - 20, housework, 2d, b. Wakefield, d/o Edwin A. Reed and Inez Dicey

Charles A. of Wakefield m. Ruth E. **Elliott** of Wakefield 12/27/1920 in Dover; H - 34, millwright, 3d, b. Wakefield, s/o James A. Drew (Brookfield, laborer) and Clara Glidden (Brookfield); W - 18, housekeeper, b. Farmington, d/o Frank Elliott (Stoneham, MA, lumbering) and Minnie Gratton (Manchester)

Clarence of Brookfield m. Cora **Remick** of Wakefield 11/23/1908; H - 22, laborer, b. Wakefield, s/o John W. Drew and Addie Tibedeau; W - 27, housework, 2d, b. Conway, d/o Harding L. Nason and Lucinda Thorn

Donald Kenneth of Sanbornville m. Viola Belle **Sprague** of Acton, ME 3/9/1940 in Acton, ME; H - 22, laborer; W - 15, at home

Enoch F. m. Florence E. **Rich** 3/19/1932 in Sanbornville

Enoch F. of Sanbornville m. Lillian **Wentworth** 4/9/1938 in West Newfield, ME; H - 31, laborer; W - 19, restaurant emp.

Frank E. m. Bessie E. **Morrison** 3/29/1925; H - 40, b. Ossipee, s/o Frank Drew and Sarah J. Eldridge; W - 23, b. Stowe, ME, d/o Fred A. Morrison and Millie M. Drew

George W. of Wakefield m. Malie E. **Stevens** of Middleton 1/1/1890 in Farmington; H - 29, carpenter, b. Exeter, s/o George W. Drew (Acton, ME, carpenter) and Lydia W. Archibald (Acton, ME, housekeeper); W - 22, housekeeper, 2d, b. Middleton, d/o Thomas Stevens (farmer) and Mary Whitehouse (housekeeper)

Leon R. of Sanbornville m. Martha **Grosmith** of Contoocook 7/10/1935 in Sanbornville; H - 27, sailor; W - 21, at home

Robert Franklin of Sanbornville m. Catherine Hagar **Aguere** of No. Conway 10/31/1965 in No. Conway; H - 29, US Navy; W - 19, tel. opr.

DRINKWATER,

Arthur C. of Dover, MA m. Anna L. **Barend** of Needham, MA 7/8/1961 in Sanbornville; H - 22, mechanic; W - 19, factory worker

DROWN,

Carroll E. of Wakefield m. Georgianna M. **Roy** of Somersworth 6/21/1917; H - 20, laborer, b. Farmington, s/o Stephen D. Drowns and Carrie C. Peavey; W - 17, housework, b. Wakefield, d/o Joseph C. Roy and Harriette E. Blouin

Edgar I. of Wakefield m. Edith I. **Newcomb** of Wakefield 5/18/1916; H - 23, teamster, b. Ossipee, s/o Stephen D. Drown and Carrie L.

Peavey; W - 19, housework, b. Westerly, RI, d/o Nathan C. Newcomb and Ellen C. Bean
Leon H. m. Myra F. Rourke 4/6/1931; H - 31, s/o Stephen D. Drown (Eaton) and Carrie C. Peavey (Farmington); W - 31, d/o George A. Rourke (Noyan, PQ) and Erie E. Nichols (Bedford)
Paul Arnold of Wakefield m. Wava Patricia Walsh of Wakefield 11/20/1955; H - 20, laborer; W - 20, clerk

DRUGG,
Charles J., Jr. of Winchester m. Mary Elizabeth Garvin of Wakefield 6/19/1949 in Sanbornville; H - 27, mill manager; W - 24, secretary

DUCHANO,
Norman Peter of Acton, ME m. Barbara Joan Laskey of Sanbornville 7/4/1962 in Sanbornville; H - 20, carpenter; W - 18, at home
Omer A. of Sanbornville m. Marjorie W. Williams of Sanbornville 8/10/1946 in Sanbornville; H - 27, laborer; W - 19, housework
Omer J.A. of Sanbornville m. Muriel Thermas Wiggin of Ossipee 10/16/1938 in Sanbornville; H - 19, laborer; W - 17, at home
Robert J. of Sanbornville m. Gloria M. Paolucci of Wolfeboro 8/11/1951 in Wolfeboro; H - 20, car salesman; W - 21, bookkeeper

DUDLEY,
Kenneth A. of Union m. Lisa M. Glennon of Sanbornville 2/13/1982
Richard L. of Union m. Constance M. Turgeon of Somersworth 9/13/1970 in Somersworth
Winburn T. m. Pauline Moulton 10/10/1925; H - 25, b. W. Newbury, MA, s/o Fred W. Dudley and Harriet Tole; W - 18, b. Centre Sandwich, d/o Arthur P. Moulton and Maud B. Shabott

DUFF,
Warren G. of Brockton, MA m. Nancy A. Tavares of Fall River, MA 11/22/1969

DUFFY,
Mark Peter of Sanbornville m. Linda Marie Brown of Sanbornville 8/10/1991 in Rochester

DUGAS,
Jeffrey A. of Wakefield m. Pamie L. Hill of Wakefield 5/23/1987

DUHY,
Walter R. m. Lena May Storey 12/27/1930; H - 32, s/o Clarence P. Duhy (Balsbury, NB) and Lillian E. ----- (Dorchester); W - 25, d/o William J. Storey (Wakefield) and Josie B. Glidden (Wakefield)

DUKE,
Fred E. of Wakefield m. Lena B. Carpenter of Manchester 7/13/1921; H - 37, teamster, b. Livermore Falls, ME, s/o Marshall Duke (Canada, mill hand) and Matilda Duke; W - 24, mill worker, b. Manchester, d/o Joe Carpenter (Canada, mill hand)

DUMAS,
Phillip H. of Salem m. Mary A. Smith of Wakefield 1/7/1972

DUNCKLEE,
Charles F. of Nashua m. Mary Theresa Soucy of Sanbornville 8/20/1955 in Sanbornville; H - 24, public serv.; W - 23, reg. nurse

DURGAN,
Frank J. of Wakefield m. Brenda J. Cust of Wakefield 8/29/1980

DURGIN,
Willard Perrin of Danvers, MA m. Barbara Ellen Harris of Danvers, MA 10/11/1958 in Sanbornville; H - 40, clerk; W - 34, clerk

DUVAL,
Kevin Daniel of Wakefield m. Ingrid Erica Lindberg of Wakefield 9/7/1996 in New Durham

DWYER,
Gerald Paul of East Wakefield m. Candace Marie Morrill of East Wakefield 7/19/1997 in Milton
Jeremiah P. of Lynn, MA m. Ann Dyer of Lynn, MA 7/13/1985

EASTMAN,
David Gale of Somersworth m. Esther Stevens Drew of Union 6/12/1954 in Union; H - 33, physician; W - 31, therapist
Harry H., Jr. of Union m. Karen E. Karcher of Sanbornville 6/18/1966 in Sanbornville; H - 20, mason; W - 19, student

Harry Hanson of Middleton m. Evelyn May Holman of Wakefield 12/29/1945 in Farmington; H - 30, truck driver; W - 18, store clerk

Lloyd R. of Middleton m. Lucille I. Beamis of Union 12/23/1944 in Sanford, ME; H - 28, saw mill worker; W - 16, at home

Raymond A. of North Conway m. Marion E. Haskell of Wakefield 11/25/1936 in Sanbornville; H - 31, hoisting engineer; W - 24, at home

EATON,

David E. of Wakefield m. Wendy L. Davis of Wakefield 6/18/1983 in Wolfeboro

Gilbert D., Jr. of Effingham m. June Elizabeth Scott of Wakefield 12/1/1945 in Sanbornville; H - 26, clerk; W - 24, reg. nurse

Lawrence Pray of Sanford, ME m. Helen Sylvia Hill of Union 7/13/1938; H - 28, mill worker; W - 21, at home

EBARE,

Clint R. of Wakefield m. Glorence I. Moody of Wakefield 10/22/1988 in Somersworth

ECKERT,

Glenn M., Jr. of Ayr, ND m. Lorraine E. Nason of Union 10/28/1967; H - 23, US Navy; W - 34, mill emp.

EDWARDS,

Carroll Richard of Wakefield m. Barbara Ann Sanborn of Wakefield 7/2/1977

Joseph H. of Wakefield m. Lillian S. Rogers of Wakefield 8/2/1910; H - 37, school teacher, b. Boston, MA, s/o Joseph H. Edwards and Sarah Bassett; W - 47, farmer, 2d, b. Wakefield, d/o John W. Sanborn and Almira J. Chapman

ELDRIDGE,

Ernest F. of Ossipee m. Elva I. Nason of Wakefield 4/21/1908 in Acton, ME; H - 21, teamster, b. Ossipee, s/o Frank J. Eldridge and Abbie J. Hodsdon; W - 20, housework, b. Wakefield, d/o Harding L. Nason and Lucinda Thorn

ELLIOTT,
Charles of Wakefield m. Sarah Whitten of Wakefield 9/6/1914 in Brookfield; H - 50, millman, 2d, b. Wolfeboro, s/o George W. Elliott and Belinda W. Bryer; W - 42, housework, b. Wolfeboro, d/o Martin V. Whitten and Mary J. Boston

Henry Almon, Jr. of Wolfeboro m. Donna Bell Drew of Sanbornville 1/16/1959 in Rochester; H - 20, logging; W - 17, at home

Mark Alan of Wakefield m. Laura J. Nason of Wakefield 12/12/1987 in Milton Mills

ELLIS,
Henry P. of Wakefield m. Bertha E. Tibbetts of Wakefield 1/1/1903; H - 19, farmer, b. Gilmanton, s/o Horace D. Ellis and Ella A. Page; W - 17, housework, b. Wakefield, d/o Thomas B. Tibbetts and Etta Hamilton

Henry P. of Wakefield m. Leila I. Herrick of Newfield, ME 8/9/1918; H - 35, laborer, 2d, b. Gilmanton, s/o Horace D. Ellis and Ella A. Page; W - 35, housework, 2d, b. Newfield, ME, d/o Albert Patch and Rose Patch

James R. of Milton m. Carleen E. Nicholson of Wakefield 8/7/1971 in Milton

EMERSON,
Alden C. of Portland, ME m. Phyllis L. Trott of Portland, ME 12/27/1936 in Sanbornville; H - 26, carpenter; W - 20, cashier

ESSIGMANN,
Harold E., Jr. of Woburn, MA m. Linda M. Fonseca of Burlington, MA 9/3/1983

EVANS,
Albert L. of Wakefield m. Mary A. Wadleigh of Wakefield 5/2/1888; H - 44, farmer, 2d, b. Wakefield, s/o Joseph G. Evans (Rochester) and Abigail D. Pickering (Rochester); W - 32, b. Wakefield, d/o Elijah Wadleigh (Hampton) and Charlotte Atkinson (Dover)

Albert L. of Wakefield m. Anna M. Swenson of Salem, MA 6/5/1900 in Boston, MA; H - farmer, 3d, b. Wakefield, s/o Joseph Evans (Rochester) and Abbie Pickering (Rochester); W - housework, b. Sweden, d/o Mons Swenson (Sweden, master builder) and Ingar Theula (Sweden, housewife)

Calvin J. of Wakefield m. Flora B. Rines of Milton 1/2/1899; H - 24, farmer, b. Wakefield, s/o John W. Evans of Wakefield (Wakefield, 58, farmer) and Melvina Farnham (Wakefield, 52, housewife); W - 24, housework, b. New Durham, d/o William T. Rines of Milton (New Durham, 53, farmer) and Ellen Boston (Lunenburg, VT, 61, housewife)

Clarence D. of Wakefield m. Gertrude L. Perry of Wakefield 12/23/1902; H - 24, farmer, b. Wakefield, s/o John W. Evans and Melvina Farnham; W - 25, housework, b. Topsfield, MA, d/o John Perry and Priscilla A. Crowdis

J. Garfield of Wakefield m. Grace E. Dorr of Milton 4/21/1908; H - 27, farmer, b. Wakefield, s/o John W. Evans and Malvina Farnham; W - 30, housework, b. Milton, d/o James F. Dorr and Sarah E. Maddox

Michael Travis of Slaidell, LA m. Donna Marie Trainor of East Wakefield 9/21/1991

Victor C. of Wakefield m. Mattie Weeks of Wakefield 5/21/1907 in Milton; H - 23, farmer, b. Wakefield, s/o John W. Evans and Melvina Farnham; W - 20, housework, b. Wakefield, d/o Brackett M. Weeks and Matilda Allen

EVELETH,

William A. of Wakefield m. Rebecca G. Sykie of Wakefield 4/4/1980 in Milton

FAGAN,

Mark W. of NY m. Patricia L. Wentworth of NY 7/30/1988 in Sanbornville

FALES,

William Henry m. Bessie G. Greuenler 9/9/1933 in Union

FANTASIA,

Daniel Joseph of Farmington m. Stacey Linda Muise of Sanbornville 10/6/1996 in Farmington

FARINA,

John E. of East Wakefield m. Jody L. Pillsbury of East Wakefield 8/12/1995 in Sanbornville

FARLEY,
Charles A. of Saugus, MA m. Florence E. Warnock of Wakefield, MA 8/23/1947; H - 37, inspector; W - 24, stenographer

FARNHAM,
Albert J. of Wakefield m. Lena M. Loud of Milton Mills 10/2/1901 in Milton Mills; H - 29, carpenter, b. Wakefield, s/o Edward B. Farnham (Wakefield, farmer) and Jennie H. Watts (So. Durham, Canada, housekeeper); W - 22, shoe stitcher, b. Acton, ME, d/o Clinton S. Loud (Acton, ME, shoe mfgr.) and Cora M. Ricker (Dover, housekeeper)

Arthur E. of Acton, ME m. Martha F. Horn of Acton, ME 5/21/1904; H - 25, farmer, 2d, b. Acton, ME, s/o Joseph Farnham and Sarah H. Snow; W - 23, housework, b. Wakefield, d/o Samuel C. Horn and Augusta A. Horn

John F. of Wakefield m. Emma R. Libbey of Chelsea, MA 4/18/1888 in Chelsea, MA; H - 57, farmer, 2d, b. Wakefield, s/o John Farnham (Acton, ME) and Betsy Berry (Milton); W - 43, housework, 2d, b. Wakefield, d/o ----- Ells and ----- Coleman

John H. of Wakefield m. Edith N. Dunnells of Newfield, ME 9/19/1898 in Rochester; H - 23, RR fireman, b. Wakefield, s/o John F. Farnham of Wakefield (Wakefield, 66, farmer) and Mary F. Nason (Alfred, ME, deceased); W - 29, housekeeper, b. Newfield, ME, d/o Morrill Dunnells of Newfield, ME (Newfield, ME, farmer) and Julia A. Giles (Newfield, ME, deceased)

Norris Elton of Sanbornville m. June Gertrude Rogers of Rochester 6/17/1950 in Rochester; H - 43, carpenter; W - 27, at home

William A. of Wakefield m. Annie A. Patch of Newfield, ME 3/9/1898; H - 31, laborer, b. Boston, MA, s/o John F. Farnham of Wakefield (Wakefield, 66, farmer) and Mary F. Nason (Alfred, ME, deceased); W - 30, housekeeper, b. Newfield, ME, d/o David R. Patch (Shapleigh, ME, deceased) and Elizabeth McFillian of Newfield, ME (Philadelphia, PA, housekeeper)

FARR,
Ronald Arthur, Jr. of Westbrook, ME m. Jane Vendituoli of Westbrook, ME 10/3/1998 in Sanbornville

FARRELL,
John F., Jr. of Wakefield m. Kathleen R. Dee of Milton 5/9/1970 in Sanbornville

FELIPE,
F. Chagas of Quincy, MA m. Elizabeth Ann Gamache of Quincy, MA 9/9/1983

FELIX,
Kirk Edward of Sanbornville m. Sheila Jones Anthony of Sanbornville 11/23/1996 in Eaton

FEYLER,
Harlan Ernest of Wolfeboro m. Louise Mae Garland of Wakefield 1/10/1942 in Wolfeboro Falls; H - 17, tractor driver; W - 16, shoe worker

FIELDS,
Frank L. of Wakefield m. Sylvia M. Hooper of Wakefield 12/10/1912 in Rochester; H - 28, freight brakeman, b. Albany, s/o James Fields and Bessie Tibadeau; W - 22, waitress, 2d, b. Brookfield, d/o Warren E. Stevens and Etta Eaton

FIFIELD,
Charles H. of Wakefield m. Agnes E. Skinner of Somerville, MA 5/25/1903; H - 24, farmer, b. Conway, s/o Frank F. Fifield and Rosina Thurston; W - 29, operative, 2d, b. Boston, MA, d/o John C. Pelton and Mary A. Sisson
Charles R., Jr. of Union m. Judith L. Turbide of Dover 5/23/1967; H - 25, Davidson Rubber; W - 17, at home
Francis Henry of Wakefield m. Marjorie V. Woodes of Milton 11/3/1945 in Milton; H - 27, shoe worker; W - 23, shop worker
Frank F. of Wakefield m. Florence Douglass of Wakefield 6/23/1897; H - 22, farmer, b. Conway, s/o Francis H. Fifield (Conway, deceased, farmer) and Rose Thurston of Wakefield (Eaton, 42, housewife); W - 19, housekeeper, b. Albany, d/o William Douglass of Wakefield (Bridgton, ME, 41, farmer) and Alberta Douglass of Conway (Albany, housekeeper)
George R. of Wakefield m. Blanche E. Penney of Lebanon, ME 12/28/1912; H - 27, farmer, b. Conway, s/o Frank F. Fifield and

Rose A. Thurston; W - 20, housework, b. Portland, ME, d/o Charles A. Penney and Etta M. Burrows

George R., Jr. of Union m. Lavina Brewer of Middleton 9/14/1950; H - 25, laborer; W - 19, at home

Leslie H. of Wakefield m. Cynthia G. Thomas of Wakefield 4/25/1981

FISCHER,

Joseph Carl of Skowhegan, ME m. Ruth Evelyn Fischer of Newfield, ME 8/26/1949; H - 40, cook; W - 38, millworker

FISHER,

Harold Percy, Jr. of Wakefield m. Judith Ann Gould of Wakefield 11/8/1975

John F. of Wakefield m. Mary L. Welch of Porter, ME 10/26/1974 in Cornish, ME

Robert Francis of Waltham, MA m. Dorothy Olioeann Chase of Waltham, MA 4/6/1957 in Sanbornville (but see Lawrence Amos Swinerton); H - 31, inspector; W - 38, tel. opr.

FITZ,

Harold A. of Wakefield m. Inez E. Campbell of Wakefield 6/28/1911; H - 24, locomotive fireman, b. Corinth, ME, s/o Amos G. Fitz and Lizzie M. Fitz; W - 18, housework, b. Milton, d/o Ernest C. Campbell and May E. Perkins

Mark S. of Wakefield m. Augusta S. Rines of Wakefield 7/16/1890; H - 26, engineer, b. Salisbury, MA, s/o Jacob B. Fitz and Harriette N. Gale (Salisbury, MA); W - 22, seamstress, b. Wakefield, d/o C. Wesley Rines (Middleton, engineer) and Mary A. Roberts (Wakefield, housekeeper)

FLANDERS,

John Walter of Saugus, MA m. Dorothy Joan Littlefield of Saugus, MA 6/30/1956 in Sanbornville; H - 29, truck driver; W - 21, office clerk

FLEMING,

Frederick Joseph of Lynn, MA m. Edith Geraldine O'Keefe of Lynn, MA 7/24/1953; H - 37, setup work; W - 33, at home

FLETCHER,
Richard I. of Sanbornville m. Diane R. Dodier of Sanbornville 6/14/1969

FLYNN,
Stanley A. of Sanbornville m. Reta E. Garland of Sanbornville 1/5/1946 in Wolfeboro; H - 27, elec. lineman; W - 20, at home

FOGELIN,
Richard A. of Wakefield m. Margaret J. Truax of Wakefield 8/3/1985

FOGG,
Austin of Wolfeboro m. Ellen Whittier of Sanbornville 1/3/1922 in Sanbornville; H - 26, mill man, 2d, b. Ossipee, s/o Daniel Fogg and Julia M. Collins; W - 22, housework, 2d, b. Brookfield, d/o Arthur Sceggel and Emma Wentworth
Israel H. of Springvale, ME m. Mercy J. Cloutman of Wakefield 5/8/1892; H - 72, carpenter, 3d, b. Limington, ME, s/o Lemuel Fogg (Scarboro, ME, dead) and Rebecca Powers (Sanford, ME, dead); W - 59, housework, 3d, b. Sanford, ME, d/o Royal Morrison (Sanford, ME, dead) and Abigail Crawford (Wells, ME, dead)
Kenneth R., II of Sanbornville m. Michelle D. Mooney of Sanbornville 2/23/1991 in Union
Kenneth R., II of Union m. Dolores V. Inglese of Union 8/17/1996 in Wolfeboro
Kenneth Robert of East Wolfeboro m. Sandra Ann Nason of Sanbornville 8/4/1962 in Sanbornville; H - 19, marine; W - 18, at home
Nathan R. of Wakefield m. Deborah A. Otto of Manchester 4/25/1987
Relf G. of Wakefield m. Annette R. Propp of Wakefield 12/10/1983

FOLEY,
Kevin M. of Sanbornville m. Deborah A. Grenlaw of Sanbornville 7/28/1984 in Union

FOLLMER,
Samuel Freas of Benton, PA m. Margaret Helen Holman of Union 1/5/1962 in Union; H - 20, USAF; W - 22, hair dresser

FORBES,
Thomas M. of Sanbornville m. Holly A. Leighton of Sanbornville 5/23/1992 in Laconia

FORD,
Paul R. of Wakefield m. Kelly J. Bickford of East Wakefield 7/2/1983

FORDER,
John Robert of Middleton m. Shirley Dixon of Union 9/16/1950 in Sanbornville; H - 22, US Army; W - 23, office worker

FORTIER,
David Allen of East Wakefield m. Angela Dorothea Schettino of East Wakefield 6/28/1998 in Rochester

FOSKETT,
Paul E. of Lynn, MA m. Dorothy A. Rose of Peabody, MA 11/23/1974

FOSS,
Richard G. of Brookfield m. Tina M. Marston of Wakefield 12/9/1979; H - 22; W - 20

FOSTER,
Augustus m. Daisy Libby 4/14/1929; H - 61, s/o Peter Foster (Lawrence, MA) and Marie Paterson (England); W - 47, d/o Butler Hanson (Leeds, England) and Susan Hoskins (Colebrook)
Scott Edward of Rochester m. Coree Anne Wright of Sanbornville 5/26/1996 in Rochester

FOUST,
Charles of Seminole, FL m. Marguerite D. Nihan of Newburyport, MA 9/27/1979; H - 71; W - 60

FOX,
Arthur H. of Wakefield m. Isabelle Taft of Wakefield 6/7/1922 in Union; H - 25, bookkeeper, b. Acton, ME, s/o George E. Fox and Lizzie Hart; W - 20, at home, b. Wakefield, d/o Arthur L. Taft and Nellie Dunham
Harvey D. of Union m. Myra J. Furbish of Wakefield 2/23/1974 in Union
Harvey D. of Wakefield m. Elizabeth A. Dower of Wakefield 11/25/1981
Harvey Dunham of Union m. Elinor Flora Arlin of Rochester 6/19/1954 in Rochester; H - 20, manufacturer; W - 20, stenographer
Kerry M. of Union m. Annette L. Gagnon of Rochester 9/4/1984 in Rochester

Marshall Hart of Union m. Priscilla Pauline Drew of Union 7/16/1955; H - 25, air craft mech.; W - 22, nurse

William Joseph of Belmont, MA m. Vicky Van Vleet of Woburn, MA 3/27/1993

FRANCIS,

Felton G. of Wakefield m. Margaret Perna of Wakefield 7/29/1988 in Rochester

Glen A. of East Wakefield m. Robin B. Coran of East Wakefield 10/13/1990 in East Wakefield

FRANKLIN,

David J. of Wakefield m. Brenda L. Cameron of Middleton 8/6/1983

FRECHETTE,

Donald E. of Wakefield m. Cheryl L. Flint of Allston, MA 8/3/1985 in Dover

Robert Joseph of Dover m. Bernice D. Leighton of Union 8/21/1965 in Somersworth; H - 38, watchman; W - 29, nurse's aid

FREEMAN,

Everett K. of Wakefield m. Helen M. Fursden of Conway 6/5/1895 in Cornish, ME; H - 26, clerk, b. Kempt, NS, s/o Zenas W. Freeman of Kempt, NS (NS, 59, farmer) and Bessie C. Kempton (Kempt, NS, 51, housekeeper); W - 26, seamstress, b. Fredericton, NB, d/o Thomas Fursden (England, deceased) and Mary J. Blatchford of Conway (England, 50, housekeeper)

FRENCH,

Clyde Maurice of Manchester m. Norma Elizabeth Barnes of Berlin 11/9/1941 in Gorham; H - 34, salesman; W - 31, at home

Robert M. m. Elaine A. Robinson 8/13/1966 in Greenland; H - 23, store clerk; W - 24, bank teller

Wilford A. m. Harriet Allard 6/24/1928; H - 24, s/o Alden C. French (Middleton) and Lauratina Runnels (New Durham); W - 21, d/o Stephen Allard (Eaton) and Edith Stuart (Eaton)

FREY,

Louis Joseph of Sanbornville m. Carrie Frances Teter of Sanbornville 5/26/1953 in Sanbornville; H - 53, cabin prop.; W - 57, nurse

FRISBEE,
Jesse E. of Kittery, ME m. Selina Bennett of Southampton, England 9/8/1908; H - 70, hotel keeper, 2d, b. Kittery, ME, s/o Daniel Frisbee and Permelia Parker; W - 41, bookkeeper, b. Cornwall, England, d/o Charles H. Bennett and Mary E. Bennett

FRISCO,
George C. of Wakefield m. Bessie M. Davis of Wakefield 5/14/1918; H - 34, sta. engineer, b. Philadelphia, PA, s/o William Frisco and Jennie Ross; W - 31, at home, b. Strafford, d/o Wilbert S. Davis and Annie J. Montgomery

FROST,
Steven W. of Wakefield m. Elizabeth R. Goodfield of Wakefield 7/28/1979 in Rochester; H - 20; W - 19

FROTHINGHAM,
Scott Alan of East Wakefield m. Kathryn Ann Garland of East Wakefield 9/28/1997 in Eaton

FULLER,
Roy of East Wakefield m. Elsie Buchan Hamm of Beverly, MA 5/29/1965; H - 70, retired; W - 67, retired

GAGNE,
Harold P., Jr. of Acton, ME m. Frances May Weeman of Union 7/5/1950 in Milton; H - 18, woodsman; W - 17, at home

GAGNON,
Albert J. of Sanbornville m. Marie R. Buchette of Lynn, MA 4/29/1934 in Lynn, MA; H - 25, truck driver; W - 24, house work

Amedie of Wakefield m. Demerise Lamie of Wakefield 8/13/1907; H - 29, laborer, b. Canada, s/o George Gagnon and Delphine Aubuth; W - 19, mill operative, b. Wakefield, d/o Mose Lamie and Lea Currier

Arnart of Wakefield m. Georgia Legare of Wakefield 7/9/1889 in Rochester; H - 22, laborer, b. Canada, s/o George Gagnon (Canada, laborer) and Delphine ----- (Canada, housework); W - 17, housekeeper, b. Wakefield, d/o Joseph Legare (Canada, laborer) and Adaline ----- (Canada, housework)

Arthur of Wakefield m. Delline Patry of Wakefield 9/12/1892 in Rochester; H - 23, laborer, b. Canada, s/o George Gagneon (sic) (Canada, carpenter) and Delphine Obay (Canada, housework); W - 19, housework, b. Canada, d/o Filiase Patry (Canada, dead) and Marie Lachance (Canada, housework)

Arthur E. of Wakefield m. Grace Levertu of Wakefield 10/26/1920 in Sanbornville; H - 27, brakeman, b. Wakefield, s/o Ernest Gagnon (Canada, laborer) and Georgianna Legary (Wakefield); W - 21, housework, b. Wakefield, d/o Ludger Levertu (Canada, laborer) and Margaret Moore (Canada)

Ernest of Sanbornville m. Eda F. Miller of New Durham 8/8/1934 in Farmington; H - 29, laborer; W - 21, shoe worker

Oscar of Wakefield m. Eva Drew of Union 10/25/1924 in Milton Mills; H - 28, laborer, 2d, b. Wakefield, s/o Ernest Gagnon and Georgenia Legary; W - 28, domestic, 3d, b. Union, d/o Edwin Reed and Inez Dicey

Oscar Ernest of Wakefield m. Viola Downs Caverly of Wakefield 11/10/1939 in Wolfeboro; H - 42, mill employee; W - 32, housekeeper

Ronald Alfred of Wakefield m. Janet Arlene Lamper of Wolfeboro 10/10/1964; H - 29, USAF; W - 27, secretary

GALE,

Parkman D. of Wakefield m. Lucille M. Gray of Whitefield 4/18/1934 in Sanbornville; H - 25, chauffeur; W - 26, dietitian

GALLANT,

Arthur J. of Springvale, ME m. Irma K. Faber of Springvale, ME 6/28/1980

GALVIN,

James Michael of Everett, MA m. Teresa E. McDonald of Everett, MA 4/5/1952 in Sanbornville; H - 47, chauffeur; W - 46, tel. oper.

GARLAND,

Arthur A. of Wakefield m. Ophelia Allen of Bartlett 12/8/1907; H - 25, shoemaker, b. Wakefield, s/o Albert F. Garland and Malissa Drown; W - 17, clerk, b. Bartlett, d/o Archie Allen and Clistie Drown

Arthur A. of Wakefield m. May L. Drew of Tuftonboro 6/9/1920; H - 37, shoemaker, 2d, b. Wakefield, s/o Albert F. Garland (Ossipee, shoemaker) and Melissa J. Drown (Bartlett); W - 21, housework, b. Wolfeboro, d/o Charles H. Drew (painter) and Ida M. Waldron (Tuftonboro)

Arthur A. of Sanbornville m. Marion L. Davis of Sanbornville 8/12/1936 in Sanbornville; H - 53, shoe dealer; W - 31, housekeeper

Brian A. of Sanbornville m. Janice L. Golden of Sanbornville 3/14/1992 in Chocorua

Charles H. of Wakefield m. Sophie S. Drisko of Addison, ME 12/16/1888; H - 28, meat dealer, b. Tuftonboro, s/o John T. Garland (Ossipee, meat dealer) and Fannie N. Ricker (Dover, housework); W - 21, housework, b. Addison, ME, d/o Morrison F. Drisko (Addison, ME, carpenter) and Evelina A. Wass (Addison, ME)

Earl F. of Sanbornville m. Gloria I. McNally of Sanbornville 11/22/1947 in Sanbornville; H - 22, laborer; W - 20, at home

Forrest A. of Sanbornville m. Patricia A. Witham of Milton 12/24/1946 in Milton; H - 26, machinist; W - 23, mach. opr.

Forrest A. of Sanbornville m. Erika A. Guldbrandsen of Jamaica, NY 12/14/1960; H - 40, cabinet maker; W - 37, hairdresser

Forrest A. of Sanbornville m. Portia J. Nadeau of Somersworth 2/4/1967; H - 46, retired; W - 21, housework

Forrest Arthur of Wakefield m. Rita Elizabeth Bean of Wakefield 3/29/1942 in Sanbornville; H - 21, store clerk; W - 17, at home

Fred of Wakefield m. Hattie M. West of Wakefield 7/25/1897; H - 19, laborer, b. Brookfield, s/o John T. Garland of Brookfield (Ossipee, farmer) and Fannie N. Ricker of Wakefield (Greenland, housewife); W - 19, housekeeper, b. Brookfield, d/o Charles F. West of Wakefield (Brookfield, laborer) and Betsey J. Whitehouse (Tuftonboro, deceased)

Fred E. of Wakefield m. Verlie E. Tufts of Wakefield 8/10/1920 in Union; H - 19, laborer, b. Wakefield, s/o Fred Garland (Brookfield, laborer) and Hattie M. West (Brookfield); W - 16, housekeeper, b. Wakefield, d/o Frank Tufts (Somersworth, painter) and Fannie S. Thompson (Andover)

George F. of Wakefield m. Idella M. Piper of Wakefield 5/24/1899; H - 31, physician, b. Wakefield, s/o John F. Garland (Wakefield, farmer) and Nellie B. Watts (Canada, deceased); W - 29, teacher, b. Wakefield, d/o George F. Piper (Wakefield, farmer) and Mary E. Jenness (Wakefield, housekeeper)

Guy W. m. Annie L. Smith 12/10/1925; H - 27, b. Wakefield, s/o Fred Garland and Hattie M. West; W - 28, b. Brookfield, d/o Charles R. Smith and Ida Foss

Howard A. of Sanbornville m. Eunice Henrietta Hill of Bartlett 4/23/1949 in Sanbornville; H - 27, truckman; W - 21, at home
Howard A. of Sanbornville m. Catherine Pelletier of Barrington 7/21/1967 in Sanbornville; H - 45, mach. operator; W - 42, shoe worker
Howard A. of Sanbornville m. Joan E. Healy of Brookfield 2/17/1974
John F. of Wakefield m. Louise Turner of Pernambuco, Brazil 9/17/1894 in Nashua; H - 49, farmer, 2d, b. Wakefield, s/o Franklin Garland (Wakefield, farmer) and Mary Goodwin (Milton, housework); W - 37, governess, 2d, b. Sackville, NB, d/o Harras Sears (Sackville, NB, tanner) and Sinthy Anderson (Sackville, NB, housework)
Kenneth Warren of Sanbornville m. Carole Lee Hathaway of Rochester 6/18/1955 in Rochester; H - 20, US Air Corp.; W - 18, secretary
Paul D. of Wakefield m. Barbara M. Dion of Wakefield 8/14/1982
Robert I. of Sanbornville m. Judith M. Robinson of Sanbornville 4/3/1960; H - 21, machinist; W - 17, shoe worker
Robert I. of Wakefield m. Marianne LaBranche of Wakefield 9/21/1983
Robert Warren of Wakefield m. Kathryn Ann Donnelly of Wakefield 6/24/1978; H - 17; W - 18
Russell A. of Chelmsford, MA m. Edithann F. Ensley of Marlboro, MA 6/22/1985
Russell William of Sanbornville m. Rita Arlene Champany of Sanbornville 9/17/1938 in Sanbornville; H - 25, laborer; W - 22, housework
Timothy R. of Wakefield m. Lynn M. Stevens of Union 11/5/1988
Wilbur of Wakefield m. Hattie M. Avery of Wolfeboro 9/17/1893 in Rochester; H - 23, butcher, b. Brookfield, s/o John T. Garland (Ossipee, farmer) and Fanny N. Ricker (Greenland, housework); W - 19, housework, b. Wolfeboro, d/o Nathaniel F. Avery (Wolfeboro, farmer) and Lydia A. Bassett (Tuftonboro)
Willis F. of Sanbornville m. Virginia R. Wilson of Sanbornville 12/31/1945 in Sanbornville; H - 23, mechanic; W - 17, at home

GARNETT,
Karl E. of Barrington m. Ramona A. Randall of Wakefield 9/17/1983

GARNIEWICZ,
Charles Alexander of No. Wakefield m. Mary Priscilla Dean of Randolph, MA 12/12/1964 in Sanbornville; H - 21, student; W - 26, housework

GARRATT,
- Hugh B. of Wakefield m. Eunice T. Massin of Milton 10/29/1937; H - 46, decorator; W - 43, at home

GARVER,
- James M. of Pawtucket, RI m. Yvette D. Fletcher of Pawtucket, RI 7/7/1971

GARVIN,
- Jeffrey S. of East Wakefield m. Lynn D. MacKay of Rochester 10/1/1983 in East Rochester
- John H. of Wakefield m. Kate P. Dow of Philadelphia, PA 9/22/1896; H - merchant, b. Wakefield, s/o E. Garvin (Wakefield, deceased, farmer) and Almira Lang of Wakefield (Brookfield, 72, housekeeper); W - b. Salem, MA, d/o Josiah Dow of Philadelphia, PA (Brooklyn, NY, engineer) and K. W. Downing (Salem, MA, deceased)
- John H., Jr. of Wakefield m. Grace E. Dowd of Wakefield 6/14/1923 in Sanbornville; H - 26, dealer, b. Sanbornville, s/o John H. Garvin and Katherine P. Dow; W - 25, at home, b. Holyoke, MA, d/o Patrick J. Dowd and Mary O'Neil
- Samuel F. of Canada m. Ina E. Brackett of Wakefield 6/24/1914; H - 28, civil engineer, b. Wakefield, s/o James W. Garvin and Charlotte J. Garvin; W - 26, librarian, b. Wakefield, d/o Asa M. Brackett and Alma E. Kenerson

GARYAIT,
- Barry Lee of Wakefield m. Gloria Marie Soucy of Wakefield 7/9/1977 in Milton

GATCHELL,
- John D. of No. Conway m. Christine K. Feddern of Wakefield 10/24/1987 in Wolfeboro

GAUDREAU,
- Joseph R., Jr. of Wakefield, MA m. Natalie A. Cicci of Malden, MA 5/1/1974 in Manchester

GAUTHIER,
- Armand J. of Sanbornville m. Pauline S. Welch of Sanbornville 7/13/1948 in Sanbornville; H - 21, RR employee; W - 16, at home

Leo Joseph of Sanbornville m. Orana Champagne of Wolfeboro
10/16/1937; H - 20, shoe shop op.; W - 20, shoe shop op.

GAYTON,
Gardner Frederick of New Bedford, MA m. Shirley Marie Campbell
of Fairhaven, MA 6/11/1955; H - 36, plumber; W - 30, secretary

GEARY,
Daniel F., III of Beverly, MA m. Diane K. Foster of Beverly, MA
8/10/1974
John Joseph of Salem, MA m. Gertrude Lucille LaVallee of Salem, MA
8/31/1959 in Sanbornville; H - 29, RR emp.; W - 30, presser

GEIST,
Lincoln A. of Wakefield m. Bernice I. Runnells of Wakefield 3/27/1983

GELINAS,
Albert L. of Farmington m. Mildred E. Drown of Farmington 8/18/1951 in
Sanbornville; H - 20, machinist; W - 24, nurse
Robert Eugene of Farmington m. Gloria Anne Swinerton 5/11/1957
in Sanbornville; H - 24, store mgr.; W - 23, tel. opr.

GELSLINGER,
Stephen G. of Chelsea, MA m. Alison N. Paul of Chelsea, MA 9/19/1989

GEMAS,
Mark Wayne of Sanbornville m. Lorie L. Zimbouski of Dover 4/29/1990
in Rochester
William Joseph of Sanbornville m. Lynda Jane Webster of Sanbornville
2/11/1995 in Sanbornville

GEORGE,
John M. of Fredericksburg, VA m. Lena A. Croff of Malone, NY
9/26/1917; H - 54, wood calker, b. Spotsylvania, PA, s/o John M.
George and Rebecca Sands; W - 43, agent, b. Malone, NY, d/o Abner
Croff and Augusta Childs

GEORGES,
Herbert F. of Toccoa, GA m. Justine Helena Flint of Worcester, MA
6/11/1942; H - 36, radio sta. exec.; W - 22, writer

GERAIGERY,
Nicholas John, Jr. of Malden, MA m. Kimberly Irene Sharp of Malden, MA 2/4/1995

GERARD,
Randolph J. of Woburn, MA m. Phyllis E. Drown of Wakefield 12/12/1944 in Sanbornville; H - 25, US Army; W - 22, def. worker
Randolph J., Jr. of Wakefield m. Linda Ann Mooney of Sanbornville 2/10/1968 in Wolfeboro
William P. of Wakefield m. Wanda M. Soucy of Somersworth 12/5/1970 in Sanbornville
William P. of Wakefield m. Katherine A. Elwell of Milton 11/3/1973 in Sanbornville

GIFFIN,
Dean Lamont of Sanbornville m. Kathleen Frances Dirth of Palmer, MA 9/3/1965 in Hartford, CT; H - 22, repairman; W - 22, reg. nurse

GIFFORD,
Paul C. of Boxford, MA m. Patricia Desmond of Wakefield 5/18/1985

GILMAN,
John B. of Ossipee m. Ethel M. Lane of Wakefield 4/30/1889; H - 20, merchant, 2d, b. Ossipee, s/o I. H. Gilman (Tamworth, merchant) and Mary E. Hobbs (Ossipee, housework); W - 20, housekeeper, b. Exeter, d/o Frank Lane (farmer) and Annie M. ----- (shoemaker)

GILSON,
David Sheffield of Melrose, MA m. Janice A. Garratt of Wakefield, MA 11/24/1949; H - 21, student; W - 18, student

GLENNON,
Patrick William of Wakefield m. Valerie Joanne Hall of Brookfield 10/30/1976 in Brookfield
Richard M. of Sanbornville m. Patricia J. Brochu of Rochester 7/16/1973 in Sanbornville
Walter E. of Malden, MA m. Catherine M. Barry of Brockton, MA 7/7/1979; H - 59; W - 51
Wesley J. of Sanbornville m. Harriette L. Karcher of Sanbornville 11/21/1947 in Sanbornville; H - 24, millworker; W - 20, shoeworker

Wesley J., Jr. of Sanbornville m. Helen M. Luscomb of Milton Mills 5/2/1967 in Milton; H - 19, laborer; W - 17, student

GLIDDEN,

Dale R. of Sanbornville m. Brenda L. Johnson of Sanbornville 8/26/1995 in Rochester

Eugene of Wakefield m. Nettie I. Nason of So. Berwick, ME 11/16/1895; H - 26, fireman, 2d, widower, b. Wakefield, s/o John H. Glidden (Effingham, deceased) and Abbie Y. Young of Wakefield (Wakefield, 66, housework); W - 17, housework, b. So. Berwick, ME, d/o Elwell Nason of So. Berwick, ME (So. Berwick, ME, 49, mill operative) and Melissa Boyle (Lebanon, ME, 52, housekeeper)

Eugene E. of Wakefield m. Tillie A. Libby of Wakefield 12/17/1890; H - 21, watchman, b. Wakefield, s/o John H. Glidden (Effingham) and Abbie Y. Young (Wakefield, housekeeper); W - 24, housekeeper, b. Brookfield, d/o Henry M. Libby (Porter, ME, wheelwright) and Mary A. Chamberlin (Brookfield, housekeeper)

Herman N.F. of Wolfeboro m. Zilla M. Barter of Manchester 9/3/1920 in Rochester; H - 39, engineer, 2d, b. Tamworth, s/o Frank Otis (Calais, ME, teamster) and Margaret A. Woodman (Sandwich); W - 45, cook, b. Manchester, d/o John S. Barter (St. Johns, Newfoundland, machinist) and Anna M. McCarty (Manchester)

James A. of Holden, MA m. Jill E. Long of Holden, MA 7/18/1998

Loren J. of Wakefield m. Alberta L. Wadleigh of Wakefield 4/29/1893; H - 30, farmer, b. Wakefield, s/o John H. Glidden (Wolfeboro, farmer) and Abigail Young (Wakefield, housework); W - 24, housekeeper, 2d, b. Saco, ME, d/o Samuel Moors (Newfield, ME, farmer) and Lucy Miles (housework)

Michael P. of Wakefield m. Brooke H. Willett of Wakefield 9/12/1987 in Wolfeboro

William R. of Hampton Beach m. Greer G. Larson of Wakefield 11/7/1981 in Milton

GODWIN,

Floyd S. of Woburn, MA m. Elizabeth S. Pelton of Woburn, MA 8/1/1947; H - 32, salesman; W - 27, at home

GOLDSMITH,
Leland John of East Wakefield m. Wilma Horne of W. Newfield, ME 6/24/1977

GOLDSTEIN,
David Allen of Sanbornville m. Tammy Lee Bertholdt of Sanbornville 5/29/1994 in Sanbornville

GOODRICH,
Donald m. Hazel Thompson 8/28/1926; H - 21, b. Sanford, ME, s/o Bert C. Goodrich and Alice Johnson; W - 18, b. Sanford, ME, d/o Frank Thompson and Marguretta Libby

Frank P. of Newfield, ME m. Alma Rhodes of Lancaster, MA 2/19/1904; H - 23, teamster, b. Newfield, ME, s/o Joseph Goodrich and Abbie E. Page; W - 18, housework, d/o Charles Rhodes and Annie Butcher

GOODRO,
Paul of Wakefield m. Malvina Derveher of Milton Mills 4/1/1890; H - 31, laborer, 2d, b. Hancock, MI, s/o John Goodro (Three Rivers, PQ, farmer) and Rosy Miganiss (Three Rivers, PQ, housekeeper); W - 18, housekeeper, b. Montreal, PQ

GOODWIN,
Leon H. of Wakefield m. Alice M. Lowd of Milton 9/20/1905 in Sanbornville; H - 20, clerk, b. Wakefield, s/o Hilton S. Goodwin and Estella Campbell; W - 19, b. Jamaica Plains, MA, d/o Freeman H. Lowd and Fanny Miller

Malcolm R. m. Marjorie R. Hollihan 6/5/1966 in East Wakefield; H - 34, laborer; W - 29, housewife

Payson Henry of Wakefield m. Sylvia Allen Bibber of Wakefield 5/16/1976

Ray T. of Wakefield m. Ruth E. Mee of Acton, ME 10/6/1909; H - 21, teamster, b. Wakefield, s/o Hilton S. Goodwin and Estella L. Campbell; W - 18, housework, b. Wakefield, d/o John H. Mee and Agnes Libbey

Theodore T. of Marblehead, MA m. N. Lorraine Fry of Beverly, MA 8/31/1935 in Sanbornville; H - 28; W - 29, nurse

GORDON,
Merle Henry, Jr. of Newton, MA m. Maureen Anne O'Donnell of Allston, MA 2/15/1962 in Sanbornville; H - 26, sales mgr.; W - 22, at home

GORTON,
Isborn W. of Union m. Ellen E. Adjutant of Union 11/23/1936 in Rochester; H - 40, truckman; W - 47, housework

GOSSELIN,
Raymond Leo of Kennebunk, ME m. Gertrude Martha Williams of Union 6/27/1953 in Rochester; H - 22, shoe cutter; W - 18, at home

GOULD,
Barton of Wakefield m. Flora M. Grace of Milton 5/8/1924 in Union; H - 22, mill hand, b. Lisbon, s/o Louis S. Gould and Belle Sweet; W - 28, at home, 2d, b. Albany, d/o Frank L. Grace and Lizzie B. Willey

GOYETTE,
Donald James of Portsmouth m. Lydia Conrad Marshall of Union 7/23/1975 in Union

GRANT,
Bruce Charles of Westerly, RI m. Dena Anne Delillo of Waterford, CT 10/4/1997 in Eaton

Charles H. of Biddeford, ME m. Kate F. Griffin of Saco, ME 8/28/1900 in Sanbornville; H - 30, farmer, 2d, b. Biddeford, ME, s/o George A. Grant (Lewiston, ME, shoemaker) and Kate Tuttle (Saco, ME, housewife); W - 32, housekeeper, 2d, b. Cornish, ME, d/o Albert Day (Cornish, ME, farmer) and Abbie Stanley (Porter, ME)

Orin B. of Acton, ME m. Jennie V. Prescott of Wakefield 12/26/1897; H - 27, farmer, b. Acton, ME, s/o Horatio Grant of Acton, ME (Acton, ME, 54, farmer) and Almeda Ham (Shapleigh, ME, deceased); W - 18, housework, b. Northwood, d/o John W. Prescott of Wakefield (Dover, 50, postmaster) and Addie Jewett (Milton, 48, housewife)

GRAVES,
Edward Henry, Sr. of Sanbornville m. Unamarie C. Kozachuk of Sanbornville 7/18/1992

GRAY,
Allan R. of Union m. Juanita J. Boyum of Flatwoods, KY 1/15/1983
Craig R. of Union m. Kirsten E. Lygren of Union 6/10/1989 in Union
Donald F. of Union m. Charlene B. Hall of Milton 4/6/1981 in Milton
Robert S. of Wakefield m. Marion R. Morrison of Wakefield 12/25/1915;
H - 19, carpenter, b. Gonic, s/o Charles E. Gray and Etta F.
Southard; W - 18, at home, b. Somerville, MA, d/o Charles L.
Morrison and Minnie Savage

GREENE,
Douglas A. of Milton m. Genny P. Frase of Wakefield 6/25/1966 in
Sanbornville; H - 23, mill emp.; W - 24, teacher
Ernest of New York, NY m. M. H. Dow of Brooklyn, NY 10/8/1896;
H - 32, architect, b. Brooklyn, NY, s/o R. G. Greene of New York,
NY (E. Haddam, CT, clergyman) and Augusta ---- (Brooklyn, NY,
housewife); W - 25, b. Brooklyn, NY, d/o Abbot L. Dow of
Brooklyn, NY (Brooklyn, NY) and C. L. Herriman (Brooklyn, NY,
deceased)
William Lee of Groveland, IL m. Denise R. Wagner of Groveland, IL
4/23/1983

GREENFIELD,
Bernard S. of Wakefield m. Rachel Jeannine L'Hereux of Sanford, ME
6/6/1993 in Wentworth Location

GREGOIRE,
Eric Scot of Union m. Sarah Anne Wilkinson of Union 9/9/1995

GREGSON,
Robinson m. Nellie F. Willey 1/5/1933 in Dover

GRIFFIN,
Sterling C. of Kennebunk, ME m. Emma A. Abbott of Shapleigh, ME
9/11/1899; H - 49, merchant, b. Hampstead, s/o William Griffin
(Sandown, carpenter) and Marion Colby (Bow, deceased); W - 47,
dressmaker, b. Shapleigh, ME, d/o Jacob Abbott (Shapleigh, ME,
deceased) and Eliza ----

GRIFFITH,
Barry E. of No. Bennington, VT m. Barbara J. Pratt of Wakefield 7/17/1971 in Union
Weston H. of Union m. Nancy L. Wiggin of Wakefield 2/20/1966 in Newington; H - 17, student; W - 17, student

GRIGAS,
Michael P. of Farmington m. Gale A. Haley of Union 9/29/1968 in Farmington

GRONDIN,
Leo V. of Wakefield m. Lauren Rae Colbroth of Wakefield 5/26/1988 in East Rochester

GROVER,
Henry John, Jr. of Sanbornville m. Nancy Ruth Whiting of Sanbornville 5/31/1997 in Wolfeboro

GULDBRANDSEN,
Fred W. of Wakefield m. Roxanne M. LeClair of Rochester 8/5/1972
Heinz W. of Wakefield m. Linda R. Labbe of Rochester 2/9/1974
Walter F.H. of New Milford, CT m. Erika K. Cotton of Sanbornville 5/27/1994 in Sanbornville

GUTTADAURIS,
James T. of Wakefield, MA m. Janice K. Smith of Malden, MA 4/29/1971

HACKETT,
George W. of W. Peabody, MA m. Mary I. Mathews of Wakefield 11/12/1894 in Ossipee; H - 30, farmer, b. W. Peabody, MA, s/o John Hackett (Brookfield, farmer) and Caroline Wheeding (Winterport, ME, housework); W - 27, clerk, b. Wakefield, d/o John W. Mathews (Ossipee, farmer) and Elizabeth Emerson (Wakefield, housework)
Norman L. of Sanbornville m. Ethel M. Clark of Sanbornville 6/19/1948 in Sanbornville; H - 31, RR employee; W - 26, at home
Thomas J. of Wakefield m. Susan E. Morrill of Wolfeboro 5/23/1987 in Effingham

HALDERMAN,
Richard D. of Wakefield m. Brenda G. Jones of Wakefield 7/8/1983 in Portsmouth

HALE,
Donald A. m. Martha P. Runnels 7/18/1931; H - 29, s/o Arthur M. Hale (Rindge) and Ida Emerson (Rindge); W - 24, d/o Samuel Runnels (Wakefield) and Mary R. Harriman (Madison)

HALL,
Frank G. of Boston, MA m. Laura C. Wells of Boston, MA 6/28/1920; H - 46, hotel prop., b. Boston, MA, s/o Frank G. Hall (Bristol, RI, hotel prop.) and Isabelle M. Robinson (Fairhaven, MA); W - 46, b. Horne's Mills, d/o Frank W. Wells (W. Buxton, ME, lawyer) and Susan A. Horne (Wakefield)

Gregory W. of Wakefield m. Denise E. Joy of Wakefield 7/24/1982

James H., III of Wakefield m. Virginia R. Berglund of Wakefield 8/6/1988

James Henry, Jr. of Cambridge, MA m. Amy Joan Marie Walsh of Cambridge, MA 11/26/1955; H - 27, carpenter; W - 25, office work

John A. of Wakefield m. Laura E. Willey of Milton 4/28/1908 in Acton, ME; H - 48, heel manufacturer, b. Wakefield, s/o Andrew G. Hall and Harriet A. Moulton; W - 26, housework, b. Milton, d/o Joseph F. Willey and Mary J. Laskey

Orman W. of Sanbornville m. Donna M. Gray of Sanbornville 10/10/1992 in Sanbornville

Percy E. of Wakefield m. Annie M. Evans of Wakefield 1/14/1901; H - 39, merchant, b. Wakefield, s/o Andrew G. Hall (Wakefield, merchant) and Harriette Moulton (Wakefield, housekeeper); W - housework, 2d, b. East Rochester, d/o John D. Pillsbury (Newburyport, MA, machinist) and Sarah Johnson (Stowe, ME, housewife)

Perley of Wakefield m. Mattie E. Sprague of Effingham 12/17/1903 in Sanbornville; H - 21, mill hand, b. Sawyer's River, s/o Edward Hall and Ora Hall; W - 17, housework, b. Newfield, ME, d/o Charles Sprague and Annie Pillmington

HALLSWORTH,
Robert W. of Plymouth, MA m. Janet S. Smith of Plymouth, MA 10/2/1972

HAM,
LeRoy H. m. Minnie G. Wentworth 11/12/1932 in Rochester
Richard E. of Acton, ME m. Dolores J. Rand of Sanbornville 9/28/1946 in Sanbornville; H - 20, lumberman; W - 18, at home

HAMILTON,
Ernest E. of Wakefield m. Sarah L. Collins of Wakefield 8/9/1919 in Milton; H - 28, shoe stitcher, b. Wakefield, s/o John E. Hamilton (Conway, RR truckman) and Sadie M. Doyle (Wakefield); W - 28, shoe packer, b. Ireland, d/o John Collins (Ireland) and Mary Murphy (Ireland)

Fitz Edgar m. Rose A. Hatch 3/13/1928; H - 72, s/o Fitz Henry Hamilton (Middleton) and Nancy Guptill (Milton Mills); W - 72, d/o Oliver Patch and Mary Patch (Newfield, ME)

John E. of Wakefield m. Sadie M. Doyle of Wakefield 10/8/1890; H - 24, laborer, b. Conway, s/o Joseph H. Hamilton (Conway, farmer) and Betsy J. Hart (Eaton, housekeeper); W - 16, housekeeper, b. Wakefield, d/o John Doyle (NY, watchman) and Amanda Wentworth (Wakefield, housekeeper)

Wendall J. of Waterboro, ME m. Mary Louise Valcourt of Wakefield 12/15/1945; H - 28, millworker; W - 18, housework

HAMM,
Bertram Charles of Wakefield m. Bertha Maude Hamm of Wakefield 11/1/1953 in Province Lake; H - 67, retired; W - 71, at home

HAMMOND,
Carl W. of Union m. Pauline Lapointe of Somersworth 10/14/1922 in Somersworth; H - 20, machinist, b. Union, s/o George L. Hammond and Lena Hill; W - 19, at home, 2d, b. Sagamore, MA, d/o William H. Gibbs and Pauline D. Fleck

Earl Stanley of Wakefield m. Ida Payson Buffum of New Boston 4/16/1938 in Milton; H - 39, lumberman; W - 43, housework

Edwin F. of Wakefield m. Lillian Chamberlin of Wakefield 11/5/1892; H - 22, bookkeeper, b. Tamworth, s/o W. Hammond (Ossipee, dead) and Almeretta Neally (Tamworth, housework); W - 22, housework, b. Charlestown, MA, d/o S. G. Chamberlin (Greenwood, ME, farmer) and Helen M. Lang (Falmouth, ME, housework)

Frank E. of Wakefield m. Mahala Miller of Acton, ME 9/18/1894 in
Milton Mills; H - 21, blacksmith, b. Dover, s/o Daniel S. Hammond
(Bangor, ME, shoemaker) and Susan Chase (Albany, housework); W -
26, housework, b. Milton, d/o Elias Miller (Milton, farmer) and Mary
----- (Milton, housework)

George L. of Wakefield m. Lena A. Hill of Wakefield 3/18/1900 in
Sanbornville; H - 23, clerk, b. Chocorua, s/o Wentworth Hammond
(Chocorua) and Almeretta Nealley (Madison, housekeeper); W - 20,
housework, b. Parsonsfield, ME, d/o Leonard Hill (Parsonsfield, ME,
heel cutter) and Gertrude Varney (Lebanon, ME, housewife)

George L. of Wakefield m. Georginia Baldwin of Chelsea, MA
2/8/1909; H - 32, mail carrier, 2d, b. Tamworth, s/o Wentworth
Hammond and Almeretta Hammond; W - 25, shoe shop, 2d, b.
Newfoundland, d/o William Best and Harriette Pike

John William of Sanbornville m. Roberta Abbie Leighton of
Rochester 2/5/1965 in Rochester; H - 18, mill emp.; W - 17, at home

Robert Tear of Acton, ME m. Lillian May Fifield of Wakefield
10/30/1943 in Sanbornville; H - 40, mail carrier; W - 34, at home

HANNAN,

Quincy F. of Liberty, ME m. Abbie J. Evans of Wakefield 8/17/1893;
H - 26, merchant, b. Liberty, ME, s/o Joseph Hannan (Liberty, ME,
farmer) and Julia A. Nash (Liberty, ME, housework); W - 21,
housework, b. Wakefield, d/o Albert L. Evans (Wakefield, farmer)
and Hattie M. Goodale (Danvers, MA)

HANSCOM,

Harold D. of Salem, MA m. Alice L.O. Donnell of Salem, MA
7/25/1937 in Portsmouth; H - 23, clerk; W - 21, lamp tester

Tobey Allen of Sanbornville m. Cheryl Tina Wentworth of
Sanbornville 6/27/1998 in Rochester

HANSEN,

John W. of Wakefield m. Diane M. Conroy of Wakefield 8/11/1978;
H - 24; W - 29

William of Sanbornville m. Fanny Ellen Fletcher of Milton Mills
10/9/1943 in Sanbornville; H - 25, dairy farmer; W - 23, secretary

HANSON,
- Allen Lewis of Effingham m. Tina Marie Marston of Sanbornville 7/4/1976 in Effingham
- Donald Karl of Sanbornville m. Dorothy May Lee of Malden, MA 6/25/1950 in Sanbornville; H - 25, accountant; W - 19, secretary
- Edward of Sanford, ME m. Tamara E. Kiernan of Sanford, ME 7/5/1991
- George of Wakefield m. Mary Perkins of Wakefield 5/1/1892; H - 67, farmer, b. Brookfield, s/o Reuben Hanson (Brookfield, dead) and Mary Watson (Brookfield, dead); W - 65, housework, 2d, b. Wakefield, d/o Joseph H. Pike (Wakefield, dead) and Elmira Lyford (Brookfield, dead)
- Harry Donald of Wakefield m. Gloria Marie Manganello of Warner 10/30/1957 in Warner; H - 17, lineman; W - 18, at home
- Lafayette of Wakefield m. Addie M. Shackford of Wakefield 7/2/1899 in Springvale, ME; H - 28, mill hand, b. Ossipee, s/o John Hanson (Ossipee, farmer) and Lydia E. Peavey (Ossipee, housekeeper); W - 21, housekeeper, b. Wakefield, d/o Frank Shackford (Eaton, farmer) and Ada L. Smith (Belfast, ME, housekeeper)
- Lafayette of Wakefield m. Lettie L. Hanson of Ossipee 5/6/1911; H - 40, mill hand, 2d, b. Ossipee, s/o John Hanson and Lydia E. Peavey; W - 40, dressmaker, 2d, b. Ossipee, d/o William H. Eldridge and Rosina Welch
- Philip S. of Sanbornville m. Ruth E. Horne of Sanbornville 12/9/1935 in Sanbornville; H - 21, clerk; W - 20, at home
- Ralph W. of Wakefield m. Marion A. McCrillis of Wakefield 8/31/1913 in Portsmouth; H - 21, clerk, b. Wakefield, s/o Sidney I. Hanson and Mary T. Johnson; W - 20, at home, b. Wakefield, d/o Frank G. McCrillis and Sarah E. McCrillis
- Ralph W. of Wakefield m. Lois M. Knight of Wakefield 4/20/1919 in Sanbornville; H - 27, watchman, 2d, b. Wakefield, s/o Sidney I. Hanson (Brookfield, RR brakeman) and Mary T. Johnson (Wakefield); W - 20, telephone op'r, b. Wakefield, d/o Marshall E. Knight (Salmon Falls, tel. operator) and Elizabeth Brackett (Wakefield)
- Ralph W., Jr. of Rochester m. Carol N. Bickford of Dover 4/8/1980
- Ralph Waldo, Jr. of Sanbornville m. Arline F. Gallagher of North Conway 11/13/1943 in Sanbornville; H - 21, US Army; W - 28, tel. operator

HARDIN,
Charles W. of Wakefield m. Mary A. Copp of Wakefield 10/8/1887; H - 37, farmer, 2d, b. Burlington, VT, s/o James Hardin (Burlington, VT, farmer) and Emily Sweet (Burlington, VT, housekeeper); W - 16, housework, b. Wakefield, ----- Copp and Josephine M. Daniel (Wakefield, housekeeper)

HARDING,
Richard Bennett of Sanbornton m. Virginia Elizabeth Souter of Union 8/27/1954; H - 23, salesman; W - 19, student

HARMON,
John M. of Wakefield m. Sarah Eaton of Brookfield 12/23/1887; H - 18, farmer, b. Freedom, s/o Reuben Harmon (Madison, farmer) and Olive Moulton (Freedom, housekeeper); W - 23, housework, b. Brookfield, d/o Samuel Eaton (farmer) and ----- Smith (Wolfeboro, housekeeper)

HARPER,
Charles of Wiscasset, ME m. Emma P. Avery of Union 6/21/1934 in Wiscasset, ME; H - 65, caretaker; W - 48, chef

HARRIS,
Jack Dash of Penn Yan, NY m. Deborah Gilbert Davis of Penn Yan, NY 8/4/1976
Kenneth W. of Milton m. Emilia Jean Harris of Sanbornville 7/2/1966; H - 18, shoe worker; W - 16, at home
Rex Wendell of Wakefield m. Jennie Mae Pichette of Lynn, MA 4/9/1939 in Sanbornville; H - 21, lumberman; W - 22, at home
Russell Lionel of Union m. Gladys Mary Reed of Union 9/30/1938 in Sanbornville; H - 25, undertaker asst.; W - 22, post office clerk
Walter S. of Wakefield m. Maureen A. Pingree of Wakefield 9/7/1996

HART,
George E. of Wakefield m. Ita Belle Carter of Milton 9/1/1887 in Milton; H - 27, manufacturer, b. Milton, s/o Edward Hart (Milton) and Sally ---- (Acton, ME, housekeeper); W - 21, music teacher, b. Lyman, d/o Alba B. Carter (Littleton) and Eliza A. ----- (Landaff, housekeeper)
James Michael of Akron, OH m. Lois Seibert of Wakefield 7/3/1977
Walter H. of Wakefield m. Hazel R. Ham of Farmington 10/15/1921 in Union; H - 29, brakeman, b. Wakefield, s/o Loammi Hart (Conway,

farmer) and Ursha Hammond (Eaton); W - 22, school teacher, b. Farmington, d/o ----- Ham (Farmington, shoe operative) and Carrie Ham

HASKELL,
P. T. of Wakefield m. M. A. Blake of Wakefield 10/28/1896; H - 28, physician, b. Deering, ME, s/o W. H. Haskell of Falmouth, ME (Greene, ME, 63, clergyman) and Ellen M. Carey (Wayne, ME, 59, housekeeper); W - 21, teacher, b. Woburn, MA, d/o Simon Blake of Wakefield (Brookfield, 63, farmer) and Ellen M. Sargent (Goshen, deceased)

HASKINS,
William C. of Sanbornville m. Tina L. Couture of Sanbornville 11/29/1990 in Sanbornville

HASSANOS,
Peter J. of Lynn, MA m. Geraldine K. Lang of Lynn, MA 7/9/1944 in North Wakefield; H - 24, def. worker; W - 26, def. worker

HASTINGS,
Richard Joseph of Sanbornville m. Geraldine Barbara Maloney of East Rochester 9/26/1964 in Rochester; H - 39, mechanic; W - 34, shoe worker

HATCH,
Maurice Albert of Durham m. Ann Carpenter Paul of Wakefield 6/21/1958 in Durham; H - 25, herdsman; W - 29, research

Robert W. of Sanbornville m. Doris B. Towle of Sanbornville 8/9/1946 in Portsmouth; H - 27, RR emp.; W - 22, at home

HAUSER,
Jerry G. of Wakefield m. Penny A. Aubuchont of Wakefield 7/15/1979 in Milton; H - 34; W - 28

HAWKES,
Frank W. of East Wakefield m. Kimberly A. Kelliher of East Wakefield 9/4/1993

HAWKINS,
Donald Smith, Jr. of Rochester m. Ramona Enola Sprague of Union 3/1/1958; H - 21, US Navy; W - 20, office work

HAWTHORNE,
Christopher Mark of Sanbornville m. Jennifer Marie Nolin of Somersworth 8/30/1997 in Portsmouth

HAYDEN,
Donald Roy of Winthrop, MA m. Mary Elizabeth Cavanaugh of Winthrop, MA 7/10/1965 in Sanbornville; H - 27, machinist; W - 19, secretary

HAYNES,
Clarence L. of Wakefield m. Verna E. Merrow of Ossipee 9/1/1908 in Rochester; H - 24, clerk, b. Wakefield, s/o John M. Haynes and Elvira Hilland; W - 21, stenographer, b. Bridgton, ME, d/o Elmer E. Merrow and Lizzie Brooks

Edwin M. of Wakefield m. Mamie Fields of Sanbornville 9/23/1905 in Sanbornville; H - 24, tinsmith, b. Laconia, s/o John M. Haynes and Elvira Hillard; W - 17, b. Conway, d/o James Fields and Bessie Thibodeau

HAYWARD,
Alden Frederick of Union m. Janna Marie Jerome of Rochester 8/4/1990 in Rochester

Donald H. of Wakefield m. Jennifer M. Downs of Wakefield 11/28/1981 in Union

HAZEN,
Howard Wellington of Newfield, ME m. Margaret A. Rogers of Newfield, ME 3/31/1949 in Sanbornville; H - 41, sta. fireman; W - 41, at home

HEALY,
Timothy E. of Wakefield m. Candace L. Loring of Wakefield 8/14/1988 in Sanbornville

Victor Nelson of Sanbornville m. Robin Lynne Pehowic of Sanbornville 10/5/1996 in Wolfeboro

HEBERT,
Daniel P. of Wakefield m. Julie Silcox of Wakefield 5/6/1978 in
Wolfeboro; H - 19; W - 25
Loren David of Sanbornville m. Jennifer Joy Challinor of Putnam, CT
8/26/1994 in Concord

HECK,
Edward V. of New Orleans, WI m. Judith A. Nordberg of New Orleans,
WI 8/8/1981
Frank Joseph of Rochester, MN m. Louise Mary Paul of Wakefield
12/29/1952; H - 55, physician; W - 53, physician

HELANDER,
Carl Frederick, Jr. of Sanbornville m. Nancy Elaine Willis of Whitman,
MA 9/12/1964 in Whitman, MA; H - 24, govt. work; W - 18, office
work

HENDERSON,
Robert W. of East Wakefield m. Elise B. Rutherford of East Wakefield
9/7/1996 in East Wakefield

HENNER,
Roland J., Jr. of Milton m. Shirley Louise Smith of Union 11/9/1963 in
Milton; H - 21, mechanic; W - 17, student

HENNESSEY,
John F., Jr. of Southbury, CT m. Judith M. Brakeville of Union 8/17/1968
in Sanbornville

HERBERT,
Gene L. of Union m. Gloria P. Drapeau of Rochester 7/22/1961 in Union;
H - 34, linotype opr.; W - 35, shoe worker
Merland R. of Union m. Norma Jane Coran of Rochester 6/6/1952 in
Rochester; H - 19, at home; W - 23, lift opr.

HERRERA,
Paul Lago of Wakefield m. Gloria M. Talbot of Wakefield 10/5/1968

HERRICK,
George A. m. Edith M. Floyd 7/15/1933 in Wolfeboro

George S. m. Nellie M. Clark 4/8/1929; H - 25, s/o George S. Herrick (Portland, ME) and Lena V. Patch (W. Newfield, ME); W - 18, d/o James E. Clark (Tuftonboro) and Mattie A. Hoyt (Rochester)

HERSEY,
Gardner D. of East Wakefield m. Jacqueline Collins of East Wakefield 7/7/1990 in East Wakefield

HERSOM,
Ivory W. of Acton, ME m. Nettie Libbey of Wakefield 3/26/1898; H - 43, farmer, 2d, divorced, b. Acton, ME, s/o Eben J. Hersom of Acton, ME (Lebanon, ME, 75, farmer) and Mahala Wentworth (Effingham, deceased); W - 19, housework, b. Ossipee, d/o DeWitt Carter of Ossipee (Ossipee, 53, lawyer) and Dora Libbey of Wakefield (40, housekeeper)

HEWEY,
Willis G. of Sanbornville m. Marcia Berry of Fryeburg, ME 1/14/1934 in St. Petersburg, FL; H - 33, novelty mfg.; W - 24, secretary

HICKEY,
Daniel James of Wakefield m. Constance Ann Kastberg of W. Lebanon, ME 9/25/1976 in Sanbornville

HILDRETH,
John H. of Union m. Sally Ann Cole of Union 2/14/1996 in Union

HILENSKI,
John H., Jr. of Boston, MA m. Sophia V. Paulowski of Sanbornville 7/31/1937 in Sanbornville; H - 23, soldier; W - 22, housework

HILL,
Alfred James of Wakefield, MA m. Dorothy Adelle Smith of Wakefield 9/4/1953 in East Rochester; H - 23, printer; W - 16, at home

Almond D. of Wakefield m. Hattie M. Robinson of Wolfeboro 3/13/1897 in Wolfeboro Falls; H - 26, blacksmith, b. Wakefield, s/o Asa W. Hill of Wakefield (Wakefield, 63, farmer) and Matilda F. Jones (Wakefield, 45, housewife); W - 22, housework, b. Wolfeboro, d/o John F. Robinson of Effingham (Hiram, ME, laborer) and Alice M. Thompson (Ossipee, deceased)

Charles Ellsworth of Haverhill, MA m. Bertha May Lindsey of Haverhill, MA 6/13/1938 in Sanbornville; H - 27, salesman; W - 32, nurse

Claudian F. of Wakefield m. Ella M. Hart of Wakefield 7/28/1912 in Ossipee; H - 24, clerk, b. Boston, MA, s/o Wilbur M. Hill and Fannie M. Frost; W - 16, housework, b. Wakefield, d/o Loammi Hart and Ursha H. Harmon

Edwin E. of Wakefield m. Sarah A. Reed of Wakefield 7/26/1896 in Newfield, ME; H - 23, painter, 2d, widower, b. Newfield, ME, s/o Josiah J. Hill of Wakefield (Wakefield, 68, laborer) and Rachel A. Heath (Newfield, ME, deceased); W - 25, housekeeper, b. Wakefield, d/o Ammon S. Reed of Wakefield (Newfield, ME, carpenter) and Elizabeth Waldron (Acton, ME, housekeeper)

Joshua E. of Wakefield m. Ora A. Tibbetts of Wakefield 7/31/1898; H - 30, farmer, b. Wakefield, s/o Thomas W. Hill (Wakefield, deceased, farmer) and Laura A. Tibbetts (Brookfield, deceased, housework); W - 16, housework, b. Wakefield, d/o J. D. Tibbetts of Wakefield (Wolfeboro, 55, farmer) and Jennie M. Gale (Dover, 52, housewife)

Leon of Wakefield m. Ellen Willey of Wakefield 8/4/1904; H - 20, brass finisher, b. Parsonsfield, ME, s/o Leonard Hill and Gertrude Varney; W - 15, housework, b. Wakefield, d/o Edwin R. Willey and Sarah Patch

Leon of Wakefield m. Florence E. Lord of Wakefield 8/18/1906; H - 22, brass finisher, 2d, b. Parsonsfield, ME, s/o Leonard Hill and Gertrude Varney; W - 16, housework, b. Shapleigh, ME, d/o Hiram Lord and Lillian Temple

Leon of Wakefield m. Catherine Shaw of Wakefield 10/17/1912; H - 28, brass finisher, 3d, b. Parsonsfield, ME, s/o Leonard Hill and Gertrude Varney; W - 38, housekeeper, 2d, b. Cork, Ireland, d/o Joseph Shannessy and Catherine Shannessy

Leslie of Wakefield m. Ellen Willey of Wakefield 11/7/1906; H - 23, brass founder, b. Parsonsfield, ME, s/o Leonard Hill and Gertrude Varney; W - 17, housework, 2d, b. Wakefield, d/o Edwin R. Willey and Sarah Patch

Lorin T. of Waterboro, ME m. Emma Hill of Waterboro, ME 2/27/1911; H - 55, farmer, 2d, b. Lyman, ME, s/o Thomas J. Hill and Sarah Hill; W - 60, housework, 4th, b. Kennebunk, ME, d/o Charles Treadwell and Susan Williams

Norman Warren of Beverly, MA m. Eleanor J. Herbert of Union 7/7/1952 in Milton; H - 25, asst. engr.; W - 21, at home

Owen Reginald of Union m. Annie May M. Rogers 6/20/1949 in Sanbornville; H - 39, laborer; W - 45, housework

Reginald Alvin of Acton, ME m. Priscilla Hazel Rand of Sanbornville 4/21/1956; H - 35, accountant; W - 23, shoe worker

Roland G. of Wakefield m. Joyce L. Hayward of Wakefield 9/15/1972

Waldo L. of Union m. Anna B. Eastman of Union 8/19/1946 in Milton; H - 41, logging cont.; W - 32, housework

Wallace Freeman of Middleton m. Pauline A. Dodier of Sanbornville 7/4/1945 in Wolfeboro; H - 20, laborer; W - 19, student

Wayne E. of Sanbornville m. Anna M. Blomstrom of E. Walpole, MA 9/5/1970 in Sanbornville

HILLIARD,
Daniel J. of Rochester m. Mahala J. Houle of Wakefield 9/24/1983

HILMAN,
Carl Thomas of Sanbornville m. Melissa Dawn Wallace of Sanbornville 8/17/1991 in Sanbornville

HILTZ,
David W. of East Wakefield m. Barbara J. Gaudet of Las Vegas, NV 6/4/1993 in Dixville Notch

HIMES,
Edwin A. of Wakefield m. Jennie A. Brackett of Wakefield 6/30/1892; H - 27, clerk, b. Buchanan, MI, s/o Edwin T. Himes (Boston, MA, dead) and Addie A. Vincent (St. Johns, NB, housework); W - 28, seamstress, b. Wakefield, d/o Charles E. Brackett (Acton, ME, farmer) and Lizzie R. Wiggin (Wakefield, housework)

Vaughan V. of Sanbornville m. Sarah L. Dudley of Concord 12/29/1923 in Concord; H - 53, fruit grower, b. St. Paul, MN, s/o William L. Himes and Adelaide H. Vincent; W - 50, no occ., 2d, b. Concord, d/o Charles W. Clarke and Clara F. Brown

HINKLEY,
Frank of Wakefield m. Minnie Blue of Wakefield 2/16/1901; H - 21, teamster, b. Phillips, ME, s/o Hezekiah Hinkley (Phillips, ME, farmer) and Emma Parker (Phillips, ME, housewife); W - 21, housework, b. Ossipee, d/o Charles Blue (wood chopper) and Susie Parker (Ossipee, housewife)

HOBBS,
Harley R. of Rochester m. Tammy J. Marston of Wakefield 8/4/1984
Howard Gordon of Boston, MA m. Violet Hacker Kimball of Sanbornville 6/23/1956; H - 41, parts clerk; W - 28, teacher

HODGES,
Michael Alan, Sr. of East Wakefield m. Misty Lorraine Mayzak of East Wakefield 7/4/1993 in East Wakefield

HODSDON,
Elliott E. of Wakefield m. Eva May Hussey of Berwick, ME 4/10/1918; H - 23, shoe cutter, b. Wakefield, s/o Horace S. Hodsdon and Terese Harmon; W - 26, at home, b. Newburyport, MA, d/o Clarence L. Hussey and Martha Vaughan

Harold E. of Wakefield m. Helen C. Connor of Ossipee 5/28/1920 in Wolfeboro; H - 26, carpenter, b. Wakefield, s/o George H. Hodsdon (Biddeford, ME, carpenter) and Sarah S. Glidden (Wakefield); W - 21, teacher, b. Exeter, d/o Edwin Connor (Ossipee, teacher) and Mary Blake (Q'ns Prov., Canada)

Harold E. m. Marie Belanger 6/28/1927; H - 34, s/o George Hodsdon (Wakefield) and Sarah Glidden; W - 30, d/o Louis Belanger (Salem, MA) and Anistin St. Pierre

William F. of Wakefield m. Emilie G. Rickly of Wakefield 5/27/1914; H - 22, stock fitter, b. Wakefield, s/o Horace S. Hodsdon and Terese Harmon; W - 24, housework, b. Manasquam, NJ, d/o Jacob Rickly and Rosena Witschi

HOLDEN,
Dudley F. of Wakefield, MA m. Barbara A. Connolly of Revere, MA 9/22/1961; H - 20, mechanic; W - 18, nurse's aide

HOLMES,
Ronald Ervin of Rochester m. Martha Elizabeth Karcher of Sanbornville 12/31/1955 in Sanbornville; H - 21, spray gun oper.; W - 20, office work

HOLT,
Bradley G. of Barrington m. Mary J. Shea of Wakefield 8/6/1978 in Durham; H - 23; W - 23
David M. of Wakefield m. Lisa E. Libby of Wakefield 7/12/1986

Mark F. of Wakefield m. Constance A. Springs of Wakefield 9/30/1983

HOOPER,
John E. of Wakefield m. Edna A. Wilkins of Wakefield 12/30/1908; H - 29, locomotive fireman, b. Boxford, MA, s/o John L. Hooper and Christina Frasier; W - 19, school teacher, b. Acton, ME, d/o Homer W. Wilkins and Mary Hutchins

John W. of Wakefield m. Grace Connolly of Milton 9/20/1905 in Somersworth; H - 23, laborer, b. Wakefield, s/o Charles E. Hooper and Nellie Downs; W - 21, mill operative, b. Milton, d/o Timothy Connolly and Clara Lowd

Randy P. of Wolfeboro m. Karen S. Nason of Wakefield 7/9/1983 in Wolfeboro

Roy E. of Wakefield m. Sylvia M. Stevens of Brookfield 11/3/1906; H - 20, carpenter, b. Wakefield, s/o Everett Hooper and Nellie J. Downs; W - 18, housework, b. Brookfield, d/o Warren E. Stevens and Etta Eaton

Roy E. of Wakefield m. Nellie E. Roles of Wakefield 6/6/1916; H - 29, RR brakeman, 2d, b. Wakefield, s/o Charles E. Hooper and Nettie Downs; W - 29, housework, b. Ossipee, d/o John H. Roles and Laura A. Dore

Rufus Roy of Wakefield m. Florence E. Adjutant of Wolfeboro 6/22/1907; H - 18, teamster, b. Wakefield, s/o Charles E. Hooper and Nellie J. Downs; W - 17, housework, b. Wolfeboro, d/o Martin Adjutant and Ella M. Tibbetts

Sidney E. m. Bernice E. Cate 3/8/1933 in Rochester

HOPEWELL,
William J. of Roxbury, MA m. Mary Dorothy Riley of Roxbury, MA 10/28/1950 in Sanbornville; H - 24, manager; W - 26, timekeeper

HORNE,
Archie Ashton of Wolfeboro m. Mary Erna Hansen of Sanbornville 3/28/1942 in Sanbornville; H - 27, prof. baseball; W - 22, at home

Charles E. of Wakefield m. Mattie M. Nielsen of Wakefield 12/17/1980

Charles F. of Wakefield m. Ethel M. Clapham of Winthrop, MA 4/11/1914 in Winthrop, MA; H - 24, RR brakeman, b. Shapleigh, ME, s/o Arthur C. Horne and Ada B. Cook; W - 21, trained nurse, b. Albany, NY, d/o Edward F. Clapham and Emma J. Lathrop

Edwin J. of Wakefield m. Hannah Runnels of Wakefield 11/20/1888 in Portsmouth; H - 25, RR fireman, b. Wakefield, s/o Jackson Horne (Acton, ME, carpenter) and Mary Quimby (Newfield, ME, housework); W - 23, housework, d/o Alvah Runnels (farmer) and Martha Wentworth

George E. of Newfield, ME m. Lulu P. Trainor of Wakefield 11/12/1917 in Newfield, ME; H - 52, farmer, 2d, b. Acton, ME, s/o Joseph D. Horne and Rosina E. Pickering; W - 34, housework, 2d, b. Wakefield, d/o Loammi Hart and Ursha H. Harmon

Robert D. of East Wakefield m. Bernice M. Almond of Rochester 10/26/1946 in Rochester; H - 23, carpenter; W - 21, reg. nurse

HOUDE,
Edward J. of Wakefield m. Anna Drapeau of Wakefield 5/3/1909; H - 26, clerk, b. Wakefield, s/o Edward Houde and Adele Pouliot; W - 21, housework, b. Wakefield, d/o Eusebe Drapeau and Aurelie Carrier

HOULE,
Richard Donald of Sanbornville m. Ethel Marjorie Floyd of Sanbornville 11/12/1994

HOWARD,
Edward L. of Wakefield m. Linda E. Pelletier of Wakefield 12/9/1960 in Farmington; H - 22, laborer; W - 18, at home

Michale L. of Wakefield m. Cynthia M. Rouleau of Wakefield 7/21/1979; H - 28; W - 22

Timothy Alan of Roxbury, MA m. Carla Marie Bailey of Sanbornville 6/25/1994 in Durham

HOWARTH,
Paul D. of Sanbornville m. Brenda White of Sanbornville 5/28/1994 in Sanbornville

HOWE,
Charles W. of W. Newfield, ME m. Florence G. Davis of Newfield, ME 4/17/1895 in Ossipee; H - 42, mill man, b. W. Newfield, ME, s/o Samuel Howe of W. Newfield, ME (W. Newfield, ME, 73, farmer) and Mary N. Peaslee (Dover, 78, housekeeper); W - 32, teacher, 2d, widow, b. Crystal Springs, MI, d/o Peterson E. Goodwyne

(Richmond, VA, deceased) and Canrilla M. Adams of W. Newfield, ME (W. Newfield, ME, 70, housekeeper)

Frederic Wayland of Revere, MA m. Alva Perley of Lynnfield, MA 6/8/1940; H - 54, sales supervisor; W - 46, at home

Magloire F. of Somersworth m. Mabel I. McDonald of Wakefield 2/10/1934 in East Rochester; H - 40, chef; W - 32, at home

Melvin P. of Newfield, ME m. Harriet M. York of Newfield, ME 12/7/1898; H - 42, milling, b. Newfield, ME, s/o Samuel Howe (Newfield, ME, deceased, farmer) and Mary N. Peaslee (Dover, 81, housekeeper); W - 17, housework, b. Parsonsfield, ME, d/o George H. York of Newfield, ME (Newfield, ME, 49, farmer) and Harriet Lord (Limerick, ME, 43, housewife)

HOWLAND,

Arthur C. of Salisbury, MA m. Belle R. Gould of Wakefield 11/21/1914; H - 43, blacksmith, 2d, b. Franconia, s/o Israel C. Howland and Colista Plante; W - 36, teacher, 2d, b. Sugar Hill, d/o Ezra Smith and Effie Lafoe

HUBBARD,

John M. of East Wakefield m. Tammie E. Stevens of Kingston 10/28/1983 in Kingston

HUDSON,

William A. of Wakefield m. Ella M. Evans of Lempster 6/14/1899 in Lempster; H - 26, clergyman, 2d, b. Chesterton, MD, s/o George Hudson (Snow Hill, MD, clergyman) and Elvira Phoebus (Monie, MD, deceased); W - 29, housekeeper, b. Lempster, d/o James A. Evans (Alstead, shoemaker) and Electa Fay (Alstead, deceased)

HUFF,

Raymond George of Sanbornville m. Stacey Ann Mattress of Sanbornville 7/26/1997 in Sanbornville

HUGHES,

Guy Robert of Union m. Norma Jean Emack of Union 9/4/1993 in Wolfeboro

William C. of Braintree, MA m. Lorrie L. Boucher of Sanbornville 6/3/1989

HULL,
Dana E. of Sanbornville m. Lolene L. Palmer of Sanbornville 12/31/1991 in Durham

HUNT,
Donald P. of Wakefield m. Lavina Young of Wakefield 7/1/1978; H - 42; W - 48

HUNTLEY,
George E. of Wakefield m. Margaret E. Holland of Wakefield 8/6/1912 in Rochester; H - 42, laborer, 2d, b. Oakland, ME, s/o Richard Huntley and Sarah J. Trafton; W - 24, housekeeper, 2d, b. Dover, d/o Richard Holland and Julia A. Morrow

HURD,
Isaac of Wakefield m. Rosy Marcoux of Wakefield 8/14/1899; H - 23, laborer, b. Canada, s/o Alfred Hurd (Canada, laborer) and Mary Duriend (Canada, deceased); W - 16, housekeeper, b. Wakefield, d/o Oliver Marcoux (Canada, laborer) and C. Marshall (Canada, housekeeper)

HURLEY,
Daniel J. of Waltham, MA m. Mary E. Walsh of West Newton, MA 8/16/1981

HUSSEY,
Ted of Sanbornville m. Melanie Jackson of Sanbornville 6/6/1992

HUTCHESON,
John Goreham of Needham, MA m. Martha Shattuck Mahard of Natick, MA 4/18/1942; H - 22, photographer; W - 20, student

HUTCHINS,
Edwin H. of Sanbornville m. Gloria J. Clough of Milton Mills 7/27/1947 in Milton; H - 20, farmer; W - 16, spooler
Everett E. of Union m. Anita M. Stone of Union 3/13/1994 in Union
Joseph H. m. Marguerite O. Grant 11/4/1933 in Auburn
Paul Bernard of Sanbornville m. Carolyn Mae Welch of Sanbornville 12/24/1953; H - 25, laborer; W - 21, at home

Richard W. of Sanbornville m. Ronda E. Walker of Sanbornville 7/4/1996 in Sanbornville

Robert Louis of Acton, ME m. Paula Louise Stevens of Union 12/20/1953 in Union; H - 28, mill work; W - 21, shop work

Verner O. of Malden, MA m. Mildred Eaton of Malden, MA 8/15/1920 in Sanbornville; H - 27, draftsman, b. Palatea, FL, s/o Frank Hutchins (ME, carpenter) and Martha Virginia (VA); W - 27, teacher, b. Amesbury, MA, d/o Gilbart O. Eaton (Hingham, MA, market business) and Caddie L. Carter (Randolph, VT)

HYNES,
Albert R. of Wakefield m. Joan B. Garland of Wakefield 8/10/1985

IRVING,
James Gordon of Wakefield m. Kathleen Jordan Knight of Wakefield 7/29/1978; H - 25; W - 25

JACKSON,
Alexander of Wakefield m. Kathleen H. Winn of Wakefield 7/17/1982

Roy of Union m. Gertrude Stevens of Union 12/24/1906 in Union; H - 25, lumberman, b. NS, s/o Thomas Jackson and Annie McKay; W - 17, housework, b. Yonkers, NY, d/o Robert Stevens and Julia Evans

Warren Herman of Melrose, MA m. Norma Jane Hofer of Melrose, MA 12/14/1963; H - 33, salesman; W - 31, at home

JACOBS,
Wilmouth J. of Natick, MA m. Margaret Wiggin of Wakefield 6/25/1918 in Natick, MA; H - 24, teacher, b. Natick, MA, s/o Irving I. Jacobs and Grace Mansfield; W - 22, food expert, b. Wakefield, d/o Luther E. Wiggin and Carrie E. Wentworth

JAGGER,
Dana C. of Wakefield m. Gwendoline H. Cram of Wolfeboro 3/3/1983 in Center Ossipee

JANIS,
James A. of Johnston, RI m. Vivian P. Lajoie of Wakefield 6/6/1981 in Sanbornville

JEDREY,
Paul F. of Sanbornville m. Beverly Lena Riley of Sanbornville 8/10/1991 in Rochester

JEFFREY,
Roy W. of Walpole m. Carolyn P. Lang of Sanbornville 6/23/1946 in Sanbornville; H - 23, clerk; W - 22, school teacher

JENNESS,
Myron Ellsworth of Salem, MA m. Mary Elizabeth Whitney of Salem, MA 7/23/1942 in Sanbornville; H - 35, tester; W - 34, store keeper
Perley A. of Wakefield m. Blanche I. Hart of Wakefield 5/13/1906 in Ossipee; H - 28, teamster, b. Wakefield, s/o Charles H. Jenness and Lizzie M. Weeks; W - 17, housework, b. Wakefield, d/o Loammi Hart and ----- H. Harmond

JENSEN,
Paul Douglas of Granville, MA m. Patricia Diane Libby of Granville, MA 8/7/1976 in Sanbornville

JETTE,
Romeo Arthur of Sanbornville m. Virginia Ruth Stevens of Sanbornville 10/10/1940 in Sanbornville; H - 26, clerk; W - 23, at home

JEWETT,
Walter H. of East Wakefield m. Bertha A. Hill of East Wakefield 10/19/1946 in Sanbornville; H - 23, woodsman; W - 18, at home

JOHNSON,
Albert R. of Wakefield m. Hattie M. Evans of Wakefield 6/16/1897; H - 24, brass moulder, b. Conway, s/o Joseph L. Johnson of Wakefield (Brighton, ME, 64, stone mason) and Sarah F. Tibbetts (Wolfeboro, 64, housewife); W - 17, weaver, b. Stoneham, ME, d/o Eugene Evans of VA (Stoneham, ME, 43, farmer) and Armia Pillsbury of Wakefield (Rochester, 37, dressmaker)
Clarence I. of Wakefield m. Angie L. Nutter of Effingham 10/26/1898; H - 27, brass worker, b. Stowe, ME, s/o Joseph L. Johnson of Wakefield (Bridgton, ME, 64, stone mason) and Sarah Tibbetts (Wolfeboro, 64, housewife); W - 26, housework, b. Effingham, d/o Melvin H. Nutter

of Effingham (Newfield, ME, 45, farmer) and Ella M. Titcomb (Effingham, 42, housework)

Frederick W. of Wakefield m. Doris A. **Hayes** of Wakefield 5/18/1918 in Rochester; H - 24, lumberman, b. New York, NY, s/o William P. Johnson and Annie M. McCann; W - 20, at home, b. Wakefield, d/o Joseph E. Hayes and Grace L. Haines

Freeman L. m. Myrtie M. **Moulton** 3/6/1925; H - 59, b. Stowe, ME, s/o Joseph L. Johnson and Sarah F. Tibbetts; W - 45, b. North Conway, d/o Moses G. Brown and Chestina Robbins

Harold C. of Portland, ME m. Bergliot M. **Purinton** of Portland, ME 10/19/1935; H - 39, contractor; W - 42, at home

John M. m. Katherine L. **Paul** 10/3/1932

Mark Lester of Union m. Tracy Lynn **Gray** of Union 6/29/1991 in Middleton

Myron L. of Wakefield m. Winnifred **Giles** of Ossipee 9/6/1911 in Rochester; H - 54, marble dealer, 2d, b. Stowe, ME, s/o Joseph L. Johnson and Sarah F. Tibbetts; W - 28, housework, b. Kearsarge, d/o John Gile and Lizzie A. Smart

Norman H. of Milton m. Darlene L. **Joy** of Union 6/22/1974 in Union

Paul A. of Walpole, MA m. Ruth V. **Cummings** of Dedham, MA 12/7/1967; H - 22, electronics; W - 21, billing clerk

Richard George of Wakefield m. Wanda Gail **Keller** of Wakefield 2/5/1977

Walter Lawrence of Boston, MA m. Ruth Fuller **Morin** of Sanbornville 4/14/1956 in Farmington; H - 41, body man; W - 36, shoe worker

JOHNSTON,

George E. of Wakefield m. Jan K. **Kelly** of Wakefield 10/10/1987

Harrison A. of Wakefield m. Virginia **Tingley** of Dedham, MA 2/22/1912; H - 54, farmer, 4th, b. Boston, MA, s/o John L. Johnston and Murvia Clapp; W - 53, housework, 2d, b. Franklin, MA, d/o Maxim Francoeur and Tillie -----

JONES,

Frank E. of Orange, NJ m. Minnie F. **Harriman** of Wakefield 7/2/1912; H - 40, teacher, b. Orange, NJ, s/o Joel Jones and Cornelia Ann Canham; W - 38, teacher, b. Tamworth, d/o Adams Harriman and Elizabeth Fisk

Harry W. of Wakefield m. Bertha A. **Brierly** of Acton, ME 10/21/1903 in Acton, ME; H - 26, RR brakeman, b. Wakefield, s/o Hiram Jones and

Lizzie A. Libbey; W - 22, bookkeeper, b. Acton, ME, d/o E. J. Brierley and Lizzie Lowd
Robert G. of Madison m. Karen A. Warner of Wakefield 8/10/1985

JOOSE,
Emil F. of Lynn, MA m. Emma B. Chase of Newfield, ME 9/18/1906; H - 30, instrument maker, b. Germany, s/o Joseph W. Joose and Elizabeth O. Shoelfeld; W - 23, housework, b. Newfield, ME, d/o William N. Chase and Jennie E. Woodman

JORDAN,
Peter A. of Wakefield m. Diane M. Jordan of Wakefield 7/29/1972

JOSLYN,
David R. of Springvale, ME m. Joanne L. Hussey of Springvale, ME 7/9/1983

JOY,
Abbott Leon of Union m. Pearl Edythe Johnson of Lebanon, ME 9/27/1940 in Acton, ME; H - 21, fibre millworker; W - 18, at home
Abbott Leon of Union m. Dorothy Annie Hersey of East Rochester 9/26/1962 in East Rochester; H - 45, maintenance; W - 42, dresser
David A. of Union m. Jacquelyn L. Putney of Middleton 7/27/1984
Donald A. of Union m. Gayle J. Merrill of Milton 9/9/1974 in Union
Donald Alan of Sanbornville m. Avis Jean Young of Farmington 6/8/1956 in West Milton; H - 20, lumberman; W - 16, at home
Douglas E. of Union m. Cheryl L. Davis of Milton Mills 4/15/1960; H - 17, laborer; W - 16, at home
Lester Eugene of Union m. Marian E. Wentworth of Union 2/22/1936 in Rochester; H - 22, counter packer; W - 21, at home
Mason G. of Union m. Mildred M. Joy of Union 11/10/1956; H - 40, lumberman; W - 36, at home
Mason I. of Union m. Mildred M. Berry of Middleton 3/12/1935 in Rochester; H - 18, laborer; W - 14, at home
Nelson M. of Union m. Mildred Pike of Rochester 7/21/1935 in Milford; H - 29, mill operator; W - 30, clerk
Oscar K. of Union m. Jessie A. Herbert of Union 7/7/1951 in Union; H - 28, mach. opr.; W - 19, at home
Philip Stephen of Wakefield m. Ann Marie Patch of Wakefield 7/25/1998 in Middleton

Richard I., Jr. of Wakefield m. Robin A. Bernier of Wakefield 4/25/1987
Richard Irving of Union m. Sylvia Lorraine Smith of Union 6/30/1956; H - 21, sample maker; W - 18, at home
Stephen P. of Union m. Lucinda E. Hicks of Milton 2/30/1974 in Union (sic)
Stephen P. of Wakefield m. Emmie L. Fulcher of Wakefield 9/26/1981 in Union

JUDD,
Douglas W. of Lowell, MA m. Marie H. Riley of Wakefield 9/25/1983

JUDGE,
William J. of Sanbornville m. Pamela A. Robinson of Sanbornville 12/31/1989 in Sanbornville

JUNEAU,
James S. of Morrisville, NY m. Cynthia A. Bridges of Shrewsbury, MA 11/28/1987

JUPINKO,
Stephen L. of Wakefield m. Roberta B. Paradis of Rochester 5/22/1982 in Rochester

KANE,
Stanley John of Augusta, ME m. Doris Elizabeth Cannon of Augusta, ME 12/27/1975 in Sanbornville

KANNHEISER,
Ronald Leslie of Stoneham, MA m. Judith A. Bowdidge of Stoneham, MA 8/29/1975

KARCHER,
Charles E. of Sanbornville m. Marion T. Randall of Sanbornville 7/13/1946 in Henniker; H - 21, mechanic; W - 20, at home
William A., Jr. of Wakefield m. Maryanne Soucy of Wakefield 5/12/1945 in Wolfeboro; H - 24, US Army; W - 20, office worker

KARDINAL,
Henry Herman of Boston, MA m. Catherine Elizabeth Maguire of New York, NY 8/11/1941 in Sanbornville; H - 38, mason; W - 39, teacher

KARRICK,
Christopher M. of Springfield, IL m. Sandra L. Witham of Haverhill, MA 6/3/1981 in Sanbornville

KASPRZYK,
Peter M. of Sanbornville m. Elizabeth P. Kierstead of Hampton Falls 9/7/1991 in Conway

KATWICK,
Arthur David, II of East Wakefield m. Catherine Mary Katwick of East Wakefield 1/15/1977 in Milton

KEATING,
James F., III of Sanbornville m. Rebbecca G. Andrews of Sanbornville 8/11/1974

KEEFE,
Wilfred E., Jr. of Sanbornville m. Chyrel L. Grondin of Sanbornville 6/28/1996 in Milton

KEKOA,
Ronald Kekaulani of Hilo, HI m. Karen Susanne Johnson of So. Wakefield 9/4/1965; H - 21, US Army; W - 17, at home

KELLEY,
Asa B. of Middleton m. Ruth B. Yeaton of Wakefield 9/29/1915; H - 50, farmer, 3d, b. Salem, s/o Asa Kelley and Charlotte J. Smith; W - 35, farmer, 2d, b. Wakefield, d/o Alvah S. Garland and Priscilla Lothrop
Jerry Maurice of Dover m. Tess Garrett of Union 10/21/1988 in Union
Michale J. of Siloam Springs, AR m. Linda L. Littlefield of Union 1/7/1966 in Sanbornville; H - 21, US Army; W - 19, at home
Thomas Walter of Cambridge, MA m. Rosemary F. Novello of Arlington, MA 8/5/1967 in Sanbornville; H - 23, student; W - 19, student

KELLY,
Dennis Bartley of Sanbornville m. Eileen Louise Hickey of Sanbornville 9/4/1965 in Sanbornville; H - 20, laborer; W - 18, student
Douglas Paul of Sanbornville m. Sara Ann Hoskinson of Peabody, MA 4/26/1975 in Sanbornville

KENERSON,
Ivory of Wakefield m. Martha Randall of Wakefield 12/24/1903 in Sanbornville; H - 45, blacksmith, 2d, b. Albany, s/o Job Kenerson and Rhoda Head; W - 28, housework, 2d, b. Wakefield, d/o Jay Runnell and Margaret Jack

KENNETT,
John Elliot m. Hazel Abbie Farnham 10/21/1933 in Union
Ralph R. of Wakefield m. Emma S. Jewett of Milton 11/2/1910 in Somerville, MA; H - 20, mail carrier, b. Madison, s/o Charles H. Kennett and Abbie Davis; W - 20, housework, b. Milton, d/o Haven R. Jewett and Nellie Sibley
Ralph R. of Sanbornville m. Lydia M. Mulvey of Wolfeboro 6/11/1938 in Sanbornville; H - 47, undertaker; W - 40, housework

KENNEY,
James H. of Wakefield m. Annie A. Lombard of Wakefield 11/5/1899; H - 44, teamster, 2d, b. St. Johns, NB, s/o James Kenney (NB, deceased) and Catharine Taylor (NS, deceased); W - 21, housekeeper, b. Biddeford, ME, d/o James Lombard (England, machinist) and Kate Desmond (Ireland, deceased)
John T., Jr. of Wakefield m. Sandra J. Buswell of Wakefield 1/6/1973 in Sanbornville
Luther W. of Wakefield m. Helen M. Lucy of Conway 12/15/1908 in Conway; H - 24, RR brakeman, b. Wolfeboro, s/o Frank B. Kenney and Carrie B. Twombly; W - 23, school teacher, b. Conway, d/o Frank Lucy and Rose E. Stuart

KENT,
Ralph W., Jr. of Holliston, MA m. Carol V. Dinn of Holliston, MA 2/9/1967; H - 27, lab. worker; W - 26, clerk

KERSHAW,
Thomas A. of Boston, MA m. Dianne Rogers of Sanbornville 4/29/1967 in Wolfeboro; H - 28, market manager; W - 28, secretary

KEY,
John M. of Wakefield m. Jean M. Maginnis of Dorchester, MA 9/2/1983

KIMBALL,
Cummings m. Marion Evans 10/25/1925; H - 23, b. Presque Isle,
ME, s/o John Kimball and Violet Cummings; W - 20, b. Milton, d/o
Calvin Evans and Flora Rhines
David L. of Middleton m. Barbara A. Hodsdon of Union 4/16/1971
Frank, Jr. of Wakefield m. Grace Bagley of New York 9/18/1908 in
Rochester; H - 21, lumberman, b. W. Newfield, ME, s/o Frank
Kimball and Annie Patch; W - 28, cook, 2d, b. Sonegal, Ireland, d/o
Andrew Bagley and Anne Leonard
Gordon Lester of Portland, ME m. Bertha R. Thompson of Portland, ME
8/20/1949; H - 23, service station; W - 22, laundry worker
Herbert Lord of Acton, ME m. Patricia Ethel Mack of Acton, ME
6/21/1941 in Sanbornville; H - 29, soldier; W - 24, school teacher
John W. of Wakefield m. Alta S. Pike of Middleton 2/13/1897 in
Springvale, ME; H - 40, farmer, b. Wakefield, s/o Ward W. Kimball
of Wakefield (Wakefield, farmer) and S. A. Watson (Wakefield,
deceased); W - 25, housekeeper, b. Middleton, d/o James L. Pike of
Middleton (New Durham, farmer) and Susan L. Cloutman (Middleton,
housekeeper)
John W. of Wakefield m. Violet H. Cummings of Fort Fairfield, ME
9/20/1900 in Brookfield; H - 45, farmer, 2d, b. Wakefield, s/o Ward
W. Kimball (Wakefield, farmer) and Sarah A. Watson (Wakefield); W
- 36, housekeeper, b. Fort Fairfield, ME, d/o Bradford Cummings
(Freedom, ME, farmer) and Martha K. White (Winthrop, ME)
John Ward of Sanbornville m. Sylvia May Littlefield of Union 7/6/1951 in
Sanbornville; H - 24, truck driver; W - 24, at home
Mark R. of Wakefield m. Pauline I. Rines of Dover 10/14/1979; H - 18; W
- 21
Mark Robert of Sanbornville m. Lisa Ann Pouliot of Sanbornville
9/22/1990 in Rochester
Oscar F. of Middleton m. Florence G. Runnels of Wakefield 4/11/1905 in
Sanbornville; H - 22, brakeman, b. Middleton, s/o George W.
Kimball and Eliza S. Hanscom; W - 21, teacher, b. Worcester, MA,
d/o Samuel Runnels and Edna Pratt
Raymond of Wakefield m. Louise Pippin of Wakefield 4/21/1908 in
Rochester; H - 19, laborer, b. Newfield, ME, s/o Frank Kimball and
Annie Patch; W - 19, housekeeper, b. Wakefield, d/o Victor Pippin
and Susan Tibedeau
Wallace Osborne of Boston, MA m. Barbara G. Hammond of Boston, MA
9/5/1943 in Union; H - 21, lab. tech.; W - 24, stenographer

Walter S. of Wakefield m. Addie M. Hanson of Wakefield 1/1/1909 in Milton; H - 30, brass worker, b. Middleton, s/o David Kimball and Nellie Hanscomb; W - 27, housework, 2d, b. Portland, ME, d/o Stephen F. Shackford and Ada L. Smith

KINCEL,
Frank John of Morrisville, PA m. Patricia Mae Hill of Sanbornville 6/12/1965; H - 20, machinist; W - 18, student

KINE,
William S., Jr. of Naples, FL m. Dorothy R. Walker of Wakefield 7/25/1981

KING,
Harry E. of Sanbornville m. Anita L. Charles of Sanbornville 7/2/1994 in Sanbornville
Johnathan W. of Wakefield m. Marianne Abbott of Wakefield 6/14/1986 in Walpole
Jonathan E. of Sanbornville m. Cheryl L. Madaferi of Sanbornville 9/9/1992 in Ossipee
William Irvine of Portland, ME m. Ruth Peterson Steady of Portland, ME 7/4/1940 in Sanbornville; H - 34, salesman; W - 31, at home

KINNON,
Lee A. of Belchertown, MA m. Lynne M. McWilliams of Belchertown, MA 8/28/1982

KINSELLA,
Richard C. of Wakefield m. Shirley M. Tice of Wakefield 12/16/1980

KINVILLE,
Christopher Michael of Union m. Kate Laurel Martin of Union 7/12/1997 in Sanbornville
Ralph E. of Wakefield m. Caroline E. Young of Wakefield 7/20/1996
Randy M. of Sanbornville m. Elaine A. Fillion of Somersworth 9/12/1969 in Somersworth
Richard N. of Sanbornville m. Gloria C. Stephens of Rochester 6/20/1970 in Rochester
Robert W. of Sanbornville m. Cathy A. Thompson of Sanbornville 11/29/1969 in Sanbornville

Ronald G., Jr. m. Sheila L. **Burns** 9/16/1966; H - 25, engineer; W - 24, teacher

Scot Alan of Sanbornville m. Jennifer Anne **Gray** of Sanbornville 7/1/1995 in Sanbornville

KIRBY,
Kenelma H. of Worcester, MA m. Mary C. **Brenn** of Worcester, MA 9/1/1934 in Sanbornville; H - 23, chauffeur; W - 22, at home

KIRK,
Arthur M. of Gilford m. Sally A. **Clifford** of Sanbornville 3/23/1968 in Sanbornville

Kirk A. of Wakefield m. Wendy J. **Grover** of Wakefield 9/30/1989

KITTELL,
Nicholas Charles of Lakewood, OH m. Helen Louise **Flickinger** of Cuyahoga Falls, OH 8/9/1958; H - 58, retired; W - 49, teacher

KNAPP,
Arthur C. of Wakefield m. Minnie L. **Tappan** of Ossipee 3/17/1935 in Ossipee; H - 39, millman; W - 16, house work

George B. m. Leda B. **Eldridge** 8/30/1930; H - 22, s/o Samuel L. Knapp (Norton, KS) and Hannah Nickerson (Norton, KS); W - 22, d/o Charles M. Eldridge (Ossipee) and Nettie Nichols (Ossipee)

KNIGHT,
Cecil Everett of Sanbornville m. Dorcas Louise **Marsh** of Malden, MA 11/12/1938 in Sanbornville; H - 27, dairyman; W - 18, at home

John A. of Wakefield m. Sandra L. **Evenson** of Barrington 6/9/1985 in Strafford

M. E. of Wakefield m. Elizabeth B. **Brackett** of Wakefield 10/14/1897; H - 24, telegrapher, b. Salmon Falls, s/o Gilman Knight of Salmon Falls (No. Berwick, ME, 67, carpenter) and Mary Pinder (Ossipee Valley, 64, housewife); W - 21, housework, b. Wakefield, d/o Charles E. Brackett of Wakefield (Acton, ME, 69, farmer) and Elizabeth R. Wiggin (Wakefield, 62, housewife)

Marshall E. of Wakefield m. Elizabeth B. **Doyle** of Wakefield 6/18/1910; H - 37, telegraph operator, 2d, b. Salmon Falls, s/o Gilman Knight and Mary C. Pender; W - 28, housework, b. Wakefield, d/o John Doyle and Amanda E. Wentworth

KNOWLES,
Duron W. of Union m. Addie M. Whitney of Union 7/29/1944 in Union: H - 30, mill worker; W - 24, at home

KOCH,
William M. of Winooski, VT m. Elizabeth J. Abbott of Winooski, VT 7/20/1985

KOLB,
Mark R. of Sanbornville m. Anita M. Randall of Sanbornville 9/12/1992

KOSINSKI,
Edward J. of Acton, MA m. Nancy L. McKay of Concord, MA 9/4/1970

KRABEK,
Axel of Wakefield m. Florence L. Burleigh of Middleton 1/19/1907; H - 23, merchant, b. Denmark, s/o Andreas H. Krabek and Annie Misselsen; W - 20, housekeeper, b. Wakefield, d/o George W. Burleigh and Alice Powell

KRIPPNER,
Paul D. of Tariffville, CT m. June E. Bucchiere of Ipswich, MA 6/17/1989

KRYWICKI,
David Shepard of Sanbornville m. Julia Patricia Ellis of Gilford 6/5/1993

KRYZAK,
Theodore J., Jr. of Acton, ME m. Deborah A. Phylis of Acton, ME 11/20/1982

LABRAREE,
Clinton L., III of Sanbornville m. Gail M. Calderone of Sanbornrnville 9/13/1998 in Sanbornville

LABRIE,
Conrad G. of Bedford m. Jean M. Knisley of Wakefield 5/12/1984 in Bedford
Gabriel Dominic of Sanbornville m. Angela Jean Horning of Sanbornville 10/12/1996 in Sanbornville

LACASIA,
Guiseppi J. of Winchester, MA m. Namiko H. **Standbridge** of Reading, MA 8/16/1969 in Sanbornville

LACASSE,
Antoine J. of Wakefield m. Leda **Cormier** of Somersworth 11/26/1906 in Somersworth; H - 20, RR employee, b. Buckland, Canada, s/o Joseph Lacasse and Orelie Patrie; W - 19, mill operative, b. St. Angel, Canada, d/o David Cormier and Zenaide LeBlanc

Joseph of Wakefield m. Mary E. **Carrier** of Wakefield 6/12/1911; H - 51, laborer, 2d, b. Canada, s/o Joseph Lacasse and Genevieve Mercier; W - 57, housework, 2d, b. Canada, d/o George Belanger and Camile Dellerre

LAFOREST,
Leon L. of Sanbornville m. Olga **Delan** of Sanbornville 8/17/1936 in Sanbornville; H - 40, cook; W - 28, at home

Leon Louis of Sanbornville m. Effie Elizabeth **White** of Sanbornville 12/31/1943 in Milton Mills; H - 47, cook; W - 40, waitress

LAHTI,
Matthew of Medfield, MA m. Dorothy W. **Lahti** of Sanbornville 8/4/1948 in Ossipee; H - 57, inv. banker; W - 46, at home

LAMIE,
Joseph A. of Wakefield m. Marie E. **Vigneault** of Somersworth 6/10/1907 in Somersworth; H - 29, baggage master, b. Somersworth, s/o Moses Lamie and Lea Currier; W - 22, operative, b. Ossipee, d/o Joseph N. Vigneault and Rose A. Marchand

LAMONTAGNE,
Robert P. of Rochester m. Judith A. **Morrill** of Sanbornville 8/4/1973

Roger R. of Hampton m. Cheryl A. **Sparks** of Wakefield 11/11/1978; H - 22; W - 22

Thomas P. of Wakefield m. Cynthia L. **St. Cyr** of Wakefield 12/19/1980

William A. of Wakefield m. Sadie **Keniston** of Wakefield 11/9/1908; H - 21, RR employee, b. Canada, s/o Joseph Lamontagne and Annie Joyce; W - 19, housework, b. Effingham, d/o Joseph Keniston and Jennie Varney

William A. of Wakefield m. Lena B. Blaisdell of East Rochester 10/2/1919 in Milton; H - 32, laborer, 2d, b. St. Jarvis, PQ, s/o Joseph Lamontagne (Canada, laborer) and Annie Joice (Montreal, PQ); W - 33, 3d, b. Wolfeboro, d/o Charles Burke (Milton, farmer) and Hattie Tebbetts (Wolfeboro)

LANCTOT,
Thomas C., Jr. of Sanbornville m. Deborah J. White of Sanbornville 10/15/1994 in Ossipee

LANDERS,
William P. of Wenham, MA m. Ellen L. Albanese of So. Hamilton, MA 10/23/1971 in Sanbornville

LANE,
Charles T. of Wakefield m. Mary G. Sanborn of Acton, ME 1/25/1899; H - 28, farmer, b. Dover, s/o Samuel F. Lane (Wakefield, farmer) and Ada Fitzgerald (Dover, housekeeper); W - 20, housekeeper, 2d, b. Acton, ME, d/o Joshua Brackett (Acton, ME, farmer) and Emeline Blaisdell (Acton, ME, housekeeper)
George F. of Wakefield m. Ida M. Davis of Tamworth 8/20/1903; H - 21, hostler, b. Wakefield, s/o Samuel F. Lane and Addie Fitzgerald; W - 23, housework, b. Tamworth, d/o Eli Davis and Rubie Perkins
Harris Linwood of Sanbornville m. Alma R. MacKinnon of Lawrence, MA 9/24/1945 in Dover; H - 41, carpenter; W - 45, mill worker
Harry L. of Wakefield m. Emma Watson of Wakefield 9/30/1903; H - 26, teamster, b. Dover, s/o Samuel F. Lane and Addie A. Fitzgerald; W - 25, housework, b. Waltham, MA, d/o John Watson and Ellen Thornton
William H. of Wakefield m. Mary Kimball of Wakefield 11/28/1917; H - 82, farmer, 2d, b. Wakefield, s/o Samuel Lane and Mary Dearborn; W - 60, housework, 2d, b. Waterboro, ME, d/o Samuel Patch and Mary Patch

LANG,
Gerald Forrest of Sanbornville m. Evelyn Pauline Clough of Rochester 1/11/1959 in Rochester; H - 20, USAF; W - 19, clerk
Reuben P. of Wakefield m. Almira P. Lyons of Exeter 5/3/1947 in Winchester, MA; H - 53, caretaker; W - 50, at home
Thomas A. of Wakefield m. Mary E. Moore of Wakefield 7/29/1972

LANGDON,
William R. of Acton, ME m. Dorothy A. Wentworth of Wakefield 2/11/1948 in Wolfeboro; H - 24, lumberman; W - 18, clerk

LANGLEY,
David James of Acton, ME m. Wendy Lynn McDormand of Wakefield 10/18/1997 in Sanbornville

Lawrence A. of Acton, ME m. Diana L. Gammon of Acton, ME 1/19/1986

Thomas H. of Acton, ME m. Emily Bradley of Malden, MA 11/2/1911; H - 45, farmer, b. Acton, ME, s/o William H. Langley and Mary A. Fernald; W - 43, housework, b. Broseley, England, d/o Thomas Bradley and Emma Pugh

LANOWETT,
George of Wakefield m. Philomene Pouliott of Wakefield 2/17/1900 in Sanbornville; H - 28, laborer, b. Franklin, s/o John Lanowett (Canada, retired) and Agnes Rogers; W - 23, housekeeper, b. Wakefield, d/o Edward Pouliott (St. Ansemme, PQ, carpenter) and Silena Boiseneail (St. Bernard, PQ)

LAPOINTE,
George J. of Springvale, ME m. Pauline A. Gibbs of Wakefield 9/25/1920 in Union; H - 18, on railroad, b. Wolfeboro, s/o John Lapointe (Canada, on railroad) and Olive Marcoux (Canada); W - 17, at home, b. Sagamore, MA, d/o William H. Gibbs (Sagamore, MA, foundry oper.) and Pauline Delva Fleck

LARSON,
David Evald of Santa Fe, NM m. Ruth Leslie Burton of Santa Fe, NM 7/27/1991

LASKEY,
Alan L. of Milton m. Barbara L. Beckwith of Sanbornville 9/16/1967 in Sanbornville; H - 19, const. worker; W - 16, at home

Clyde of Milton m. Eva M. Richards of Wakefield 7/21/1934 in Rochester; H - 28, farmer; W - 20, mill employee

Kenneth Morton of Milton m. Arlene Frances Bumford of Sanbornville 5/23/1942 in Sanbornville; H - 27, mechanic; W - 23, waitress

LAUTH,
Les H. of North Wakefield m. Melanie A. Horne of North Wakefield 2/3/1990

LAVERTUE,
Dale R. of Sanbornville m. Karen L. Staines of Sanbornville 9/21/1996 in Somersworth
John Francis of Union m. Phyllis LaDell Morrill of Union 4/21/1957 in Sanbornville; H - 18, log surveyor; W - 16, at home
Norman Daniel of Union m. Nancy Joyce Glidden of East Wolfeboro 8/13/1959; H - 20, laborer; W - 18, at home
Randy of Wakefield m. Jennifer H. Boisvert of Wakefield 9/12/1987 in East Wakefield
William John of Union m. Cecile Demers of So. Berwick, ME 9/4/1954 in So. Berwick, ME; H - 21, mill employee; W - 23, shoe shop

LAVOIE,
Charles of Wakefield m. Deyulda Breton of Newmarket 7/22/1918 in Newmarket; H - 63, mill hand, 2d, b. Canada, s/o Augustine Lavoie and Lea St. Lauraine; W - 41, mill hand, b. Canada, d/o Francis Breton and Philomene Bretber
William A. of Wakefield m. Rose D. Ramie of Wakefield 9/4/1906 in Gonic; H - 24, laborer, b. Hollis, s/o Charles Lavoie and Mary Raymond; W - 23, housework, b. St. Pie, Canada, d/o Louis Ramie and Emelie Tetreault

LAWRENCE,
Lester A. of Palestine, IL m. Elizabeth Dudley of Wakefield 8/17/1922 in East Ware; H - 24, clerical, b. Palestine, IL, s/o John Lawrence and Cora Duke; W - 23, teacher, b. West Newbury, MA, d/o Fred W. Dudley and Harriet D. Towle

LAWS,
Michael E. of Wakefield m. Lucy A. Adjutant of Wakefield 12/24/1982

LEADEN,
John C. of Stoneham, MA m. Sheila M. Wilson of Stoneham, MA 9/15/1990

LEDUC,
Roger B. of Woonsocket, RI m. Germaine J. Valois of Pawtucket, RI 5/24/1966 in Sanbornville; H - 63, office mgr.; W - 56, office clerk

LEE,
Mark David of Dover m. Monique Marie Rancourt of Union 9/28/1991 in Dover

LEEMAN,
Stanwood S. of York, ME m. Marylin L. Drown of Sanbornville 7/14/1951 in Rochester; H - 21, US Army; W - 18, at home

LEHORILLER,
Gerard R. of Biddeford, ME m. Nancy C. Ouellette of Biddeford, ME 8/1/1969

LEIGHTON,
Edwin P. of Union m. Abbie J. Armstrong of Dunbarton 10/18/1945 in Grasmere; H - 20, farmer; W - 18, at home
Edwin Presco of Wakefield m. Irene May Goodwin of Farmington 3/10/1976 in Dover
Francis E. of Sanbornville m. Margaret E. Palmer of Rochester 7/22/1960; H - 21, carpenter; W - 23, office work
Gregory D. of Wakefield m. Lisa E. Agans of Wakefield 11/29/1986
Richard Lloyd of Wakefield m. Heidi Marie Pheasant of Rochester 8/13/1977 in Sanbornville
Robert C. of Union m. Kathy A. Gardner of Milton 2/23/1974 in Rochester
Robert Norton of Sanbornville m. Ann Dodge Stevens of Sanbornville 5/13/1951 in Sanbornville; H - 22, electrician; W - 23, bookkeeper

LEMAN,
Russell J. m. Gertrude Hayden 7/20/1930; H - 23, s/o Charles I. Leman (Germany) and Sarah Amers (NS); W - 20, d/o Ellis R. Hayden (Ashland, MA) and Gertrude Phillips (Lynn, MA)

LENNON,
John Edward, 3d of Boston, MA m. Kathleen Patricia Hickey of Sanbornville 12/28/1963 in Sanbornville; H - 26, student; W - 22, librarian

LEROUX,
Joseph A.A. m. Marie Adele Langlois 7/20/1929; H - 53, s/o Francois Leroux (Canada) and Hermine Dubois (Canada); W - 58, d/o Hubert Roy (Canada) and Salomie Lachante (Canada)

LESPERANCE,
Donald P., Jr. of Gonic m. LeeAnn Beaupre of Sanbornville 9/28/1984 in Rochester

LESSARD,
Forrest G. of Wakefield m. Joan L. Jewell of Wakefield 2/28/1961 in Sanbornville; H - 31, construction; W - 18, at home
Leo W. of Rochester m. Christine E. Karcher of Sanbornville 4/27/1947 in Sanbornville; H - 31, spinner; W - 22, spinner

LETENDRE,
John of Newfield, ME m. Ida Florence Goodwin of Newfield, ME 10/16/1937; H - 52, laborer; W - 54, housework

LEUCHTNER,
Thomas Grant of Palo Alto, CA m. Mandi Lee Toutsch of Palo Alto, CA 6/19/1993

LEWIS,
Frank T. of Wakefield m. Marion B. Southack of Lincoln, MA 9/1/1974 in Sanbornville
Richard S. of Topsfield, MA m. Jean E. Swanstrom of Lexington, MA 11/11/1967; H - 51, candy mfg.; W - 34, secretary

LIBBY,
Arthur Leroy of Sanbornville m. Beatrice Nelda Reid of Sanford, ME 4/6/1957; H - 40, carpenter; W - 31, factory worker
Edward E. of Sanbornville m. Winnifred M. Gauthier of Sanbornville 4/29/1961 in Sanbornville; H - 18, USAF; W - 17, at home
Fred I. of Sanford, ME m. Dorothea D. Stanley of Sanford, ME 7/22/1967 in Sanbornville; H - 37, bookkeeper; W - 49, housewife
Lucian V.B. of West Newfield, ME m. Ola A. Junkins of Lebanon, ME 1/14/1905 in Sanbornville; H - 20, blacksmith, b. W. Newfield, ME, s/o John J. Libby and Cora B. Glidden; W - 20, school teacher, b. Somersworth, d/o Frank H. Junkins and Annie B. Fleer

Nathan J. of Wakefield m. Eliza B. Wilkinson of Laconia 12/11/1901 in Laconia; H - 28, carpenter, b. Wakefield, s/o Washington Libby (Wakefield, farmer) and Ellen M. Farnham (Wakefield, housewife); W - 28, bookkeeper, b. Laconia, d/o Henry L. Wilkinson (Holderness, hotel proprietor) and Nell L. Howell (Goldsboro, NC, housekeeper)

Steven R. of Wakefield m. Brenda L. Tuttle of Wakefield 2/14/1987 in Milton Mills

LINCOLN,
Joseph Bartlett of Wakefield m. Tricia Lee Segeberg of Wakefield 4/1/1997

Raymond Henry, Jr. of Union m. Colleen J. Nelson of Union 10/1/1965 in Union; H - 33, laborer; W - 26, billing clerk

LINEHAM,
David A. of Wakefield m. Kathleen M. Richards of Wakefield 6/25/1983

David Alan of Christiansted m. Kay Marie Morgan of Christiansted 7/3/1997 in Sanbornville

LITTLE,
Adam Enos of Boston, MA m. Florence Martin of Wakefield 11/28/1942 in East Wakefield; H - 64, cons't builder; W - 43, housework

LITTLEFIELD,
Delbert W. of Union m. Constance M. Mallica of Milton 12/31/1971 in Union (also listed as 1/3/1972 in Wakefield)

Henry H. of Wakefield m. Ada V. Lord of Wakefield 6/5/1919 in Union; H - 24, section hand, b. Somerville, MA, s/o Daniel L. Littlefield (No. Shapleigh, ME, teamster) and Maria Haney (ME); W - 19, b. Acton, ME, d/o Harvey L. Lord (Acton, ME, sawyer) and Clara Nichols (Ossipee)

Holsea M. of Waterboro, ME m. Dorothy E. Pike of Shapleigh, ME 11/23/1903; H - 60, merchant, 3d, b. Waterboro, ME, s/o William Littlefield and Anna Mildram; W - 60, domestic, b. Waterboro, ME, d/o Joseph Pike and Eunice Thyng

Nathan L. of Wakefield m. Grace F. Eastman of Wakefield 9/5/1908; H - 23, clerk, b. York, ME, s/o Jothan L. Littlefield and Martha E. Allen; W - 23, bookkeeper, b. Fort Fairfield, ME, d/o Edward P. Eastman and Eliza M. Sawyer

Nicholas Guild of Wakefield m. Ann Louise Rose of Wakefield 11/24/1976

Payson Eastman of Union m. Frances Lillian Henderson of Union 6/26/1953; H - 43, laborer; W - 38, shoe worker

Richard Preble of Union m. Lorraine Ellen Wilson of Union 4/11/1953; H - 24, truck driver; W - 19, at home

LIVERMORE,

Edwin J. of Wakefield m. Ellen McDonald of North Sydney, NS 9/25/1902 in Bartlett; H - 29, brakeman, b. Hudson, MA, s/o Thomas Livermore and Ellen -----; W - 29, housework, b. North Sydney, NS, d/o John McDonald and Susan -----

LJUNGGREN,

Ove William of Medford, MA m. Marjorie Ethelynd Johnson of Cambridge, MA 9/8/1956 in Sanbornville; H - 32, sign const.; W - 37, at home

LOCKE,

Austin P. of Allston, MA m. Imogene Tibbetts of Wakefield 2/22/1897; H - 25, conductor, b. Portsmouth, s/o John H. Locke (Barrington, deceased) and Sarah L. Webster (Rye, deceased); W - 25, teacher, b. Wakefield, d/o Benjamin F. Tibbetts of Wakefield (Porter, ME, 58, farmer) and Emily J. Abbott (Porter, ME, 56, housewife)

S. Ellsworth of Sanbornville m. Flora Thibeault of Center Ossipee 1/27/1940 in Porter, ME; H - 33, mechanic; W - 26, at home

LOCKER,

Walter L. of Andover m. Loraine Martin of Wakefield 2/9/1979; H - 44; W - 46

LODGE,

Bruce D. of Wakefield m. Elizabeth M. Marshall of Wakefield 2/9/1980

LOMBERTO,

Roger Paul of Franklin, MA m. Doris Gertrude Fiske of Franklin, MA 11/29/1958 in Sanbornville; H - 21, press. opr.; W - 18, typist

LONCARIC,

Russell James of Sanbornville m. Kathleen Julia Chick of East Wakefield 6/2/1993

LONDO,
Thomas of Wakefield m. Alice M. Patch of Newfield, ME 12/14/1902 in East Wakefield; H - 35, fireman, 2d, b. Portland, ME, s/o Abel M. Londo and Julia Gauthier; W - 24, housework, b. Newfield, ME, d/o Albert H. Patch and Rose A. Patch

LONG,
Donald A. of Milton Mills m. Joan M. Hall of Wakefield 10/31/1987 in Milton

LONGLEY,
Leon M. of Norway, ME m. Edna M. Sibley of Wakefield 12/26/1899; H - 30, plumber, b. Raymond, ME, s/o Luther Longley (Raymond, ME, farmer) and Sophia D. Butler (Flagstaff, ME, teacher); W - 30, stitcher, b. Wakefield, d/o R.F.D. Sibley (Wakefield, deceased) and Emma B. Buzzell (Acton, ME, housekeeper)

LONGO,
David C. of Lanham, MD m. Deborah A. Mallonee of Lanham, MD 10/3/1982

LORING,
Russell G. of Ossipee m. Mary L. Brooks of Union 1/26/1974
Russell George of Center Ossipee m. Nancy Jeanne Doe of Wakefield 12/5/1965; H - 18, laborer; W - 17, student

LOUD,
Ivory S. of Wakefield m. Amanda L. Waldron of Wakefield 3/22/1887 in Portsmouth; H - 46, station agent, 2d, b. Newfield, ME, s/o Nathan N. Loud (Newfield, ME, farmer) and Mary Jane ----- (Newfield, ME, housekeeper); W - 32, housework, b. Wakefield, d/o Hiram R. Waldron (Acton, ME, trader) and Sarah P. ----- (Newfield, ME, housekeeper)

LOVECCHIO,
Joseph M. of Wolfeboro m. Christene Ann Benner of Sanbornville 11/9/1996 in Wolfeboro

LOVER,
Charles J. of Wakefield m. Elizabeth S. Thebideau of Danvers, MA 11/28/1905 in Gonic; H - 25, box manufacturer, b. Wakefield, s/o John Lover and Celina M. Cloutier; W - 24, b. NS, d/o John Thibideau and Sarah E. Tebo
Fred A. of Wakefield m. Nellie A. Downs of Wakefield 4/4/1920 in Milton; H - 24, core maker, b. Wakefield, s/o Charles Lover (Canada, mill hand) and Mary Raymond (Gorham, ME); W - 16, housework, b. Wakefield, d/o Harry A. Downs (Wolfeboro, farmer) and Agnes Sawyer (Caribou, ME)
Peter J. of Union m. Alice M. Downs of Union 5/3/1905 in Gonic; H - 19, laborer, b. Union, s/o Augusten Lover and Celina Cloutier; W - 18, weaver, b. Sanbornville, d/o Charles Downs and Lizebelle Ellis

LUBESKI,
William L. of Lawrence, MA m. Sheila M. Daggett of Wakefield 7/15/1984 in East Wakefield

LYNCH,
Dennis P. of Plainville, CT m. Jean E. Pratt of Union 6/16/1973 in Union

LYNN,
Ernest E. of Fall River, MA m. Jennie Meikle of Wakefield 3/26/1898; H - 49, engraver, 3d, b. England, s/o Edward Lynn (England, deceased) and Martha Atkinson (England, deceased); W - 39, pantographer, b. Milford, d/o John Meikle of Wakefield (Scotland, 64, calico printer) and Mary McArthur (Scotland, 60, housewife)

LYONS,
Donald Henry of Sanbornville m. Helen E. Herrick of Sanbornville 9/10/1950 in Sanbornville; H - 23, student; W - 18, shoe opr.
Edward Palmer of Sanbornville m. Nancy S. Churchill of Brookfield 12/24/1950 in Sanbornville; H - 19, student; W - 15, student

MACCORMAC,
Harry H. of East Wakefield m. Doris A. Walley of Farmington 5/21/1960 in East Wakefield; H - 67, retired; W - 52, factory worker

MACDONALD,
Jamis Erwin of Rochester m. Linda Shirley Boutidier of Sanbornville 11/16/1963 in Dover; H - 30, asst. foreman; W - 22, housework

MACE,
Donald Hanscom of Lebanon, ME m. Jane Eva Keating of Sanbornville 6/13/1953 in Sanbornville; H - 21, US Army; W - 18, at home

MACGREGOR,
Mark Arthur of East Wakefield m. Wendi J. Coran of East Wakefield 6/11/1994 in East Wakefield
Robert B. of Union m. Maryellen Cormier of Union 7/31/1985

MACINTOSH,
Roger E., Jr. of Attleboro, MA m. Kimberly A. Habersack of Norton, MA 12/20/1986

MACKENZIE,
Samuel Peel of Wakefield m. Alice Bertha Ward of Manchester 9/1/1942 in Union; H - 65, filling sta. prop.; W - 52, office worker

MACKIE,
George A. of Union m. Florence M. Stevens of Union 6/1/1946 in Union; H - 27, shoeworker; W - 25, secretary
George R. of Wakefield m. Olive M. Lover of Wakefield 4/9/1895; H - 24, mill operative, b. Portland, ME, s/o George F. Mackie of Portland, ME (Portland, ME, merchant) and Ellen E. Kinney (Sebago, ME, deceased); W - 17, mill operative, b. Wakefield, d/o John Lover of Wakefield (Canada, mill operative)

MACLELLAN,
Roderick J. m. Rosa Mary Dodier 2/25/1933 in Sanbornville

MACLEOD,
Joel Hayden of Wakefield m. Maryellen T. Stoddard of Wakefield 2/22/1977

MACNEILL,
Robert of Ipswich, MA m. Michelle A. Higgins of Ipswich, MA 5/1/1987

MADDIX,
Forrest N., Jr. of Brookline, MA m. Lois E. **Harrington** of Natick, MA 8/10/1946 in Sanbornville; H - 25, physician; W - 22, physiotherapist

MAILLETT,
Glen Patrick of East Wakefield m. Victoria Lorraine Davis of East Wakefield 4/28/1990 in Sanbornville

MALEHAM,
Charles H. of Wakefield m. Grace M. **Burroughs** of Brookfield 2/1/1899 in Rochester; H - 24, engine wiper, b. Wakefield, s/o William H. Maleham (Wakefield, carpenter) and Sarah L. Farnham (So. Boston, MA, housekeeper); W - 20, housekeeper, b. Wakefield, d/o Howard Burrows (Brookfield, engineer) and May Willey (Wakefield, deceased)
Elmer B. m. Hazel **Downs** 10/23/1927; H - 21, s/o Charles H. Maleham (Portsmouth) and Grace May Burroughs; W - 20, d/o Harry Downs (Wakefield) and Agnes Sawyer
Herbert W. m. Elsie M. **Hodsdon** 6/27/1928; H - 26, s/o Charles H. Maleham (Wakefield) and Grace Burroughs (Brookfield); W - 19, d/o Frank Hodsdon and Ella Spaulding (West Somerville, MA)
William H. of Wakefield m. Darlene J. **Davis** of East Wakefield 8/1/1984
William H. of East Wakefield m. April J. **Geary** of East Wakefield 1/4/1997 in Gilford

MALSTON,
Douglas R. of Ontario, WI m. Virginia F. **Wiedeman** of Sanbornville 9/19/1969
Douglas R. of Ontario, WI m. Virginia F. **Wiedeman** of Sanbornville 6/11/1970 in Sanbornville

MANCUSO,
Todd J. of Wakefield m. Karen M. **Vachon** of Wakefield 6/27/1981 in Union

MANSUR,
H. Wesley of Wakefield m. Emma F. **Sibley** of Charlestown, MA 12/26/1888; H - 25, carpenter, b. Wakefield, s/o Hiram P. Mansur (Monroe, ME, clergyman) and Nancy Hutchins (Wakefield, housework); W - 23, housework, b. Medford, MA, d/o John Sibley (Wakefield) and Lizzie ----- (Charlestown, MA, housework)

MARCOUX,
Archil of Wakefield m. Rose Brouillard of Wakefield 9/21/1892 in
 Rochester; H - 26, laborer, b. Canada, s/o Marc Marcoux (Canada,
 carpenter) and Loce Beador (Canada, dead); W - 16, housework, b.
 Canada, d/o Isadore Brouillard (Canada, laborer) and Rose Belimer
 (Canada, housework)
Arthur Pierre of Sanbornville m. Sharon Lee Bergeron of Sanbornville
 8/3/1991 in Rochester
Henry of Sanbornville m. Lucia Willette of Rochester 10/11/1920 in
 Rochester; H - 33, blacksmith, b. Wakefield, s/o Oliver Marcoux
 (Canada, stone mason) and Celada Marchand (Canada); W - 23,
 housework, b. Quincy, MA, d/o Joseph Willette (Canada, contractor)
 and Philones Lafevre (Canada)

MARGERISON,
Thomas of Wakefield m. Marjorie F. Dearborn of Wakefield 8/14/1981

MARSH,
Lester m. Muriel Hagerman 10/24/1931; H - 22, s/o George Marsh
 (Acton, ME) and Eva Burrows (Milton); W - 21, d/o Miles Hagerman
 (W. Lebanon, ME) and Margaret Condor (Littleton)
Paul C. of Sanbornville m. Barbara May Hemmer of Sanbornville 8/9/1997
Robert E. of West Medford, MA m. Mary Elizabeth Tucker of
 Sanbornville 8/14/1937; H - 30, salesman; W - 31, clerk

MARSHALL,
David Scott of Dedham, MA m. Dawn Patricia Lee of Canton, MA
 10/27/1990
Edward Roy of Rochester m. Ruth Amelia Hill of Sanbornville 5/27/1965
 in Gilmanton; H - 81, retired; W - 72, home
Frank, Jr. of Wakefield m. Phoebe Littlefield of Wakefield 7/18/1903 in
 Sanbornville; H - 27, butcher, b. Wakefield, s/o Frank Marshall and
 Phoebe Puliott; W - 22, housework, b. Brookfield, d/o John Littlefield
 and Phoebe Clark
G. Conrad of York, ME m. Ruth E. Clark of Sanbornville 3/13/1937 in
 Wolfeboro; H - 26, bus operator; W - 18, at home
Joshua of Salisbury, MA m. Louise B. Dow of Salisbury, MA 12/20/1919;
 H - 38, shoemaker, b. Seabrook, s/o Joseph H. Marshall (Seabrook,
 shoemaker) and Almira Eaton (Seabrook); W - 45, 2d, b. Seabrook,

d/o Owen P. Sargent (Newburyport, MA, shoemaker) and Sally A. Eaton (Seabrook)

Samuel E. m. May F. Tilton 11/11/1933 in Rochester

MARSTON,

Wilbur C. of Wakefield m. May E. Hurd of Madison 4/12/1906; H - 26, farmer, 2d, b. Brownfield, ME, s/o Joseph Marston and Sarah E. Burnell; W - 18, housework, b. Madison, d/o Aaron Hurd and Emma Danforth

MARTELL,

Alphie N. m. Palphy M. Johnson 10/25/1925; H - 24, b. Sanford, ME, s/o Edward Martell and Maud Cote; W - 21, b. Parsonsfield, ME, d/o Asa Johnson and Mary Crawford

Peter B. of Sanbornville m. Cheryl A. Sparks of East Wakefield 10/26/1974

MARTIN,

Albert Delbert of Springvale, ME m. Marie Anne Alexandre of Sanford, ME 9/28/1975

David Paul of Sanbornville m. Rita Anne Berry of Sanbornville 8/8/1998 in Rochester

George R. of Sanbornville m. Margaret L. Martin of Wakefield 8/17/1947 in Sanbornville; H - 21, RR telegrapher; W - 23, nurse

James D. of Wakefield m. June J. Sprague of Wakefield 1/12/1980

James D., Jr. of Wakefield m. Diana L. Sprague of Wakefield 3/11/1984 in Wolfeboro

James Daniel of Sanbornville m. Ruth Emma Dodier of Sanbornville 9/29/1962; H - 24, garage worker; W - 32, housewife

Wayne R. of Sanbornville m. Teri JoAnn Cleary of Sanbornville 3/27/1971 in Wolfeboro

MARUSA,

Anthony J. m. Bernice Paulowski 1/2/1933 in Sanbornville

MARX,

George E. of Canaan, NY m. Lilla R. Burleigh of Wakefield 10/5/1892; H - 28, reformatory officer, b. Germany, s/o George J. Marx (Germany, theatricals) and Amelia ----- (Germany, housework); W - 28, dressmaker, b. Wakefield, d/o Jonathan M. Burleigh (Wakefield, farmer) and Rosilla Wedgwood (Effingham, dead)

MASTRO,
Richard L. of Wakefield m. Corinne E. Thomas of Wakefield 12/22/1972

MASURY,
Charles F. of Beverly, MA m. Lena E. Davis of Wakefield 6/1/1898; H - 24, shoe cutter, b. Beverly, MA, s/o John F. Masury (Beverly, MA, deceased) and Sarah A. Young of Beverly, MA (Beverly, MA, 54); W - 19, b. Acton, ME, d/o Frank E. Davis of Wakefield (Wakefield, 53, farmer) and Mary O. Bearce (Springvale, ME, 46, housewife)

MATHIESON,
Michael A. of Lincolnville, ME m. Cynthia A. Wilson of Acton, ME 8/24/1969

MATTINA,
John Joseph of Abington, MA m. Marjory Snyder of Charlotte, NC 8/16/1964; H - 33, sen. tech.; W - 30, at home

MATTRESS,
John E. of Sanbornville m. Patsy L. Overlook of Rochester 9/25/1970 in Union
John E. of Wakefield m. Linda L. Colby of Rochester 4/8/1972 in Milton

MAXFIELD,
Danny Martin of Wakefield m. Lori Marie Stevens of Wakefield 12/3/1977

MAY,
Huston of Wakefield m. Katie Emerson of Salmon Falls 8/2/1889; H - 64, carpenter, b. Northfield, VT, s/o Joseph May and Mary Langley; W - 36, weaver, b. Scotland, d/o John Durgin and Mary Moulton

MAYRANEN,
Martin Allan of Sanbornville m. Heidi Kim St. Cyr of Sanbornville 9/16/1995 in Sanbornville

McCARTHY,

Francis W., Jr. of Wakefield m. Gloria J. Bozek of Wakefield 11/9/1987 in East Wakefield

William J. of Everett, MA m. Constance Fuller of Marblehead, MA 7/3/1946; H - 34, salesman; W - 30, at home

McCARTY,

Frank Joseph of Springfield, MA m. Mary Leontine Dodier of Sanbornville 9/28/1962 in Sanbornville; H - 67, retired; W - 64, d. room

McCONNELL,

Perley S. m. Mary Lizzie Cottle 7/13/1926; H - 41, b. No. Stratford, s/o David J. McConnell and Elizabeth Nelson; W - 68, b. Brookfield, d/o Josiah Cottle and Martha Weeks

McCRILLIS,

Harry H. of Wakefield m. Ethel M. Willey of Wakefield 11/24/1908; H - 32, locomotive engineer, b. Rochester, s/o Frank G. McCrillis and Sarah McCrillis; W - 28, music teacher, b. Wakefield, d/o William H. Willey and Sarah F. Brown

Ora F. of Wakefield m. Ruth F. Meikle of North Conway 3/28/1914 in Dover; H - 39, RR conductor, b. East Rochester, s/o Frank G. McCrillis and Sarah E. McCrillis; W - 22, at home, b. North Conway, d/o Andrew Meikle and Nellie Francis

McDANIEL,

Robert C. of Wakefield m. Elizabeth Aspernall of Wakefield 12/9/1888; H - 73, shoemaker, 2d, b. Pembroke, s/o Robert McDaniel and Nancy Keniston; W - 66, seamstress, 2d, b. Truro, NS, d/o ----- Morrison

McDONALD,

Arthur of Wakefield m. Leona Hill of Wakefield 6/8/1901 in East Wolfeboro; H - 20, section man, b. Wakefield, s/o Malcolm McDonald (PEI, section man) and Amanda Crockett (Mechanics Falls, ME, housewife); W - 18, housework, b. Chatham, d/o Edward Hill (Canada, farmer) and Ora ----- (Canada, housewife)

Carroll W. of Wakefield m. Alice J. Lavine of Wakefield 12/26/1913 in Dover; H - 20, laborer, b. Wakefield, s/o Malcolm McDonald and Amanda Crockett; W - 20, housework, b. Portsmouth, d/o Peter E. Lavine and Alice J. Sprood

James J. of Sanbornville m. Dorothy M. Clark of Sanbornville 7/16/1935 in Sanbornville; H - 23, truck driver; W - 21, nurse

James Joseph, 3d of Sanbornville m. Paula Arlyne Stevens of Sanbornville 7/11/1959 in Sanbornville; H - 23, USAF; W - 35, mgr.

John A. of Wakefield m. Minnie E. Quimby of Wakefield 6/10/1916 in Springvale, ME; H - 24, laborer, b. Wakefield, s/o Malcolm McDonald and Amanda D. Crockett; W - 35, housework, 2d, b. Derry, d/o Fred Duprey and Emma Quimby

John A. of Wakefield m. Minnie Quimby of Wakefield 8/23/1924; H - 34, laborer, 2d, b. Wakefield, s/o Malcom McDonald and Amanda D. Crockett; W - 49, domestic, 3d, b. Derry, d/o Fred Duprey and Emma Quimby

Malcolm, Jr. of Wakefield m. Ethel A. McClary of Wakefield 1/26/1919 in North Wakefield; H - 43, sectionman, b. Wakefield, s/o Malcolm McDonald (PEI, foreman) and Amanda D. Crockett (Mechanic Falls, ME); W - 45, b. Gilmanton, d/o Joseph E. McClary (Alexandria, farmer) and Frances A. Adams (Bristol)

Scott of Wakefield m. Elsie M. Duke of Wakefield 12/6/1913; H - 19, laborer, b. Wakefield, s/o Malcolm McDonald and Amanda Crockett; W - 19, housework, b. Fall River, MA, d/o Marshall Duke and Matilda Hall

McDOUGAL,

Stephen G. of Sanbornville m. Donna L. Granigan of Sanbornville 2/15/1992 in North Conway

Stephen Gerald of Union m. Ruby Ann Hubbard of Union 11/11/1995 in Union

McFARLAND,

Walter Francis of Allston, MA m. Jean Frances Boardman of Brighton, MA 10/10/1965; H - 39, mail carrier; W - 21, clerk

McGINNIS,

Robert C. of Wakefield m. Susan S. Hackett of Wakefield 4/1/1978 in Farmington; H - 63; W - 34

McGRATH,

John F. of Sanbornville m. Jane A. Colbath of Sanbornville 9/25/1948; H - 20, woodsman; W - 18, shoeshop emp.

MCHAN,
Alan Dwayne of Wakefield m. Marie A. Lichorobiec of Wakefield 3/26/1989 in Milton

McINTIRE,
Robert E. of Milton m. Lena I. Smith of Union 10/4/1958 in Wolfeboro; H - 19, US Navy; W - 18, at home

McKAY,
Ronald J. of Boxboro, MA m. Kathleen M. Lang of Wakefield 6/29/1985

McKENNA,
Raymond F. of Union m. Carolyn A. Gosselin of Union 6/6/1960; H - 22, truck driver; W - 18, at home

McKENNEY,
Christopher B. of Sanbornville m. Deborah J. Doyon of Rochester 3/21/1981 in Rochester

McKINNEY,
Brian P. of Wakefield m. Lorie A. Wellington of Wakefield 12/30/1980
Stewart E. of Union m. Shirley M. McKuhen of Rochester 6/30/1978; H - 57; W - 44
William John of Union m. Cheryl Elaine Bosley of Union 10/4/1975 in Union

McKUHEN,
Alan W. of Sanbornville m. Robin A. St. Hilaire of Somersworth 5/15/1982 in Somersworth

McLAUGHLIN,
Charles Kenneth of East Wakefield m. Charletta Lee Charles of East Wakefield 12/31/1997 in Hampton

McLEAN,
Kenneth M. of Louisville, CO m. Lorraine A. Joy of Louisville, CO 10/9/1982 in Union

McLELLAN,
Corey of Rochester m. Amy L. Garland of Sanbornville 2/8/1992

McLEOD,
Donald Ole of Rockland, MT m. Marjorie F. Lougee of Camden, ME 8/10/1974

McMAHON,
Martin S. of Revere, MA m. Joyce N. Kermander of Woburn, MA 6/16/1961 in Union; H - 21, US Navy; W - 21, typist

McNALLY,
James C. of Sanbornville m. Frederica H. Keniston of Wolfeboro 6/13/1953 in Sanbornville; H - 22, US Air Force; W - 18, at home

McPHERSON,
Kenneth Earl of Middleton m. Carol Elizabeth Booth of Sanbornville 9/26/1965 in Sanbornville; H - 20, shoe worker; W - 17, at home
Norman L. of Wakefield m. Marie A. Adjutant of Union 6/13/1969

MEADER,
William Lewis of Saugus, MA m. Beatrice Elizabeth Brandt of Saugus, MA 6/2/1956 in Sanbornville; H - 26, cabinet maker; W - 22, tester

MEAKIN,
John G. of Los Gatos, CA m. Dian Sue Doss of Los Gatos, CA 9/25/1993

MEDINA,
Ricardo of Westfield, MA m. Cynthia Fifield of Westfield, MA 5/25/1991 in Union

MEE,
John H. of Wakefield m. Agnes E. Libbey of Wakefield 9/23/1888; H - 21, RR section, b. England, s/o John Mee (England) and Ellen Smith (England, housework); W - 20, housework, b. Wakefield, d/o Washington Libbey (Wakefield, farmer) and Ellen M. Farnham (Wakefield, housework)
Robert of Wakefield m. Ella M. Remick of Brookfield 2/3/1889; H - 24, RR fireman, b. England, s/o John Mee and Ellen Smith (England, housework); W - 19, housekeeper, b. Brookfield, d/o Mark Remick (stonecutter) and Sarah Young (Wakefield, housework)
Victor H. of Acton, ME m. Louise I. Pillsbury of Acton, ME 5/17/1935 in Sanbornville; H - 20, laborer; W - 18, at home

MEISNER,
C. Boyd of Georgetown, MA m. Leota M. Brennan of Reading, MA 7/12/1968 in Salem

MELANSON,
Carroll T. of Brookfield m. Hazel Sibley of Wakefield 4/19/1924; H - 21, teamster, b. Canaan, s/o Thomas D. Melanson and Jennie B. Elliott; W - 19, housework, b. Haverhill, MA, d/o Ernest Sibley and Ethel Richards

MENARD,
Edmund of Wakefield m. Ethel Fellows of Wakefield 2/12/1907; H - 23, laborer, b. Wakefield, s/o Buzzell Menard and Adeline Theoret; W - 16, housekeeper, b. Wakefield, d/o Horatio B. Fellows and Belle F. Tibbetts

Edmund of Wakefield m. Sophia Flagg of Perry, ME 6/14/1911 in Rochester; H - 27, moulder, 2d, b. Wakefield, s/o Basil Menard and Adeline Nealley; W - 18, machine operator, b. Perry, ME, d/o William P. Flagg and Fannie E. Denison

MERCER,
Scott E. of East Wakefield m. Nicki L. Lavanway of East Wakefield 4/23/1994

MERRICK,
Clayton Milton, III of Halifax, MA m. Lynn M. Hanson of Plymouth, MA 5/17/1978; H - 19; W - 20

MERRILL,
Asa of Wakefield m. Susan S. Titcomb of Milton 10/25/1904 in Milton Mills; H - 74, farmer, 2d, b. Acton, ME, s/o Nathan Merrill and Sarah Brackett; W - 66, housekeeper, 2d, b. Somersworth, d/o Benjamin Randall and Melinda Stillings

Vincent N. of Sanbornville m. Natalie Ames Prentice of Sanbornville 8/17/1997 in Sanbornville

MESERVE,
Clarence O. of Wakefield m. Lillian M. Look of Wakefield 4/27/1910; H - 26, farmer, b. Wakefield, s/o Joseph H. Meserve and Emma E. Fall;

W - 24, housework, b. Boston, MA, d/o Hollis J. Look and Ellen J. Avery

Clarence O. of Wakefield m. Pauline Carter of Wakefield, MA 2/2/1924 in Rochester; H - 39, farmer, 2d, b. Wakefield, s/o Joseph H. Meserve and Emma Fall; W - 18, music teacher, b. Wakefield, MA, d/o Louis E. Carter and Maude I. Heath

Edward H. of Wakefield m. Sarah B. Mackie of Norwood, MA 4/5/1952; H - 24, factory emp.; W - 21, ldy. worker

Irving E. of Milton m. Joan B. Dodge of Sanbornville 10/4/1947 in Milton; H - 18, woolen mill emp.; W - 16, at home

METTER,

Craig A. of Sanbornville m. Lisa Steedman of Sanbornville 6/24/1989 in Center Ossipee

MEYER,

Fred A., III of Milton m. Wanda G. Keller of Wakefield 4/15/1972 in Sanbornville

Frederick Augustus, III of Milton m. Patricia Louise Parker of Wakefield 11/27/1976

Gary James of Livingston, NJ m. Joan Carol Wentworth of Union 1/5/1974 in Union

MEYERS,

Daniel A. of East Wakefield m. Carla J. Schmelzer of Concord 12/5/1986 in Concord

MEYNENDONCKX,

Stefan of Belgium m. Angela C. Cole of North Wakefield 7/19/1996

MICHALSKY,

Stephen of Wakefield m. Patricia J. Golden of Brookfield 8/15/1986

MICK,

Vincent of Wolfeboro m. Gladys D. Moulton of Wakefield 8/6/1948 in Sanbornville; H - 63, oil merchant; W - 50, at home

MIGNEAULT,

Leonard R. of Wakefield m. Jessica L. Pike of Wakefield 8/2/1975 in Union

MILINER,
Bernard William of Sanbornville m. Mildred Josephine Senter of Rochester 7/6/1959 in Hampton; H - 29, shoe operator; W - 30, waitress
David V. of Sanbornville m. Janet L. Archambault of Rochester 3/13/1981 in Rochester
Elmor of Sanbornville m. Frances M. Corson of Sanbornville 1/2/1943 in Concord; H - 23, woodsman; W - 21, stenographer
Gary L. of Wakefield m. April J. Welch of Farmington 9/29/1978; H - 26; W - 21
James W. of Sanbornville m. Sandra L. Dudley of Union 6/18/1966 in Sanbornville; H - 19, USAF; W - 18, at home
Keith E. of Sanbornville m. Sandra J. Taylor of East Rochester 12/21/1968 in East Rochester
Paul A. of Dover m. Lorrie A. Weeks of Wakefield 8/6/1982 in Dover
Vinton of Sanbornville m. Olida D. Soucy of Berlin 1/19/1946 in Berlin; H - 25, state highway employee; W - 23, reg. nurse

MILLER,
George Wilbur of Acton, ME m. Jennie Louise Pippin of Union 9/1/1956; H - 26, orchardist; W - 17, at home
Henry F., Jr. of Wakefield, MA m. Doris E. Allen of Wakefield, MA 8/25/1934 in Union; H - 21, weavers helper; W - 19, at home

MILLIKEN,
Harry S. of West Baldwin, ME m. Letitia A. Vance of W. Somerville, MA 5/18/1935 in Union; H - 50, carpenter; W - 42, nurse

MILLS,
Allan W. of Springfield, MA m. Marion E. Chapman of Gardiner, ME 2/7/1948 in Sanbornville; H - 34, engineer; W - 28, asst. plant mgr.
Fred W. m. Agnes Downs 5/5/1927; H - 52, s/o William Mills (Madbury) and Nancy Foss; W - 42, d/o Ozro Sawyer (Limestone, ME) and Emma Butler
Ralph P. of Wakefield m. Irene I. Weeks of Wakefield 12/17/1921 in Union; H - 23, trackman, b. Milton, s/o Fred W. Mills (Madbury, RR foreman) and Annie L. Eaton; W - 16, at home, b. Wakefield, d/o William G. Weeks (Wakefield, liveryman) and Emily Robinson (Wolfeboro)

MILTNER,
Peter William of Rochester m. Lori Ann Philpot of Sanbornville 1/13/1990 in Rochester

MINICHIELLO,
James Edmund of Wakefield m. Wendy Elizabeth Stavseth of Wakefield 10/15/1977 in Westmoreland

MINKLER,
Edward of Dover m. Ilene J. Hill of Fitzwilliam 10/12/1921 in Fitzwilliam; H - 21, lineman, b. Canada, s/o Ernest N. Minkler (Canada, farmer) and Dorris Converse (Rindge); W - 19, at home, b. Finland, d/o Sefon Hill (Finland, quarryman) and Hilda Syri (Finland)

MONAHAN,
Francis T. of Wakefield m. Lumina Lover of Wakefield 4/17/1907; H - 22, core maker, b. Cambridge, MA, s/o Alexander Monahan and Mary McGurk; W - 18, mill operative, b. Wakefield, d/o Charles Lover and Mary Raymond

MONTGOMERY,
Joseph Howard of Wakefield m. Sandra Jewell Montgomery of Wakefield 10/9/1976

MOODY,
Daniel P. of Wakefield m. Lois E. Smith of Wakefield 6/26/1987 in Union
Edwin V. of Wakefield m. Bernice Estelle Walter of Wolfeboro 7/30/1924 in Wolfeboro; H - 25, laborer, b. Wolfeboro, s/o Arthur Moody and Marcia Dorr; W - 22, household, b. Wolfeboro, d/o Elmer C. Walter and Lizzie Mitchell
Harland P., Jr. of Bristol, CT m. Charlotte E. Byron of Newburyport, MA 7/9/1951 in Sanbornville; H - 33, machinist; W - 21, at home
Jamie D. of Wakefield m. Deborah L. Bodwell of Wakefield 3/6/1982
Ronald A. of Milton m. Susan L. Bennett of Sanbornville 6/2/1973 in Sanbornville

MOOERS,
Rodney Scott of Wakefield m. Joanne Nicholson of Wakefield 9/17/1977 in East Wakefield

MOONEY,
Earle G. of Wakefield m. Gladys M. **Eastman** of Lynn, MA 5/12/1919 in Milton Mills; H - 22, RR brakeman, b. Kingfisher, OK, s/o George Mooney (Madison, teamster) and Clara Griffin (Wakefield); W - 22, tel. operator, b. Beverly, MA, d/o William Eastman (Meredith, shoe laster) and Annie Harper (Lynn, MA)

James G. of Wakefield m. Harriet L. **Drury** of Salem 2/22/1935 in Sanbornville; H - 24, laborer; W - 26, at home

Stanley E. of East Wakefield m. Karen K. **Luscomb** of Milton Mills 10/18/1969

Stanley E. of Wakefield m. Dorene N. **Brown** of Wakefield 7/8/1978; H - 29; W - 22

Stanley Everett of East Wakefield m. Nancy Clare **Goodwin** of Plymouth 8/22/1962 in Sanbornville; H - 17, US Navy; W - 19, trimmer

MOORE,
Frank H. of Wakefield m. Hattie S. **Burleigh** of Wakefield 4/30/1898; H - 33, brakeman, b. Effingham, s/o John F. Moore of Wakefield (Parsonsfield, ME, carpenter) and Sarah A. Leavitt (Effingham, housewife); W - 33, housekeeper, b. Brookfield, d/o Thomas C. Burleigh (Brookfield, deceased) and Susan F. Moulton (Brookfield, deceased)

George S. of Bellingham, WA m. Charlene R. **Hazelwood** of East Wakefield 7/9/1966; H - 26, US Navy; W - 24, at home

Keith A. of Wakefield m. Morna E. **Messier** of Wakefield 9/6/1986 in Somersworth

Malcolm J. of Wakefield m. Lillian M. **Harden** of Wakefield 10/14/1897 in Farmington; H - 22, clerk, b. Effingham, s/o John F. Moore of Wakefield (Parsonsfield, ME, 66, carpenter) and Sarah A. Leavitt of Wakefield (Effingham, 70, housewife); W - 20, weaver, b. Rochester, d/o Charles Harden of Wakefield (laborer) and Eva Baker (deceased)

Maurice M. of Minneapolis, MN m. Olive **Brown** of Wakefield 12/23/1919; H - 35, lawyer, b. Grand Rapids, MI, s/o Malcolm M. Moore (No. Anson, ME, lawyer) and Margaret L. Ballard (Grand Rapids, MI); W - 24, b. Wakefield, d/o Daniel R. Brown (Wakefield, physician) and Mary A. Paul (Wakefield)

Steven Harrison of Wolfeboro m. Lora Lee **Ulmer** of Wakefield 8/18/1979 in Wolfeboro; H - 20; W - 20

William R. of Wakefield m. Carol A. **Moran** of Wakefield 5/23/1987

MOORS,
Leon F. of Wakefield m. Gladys May **Sanborn** of Newfield, ME 2/5/1916 in Newfield, ME; H - 29, laborer, b. Biddeford, ME, s/o Almon Wentworth and Nellie May Miles; W - 19, housework, b. Newfield, ME, d/o Joseph J. Sanborn and Edith May Reed

MOREAU,
Bruce E. of Wakefield m. Marjorie L. **Smart** of Wakefield 6/12/1982

MORIARTY,
William E., III of Wakefield m. Charlene **McGovern** of Wakefield 9/26/1987 in Sanbornville

MORIN,
Henry Peter of Sanbornville m. Ruth Fuller **Garland** of Sanbornville 6/15/1951; H - 59, mason; W - 31, reg. nurse
Paul D. of Amesbury, MA m. Beth E. **Shellnut** of Amesbury, MA 4/8/1989 in East Wakefield

MORRELL,
Ralph R., II of East Wakefield m. Susan M. **Wright** of East Wakefield 10/15/1994

MORRILL,
Daniel P. of Wakefield m. Roxanne **Dore** of Ossipee 9/4/1982
Donald Willene of Sanbornville m. Norene Alberta **Warren** of Sanbornville 3/31/1950; H - 17, laborer; W - 17, at home
Fred R. of Wakefield m. Eva C. **Meyer** of Milton Mills 9/2/1948; H - 18, truck driver; W - 17, at home
George W. m. Charlotte H. **Eastman** 11/12/1928; H - 65, s/o William Morrill (Moultonboro) and Susan E. Brown (Tuftonboro); W - 46, d/o Edward P. Eastman (North Conway) and Eliza N. Sawyer (Woodfords, ME)
John L., III of Wakefield m. Jayme A. **Hall** of Wakefield 9/20/1985
Michael V., Jr. of Sanbornville m. Judith Anne **Smith** of Sanbornville 9/16/1995 in Wolfeboro
Paul S. of Wakefield m. Laurel A. **Bell** of Wakefield 2/14/1987 in Rochester
Richard Tristram of Union m. Stephanie Alice **Wilkinson** of Union 7/1/1995 in Union

Robert L. of Wakefield m. Lisa A. Watson of Wakefield 10/31/1985

MORRISON,
George W. of Wakefield m. Clara B. Hamlin of Wakefield 9/13/1893; H - 24, mechanic, b. Moultonboro, s/o John D. Morrison (Tuftonboro, farmer) and Sarah E. Brown (Moultonboro, housework); W - 18, housework, b. S. Newmarket, d/o Edwin F. Hamlin (Boston, MA, mechanic) and Josie S. Littlefield (Portsmouth, housework)

Roger H. of Wakefield m. Mary L. Corson of Milton 6/3/1922 in Milton; H - 23, dental student, b. Boston, MA, s/o George W. Morrison and Clara Bell Hamlin; W - 21, stenographer, b. Milton, d/o John N. Corson and Eva M. Postleton

MORROW,
T. N. of Wakefield m. Minnie A. Ham of Wakefield 12/31/1896 in Farmington; H - 30, brass finisher, b. Dover, s/o T. H. Morrow (Scotland, deceased) and M. A. Armstrong of Dover (Scotland, 70, housekeeper); W - 19, housework, b. Farmington, d/o Natt F. Ham (New Durham, deceased) and Sarah E. Stevens of Wakefield (Rochester, 46, housekeeper)

MORSE,
David B. of Malden, MA m. Delia M. Dodier of Wakefield 9/18/1920 in Sanbornville; H - 26, mech. sig. man., 2d, b. So. Paris, ME, s/o George S. Morse (Oldtown, ME, carpenter) and Georgianna Doyle (Leeds, ME); W - 26, housework, b. Somersworth, d/o Joseph H. Dodier (Canada, railroad emp.) and Edith M. Perron (Canada)

MOSELEY,
Arthur C. of Westfield, MA m. Eliza H. Rust of Westfield, MA 8/4/1897; H - 34, plumber, b. Westfield, MA, s/o John M. Moseley (Westfield, MA, deceased) and J. Alma Holcomb of Westfield, MA (Granby, CT, 60, housekeeper); W - 32, teacher, b. Charlestown, MA, d/o George Burbank (deceased) and Hannah J. Rust of Wolfeboro (Wolfeboro, 56, housekeeper)

MOYNIHAN,
Sean Patrick of Rochester m. Amy Elizabeth Hall of Union 6/25/1994 in Rochester

MUNFORD,
Walter Ferdinand, Jr. of Chatham, MA m. Elizabeth Caroline Cain of Hyannis, MA 12/14/1962 in Sanbornville; H - 33, self emp.; W - 34, at home

MUNROE,
Robert S. of Wakefield m. Susan A. Dube of Wakefield 1/19/1979; H - 49; W - 28

MURPHY,
Frank Rainer of Wakefield m. Gail Eve Flynn of Beverly, MA 3/26/1977
Richard John, Jr. of Sanbornville m. Roberta Ann Capillo of Sanbornville 4/30/1993

MURRAY,
Boyd F. of Sanbornville m. Doris M. Hamilton of Rochester 4/16/1960 in Rochester; H - 53, letter carrier; W - 46, stitcher
David of Wolfeboro m. Natalie A. Spinney of Wakefield 7/9/1960; H - 20, student; W - 25, reg. nurse
Justin C. of Wakefield m. Staci Elizabeth Lincoln of Wakefield 9/13/1997 in Rochester
Lloyd of Springvale, ME m. Jennie Wilkinson of Springvale, ME 1/1/1896; H - 28, overseer, b. Springvale, ME, s/o Ham W. Murray of Springvale, ME (Emery's Mills, ME, 65, shoemaker) and Olive O. Boston (Shapleigh, ME, 63, housekeeper); W - 26, stitcher, b. Springvale, ME, d/o Jerre D. Wilkinson of Springvale, ME (63) and Eliza Goodwin (Springvale, ME, 64, housekeeper)
Peter Joseph of West Lynn, MA m. Nancy Carlyne Drew of Sanbornville 12/27/1958 in Sanbornville; H - 21, salesman; W - 18, student

MUSREAU,
Edward of Wakefield m. Gene Pudveau of Dover 2/9/1896 in Dover; H - 25, operative, b. NB, s/o Edward Musreau of NB (NB, 65, pilot) and Mary McIntire (deceased); W - 25, stitcher, b. Canada, d/o ---- Pudveau of Dover (Canada, 50, operative) and ----- (Canada, housekeeper)

MYERS,
John J. m. Ruth A. **Bach** 2/7/1931; H - 40, s/o John P. Myers (Holyoke, MA) and Catherine Clark (Ireland); W - 38, d/o Kraig J. Yoerg (Holyoke, MA) and Nellie A. Duffy (Dalton, MA)

NADLER,
Harvey W. of Malden, MA m. Linda A. **Padova** of Malden, MA 7/13/1985

NANCE,
Carl E. of Wakefield m. Kathrina **Hamner** of Wakefield 2/18/1989

NAPLIN,
Roger J. of Farmington m. Maria M. **Mailhot** of Union 3/9/1991

NASON,
Almond L. of Wakefield m. Nancy J. **Streader** of Wakefield 7/2/1904 in Brookfield; H - 25, teamster, b. Bridgton, ME, s/o Harding L. Nason and Lucinda Thorn; W - 19, housework, 2d, b. Wakefield, d/o Joseph Streader and Valaria Dyer

Bruce Richard of Sanbornville m. Glenn Marie **Ashford** of Sanbornville 7/30/1975 in Rindge

Clarence C., Jr. of Sanbornville m. Kelly Ann **Adjutant** of Sanbornville 2/24/1996 in Milton

Daniel Gary of Bedford m. Josephine Ann **Morrison** of Manchester 6/12/1977 in Union

David A. of Wakefield m. Lisa G. **Weeks** of Wakefield 1/10/1987

David Harry of Sanbornville m. Nancy Lee **Dodier** of Sanbornville 11/17/1962; H - 19, laborer; W - 17, at home

Dean F. of Wakefield m. Robin **Kachoris** of Wakefield 9/20/1986

Donald Robert of Sanbornville m. Marion E. **Walter** of Wolfeboro 9/9/1950 in Wolfeboro; H - 23, RR emp.; W - 18, at home

Edward B. of Brookfield m. Arline M. **Zalenski** of Wakefield 2/24/1961 in Sanbornville; H - 22, mechanic; W - 18, student

Edward J. of Wakefield m. Tina M. **Sargent** of Ctr. Ossipee 8/24/1985

Edward R. of Sanbornville m. Ida M. **Drapeau** of Sanbornville 10/26/1935 in East Rochester; H - 23, laborer; W - 19, at home

Ernest E. of Sanbornville m. Dorothy M. **Cate** of Brookfield 9/18/1937 in Sanbornville; H - 21, laborer; W - 19, at home

Ernest Everett of Sanbornville m. Catherine **Garland** of Sanbornville 4/18/1975

Ernest R., Jr. of Wakefield m. Chris A. **Moody** of Wakefield 3/6/1982

Fred Eugene of Sanbornville m. Mary Jean **Bailey** of Sanbornville 4/19/1959; H - 30, truck driver; W - 22, nurse's aide

Fred H. m. Evelyn P. **Weymouth** 3/16/1927; H - 20, s/o Almon Nason (Wakefield) and Nancy Streeter; W - 18, d/o John Weymouth (So. Boston, MA) and Emma Ryer

Glendon R. of Union m. Marion R. **Stevens** of Union 10/9/1944 in Sanford, ME; H - 21, US Army; W - 19, shoe shop

Johnnie W. of Union m. Winnifred **Downs** of Union 3/1/1946 in Milton; H - 23, mill emp.; W - 24, office emp.

Larry M. of Union m. Donna M. **Watson** of Rochester 4/27/1985 in Rochester

Lawrence C. of Sanbornville m. Marilyn E. **French** of Milton 10/30/1948; H - 18, RR emp.; W - 18, at home

Robert Almond of Wakefield m. Judith Ann **Patriquin** of Wakefield 11/12/1977

Robert Francis of Brookfield m. Lorraine Ellen **Littlefield** of Wakefield 2/16/1957; H - 22, tannery worker; W - 23, at home

Todd C. of Wakefield m. Christine M. **DiPrizio** of Middleton 8/4/1985

Willis L. of Wakefield m. Maud Eva **Reed** of Wakefield 9/8/1920 in Milton Mills; H - 18, lumberman, b. Wakefield, s/o Almon L. Nason (Bridgton, ME, board sawyer) and Nancy J. Streader (Wakefield); W - 21, mill operative, b. Wakefield, d/o Edward S. Reed (Effingham, mill operative) and Inez Dicey

NEAL,

Ernest C. of Sanbornville m. Patience A. **Martell** of East Wakefield 1/1/1971 in Sanbornville

Ernest Charles of Sanbornville m. Julia Etta **Hollenbeck** of Canaan 6/25/1950 in Canaan; H - 23, shoe shop; W - 19, elec. worker

NEALLEY,

Buzzell P. of Wakefield m. Jane W. **Perry** of Bartlett 4/3/1907 in Bartlett; W - 27, laborer, b. Wakefield, s/o Henry Nealley and Flora Bishop; W - 18, housekeeper, b. PEI, d/o Joseph T. Perry and Caroline Botts

Henry L. of Wakefield m. Elsie E. **Nichols** of Wakefield 10/12/1906 in Lynn, MA; H - 28, printer, b. Salmon Falls, s/o Henry Nealley and

Flora Bishop; W - 26, housework, b. Wakefield, d/o Hiram W. Nichols and Sarah W. Lane

Stuart Jay of Bartlett m. Kathleen Ann Goodnow of East Wakefield 9/6/1975 in No. Conway

NEILY,

Guy E. m. Jean F. Murray 8/30/1926; H - 30, s/o Robert Neily and Leah Hutt; W - 24, b. Halifax, NS, d/o George R. Murray and Ida Mabel Robinson

Kennett Winston of Wakefield m. Judith Linsey Churchill of Brookfield 1/30/1953; H - 20, mechanic; W - 16, student

NELSON,

Ferdinand of Wakefield m. Alice L. Edwards of Effingham 5/3/1892; H - 31, farmer, 2d, b. Denmark, s/o ----- Nelson (Denmark, farmer); W - 18, housework, b. Wolfeboro, d/o Augustus Edwards (dead) and Marcia Williams (housework)

Rufus Lawrence, Jr. of Concord m. Cynthia June Knight of Sanbornville 1/10/1959; H - 20, salesman; W - 18, housework

NEVERS,

Lloyd E. m. Isabel M. Wiggin 11/8/1928; H - 43, s/o William Nevers (Newfield, ME) and Augusta Farnham (Wakefield); W - 42, d/o Samuel McIntyre (Wolfeboro) and Isabel Sanborn (Milton)

NEWCOMB,

Glenn C. of Wakefield m. Karen L. Pratt of Wakefield 9/13/1986

NEWMAN,

David of No. Miami Beach, FL m. Christine Brudevold of Newton, MA 8/26/1978; H - 22; W - 24

NICHOLS,

Earle E. of Sanbornville m. Rosina Ashby of Sanbornville 10/17/1948 in Sanbornville; H - 28, millman; W - 43, housework

Ernest C. of Sanbornville m. Bertha A. Harmon of Ossipee 10/14/1947 in Sanbornville; H - 37, sawyer; W - 28, at home

Leigh A. of Union m. Stephanie A. Foss of Union 7/29/1989 in Union

Lorenzo D. of Wakefield m. Anstriss Fellows of Wakefield 9/9/1899; H - 25, sectionman, b. Wakefield, s/o Hiram W. Nichols (Wakefield, section man) and Sarah W. Lane (Wakefield, housekeeper); W - 25, teacher, b. Wakefield, d/o Horatio B. Fellows (Wakefield, farmer) and Belle Tibbetts (Newfield, ME, housekeeper)

Mose O. of Union m. Mabel York of Farmington 2/4/1934 in Sanbornville; H - 21, truck driver; W - 22, at home

Rupert L. of Sanbornville m. Icona L. Dodge of Sanbornville 5/30/1934 in Sanbornville; H - 22, clubwork; W - 24, saleslady

William H. of Wakefield m. Emma E. Moulton of Wolfeboro 6/26/1920 in Wolfeboro; H - 49, track foreman, b. Wakefield, s/o Hiram W. Nichols (Wakefield, RR employee) and Sarah N. Lane (Wakefield); W - 45, housekeeper, 2d, b. Wolfeboro, d/o John D. Waldron (Rochester, grocer) and Jennie Stevens (Wolfeboro)

NICKERSON,

Edwin O. of Rochester m. Florence E. Lawrence of Wakefield 6/30/1934 in Rochester; H - 62, painter; W - 46, housework

NICKLESS,

Arthur Henry, Sr. of Wakefield m. Jillian Louise Watson of Wakefield 1/23/1988 in Sanbornville

NIELSON,

Paul Bernard, Jr. of Newfield, ME m. Karen Louise Mann of Acton, ME 6/26/1965; H - 24, lineman; W - 19, secretary

NOEL,

Frank T. of Wakefield m. Lee M. Meisner of Georgetown, MA 9/12/1980

Harold Bennett of Newmarket m. Helena Mary Wycik of Newmarket 6/19/1940 in Sanbornville; H - 30, store manager; W - 24, telephone op.

NOLAN,

John F. of Joplin, MO m. Sally E. Dean of North Wakefield 9/2/1969

Robert Louis of Brighton, MA m. Joan Elaine O'Donnell of Brighton, MA 7/3/1965; H - 30, chemist; W - 25, secretary

Stephen J. of Wakefield m. Wanda G. Crawford of Wakefield 2/2/1974

NORRISH,

Stephen E. of Milton m. Tammy A. Champy of Wakefield 11/14/1987 in Milton

NOTT,
John R. of Boston, MA m. Bjorg L. Lygren of Boston, MA 2/19/1966 in Sanbornville; H - 23, acct. asst.; W - 23, stewardess

NUCHTEN,
Walter Herman of Sanford, ME m. Lena Ashworth of Sanford, ME 9/6/1957; H - 57, printer; W - 63, office worker

NUTE,
Charles E. of Wakefield m. Bertha F. Garland of Wakefield 8/23/1911 in Brookfield; H - 23, farmer, b. Farmington, s/o Charles E. Nute and Emma Pike; W - 17, housework, b. Wolfeboro, d/o George Garland and Mary E. Stillings

Fred S. of Wakefield m. Josephine A. Hanson of Wakefield 5/30/1896; H - 28, mill hand, b. Milton, s/o Sidney Nute of Milton (Dover, 49, shoe maker) and Emma Morrill (Dover, 46, housekeeper); W - 31, housework, 2d, divorced, b. VT, d/o Royal J. Pike of Wakefield (Ossipee, 82, farmer) and Mary Hawthorne (Reading, VT, 67, housekeeper)

Fred S. of Wakefield m. Olive A. Garland of Wakefield 12/19/1914; H - 47, mill operative, 2d, b. Milton, s/o John S. Nute and Emma L. Hardy; W - 20, housework, b. Wolfeboro, d/o George Garland and Mary E. Stillings

Wilfred S. of Union m. Jinnie A. Marsh of Farmington 10/1/1944 in Farmington; H - 28, mill worker; W - 22, at home

NUTTER,
Charles A. of Wakefield m. Emma F. Ham of Wolfeboro 12/12/1888 in Parsonsfield, ME; H - 36, attorney, b. Lancaster, s/o Oliver Nutter (Wakefield, farmer) and Roxana Wentworth; W - 37, housework, b. Wolfeboro, d/o Hiram Ham

Ralph A. m. Ruth M. Morrison 2/20/1926; H - 22, b. Farmington, s/o Freeman J. Nutter and Lillian Babb; W - 22, b. Wakefield, d/o George W. Morrison and Clara Hamlin

NUTTING,
Leslie J. of Beverly, MA m. Lillian J. Whitlock of Winnipeg, Canada 8/16/1986

Richard Mark of East Rochester m. Nancy Louise Brown of Sanbornville 6/29/1991 in Union

O'BRIEN,
David J. of Waltham, MA m. Mary M. Giers of Dorchester, MA 8/5/1967 in Sanbornville; H - 27, pile driver; W - 25, secretary

O'CONNELL,
John of Wakefield m. Edith Evans of Wakefield 1/1/1898; H - 34, mill operative, b. Ireland, s/o Dennis O'Connell of Leicester, MA (Ireland, 76, farmer) and Elizabeth McMerrer (Ireland, deceased); W - 20, mill operative, b. Wakefield, d/o Eugene Evans of VA (Stoneham, ME, 45, farmer) and Annie Pillsbury of Wakefield (Rochester, dressmaker)

O'CONNOR,
Jeremiah J. of Sanbornville m. Kim E. Jones of Sanbornville 4/25/1992 in Rochester

O'HALLORAN,
Michael J. of Boston, MA m. Deborah E. Singelais of Sanbornville 9/--/1989 in Sanbornville

OLESON,
William H. of Wakefield m. Barbara Liberty of Farmington 11/16/1980

OLIMPIO,
Marc A. of Wakefield m. Melanie S. Wade of Wakefield 8/22/1982

OLIVER,
Terence Brian of Framingham, MA m. Susan Lee Cloutman of Wakefield 1/9/1994

OSMER,
Larry J. of Weymouth, MA m. MaryEllen LaBelle of Weymouth, MA 7/18/1998 in Sanbornville

OTIS,
Charles G. of Wakefield m. Mabel L. Richards of Wakefield 4/29/1911 in North Berwick, ME; H - painter; W - housework, b. Wakefield, d/o Charles Richards

OUELLETTE,
Maurille F. of Sanbornville m. Marie A. Soucy of Sanbornville 6/16/1934 in Sanbornville; H - 23, truck driver; W - 22, counter moulder
Steven R. of Wakefield m. Maryellen Grondin of Wakefield 12/12/1981

OUILLETTE,
Armand of Wakefield m. Lida Lamontagne of Wakefield 8/6/1907; H - 30, laborer, b. Canada, s/o David Ouellette and Helmina Pinette; W - 30, housekeeper, b. Canada, d/o Joseph Lamontagne and Annie Joyce
Roland J. of Sanbornville m. Winona H. Karcher of Sanbornville 9/24/1934 in Sanbornville; H - 26, store clerk; W - 17, at home

OULETTE,
David R. of Wakefield m. Karen Mooney of Wakefield 10/10/1987 in Lee

PACKARD,
Everard L. of Wakefield m. Flora L. Dickinson of East Charlemont, MA 3/31/1894 in East Charlemont, MA; H - 52, farmer, 2d, b. Conway, MA, s/o Joseph Packard (Conway, MA, farmer) and Submit M. Brown (Haverhill, housework); W - 38, housework, 2d, b. Granville, IL, d/o Lary Davis (NY, farmer) and Mary Leavitt (MA, housework)

PAEY,
David Gene of Milton m. Dorothy May Christie of Sanbornville 8/14/1959 in Milton; H - 23, US Navy; W - 24, mill emp.

PAGE,
Bret Alan of Barrington m. Amy-Lyn Geraldine Macedo of East Wakefield 10/11/1998 in Exeter
Frederick Stover of East Boston, MA m. Elaine Margaret Famolare of East Boston, MA 11/25/1962; H - 24, laborer; W - 18, operator

PAINTER,
Verne David of Sanford, ME m. Lena Bell Miller of Sanford, ME 8/24/1957; H - 52, tool die mkr.; W - 40, housework

PALETSKY,
Robert John of Sanbornville m. Groellen Nelson of Sanbornville 3/24/1998

PALMER,
Robert T. of Wakefield m. Charlotte Amelia Brown of Farmington 6/14/1949 in Farmington; H - 33, merchant; W - 23, shoe shop emp.
Rodney W. of Milton Mills m. Janet M. Forsythe of Union 9/16/1961 in Sanbornville; H - 25, grinder; W - 17, at home

PALMISANO,
Timothy James of Wakefield m. Michelle Paulette Lemonds of Wakefield 2/26/1994

PARENT,
Paul M. of Rochester m. Joanne L. Keating of Wakefield 5/1/1971 in Sanbornville
Paul M. of Sanbornville m. Sharon L. Gadapee of Sanbornville 8/22/1992 in Rochester

PARK,
Leslie H. of Milton, MA m. Brenda L. Bourne of Brockton, MA 7/6/1974
Robert David, Jr. of Union m. Dawn Jo-Ann Stetson of Union 9/6/1997

PARKER,
Franklyn S. of Cambridge, MA m. Patsy J. Welch of Wakefield 6/25/1960; H - 27, tree work; W - 19, waitress
Lauren E. of Wakefield m. Evelyn F. Morrill of Wakefield 7/8/1923 in Rochester; H - 27, mill operative, b. Manchester, s/o Elmer Parker and Minnie Graton; W - 21, mill operative, b. Rochester, d/o William O. Morrill and Victoria Berry

PATIGNANO,
Patrick J. of Hasbrouck Hts., NJ m. Grace M. Flanagan of Montclair, NJ 9/9/1950 in Sanbornville; H - 27, salesman; W - 22, dept. store

PAUL,
Samuel H. m. Julia H. Bishop 9/26/1927; H - 30, s/o Arthur H. Paul (Wakefield) and Annie H. Nairn; W - 28, d/o Stanley Bishop (Gray, ME) and Martha A. Carpenter

PAWLOSKY,
Robert E. of Sanbornville m. Tremace A. Kelly of Sanbornville 7/15/1989 in Sanbornville

PEACOL,
Fred of Wakefield m. Florence E. Bragdon of Wakefield 7/2/1902 in Ossipee; H - 22, jobber, b. Brattleboro, VT, s/o George Peacol and Mary J. Wright; W - 19, housework, b. Philadelphia, PA, d/o Orin D. Bragdon and Florence E.J. Bragdon

PEARCE,
George M. of East Wakefield m. Cassandra M. Coolidge of East Wakefield 5/20/1995 in Sanbornville
James C. of Wakefield m. Rita L. McDonald of Wakefield 11/3/1979; H - 18; W - 17
Kenneth R. of Saudi Arabia m. Nancy L. Green of Saudi Arabia 8/6/1985
Nelson L. of Peabody, MA m. Margaret A. Viel of Salem, MA 8/4/1923 in Sanbornville; H - 26, jeweler, b. Bainbridge, NY, s/o William H. Pearce and Tilley Johnston; W - 20, housewife, b. Salem, MA, d/o Hilaire Bier and Georginia Belanger

PEASLEE,
Robert Arthur of Farmington m. Ute Marianna Kolb of Wakefield 9/2/1962; H - 27, undertaker; W - 21, clerk

PEAVEY,
Allen W. of South Wakefield m. Ellen M. Hutchins of Sanbornville 10/31/1973
Allen Wayne, Jr. of Sanbornville m. Laurie Jean Rourke of Rochester 9/8/1997 in Sanbornville
Paul Edward of Wakefield m. Nancy Lee Hutchins of Wakefield 3/12/1976
Paul Edward of Sanbornville m. Cheryl A. Corbett of Middleton 2/3/1991 in Barrington

PEDERSEN,
Craig J. of NE m. Mary Ellen McNally of MA 7/2/1988

PEHOWIC,
Edward of Sanbornville m. Robin Hilman of Sanbornville 5/12/1991 in Wolfeboro

PERCH,
John of Wakefield m. Gertrude M. Clarke of Wakefield 4/5/1892 in Milton; H - 23, farmer, b. Newfield, ME, s/o Samuel Perch

(Shapleigh, ME, farmer) and Mary Perch (Shapleigh, ME, housework); W - 14, housework, b. Alton, d/o Frank Clarke (Madison, farmer) and Fanny Smith (Alton, housework)

PERILLO,
Randy Thomas of New Durham m. Vanessa Smith of East Wakefield 9/1/1990 in Wolfeboro

PERKINS,
Daniel James of Watertown, MA m. Honora Rose Fitzsimmons of Waltham, MA 11/23/1957; H - 26, truck driver; W - 29, at home
Edward James of East Wakefield m. Joanne Darlene Pedneault of Westbrook, ME 3/27/1965 in Milton; H - 24, mill worker; W - 20, at home
Guy S. of Acton, ME m. Florence E. Knight of Wakefield 12/31/1918; H - 27, mill hand, b. Hampton, s/o Andrew C. Perkins and Ida E. Hanson; W - 20, housework, b. Wakefield, d/o Marshall E. Knight and Belle Brackett
Henry M. of Wakefield m. Daisy Hayes of Freedom 10/9/1894; H - 27, farmer, b. Wakefield, s/o William H. Perkins (Wakefield, farmer) and Susana J. Moody (Newfield, ME, housework); W - 22, seamstress, b. Haverhill, MA, d/o James Hayes (Eaton, farmer) and Mary Perkins
James A. of Wakefield m. Marguerite Swinerton of Milton 4/20/1918 in Farmington; H - 22, farmer, b. Wakefield, s/o Samuel Perkins and Bridget McNamara; W - 17, shoe operative, b. Milton, d/o Jacob M. Swinerton and Emma A. Melville
Jeffrey A. of Wakefield m. Nancy J. Clark of Wakefield 6/28/1980
Otis I. m. Hattie Twombly 6/20/1931; H - 31, s/o Charles E. Perkins (Middleton) and Jennie M. Piper (Wolfeboro); W - 20, d/o Clarence Twombly (Conway) and Bessie Douns (Wolfeboro)
Ralph Carl of Wakefield m. Shirleen Tutt of Meredith 4/26/1964 in Milton; H - 16, student; W - 17, student

PERLES,
Richard Stanley of New York, NY m. Janice Clare Griffith of New York, NY 2/16/1975 in Union

PERRY,
Frederic F. of Boston, MA m. Joan Mahard of Natick, MA 8/4/1941; H - 22, chemist; W - 21, at home

John m. Hazel May Drew 9/7/1932 in Union

Perley D. of Wakefield m. Gladys B. Fogg of Wakefield 2/17/1919 in Sanbornville; H - 20, shoe trimmer, b. Brookfield, s/o John Perry (Wolfeboro, farmer) and Lena Eaton (Brookfield); W - 17, b. Deerfield, d/o Herbert Fogg (Deerfield, mill hand) and Lizzie Witham (Deerfield)

Perley D. of Wakefield m. Inez E. Garland of Wakefield 8/29/1923 in Milton; H - 24, railroad employee, 2d, b. Brookfield, s/o John Perry and Lena Eaton; W - 20, at home, b. Brookfield, d/o Fred Garland and Hattie West

Shawn Nicholas of Union m. Annette Lynn George of Union 3/23/1996 in Union

William D., Jr. of Sanbornville m. Suzanne Garland of Sanbornville 5/18/1991 in Sanbornville

PETERS,

Gilbert Arthur of Benton Station, MI m. June Loretta Totman of Fairfield, ME 8/20/1938; H - 21, college student; W - 18, college student

Merrill Strout of Limington, ME m. Pasqua Di Censo of Portland, ME 8/2/1952; H - 36, woodsman; W - 45, packer

PETKEVITCH,

Alexander D. of Wakefield m. Cheryl A. Greenfield of Wakefield 5/19/1989 in Ossipee

PETRIE,

Edgar H. of Monroeville, PA m. Barbara A. Haggerty of Winchester, MA 9/28/1974

PHELAN,

Robert J. m. Sharon L. Libby 11/8/1966 in Wolfeboro; H - 21; W - 19

PHILBRICK,

George S. of Wakefield m. Emma Lafayette of Ossipee 6/11/1889 in Ossipee; H - 26, carpenter, b. Wakefield, s/o John S. Philbrick (Wakefield, carpenter) and Mary Small (Ossipee); W - 37, housekeeper, 2d, b. Ossipee, d/o Jonathan Woodman (Wakefield, trader) and Jane Goudy (Ossipee, housework)

Henry of Milton m. Lucy A. Blaisdell of Effingham 12/12/1900 in Effingham; H - 61, farmer, 3d, b. Freedom, s/o Frederick Philbrick

(Freedom, farmer) and Clarissa Young (Freedom, housewife); W - 55, housekeeper, 2d, b. Littleton, MA, d/o Benjamin Fletcher (Littleton, MA, shoemaker) and Mary E. Blaisdell (Lebanon, ME, housework)

Wesley Austin, Jr. of Farmington m. Georgia Diane Perkins of Sanbornville 7/24/1965 in Gonic; H - 17, laborer; W - 16, at home

PHILLIPS,

Horace Wyman of Portland, ME m. Ida May Meserve of Wakefield 9/20/1905; H - 26, bookkeeper, b. Saco, ME, s/o Edwin T. Phillips and Forestine Libby; W - 27, housework, b. Brownfield, ME, d/o Alexander Meserve and Mary E. Thurston

PICKERING,

B. Frank of Wakefield m. Viola E. Brackett of Wakefield 5/1/1909 in Portsmouth; H - 51, railroad official, 2d, b. Wakefield, s/o Thomas L. Pickering and Ann T. Wiggin; W - 28, housework, 2d, b. Brookfield, d/o Warren J. Stevens and Etta Eaton

David W. of Plymouth m. Christine E. Hayward of Union 11/30/1974 in Union

Frank M. of Wakefield m. Louise A. Rand of Rye 12/29/1923 in Rye; H - 30, brakeman, b. Wakefield, s/o B. Frank Pickering and Nettie L. Sanborn; W - 23, at home, b. Rye, d/o Jedidiah Rand and Edith C. Foss

Fred E. of Wakefield m. Anna E. Dennison of Dorchester, MA 6/11/1917; H - 28, clerk, Wolfeboro, s/o Frederick W. Pickering and Lillian E. Earle; W - 30, bookkeeper, b. Dorchester, MA, d/o Hiram A. Dennison and Carrie Smith

PIERCE,

Carl Henry of Union m. Mary Ellen Drew of Milton 7/31/1943 in Milton Mills; H - 29, painter; W - 18, at home

PIERSON,

Howard Ross of Lisbon m. Elizabeth Stetson Alley of Union 9/18/1940 in Union; H - 48, mechanic; W - 30, at home

PIGEON,

Moses B. of Wakefield m. Ruth Chick Doen of Wakefield 2/28/1920 in Rochester; H - 31, fireman, b. Montreal, PQ, s/o Thomas Pigeon (Montreal, PQ, farmer) and Mary Logan (Montreal, PQ); W - 25, teacher, 2d, b. Wakefield, d/o George H. Chick (Waterboro, ME, mill man) and Nellie Waldron (Wakefield)

PIKE,

David C. of Wakefield m. Mary E. Miller of Wakefield 12/19/1889; H - 24, farmer, b. Middleton, s/o George C. Pike (Middleton) and Maria S. Cook (Middleton, housework); W - 20, housekeeper, b. Lawrence, MA, d/o Benjamin Miller (Acton, ME, farmer) and Mary Ross (Lebanon, ME, housework)

Floyd Gerry of Wakefield m. Marylin Loretta Williams of Milton 8/21/1954; H - 21, farmer; W - 18, clerk

Forrest S. m. Lois F. Robinson 1/1/1931; H - 33, s/o Winthrop W. Pike (Stoneham, MA) and Sarah A. Tibbetts (Wolfeboro); W - 21, d/o Frank R. Robinson (Wakefield) and Bertha E. Hart (Wakefield)

John W. of Hanson, MA m. Viola M. Holland of Hanson, MA 7/19/1969

Kevin L. of Wakefield m. Dorothy B. Nason of Wakefield 8/1/1987

Kevin R. of Milton Mills m. Sherrylee M. Ganther of Sanbornville 2/17/1968 in Milton

L. Gerry of Barrington m. Carol-Anne Randall of Wakefield 9/12/1981 in Sanbornville

Lincoln A. of Wakefield m. Mary M. Birch of Parsonsfield, ME 3/25/1899; H - 37, mill hand, b. Plymouth, VT, s/o Royal J. Pike (Ossipee, carpenter) and Mary Hawthorne (Reading, VT, housekeeper); W - 30, mill hand, 2d, b. Parsonsfield, ME, d/o Edwin Wentworth (Acton, ME, farmer) and Fannie M. Hurd (Ossipee, housekeeper)

Loring Robinson of Wakefield m. Georgia Sue Promise of Brookfield 9/15/1964; H - 20, R mgr.; W - 19, at home

Richard A. of Wakefield m. Jeanne M. O'Neill of Wakefield 3/11/1988

Richard A. of Sanbornville m. Emily J. Pearce of Milton 12/23/1995 in Sanbornville

Roland S. of Milton m. Carolyn M. Drew of Milton 6/7/1947 in Union; H - 22, mechanic; W - 19, student

Smith of Wakefield m. Maud Gilman of Wakefield 9/15/1895; H - 26, conductor, b. Middleton, s/o Ebenezer Pike of Middleton (Middleton, farmer) and Mary E. Pike (Middleton, seamstress); W - 25, housekeeper, second, divorced, b. Wakefield, d/o Frank Lane of Wakefield (Wakefield, farmer) and Annie M. ----- of Exeter (Exeter, seamstress)

Smith of Wakefield m. Minnie A. Sanborn of Wakefield 11/16/1909 in
Exeter; H - 40, RR conductor, 2d, b. Middleton, s/o E. S. Pike and
Mary E. Pike; W - 38, housework, 2d, b. Wakefield, d/o Josiah W.
Wiggin and Mary W. Rines

Smith of Wakefield m. Ethel M. Pike of Wakefield 12/24/1919 in
Rochester; H - 50, RR conductor, 3d, b. Middleton, s/o Ebenezer S.
Pike (Middleton, farmer) and Mary E. Pike (Middleton); W - 49, 3d,
b. Wakefield, d/o Frank Lane (Wakefield, farmer) and ----- Bartlett
(Exeter)

PIPER,

James A. of Wakefield m. Laura A. Evans of Wakefield 10/16/1887; H -
29, RR section boss, b. Newfield, ME, s/o Mark F. Piper (Newfield,
ME, wheelwright) and Elizabeth C. Davis (Newfield, ME,
housekeeper); W - 19, housework, b. Wakefield, d/o John W. Evans
(Wakefield, farmer) and Malvina Farnham (Wakefield, housekeeper)

PIPPIN,

Frank of Wakefield m. Janie Parker of Middleton 9/5/1909; H - 22,
fireman, b. Wakefield, s/o Victor Pippin and Susan Tibidore; W - 15,
housework, b. Manchester, d/o Elmer Parker and Minnie Graton

Harold F. of Union m. Dorothy E. Wentworth of Union 12/5/1934 in
Rochester; H - 23, truck driver; W - 18, at home

Victor, Jr. of Wakefield m. Florida Carrier of Acton, ME 6/30/1913; H -
30, teamster, b. Wakefield, s/o Victor Pippin and Susan Tibidore; W -
18, weaver, b. Ossipee, d/o Joseph Carrier and Delia Matias

PIRKENS,

Cecil Hanson of Kittery, ME m. Alma Mary Lamb of Kittery, ME
12/31/1950 in Sanbornville; H - 61, edgerman; W - 49, bank clerk

PLACE,

Percy of Wakefield m. Freena Lover of Wakefield 2/15/1905 in Rochester;
H - 20, mill hand, b. Farmington, s/o William Place and Lydia
Whitehouse; W - 21, mill hand, b. Wakefield, d/o Augustine Lover
and Cilena Cloutier

PLANT,

Darrell E. of Wakefield m. Ann M. Craigue of Wakefield 6/14/1982 in
Wolfeboro

Darrell E. of Brookfield m. Judith A. **Ruff** of Wakefield 7/11/1995

Eli J. of Wakefield m. Elsie **McDonald** of Wakefield 7/1/1904; H - 23, laborer, b. Elisville, ME, s/o Joseph Plant and Ellen M. Morrow; W - 16, housework, b. Wakefield, d/o Malcolm McDonald and Amanda Crockett

PLANTE,

Michael R. of MA m. Patricia A. **Burke** of MA 7/23/1988 in Sanbornville

PLATT,

Albert R. of Fall River, MA m. Natalie M. **Quinen** of Fall River, MA 12/7/1973

PLIMPTON,

Warren O. of NY m. Harriet M. **Stevens** of Wakefield 9/23/1890; H - 32, doctor, b. Litchfield, ME, s/o A. W. Plimpton (Litchfield, ME, manufacturer) and Hattie E. Plimpton (Gardiner, ME, housekeeper); W - 35, teacher, b. Wakefield, d/o J. G. Stevens (Middleton, farmer) and Amanda H. Stevens (Wakefield, housekeeper)

PLUMMER,

E. O. of Wakefield m. Luella **Goldthwait** of Wakefield 7/28/1921 in Sanbornville; H - 44, shoe operative, b. Farmington, s/o Lorenzo Plummer (Farmington, retired) and Ella Osborne (London); W - 36, housekeeper, 2d, b. Boston, MA, d/o George Richardson (Boston, MA, policeman) and Ella Perigny (Boston, MA)

F. Harrison of Sanbornville m. Ellen P. **Pratt** of Sanbornville 11/30/1937 in Sanbornville; H - 23, sign painter; W - 23, housework

George W. of Bennington, VT m. Geneva M. **Dexter** of Wakefield 2/19/1951 in Sanbornville; H - 40, chef; W - 22, housework

James Lawrence of Sanbornville m. Linda Shirley **Robinson** of Sanbornville 5/21/1959; H - 21, US Navy; W - 18, at home

Thomas O. of Sanbornville m. Alice T. **Hanscom** of Berwick, ME 6/12/1942 in Berwick, ME ; H - 58, carpenter; W - 44, mill worker

POINDEXTER,

C. W. of Sanford, ME m. Minnie E. **Guptil** of Waterboro, ME 10/12/1887; H - 32, farmer, b. Cornish, ME, s/o Samuel Poindexter (Cornish, ME, farmer) and Ruth Wadsworth; W - 19, b. Waterboro,

ME, d/o James Guptill (Waterboro, ME) and Matilda Kimball
(Waterboro, ME, housekeeper)

POISSON,
James Michael of Sanbornville m. Amy Elizabeth Clarke of Sanbornville 8/29/1998 in Rochester
Norman Rene of Rochester m. Jean Claire Dodier of Sanbornville 9/25/1954 in Sanbornville; H - 24, carpenter; W - 17, at home

POLIQUIN,
Raymond J. of Sanbornville m. Candace E. Lee of Sanbornville 10/14/1989 in Sanbornville

POLLARD,
David of Stoneham, MA m. Lorraine Seibert of Stoneham, MA 11/24/1984

POTRIN,
Raymond J. of Somerset, MA m. Eileen M. Olivua of Somerset, MA 4/17/1971

POULIN,
Alfred Joseph of Union m. Kathryn Louise Walker of Sanbornville 12/14/1974 in Sanbornville
Jaime P. of East Wakefield m. Lisa Ann Purple of East Wakefield 2/7/1998 in Wolfeboro

POULIOT,
Edward J. of Sanbornville m. Enid M. Watson of Sanbornville 10/13/1951 in Sanbornville; H - 73, retired; W - 58, ret. tel. oper.

PRATT,
George H. of Wakefield m. Ruth L. Wentworth of Wakefield 5/12/1917; H - 22, farmer, b. Townsend, VT, s/o George I. Pratt and Bessie A. Wilson; W - 17, housework, b. Wakefield, d/o Charles E. Wentworth and Clara L. Place
John C., Jr. of Wakefield m. Paula A. Menegoni of Milton 7/28/1979 in Milton; H - 23; W - 23
John Charles of Wakefield m. Martha Ann Bailey of Wakefield 6/17/1945 in Union; H - 21, carpenter; W - 19, secretary

Robert Harrison of Union m. Mary Lillian Moulton of Somerville, MA 3/28/1943 in Union; H - 24, soldier; W - 24, secretary
William Clifford of Stoneham, MA m. Frances Margaret Lucas of Winchester, MA 7/16/1965; H - 30, truck driver; W - 32, at home

PRESCOTT,
Franklin L. of Union m. Anita M. Boulard of Pelham 6/24/1973 in Pelham

PRIDE,
Robert of Belmont, MA m. Ida G. Woolfrey of No. Wakefield 8/24/1946 in No. Conway; H - 59, carpenter; W - 56, at home

PRIDHAM,
Lawrence M., Jr. of Sanbornville m. Krystle M. Fry of Sanbornville 6/17/1989 in Sanbornville

PROVENCHER,
Antonio E. m. Draxa Corson 8/20/1932 in Sanbornville
Donat of Wakefield m. Malvina Huard of Wakefield 9/6/1910; H - 24, laborer, b. Canada, s/o Hyacinthe Provencher and Mary Lacharite; W - 29, mill operative, b. Canada, d/o Alfred Huard and Melle Durand
Edward A. of Rochester m. Lillian S. Shonyo of Wakefield 12/2/1960 in Durham; H - 48, shoeworker; W - 40, shoe worker
Ernest L. of Sanford, ME m. Odelie M. Bisson of Sanford, ME 9/18/1948 in Sanbornville; H - 54, carpenter; W - 56, millworker

PULEO,
Stephen J. of Belmont, MA m. Linda A. Renner of Belmont, MA 1/10/1967; H - 21, student; W - 19, student

PULIOTT,
Edward F., Jr. of Wakefield m. Exzelia Sturgeon of Milton Mills 10/27/1904 in Milton Mills; H - 25, watchman, b. Wakefield, s/o Edward F. Puliott and Celenia Bosonio; W - 21, weaver, b. Acton, ME, d/o Henry Sturgeon and Dorothie Chauvette

PUSHOR,
Carl L. of Portland, ME m. Evelyn R. Thompson of Portland, ME 5/19/1951 in Sanbornville; H - 33, garageman; W - 27, seamstress

QUARNSTROM,
Ralph Harold of Cambridge, MA m. Diana Greaves of Lexington, MA 9/1/1956 in Sanbornville; H - 53, plumber; W - 41, grad. nurse

QUIMBY,
Forest E. of Wakefield m. Carrie E. Pinkham of Middleton 7/16/1902 in Union; H - 19, mill hand, b. Newfield, ME, s/o Joseph W. Quimby and Ella A. Wentworth; W - 27, housework, b. Middleton, d/o George Pinkham and Laura Main

QUINN,
Steven C. of Wakefield m. Michelle L. Erbacher of Wakefield 8/20/1988

QUINTAL,
Roland E., Jr. of Wakefield m. Rhonda L. Coleman of Wakefield 9/20/1988

RAINAUD,
Warren m. Dora M. Whitten 10/1/1925; H - 25, b. Haverhill, MA, s/o Alfred Reinaud (sic) and Mary King; W - 20, b. So. Berwick, ME, d/o Daniel A. Whitten and Annie Pelletier

RAMIE,
Elucide of Wakefield m. Marie Lavoie of Wakefield 2/1/1905 in Union; H - 24, laborer, b. Canada, s/o Louis Ramie and Aralia Taitraux; W - 20, operative, b. Wakefield, d/o Charles Lavoie and Mary Raymond

RAMSAY,
William D. of Boston, MA m. Bessie A. Richardson of Minot Cor., ME 9/26/1906; H - 29, teamster, b. PEI, s/o Donald M. Ramsay and Christiana McCullom; W - 19, housework, b. Conway, d/o John A. Richardson and ----- Carter

RAMSEY,
George William of Ashland m. Isabelle Bertha Kachanian of Ashland 10/9/1962 in Sanbornville; H - 58, laborer; W - 46, nurse

RAND,
Forrest E. of Wakefield m. Jane M. Gullage of Wakefield 2/14/1984

Frank H. of Wakefield m. Bertha J. Fellows of Wakefield 9/14/1906; H - 36, laborer, b. Hollis, ME, s/o Charles Rand and Serena L. Dunn; W - 20, housework, b. Wakefield, d/o Horatio B. Fellows and Belle F. Tibbetts

Joseph D. of New Durham m. Dorothy M. Garland of Sanbornville 2/15/1935 in Sanbornville; H - 27, mechanic; W - 19, housework

Lester E. m. Blanche I. Elliott 4/28/1929; H - 19, s/o Frank H. Rand (W. Buxton, ME) and Bertha J. Fellows (Wakefield); W - 19, d/o Frank Elliott (Warren) and Minnie Grafton (Manchester)

RANDALL,

David E. of Sanbornville m. Nancy K. Cram of Lebanon, ME 8/16/1969 in Milton

Earl F. of Wakefield m. Pearl G. Mooney of Wakefield 11/3/1917; H - 22, farmer,. b. Wakefield, s/o Frank W. Randall and Martha Runnels; W - 20, teacher, b. Kingfisher, OK, d/o James S. Mooney and Clara M. Griffin

Earl F. of Wakefield m. Mabel Weeks of Milton Mills 5/26/1920 in Union; H - 25, farmer, 2d, b. Wakefield, s/o Frank W. Randall (Brownfield, ME, hotel) and Martha Runnels (Wakefield); W - 18, mill operative, b. Milton Mills, d/o Frank L. Weeks (Kezar Falls, ME, physician) and Minnie Allie (Kezar Falls, ME)

Edgar E. of Sanbornville m. Kathy J. Logan of Milton 8/19/1967 in Milton; H - 20, mechanic; W - 19, at home

Frank W. of Wakefield m. Martha C. Runnels of Wakefield 11/3/1894 in Somersworth; H - 22, iceman, b. Brownfield, ME, s/o Frederick W. Randall (Limerick, ME, shoemaker) and Lydia Grafton (Porter, ME, housework); W - 19, housework, b. Wakefield, d/o Jay Runnels (blacksmith)

Fred B. of Sanbornville m. Ruth V. Drown of Wakefield 3/28/1947 in Sanford, ME; H - 22, farmer; W - 21, at home

Fred B., Jr. of Sanbornville m. Kathryn E. Miller of Sanbornville 10/24/1969 in East Rochester

Gary Frank of Sanbornville m. Sylvia Louise Hopkins of Beverly, MA 1/25/1975

Michael David of Sanbornville m. Danielle Marie Ferland of Sanbornville 4/12/1997 in Rochester

Raymond A. of Sanbornville m. Barbara J. Eldridge of Tuftonboro 9/2/1950 in Ctr. Ossipee; H - 22, teamster; W - 15, at home

Raymond A., Jr. of Sanbornville m. Ann M. Sargent of Effingham

11/11/1967 in Wolfeboro; H - 16, student; W - 18, student
Richard Jay of Sanbornville m. Eunice Sybil Resnick of Springfield, MA 4/1/1975

RAUSCHNOT,
Anthony N., Jr. of East Wakefield m. Lynn M. McIntire of Wakefield 5/12/1979; H - 20; W - 20
Henry A. of Wakefield m. Cheryl L. Gerard of Wakefield 10/26/1985

RAY,
Kevin L. of Barker, NY m. Evelyn U. Guldbrandsen of Sanbornville 8/4/1973 in Sanbornville

RAYMOND,
Edward Louis of Springfield, MA m. Ruth Agatha Myers of Holyoke, MA 6/24/1940 in Wolfeboro; H - 45, salesman; W - 47, at home

READE,
Gordon Alvah of Newfield, ME m. Arlene Patricia Horne of Acton, ME 7/30/1949; H - 23, student; W - 19, student

REARDON,
Alfred L. of Wakefield m. Jane E. LaCoss of Conway 12/31/1968 in Littleton

REBER,
Dale Leonard of Wakefield m. Susan E. Waters of Wakefield 10/6/1978; H - 41; W - 33

REED,
Andrew L. of Wakefield m. Janis L. Hall of Wakefield 5/2/1987 in Milton
Arthur W. of West Newfield, ME m. Marjorie M. Davis of Wakefield 3/18/1934 in Rochester; H - 20, farmer; W - 18, at home
Austin P. of Wakefield m. Gertrude M. Smith of Newfield, ME 11/29/1907; H - 20, teamster, b. Wakefield, s/o Ammon S. Reed and Elizabeth Waldron; W - 18, housework, b. Newfield, ME, d/o Fred Smith and Nellie Sanborn
Elmer E. of Wakefield m. Cora Martin of Wakefield 11/20/1901; H - 30, farmer, b. Dover, s/o Henry A. Reed (Acton, ME, farmer) and Hannah E. Moore (Dover, housewife); W - 17, housework, b. Acton,

ME, d/o Alick Martin (Canada, laborer) and Ruth McGill (Acton, ME, housewife)

Everett W. of Wakefield m. Millie B. Scruton of Strafford 11/26/1905 in Strafford; H - 36, laborer, b. Dover, s/o Henry A. Reed and Hannah Moore; W - 33, housekeeper, b. Strafford, d/o George B. Scruton and Margaret Stanton

George H. m. M. Florence Benson 12/11/1932 in Strafford

Lester H. of Newfield, ME m. Kate L. Gray of Brownfield, ME 7/8/1909; H - 24, painter, b. Newfield, ME, s/o Orion L. Reed and Alice A. Googins; W - 24, housework, b. Brownfield, ME, d/o Angvine W. Gray and Fannie Bickford

Lester Haven of Newfield, ME m. Harriet Mildred Chase of Newfield, ME 12/28/1955; H - 71, farmer; W - 74, at home

Lester Haven, Jr. of Wellesley, MA m. Evelyn Florence McDonald of North Wakefield 8/20/1938 in Rochester; H - 26, painter; W - 18, at home

Norman E. of East Wakefield m. Marjorie F. Chick of Wolfeboro 5/18/1946 in Wolfeboro; H - 26, arborist; W - 18, at home

Theodore E. of Union m. Exzena Garyalt of Rochester 6/25/1937 in Farmington; H - 30, wood turner; W - 31, shoe shop op.

Warren B. of Newfield, ME m. Grace I. Gilpatrick of Limerick, ME 10/25/1908; H - 19, farmer, b. Newfield, ME, s/o Orion Reed and Alice Gogings; W - 30, school teacher, b. Limerick, ME, d/o Horace Gilpatrick and Lottie McCusick

REGAN,
James Victor m. Dorothy Adeline Otis 3/2/1933 in Alton

REID,
James R. of Sanbornville m. Leola Blackwood of East Wakefield 6/8/1974 in Portsmouth

James R., Jr. of Wakefield m. Cynthia A. Webster of Wakefield 11/26/1982

James Richard of Sanbornville m. Jacqueline Lois Libby of Sanbornville 5/3/1957 in Wolfeboro; H - 28, carpenter; W - 32, at home

James Richard of Wakefield m. Anna Caroline Plant of Wakefield 3/27/1976 in Wolfeboro

James Richard, Jr. of Wakefield m. Kathleen-Jean Long of Wakefield 11/4/1977 in Sanbornville

Steven Roy of Newington m. Karen Diana Giffin of Sanbornville 3/25/1990 in Portsmouth

REISSFELDER,
Bruce Thomas of Lyman, ME m. Barbara J. Wentworth of Wakefield 8/12/1978; H - 32; W - 30

REMICK,
Crosby B. of Wakefield m. Emma M. Gale of Wakefield 9/16/1904 in Concord, MA; H - 55, hotel proprietor, 2d, b. Milton, s/o Moses H. Remick and Clara Wentworth; W - 42, domestic, 2d, b. Boston, MA, d/o William Henry and Elizabeth Howell

Mark A. of Wakefield m. Blanche M. Bassett of Dover 10/23/1917; H - 18, carpenter, b. Wakefield, s/o Alonzo M. Remick and Harriette M. Maleham; W - 20, b. Dover, d/o Thomas Bassett and Mabel Collins

REYNOLDS,
Henry Charles of Wakefield m. Adelaide G. Colangelo of Wakefield 8/25/1952 in West Milton; H - 28, mechanic; W - 35, housework

John Francis of Milton, MA m. Rita LaVerne Grace of Roxbury, MA 12/10/1955; H - 24, driver; W - 15, at home

RHOADES,
Charles Campbell of Ft. Collins, CO m. Susan Paulette Miller of Morgantown, WV 9/19/1998 in Tamworth

Steven William of Rochester m. Joanne M. Nason of Wakefield 7/30/1978 in Rochester; H - 20; W - 18

RHODES,
Charles H. of Milton Mills m. Deborah A. Adjutant of Union 7/4/1970 in Acton, ME

RICHARDS,
Albert L. of Wakefield m. Inez M. Colbath of Wakefield 6/9/1909; H - 23, clerk, b. Haverhill, MA, s/o Silas F. Richards and Jennie M. Ford; W - 20, housework, b. Wakefield, d/o Walter G. Colbath and Emma B. Knox

Allen William of Wakefield m. Gayle Wareham of Marblehead, MA 5/22/1976

Charles Walter of Wakefield, MA m. Bernice Robbins King of Union 4/5/1965 in Sanbornville; H - 61, fire fighter; W - 56, clerk
Douglas C. of Sanbornville m. Peggy A. Moody of Milton 5/22/1970

RICHARDSON,
David E. of Wakefield m. Jean M. VanDerKar of Pelham, NY 2/2/1974
Kenneth C. of Topeka, KS m. Stephanie J. Jacobs of Topeka, KS 7/30/1983

RICKER,
Fred A. of East Wakefield m. Linda J. Wisnioski of East Wakefield 8/17/1996 in East Wakefield
Fred R. of Wakefield m. Bertha E. Allen of Brookfield 6/3/1901; H - 27, hostler, b. Wakefield, s/o John R. Ricker (Wakefield, farmer) and Emma J.L. Ricker (Wakefield, housewife); W - 20, housework, b. Brookfield, d/o Samuel M. Allen (Brookfield, mason) and Emma Cummings (Brookfield, housewife)

RIDGE,
William J., IV of Clintondale m. Patricia Anne Duff of Pine Hill, NY 12/27/1988

RIDLON,
Arnold L. of Tuftonboro m. Hazel Louise Beale 10/24/1945 in Rochester; H - 30, carpenter; W - 22, at home

RINES,
Charles W. of Wakefield m. Edna F. Fletcher of Wakefield 12/3/1904; H - 58, farmer, 2d, b. Middleton, s/o Charles F. Rines and Amelia Jones; W - 44, housekeeping, b. New Durham, d/o George W. Fletcher and Julia A. Willey
Philip Harry of Brookfield m. Frances M. Colman of Sanbornville 3/6/1942 in Concord; H - 22, student; W - 21, student
Walter F. of Brookfield m. Grace N. Spiller of Wakefield 6/17/1918 in Farmington; H - 32, farmer, b. Brookfield, s/o Elihu M. Rines and Mary E. Dearborn; W - 32, housekeeper, 2d, b. Ossipee, d/o Charles A. Nichols and Emma A. Williams

RING,
Daniel E. of East Wakefield m. Debra A. Nettelbladt of Wakefield 8/12/1984
Kevin E. of Wakefield m. Patsy A. Weeks of Wakefield 8/8/1981

RINGER,
Kenneth C. of Union m. Viola B. Drew of Union 10/25/1969

RIPLEY,
Walter S. of Wakefield m. Luella A. Morrison of Wakefield 3/28/1908; H - 48, telegraph operator, 2d, b. Bethel, ME, s/o Hosea Ripley and Julia Sturgis; W - 23, housework, 2d, b. Jefferson, MA, d/o Peter Rainville and Alma Beaudio

ROBBINS,
Charles P. of Wakefield m. Ann M. Surette of Wakefield 8/21/1983
Verne E. of Wakefield m. Charlene M. Pappas of Wolfeboro 10/1/1983

ROBERGE,
Roger Claude of Newport, VT m. Judith Ann McDonald of Sanbornville 6/25/1955; H - 23, USMC; W - 18, at home

ROBERTS,
Frederick S. of Wakefield m. Laura E. Simes of Milton 12/7/1892; H - 38, real estate agent, b. NY, s/o Samuel W. Roberts (Alfred, ME, dead) and Lydia J. Burnham (Kennebunk, ME, housework); W - 19, housework, b. Milton, d/o Edward Simes (Milton, farmer) and Mary E. Loud (Acton, ME, housework)
John S. of Wakefield m. Sadie N. Moulton of Wakefield 5/20/1893; H - 28, farmer, b. Wakefield, s/o Samuel W. Roberts (Alton, physician) and Elizabeth Smith (Ossipee, housework); W - 27, housework, b. Wakefield, d/o Herschel Moulton (Wakefield, fireman) and Mary E. Thompson (Eaton, housework)
William R. of Wells, ME m. Sheryl L. Edwards of W. Newfield, ME 5/8/1983

ROBERTSON,
George A. of Waltham, MA m. Louise M. Hanson of Wakefield 7/14/1923 in Sanbornville; H - 22, watch maker, b. Boston, MA, s/o George A.

Robertson and Annie Kelley; W - 22, watch maker, b. Acton, ME, d/o John Hanson and Alice Watson

Leonard of Sanbornville m. Winnifred R. Wood of Dover 1/7/1946 in Dover; H - 24, carpenter; W - 23, stenographer

ROBINSON,

Burton G. m. Josephine Lasky 6/15/1933 in Sanbornville

David B. of No. Reading, MA m. Ruth J. Davis of No. Reading, MA 4/2/1983

Dennis A. of Sanbornville m. Loretta M. Blomstrom of E. Walpole, MA 5/16/1970 in Sanbornville

Donald F. of Wakefield m. Frances L. Meserve of Wakefield 7/1/1937; H - 25, laborer; W - 28, at home

Frank Carl Chase of Acton, ME m. Virginia Clark of Sanbornville 10/15/1962 in Sanbornville; H - 67, retired; W - 46, at home

Frank R. of East Wakefield m. Bertha E. Hart of Wakefield 11/4/1905; H - 23, teamster, b. Wakefield, s/o Frank Robinson and Alice Thompson; W - 18, housekeeper, b. Wakefield, d/o Loammi Hart and L. Hammond

Frank R. of Sanbornville m. Anna M. Renfrow of Dover 3/20/1960; H - 22, US Army; W - 22, mill emp.

Raymond Leroy of Wakefield m. Nellie Frances Karcher of Wakefield 5/29/1939 in Sanbornville; H - 32, millworker; W - 24, housework

Richard Alan of Wakefield m. Linda Roberts Peterson of Arlington, MA 7/31/1976 in Sanbornville

Samuel M. of Wakefield m. Minnie McLean of Wakefield 4/8/1920; H - 55, farmer, 3d, b. Chelsea, MA, s/o Charles Robinson (Dundee, Scotland, sea captain) and Emma Ellis (Fredericton, NB); W - 33, housework, 2d, b. PEI, d/o John Kennedy (PEI, farmer) and Annie Naoning (PEI)

Stephen J. of Wakefield m. Rena L. Drew of Wakefield 11/13/1971 in Middleton

Wayne A., Jr. of Wakefield m. Lisa M. Jerome of Rochester 6/25/1988

Wayne Albert of Sanbornville m. Pamela Ann Wiggin of Wakefield 7/24/1965 in Sanbornville; H - 20, US Army; W - 18, clerk

William A. of Sanbornville m. June Valley of Milton Mills 10/16/1948 in Sanbornville; H - 21, mechanic; W - 18, at home

William A., Jr. of Sanbornville m. Vicki A. Billings of Berwick, ME 6/14/1970

William A., Jr. of Rochester m. Martha E. Couture of Rochester
    4/26/1981 in Dover
William B. m. Susie M. Davis 10/22/1932 in Sanbornville

RODNEY,
Todd R. of Wakefield m. Christine V. Leonardi of Wakefield 10/7/1995

ROGERS,
James M. of Rochester m. Patricia A. Dennison of Wakefield 9/5/1981
Vincent D. m. Marion A. Hickman 8/19/1933 in New London
Walter E. m. Irma Grover 10/13/1931; H - 34, s/o Herbert Rogers
    (Wolfeboro) and Lillian Sanborn (Wakefield); W - 28, d/o J. Frank
    Grover (Rochester) and Maud Allen (Rochester)

ROM,
Kenneth B. of Pittsburgh, PA m. Beth A. Graden of Pittsburgh, PA
    8/17/1991

ROSE,
Gerald A. m. Beulah H. Morse 9/16/1966; H - 64, retired; W - 64, at home

ROSS,
Richard Andre of Biddeford, ME m. Patricia Ann Fee of Sanbornville
    4/14/1990

ROULEAU,
Samuel J., Jr. of Milton m. Barbara M. Herrick of Sanbornville 6/26/1948
    in Lebanon, ME; H - 19, RR employee; W - 17, at home
Syd of Sanbornville m. Rebecca Thompson of Sanbornville 4/27/1991 in
    Sanbornville

ROUSSEAU,
Carlton J. of Wakefield m. Laura J. Adams of Wakefield 7/30/1983

ROY,
Leslie A. of Danvers, MA m. Jean Vigliotta of Saugus, MA 8/11/1973 in
    Sanbornville
Timothy Scott of No. Berwick, ME m. Carol Ann Stier of Wakefield
    5/29/1993 in Moultonboro

ROYLE,
Stephen F. of Wakefield m. Lauree Fletcher of Wakefield 3/4/1989

RUNNELLS,
Othello Dean of Milton m. Bernice Irene Goodwin of Sanbornville 4/13/1975

Robert Dean of Milton Mills m. Virginia S. Worster of Wakefield 7/21/1951 in Milton; H - 19, Navy Yard worker; W - 20, at home

RUNNELS,
Alvah of Wakefield m. Elizabeth Harriman of Tamworth 11/29/1888 in Tamworth; H - 63, farmer, 2d, b. Acton, ME, s/o Samuel Runnels and Hannah Farnham; W - 53, housework, 2d, b. NY

Samuel of Wakefield m. Mary R. Knox of Wakefield 6/30/1892; H - 36, manufacturer, 2d, b. Wakefield, s/o Alvah Runnels (Acton, ME, farmer) and Martha Wentworth (Milton, dead); W - 29, seamstress, 2d, b. Madison, d/o Adams F. Harriman (Madison, dead) and Elizabeth Fisk (Moira, NY, housework)

RUSH,
Harry G. of Wakefield m. Phoebe Crateau of Wakefield 10/16/1916; H - 22, shoe cutter, b. Londonderry, s/o John J. Rush and Delia Peney; W - 23, shoe stitcher, b. Wakefield, d/o Edward Crateau and Emile Robenhymer

RUSSELL,
James Arthur of Wakefield m. Iva May Gagnon of Wakefield 12/24/1939 in Sanbornville; H - 33, woodsman; W - 43, moulder

Jonathan L. of Sanbornville m. Ruth Marie Ricci of Rochester 5/7/1996 in Rochester

RYAN,
Robert H. of Baltimore, MD m. Margaret E. Taliano of Wrentham, MA 6/14/1986

ST. CYR,
James R. of Lynn, MA m. Lauren S. Wilson of Beverly, MA 7/22/1973 in East Wakefield

James R. of East Wakefield m. Barbara A. Williams of Hampton 10/16/1981

Leo A. of Wakefield m. Leigh A. McDormand of Wakefield 11/14/1987 in Sanbornville

ST. LAURENT,
Norman P. of Lawrence, MA m. Margaret Lucille Burton of Lawrence, MA 8/31/1940 in Wolfeboro; H - 23, salesman; W - 21, reg. nurse

SADLER,
Franklin W. of Pittsburgh, PA m. Murial A. Shuler of Pittsburgh, PA 10/23/1972 in Sanbornville

SADLIER,
Paul W. of Wakefield m. Ruth L. Dwyer of Wakefield 9/2/1972 in Rindge

SAMPSON,
Arthur C. of Lewiston, ME m. Emma B. Willey of Wakefield 6/1/1895; H - 23, clerk, b. Wayne, ME, s/o Osgood M. Sampson of Lewiston, ME (W. Gardiner, ME, 58, machinist) and Luella Dearborn (Hallowell, ME, 51, housekeeper); W - 21, housework, b. Wakefield, MA, d/o Osgood E. Willey (Bingham, ME, deceased) and Augusta E. Barron of Skowhegan, ME (Harmony, ME, 48, housekeeper)

SANBORN,
Carlton I. m. Myrtle M. Nute 9/1/1933 in Rochester

Carlton Wilbur, Jr. of Sanbornville m. Janice Maria Glennon of Sanbornville 10/25/1975 in Sanbornville

Dyer H. of Wakefield m. Minnie A. Wiggin of Wakefield 6/11/1887 in Newington; H - 28, sawyer, b. Wakefield; John G. Sanborn (Acton, ME, lumber dealer) and Mary E. Garvin (Acton, ME, housekeeper); W - 17, b. Wakefield, d/o Josiah W. Wiggin (Wakefield, farmer) and Mary A. Rines (Middleton, housekeeper)

George Buron of Salisbury m. Cora May Drew of Sanbornville 8/5/1950 in Milton Mills; H - 66, retired; W - 63, at home

Harley Nason of Wakefield m. Daisy Alma Dyer of Dorchester, MA 6/22/1958; H - 46, mill emp.; W - 31, c. work

Henry S. of Newfield, ME m. Alice E. Shepard of Newfield, ME 11/13/1907; H - 19, laborer, b. Newfield, ME, s/o Charles H. Sanborn and Ada Reed; W - 21, housework, b. Brockton, MA, d/o Charles E. Ford and Annie Murphy

J. Frank of Salem, MA m. Isabel L. **Perkins** of Salem, MA 7/3/1907; H - 45, engineer, 2d, b. Newfield, ME, s/o Joseph Sanborn and Mercy J. Moody; W - 55, housekeeper, 2d, b. Peabody, MA, d/o Mark Merrow and Ruhannah Baldwin

John G. of Wakefield m. Ida B. **Mann** of Shapleigh, ME 10/18/1892 in Milton Mills; H - 70, farmer, 2d, b. Acton, ME, s/o Henry Sanborn (Shapleigh, ME, dead) and Elizabeth French (Epping, dead); W - 32, housework, b. Shapleigh, ME, d/o John Mann (Shapleigh, ME, farmer) and Betsy Thyng (Shapleigh, ME, dead)

John Gilman of Sanbornville m. Anna Leona **Fay** of Newton, MA 8/15/1952 in Wolfeboro; H - 19, shoeworker; W - 18, cook

John W. of Wakefield m. Julia A. **Thurston** of Freedom 9/10/1896 in Freedom; H - 74, RR superintendent, 2d, widower, b. Wakefield, s/o D. H. Sanborn (Wakefield, deceased, farmer) and Lydia Dore (Acton, ME, deceased, housekeeper); W - 53, housework, 3d, b. Hiram, ME, d/o Daniel Prime of Hiram, ME (Woburn, MA, farmer) and Abagail Hancock (Buxton, ME, housework)

Norris R. m. Margaret K. **Regan** 9/23/1933 in Farmington

Richard D. of Sanbornville m. Bernice F. **McCrillis** of Sanbornville 6/23/1935 in Sanbornville; H - 21, filling sta. prop.; W - 22, book keeper

Richard D. of Wakefield m. Florence E. **Roberts** of Medfield, MA 9/22/1981

Richard Dyer, Jr. of Sanbornville m. Elizabeth Ann **Richardson** of Gonic 1/19/1957 in Rochester; H - 20, student; W - 21, student

Wilbur F. of Wakefield m. Lillian M. **Johnson** of Lowell, MA 10/5/1910; H - 36, farmer, b. Newfield, ME, s/o Luther M. Sanborn and Ellen C. Blake; W - 24, housework, b. Lowell, MA, d/o Mathew R. Johnson and Abigail G. McElman

Winfield S., III of Sanbornville m. Joanne M. **Stewart** of Sanbornville 7/12/1997 in Sanbornville

SANDERS,
Charles L. m. Florence D. **Leavitt** 10/20/1926; H - 67, b. Ossipee, s/o J. L. Sanders and Elizabeth Leighton; W - 65, b. Effingham, d/o Joseph Durgin and Mary F. Taylor

SANTOS,
Paul S. of Wakefield m. Carol A. **Speed** of Wakefield 9/22/1988

SARGENT,
Alan Wayne of Ctr. Ossipee m. Carole Joyce Duchano of Sanbornville 11/1/1962; H - 16, laborer; W - 16, student
John A. of Wakefield m. Winifred McCormack of Wolfeboro 7/12/1916; H - 29, shoe cutter, b. Wolfeboro, s/o Louis A. Sargent and Ida F. Hinds; W - 30, housekeeper, b. Ireland, d/o Luke McCormack and Mary Quenn

SAWYER,
Charles E., Jr. of Boxford, MA m. Cheryl L. Hoyt of Boxford, MA 8/17/1991
Fred E. of Waterville, ME m. Mary L. Dyer of Waterville, ME 6/21/1910; H - 49, confectioner, 2d, b. Wakefield, s/o George W. Sawyer and Hannah Young; W - 36, housework, b. Burnham, ME, d/o Benjamin Dyer and Fidelia Stevens

SCALA,
Dino Anthony of Sanbornville m. Beth Marie Hayes of Sanbornville 11/25/1995 in Sanbornville

SCEGGEL,
Charles B. of Ossipee m. Roxie Earle of Wakefield 10/8/1899; H - 32, painter, 2d, b. Ossipee, s/o Roswell J. Sceggel (Ossipee, painter) and Hannah B. ---- (Ossipee, housekeeper); W - 31, housekeeper, 2d, b. Madison, d/o Samuel J. Hanson (mill hand) and A. G. Thompson

SCEGGELL,
Stephen Howard of Milton m. LuAnn B. Pratt of Wakefield 6/11/1977 in Milton
Stephen Howard of East Wakefield m. Kimberly Ann Mendell of East Wakefield 10/3/1993 in East Rochester

SCHNEIDER,
David A. of Providence, RI m. Marjorie Salinger of Providence, RI 10/12/1985

SCHNURBUSH,
Daniel Bernard of East Wakefield m. Barbara M. Schroeder of East Wakefield 11/22/1994

SCHOONMAKER,
Weld Day of Rochester m. Evelyn Clapham Horne of Acton, ME 6/28/1941 in Rochester; H - 29, supt.; W - 25, at home

SCHUCHMAN,
Walter of Marshall, PA m. Agnes L. Cowper of New York, NY 6/30/1919 in Sanbornville; H - 35, manager, b. Homestead, PA, s/o Frederick Schuchman (Pittsburgh, PA, manufacturer) and Virginia Ruth (Pittsburgh, PA); W - 35, trained nurse, b. Northfield, VT, d/o Fred C. Cowper (Brazil, clergyman) and Emma A. Kidd (NS)

SCHULTIES,
John H. of Wakefield m. Candace M. Fenna of Laconia 7/13/1979 in Gilford; H - 35; W - 27

SCHWEIZER,
David E. of Marblehead, MA m. Adele C. Sparhawk of East Wakefield 6/28/1969 in Sanbornville

SCHWIETERMAN,
Eugene L. of Coldwater, OH m. Bonnie L. Booth of Wakefield 2/6/1966 in Sanbornville; H - 21, US Navy; W - 16, student

SCIROCCO,
Thomas J., Jr. of Wakefield m. Linda Bibber of Wakefield 12/24/1978; H - 26; W - 32

SCOTT,
Daniel M. of W. Newfield, ME m. Rachael Alexander of W. Newfield, ME 4/9/1983
Frank Alexander of Auburn, ME m. June Elizabeth Kennett of Sanbornville 4/20/1943 in Sanbornville; H - 26, US Army; W - 22, reg. nurse
Sumner Sterling of Sanbornville m. Theresa Marie Lepene of Sanbornville 6/30/1990 in East Wakefield

SCOWCROFT,
Thomas W. of Warwick, RI m. Karen E. Steadman of Wakefield 1/15/1972 in Sanbornville

SCRIBNER,

Neil Robert of Rochester m. Maureen Theresa **Flanagan** of Sanbornville 6/14/1997 in Rochester

Walter M. of Wakefield m. Margaret E. **Rose** of Wakefield 7/10/1960; H - 24, carpenter; W - 22, secretary

SCULLY,

Robert M. of Wakefield m. Clara E. **LeBosquet** of Haverhill, MA 11/26/1968

SEARS,

Philip J. of Sanbornville m. Roberta E. **Marsh** of Wakefield, MA 7/14/1968 in Sanbornville

SEEBER,

Knut M. of Cambridge, MA m. Barbara N. **Wagner** of Somerville, MA 10/13/1979; H - 43; W - 33

SEIBERT,

Bruce A. of Littleton, MA m. Carolyn **Abbott** of Littleton, MA 10/12/1985 in Brookfield

SENNOTT,

Frederick Joseph of Arlington, MA m. Marjorie Maude **Sparks** of Arlington, MA 9/19/1964 in Sanbornville; H - 60, sales; W - 61, secretary

SERSON,

Harold V. of Ottawa, Canada m. Eva F. **Horne** of Spuyten Duyvil, NY 9/24/1919 in Sanbornville; H - 36, civil engineer, b. Kinburn, ON, s/o William Serson (ON, farmer) and Martha Scott (ON); W - 34, mus. governess, b. Acton, ME, d/o Henry A. Horne (Acton, ME, farmer) and Ida Sanborn (Dover, MA)

SEWELL,

Robert Franklin of Saugus, MA m. Martha Sue **Faulkner** of Saugus, MA 10/27/1962; H - 21, peace corps; W - 18, at home

SHACKFORD,
E. D. of Wakefield m. Edna Drew of Eaton 12/12/1896; H - 20, teamster, b. Eaton, s/o S. F. Shackford of Wakefield (Eaton, 41, farmer) and Ada L. Smith (Belfast, ME, 36, housewife); W - 27, housework, b. Eaton, d/o Edward Drew of Eaton (Eaton, 81, farmer) and Rose Allard (Freedom, 82, housekeeper)
Mark D. of Sanbornville m. Richelle R. Zalenski of Sanbornville 6/13/1992

SHARP,
Frank of Wakefield m. Ethel S. Cook of Wakefield 3/21/1909 in Milton; H - 27, teamster, s/o Gideon Sharp and Ruth McGill; W - 16, housework, b. Wakefield, d/o Elmer M. Cook and Lillian Clow

SHAUGHNESSY,
Stephen J., Jr. of Wakefield m. Lorraine M. Jordan of Wolfeboro 8/11/1957 in Wolfeboro; H - 22, tel. co.; W - 16, at home

SHAW,
Herbert E. of Wakefield m. Nellie I. Elliott of Wakefield 7/6/1920 in Ossipee; H - 21, mill hand, b. Tuftonboro, s/o Daniel W. Shaw (Tuftonboro, teamster) and Margaret Philbrick (Tuftonboro); W - 16, housekeeper, b. Candia, d/o Frank Elliott (Stoneham, MA, teamster) and Minnie Graton (Manchester)
Lee Walter m. Mary Elizabeth Woods 6/22/1929; H - 27, s/o Elijah Shaw (Wakefield, NB) and Susan Lovely (Presque Isle, ME); W - 24, d/o Frank E. Woods (WI) and Clara E. Hill (Wakefield)
Rexford N. of Salem, MA m. Suzan L. Stevens of Salem, MA 6/20/1992

SHEA,
Alfred H. of Union m. Lois J. Colby of Milton 6/10/1935 in Milton Mills; H - 21, laborer; W - 23, at home
Carroll J. of Union m. Susan G. Burns of Milton 2/8/1974 in Union
Patrick J. of Wakefield m. Florence Reed of Wakefield 6/21/1909 in Brookfield; H - 26, brass finisher, b. Boston, MA, s/o Daniel Shea and Abbie Laughton; W - 18, housework, b. Wakefield, d/o Edwin S. Reed and Inez Dicey

SHEEHAN,

Thomas of Wakefield m. Kate Myers of Boothbay, ME 1/11/1896; H - 34, florist, b. Lynn, MA, s/o John Sheehan of Lynn, MA (Ireland, 84, florist) and Mary Ellard (Ireland, deceased); W - 33, housekeeper, 2d, widow, b. Boothbay, ME, d/o Thomas Murphy (Boothbay, ME, deceased) and Mary Digdon (Boothbay, ME, deceased)

SHEHAN,

William P. of Providence, RI m. Mae E. Greene of Providence, RI 8/31/1935 in Sanbornville; H - 21, architect; W - 21, at home

SHELATO,

Jerry L. of Sanbornville m. Evelyn M. Gautreau of Sanbornville 8/26/1995 in Milton

SHERMAN,

Jack M. of Wakefield m. Peggy A. Canavan of Wakefield 12/29/1984

SHERR,

Michael Bruce of Wakefield m. Nancy Mildred Powers of Peabody, MA 8/20/1977

SHETLER,

Steven Charles of Medford, MA m. Leslie Gabrielle Jonas of Medford, MA 8/29/1998 in Sanbornville

SHORTRIDGE,

Everett D. of Wakefield m. Alice J. Thompson of Effingham 10/2/1894; H - 29, typesetter, b. Wolfeboro, s/o James H. Shortridge (Wolfeboro, farmer) and Mary J. Twombly (Wolfeboro, housework); W - 21, housework, b. Ossipee, d/o Thatcher Thompson (Newfield, ME, farmer) and Fannie H. Tibbetts (Madison, housework)

SIBLEY,

Ernest R. of Wakefield m. Ethel M. Richards of Wakefield 4/1/1905 in Sanbornville; H - 23, farmer, b. Wakefield, s/o Richard F.D. Sibley and Emma B. Buzzell; W - 22, housework, b. Wakefield, d/o Charles C. Richards and Keziah F. Quimby

Forrest F. of Wakefield m. L. Mabel Buzzell of Peabody, MA 10/17/1906 in Everett, MA; H - 42, farmer, b. Wakefield, s/o Richard F.D.

Sibley and Emma B. Buzzell; W - 40, housework, 2d, b. Wakefield, d/o Thomas Cloutman and Mary E. Sanborn

Forrest F. of Sanbornville m. Carrie A. Hooper of Sanbornville 11/22/1938 in Sanford, ME; H - 74, farmer; W - 61, housework

Fred D. of Wakefield m. Sarah A. Langley of Raymond, ME 9/18/1901 in Norway, ME; H - 25, carpenter, b. Boston, MA, s/o Richard F.D. Sibley (Wakefield, farmer) and Emma Buzzell (Acton, ME, housekeeper); W - 28, shoe stitcher, b. Flagstaff, ME, d/o Luther M. Langley (Raymond, ME, farmer) and Sophia L. Butler (Flagstaff, ME, housekeeper)

SILCOCKS,
Donald W. of Wakefield m. Jane E. Schnurbush of Wakefield 8/1/1981

SIMMONS,
Daniel Leroy of Sanford, ME m. Nancy Christine Leach of Sanford, ME 10/9/1976

SIMONAULT,
Alfred of Alfred, ME m. Annie C. Hall of Wakefield 12/1/1910 in Portland, ME; H - 22, millwright, b. Lawrence, MA, s/o Edward Simonault and ----- Brisson; W - 23, housework, b. Baldwin, ME, d/o Edward Hall and Mary Hall

SINAPUIS,
Daniel R. of Sanbornville m. Tammy J. Carter of Sanbornville 9/21/1996 in Sanbornville

SINCLAIR,
Clarence of East Rochester m. Elizabeth Blanchard of Wakefield 12/8/1923 in Portsmouth; H - 23, mill operative, b. Dover, s/o Colon Sinclair and Etta Burse; W - 27, teacher, b. Lebanon, ME, d/o Frank Blanchard and Susan Quint

SKALTSIS,
Peter J. of Middleton m. Michelle A. Bilodeau of Wakefield 4/13/1987

SKILLIN,
Alexander W. of Falmouth, ME m. Florence M. Corson of Union 9/4/1924 in Sanford, ME; H - 22, bank clerk, b. Falmouth, ME, s/o Alexander

Skillin and Susie M. Winslow; W - 22, teacher, b. Union, d/o John E. Corson and Idella Wiggin

SKINNER,
Harold E. of Wakefield m. Olga Bell **Laforest** of Wakefield 1/15/1944 in Rochester; H - 50, store manager; W - 35, at home

SLEDGE,
Colin J. of Belmont, MA m. Diana M. **Vaughn** of Belmont, MA 10/21/1989

SMART,
James Woodrow of Woodman m. Etta Lenora **Clark** of Springvale, ME 11/5/1938 in Porter, ME; H - 23, laborer; W - 21, mill operative
Leonard E. of Woodman m. Isabelle K. **Ringer** of Newfield, ME 8/15/1936 in Sanbornville; H - 24, laborer; W - 28, waitress

SMITH,
Alverton m. Barbara **Hoage** 1/24/1932 in Union
Arthur E. m. Verna B. **MacDonald** 7/28/1929; H - 27, s/o Andrew T. Smith (Boston, MA) and Agnes G. Murphy (Boston, MA); W - 17, d/o Arthur MacDonald (North Wakefield) and Leona Hall (Sawyer's River)
Charles A. of Boston, MA m. Maria J. **Hackett** of Wakefield 2/10/1897; H - 23, clerk, b. Kingston, NY, s/o Hiram Smith of Ansonia, CT (Rosendale, NY, 59, veterinary) and Sarah E. Nutting (Napahanock, NY, 59, housewife); W - 20, b. Brookfield, d/o Charles A. Hackett of Wakefield (Brookfield, 53, carpenter) and Maria A. Trask (Wolfeboro, deceased)
Charles R. of Wakefield m. Ida **Foss** of Brookfield 8/16/1887 in Rochester; H - 27, farmer, b. Digby, NS, s/o Jacob Smith (farmer) and Olive Worthylake; W - 26, housework, b. Stow, ME, d/o Nathaniel Foss (Strafford, farmer) and Abigail B. ----- (Stow, ME)
Chellis W., Jr. of East Wakefield m. Cynthia L. **Bibeault** of East Wakefield 5/3/1997
David G. of Wakefield m. Renee D. **Hill** of Wakefield 12/18/1971
Henry V. of Everett, MA m. Beatrice M. **Butters** of Medford, MA 6/23/1935 in Sanbornville; H - 21, stockman; W - 20, at home
Norman A. of Wakefield m. Julie C. **Pappas** of Wakefield 7/17/1981 in Ossipee

Patrick A. of Wolfeboro m. Susan L. Moody of Wolfeboro 3/12/1983
Patrick M. of Hyde Park, MA m. Deborah J. Ridlon of Hyde Park, MA 8/15/1987
Paul Francis of Saugus, MA m. Dolores Mary Choate of Lynn, MA 10/3/1964; H - 21, cook; W - 19, packer
Raymond of Montpelier, VT m. Carol Hooper of Sanbornville 2/24/1940 in Sanbornville; H - 26, poultry expert; W - 24, at home
Richard A. of Union m. Christine L. Jasztal of Union 9/12/1969 in Sanbornville
Richard Arthur of Wakefield m. Janette Houston Morrill of Milton Mills 9/3/1977 in Rochester
Robert A. of Wakefield m. Cecile M. Glaude of Wakefield 9/7/1983
Robert Andrew, Jr. of Brookfield m. Rita Mary Phelan of Sanbornville 9/25/1976
Robert J. of Houston, TX m. Karen Ann Soucy of Houston, TX 5/28/1980
Ronald Clark of Beverly, MA m. Joanne Alyce Pickos of Beverly, MA 6/29/1962 in Sanbornville; H - 26, ret. sales; W - 25, teacher
Thomas A. of Wakefield m. Helen L. Joy of Wakefield 6/13/1987 in Union
Timothy James of Sanbornville m. Joyce Elizabeth Randall of Sanbornville 10/3/1998 in Chocorua
William J. of Sanbornville m. Katherine H. Drew of Sanbornville 10/7/1984

SONGER,
John S. of Emporium, PA m. Jessie M. Kimball of Wakefield 9/23/1907; H - 26, laborer, b. Brookville, PA, s/o Edmund Songer and Elizabeth Greime; W - 16, housekeeper, b. Wakefield, d/o Frank E. Kimball and Annie Patch

SORRELL,
Lewis of Dover m. Abbie T. Allen of Wakefield 4/19/1948 in Dover; H - 83, retired; W - 69, at home

SOUCEY,
Joseph F.D. m. Marion A. Gagnon 5/20/1929; H - 22, s/o Alphonse Soucey, Sr. (St. Anne, PQ) and Leopaldine Potvine (Matane, Canada); W - 22, d/o Ernest Gagnon (Canada) and Georgiana Legany (Wakefield)

SOUCY,
- Alfonse, Jr. of Wakefield m. Rosanna **Lavertu** of Wakefield 9/19/1921 in Sanbornville; H - 21, on ice, b. Salem, MA, s/o Alfonse Soucy (Canada, machinist) and Pauline Perdvain (Canada); W - 21, b. Wakefield, d/o Ludger Lavertu (Canada, farmer) and Margaret Moore (Canada)
- Alphonse J. of Sanbornville m. Marjorie L. **Partington** of Keene 7/8/1950 in Sanbornville; H - 28, teacher; W - 22, teacher
- Armond Joseph of Sanbornville m. Louise L. **Swinerton** of Sanbornville 6/24/1950 in Sanbornville; H - 21, blacksmith; W - 18, at home
- John Jeffrey of Sanbornville m. Cecile A.M. **Minnon** of Manchester 7/6/1962 in Manchester; H - 20, barber; W - 19, stitcher
- Leo Paul of Wakefield m. Phyllis Winch **Marsh** of Malden, MA 11/8/1941; H - 22, soldier; W - 19, filing clerk
- Mark F. of Wakefield m. Laurianne **Hall** of Wakefield 5/25/1984 in Milton
- Mark Francis of Brookfield m. Sally Marie **Stevens** of Wakefield 3/11/1978; H - 20; W - 19
- Oscar Joseph of Sanbornville m. Dora Mae **Davenport** of Sanbornville 9/19/1942 in Sanbornville; H - 17, rigger; W - 15, housework
- Oscar J., Jr. of Sanbornville m. Roberta C. **Marcoux** of Milton 9/9/1961 in Milton; H - 17, shoe worker; W - 24, shoe worker
- Thomas S. of Brookfield m. Susan E. **Abbott** of Wakefield 10/13/1979; H - 20; W - 20

SPARHAWK,
- William Norwood, III of Wakefield m. Karen Leslie **Ouellette** of Wakefield 12/13/1975

SPARKS,
- Bernie G., III of East Wakefield m. Anna-Marie **Desilets** of Merrimack 6/19/1978 in Merrimack

SPAULDING,
- Henry Otis, Jr. of Portsmouth m. Florence May **Adjutant** of Union 5/10/1942 in Union; H - 22, soldier, US Army; W - 19, at home

SPENCER,
- Frank P. of Wakefield m. Ettie M. **Wentworth** of Parsonsfield, ME 2/2/1915 in Dover; H - 50, farmer, b. Waterboro, ME, s/o Joseph C.

Spencer and Sarah Thing; W - 62, housekeeper, 2d, b. Hallowell, ME, d/o Silas May and Hannah Goodwin

Frank P. m. Georgianna Robinson 11/12/1932 in Dover

Fred of Wakefield m. Sophia Drisco Garland of Wakefield 6/14/1903; H - 42, brass moulder, b. Liverpool, England, s/o Thomas Spencer and Susan Fielding; W - 36, housekeeper, 2d, b. Addison, ME, d/o F. M. Drisco and Alice E. Wass

SPILLER,

Albert C. of Wakefield m. Grace E. Nichols of Effingham 3/30/1908 in Brookfield; H - 22, farmer, b. Shelburne, s/o Isaiah W. Spiller and Emma Tyler; W - 22, housework, b. Ossipee, d/o Charles Nichols and Emma Williams

Robert O. of Wakefield m. Jennie M. Palmer of Wakefield 3/25/1907 in Brookfield; H - 26, laborer, b. Shelburne, VT, s/o Isiah W. Spiller and Emma Tyer; W - 30, housekeeper, b. Boston, MA

SPINNEY,

Ernest O. of Sanbornville m. Ruth E. Shaw of Union 4/8/1967 in Milton; H - 57, laborer; W - 55, retired

George M. of Wakefield m. Addie M. Nason of Wakefield 2/4/1888; H - 18, farmer, b. Wakefield, s/o James T. Spinney (Wakefield, farmer) and Mary A. Farnham (Milton, housework); W - 18, housework, b. Bridgton, ME, d/o Hardin L. Nason (Bridgton, ME, laborer) and Lucinda Nason (Bridgton, ME, housework)

George M. of Sanbornville m. Hattie P. Paul of Portsmouth 10/26/1921 in Milton; H - 51, carpenter, 2d, b. Wakefield, s/o James T. Spinney (Wakefield, farmer) and Mary A. Farnham (Milton); W - 50, b. Charlestown, MA, d/o Stephen W. Paul (Eliot, ME) and Henrietta H. Ross (Rockport, ME)

SPRAGUE,

Louis E. of Acton, ME m. Madeline Adjutant of Union 8/27/1934 in Acton, ME; H - 18, laborer; W - 17, at home

Louis Ronald of Union m. Cynthia Ruth Paey of Milton 5/12/1956; H - 21, machine oper.; W - 16, at home

Simon of Shapleigh, ME m. Annie James of Wakefield 4/15/1892 in Newfield, ME; H - 22, farmer, b. Shapleigh, ME, s/o Hugh H. Sprague (Shapleigh, ME, farmer) and Emerline Tredwell (Kennebunk, ME, housework); W - 19, housework, b. Springvale, ME, d/o Miles

James (Biddeford, ME, farmer) and Lucy Fogg (Springvale, ME, dead)

STABLERLAW,
William m. Ruth Elizabeth Shenton 5/26/1933 in Nashua

STALNAKER,
William R. m. Evelyn G. Shea 12/14/1932 in Union

STEADMAN,
Charles L. of Rochester m. Cindy L. Garland of Wakefield 9/9/1979; H - 21; W - 18
William Howard, Jr. of Wakefield m. Lauretta Pamela Glennon of Rochester 12/11/1976 in Rochester

STEELE,
David C. of Sanbornville m. Kathleen E. Flynn of Sanbornville 6/21/1969 in Sanbornville

STENGEL,
Mark H. of Sanbornville m. Susan L. Smith of Sanbornville 9/23/1989

STEPHEN,
Sanders Hill of Wakefield m. Mary Bradley Lund of Lancaster 6/11/1957 in Lancaster; H - 21, student; W - 20, student

STEVENS,
Dan H. of So. Lebanon, ME m. Darlene A. Maleham of Wakefield 12/14/1968
David S., Jr. of Wakefield m. Kathy M. Therrien of Rochester 8/29/1981 in Rochester
David Spencer of Sanbornville m. Beverly Ann Dodier of Sanbornville 9/3/1955 in Sanbornville; H - 25, lbr. surveyor; W - 20, secretary
Frank L. of Wakefield m. Myrtle M. Johnson of Wakefield 4/8/1903 in Lebanon, ME; H - 19, mill hand, b. Brookfield, s/o Warren J. Stevens and Etta L. Eaton; W - 17, housework, b. Wakefield, d/o Myron L. Johnson and Ellen F. Durgin
Gary Paul of Union m. Roberta Lyn St. Cyr of East Wakefield 6/28/1975 in Union

George W. of Sanbornville m. Mary L. **Drapeau** of Sanbornville 10/16/1944 in Farmington; H - 39, US Army; W - 59, at home

Guy W. m. Callie M.D. Peters 5/23/1932 in Pawtucket, RI

John A. of Wakefield m. Nellie M. **Kimball** of Wolfeboro 9/26/1911 in Milton; H - 38, physician, 2d, b. Wakefield, s/o John G. Stevens and Harriet A. Moulton; W - 28, housework, b. Wolfeboro, d/o Woodbury H. Kimball and Lucy E. Chase

John P. m. Lillian M. **Cooke** 3/28/1929; H - 60, s/o Jacob B. Stevens (Middleton) and Elizabeth Burleigh (Newmarket); W - 41, d/o Thomas A. Cooke (Amesbury, MA) and Caroline Sherman (England)

Kenneth D. of Wakefield m. Shelley R. **Turgeon** of Strafford 3/10/1979; H - 19; W - 17

Kenneth D. of Wakefield m. Lisa L. **Bush** of Wakefield 8/23/1986

Lloyd E. of Wakefield m. Dorothy A. **Dodge** of Wakefield 3/5/1916; H - 22, barber, b. Wakefield, s/o Everett W. Stevens and Lizzie A. Glidden; W - 18, housework, b. Raymond, d/o John W. Dodge and Nettie P. Healy

Mark E. of Union m. Alice F. **Bush** of Rochester 5/4/1985 in Union

Michael K. of Union m. Stephanie A. **Wilkinson** of Union 10/25/1986

Philip L. of Wakefield m. Olive D. **Averill** of Wolfeboro 7/13/1935 in Alfred, ME; H - 29, RR clerk; W - 27, hair dresser

Ralph W. of Wakefield m. Helen R. **Weeks** of Wakefield 2/1/1906 in Parsonsfield, ME; H - 22, laborer, b. Newfield, ME, s/o Calvert R. Stevens and Delia Benson; W - 19, housework, b. Wakefield, d/o N. O. Weeks and Florence Shorey

Reginald W. of Wakefield m. Elizabeth A. **Saunders** of Madison, WI 11/21/1936 in Claremont; H - 25, salesman; W - 21, at home

Richard E. of Wakefield m. Linda A. **Adams** of Wakefield 1/14/1984

Roscoe J. of Wakefield m. Laura L. **Loud** of Wakefield 9/16/1899; H - 23, tel. operator, b. Parsonsfield, ME, s/o Calvin R. Stevens (Newfield, ME, farmer) and Delia J. Benson (Parsonsfield, ME, housekeeper); W - 29, tel. operator, b. Wakefield, d/o Ivory S. Loud (Newfield, ME, station agent) and Ella Davis (Newfield, ME, deceased)

Roscoe J. of East Wakefield m. Hazel F. **Gerrish** of Somersworth 10/9/1944 in Somersworth; H - 66, carpenter & painter; W - 51, bleachery emp.

Roy Albert of Union m. Barbara Ann **Hanson** of Farmington 9/3/1955 in Farmington; H - 28, fireman; W - 19, shoe worker

Thomas W. of Union m. Priscilla A. **Wentworth** of Farmington 10/19/1974 in Farmington

Timothy W. of Union m. Susan L. Miliner of Union 5/2/1998 in Rochester
William H. of Middleton m. Kathleen E. Sprague of Union 12/6/1952; H - 20, lumberman; W - 16, at home

STEVENSON,

Myron L. m. Hazel Weeks 8/20/1928; H - 22, s/o Robert L. Stevenson (Scotland) and Gertrude V. Fogg (Ossipee); W - 21, d/o Herbert L. Weeks (Porter, ME) and Alice E. Brooks (East Boston, MA)

STEWART,

Albert A. of Sanbornville m. Ernestine B. Dimond of Sanbornville 8/24/1946; H - 32, lumberman; W - 18, at home

Albert A. of Sanbornville m. Theresa L. Montgomery of Sanbornville 9/8/1951 in Sanbornville; H - 37, lumberman; W - 31, stitcher

Carl E. of Wakefield m. Joanne M. Rhoades of Wakefield 2/14/1987 in Rochester

Richard R. of Sanbornville m. Dianne M. Nason of Sanbornville 5/16/1970 in Sanbornville

STILLMAN,

Gerald C. of Salem, MA m. Mary B. Wilcock of Dorchester, MA 11/14/1970 in Sanbornville

STINCHFIELD,

Stuart Ralph of Wakefield m. Jule Ann Contois of Wakefield 6/27/1998 in Wofeboro

STITSON,

Carl R. of Parsonsfield, ME m. Carolyn L. Beckman of East Wakefield 8/21/1970 in Sanbornville

STOCKER,

Robert H. of Shapleigh, ME m. Betty Lou Dow of Sanbornville 8/22/1970 in Sanbornville

STOKES,

Edgar F. m. Edythe S. McDonald 10/24/1927; H - 21, s/o John H. Stokes (Boston, MA) and Gertrude Hodgdon; W - 18, d/o Arthur W. McDonald (Wakefield) and Leona M. Hall

STONE,
- Edgar L. of Wakefield m. Mary Megahan of Wakefield 8/30/1893; H - 27, laborer, b. Parsonsfield, ME, s/o Lewis G. Stone (Newfield, ME) and Mary E. ----- (Wakefield); W - 28, housework, b. Cootehill, d/o John Megahan (Cootehill) and Mary -----
- Joseph Whelden m. Amy Alice Pinfold 10/1/1929; H - 62, s/o Henry A. Stone (New Bedford, MA) and Robie W. Keen (Fairhaven, MA); W - 38, d/o William Pinfold (Reading, England) and Annie E. Lewis (Reading, England)

STOVER,
- Ernest of Wakefield m. Mabel Chick of Wakefield 10/3/1901; H - 35, teamster, b. Lovell, ME, s/o Alvin Stover (Lovell, ME, farmer) and Lucy Caldwell (Lovell, ME, housewife); W - 31, housework, d/o Stephen Chick (Limerick, ME, farmer) and Abbie Edwards (Parsonsfield, ME, housewife)

STOWELL,
- Donald I. of Milton m. Betty Lou Gallagher of Sanbornville 9/27/1958 in Gorham; H - 22, laborer; W - 19, bookkeeper

STRATTON,
- Gene of Cumberland, ME m. Carol Mae Greer of Portland, ME 12/29/1950; H - 22, logger; W - 18, sales clerk

STREADER,
- William H. of Wakefield m. Sarah A. Jones of Wakefield 2/10/1914 in Brookfield; H - 25, laborer, 2d, b. Wakefield, s/o Joseph Streader and Valeria Dyer; W - 32, housework, 2d, b. Epping, d/o Jacob M. Bly and Lydia A. Tuttle
- William T. of Wakefield m. Octavia Knowlton of Winchester, MA 7/2/1906 in Brookfield; H - 19, laborer, b. Wakefield, s/o Joseph Streader and Velaria I. Dyer; W - 18, mill operative, b. Winchester, MA, d/o Edmund Knowlton and Josephine Elmore

STROUT,
- James Augustus of No. Waterboro, ME m. Alice Elizabeth Shoemaker of No. Waterboro, ME 6/21/1958 in Sanbornville; H - 84, retired; W - 62, at home

STRUM,
Frederick L. of Wakefield m. Patricia A. Hanley of Wakefield 5/4/1984

STUART,
Jerald Jackson of East Wakefield m. Patricia Myrtle Dexter of Farmington 11/10/1956; H - 24, US Army; W - 19, at home

SULLIVAN,
Daniel Brian of Union m. Patricia Lynn Perry of Union 8/30/1998 in Union
John M. of Peabody, MA m. Laureen Devlin of Georgetown, MA 4/5/1980
Mortimor F. of Farmington m. Gloria Losetta Anderson of Sanbornville 6/3/1955 in East Rochester; H - 23, shoe cutter; W - 27, shoe worker

SUSAN,
Bernard Everett of Union m. Mary Lorraine Bryant of Sandwich 12/9/1949; H - 21, USMC; W - 20, at home

SWANSON,
David E. of Sanbornville m. Kathryn C. Saunder of Sanbornville 8/13/1994 in Sanbornville

SWEENEY,
Richard W. of MA m. Carol-Lynn H. Rice of Salem 7/3/1988 in East Wakefield

SWETT,
William of Wakefield m. Alice Martin of Wakefield 7/27/1912 in Brookfield; H - 60, carpenter, 3d, b. Standish, ME, s/o Bernace Swett and Jane Thorn; W - 18, housework, d/o Alex Martin and Ruth ----

SWIFT,
Harry I. of Wakefield m. Elizabeth E. Cronin of Milton 1/1/1920 in Union; H - 23, mill hand, b. Waterford, ME, s/o Arthur J. Swift (Windham, ME, laborer) and Maude R. Morse (Skowhegan, ME); W - 17, at home, b. Acton, ME, d/o William Cronin (Portsmouth, laborer) and Kate Winch (Charlestown, MA)

SWINERTON,
Alan James of Sanbornville m. Sherrie Ann Maxwell of Sanbornville 5/24/1975
John B. of Chelsea, MA m. Phyllis J. **Friedman** of Revere, MA 2/25/1944 in Sanbornville; H - 40, ropemaker; W - 19, machine opr.
Lawrence Amos of Wakefield m. Dorothy Olioeann **Chase** of Milton 4/13/1957 (but see Robert Francis **Fisher**); H - 43, mill worker; W - 33, at home

TALBOT,
Frederick C. of Riverside, RI m. Gail O. **Dufour** of East Wakefield 5/6/1995 in Sanbornville

TANNER,
Lloyd Cecil of Middleton m. Sarah Jane **Fifield** of Wakefield 5/19/1945; H - 26, machine oper.; W - 22, assembler

TAYLOR,
Robert A. of Wakefield m. Suzanne M. **Koshuta** of Wakefield 9/6/1985

TEBBETTS,
John E. of Berwick, ME m. H. Aromine **Darling** of Malone, NY 9/25/1907; H - 25, merchant, b. Berwick, ME, s/o John A. Tebbetts and Harriette E. Worster; W - 30, operative, b. Malone, NY, d/o James G. Darling and Harriette S. Slack

TEMPLE,
Leroy Ernest of Concord, MA m. Janet Camnon **Saunders** of Boston, MA 6/14/1964; H - 22, student; W - 24, jewelry rep.
Willie M. of Shapleigh, ME m. Etta M. **Young** of Shapleigh, ME 12/6/1889; H - 22, farmer, b. Waterboro, ME, s/o William H. Temple (Waterboro, ME, housework) and Sarah J. Smith (Waterboro, ME, housework); W - 17, housekeeper, b. Waterboro, ME, d/o Hiram H. Young (Waterboro, ME, farmer) and Mary M. Ham (Somersworth, housework)

TEMPLETON,
Harold of Wakefield m. Theodora C. **Libby** of Middleton 4/5/1949 in Milton; H - 42, mechanic; W - 34, at home
Ralph Richard of Wakefield m. Ruth Donna **Bodge** of Center Ossipee

5/28/1938 in Sanbornville; H - 20, sawmill emp.; W - 20, at home

TENAGLIA,
Mario F. of Saugus, MA m. Marion D. **Romsey** of Gloucester, MA 1/26/1964 in Sanbornville; H- 47, mfg.; W - 43, clerk

TESSIER,
George E. m. Marjorie E. **Hatch** 5/30/1931; H - 21, s/o Louis E. Tessier (Suncook) and Lucy Pouliot (Sanbornville); W - 22, d/o Herbert O. Hatch (Wolfeboro) and Ethel G. Nute (Milton)
George E. of Sanbornville m. Edna Ellen **Mills** of Lee 11/16/1974

TESTA,
Robert G. of Wakefield m. Charlotte M. **Miller** of Wakefield 2/20/1993

TEWKSBURY,
Fred Arthur of Wakefield m. Pearle Leona **Nichols** of Wakefield 1/3/1942; H - 44, truck driver; W - 21, housework
R. S. of Wakefield m. Jennie **Hill** of Bartlett 7/2/1896; H - 24, carpenter, b. Tamworth, s/o W. Tewksbury (Tamworth, deceased, farmer) and Adaline Mack (Madison, housekeeper); W - 27, housekeeper, b. Bartlett, d/o Jacob Hill of Bartlett (farmer) and Mary J. Eastman (Bartlett, housekeeper)

THIBEAULT,
George P. of Wakefield m. Mary E. **Ferrarini** of Wakefield 8/15/1992 in Seabrook

THIBODEAU,
Erland Ambrose of Roxbury, MA m. Natalie Frances **Nash** of Jamaica Plains, MA 6/13/1964; H - 51, carpenter; W - 42, nurse

THOMAS,
Alexander of Hyde Park, MA m. Anna K. **Paulowski** of Sanbornville 9/3/1934 in Sanbornville; H - 31, painter; W - 24, maid
James Donald of Sanbornville m. Denise Lorraine **Turbitt** of Sanbornville 7/25/1998 in Sanbornville
James Guilford of Milton m. Corinne Eleanor **Dame** of Union 2/14/1959; H - 18, electronics; W - 19, millworker

Kenneth G. of Wakefield m. Kathleen J. Towle of Wakefield 5/12/1979; H - 20; W - 17

Walter F., Jr. of Wakefield m. Dorothy G. Colman of Wakefield 3/20/1948 in Sanbornville; H - 33, student; W - 35, teacher

THOMPSON,

Barry Jon of Wakefield m. Pamela Jean Beaudoin of Rochester 5/14/1977 in Sanbornville

George of Wakefield m. Dorothy M. Hill of Wakefield 12/28/1920; H - 43, RR coal shed, b. Ossipee, s/o Charles Thompson (Ossipee, on railroad) and Mary A. Bean (Ossipee); W - 20, housework, b. W. Newfield, ME, d/o Louis Hill (Brunswick, ME, farmer) and Rose ----- (W. Newfield, ME)

Morris E. of Quaker Hill, CT m. Isabelle P. Beebe of Waterford, CT 7/26/1978; H - 48; W - 51

Perley E. of Effingham m. Patti A. Ring of Wakefield 12/7/1985

THORNTON,

Roswell P. of Lawrence, MA m. Alice F. Pearl of Lawrence, MA 9/5/1888; H - 31, florist, 2d, b. Lawrence, MA, s/o George Thornton and Elizabeth ----- (housework); W - 34, housework, b. Anson, ME, d/o Nathaniel H. Pearl and Hannah Murch (Stark, ME, housework)

THURSTON,

Donald Herbert of Farmington m. Geraldine Theresa Avery of Union 1/2/1954 in Farmington; H - 23, shoe worker; W - 18, housework

Lee John of Wakefield m. Alice W. Danforth of Wakefield 6/25/1988 in East Wakefield

TIBBETTS,

Arthur D. of Wakefield m. Jerusha Spencer of Parsonsfield, ME 4/9/1898; H - 28, farmer, b. Wolfeboro, s/o J. D. Tibbetts of Wakefield (Wolfeboro, 55, farmer) and Jennie M. Gale (Dover, 52, housewife); W - 38, housework, b. Waterboro, ME, d/o Joseph C. Spencer of Parsonsfield, ME (Waterboro, ME, 71, farmer) and Electra C. Thyng (Waterboro, ME, deceased)

David S. of Farmington m. Beatrice M. Carberry of Sanbornville 8/30/1968 in Center Ossipee

Fred of Wakefield m. Lucy P. Maleham of Wakefield 7/27/1892; H - 32, engineer, b. Porter, ME, s/o Benjamin F. Tibbetts (Porter, ME, farmer) and Emily J. Roberts (Porter, ME, housework); W - 35, milliner, b. Wakefield, d/o William A. Maleham (Wakefield, farmer) and Nancy Pike (Brookfield, dead)

James E. of Union m. Brenda L. **Tucker** of Hopkinton 10/7/1967 in Hopkinton; H - 22, accountant; W - 21, ser. rep.

Willis F. of Portsmouth m. Grace M. **Tuttle** of Wakefield 12/23/1917; H - 24, machinist, b. Wakefield, s/o Fred Tibbetts and Lucy P. Maleham; W - 22, teacher, b. Wakefield, d/o Horace B. Tuttle and Kate V. Weeks

TILESTON,

Alden S. of Wakefield m. Clara E. Mee of Wakefield 10/29/1910; H - 28, civil engineer, b. Dorchester, MA, s/o George C. Tileston and Amelia T. Gless; W - 19, housework, b. Lynn, MA, d/o Robert Mee and Emma Remick

TIMPERLEY,

Robert H. of MA m. Regina E. **Spears** of MA 8/27/1988 in East Wakefield

TINKER,

Scott M. of Wakefield m. Gail S. **Tinker** of Wolfeboro 7/2/1987

TITCOMB,

Leon H. of Wakefield m. Helen M. **Remick** of Wakefield 2/25/1914; H - 25, farmer, b. Wakefield, s/o John F. Titcomb and Abbie M. Morse; W - 23, teacher, b. Wakefield, d/o Alonzo M. Remick and Hattie Maleham

TITUS,

John Joseph of Salem, MA m. Lucy C. **Santarella** of Peabody, MA 5/9/1952; H - 32, machinist; W - 31, lea. worker

TODD,

Robert W., Jr. of East Wakefield m. Sonia A. **Wilkinson** of East Wakefield 6/24/1989

TOWLE,

Durward William of Rochester m. Doris **Bean** of Sanbornville 9/4/1943 in Sanbornville; H - 24, truck driver; W - 19, cashier

Raymond D. of Wakefield m. Ritta E. Brown of Brookfield 5/5/1906 in Brookfield; H - 21, painter, b. Dover, s/o Hiram G. Towle and Martha A. Davis; W - 18, housework, b. Brookfield, d/o Langdon D. Brown and Alfretta Drew

TOWNSEND,
Edward of East Providence, RI m. Frances Ellis Parker of Boston, MA 9/12/1905 in Union; H - 33, commercial traveler, b. East Providence, RI, s/o A. N. Townsend and Sarah E. Townsend; W - 32, nurse, b. Lebanon, CT, d/o Gilbert Parker and Minnie Frink

TRAFTON,
Ashton R. of Union m. Bertha M. Lord of Union 3/31/1905 in Milton Mills; H - 22, mill hand, b. Wakefield, s/o Charles W. Trafton and Susan E. Archibald; W - 16, housework, b. Shapleigh, ME, d/o Hiram Lord and Lill M. Temple
Charles W., Jr. of Portsmouth m. Mary Theresa Herbert of Hampton 1/24/1942 in Sanbornville; H - 28, insurance broker; W - 26, waitress
Eugene C. of Milton m. Marion E. Maleham of Wakefield 3/5/1966 in Sanbornville; H - 19, highway emp.; W - 18, student
Everett E. of Sanford, ME m. Myra E. Wentworth of Wakefield 5/26/1887; H - 24, painter, b. Shapleigh, ME, s/o George W. Trafton (Shapleigh, ME, carpenter) and Mary E. Stiles (Shapleigh, ME, housekeeper); W - 27, housework, 2d, b. Wakefield, d/o Stephen M. Willey and Sarah A. Willey (Wakefield, housekeeper)
Ralph Bradley of Boston, MA m. Glenna Mae Hallock of Boston, MA 10/20/1962 in Sanbornville; H - 21, accountant; W - 22, secretary
Reuben B. of Wakefield m. Iva M. Ham of Wakefield 4/22/1897 in Milton; H - 22, mill operative, b. Wakefield, s/o Charles W. Trafton of Wakefield (Acton, ME, 46, laborer) and Susan E. Archibald (Wakefield, 54, housekeeper); W - 19, housework, b. Farmington, d/o Natt F. Ham (New Durham, deceased) and Susan E. Stevens (Rochester, deceased, housekeeper)

TRAINOR,
James M. of Brownfield, ME m. Lulu P. Hart of Wakefield 3/5/1905 in Ossipee; H - 23, farmer, b. Brownfield, ME, s/o Michael Trainor and Ruth T. Hartford; W - 16, housekeeper, b. Wakefield, d/o Loammi Hart and Hannah M. Harmon

TREFRY,
Wayne Allen of MA m. Cynthia Lynn Elliott of Wolfeboro 4/2/1988 in Union

TRENTSCH,
Scott D. of Sanbornville m. Cynthia J. D'Amico of Lynn, MA 9/2/1994 in Sanbornville

TRIDHAN,
Lawrence M. of Wakefield m. Paula A. Laney of Wakefield 1/14/1961 in Farmington; H - 17, shoeworker; W - 17, at home

TRIPP,
Francis of Medford, MA m. Madeline G. Pigott of Medford, MA 5/16/1936 in Sanbornville; H - 28, chemist; W - 28, biological chemist

TROTT,
Leander M. of Wakefield m. Hazel M. Cook of Wakefield 9/20/1909; H - 25, merchant, b. Portland, ME, s/o Thayer S. Trott and Emma Mathews; W - 16, housework, b. Wakefield, d/o Elmer M. Cook and Lillian Clough
Winfred of Boston, MA m. Effie M. McDonald of Wakefield 4/22/1903 in Sanbornville; H - 21, conductor electric RR, b. Peaks Island, ME, s/o Charles Trott and Flora Mathews; W - 17, housework, b. Wakefield, d/o Malcolm McDonald and Amanda Crockett

TRUSLOW,
James L. m. Anna Leigh Kendall 7/30/1930; H - 29, s/o Henry A. Truslow (Santiago, Cuba) and Jane Auchincloss (Wilmington, DE); W - 23, d/o Eugene Kendall (NJ) and Mabel Congdon (Lawrence, MA)

TUCKER,
Earl M., Jr. of Plymouth, MA m. Priscilla C. Bohmiller of No. Carver, MA 7/27/1973 in Sanbornville
Emerson Leroy of Wakefield m. Anne Irene Peterson of Wakefield 5/20/1977
Harris Wiggin of Wakefield m. Dorothy C. Mason of Haverhill, MA 10/29/1978 in Melvin Village; H - 76; W - 61

James F. of Wakefield m. Sarah E. Stevens of Boston, MA 7/17/1910; H - 55, engineer, 2d, b. Somersworth, s/o James Tucker and Mary E. Hale; W - 53, housework, 3d, b. Bridgewater, MA, d/o James S. Keane and Nancy Shaw

Thomas R. of Lynn, MA m. Frances A. Moon of Ipswich, MA 6/15/1974

Willis F. of Wakefield m. Helen G. Currell of Reading, MA 4/13/1921 in Portsmouth; H - 20, clerk, b. Wakefield, s/o James F. Tucker (Somersworth, engineer) and Mary F. Brackett (Wakefield); W - 18, stenographer, b. Reading, MA, d/o Elias B. Currell (Bridgetown, NS, contractor) and Uella Messenger (Digby, NS)

TUFTS,

Charles F. of Sanbornville m. Almira M. Karcher of Sanbornville 11/29/1934 in Milton; H - 29, painter; W - 21, shoe worker

Charles F. of Wakefield m . Almira M. Wentworth of Rochester 11/11/1978 in Tuftonboro; H - 73; W - 65

Frank J. of Wakefield m. Fannie L. Thompson of Wakefield 5/15/1904; H - 26, railroad employee, b. Somersworth, s/o James W. Tufts and Carrie E. Wyatt; W - 19, housework, b. Andover, d/o Rosto H. Thompson and Jennie P. Godfrey

TURSCHMANN,

Emil H. of Somersworth m. Blanche T. Wentworth of Union 8/29/1952 in Rochester; H - 66, mill hand; W - 54, housework

TUTTLE,

Horace B. of Wakefield m. Kate V. Weeks of Wakefield 10/2/1888; H - 23, RR fireman, b. Wakefield, s/o James Tuttle (Strafford, farmer) and Deborah Howard (Strafford); W - 36, housework, b. Wakefield, d/o Nathan J. Weeks (Wolfeboro) and Salome C. Weeks (Wakefield)

Irving D. of Wakefield m. Ruth E. Johnson of Wayland, MA 7/27/1919 in Waltham, MA; H - 21, farmer, b. Wakefield, s/o Daniel N. Tuttle (Wakefield, farmer) and Ora F. Tuttle (Wolfeboro); W - 21, proof reader, b. Waltham, MA, d/o Elmer E. Johnson (Cambridge, MA, RR employee) and Catherine Wilson (Waltham, MA)

Irving D., Jr. of Wakefield m. Jean Robertson of Acton, ME 6/19/1948 in Brookfield; H - 24, carpenter; W - 29, at home

John C. of Wakefield m. Clara L. Estey of Brookfield 11/3/1903; H - 24, carpenter, b. Wakefield, s/o Daniel N. Tuttle and Ora F. Tibbetts; W

- 28, housework, 2d, b. Boston, MA, d/o Wilder F. Hutchins and Georgiana Jellison
Randal C. of Wakefield m. Pamela J. Hooper of Tuftonboro 7/26/1979; H - 20; W - 20

TWOMBLEY,
Lawrence Ward of Sanbornville m. Kathy Leah Moody of Milton Mills 8/22/1964 in Sanbornville; H - 20, group foreman; W - 18, at home
Philip Douglas of Sanbornville m. Constance Marie Gagnon of Sanbornville 6/15/1962 in Sanbornville; H - 20, USAF; W - 20, clerk

TWOMBLY,
Clarence H. of Conway m. Bessie L. Downs of Wakefield 8/23/1910 in Brookfield; H - 24, farmer, b. Conway, s/o William C. Twombly and Addie M. Burbank; W - 26, housework, b. Wakefield, d/o Thomas J. Downs and Cora L. Hamilton
Nelson F. of Wakefield m. Emma E. Burleigh of Ossipee 2/7/1894 in Ossipee; H - 29, painter, 2d, b. Wolfeboro, s/o Sylvester Twombly (Wolfeboro, painter) and Lydia J. Moody (Tuftonboro, housework); W - 32, teacher, b. Ossipee, d/o Samuel Burleigh (Ossipee, farmer) and Mary S. Bickford (Wolfeboro, housework)
Paul J. of Sanbornville m. Janet M. Waite of Malden, MA 6/4/1960; H - 24, supt.; W - 19, prod. work

TYLER,
Dennis L. of Wakefield m. Marcia A. Tutein of Wakefield 11/5/1988 in Rochester

UZMANN,
Joseph R. of Boothbay Harbor, ME m. Deborah A. Magyar of Boothbay Harbor, ME 7/18/1970

VACHON,
Bruce W. of Farmington m. Therese C. Downs of Wakefield 8/1/1987 in Milton
James Robert of Sanbornville m. Noi Thi Jagielski of Sanbornville 9/10/1994 in Sanbornville
Joseph of Wakefield m. Inez B. Elliott of Gilmanton 1/26/1924 in Alton; H - 34, laborer, 2d, b. Lancaster, s/o Deneth Vachon and Fliedo Cotue;

W - 18, at home, b. Gilmanton, d/o William D. Elliott and Bertha C. Plummer

Joseph Zoel, Jr. of Sanbornville m. Catherine M. Kimball of Sanbornville 8/19/1995

Leo A. m. Pearl E. Goodfield 12/17/1966 in Sanbornville; H - 35, lumber; W - 26, shoeworker

Leo A. of Wakefield m. Shirley J. Nobis of Wakefield 12/31/1978; H - 47; W - 34

Robert A. of Milton m. Theresa M. Duchesneau of Sanbornville 8/30/1947 in Sanbornville; H - 19, boxmaker; W - 18, waitress

VALLEE,

Henry Joseph of Sanford, ME m. Dawn Victoria LeClair of Waterboro, ME 8/30/1958 in Sanbornville; H - 20, hgy. worker; W - 23, clerk

VALLEY,

David of Wakefield m. Addie Patrie of Wakefield 12/27/1898; H - 27, laborer, b. Canada, s/o Frank Valley of Canada (Canada, 80, farmer) and Caroline Lacox (Canada, deceased); W - 25, housework, b. Canada, d/o Feriole Patrie (Canada, deceased) and Marie Lachance of Canada (Canada, 50, housework)

Paul G. of Ossipee m. Mildred R. Weeks of Milton Mills 6/30/1923 in Wolfeboro; H - 26, woodsman, b. Ossipee, s/o Maude Valley; W - 23, housekeeper, 2d, b. Milton Mills, d/o Frank S. Weeks and Minnie L. Weeks

VALLIERE,

George Faye of Moultonboro m. Mary Elizabeth Knight of Sanbornville 9/18/1965 in Sanbornville; H - 19, surveyor; W - 17, at home

VAN,

Ronald David of Natick, MA m. Patricia Leslie Cleary of Wakefield 5/15/1976

VAN DOORN,

Roger A. of Wakefield m. Nancy E. Anderson of Milton 7/8/1961; H - 23, US Navy; W - 20, waitress

VAN DYKE,

Bruce E. of Ossipee m. Velma J. Hobbs of Brookfield 1/20/1973

VAN TUYL,
Robert C. of Portland, ME m. Irene A. Moriarty of Springfield, MA 6/12/1937 in Sanbornville; H - 23, salesman; W - 27, at home

VANDORI,
William R. of Jenkintown, PA m. Janna Rebecca Kolb of Jenkintown, PA 8/20/1994

VARNEY,
Charles C. of Wakefield m. Mary Eastmault of Wakefield 4/23/1910; H - 25, laborer, b. Wakefield, s/o J. Frank Varney and Nancy M. Prescott; W - 25, housework, b. Wakefield, d/o Cyrus Eastmault and Madaline Dereau

Frank W. of Ctr. Ossipee m. Jennifer R. Ouellette of Sanbornville 9/4/1993 in Ossipee Valley

Franklin Parker of Wakefield m. Virginia Inez Nason of Wakefield 6/18/1939 in Union; H - 26, RR employee; W - 18, at home

Guy G. of Wakefield m. Eliza E. Jenness of Milton 12/1/1909 in Milton; H - 20, brass finisher, b. Wakefield, s/o J. Frank Varney and Nancy N. Prescott; W - 17, housework, b. Milton, d/o Edwin P. Jenness and Ella Hawkins

Stanley M. of Wakefield m. Hazel L. Livermore of Wakefield 12/16/1972

Stanley Maurice of Wakefield m. Esther Louise McCrillis of Wakefield 9/12/1941; H - 26, soldier; W - 31, store clerk

VELTSOS,
Donald P. of Haverhill, MA m. Lorraine R. Woods of Haverhill, MA 6/10/1972

VENO,
William of Wakefield m. Mary Lavertu of Wakefield 10/9/1911; H - 21, flagman, b. Ossipee, s/o Joseph Veno and Rosie Marshall; W - 19, housework, b. Canada, d/o Joseph Lavertu and Margaret Moore

VERGARA,
Gustavo J. of Winter Park, FL m. Sandra A. St. Laurent of Sanbornville 9/7/1996 in Durham

VESESKIS,
Mark Anthony of Wakefield m. Young Ok Yun of Wakefield 6/4/1983

VISELLI,
Antonio A. of East Wakefield m. Leanne M. Donahue of East Wakefield 8/8/1991

VORTEAU,
Ranceford of Wakefield m. Maud E. Heath of Wakefield 10/14/1899 in Newburyport, MA; H - 24, laborer, b. Shediac, NB, s/o Phillip Vorteau (Shediac, NB, farmer) and Valentine Arseno (Shediac, NB, housekeeper); W - 18, housekeeper, b. Amesbury, MA, d/o Frank S. Heath (Merrimac, MA, carpenter) and Jennie S. Nutter (Amesbury, MA, housekeeper)

WADE,
George E., Jr. of Rochester m. Beulah S. Winship of Sanbornville 6/29/1968 in Rochester

WADLEIGH,
J. Elijah of Wakefield m. Edwina E. Fox of Milton Mills 11/21/1917 in Milton Mills; H - 28, farmer, b. Lynn, MA, s/o Frank F. Wadleigh and Mary J. Gilmore; W - 24, teacher, b. Milton Mills, d/o Charles D. Fox and Hattie Fox

WADSWORTH,
Harold H. m. Mabel E. Marston of Parsonsfield, ME 11/3/1946 in Union; H - 38, spinner; W - 22, spinner

WAKEFIELD,
George Henry of Wakefield m. Allura M. Burrows of Middleton 9/6/1924 in North Wakefield; H - 23, mechanic, b. Meredith, s/o William Wakefield and Bessie Canning; W - 18, household, b. Farmington, d/o William Burrows and Emma Knowles

WALDRON,
Bertwell T. of Wakefield m. Mattie A. Lewis Clough 8/26/1903 in West Parsonsfield, ME; H - 26, teamster, b. Wakefield, s/o John D. Waldron and Anna E. Reed; W - 29, housework, 2d, b. Stoneham, MA, d/o Frederick Lewis and Laura G. Sturtevant

Charles D. of Wakefield m. Mary F. Philbrick of Wakefield 10/30/1895 in Ossipee; H - 38, merchant, b. Wakefield, s/o Hiram R. Waldron of Wakefield (Acton, ME, merchant) and Sarah P. Woodman (Newfield, ME, housekeeper); W - 21, housework, b. Wakefield, d/o John D. Philbrick of Newfield, ME (Wakefield, carpenter) and Harriette E. Champion (Effingham, housekeeper)

Hiram E. of Wakefield m. Rose Billedeau of Wakefield 12/26/1898; H - 25, laborer, b. Cambridge, MA, s/o J. Drew Waldron of Wakefield (Acton, ME, 71, farmer) and Anna E. ----- (Newfield, ME, 63, housewife); W - 16, housework, b. Salem, MA, d/o Felix Billedeau of Wakefield (Canada, 38, laborer) and Phebe ----- (Canada, 40, housewife)

Homer J. m. Lucy S. Daggett 5/25/1929; H - 57, s/o Albert H. Waldron (Taunton, MA) and Fannie Howard (Gilsum); W - 60, d/o William Kimball (Lyman, ME) and Melissa Ross (West Newfield, ME)

Roger H. of Wakefield m. Alice H. Ganong of Wakefield 7/19/1924 in Wolfeboro; H - 28, baggage master, b. Wakefield, s/o Charles D. Waldron and May Philbrick; W - 28, bookkeeper, b. Long Island, NY, d/o Arthur Ganong and Lena E. Conner

WALKER,

Charles Brewster, III of Wakefield m. Judith Mary McCoy of Wakefield 7/2/1995

Richard J., Jr. of Sanbornville m. Nancy K. Jones of Sanbornville 7/27/1973 in Sanbornville

Steven Scott of Tamworth m. Deborah Jean Beckwith of Sanbornville 5/10/1975 in Sanbornville

WALLACE,

Charles P. of Ossipee m. Nancy H. Storer of Wakefield 1/11/1888; H - 28, laborer, 2d, b. Ossipee, s/o Simeon P. Wallace (Ossipee, merchant) and Mehitable Welch; W - 15, housework, b. Brownfield, ME, d/o John Storer (Brownfield, ME, laborer) and Ida Copp (Wakefield, housework)

Jeffrey Todd of Annandale, VA m. Judianne Sisson of Arlington, VA 5/20/1989

John H. of East Wakefield m. Rosemarie Wallace of East Wakefield 8/31/1991

WALLINGFORD,
Collis E., Jr. of Rochester m. Abbie E. Sears of Sanbornville 9/21/1946 in Rochester; H - 23, stitcher; W - 26, at home
Wayne D. of Gonic m. Mamie M. Stewart of Sanbornville 1/18/1947 in Rochester; H - 21, box shop emp.; W - 21, at home

WALSH,
Thomas J. of Wellsville, NY m. Julia R. Hamilton of Angelica, NY 5/8/1967; H - 20, USMC; W - 19, at home

WALTER,
Frank J. of Sanbornville m. Rita A. Kinville of Sanbornville 7/11/1992 in Sanbornville

WANSOR,
Edward M. of Wakefield m. Mary Erna Horne of Sanbornville 10/1/1950 in Sanbornville; H - 30, woodworker; W - 30, at home

WARD,
John Curtiss of W. Columbia, SC m. Lanier Lana Roberts of Sanbornville 4/15/1989 in Wolfeboro
Samuel of Wakefield m. Mamie E. McDonald of Wakefield 10/5/1890 in Ossipee; H - 23, laborer, b. Madison, s/o Samuel Ward (Madison, farmer) and T. Shaw (Freedom, housekeeper); W - 17, housekeeper, b. Wakefield, d/o Malcolm McDonald (PEI, RR section) and Amanda Crockett (Minot, ME, housekeeper)

WARREN,
Elvin M. m. Grace B.P. Stone 10/15/1932 in Union
James of Melrose, MA m. Beverly F. Shaw of Malden, MA 11/17/1946; H - 21, truck driver; W - 18, tel. operator

WASSON,
Leslie m. Marion E. Johnson 10/29/1933 in Tamworth

WATKINS,
Roy W. of Pittsburgh, PA m. Edith M. Cowper of Wakefield 7/3/1913; H - 23, real estate, b. Millville, PA, s/o Thomas A. Watkins and Mattie Bigham; W - 23, school teacher, b. Washington, PA, d/o Frederick C. Cowper and Emma A. Kidd

WATSON,
Alfred m. Helen Dawes 8/28/1931; H - 23, s/o Fredrick Watson (Lancashire, England) and Alice J. Stevens (Bristol, England); W - 22, d/o Frank A. Dawes (No. Anson, ME) and Mollie Henderson (Brooklyn, NY)
David Jack of Arlington, VA m. Pamela Marie Rowe of Arlington, VA 6/20/1998
John M. of Wakefield m. Nettie H. Wishart of Wakefield 3/26/1905 in North Wakefield; H - 40, blacksmith, b. Wakefield, s/o Isaac D. Watson and Ester J. Tear; W - 39, housekeeper, 2d, b. East Boston, MA, d/o Edward G. Tarbox and Miriam G. Haley

WEAVER,
Frank W., Jr. of Lynn, MA m. Ethel M. Nunes of Lynn, MA 11/10/1961; H - 21, cook; W - 18, at home

WEBSTER,
Charles Stanley of Ossipee m. Cynthia Ann Hutchins of Sanbornville 6/14/1975

WEEKS,
Almon F. of Wakefield m. Gladys H. Bennett of Wakefield 10/14/1913; H - 29, chauffeur, b. Wakefield, s/o John H. Weeks and Ora Fernald; W - 23, school teacher, b. Watertown, MA, d/o George A. Bennett and Abbie V. Hartford
Alfred R. of Wakefield m. Marilyn H. McKernan of Wakefield 6/5/1982 in Dover
Arthur A. of Wakefield m. C. Marion Wallace of Wakefield 8/9/1915; H - 21, stable keeper, b. Wakefield, s/o Nathan O. Weeks and Florence E. Shorey; W - 19, telephone operator, b. Boston, MA, d/o Warren Wallace and Anna O'Brien
Guy B. of Wakefield m. Margaret Stevens of Middleton 12/25/1919 in Union; H - 19, chauffeur, b. Wakefield, s/o William G. Weeks (Wakefield, stable keeper) and Millie C. Robinson (Ossipee); W - 20, b. Middleton, d/o Albert Stevens (Middleton, farmer) and Bernice Tufts (Middleton)
Guy Brackett of Wakefield m. Clara Reed Bickford of Wakefield 3/17/1945 in Rochester; H - 44, truck driver; W - 18, at home
Harry G. of Wakefield m. Bessie A. Taylor of Wakefield 9/11/1987 in East Wakefield

Lawrence Paul of Union m. Bertha Hannah Taylor of Wolfeboro Falls
9/15/1956 in Wolfeboro Falls; H - 34, tel. equip. inst.; W - 28,
bookkeeper

Nathan O. of Wakefield m. Olive L. Young of Wakefield 12/25/1904 in
Parsonsfield, ME; H - 49, farmer, 3d, b. Wakefield, s/o Algneron S.
Weeks and Sarah J. Rogers; W - 30, school teacher, b. Wakefield, d/o
Peter C. Young and Mary Farnham

Richard F. of Wakefield m. Martha L. Hackett of Wakefield 10/15/1983

Rufus J. of Wakefield m. Agnes E. Tufts of Middleton 7/3/1920; H - 27,
farmer, b. Wakefield, s/o Nathan O. Weeks (Wakefield, lumber
dealer) and Florence Shorey (Wakefield); W - 26, nurse, b.
Middleton, d/o George Tufts (Middleton, farmer) and ----- Whitehouse
(Farmington)

Rufus James of North Wakefield m. Margaret Lillian Trott of Ossipee
9/30/1938 in Rochester; H - 45, farmer; W - 24, at home

Satchell of Wakefield m. Susie Proctor of Barnstead 6/5/1888; H - 59,
farmer, 3d, b. Wolfeboro, s/o Nathan Weeks and Sally Clark; W - 40,
housework, b. Barnstead, d/o Joseph Proctor and Sarah Ayers

Thomas F. of Wakefield m. Lynne M. Twombley of Wakefield 10/8/1983

William G. of Wakefield m. Emily C. Robinson of Ossipee 1/13/1900; H -
22, teamster, b. Wakefield, s/o Brackett M. Weeks (Wakefield,
farmer) and Matilda Allen (ME, housewife); W - 22, housework, b.
Wolfeboro, d/o Frank Robinson (Hiram, ME, teamster) and Alice
Thompson (Ossipee, housewife)

WEEMAN,

Howard A. of Bristol, CT m. Ella F. Smith of Wakefield 5/13/1920 in
Rochester; H - 24, brass worker, b. Bar Mills, ME, s/o Horatio H.
Weeman (E. Limington, ME, farmer) and Belle F. Mackie (E.
Limington, ME); W - 20, housework, b. Acton, ME, d/o Irving A.
Smith (Acton, ME, farmer) and Amanda Wells (Acton, ME)

Howard A., Jr. of Union m. Hazel E. Hodgman of E. Windsor, CT
9/1/1950 in E. Windsor, CT; H - 23, laborer; W - 24, mach. opr.

Roger R. of Union m. Carol E. Jenness of Rochester 2/5/1966 in Union; H
- 24, wood heel; W - 18, wood heel

WEINER,

Thomas of Poughkeepsie, NY m. Barbara A. Aiken of Wakefield
8/20/1983

WELCH,
Dana E. of Springvale, ME m. Susan M. Lord of Springvale, ME 10/15/1983

Thomas D. of Weymouth, MA m. Maureen C. Hickey of Sanbornville 10/29/1960 in Sanbornville; H - 20, US Army; W - 18, at home

WELLS,
E. James of Sanbornville m. Deborah Jean Cummings of Colebrook 10/20/1990 in Colebrook

WENTWORTH,
Adrial T. of Wakefield m. Ellen T. Burbank of Wakefield 5/1/1920; H - 67, laborer, 3d, b. Wakefield, s/o Thomas L. Wentworth (Wakefield, farmer) and Olive I. Farnham (Wakefield); W - 64, housekeeper, 3d, b. Oldtown, ME, d/o George Morell (Quebec, mill hand) and Catherine E. Burton

Alan E. of Union m. Barbara J. Laskey of Union 8/2/1970 in Union

Alan Earl of Union m. Joan Marie Comeau of Union 5/16/1975 in Farmington

Arnold H. of Wakefield m. Rachael Downs of Wakefield 5/2/1941 in Sanford, ME; H - 25, shoeworker; W - 21, shoeworker

Austin B. m. Lulu McDonald 10/9/1933 in Union

E. H., Jr. of Wakefield m. Lydia W. Kenison of Wakefield 1/23/1889 in Farmington; H - 38, farmer, 2d, b. Boston, MA, s/o E. H. Wentworth (Rockport, MA, farmer) and Susan M. Smith (Dedham, MA); W - 39, housekeeper, 2d, b. Milton, d/o Israel M. Kenison and Lavina E. Corson (Epping, housework)

Earl Roger of Milton m. Virginia Kimball of Wakefield 8/2/1941 in Union; H - 21, shipper; W - 19, at home

Frank I. of Wakefield m. Anna J. Peavey of Tuftonboro 11/15/1890; H - 24, watchman, b. Farmington, s/o David G. Wentworth (Farmington) and Nettie M. Glidden (Alton, housekeeper); W - 33, housekeeper, 2d, b. Tuftonboro, d/o Albert Peavey (Tuftonboro) and Sarah Bryant (Moultonboro, housekeeper)

George F. m. Mary E. Jose 7/28/1928; H - 19, s/o George F. Wentworth (Acton, ME) and Marion Burbank (Parsonsfield, ME); W - 20, d/o Emile Jose (Germany) and Emma Chase (Newfield, ME)

George Francis of East Wakefield m. Marguerite Wentworth of East Wakefield 6/28/1954; H - 64, bookkeeper; W - 56, clerk

Gerald Reed of Union m. Maria Enriquata Arce of Durham 6/3/1955 in Dover; H - 22, student; W - 21, student

Harry D. of Wakefield m. Lena E. Avery of Wolfeboro 4/1/1905 in Sanbornville; H - 28, farmer, b. Wakefield, s/o Orin H. Wentworth and Mary A. Leonard; W - 20, school teacher, b. Wolfeboro, d/o J. Everett Avery and Inez Dorr

Homer R. of Wakefield m. Margie V. Drown of Wakefield 4/29/1916; H - 19, teamster, b. Wakefield, s/o Charles E. Wentworth and Clara L. Place; W - 20, mill operative, b. Ossipee, d/o Stephen D. Drown and Carrie L. Peavey

J. Leon of Newfield, ME m. Marion E. Leighton of Wakefield 1/27/1912 in Newfield, ME; H - 20, farmer, b. Acton, ME, s/o J. Walter Wentworth and Etta M. Stone; W - 21, housework, b. Wakefield, d/o Frank Leighton and Ella Woodman

Linwood J. of Lebanon, ME m. Carrie S. Wentworth of Wakefield 3/5/1911; H - 22, counter moulder, b. Lebanon, ME, s/o William H. Wentworth and Emily E. Kenney; W - 18, student, b. Acton, ME, d/o Fred Wentworth and Mary C. Barker

Lloyd Roger of Union m. Miriam Louise Corson of Rochester 12/13/1940 in East Rochester; H - 21, machine operator; W - 18, at home

Ralph M. of Acton, ME m. Anita M. Finley of East Hartford, CT 7/6/1974

Richard A. of Union m. Linda E. Denton of Rochester 1/15/1966 in Rochester; H - 23, press worker; W - 21, assembly worker

Richard R. of Farmington m. Emily F. Lavertue of Union 10/25/1952 in Union; H - 30, lumberman; W - 18, housework

Robert J. of Wakefield m. Agnes L. Burroughs of Middleton 5/2/1915 in Dover; H - 19, teamster, b. Wakefield, s/o Charles E. Wentworth and Clara L. Place; W - 16, housework, b. Middleton, d/o David E. Burroughs and Nina Pinkham

Roscoe C. of Wakefield m. Blanche E. Tufts of Middleton 12/5/1914; H - 23, laborer, b. Milton, s/o Charles E. Wentworth and Clara L. Place; W - 18, waitress, b. Middleton, d/o George J. Tufts and Emma F. Whitehouse

Walter E. of Sanbornville m. Ella R. Knudsen of Rochester 2/2/1946 in North Wakefield; H - 45, drug clerk; W - 37, nurse

Will R. of Brookfield m. Myrtle B. Nute of Wakefield 1/16/1900; H - 22, barber, b. Brookfield, s/o J. Smith Wentworth (Wakefield, farmer) and Mary E. Weeks (Brookfield, housewife); W - 17, housework, b. Salmon Falls, d/o Eli W. Nute (Milton, barber) and Elvira E. Johnson (Salmon Falls, housewife)

William C. m. Blanche L. Reed 5/29/1931; H - 21, s/o Charles E. Wentworth (Acton, ME) and Clara L. Place (Middleton); W - 19, d/o James A. Reed (Lawrence, MA) and Mae A. McCullen (Nashua)

WERNER,
William P. of Boston, MA m. Christina J. Wade of Milton, MA 7/20/1942 in Wolfeboro; H - 32, accountant; W - 33, clerk

WESTFALL,
Kurt Peter of Ossipee m. Darlene Patricia Cheney of Sanbornville 7/3/1998
Michael F. of Sanbornville m. Jean P. Stawasz of Sanbornville 6/6/1992

WESTON,
Lon Martin of Pelham m. Shannon Renee Hughes of East Wakefield 10/19/1996 in Exeter

WEYMOUTH,
J. F. of Wakefield m. Sarah Campbell of Wakefield 4/21/1889 in Parsonsfield, ME; H - 27, laborer, 2d, b. Parsonsfield, ME, s/o George C. Weymouth (Parsonsfield, ME) and Cynthia J. Moulton (Albany, housework); W - 29, housekeeper, 2d, b. Lewiston, ME, d/o Reuben E. Brown (Strafford) and Betsy Evans (Strafford)
John H. of Wakefield m. Emma L. Ryer of Wakefield 12/4/1903 in Sanbornville; H - 20, laborer, b. Wakefield, s/o James F. Weymouth and Mary E. Wilkinson; W - 20, housework, b. NS, d/o Robert P. Ryer and Alice Hipson

WHALEY,
Kenneth A. of Wakefield m. Barbara H. Wooddell of Wakefield 7/2/1983

WHEELER,
Craig Richard of Wakefield m. Sandra Jeanne Vokey of Vernon, CT 9/26/1978 in Vernon, CT; H - 19; W - 19
Fred Kenneth of Conway m. Marion Louise Welch of Wakefield 9/19/1958; H - 55, mill opr.; W - 46, at home
Thomas P. of Wakefield m. Louise S. Potvin of Wakefield 9/12/1987
Thomas P. of Wakefield m. Elvira Quezon Liporada of Wakefield 1/13/1994

WHICHER,
William E. of Wakefield m. Cathleen E. Gordon of Wakefield 7/23/1988 in East Wolfeboro

WHIPPLE,
Clyde E. of Wakefield m. Blanche A. Thurston of Effingham 4/14/1906; H - 25, merchant, b. Solon, ME, s/o Charles A. Whipple and Lillian Drury; W - 24, housework, b. Effingham, d/o Josiah W. Thurston and Arvilla F. Chick

WHITE,
Alfred Preston of Parsonsfield, ME m. Karen Elaine Wicks of Wakefield, MA 5/22/1976
Charles Herbert, Jr. of Wakefield m. Gloria Frances Allaman of Milton 4/22/1978 in Milton; H - 23; W - 22
Frank P. of Wakefield m. Dora Fellows of Wakefield 6/2/1898; H - 34, RR conductor, 2d, widower, b. Madison, s/o T. C. White (Ossipee, deceased) and Jane Gannett of Madison (Tamworth, 54, housework); W - 19, housework, b. Wakefield, d/o Horatio B. Fellows of Wakefield (Wakefield, 49, farmer) and Belle Tibbetts (Newfield, ME, 45, housework)
James W. of Farmington m. Lizzie H. Reed of Wakefield 12/1/1896; H - 42, shoemaker, b. Newcastle, s/o W. White of Farmington (Newcastle, 70, carpenter) and Ann Card (Newcastle, 63, housekeeper); W - 36, housekeeper, b. Wolfeboro, d/o Ammon S. Reed of Wakefield (Newfield, ME, carpenter) and E. Waldron (Acton, ME, dressmaker)
Keith Gordon of Wakefield m. Rebecca Anne Lupien of Wakefield 8/29/1998 in Freedom
Norman Earl of Swampscott, MA m. Althea Northup Sutherland of Lynn, MA 10/11/1962; H - 47, drill spec.; W - 57, bookkeeper

WHITEHOUSE,
Merle C. of Salem, MA m. Mary C. Goundry of Salem, MA 7/14/1948 in Sanbornville; H - 47, car salesman; W - 28, at home
Richard Albert of Middleton m. Linda Dianne Drew of Sanbornville 6/5/1964 in Middleton; H - 20, grinder; W - 15, at home

WHITKENS,
David P. of Wakefield m. Lori A. Hackett of Wakefield 10/3/1992

WHITTAKER,
Albert Edward of Greenwood, MA m. Winifred Pearl of Revere, MA 8/12/1941 in Brookfield; H - 50, teacher; W - 43, teacher

WHITTEMORE,
Hadley L. of Scituate, MA m. Joyce Rita Hubbard of Acton, ME 9/2/1950 in Sanbornville; H - 22, hotel trainee; W - 22, entertainer
James F. of Sanbornville m. Nancy M. Neal of Sanford, ME 12/15/1960 in Sanbornville; H - 35, plumber; W - 26, secretary

WHITTEN,
Barry A. of Milton Mills m. Julie E. Cogswell of Sanbornville 8/5/1989
Frederick of Wakefield m. Eva M. Bell of Wakefield 1/12/1924; H - 25, laborer, b. So. Berwick, ME, s/o Daniel Whitten and Annie Peletier; W - 18, laborer, b. Lyndonville, VT, d/o Henry Bell
Fredrick B. m. Lora A. Labissonere 2/1/1932 in Somersworth
George A. of Wakefield m. Martha L. Radcliffe of Watertown, MA 3/7/1934 in Sanbornville; W - 37, laborer; W - 33, nurse
George Abner m. Hazel Bean 9/23/1926; H - 30, b. So. Berwick, ME, s/o Daniel A. Whitten and Annie Pelletier; W - 18, b. Ossipee, d/o Fred Bean and Anna Nichols

WIEDEMAN,
Richard C. of Wakefield m. Brenda G. Brenton of Foxboro, MA 9/8/1979; H - 22; W - 22

WIGGIN,
Albert W. of Wakefield m. Alice A. McMullen of Portsmouth 10/4/1903; H - 24, fireman, b. Tuftonboro, s/o John W. Wiggin and Mary A. Elliott; W - 18, housework, b. England, d/o William McMullen and Mary Ann O'Day
Charles E. of Brookfield m. Amy L. Lord of Wakefield 6/4/1898; H - 22, clerk, b. Wakefield, s/o John F. Wiggin of Brookfield (Durham, farmer) and Sarah P. Brackett (Wakefield, housework); W - 22, school teacher, b. Brookfield, d/o John B. Lord (Effingham, deceased, sawyer) and Elvira E. Stevens of Wakefield (Middleton, housework)
Clayton Robert of Rochester m. Norma Bernice Mildram of Wakefield 11/9/1957; H - 27, shoe worker; W - 23, bookkeeper
Everett F. of Sanbornville m. Mildred M. Nowlin of Sanbornville 5/18/1947 in Sanbornville; H - 38, farmer; W - 46, at home

Harvey F. of Wakefield m. Myra L. Witham of Milton 6/20/1905 in
Milton; H - 20, brakeman, b. Wakefield, s/o Frank J. Wiggin and
Augusta Farnham; W - 22, shoe stitcher, b. Milton, d/o Everett
Witham and Jennie Colomy

John Aspinwall of Wolfeboro m. Christine Hooper of Sanbornville
6/4/1938 in Sanbornville; H - 25, plumber & elec.; W - 25,
bookkeeper

John W. of Wakefield m. Anna L. Bliss of Percy 9/14/1918; H - 63,
farmer, 2d, b. Acton, ME, s/o Alonzo L. Wiggin and Hannah
Witham; W - 48, compositor, b. Hamilton, NY, d/o Oliver Bliss and
Cornelia A. Turner

John W. m. Mary J. Lane 8/12/1927; H - 72, s/o Alonzo L. Wiggin
(Acton, ME) and Hanna W. Whithem; W - 85, d/o Samuel Patch
(Parsonsfield, ME) and Mary Patch

Lester A., Jr. of Rochester m. Audrey Elizabeth Drew of Union 5/15/1943
in Rochester; H - 22, US Navy; W - 23, stenographer

Luther E. of Wakefield m. Carrie E. Wentworth of Milton 6/20/1895 in
Milton Mills; H - 29, lumberman, b. Boston, MA, s/o Luther P.
Wiggin of Wakefield (Wakefield, 62, lumberman) and Margaret
McCully (NS, 65, housekeeper); W - 20, housework, b. Milton, d/o
Edgar Wentworth of Milton (Milton, 39, teamster) and Sarah Platt (N.
Andover, MA, deceased)

Richard Arthur of Tamworth m. Katherine F. Tuttle of Wakefield
6/13/1942; H - 23, mechanic USA; W - 20, at home

Richard Arthur of Sanbornville m. Mary Roberts of Union 8/25/1962 in
Union; H - 44, auto dealer; W - 29, teacher

Richard I. of Rochester m. Constance R. Drew of Union 10/21/1944 in
Union; H - 28, US Army; W - 21, nurse

William P. of Wakefield m. Winifred R. Barnard of Wellesley, MA
6/16/1920 in Nashua; H - 38, merchant, 2d, b. Brookfield, s/o George
A. Wiggin (Durham, farmer) and Amy F. Ordway (Lincoln, ME); W
- 35, cook, b. Granville, MA, d/o Edwin J. Barnard (Hartford, CT,
farmer) and Evelyn G. Green (Lee, MA)

WIKERS,
Roger T. of Charlestown, MA m. Sally R. Bickel of Boston, MA
8/10/1987

WILBUR,
Joseph Michael of Rochester m. Lisa April Loring of Union 6/11/1995 in Barrington
William Joseph of East Wakefield m. Carlene Elizabeth Fenton of Atkinson 5/14/1954 in Atkinson; H - 21, bookkeeper; W - 19, student nurse

WILCOX,
Raymond M. m. Doris E. Hodsdon 1/19/1930; H - 30, s/o Otis M. Wilcox (Malden, MA) and Alice Tuck (Peabody, MA); W - 30, d/o George H. Hodsdon (Wakefield) and Sarah Glidden (Wakefield)

WILFERT,
Joseph Paul of Franklin, MA m. Eleanor May Kell of Franklin, MA 11/29/1958 in Sanbornville; H - 21, baker; W - 19, typist

WILKINS,
Homer W. of Wakefield m. Abbie J. Crawford of Wakefield 2/9/1916; H - 49, farmer, 2d, b. Acton, ME, s/o Myron Wilkins and Eliza A. Horn; W - 44, housekeeper, 3d, b. Wakefield, d/o Albert L. Evans and Hattie Goodell
Timothy M. of Sanbornville m. Nadean J. Lemoyne of Sanbornville 6/15/1991
Timothy M. of Sanbornville m. Denise A. Burke of Sanbornville 2/17/1996 in Middleton

WILKINSON,
Durwood F. of Milton Mills m. Linda M. Worster of Union 7/8/1966; H - 21, const. worker; W - 18, at home
George William of Sanbornville m. Judith Lee Sands of Wolfeboro 8/17/1962 in Wolfeboro; H - 20, Navy; W - 20, clerk
James E. of Wakefield m. Jo-Ann A. Bates of Wakefield 2/22/1997
Kenneth Albert of Wakefield m. Waneta Victoria Karcher of Wakefield 8/2/1941 in Effingham; H - 30, millworker; W - 22, housework
Melbourne O. of Wakefield m. Edwina M. Young of Middleton 11/18/1937 in West Milton; H - 21, truck driver; W - 18, at home
Raymond E. of Andover, MA m. G. Estelle Willey of Sanbornville 2/27/1937 in Milton; H - 23, mill hand; W - 23, at home
Wilfred Arthur of Wakefield m. Yvonne Frances Bullis of Middleton 11/18/1939 in Milton; H - 26, laborer; W - 18, at home

WILLEY,
- Chandler Clarence of Wakefield m. Leah Etta Young of Acton, ME 11/4/1939 in Sanford, ME; H - 27, millhand; W - 24, mill employee
- Charles Parsons of Sanbornville m. Marion E. Lowd of Acton, ME 2/8/1945 in Acton, ME; H - 41, farmer; W - 36, bookkeeper
- Clarence D. of Wakefield m. Charlotte G. Twombly of Wakefield 7/29/1908; H - 25, farmer, b. Wakefield, s/o John D. Willey and Olivia E. Demeritt; W - 19, housework, b. Wolfeboro, d/o Nelson F. Twombly and Estella A. Drake
- Cortez W. of Wakefield m. Bertha W. Grant of Dover 6/30/1908 in Acton, ME; H - 24, farmer, b. Wakefield, s/o William H. Willey, 2d and Maria J. Jones; W - 19, teacher, b. Dover, d/o Edward Grant and Nellie C. Reynolds
- Edwin R. of Wakefield m. Sarah F. Woodman of Milton 10/7/1887; H - 35, mason, b. Wakefield, s/o Stephen Willey and Sarah A. Willey (Brookfield, housekeeper); W - 24, housework, b. Newfield, ME, d/o Samuel Patch (Newfield, ME, laborer) and Mary ----- (Newfield, ME, housekeeper)
- Joseph A.C. of Wakefield m. Susie A. Perkins of Milton 8/7/1911 in Laconia; H - 21, farmer, b. Wakefield, s/o William H. Willey, 2d and Marie J. Jones; W - 20, housework, b. Milton, d/o George D. Perkins and Anna Gardner
- Nelson F. m. Julia W. Karcher 3/27/1932 in Milton
- William H. of Wakefield m. Sarah A. Rand of Lakeport 1/9/1905 in Laconia; H - 60, merchant, 3d, b. Brookfield, s/o William Willey and Susan R. Henderson; W - 56, housekeeper, 2d, b. Wolfeboro, d/o Levi B. Sanborn and Sarah A. Thurston
- William H., Jr. of Wakefield m. Ethel E. Quimby of Groveland, MA 4/10/1908 in Groveland, MA; H - 24, merchant, b. Wakefield, s/o William H. Willey and Sarah F. Brown; W - 21, clerk, b. Sandwich, d/o Preston Quimby and Dell Alma Banks

WILLIAMS,
- Barney J. of Wakefield m. Nancy L. Davis of Wakefield 11/22/1986 in Rochester
- Barney Joseph, Jr. of Sanbornville m. Jane Marie McNelley of Sanbornville 7/3/1965 in Sanbornville; H - 21, laborer; W - 21, record lib.
- Bernard Joseph of East Wakefield m. Teresa Ann Glidden of East Wakefield 11/2/1991

George H. of Wakefield m. Florence B. Murray of Ossipee 3/7/1944 in Dover; H - 35, truckman; W - 39, nurse

Harold L. of Saugus, MA m. Pearl S. Reny of Saugus, MA 6/25/1944 in Union; H - 35, bus operator; W - 26, waitress

Harry C. of Wakefield m. Blanche Colbath of Wakefield 6/17/1896; H - 27, painter, b. Somerville, MA, s/o George A. Williams (deceased) and Nancy E. Davis (Oakland, ME); W - 18, housework, b. Wakefield, d/o Walter G. Colbath of Wakefield (Brookfield, railroad master) and Emma B. Knox (Ossipee, housekeeper)

Jefferson m. Cora Mary Drew 4/9/1933 in Union

Joseph B. of Sanbornville m. Anne Marie Bilodeau of Sanbornville 9/12/1997

Kent of Wakefield m. Carolyn Hayward of Concord 2/11/1961 in Concord; H - 28, state police; W - 23, comm. clerk

Richard J. of Sanbornville m. Jane M. Williams of Sanbornville 7/27/1968 in Sanbornville

WILLIAMSON,

Albert W. of Portland, ME m. Martha R. Hale of Wakefield 10/22/1972 in Hanover

Bradford N. of Sanbornville m. Janet S. Morgan of Thornton 3/23/1991 in Portsmouth

WILSON,

Daniel Hall m. Florence Ellen Drew 6/24/1933 in Rochester

David Donald of Wakefield m. Andrea Josephine Seiver of Wakefield 6/23/1977

Kenneth H. of Union m. Donna Lee Drew of Sanbornville 12/29/1961 in Union; H - 23, US Army; W - 17, student

Silas C. of Hyde Park, MA m. Lizzie E. Morse of Wakefield 1/12/1899 in Milton Mills; H - 57, merchant, 2d, b. Wakefield, s/o Tristram Wilson (Acton, ME, deceased) and Mary D. Cloutman (Wakefield, deceased); W - 43, housekeeper, b. Biddeford, ME, d/o Daniel E. Morse (England, deceased) and Elizabeth M. Wiggin (Wakefield, deceased)

William J. of Wakefield m. Edith M. Hall of Wakefield 5/12/1906 in Union; H - 23, brass operative, b. Moncton, NB, s/o Daniel Wilson and Almira Lodge; W - 32, teacher, b. Wakefield, d/o Charles Hall and Lucy M. Chapman

WINKLEY,
Charles T. of Rochester m. Margie V. Wentworth of Union 1/23/1948 in Union; H - 54, box maker; W - 52, stitcher

WINSLOW,
Edward L. m. Janet P. Stenberg 9/14/1928; H - 56, s/o John L. Winslow (Nottingham) and Emma Perkins (Salem, MA); W - 42, d/o William Best and Harriet Pike

WINTON,
Gary R. of Wakefield m. Nancy L. Downs of Wakefield 7/10/1971 in Sanbornville

Kenneth A. of East Wakefield m. Paula J. Vachon of Milton 9/16/1972 in Milton

Robert D. of Wakefield m. Paula Worster of Milton 10/20/1971 in Milton

WITHAM,
Arthur J. of North Rochester m. Sylvania D. Lamie of Sanbornville 10/26/1934 in Rochester; H - 27, machine fixer; W - 19, punch press op.

WOLFE,
David Walter of Boston, MA m. Karla Rose Tibbetts of Union 9/28/1962; H - 22, engineer; W - 22, secretary

WOOD,
Fred I. of Wakefield m. Grace L. Wentworth of Newfield, ME 10/25/1890; H - 29, farmer, b. Great Falls, s/o Thomas Wood (England, farmer) and Losina M. Dore (Wakefield, housekeeper); W - 18, housekeeper, b. Newfield, ME, d/o Madison Wentworth (Wakefield, farmer) and Rose A. Merrow (Newfield, ME, housekeeper)

Robert C. of Waltham, MA m. Cheryl A. Schools of Waltham, MA 8/20/1970

Theodore Ralph, Jr. of Sanbornville m. Janet Arlene Gagnon of Wolfeboro 7/4/1975

WOODARD,
John B. of Sanbornville m. Carolyn L. Bye of Beverly, MA 12/2/1967; H - 32, US Navy; W - 26, cashier

Leonard W. m. Marcia E. Bye 11/12/1966 in Milton Mills; H - 29, roofer; W - 19, clerk

WOODBURY,
Robert J. of Somersworth m. Wanda J. Brown of Sanbornville 11/2/1991 in Sanbornville

WOODMAN,
Alphonzo of Wakefield m. Lillian Roberts of New Durham 10/10/1908; H - 26, brass finisher, b. Wakefield, s/o Frank Woodman and Sarah Patch; W - 18, housework, b. Exeter, d/o Andrew J. Roberts and Eliza Camet

Alphonzo of Wakefield m. Mary Stuart of Wakefield 2/13/1915; H - 35, mill operative, 2d, b. Middleton, s/o Frank Woodman and Sarah Patch; W - 19, housework, b. Wakefield, d/o Joseph Stuart and Addie Shackford

Clayton R. m. Olive Jellison 12/24/1927; H - 32, s/o Frank E. Woodman (Wakefield) and Maud Johnson; W - 40, d/o Martin V. Drury (Wakefield) and Charlotte Wentworth

Herman E. of Wakefield m. Susie V. Wiggins of Ossipee 3/29/1914 in Ossipee; H - 25, teamster, b. Wakefield, s/o Frank E. Woodman and Maude E. Johnson; W - 18, housework, b. Ossipee, d/o William H. Wiggins and Sophia Eldridge

Kirtland C. of Wakefield m. Dorothy G. Sprague of Effingham 12/8/1923 in Freedom; H - 23, laborer, b. Wakefield, s/o Frank Woodman and Maude Johnson; W - 18, house keeper, b. Effingham, d/o Charles Sprague and Annie Fernald

M. C. of Milton Mills m. Sarah M. Fellows of Wakefield 9/26/1896 in Milton Mills; H - 30, shoe maker, b. Alton, s/o J. Woodman (Alton, deceased) and Hannah P. Rollins of Alton (Alton, 66, housekeeper); W - 21, housework, b. Wakefield, d/o J. P. Fellows of Wakefield (Wakefield, 52, farmer) and Mary A. Pike (Middleton, 43, housekeeper)

WORSTER,
George O. of Farmington m. Lucy C. Downs of Union 6/1/1946 in Rochester; H - 20, shoeworker; W - 18, shoeworker

WRIGHT,
David M. of Union m. Gloria M. Bentzler of Union 5/23/1971 in Milton

WYMAN,
Alben of Fryeburg, ME m. Narcissa A. Stone of Wakefield 6/24/1895; H - 66, farmer, 2d, b. Chatham, s/o Abial Wyman of Chatham (Chatham, farmer) and Hannah K. Stevens (Chatham, housekeeper); W - 36, housekeeper, b. Boston, MA, d/o Thorndyke B. Stone of Boston, MA (Lynn, MA, merchant) and Anna E. Reed of Wakefield (Newfield, ME, housekeeper)

Douglas Fairbanks, Jr. of Meredith m. Carol Ann Jarvis of East Wakefield 3/27/1993

YANOSKY,
Stephen W. of Rochester m. Bethany A. Brackett of Sanbornville 6/13/1970 in Sanbornville

YEATON,
George E. of Wakefield m. Ruth B. Garland of Wakefield 9/4/1906; H - 38, machinist, b. Wakefield, s/o Enoch D. Yeaton and Jane Smith; W - 26, housework, b. Wakefield, d/o Alvah S. Garland and Priscilla Lothrop

YORK,
Fred of Wakefield m. Nellie Nealley of Wakefield 9/1/1899; H - 26, laborer, b. Canada, s/o Thomas York (Canada, farmer) and Mary Parie (Canada, deceased); W - 18, housekeeper, b. Wakefield, d/o Henry Nealley (Canada, brakeman) and ----- (Canada, deceased)

Horace B. of Wolfeboro m. Catherine LeV. Cameron of Sanbornville 9/21/1946 in Wolfeboro; H - 59, photographer; W - 34, domestic

YOUNG,
Aaron G. of Wakefield m. Celia Lilley of Stoneham, MA 4/16/1901; H - 37, farmer, b. Wakefield, s/o James Young (Wakefield, farmer) and Rosemandel Gile (Cape Cod, MA, domestic); W - 20, housekeeper, b. Stoneham, MA, d/o William Lilley (Boston, MA, shoemaker) and Martha Cullen (Boston, MA, housewife)

Albert L. of Wakefield m. Shirley E. Baldwin of Kingston 10/31/1937 in East Kingston; H - 33, carpenter; W - 22, at home

Fred R. of Middleton m. Alice E. Heath of Wakefield 6/19/1909 in Dover; H - 18, teamster, b. Middleton, s/o Charles H. Young and Etta M. Young; W - 17, housework, b. Wakefield, d/o Charles Heath and Maud Sanborn

James C. of Wakefield m. Mary A. Doyle of Wakefield 12/9/1893; H - 21, farmer, b. Wakefield, s/o DeWitt Carter (Ossipee, lawyer) and Ruth C. Young (Wakefield, housework); W - 20, housework, b. Wakefield, d/o John Doyle (NY, laborer) and Amanda Wentworth (Milton, housework)

James C. of Wakefield m. Annie G. Cameron of Ligonia, ME 9/25/1897 in Newburyport, MA; H - 25, blacksmith, 2d, widower, b. Wakefield, s/o DeWitt Carter of Ossipee (Ossipee, 45, lawyer) and Ruth C. Young of Brookfield (Wakefield, housekeeper); W - 19, housework, b. Ligonia, ME, d/o T. L. Cameron of Portland, ME (Scotland, 44, RR employee) and Katherine McDonald of Ligonia, ME (Cape Breton, 44, housewife)

James C. of Wakefield m. Harriett L. Fellows of Wakefield 12/31/1905 in Sanbornville; H - 35, blacksmith, 3d, b. Wakefield, s/o DeWitt Carter and Ruth Young; W - 31, teacher, b. Wakefield, d/o Charles S. Fellows and Ann Sherburn

Michael L. of Wakefield m. Linda L. Kelley of Wakefield 12/31/1985

Richard Allen of East Wakefield m. Glory S. Brierley of East Wakefield 10/18/1997 in Milton

Roland Wilford of Middleton m. Stella Marjorie Budroe of Wakefield 8/31/1940 in West Milton; H - 23, lumberman; W - 18, waitress

Samuel K. of Wakefield m. Viola E. Richardson of Reading, MA 7/28/1920 in Sanbornville; H - 26, RR trainman, b. Wakefield, s/o James C. Young (Wakefield, garage man) and Mary Doyle (Wakefield); W - 20, stenographer, b. Reading, MA, d/o William H. Richardson (NB, RR foreman) and Margaret ---- (NB)

Willard Junkins of Wakefield m. Beatrice L. Wilkinson of Milton 6/2/1940 in Alton; H - 21, truck driver; W - 25, telephone op.

ZAIDAN,

Joseph Elias of East Wakefield m. Marcia Elizabeth Scalfani of East Wakefield 6/29/1997 in Wolfeboro

ZALENSKI,
Alfred Joseph of Sanbornville m. Shirley Ann Hussey of Farmington 5/4/1975
Alfred L. of Wakefield m. Diane R. Fletcher of Wakefield 3/4/1972

ZANNI,
George Shackford, Jr. of Wakefield m. Elaine Theresa Thomas of Melrose, MA 4/17/1962 in Manchester; H - 31, const.; W - 29, dancing teacher

ZARSE,
John R. of Sanbornville m. Deborah L. LaRoche of Rochester 10/7/1972

ZIELFELDER,
Richard D., Jr. of Union m. Barbara Ann Routhier of Union 11/26/1994 in Dover

ZIMMER,
Albert E. m. Ruth E. Copp 2/1/1932 in Center Ossipee
Albert Edward of Wakefield m. Alice Nettie Atwood of Wakefield 2/1/1941; H - 39, mechanic; W - 29, housework

ZURHEIDE,
Robert George of Sanbornville m. Joan Dorothy Colquhoun of Boston, MA 12/10/1963; H - 31, salesman; W - 32, stewardess

DEATHS

ABBOTT,
Dorothy W., d. 8/8/1996 at 94 in Wolfeboro; James T. Jackson and Iva W. Foss
Herman E., d. 12/1/1989 at 89 in Wolfeboro; Harry Abbott and Lizzie Nichols
Orville L., d. 8/29/1961 at 82 in East Wolfeboro; b. Ossipee; Frank Abbott and Mary Libbey
Ralph Emerson, d. 2/5/1990 at 76 in Wolfeboro; Ralph E. Abbott and Blanche Brown
Wallace S., d. 11/30/1959 at 60 in Rochester; b. Effingham; Florence A. Kenniston

ADAMS,
Jacob S., d. 7/14/1901 at 72/10/14; railroading; married; b. Milton; Ebenezer Adams (Newington) and Betsy Sanborn (Wakefield)

ADJUTANT,
son, d. 1/7/1966 at 0/0/0 in Rochester; b. Rochester; Ronald H. Adjutant and Susan E. Kelly
son, d. 1/7/1966 at 0/0/0 in Rochester; b. Rochester; Ronald H. Adjutant and Susan E. Kelly
Addie E., d. 10/1/1896 at 25/1/18 in Sanbornville; housewife; married; b. Middleton; Colman E. Colbath (Middleton) and Lucinda F. Hunt (East Pittston, ME)
Annie E., d. 5/2/1901 at 21/10/17; housework; single; b. Brookfield; John F. Adjutant (Tuftonboro) and Augusta Garland (Ossipee)
Evelyn G., d. 8/2/1973 at 62 in Wolfeboro; Leslie Hill and Ellen Willey
George F., d. 3/14/1887 at 22; married; ---- Garland
John F., d. 1/15/1920 at 75/2/25; apoplexy; retired; widower; b. Tuftonboro
Joseph C., d. 8/21/1979 at 77 in Wolfeboro
Lester Ervin, d. 2/18/1992 at 53 in Sanbornville; Ervin Franklin Adjutant and Catherine P. Quimby
Rollin P., d. 10/19/1905 at 0/0/22 in Sanbornville; b. Sanbornville; Leonard Adjutant (Tuftonboro) and Lena Eaton (Brookfield)
Royal P., d. 10/14/1905 at 0/0/17 in Sanbornville; b. Sanbornville; Leonard Adjutant (Tuftonboro) and Lena Eaton (Brookfield)
Samuel B., d. 1/29/1893 at 24/7/11; laborer; single; b. Tuftonboro; John F. Adjutant (Tuftonboro) and Augusta F. Garland (Ossipee)

Samuel D., d. 8/14/1913 at 74/4; farmer; married; b. Ossipee; Samuel Adjutant

Sarah J., d. 4/2/1894 at 56; housekeeper; married; b. Randolph, VT; Thomas J. Quaid (Plattsburg, VT) and Runda Bruce (Randolph, VT)

ADLINGTON,
Ellen G., d. 2/1/1943 at 86/3/26 in Concord; b. Wakefield; Isaac F. Clark and Alma Churchill

AINSWORTH,
Charles W., d. 2/12/1902 at 0/11/10; b. Wakefield; Charles W. Ainsworth (Calais, VT) and Nellie J. Alexander (Wolcott, VT)

AKERS,
Ellen G., d. 6/6/1975 at 82 in Rochester; Orlando Hannaford and Emma F. Ladd

Lewis W., d. 11/30/1971 at 80 in Sanbornville; Lewis C. Akers and Annie Andrews

ALASKIEWICZ,
Joseph S., d. 7/6/1954 at 37 in Sanbornville; b. Salem, MA; Peter Alaskiewicz and Mary Rogowski

ALBEE,
Emma Whiting, d. 7/21/1924 at 72/9/18; no occ.; single; b. Charlestown, MA; Godfrey B. Albee (Chesterfield) and Martha L. Willard (Charlestown, MA)

ALLAIN,
Daniel G., d. 7/13/1990 at 38; Louis V. Allain and Laurette Chevalier

ALLEN,
E. George, d. 2/9/1977 at 68 in Sanbornville

George McD., d. 5/21/1948 at 88/2/27 in Union; b. Dover; John Allen and Lydia Flagg

Jennie, d. 12/16/1896 at 65/4/10; housewife; married; Henry Norton and Nancy Long

Lloyd E., d. 3/1/1987 at 67 in Concord

Mary, d. 12/25/1951 at 63/11/17 in Haverhill, MA; b. Wakefield; Frank Hutchins and Agnes Augusta Gilman

Melvin, d. 1/2/1906 at 69/6/14; farmer; married; b. Brookfield; Noah Allen and Lydia

William H., d. 5/25/1904 at 58/3/11; laborer; widower; b. Wakefield; Shedrich Allen (Wakefield) and Eleanor Heard (Acton, ME)

William H., d. 5/28/1911 at 0/2; b. Berwick, ME; William J. Allen (Enosburg, VT) and Sadie Slapter (No. Berwick, ME)

William M., d. 3/11/1957 at 86 in Union; b. Philadelphia, PA; Melvin Allen and Jennie Norton

ALLISON,
Byron G., d. 7/30/1967 at 70 in Hanover; b. Stryker, OH; Byron F. Allison and Lydia Midnerey

ALLOTT,
James Henry, d. 10/6/1937 at 34/8/2; b. Cleveland, OH; Thomas J. Allott and Rose Wilkinson

AMARAL,
Geneva L., d. 3/22/1980 at 65 in Wolfeboro; Wesley H. Trott and Gladys M. Cahoon

Joseph Francis, d. 6/19/1997 at 86 in Ossipee; Emanuel P. Amaral and Maria DePonte

AMES,
Orrin D., d. 11/29/1903 at 47/1/15; laborer; single; b. Ossipee; A. C. Ames (Ossipee) and Katie Knox (Ossipee)

Sally, d. 2/23/1894 at 86/4/18; housekeeper; married; b. Wakefield; Moses Young (Dover) and Molly Chadwick (Berwick, ME)

Samuel, d. 5/7/1906 at 72/1/6; merchant; married; b. Ossipee; Marston Ames (Tamworth) and Clarissa Moulton (Parsonsfield, ME)

Samuel B., d. 5/24/1900 at 89/3/19; farmer; widower; b. Parsonsfield, ME; Samuel Ames (Parsonsfield, ME) and Susan Glidden (Newmarket)

ANDERSON,
Catherine M., d. 10/18/1983 at 88; Thomas Hoskins and Mary ----

Elmer R., d. 11/27/1988 at 65 in Wolfeboro; Elmer E. Anderson and Selma Reenstierna

John S., d. 2/7/1904 at 45/11/7; clerk; married; b. Buxton, ME; Rishworth Anderson (Limington, ME) and Hannah Sawyer (Buxton, ME)

Joseph Michael, d. 7/3/1961 at 0/0/3 in Wolfeboro; b. Wolfeboro; Richard W. Anderson and Beatrice Duchano

Lulu I., d. 12/22/1985 at 72 in Ossipee; Erick Anderson and Freda Waljus

ANDREWS,

Charles P., d. 9/25/1924 at 65/9/28; painter; married; b. Lovell, ME; Benjamin W. Andrews (Lovell, ME) and Caroline M. Charles (Lovell, ME)

Rose E., d. 6/11/1948 at 81/11/8 in Union; b. New Durham; Charles H. Rines and Sarah L. Boston

ANGLAND,

Elizabeth A., d. 8/28/1982 at 77 in East Wakefield; Matthew J. McDonnell and Hannah Lane

ANTHONY,

Harry E., d. 1/26/1974 at 32 in Rochester; Arnold Anthony and Ruth Berry

Stephen H., d. 2/19/1958 at 54 in Union; b. Brownfield, ME; William E. Anthony and Clara Harriman

ARCHIBALD,

Evelyn M., d. 10/10/1980 at 72 in Wolfeboro

Mott L., d. 8/19/1953 at 79 in Milton; b. Acton, ME; Reuben Archibald and Abjona Davis

Oscar David, d. 4/6/1939 at 66/10/15 in Alton; b. Wakefield; Josiah E. Archibald and Charlotte Archibald

Stewart G., d. 4/8/1976 at 78 in Milton

ARLEN,

Hattie M., d. 11/13/1914 at 56; housework; widow; b. Eastport, ME

ARNOTT,

Ella T., d. 6/15/1996 at 71 in Wolfeboro; George A. Hall, Jr. and Ella May Young

George E., Sr., d. 8/31/1993 at 75 in Wolfeboro; Thomas Arnott and Myra Lee

ASHER,

Maurice L., d. 1/25/1956 at 78 in Conway; b. England; Jacob Asher and — -- Bellsie

ASPRAY,
Elizabeth I., d. 8/13/1986 at 88 in Sanford, ME

ATHERTON,
Helen P., d. 9/6/1918 at 30/6/10; housewife; married; b. Exeter; S. Albert Lawrence and Augusta A. Horne (Middleton)
Isaac H., d. 6/18/1947 at 67/4/21 in Wolfeboro; b. Houlton, ME; Howard Atherton and Katherine M. ----

ATKINSON,
Johanna C., d. 6/19/1957 at 68 in S. Wakefield; b. Brooklyn, NY; William Knickel and Henriette Schneider

ATWOOD,
Ernest P., d. 4/5/1943 at 59/3/22 in Wolfeboro; b. North Salem; John P. Atwood and Julietta Coborn

AUBIN,
child, d. 2/10/1936 at 0/0/1 in Wolfeboro; b. Wolfeboro

AUBREY,
Vera A., d. 3/4/1958 at 73 in Keene; b. Conway; Herbert B. Colbath and Clara Whitney

AUGER,
William J., Sr., d. 1/20/1990 at 75 in Haverhill, MA

AVERY,
Joseph Clifton, d. 12/31/1953 at 79 in Union; b. Wolfeboro; Joseph L. Avery and Helen M. Libbey
May E., d. 3/12/1948 at 78/11/19 in Concord; b. MA; Benjamin F. Miller and Mary Rose
Samuel E., d. 1/19/1951 at 88/10/2 in Union; b. Strafford

AYERS,
John F., d. 10/24/1910 at 53/7/10; farmer; married; b. Barrington; Joseph Ayers (Barrington) and Mary Henderson

BABB,
Florence E., d. 12/28/1941 at 74/3/2 in Arlington, MA; b. Boston, MA; John Pilton and Mary Anna Earl

BABINEAU,
Bella D., d. 1/16/1933 at 26/1/26

BACKMAN,
Hazel M., d. 3/31/1960 at 65 in Dorchester, MA

BAHM,
Mary F., d. 6/8/1947 at 59/5/17 in Wolfeboro; Chris Russell

BAILEY,
Ellen M., d. 1/30/1992 at 89 in Wolfeboro; Alexander Monroe and Helen Robertson
Ernest, d. 5/3/1948 at 61/1/8 in East Wakefield; b. Windham; Rufus H. Bailey and Mina P. Watson
William A., d. 1/20/1988 at -- in FL

BAIN,
Mary Kerwin, d. 12/2/1974 at 49 in Sanbornville; John J. Kerwin and Kathryn E. Hurld

BAKER,
Maria B., d. 10/22/1898 at 76/10/22; housework; widow; b. Conway; True Palmer (Loudon) and Betsy Emerson (Conway)
Michael William, d. 12/9/1991 at 39; Ernest Baker and Alice Roy
William Joseph, d. 1/26/1941 at 46/8/16 in Sanford, ME; b. Somerville, MA; Nicholas Baker and Catherine Fitzgerald

BALDWIN,
Annalise R., d. 10/6/1987 at 0/0/18 in Rochester; Russell T. Baldwin and Sharon Vanderhoof

BALLARD,
Jacob, d. 4/6/1899 at 85/4/22; farmer; married; b. Wakefield; Lucratus Ballard (Wakefield) and Mary Folsom (Wakefield)

BANCROFT,
Charles, d. 6/3/1982 at 76 in York, ME
Jane Cockburn, d. 5/5/1977 at 72 in Turkey, Royal Viking Sea; Waterford Marler and Jane Cockburn Vassie

BANFIELD,
Abbie J., d. 2/5/1919 at 66/11/16; chron. endocarditis; housewife; widow; b. Rowley, MA; Natt Jellison and Abigail S. Hunt (Newbury, MA)

BANKS,
Bruce Howard, Sr., d. 6/9/1997 at 86 in Sanbornville; Bruce Francis Banks and Josephine Smith

BARBER,
Charles H., d. 7/12/1976 at 58 in Sanbornville; Maurice Barber and Viotti Ingalls
Gertrude Z., d. 12/30/1978 at 48 in Wolfeboro; Albert Ziegelmayer and Gertrude Dierman

BARKER,
Elizabeth B., d. 6/10/1967 at 85 in Sanbornville; John Doyle and Amanda Wentworth
Joanne M., d. 5/21/1982 at 18 in Union; George B. Barker and Joan Pritchitt
Mary J., d. 12/4/1891 at 85/0/16; housekeeper; widow; b. Stratham; Ebenezer Robinson and Anna Avery
Robert S., d. 10/12/1952 at 79 [or 78] in Colebrook; b. Stoneham, MA; Timothy Barker and Elizabeth Morton

BARNES,
Fred E., d. 1/19/1944 at 71 in Wolfeboro; b. CT

BARRY,
Stanley, d. 2/7/1975 at 19 in East Wakefield; Stanley J. Barry and Louise Govoni

BARTER,
Herbert, d. 8/17/1945 at 76/11/28 in Wolfeboro; b. Boothbay, ME; John Barter and Georgia Decker

BATEMAN,
Charles H., d. 8/4/1930 at 85; widower; b. Dover
Lewis C., d. 11/4/1978 at 55 in Appleton, WI

BAXTER,
Marion L., d. 7/10/1969 at 74; Edwin Tinkham and Cynthia Privington

BEACHAM,
Hattie F., d. 12/15/1946 at 75/4/13 in Wolfeboro; b. Wakefield; George W. Haines and Susan Nichols
Howard A., d. 1/2/1962 at 90 in Union; b. Union; Henry K. Hunt and Mary Canney
Mary F., d. 3/10/1913 at 82/6/17; housekeeper; widow; b. Amesbury, MA; Moses B. Canney (Ossipee) and Mary Abbott (Berwick, ME)

BEAN,
Harold, d. 11/14/1960 at 56 in Ossipee
Nellie M., d. 2/25/1979 at 88 in Wolfeboro; Charles S. Ellis and Ella Thompson
Raymond, d. 5/19/1980 at 82 in Ossipee
Stephen, d. 4/6/1934 at 23/1/29 in Wolfeboro; b. Eaton; Herbert L. Bean and Etta Drown

BEAUDETTE,
son, d. 2/29/1904 at 0/0/0; b. Wakefield; Henry Beaudette (Canada) and Marie Poutrie (Canada)

BECKMAN,
Marie, d. 8/4/1987 at 64 in MA

BECKWITH,
Barbara Lillian, d. 12/24/1991 at 65 in Wolfeboro; Ralph Chick and Lillian Look
Richard L., d. 10/31/1956 at 11; b. So. Boston, MA; John E. Beckwith and Barbara Chick

BEDELL,
Dora A., d. 7/29/1964 at 78 in Wolfeboro; b. Huntington, NY; Albert S. Pettit and Harriet A. Box

BELL,
William N., d. 11/21/1937 at 60/7/24 in Sanbornville; b. Rochester; James Bell and Sophia A. Nutter

BELLANGER,
Camille, d. 1/16/1897 at 67/4; housewife; married; b. Canada; George Bellanger

BELLEAU,
Catherine M., d. 3/7/1986 at 69 in Wolfeboro; George J. Desmond and Mary H. Kobut

BELLEVEAU,
Fred, d. 1/2/1892 at 3/5; Louis Belleveau (Canada) and Eliza Marrow (Canada)

BELLIVEON,
Thomas, d. 6/30/1887 at 4/7/14; Lewis Belliveon (Canada) and Lizzie Merrow (Canada)

BELLONGE,
George, d. 6/11/1905 at 74/11/20 in Sanbornville; laborer; widower; b. Canada

BENNETT,
Hazel P., d. 1/31/1983 at 61 in Wolfeboro; Arthur Perry and Alice Fogg
James W., Sr., d. 1/10/1987 at 70; Frank S. Bennett and Eleanor Dawes
Josephene, d. 1/25/1934 at 60 in Rochester

BENSON,
Martha J., d. 1/2/1905 at 84/11/11; domestic; widow; b. Eaton; Cyrus M. Moses (Standish, ME) and Eunice Underwood (Saco, ME)

BERG,
Hugh A., d. 6/23/1971 at 76 in Wolfeboro; Herman Berg and Albertina Halverson

BERNHART,
Finn W., d. 7/11/1973 at 66 in Union; Peter Bernhart and Fanny Westelius

BERRY,
Elizabeth, d. 11/10/1912 at 69/11/21; housewife; married; b. Wakefield; John Farnham (Shapleigh, ME) and Marjorie Wiggin (Wakefield)
Eva A., d. 1/7/1942 at 51/2/10 in Sanford, ME; b. Dunbarton; Henry E. Weymouth and Lucy Weymouth
George P., d. 6/20/1896 at -- in East Wakefield; provision dealer; b. Salem, MA; George H. Berry (Salem, MA) and Lydia W. Masway (Salem, MA)
Lillie M., d. 9/25/1950 at 69 in Union; b. E. Templeton; James Cochran and Ellen E. Kelley
Martha M., d. 7/28/1930 at 79/4/3; widow; b. Wakefield; Asa Farnham and Mary Jones
Percy deR., d. 4/21/1958 at 77 in Union; b. Greenland; George Berry and Anna M. deRochemont
William, d. 4/4/1929 at 86/0/22; married; b. Wakefield; Francis Berry and Temperance Wiggin

BERTSCH,
Hattie N.A., d. 4/29/1897 at 46/7; teacher; married; b. Wakefield; Joshua Brooks (Wakefield) and Mary D. Smith (Wakefield)

BEVARD,
John W., d. 4/29/1985 at 48 in Sanbornville; Arthur Bevard and Jane Kidwell

BEZANSON,
G. Victor, d. 12/17/1969 at 71 in Wolfeboro; G. Victor Bezanson, Sr. and Annie White
Rose A., d. 1/26/1969 at 73 in Wolfeboro; George Croteau and Adelaide Juneau

BICKFORD,
Albion M., d. 6/13/1940 at 70/10/23 in Portsmouth; b. Farmington; Oliver Bickford and Almina Kenney
Arthur B., d. 10/3/1918 at 26/3/9; farmer; married; b. Wakefield, MA; George R. Bickford (Wakefield) and Lottie A. Tanner (New York, NY)
Arthur F., Sr., d. 3/28/1961 at 42 in Scarborough, ME
Bertha E., d. 6/29/1949 at 68/11/22 in Portsmouth; b. Sanbornville; Wesley Rines and Abbie Roberts

Carroll F., d. 12/6/1964 at 60 in Wolfeboro; b. Wolfeboro; Andrew
  Bickford and Marsha Dore
Carroll Freeman, d. 7/27/1944 at 8/3/1 in Wolfeboro; b. Wakefield; Carroll
  F. Bickford and Blanche Jenness
Ellen, d. 12/23/1934 at 86 in Danvers, MA; b. Cambridge, MA; J. P.
  Davis and Elizabeth Webber
Elsie M., d. 9/20/1966 at 76 in Rochester; b. Bartlett; Marshall Duke and
  Matilda Hall
Everett J., d. 4/27/1969 at 62 in Wolfeboro; Andrew F. Bickford and
  Marcia Doe
Florence H., d. 8/24/1962 at 42 in Portland, ME
George R., d. 2/9/1929 at 83/10/17; married; b. Wakefield; Capt. Charles
  Bickford and Mary Remick
Lena Durgin, d. 4/27/1938 at 64/8/11 in Sanbornville; b. Concord; Valman
  Godfrey and Alice Miranda Drake
Thomas, d. 3/12/1894 at 82; laborer; widower

BILLEVEAU,
Eddie, d. 12/9/1896 at 0/4/13; b. Wakefield; Lewis Billeveau (Canada) and
  Eliza Morrow (Canada)

BISBEE,
Mary A., d. 6/29/1987 at 74 in Wolfeboro

BISHOP,
Helen F., d. 5/1/1922 at 78/5; no occ.; widow; b. Camden, ME; Robert
  Hassen (Camden, ME) and Christina Coombs

BJORKROTH,
Eric C.W., d. 10/16/1978 at 88 in Wolfeboro

BLACKADAR,
H. Dexter, d. 5/20/1986 at 55 in Rochester; Harry D. Blackadar and Olive
  I. Banks

BLACKWOOD,
James, d. 3/5/1970 at 71 in Sanford, ME; John Blackwood and Agnes
  Snedden
Robina J., d. 3/14/1967 at 83 in Trenton, NJ

BLAIR,
Alfred C., Sr., d. 6/10/1988 at 65; Harry A. Blair and Amelia M. Clifford

BLAIS,
Ralph Frank, Jr., d. 5/31/1998 at 52; Ralph Frank Blais, Sr. and Alice Comas

BLAISDELL,
Ernest O., d. 10/4/1956 at 64 in Union; b. Farmington; Orin M. Blaisdell and Ada Jones
Frederick E., d. 5/19/1947 at 79/1/13 in Lowell, MA; b. Cambridge, MA; Edward Blaisdell and Kate Morey
Nathaniel, d. 10/7/1891 at 63/10/18; shoemaker; married

BLAKE,
Elsie M., d. 12/7/1947 at 79/0/24 in Wolfeboro; b. Woburn, MA; Simon Blake and Ellen M. Sargent
George E., d. 11/10/1905 at 65; single; b. Dover; William H. Blake (Boston, MA) and Eliza C. Rice (Portland, ME)
Georgiana P., d. 4/6/1925 at 74/2/14; widow; b. Roxbury, MA; Isiah W. Palmer and Margaret Langmaid
Herbert Irving, d. 10/16/1953 at 79 in Wolfeboro; b. Woburn, MA; Simon Blake and Ellen M. Sargent
Simon, d. 11/4/1919 at 86/11/21; ac. heart failure; farmer; married; b. Brookfield; William Blake (Wakefield) and Abigail Cook (Wakefield)

BLAKELEY,
Quincy, d. 2/25/1892 at 67/8/8; clergyman; married; b. Pawlet, VT; David Blakeley (Pawlet, VT) and Esther Edgerton (Pawlet, VT)

BLAMY,
Ernest, d. 7/17/1970 at 34 in East Wakefield; Ernest Blamy and Anne Harve

BLANCHARD,
Alfred William, d. 5/25/1994 at 55 in Union; Mayo Howard Blanchard and Lucienne Patricia Goyette
Roland S., d. 11/16/1969 at 80 in Wolfeboro; Agil Blanchard and Ellen Lane

BLANTON,
Nancy Hutchins, d. 5/25/1989 at 56 in Wolfeboro; Bernard S. Hutchins and Teresa Hayes

BLODGETT,
Albert W., d. 5/10/1934 at 68/7/24 in Rochester; b. Danvers, MA; William Blodgett and Susan Andrews

BLOMSTER,
George A., d. 5/25/1981 at 80 in Sanbornville; Alfred Blomster and Anna Erickson

BLY,
Charles, d. 6/9/1967 at 81 in Ossipee

BOARDMAN,
Rose A., d. 9/24/1968 at 61 in Hanover; Louis Hill and Rose Patch

BODWELL,
Mary Myrtle, d. 4/11/1968 at 60 in Sanford, ME

BOHM,
Jacob, d. 5/31/1926 at 74/4/21; widower; b. Denmark; Jacob Bohm and Mary Olsen
Louis F., d. 7/10/1950 at 67/11/10 in Province Lake; b. Cambridge, MA; Jacob Bohm and Johanna Olsen

BOILLARD,
Ida, d. 9/10/1925 at 52; married; b. Canada; Eamede Martin and Cloutide Durant

BOLTON,
Mae E., d. 12/17/1975 at 84 in Rochester; Lawrence Bolton and Elizabeth Thompson

BOND,
Franklin, d. 12/5/1989 at 78; Bernard Q. Bond and Jessica Edwards

BONNYMAN,
Frederick C., d. 10/27/1946 at 60/9/4 in Hanover; b. Effingham; Harry Bonnyman and Annie Monroe

BOOTH,
Gail Beverly, d. 2/27/1964 at 14 in Laconia; b. Rochester; George W. Booth, Jr. and Elizabeth Francis

BOOTHBY,
Rose, d. 5/11/1990 at 76 in ME

BORRACCI,
Leo, d. 7/3/1984 at 67 in Rochester; Evasio Borracci and Ada Tici

BOSLEY,
John Charles, d. 6/1/1975 at 18 in Milton; Charles E. Bosley and Roberta F. Nason

BOSTON,
Asa W., d. 2/4/1960 at 73 in East Rochester; b. Brookfield; Henry Boston and Susan Drew
George H., d. 12/22/1952 at 70/2/8 in Union; b. Brookfield; Henry Boston and Susan Drew

BOULE,
William, d. 9/28/1982 at 76 in North Wakefield

BOWERS,
George N., d. 7/23/1936 at 81/10/4 in Sanbornville; b. Dover; George Bowers and ----- Murray

BOWLBY,
Jessie A., d. 7/23/1985 at 90 in Rochester; William J. MacIntosh and Rachel Snow
Kenneth L., d. 1/22/1963 at 67 in Sanbornville; b. Washington, NJ; Edward E. Bowlby and Olive Wagner

BOWSER,
Edward Thomas, d. 5/29/1953 at 54 in Sanbornville; b. MA; Thomas F. Bowser and Catherine A. Kelley

BOYD,
Abbie S., d. 8/1/1895 at 22/11/6; housewife; married; b. Wakefield; George H. Gage (Wakefield) and E. Jennie Cotton (Wolfeboro)
Patricia Ann, d. 1/29/1997 at 61 in Wolfeboro; John H. Boyd and Ruth Corlis
Ruth C., d. 10/6/1898 at 4/8/24; b. Georgetown, ME; William T. Boyd (Biddeford, ME) and Abbie S. Gage (Wakefield)

BOZUWA,
Joan Mary, d. 6/12/1986 at 29; Gerard G. Bozuwa and Titia L. Wetselas

BRACKETT,
Ada A., d. 12/25/1956 at 86 in Sanbornville; b. Sanford, ME; Crosby B. Remick and Jennie B. Goodwin
Alma E., d. 4/25/1901 at 53/6/8; housewife; married; b. Albany; Job Kenerson (Albany) and Rhoda A. Head (Tamworth)
Arthur T., d. 4/13/1962 at 54 in Rockport, MA
Arthur W., d. 5/16/1893 at 6/3/22; b. Wakefield; Cecil A. Brackett (Wakefield) and Annie M. Wiggin (Wakefield)
Asa M., d. 3/7/1921 at 81/2/23; apoplexy; widower; b. Wakefield; David Brackett (Berwick, ME) and Nancy Fernald (Berwick, ME)
Charles E., d. 5/19/1902 at 73/6/17; farmer; married; b. Acton, ME; David Brackett (Berwick, ME) and Nancy Fernald (Berwick, ME)
Daniel, d. 2/18/1917 at 54/6/24; sta. engineer; married; b. Wakefield; Daniel Brackett (Acton, ME) and Hannah Cook (Wakefield)
Doris, d. 1/31/1988 at 87 in Dover; John Brackett and Mary Kenny
Elizabeth R., d. 3/2/1914 at 78/3/1; housewife; widow; b. Wakefield; Willard Wiggins and Polly Roberts
Flora P., d. 9/7/1964 at 83 in Wolfeboro; b. Wakefield; Charles E. Brackett and Mary Wiggin
Forris Linwood, d. 6/18/1944 at 76/0/22 in Sanbornville; b. Union; Asa M. Brackett and Rowena Farnham
Frank J., d. 8/16/1951 at 78 in Sanbornville; b. Sanbornville; Charles E. Brackett and Elizabeth Wiggin
George A., d. 8/30/1909 at 35/11/12; teamster; single; b. Wakefield; Charles E. Brackett (Acton, ME) and Lizzie R. Wiggin (Wakefield)
Harry L., d. 12/12/1954 at 76 in Gloucester, MA; b. Wakefield; Charles E. Brackett and Elizabeth Wiggin
Herbert C., d. 1/31/1908 at 41/2/24; laborer; married; b. Wakefield; Charles E. Brackett (Acton, ME) and Elizabeth R. Wiggin (Wakefield)

Ida F., d. 2/13/1890 at 26/1/24; housekeeper; married; b. Freedom; Ivory F. Rice (Freedom) and Mary McCartee (Porter, ME)

Jeremiah F., d. 10/10/1914 at 75/5; laborer; divorced; b. Milton Mills; Asa Brackett and Lucinda Nason

John Edward, d. 2/12/1949 at 77/8/4 in Sanbornville; b. Wakefield; Charles E. Brackett and Elizabeth Wiggin

John H., d. 5/13/1915 at 81/0/23; wheelwright; single; b. Wakefield; David Brackett (No. Berwick, ME) and Nancy Brackett (No. Berwick, ME)

John S., d. 9/15/1902 at 62/11/13; merchant; widower; b. Somersworth; Thomas Brackett (Ossipee) and Olive Hartford

Mary E., d. 10/3/1952 at 80/3/19 in Dover; b. Salem, MA; Martin Kenney and Mary McShea

May Taft, d. 7/20/1945 at 63/7/18 in Rockport, MA

Pauline M., d. 6/30/1989 at 74 in Dover; Ora F. McCrillis and Ruth F. Meikle

Peggy Ann, d. 9/17/1936 at 0/0/8 in Rochester; b. Rochester; Ralph E. Brackett and Pauline F. McCrillis

Ralph E., d. 1/7/1994 at 87 in Rochester; John Brackett and Mary Kenny

BRAGDON,
Oren D., d. 3/5/1912 at 65; lawyer; married; b. Portsmouth; Oren Bragdon (Limerick, ME) and Ann Waldron (Limington, ME)

BRAUMANN,
Hope M., d. 7/19/1984 at 79 in Wolfeboro; ---- Transeau and Carrie Schimel

BREWSTER,
George W., d. 2/4/1940 at 48 in New York, NY

Glenn, d. 2/13/1987 at 39 in Wolfeboro

Marion W., d. 8/24/1924 at 65/2/23; at home; widow; b. Wakefield; Henry L. Willard (Wakefield) and Charlotte Nason (Wakefield)

BRIDGES,
William Henry, d. 9/21/1998 at 75 in East Wakefield; Charles Edward Bridges and Laura Camelia Bushway

BRIGGS,
John D., d. 4/25/1991 at 70 in Wolfeboro; Percy Dixon Briggs and Grace Spencer

BRIGHAM,
George T., d. 4/26/1926 at 82/2/1; married; b. Southboro, MA; Taylor Brigham and Ann Jacobs

BRINTNALL,
Norman Y., d. 8/16/1926 at 65/10/24; single; b. Charlestown, MA; Norman Y. Brintnall and Julia Delaney

BRITTON,
child, d. 2/5/1942 at 0/0/5 in Wolfeboro; b. Wolfeboro; Paul Britton, Jr. and Emma Lagasse
daughter, d. 4/22/1951 at 0/0/0 in Rochester; b. Rochester; Paul J. Britton and Emma Lagace

BROAD,
James W., d. 7/5/1929 at 47/4/2; single; b. Natick, MA; Hezekiah Broad and Flora M. Corson

BROCHU,
Linda, d. 3/4/1951 at 1/7/14 in Rochester; b. Milton Mills; Paul Brochu and June Durgin

BROCK,
John B., d. 12/5/1948 at 73/3/15 in Union; b. Pittsfield; John Brock

BRODZINSKI,
Mildred A., d. 7/21/1980 at 58; Stephen Puddister

BRONSON,
Gery L., d. 12/4/1976 at 21 in Morristown, NJ

BROOKS,
Dennis Ralph, d. 11/2/1943 at 71/11/14 in Sanbornville; b. Montgomery, VT; Antoine Brooks and Delia Newcity
Joshua, d. 4/13/1892 at 76/6/14; carpenter; widower; b. Wakefield; John Brooks (Wells, ME) and Phebe Clark (York, ME)
Julia D., d. 6/27/1947 at 72/3/27 in Wolfeboro; b. No. Grafton, MA; Alfred Parent and Julia D. Parent
Kenneth Edward, Sr., d. 5/28/1997 at 75 in Wolfeboro; Edward Brooks and Gladys York

Mary D., d. 10/10/1890 at 67/8; housekeeper; married; b. Wakefield; Ephraim G. Smith and Susie G. Burbank (Newfield, ME)

BROUILLARD,
child, d. 4/18/1937 at 0/0/1 in Wolfeboro; b. Wolfeboro; Henry Brouillard and Grace King

Simon Peter, d. 6/29/1942 at 68/0/0; b. Roxton Falls, Canada; Simon Brouillard and Delina Legaud

BROWN,
Adam A., d. 9/26/1898 at 0/1/24; b. Wakefield; Plummer A. Brown (Ossipee) and Laura V. Rice (Freedom)

Anna M., d. 6/10/1955 at 80 in Union; b. England; Daniel Brooks and Comfort Marsh

Asa, d. 12/1/1910 at 84/2/1; postmaster; married; b. Roxbury, MA; Eliphalet Brown (MA) and Martha Gay (MA)

Basil I., d. 1/14/1916 at 24/14(?)/14; train hand; single; b. Wakefield; Plummer Brown (Ossipee) and Laura Rice (Freedom)

Celia F., d. 12/12/1961 at 86 in Wolfeboro; b. Sanbornville; Horatio Fellows and Belle Tibbetts

Charles Bryant, d. 10/9/1939 at 72/0/5; b. Wolfeboro; Moses E. Brown and Abigail Brown

Clara A., d. 10/2/1906 at 33/3/13; housework; married; b. So. Acton, ME; George D. Perkins (New Durham) and Sarah A. Bodwell (Acton, ME)

Edward E., d. 1/12/1947 at 81/4/8 in Union; b. Somersworth; Moses E. Brown and Abigail Bryant

Emma C., d. 10/29/1937 at 71/3/18 in Wolfeboro; b. Harmony, ME; William C. Richards and Eunice D. Dyer

George W., d. 4/13/1953 at 86 in Union; b. Tamworth

John F., d. 8/23/1896 at 59/5/8; farmer; widower; Moses H. Brown and Mary Tuttle

Joseph William, d. 5/12/1998 at 62 in Lebanon; James G. Brown and Rebecca S. Synnott

Laura V., d. 3/19/1929 at 65; widow; b. Freedom; Ivory Rice and Mary McCarter

Lillian R., d. 2/22/1993 at 90; Gudmund Rafson and Belle ----

Mabel F., d. 1/31/1963 at 89 in Ossipee

Mabel Galena, d. 12/2/1944 at 75/7 in West Newbury, MA; b. Wakefield; Gilman P. Dore and Katie C. Donovan

Mildred, d. 4/23/1938 at 16/9/15 in Lancaster, MA; b. Wolfeboro; Edwin M. Brown and Doris Morgan

Moses E., d. 9/5/1912 at 76/0/7; blacksmith; married; b. Wolfeboro; Paul Brown and Mary Neal (Brookfield)

Olive E.R., d. 6/6/1911 at 83/2/11; housewife; widow; b. Wakefield; Elisha Rollins (Lebanon, ME) and Prudence Lord (Lebanon, ME)

Plummer A., d. 5/10/1917 at 58/2/23; RR conductor; married; b. Ossipee; John F. Brown (Ossipee) and Abbie A. Wentworth (Ossipee)

Rollins, d. 4/4/1962 at 70 in Wolfeboro; b. Brooklyn, NY; Daniel R. Brown and Mary Paul

Sally Evans, d. 2/11/1896 at 91/9/13; housekeeper; b. Holderness; William Evans (Holderness) and Mary Brown (Holderness)

Susan Mary, d. 1/18/1976 at 1 in Sanbornville; Walter E. Brown and Ann L. Smith

Thomas Joseph, d. 2/2/1996 at 32 in Sanbornville; Walter Edward Brown and Ann Louise Smith

BRUCE,

David Kenneth, d. 12/14/1996 at 47 in Sanbornville; Kenneth Bruce and Marion Cole

BRULEY,

Roger S., d. 12/22/1980 at 85 in Wolfeboro; Frank Bruley and ---- Sweetser

BRYAN,

Ernest A., d. 9/26/1969 at 70 in Springfield, MA

Helen Louise, d. 3/1/1997 at 78 in Wolfeboro; Francis J. Clifton and Etta Kennedy

BRYANT,

Elizabeth, d. 1/12/1899 at 45/2/7 in Sanbornville; housewife; married; b. West Fairlee, VT; Benjamin Hurst (England) and Angeline West (West Fairlee, VT)

Ruth A., d. 12/19/1975 at 87 in Somerville, MA

BUCHANAN,

Dora Rideout, d. 4/18/1986 at 80 in Derry

BUCHMAN,
William Walter, d. 1/12/1995 at 75 in Dover; William Buchman and Ella Johnson

BUCKLESS,
George E., d. 6/22/1998 at 81; George G. Buckless and Louise Young

BUDROE,
Adelard, d. 7/19/1930 at 79/8/18; widower; b. Three Rivers, Canada
Edward, Sr., d. 5/28/1973 at 88 in Wolfeboro; David Budroe and Adelaide Goodblood

BUMFORD,
Flora A., d. 6/15/1968 at 69 in Concord; Leroy Hobbs

BURBECK,
Annie Eliza, d. 5/7/1937 at 90/11/12 in Sanbornville; George Horne and Palidia Roberts

BURGESS,
Gideon E., d. 1/21/1950 at 83/1/13 in Union; b. Canada

BURKE,
Frederick, d. 7/1/1933 at 49/5/18
Maria, d. 6/9/1951 at -- in Union

BURLEIGH,
Arthur S., d. 2/15/1986 at 91 in Ossipee; Charles J. Burleigh and Julia F. Roberts
Harry W., d. 9/9/1890 at 0/6/18; b. Wakefield; George W. Burleigh (Wakefield) and Alice L. Powell (England)
Lillian, d. 10/14/1983 at 90 in Ossipee; Andrew Mast and Julia Lyons
Susan F., d. 2/2/1898 at 65/6/12; housewife; widow; b. Wakefield; Charles Moulton (Hampton) and Olive Ayers (Greenland)
Thomas C., d. 2/22/1887 at 64/5/21; carpenter; married; b. Brookfield; Thomas Burleigh (Wakefield) and Nancy Smith (Ossipee)

BURLEY,
Jonathan M., d. 3/13/1907 at 86/4/16; farmer; married; b. Wakefield; William Burley (Wakefield) and Lydia Ames (Parsonsfield, ME)

BURNS,
Anna G., d. 1/27/1959 at 57 in Sanbornville; b. Perth Amboy, NJ; Alfred J. Peck and Carron Peterson
William F., d. 7/15/1955 at 55 in Rochester; b. Perth Amboy, NJ; Joseph G. Burns and Mitelda Simonsen

BURROUGHS,
Dana, d. 12/4/1962 at 63 in Laconia; b. Wolfeboro; Howard W. Burroughs and Mercy Kimball
Edgar H., d. 5/1/1933 at 75/11/11
Grace Ricker, d. 9/29/1941 at 89/10/13 in Wolfeboro; b. Biddeford, ME; John Ricker and Sarah Calef
Luella C., d. 4/3/1980 at 87; John I. Sanborn and Ella C. Grant
Mercy May, d. 12/15/1954 at 76 in Dover; b. Wolfeboro; Alonzo F. Kimball and Mary Parsons
Ralph J., Jr., d. 6/25/1981 at 62 in Wolfeboro

BUZZELL,
Basil A., d. 2/9/1998 at 85 in Sanbornville; Melvin Buzzell
Florence M., d. 7/27/1958 at 79 in Union; b. W. Newfield, ME; John L. Day and Susan B. Patch
Mary B., d. 5/26/1991 at 74 in Rochester; George E. Cook and Luler J. Woodbury
Raymond B., d. 6/26/1935 at 56/0/22 in So. Wakefield; b. Acton, ME; James H. Buzzell and Sarah F. Littlefield
Virgil R., d. 5/13/1919 at 0/1; congenital ichthyosis; b. Wakefield; Richard Buzzell (Pittsfield, ME) and Carrie Raymond (Palmyra, ME)

BYAM,
Harriette Finette, d. 8/20/1941 at 79/3/19; b. Newport, VT; ----- Woodard and Mary Woodard

CADDELL,
John Penney, d. 5/3/1993 at 61; John Caddell and Christine Penney

CAME,
Abbie Jane, d. 6/30/1951 at 83 in Rochester; b. Milton; George W. Came and Sarah Mills

CAMERON,
Agnes C., d. 10/21/1973 at 82 in East Wakefield; George E. Sanborn and Georgiana Junt

CAMPBELL,
Carrie M., d. 9/9/1967 at 82 in Rochester; b. Strafford; Benjamin Ellis and Emily Berry
Esther L., d. 10/24/1972 at 69 in Rochester; William Martin and Louella Fancher
Madeline, d. 7/25/1906 at 0/7/15; b. Wakefield; Ernest C. Campbell (Barnard, VT) and Mary E. Perkins (Acton, ME)
Phebe A., d. 3/1/1901 at 70/5/23 in Sanbornville; domestic; widow; b. Barnard, VT; Asa Walker (VT) and Sarah Keith (VT)
Walter F., d. 5/15/1959 at 76 in Rochester; b. Wolfeboro; John F. Campbell and Sarah Brown
Winifred M., d. 3/21/1966 at 54 in Wolfeboro

CAMPERNELL,
Peter, d. 9/9/1905 at 78/11/6; farmer; single; b. Wakefield; John Campernell (Newfield, ME) and Charity Horn (Wakefield)

CANNEY,
George, d. 8/7/1966 at 54; b. Portsmouth; Frank C. Canney and Fannie Williams
Moses A., d. 3/2/1891 at 41/10; farmer; married; b. Nottingham; James M. Canney (Nottingham) and Lydia O. Sherburn (Barrington)

CAPLETTE,
Ethel E., d. 4/24/1982 at 86 in Rochester

CARBERRY,
James F., d. 12/17/1993 at 58 in Wolfeboro; Henry Carberry and Mary Berry

CARD,
Daniel J., d. 6/21/1938 at 79/3/4; b. Dover; Andrew C. Card and Martha Howe

CAREY,
Alfred J., d. 6/23/1956 at 59; b. Somerville, MA; Alfred E. Carey and Winifred McCarty

CARLETON,
Clarence E., d. 9/8/1974 at 89 in Wolfeboro
Ellen, d. 5/29/1956 at 68 in Concord; b. Boston, MA; Edwin A. Jeffery, Jr. and Jessie MacLennan

CARRIER,
Mary, d. 1/11/1934 at 77/4/9; George Carrier and Camille Dalaire

CARSON,
John, d. 8/2/1911 at 19/0/25; moulder; single; b. Dover

CARTER,
Frank S., d. 4/27/1956 at 73; b. NB; Oscar Carter
Mary A., d. 1/5/1903 at 75; widow; b. Wakefield; Daniel Young and Betsy Cook
Mary Etta, d. 11/14/1891 at 0/11/2; b. Wakefield; William Carter (Montpelier, VT) and Carrie E. Vallie (New Durham)

CARVER,
Nancy M., d. 8/21/1920 at 84/2/27; acute bronchitis; single; b. Pawlet, VT; John Carver (Pawlet, VT)

CASANI,
Albert A., d. 9/13/1966 at 87 in Wolfeboro; b. Italy; Frank Casani and Ernesta Garbati

CASWELL,
Jean A., d. 12/8/1995 at 58 in Wolfeboro; Eustace G. Caswell and Gladys Joy

CATE,
Elizabeth B., d. 12/16/1939 at 77/11/23 in Farmington
Evelyn A., d. 1/7/1974 at 73 in Waltham, MA; Harry Cate
Flora E., d. 7/29/1985 at 95 in East Wakefield; Ansel Farnham and Lizzy M. Brown
Herbert H., d. 10/17/1946 at 65/3/11 in Brookfield

Irene L., d. 3/7/1991 at 81 in Wolfeboro
Myron J., d. 6/19/1987 at 88 in Rochester; Harry Cate and Aimee Bauie
Myrtie D., d. 3/19/1943 at 43/8/26 in Rochester; b. Gray, ME; Wendell Small and Minnie Libbey
Norris E., d. 10/23/1976 at 79 in Wolfeboro
Olive F., d. 9/8/1981 at 72 in Wolfeboro
Raymond M., d. 4/3/1965 at 73 in Wolfeboro; b. Brookfield; Harry Cate and Ami Bauge

CATES,
Pearl Francis, d. 4/20/1905 at 0/1 in Union; b. Union; Alfred A. Cates (Harrison, ME) and Florice Richardson (Magalloway, ME)

CELLA,
Steven S., d. 11/1/1969 at 17; Silvio Cella and Mary Catalda

CHADBOURNE,
J. L., d. 3/13/1921 at 70/10/18; diabetes mellitus; machinist; married; b. Waterboro, ME; Ivory Chadbourne (Waterboro, ME) and Julia Lewis (Waterboro, ME)

CHAKOUTIS,
George, d. 3/17/1991 at 70; Nicholas Chakoutis and Helen Manoulakou

CHAMBERLAIN,
Alexander, d. 1/18/1930 at 78/4/9; widower; b. Milton; Samuel Chamberlain and Mary E. Fall
Fred M., d. 5/30/1935 at 77/0/1 in Union; b. Milton; Samuel Chamberlain and Mary E. Fall
Sarah E., d. 7/11/1926 at 79/10/24; married; b. Wakefield; Roberts S. Corson and Sarah Nay

CHAMBERLAND,
Eugenie M., d. 3/12/1899 at 28; housewife; married; b. Canada; L. Marshall (Canada) and S. King (Canada)
Telesphore, d. 11/2/1909 at 42/7/29; janitor; married; b. Canada; Joseph Chamberland (Canada) and Hermine Gregois (Canada)

CHAMPION,
George, d. 9/7/1946 at 84/2/17 in So. Warren, ME; b. Effingham

Nancy, d. 8/18/1890 at 62; housewife; married; b. Meredith

CHANDLER,
Arthur L., d. 9/24/1966 at 80 in Union; b. E. Bridgewater, MA; Charles Chandler and Mary Mills
Hazel, d. 3/3/1971 at 76 in Rochester; William A. Davenport and Mabel McIntire

CHAPIN,
Nora G., d. 11/10/1954 at 68 in Rochester; b. Boston, MA; Timothy Sullivan and Nora O'Meara
Sadie J., d. 10/2/1936 at 59/11/13; b. Summer Hill, NB; William Johnson and Annie McFarland
Sarah E., d. 12/14/1952 at 93/6/10 in Brookfield; Luther P. Wiggin and Margaret McCulley

CHAPMAN,
Clarissa, d. 10/15/1897 at --; married; b. Brookfield; Samuel Lang and Lydia Thurber
Clinton H., d. 5/30/1988 at 75 in Wolfeboro; Clinton T. Chapman and Lila Burnett
Elinore A., d. 9/6/1988 at 96 in Ossipee; George Wyman and Mary Main
George Arthur, d. 9/19/1925 at 0/0/4; b. Sanbornville; Homer L. Chapman and Elinore A. Wyman
Herbert F., d. 5/6/1945 at 65/5/27 in Acton, ME; b. Charlestown, MA; Herbert S. Chapman and Maretta Swan
Homer L., d. 12/20/1975 at 87 in Natick, MA; Jonathon Chapman and Ella Snow
John H., d. 4/20/1902 at 49/7 in Sanbornville; carpenter; married; b. Wakefield; Eben Chapman (Milton) and Clarissa A. Lang (Brookfield)
Jonathan E., d. 1/6/1913 at 70/11/10; supt. ice co.; married; b. Canada; Lucius Chapman (Quebec) and Lydia Leavitt (Quebec)
Lena E., d. 10/24/1976 at 85 in Maplewood, MN
Marietta S., d. 6/20/1925 at 72/9/15; widow; b. Charlestown, MA; Aron F. Swain and Elvira Jane Greenlow
Maude A., d. 10/8/1965 at 86 in Wolfeboro; b. Rochester; Charles A. Allen and Abbie M. Randlett
Russell P., d. 8/6/1969 at 82 in Leominster, MA

CHARPENTIER,
Medora, d. 7/2/1994 at 88 in Ossipee; Joseph Levesque and Emma Demaris

CHASE,
Adeline Willey, d. 12/23/1944 at 58/11/20 in Milton
Arthur, d. 3/8/1976 at 64 in Manchester
Evelyn C., d. 12/4/1988 at 85 in Rochester; Myron R. Currier and Ellen Atwood
George H., d. 11/30/1967 at 86 in East Lebanon, ME
Gladys E., d. 7/18/1969 at 80; William Washburn and Georgia Potter
Henry, d. 1/27/1891 at 80/1/30; farmer; married; b. Wakefield; John Chase
Winfield S., d. 2/16/1925 at 58/5/19; married; b. Saco, ME; Melville B. Chase and Susan J. Gerry

CHATFIELD,
H. Wheeler, b. 2/9/1952 at 58/1/8 in Union; b. New York, NY; Arthur W. Chatfield and Alida Wheeler

CHENEY,
Cora B., d. 9/25/1868 at 0/11/12 in So. Berwick, ME (1936)
Edwin J., d. 11/25/1935 at 69/0/2 in Sanbornville; b. Freedom; Ivory F. Rice and Mary McCartee
Emma F., d. 10/16/1884 at 19/8 in So. Berwick, ME (1936)
Eva M., d. 1/13/1890 at 17/8/16 in So. Berwick, ME (1936)
Sarah N., d. 7/20/1884 at 37/4/23 in So. Berwick, ME (1936)

CHESBROUGH,
Gladys M., d. 12/31/1982 [also listed as 1/6/1983] at 84 in Wolfeboro; Charles Wentworth
Walter A., d. 6/22/1958 at 77 in Union; b. Gaines, NY; Chauncey P. Chesbrough and Jennie M. Bennett

CHESLEY,
child, d. 7/28/1968 at 0/0/0 in Rochester; Douglas N. Chesley and Lana L. Plummer
James A., d. 10/17/1895 at 71/1/14; retired naval officer; married; b. Wakefield; Isaac B. Chesley (Rochester) and Lucy B. Parsons (Parsonsfield, ME)
Lucy M., d. 9/11/1902 at 77/2/20; housewife; widow; b. Wakefield; Amasa Copp (Wakefield) and Eliza Remick

CHICK,
son, d. 9/29/1892 at 0/0/1; b. Wakefield; Charles Chick (Milton) and Verta Randall (Great Falls)
child, d. 4/20/1969 at 0/0/0 in Sanford, ME
Alma D., d. 1/1/1918 at 35/13(?)/16; housewife; married; b. Germany; Frederick C. Dohne (Germany) and Anna M. Delfs (Germany)
Beatrice Florence, d. 12/31/1963 at 66 in Sanford, ME
Cora E., d. 6/29/1887 at 26/6/16; housework; married; b. Ossipee; John F. Brown (Ossipee) and Abbie A. Wentworth (Ossipee)
George, d. 1/31/1936 at 75/11/20 in Woodman; b. Waterboro, ME; Hanson D. Chick and Mehitable Smith
George E., Jr., d. 10/11/1993 at 66 in East Wakefield; George E. Chick, Sr. and Kathleen Ringer
Lewis B., d. 4/8/1934 at 69/4/27; b. Waterboro, ME; Hanson Chick and Mehitable Smith
Lewis Sumner, d. 2/5/1968 at 77 in Sanford, ME
Lillian M., d. 6/13/1966 at 79 in Wolfeboro; b. Boston, MA
Mabel, d. 11/6/1971 at 88 in Augusta, ME
Pearl M., d. 2/3/1992 at 81 in Ossipee; Robert A. Cameron and Agnes C. ----
Ralph H., d. 9/3/1961 at 77 in Union; b. Woodman; George Chick and Jane Waldron
Russell W., d. 9/19/1991 at 82 in Wolfeboro; Harry Chick and Helen Blake
Sarah Jane, d. 12/6/1945 at 83/8/3 in Wolfeboro; b. Wakefield
Willard, d. 4/13/1964 at 67 in Arlington, MA

CHICKOPUS,
Powell, d. 2/7/1917 at 0/4/16; b. Wakefield; George Chickopus (Poland) and Annie Mingen (Poland)

CHITTICK,
Ruth Gardner, d. 5/23/1997 at 93 in No. Wakefield; Robert Nicholson Gardner and Martha Sanford

CHURCHILL,
Alice M., d. 5/27/1967 at 89 in Brookfield; b. Stowe, ME; Leonard Emerson and Marilda -----
Charles F., d. 7/2/1972 at 63 in Manchester; Charles Churchill and Melissa Battis

Guy L., d. 3/9/1946 at 59/9/4 in Wolfeboro; b. Brookfield; Lester L. Churchill and Harriet Ferguson

CLANCY,

Joseph, d. 11/29/1962 at 72 in Wolfeboro; b. Bayonne, NJ; Thomas Clancy and ----- Prial

Mabel M., d. 9/12/1975 at 85 in Sanbornville; William Macintosh and Fannie Snow

CLARK,

Dorothy M., d. 2/6/1975 at 57 in Wolfeboro; Almon Bryant and Nellie M. Ellis

Ellen N., d. 1/15/1991 at 69 in Somerville, MA

George W., d. 11/1/1910 at 43; laborer; married; b. Dover; John S. Clark (Dover) and Lucinda Gilman (Dover)

Gladys M., d. 2/20/1974 at 81 in Ossipee; Walter Pickering

Hannah L., d. 3/21/1918 at 89/5/11; housewife; widow; b. Newmarket; Eben G. Churchill (Brookfield) and Ann E. Gove (Portsmouth)

Isaac T., d. 5/26/1899 at 75/9/26; farmer; married; John Clark (Wakefield) and Betsy Cotton (Wolfeboro)

John Frank, d. 6/21/1964 at 73 in Sanbornville; b. Dover; George Clark and Mary E. Tibbetts

Kenneth Frank, d. 8/4/1959 at 44 in Victorville, CA; J. Frank Clark and Gladys Pickering

Loring Townsend, d. 12/28/1997 at 82 in Wolfeboro; Edwin Clark and Edith Loring

Mary P., d. 12/4/1978 at 57 in Wolfeboro; William Lortis and May -----

Samantha E., d. 5/31/1989 at 0/1/19 in Wolfeboro; George H. Clark III and Anne E. Lund

CLEMENTS,

Peter D., d. 4/5/1970 at 76 in Wolfeboro; Benjamin R. Clements and Louise Crosby

CLIFFORD,

daughter, d. 12/29/1893 at 0/1; b. Wakefield; Charles H. Clifford (Denmark, ME) and Eliza E. Buswell (Bridgton, ME)

Arthur Charles, d. 3/30/1988 at 82 in Ossipee

CLOUTIER,
Lenora, d. 6/2/1909 at 74/10; housework; widow; b. Canada

CLOUTMAN,
Abbie S., d. 11/19/1896 at 27/5/13; housekeeper; b. Wakefield; Timothy Cloutman (Wakefield) and Hannah Sanborn (Acton, ME)
Edna M., d. 1/1/1979 at 93 in Ossipee; James P. Fellows and Mary A. Pike
Ernest C., d. 6/3/1930 at 70/8/24; single; b. W. Milton; Charles Cloutman and Ellen Dearborn
Harriett A., d. 1/8/1922 at 88/3/8; at home; widow; b. Acton, ME; David Horne (Wakefield) and ----- Nason (Exeter)
James Daniel, d. 5/12/1943 at 86/1/4; in Wolfeboro; b. Wakefield; Thomas Cloutman and Mehitable Watson
Joshua H., d. 9/16/1892 at 62/10/19; farmer; married; b. Wakefield; Thomas Cloutman (Wakefield) and Mary Hanson (Middleton)
Nora A., d. 12/2/1913 at 52/0/16; housekeeper; single; b. Wakefield; Joshua H. Cloutman and Harriet A. Horn

CLOW,
Asa M., d. 3/22/1930 at 70/1/17; widower; b. Wolfeboro; Daniel Clow and Susan Morgan
John R., d. 10/24/1954 at 69 in Union; b. Wolfeboro; Henry Clow and Annie Philpott

COFFRIN,
Sarah W., d. 4/18/1908 at 78/9/11; housewife; widow; b. Ossipee; Cotton Hayes (Barnstead) and Melvina Danforth (Ossipee)

COGGER,
Walter Thomas, d. 9/21/1991 at 85; Charles Cogger and Rosetta Mitchell

COLBATH,
Betsy S., d. 8/14/1988 at 94 in Wolfeboro
Charles F., d. 7/15/1894 at 14/1/29; single; b. Wakefield; Charles W. Colbath (Boston, MA) and Emma Bickford (Wolfeboro)
Charles W., d. 6/17/1934 at 81/5/25 in Wolfeboro; b. Boston, MA; Mark L. Colbath and Martha Ham
Clara C., d. 7/15/1932 at 71/7/0 in Sanbornville
Clarence D., d. 7/18/1894 at 4/4/12; Charles W. Colbath (Boston, MA) and Emma Bickford (Wolfeboro)

Emily A., d. 7/3/1982 at 82 in Wolfeboro; Elmer Mansfield and Lillian Clow

Herbert B., d. 6/11/1932 at 76/3/26 in Wolfeboro

John E., d. 10/28/1985 at 91 in Wolfeboro

M. A. L., d. 3/5/1888 at 21/6/2; fireman; single; b. Brookfield; Mark A.L. Colbath (Barnstead) and Martha J. Ham (Wellington, CT)

Mark A.L., d. 4/27/1911 at 85/4/19; retired; married; b. Barnstead; Dudley C. Colbath (Newington) and Betsey Pickering (Barnstead)

Mary J., d. 8/23/1894 at 7/3/22; Charles W. Colbath (Boston, MA) and Emma Bickford (Wolfeboro)

Robert N., d. 1/23/1987 at 87 in Wolfeboro

Rossmore K., d. 2/12/1958 at 76; b. Sanbornville; Walter Colbath and Emma B. Knox

Walter G., d. 3/30/1928 at 78/8/17; widower; b. Boston, MA; Mark A.L. Colbath and Martha Ham

COLBY,

Bernadette E., d. 5/6/1977 at 63 in Sanbornville; Stanislas Fugure and Alma Robinson

Charles Wallace, d. 4/14/1988 at 69 in Rochester; Harold P. Colby and Mildred Douglass

Lawrence A., d. 5/5/1985 at 70 in Wolfeboro

COLCORD,

Harvey, d. 4/11/1900 at 46; farmer; married; b. Tuftonboro; Noah Colcord (Tuftonboro)

COLE,

Susan, d. 4/9/1887 at 40; housework; married

COLELLO,

Angelina Eileen, d. 4/27/1992 at 76 in Portsmouth; Stephano Ravaglia and Martina Paganelli

COLLINS,

Janet Lee, d. 8/15/1987 at 28 in East Lebanon, ME

Julia E., d. 5/31/1915 at 65; housekeeper; single; b. Ireland; John Collins (Ireland)

COLLYER,
Harry, d. 4/25/1981 at 58 in Rochester; Albert Collyer and Annie Moran

COLMAN,
Helene Phoebe, d. 4/26/1949 at 62/11/17 in Wolfeboro; b. Brookfield; Robert L. Chamberlain and Gertrude Hanson
Leon C., d. 9/22/1956 at 82 in Wolfeboro; b. Brookfield; Charles Colman and Salome A. Cotton
Wilson, d. 6/8/1964 at 91 in Wolfeboro; b. Brookfield; Charles Colman and Salome Cotton

COLOMY,
Cora E., d. 7/4/1952 at 77/7/26 in Union; b. Wakefield; Samuel Allen and Emma Cummings

COLSON,
Cyrus B., d. 7/30/1965 at 70 in East Wakefield; b. Newburyport, MA; Cyrus N. Colson and Marguerite B. Sweetser
Joseph B., d. 2/23/1982 at 52 in East Wakefield; Cyrus Colson and Teresa Mahoney

COMEAU,
Arthur R., d. 5/29/1963 at 58 in Lawrence, MA
Richard, d. 6/19/1988 at 48 in Lawrence, MA; Arthur Comeau and Eva Gagnon

CONDON,
Agnes, d. 3/10/1977 at 82 in Rochester; John F. Crowley and Ellen Drew

CONEY,
Carolyn M., d. 3/21/1984 at 54 in Wolfeboro; Charles Moulton and Cora Pease
Johanna, d. 9/30/1964 at 79; b. Germany; J. W. Paasch

CONNOUGHTON,
John, d. 6/5/1957 at 55 in Boston, MA

COOK,
Duane Royal, d. 1/15/1995 at 65 in Sanbornville; Eugene Staples and Helen Cook

Elizabeth W., d. 3/11/1931 at 48; married; b. Newburyport, MA; Charles
Post and Mary A.S. Page

Ellen M., d. 4/9/1891 at 57/1/18; housekeeper; married; b. Montpelier,
VT; Lyman Briggs (Keene) and Mary Stebbins (Williamstown, VT)

Elmer M., d. 10/27/1938 at 74/9/9 in Sanbornville; b. Wenham, MA;
Robert A. Cook and Emily M. Shattuck

Emily A., d. 6/26/1895 at 54; widow; b. Wenham, MA; Nathaniel Shattuck
(Andover, MA) and Sally Cook (Wenham, MA)

Emily A., d. 12/20/1909 at 73/7/6; housekeeper; single; b. Middleton; Isiah
Cook (Middleton) and Joanna Pike (Middleton)

Frank Raymond, d. 11/26/1978 at 79 in Wolfeboro; Frank C. Cook and
Annie Norton

Gilbert, d. 12/17/1953 at 86 in Concord; b. Wakefield; Peter Cook and
Sarah J. Gage

Harold M., d. 2/25/1958 at 51 in Rochester; b. Wakefield; Elmer Cook and
Lillian Cook

Haven N., d. 2/1/1893 at 60; farmer; widower; b. Wakefield; Benjamin
Cook (Wakefield) and Mary Burley (Sandwich)

Joseph L., d. 6/10/1976 at 64 in Dover; James L. Cook and Ida Richards

Lillian B., d. 9/22/1932 at 63/5/1 in Sanbornville

Lizzie S., d. 6/4/1914 at 75/8/23; housekeeper; widow; b. Acton, ME;
Luther Sanborn (Acton, ME) and Abigail Berry (Milton)

Wilfred A., d. 11/14/1935 at 63/8/10 in Sanbornville; b. Wakefield; Robert
Cook and Emily M. Shattuck

Wilheminas, d. 11/11/1989 at 87 in Rochester

COPP,

Emily S., d. 3/2/1892 at 57/8/20; housework; married; b. Wakefield; John
Paul (Sanford, ME) and Eliza Lord (Sanford, ME)

Frederick A., d. 11/6/1913 at 91/4/7; widower; b. Wakefield; George W.
Copp (Wakefield) and Sarah Palmer (Wakefield)

CORMIER,

Norma, d. 8/24/1990 at 67 in Rochester

CORNO,

Orilla S., d. 6/19/1962 at 79 in Wolfeboro; b. Epping; Ivah Thurston and
Sarah Johnson

CORRELL,
Fred C., Sr., d. 1/22/1991 at 80; Theodore Correll and Maggie Chilsom

CORSON,
Idella L., d. 1/21/1960 at 94 in Portland, ME
John Edwin, d. 8/20/1940 at 85/10/25 in Sanbornville; b. Wakefield; Robert Corson and Sarah Nay
Raymond S., d. 12/26/1960 at 66 in Manchester
Sarah, d. 2/15/1908 at 91/5/9; housewife; widow; b. Ossipee; Joseph Nay (Ossipee) and Mary Haines (Wolfeboro)
Sylvia D., d. 8/18/1984 at 89 in Wolfeboro; Nathaniel Cook and Cynthia Caverly
Vina A., d. 12/1/1960 at 85 in Wolfeboro; b. Westville, NS; Robert Simpson and Charlotte Higgins

COTE,
Eugene, d. 3/27/1952 at 83/0/13 in Union; b. St. Vesta, PQ

COTTLE,
Charles J., d. 1/10/1892 at 84/10/23; farmer; widower; b. Kittery, ME; Joshua Cottle (Eliot, ME) and Abigail Cole (Eliot, ME)
Emily A., d. 4/4/1923 at 83; housekeeper; single; b. Wakefield; Charles Cottle (Kittery, ME) and Eliza Cotton (Wolfeboro)
Martha M., d. 10/9/1924 at 77/11/27; at home; single; b. Brookfield; Joshua Cottle (Kittery, ME) and Martha Weeks (Wakefield)
Phineas O., d. 12/30/1909 at 61/3/19; retired; single; b. Brookfield; Joshua Cottle (Eliot, ME) and Martha Weeks (Wakefield)

COTTON,
Annie S., d. 11/22/1900 at 78/0/8; housewife; widow; b. Moultonboro; Joseph Richardson and Dolly B. Moulton
Charles A., d. 10/20/1979 at 54 in Sanbornville; John A. Cotton and Mary L. Neal
Henry J., d. 8/6/1970 at 49 in Sanbornville; John A. Cotton and Mary L. Neal
Mary Leona, d. 7/17/1960 at 74 in Brookfield

COUNTER,
George H., d. 4/16/1956 at 91 in Union; b. Burke, VT; Joseph Counter and Adeline Counter

COURIER,
Edward E., d. 11/20/1963 at 82 in Wolfeboro; b. Gloucester, MA; Antone J. Courier and Mary E. Moore
George, d. 3/1/1906 at 55/5/18; laborer; married; b. Liverpool, PQ; Joseph Courier (Canada) and Ange'e Levertu (Canada)

COUTURE,
Lawrier, d. 4/8/1957 at 29; b. Berlin; Antoine Couture and Alvina LaMontagne

COVEY,
Ernest Frederick, d. 7/15/1995 at 71 in Dover; Hiram Covey and Margaret Cornock

COVILLE,
Annie, d. 1/19/1930 at 75; widow; b. Lynn, MA

COWAN,
Erford O., d. 3/13/1966 at 51; b. Sanbornville; Lester Cowan and Nellie A. Libbey
Marcelle M., d. 5/6/1986 at 63 in Dover
Nellie E., d. 3/9/1955 at 66 in Brookfield

COWLEY,
Elsa, d. 10/14/1956 at 52 in Burlington, VT

COWPER,
Frances, d. 2/23/1968 at 81 in Concord; Frederick J. Cowper and Emma Kidd
Henry L., d. 5/27/1932 at 44/4/27 in Northampton, MA

COX,
Claris Grace, d. 5/5/1940 at 68/2/8 in Wolfeboro; b. NS; George Withers and Annie Rooney
Earle E., d. 7/11/1978 at 85 in East Wakefield; Henry P. Cox

COYNER,
Mark Thomas, d. 7/29/1996 at 42; Harry Regis Coyner and Patricia Kelley

CRAM,
Hope M., d. 11/20/1981 at 62; Henry LeClair and Flora McKinnon

CRANDALL,
I. Leah, d. 10/14/1977 at 90 in Wolfeboro; Edward E. Crandall

CRATEAU,
daughter, d. 6/21/1904 at 0/0/0; b. Wakefield; Edward Crateau (Canada)
child, d. 3/9/1912 at 0/0/0; b. Wakefield; Edward Crateau (Canada) and Emily Rhobinhymer (Canada)
Grace C., d. 8/9/1911 at 6/6/12; b. Wakefield; Edward Crateau (Canada) and Roben Hymer (Canada)

CRAWFORD,
Warren E., d. 11/21/1981 at 56 in East Wakefield; Irving Crawford and Gladys Lane

CREASER,
Corrie M., d. 3/17/1983 at 91 in Palmer, MA
Frank R., d. 11/9/1964 at 73 in Sanbornville; b. No. Thetford, VT; Samuel Creaser and Matilda Ritcie

CREDIFORD,
Lila I., d. 3/13/1993 at 86 in Ossipee; Freeman Langley and Kate Davis
Roger H., d. 12/20/1955 at 53 in Sanbornville; b. Shapleigh, ME; Joseph Crediford and Margaret Higgins

CRENSHAW,
Laura L., d. 7/12/1958 at 2; b. Chelsea, MA; George Crenshaw and Helen M. Crew

CRISPELL,
Patricia J., d. 9/30/1996 at 73

CRITCHERSON,
George W., d. 3/12/1976 at 68 in Brookfield; Ralph H. Critcherson and Jessie Horton

CROCKER,
Bertha J., d. 1/16/1970 at 83 in Dover

George H., d. 3/18/1925 at 52/0/26; married; b. Bangor, ME; ---- Crocker and Abbie Willey

Lydia E., d. 11/5/1913 at 45/8/18; housewife; married; b. Biddeford, ME; Elijah Drown (Eaton)

CROCKETT,
Bessie M., d. 8/25/1982 at 93 in Arlington, VA
George W., d. 8/7/1963 at 77 in Arlington, VA

CRONIN,
Louis, d. 5/31/1948 at 65/8/12 in Sanbornville; b. Bangor, ME; Daniel Cronin and Mary Jordan

CROUSE,
John Southworth, d. 10/3/1994 at 82 in Rochester; St. Claire Crouse and Edith Swindells

CROWLEY,
Mary Montogomery, d. 9/29/1990 at 79 in Wolfeboro; John Montogomery and Isabella McCay

Stephen J., d. 11/21/1965 at 62 in Norwood, MA

Teresa P., d. 2/16/1968 at 89 in Norwood, MA

William J., d. 11/14/1990 at 80 in Wolfeboro; Patrick W. Crowley and Nora O'Callahan

CRUM,
M. Eliza, b. 3/1/1947 at 79/1/6 in Union; b. Acton, ME; Josiah Witham and Abbie Willey

CURRIER,
Alfred A., d. 12/4/1892 at 0/2/11; b. Wakefield; Fred Currier (Canada) and Virginia Duval (Milton Mills)

David A., d. 10/13/1981 at 38 in York, ME

CURRY,
Harriet, d. 5/16/1942 at 67/11/12 in Ossipee; b. Milton Mills; Benjamin Goodwin and Emma A. Wentworth

John Thomas, d. 6/13/1945 at 93/1/15; b. Lenox, MA; Alex Curry and Mary Cassidy

CURTIS,
Eva M., d. 4/6/1893 at 0/8/25; b. Wakefield; Joseph S. Curtis (Brookfield) and Fannie E. Butler (Lebanon, ME)
Fannie E., d. 12/18/1904 at 42/8/25; housewife; married; b. Lebanon, ME; Francis Butler (Lebanon, ME) and Martha A. Jones (Lebanon, ME)
Mary M.W., d. 9/14/1933 at 77/5/5
Sarah A., d. 7/10/1962 at 76 in Saugus, MA
William Jascal, d. 9/18/1940 at 67/11/5 in E. Wakefield; b. Newfoundland; William Curtis and Jane Kennedy
Winfred F., d. 1/17/1958 at 73 in Saugus, MA
Winslow Sheridan, d. 4/7/1997 at 82 in Wolfeboro; Ray Curtis and Bessie Sheridan

CUTTER,
Clarence E., d. 5/29/1987 at 86 in East Wakefield; Edward A. Cutter and Lydia W. Balcom

DAGGERT,
Donald L., d. 11/21/1974 at 49 in Hancock County, ME

DAGGET,
Barbara, d. 10/30/1988 at 66 in Auburn, ME

DAMARIS,
John, d. 12/13/1937 at 80 in Sanbornville; b. Canada; Marshall Damaris and Mary Barton

DAME,
Daniel E., d. 4/4/1958 at 85 in Union; b. Portsmouth; Howard Dame and Fidelia Moore
Fred S., d. 3/11/1935 at 74/8/12 in Union; b. Rochester; Josiah Dame and Lydia Dame
Howard E., d. 12/27/1975 at 60 in Rochester; Daniel E. Dame and Josephine Pinkham
Laura J., d. 2/20/1965 at 73 in Union; b. Middleton; George Pinkham

DANFORTH,
Alfred H., d. 2/4/1952 at 91/0/2 in Union; b. Franklin; James Danforth and Lucretia Austin

DAVENPORT,
George Henry, d. 9/10/1940 at 69/1/27 in Wolfeboro; b. Tonawanda, NY; James Davenport and Mary Ryan
George Henry, d. 9/3/1992 at 71 in Wolfeboro; George H. Davenport and Wilda E. Whitten
Wilda E., d. 10/23/1985 at 87 in Ossipee; Daniel A. Whitten and Annie Pelletier

DAVIS,
son, d. 5/21/1900 at 0/0/4 in Sanbornville; b. Sanbornville; Curtis A. Davis (Bradford) and Grace E. Howland (Lyme)
Annie J., d. 2/8/1936 at 71/5/9 in Sanbornville; b. Strafford; Charles Montgomery and Mary E. Locke
Bertha T., d. 9/24/1936 at 66/7/15 in Wolfeboro; b. Wakefield; Malcolm McDonald and Amanda Crockett
Carrie B., d. 3/21/1922 at 67/2/7; housewife; widow; b. Balch Mills, ME; Winthrop Tuttle (NH) and Nancy Folsom (NH)
Charles S., d. 4/28/1962 at 73 in Wolfeboro; b. Sanbornville; Wilbert Davis and Annie J. Montgomery
Clarence E., d. 9/20/1960 at 79 in Wolfeboro; b. Wakefield; Daniel S. Davis and Martha Horn
Daniel S., d. 11/18/1917 at 77/8/3; farmer; widower; b. Newfield, ME; Timothy Davis and Belinda Knox
Ellwood, d. 1/15/1961 at 73 in Concord; b. Philadelphia, PA; James Davis and ----- Hooker
Emily S., d. 11/12/1906 at 83/11/17; housework; widow; b. Portland, ME
Frederick H., d. 12/31/1948 at 87/11/9 in Sandwich
Gertrude, d. 8/16/1953 at 84 in Concord; b. Wolfeboro; Charles E. Abbott and Alice S. Young
Harriett, d. 1/29/1986 at 70 in ME
Jonathan J., d. 5/9/1891 at 73/9/9; farmer; married; b. Nottingham
Lillian, d. 8/16/1937 at 65/1/10 in Wolfeboro; b. Alton; Daniel S. Davis and Martha Horn
Lynn R., d. 2/25/1988 at 77 in Wolfeboro
Marjorie W., d. 11/7/1998 at 81 in North Conway; Henry Walmsley and Charlotte Allerby
Martha H., d. 12/13/1893 at 57/0/16; housework; married; b. Wakefield; Stephen Horn (Wakefield) and Abigail Lord
Mayhew C., d. 8/15/1895 at 60/2/13; farmer; married; b. Wakefield; Timothy Davis (Newfield, ME) and Belinda Knox (Newfield, ME)

Minnie May, d. 11/30/1898 at 0/4/12; b. Wakefield; George Davis (Wakefield) and Fanny Reed (Milton)

Teresa Wisniewski, d. 3/11/1997 at 59 in Rochester; Stephen Walter Wisniewski and Josephine Genevieve Baron

DEALAND,
Julia A., d. 11/2/1916 at 76/0/23; housework; widow; b. New Durham; John Willey and Lovey Watson (Gilmanton)

DEAN,
Rexford Stanley, d. 7/16/1988 at 86 in North Wakefield; Austin Dean and Carrie Clayton

DEANGELIS,
Mollie L., d. 9/20/1985 at 79 in Sanbornville; Gabriel Matarazza

DEARBORN,
Nora G., d. 8/28/1909 at 50/2; housework; married; b. Lowell, MA; Nathan Chapman (Milton) and Jane Gardner (ME)

Thomas E., d. 5/10/1936 at 83/5/14 in Sanbornville; b. Candia

DEBOW,
Christopher A., d. 3/7/1973 at 7 in Sanbornville; Lawrence DeBow and Rena Stetson

DECIACCIO,
Joaquin, d. 9/15/1931

DEE,
Frederick John, d. 9/3/1982 at 2 mins. in Dover; Raymond H. Dee and Nancy Dean

DELAN,
Dora Belle, d. 1/8/1940 at 60/7/21 in Sanbornville; b. Sanbornville; Horatio B. Fellows and Belle Frances Tibbetts

DELAND,
Thomas T., d. 3/3/1904 at 83/9/6; farmer; married; b. Brookfield; John Deland (Brookfield) and May Roberts (Brookfield)

DELANO,
George W., d. 8/6/1914 at 60/6/6; farmer; married; b. Bath, ME; John
    Delano (Seguin, ME) and Catherine Gould (Wiscasset, ME)

DELOREY,
John Roger, d. 10/8/1995 at 85 in Ft. Myers, FL; William Delorey and
    Elizabeth Rogers

DEMERS,
Georgianora T., d. 1/10/1937 at 74/6/27 in Sanbornville; b. Canada; Alene
    Thiboult and Philone Fortin

DENSON,
Rena M., d. 3/5/1986 at 77 in Portland, ME

DEROCHER,
Philbert J., d. 3/3/1941 at 67/10/20; b. Canada; Joseph Derocher and
    Suffrine Derocher

DESHARNAIS,
Alfred, d. 12/24/1927 at 56/10/5; married; b. Nuthot Mills, Quebec; Lewis
    Descharnais and Celena Wood

DESROCHERS,
Henry, d. 6/18/1905 at 0/0/0 in Sanbornville; b. Sanbornville; Philibert
    Desrochers (Canada) and Marie Marcoux (Sanbornville)
Marie L., d. 7/1/1957 at 75 in Nashua; b. Sanbornville; Etienne Marcoux
    and Aledase Marchand
Mary, d. 3/17/1904 at 0/0/0; b. Wakefield; Philbert Derrochers (sic)
    (Canada) and Mary Marcoux (Wakefield)

DEVENS,
George W., d. 7/4/1963 at 91 in Wolfeboro; b. Philipsport, NY; Elias W.
    Devens and Catherine Sherwood

DEVINS,
Lizzie M., d. 6/15/1957 at 84 in Sanbornville; b. Wurthboro, NY;
    Zackariah T. Johnson and Harriet A. Bedford

DEWOLF,
Carla M., d. 3/9/1962 at 0/8/21 in Hanover; b. Wolfeboro; Donald DeWolf and Davena Rogers
Davena Rogers, d. 12/21/1993 at 59; Vincent D. Rogers and Marion Hayes

DEXHEIMER,
John P., III, d. 1/14/1979 at 78 in Hanover; John P. Dexheimer and Helen Stocum

DICK,
Roy Charles, d. 9/9/1974 at 13 in Wolfeboro; Roy Dick and Elizabeth Conover

DILLAWAY,
Arthur W., d. 8/1/1962 at 77 in Medford, MA
Langdon H., d. 10/23/1974 at 61 in Winchester, MA
Lillian M., d. 2/23/1966 at 76 in Reading, MA

DIXON,
Bessie F., d. 8/5/1959 at 60 in Union; b. Woodstock, NB; George W. Wiggin and Lillian Campbell
George R., d. 10/16/1977 at 87 in Union; George E. Dixon and Ellen Austin

DODGE,
John W., d. 1/19/1963 at 91 in Sanbornville; b. So. Berwick, ME; Everett Dodge and Sabina Ricker

DODIER,
Alcide J., d. 7/22/1962 at 58 in Portsmouth; b. Sanbornville; Joseph Dodier and Edith Perron
Alfred J., d. 7/9/1979 at 72 in Sanbornville; Joseph Dodier and Edith Parent
Archie J., d. 11/17/1987 at 79; Joseph Dodier and Edith Perron
Bessie E., d. 6/22/1894 at 0/7/5; b. Wakefield; Frank Dodier (Canada) and Georgiana Custo (Canada)
Donald R., d. 7/15/1984 at 56 in Wolfeboro; Frank Dodier and Evangeline Young
Edith, d. 3/20/1955 at 81 in Concord; b. Canada; Damien Perron and Virginia Tremblay

Edward Joseph, d. 7/8/1944 at 44/2/8 in Rochester; b. Sanbornville; Herode J. Dodier and Edith Perron
Evangeline C., d. 11/11/1967 at 71 in Rochester; b. Newfoundland; Matthew Young
Frank J., d. 4/29/1896 at 0/8 in Sanbornville; b. Sanbornville; Joseph Dodier (Canada) and Ouida Perron (Canada)
Frank Joseph, d. 3/19/1944 at 47/1/17 in Sanbornville; b. Sanbornville; Joseph Dodier and Edith Perron
Jennie, d. 10/11/1984 at 9 hrs. in Dover
Joseph H., d. 7/2/1938 at 67/3/20 in Sanbornville; b. Thetford Mines, Canada; Baptiste Dodier and Philomene Ferland
Leonard Paul, d. 8/4/1933 at 0/6/19
Lydia, d. 11/6/1895 at 5/6; b. Wakefield; Frank Dodier (Canada) and Georgia Dodier (Canada)
Ralph W., d. 8/5/1984 at 62 in Sanbornville; Frank Dodier and Evangeline Young
Wayne, d. 10/13/1972 at 21 in Farmington; Donald R. Dodier and Ruth E. Valley

DOE,
Anna Marie, d. 7/26/1949 at 64/8/29; b. Cambridge, MA; Julius C. Pawlowski and Augusta Grohn
George A., d. 1/13/1971 at 88 in Wolfeboro; Tristram Doe and Fannie Stone
Margaret P., d. 10/2/1975 at 73 in Rochester; Henry Paul and Nancy Libby

DOHERTY,
Alden J., Jr., d. 4/11/1974 at 46; Alden J. Doherty and Glenis Staples

DOLAN,
Fred, d. 5/25/1927 at 77/2/9; married; Patrick Dolan and Mary
Rose Ellen, d. 1/24/1934 at 82/8/5; b. Bartlett; Jacob Hill and Margaret Gray

DONAHUE,
Margaret F., d. 12/26/1970 at 34 in Sanbornville; Joseph Donahue and Lillian Warren
P. Joseph, d. 4/11/1986 at 73 in Rochester; Timothy Donahue and Fedora Charpentier

DONNELLY,
William F., d. 1/25/1986 at 67 in Rochester; Herbert Donnelly and Ida McKuhen

DONOLLEY,
David, d. 8/22/1978 at 24 in Ossipee

DOPHENY,
Ramie, d. 3/25/1925 at 60/9/27; widower; b. Canada

DORE,
Anna M., d. 7/26/1973 at 74 in Portsmouth; Nicholas Cole and Mary Skane
Gilman P., d. 2/8/1896 at --; carpenter; married
Harry B., d. 4/4/1962 at 76 in York, ME; b. Wakefield; Gilman Dore and Katherine Donovan
Hattie M., d. 1/15/1958 at 85 in Portsmouth; b. Sanbornville; Charles A. Rines and Mary A. Roberts
Katie C., d. 5/15/1932 at 86/5/9 in Portsmouth
Lewis G., d. 8/24/1944 at 73/3/15 in Portsmouth; b. Wakefield; Gilman P. Dore and Katie C. Donovan
William F.H., d. 7/6/1979 at 59 in Portsmouth

DORNAN,
John Wright, d. 3/26/1989 at 72 in Rochester; James L. Dornan and Amelia H. Hemmingway

DORR,
George S., d. 5/2/1907 at 55/11/20; editor; married; b. Wakefield; Charles Dorr (Milton) and Mary Shackford (Newington)

DOUCETTE,
Henry C., d. 8/5/1976 at 62 in Wolfeboro; James H. Doucette and Delima Boucher
John P., d. 11/21/1993 at 36; Lucien Doucette and Rita Carrier

DOUGLAS,
child, d. 9/10/1911 at 0/0/1; b. Wakefield; Frank Douglas (Albany) and Jennie Harmon (Brookfield)

DOUGLASS,
James W., d. 7/29/1922 at 66/3/3; farmer; married; b. Bridgton, ME; William Douglass
Rose A., d. 11/19/1923 at 69/0/11; housekeeper; widow; b. Eaton; Daniel Thurston (Eaton) and Mary Littlefield (Eaton)

DOW,
Anna DeBevoise, d. 1/1/1905 at 88/5/24; housewife; widow; b. Brooklyn, NY; Christopher Prince (Boston, MA) and Annie Duffield (Brooklyn, NY)
David Sterling, d. 5/24/1952 at 60/3/18 in Sanbornville; b. MA; David Dow and Jennie Dow
Harriette, d. 7/10/1904 at 84/8/8; spinster; single; b. Wakefield; Josiah Dow (Wakefield) and Rebecca Marie Phippin (Salem, MA)
Josiah, d. 2/14/1925 at 89/0/2; widower; b. Brooklyn, NY; George W. Dow and Anna Prince
Mary Pickering, d. 11/13/1944 at 82/3/16 in Sanbornville; b. Salem, MA; Josiah Dow and Katherine Downing

DOWD,
John F., d. 2/5/1950 at 53/0/19 in Sanbornville; b. Portsmouth; John H. Dowd and Eleanor Hutchings

DOWDEN,
Alfred L., d. 12/13/1988 at 81 in Wolfeboro; Alfred Dowden

DOWNS,
son, d. 1/9/1925 at 0/0/0; b. Wakefield; Winfred E. Downs and Carrie S. Wentworth
Abbie E., d. 4/2/1930 at 76/8/24; b. Conway; John Eastman and Martha Farnum
Carrie W., d. 11/29/1986 at 94 in Ossipee; Fred S. Wentworth and Delia Barker
Cora L., d. 4/8/1923 at 60/1/17; at home; married; b. Fryeburg, ME; Joseph Hamilton (Eaton) and Betsey G. Hart (Brownfield, ME)
Edna B., d. 5/27/1961 at 84 in Wolfeboro; b. Sanbornville; George Downs and Abbie Eastman
Eva M., d. 6/12/1960 at 74 in Milton
Floy L., d. 10/8/1918 at 25/8/8; housewife; married; b. Somerset, MA; John E. Everingham (Canada) and Florence Coleman (Portsmouth)

George E., d. 12/30/1907 at 58/1/2; laborer; married; b. Rochester; John R. Downs (Rochester) and Mary Shorey (Rochester)

James M., d. 5/21/1982 at 26 in Union; Fred W. Downs and Hilda E. Joy

John F., d. 4/14/1922 at 62/4/16; no occ.; single; b. Milton Mills; John R. Downs (E. Rochester) and Mary L. Shorey (E. Rochester)

John R., d. 6/30/1904 at 83/2; farmer; widower; b. Rochester; Aaron Downs (Rochester)

Mary A., d. 8/12/1899 at 71/1/12; housework; married; b. Lebanon, ME

Phoebe A., d. 12/2/1913 at 76/11/20; retired; widow; b. Tamworth; William Stanley and Nancy Perkins

Thomas Jefferson, d. 1/22/1940 at 80/1/25 in Sanbornville; b. Milton; John R. Downs and Mary Shorey

Winfred E., d. 11/5/1968 at 80 in Wolfeboro; Thomas J. Downs and Cora Hamilton

DOYLE,

Clayton Cecil, d. 7/5/1920 at 3/8/27; accid. drowning; b. Wakefield; Smith Pike (Milton Mills) and Mabel E. Doyle (Wakefield)

George H., d. 8/18/1946 at 68/0/17 in Rochester; b. Wakefield; John Doyle and Amanda E. Wentworth

Hannah, d. 12/17/1932 at 47/0/2 in Wolfeboro

John, d. 11/27/1922 at 83/6/18; no occ.; widower; b. New York, NY

Manda E., d. 7/7/1894 at 38/2/12; housekeeper; married; William Wentworth (Milton) and Emeline Blazo (Newmarket)

DRAKE,

Chester H., d. 5/26/1960 at 85; b. Effingham; John Drake and Julia Hardy

Oscar H., d. 1/5/1968 at 66 in Wolfeboro; Chester Drake and Grace Ward

DRAPEAU,

Aurelie C., d. 9/10/1937 at 76/10/10 in Sanbornville; b. Canada; Joseph Carrier and Angel Lavertu

Donat, d. 10/2/1903 at 0/3/2 in Sanbornville; b. Sac; Eusebe Drapeau (Canada) and Orille Corrier (Canada)

Eusebe, d. 5/23/1940 at 79 in Fall River, MA; b. Canada; Noel Drapeau

Eva, d. 1/28/1897 at 5/5; b. Wakefield; Eusebe Drapeau (Canada) and Arille Currier (Canada)

Genevieve, d. 4/15/1941 at 75 in Manchester; b. Canada

Thalia B., d. 10/13/1998 at 71 in Wolfeboro; Arthur L. Bailey and Eleanor ----

DRAPER,
Kenneth L., d. 2/15/1914 at 12/11/21; b. Greenland; Alvah E. Draper (Plymouth) and Mary A. Dustan (Salisbury)

DRESSER,
Bert A., d. 3/13/1956 at 81 in Ossipee
Mary, d. 2/27/1950 at 71/9/28 in East Wakefield; b. Portsmouth; Andrew Geddie and Annie Coville

DREW,
son, d. 6/3/1906 at 0/0/0; b. Union; John W. Drew (Cambridge, ME) and Mary A. Farrell (Ireland)
daughter, d. 5/8/1926 at 0/0/0; b. Wakefield; Harold S. Drew and Charlotte Brown
Austin F., d. 2/22/1960 at 50 in Wolfeboro; b. Ossipee; Frank Drew and Amanda Williams
Burrows, d. 2/21/1888 at 85/0/21; farmer; widower; b. VT; Daniel Drew (Middleton) and Sally Smith (VT)
Charles A., d. 4/18/1931 at 44/4/5; married; b. Wakefield; James Drew and Clara Drew
Charlotte B., d. 10/17/1977 at 80 in Union; Plummer Brown and Laura Rice
Clara A., d. 10/7/1922 at 70/3/22; at home; married; b. New Durham; Joseph Glidden (New Durham)
Clarence L., d. 2/21/1970 at 83 in Milton
Cora A., d. 6/4/1935 at 52/7/16 in Milton; b. Conway; Harding Nason and Lucinda Thorne
Edward F., d. 11/24/1928 at 0/2/6; b. Union; Charles A. Drew and Cora M. Dunn
Fannie J., d. 4/28/1893 at 1/0/20; b. Wakefield; James A. Drew (Brookfield) and Clara A. Glidden (Alton)
George, d. 11/23/1943 at 68 in Ossipee
George W., d. 6/16/1897 at 80/1/3; carpenter; widower; b. Acton, ME; Asa Drew (Acton, ME) and Mary Ricker (Acton, ME)
George W., d. 8/13/1941 at 80/9/5; b. Exeter; George W. Drew and Lydia Archibald
Harold S., d. 3/12/1974 at 78 in Rochester; George W. Drew and Malie Stevens
Harriet L., d. 8/8/1960 at 71 in Rochester; b. No. Adams, MA; Augustus Locke and Martha Perkins

Irving, d. 5/17/1903 at 24/11/8; laborer; single; b. Brookfield; Henry
Drew, Sr. (Brookfield) and Emeline Dyer (Porter, ME)
Ivory, d. 10/31/1902 at 84/11/20 in Union; farmer; widower; b. Brookfield;
Joseph Drew (Brookfield) and Susan Chamberlin (Brookfield)
Jimmie, d. 12/4/1896 at 16/11/24; day laborer; b. Brookfield; James A.
Drew (Brookfield) and Clara A. Glidden (Alton)
Joanna H., d. 4/8/1943 at 82/3/2 in Union; b. Wolfeboro; Amos E. Bradley
and Sarah F. Kenney
John Edward, d. 7/2/1953 at 68 in Union; b. Brookfield; John E. Drew and
Addie Thibodeau
John W., d. 2/16/1909 at 61/1/27; laborer; married; b. Eaton; Jefferson
Drew (Eaton) and Matilda Wilkinson (Alton)
Lydia W., d. 4/13/1892 at 70/1/9; housework; married; b. Acton, ME;
John Archibald and Sally
Lyle S., d. 10/1/1961 at 70 in Union; b. Union; George W. Drew and
Malie E. Drew
Malie E., d. 8/30/1938 at 71/0/8 in Union; b. Middleton; Thomas J.
Stevens and Mary Whitehouse
Maude, d. 2/22/1967 at 74 in Concord; b. Kingfisher, OK; George Mooney
and Clara Giffin
Rebeccah F., d. 4/20/1990 at 0/4/8 in Plattsburgh, NY
Robert F., d. 7/18/1937 at 64/2/15 in Sanbornville; b. Madison; Enoch L.
Drew and Mary E. Frost
William H., d. 11/14/1891 at 42/1/11; foreman; widower; b. Wakefield;
Burrows Drew and Betsy Wentworth (Ossipee)

DROUIN,
Amanda, d. 11/10/1906 at 39/1/3; mill operative; married; b. Canada;
Pierre Drouin (Canada) and Cezaire Routhier (Canada)

DROWN,
Alice H., d. 3/10/1986 at 81 in Rochester; William C. Haskell and Alice G.
Hotchkiss
Carrie C., d. 10/28/1938 at 66/3/25 in Wolfeboro; b. Farmington;
Benjamin Peavey and Mary Lougee
Carroll E., d. 10/13/1918 at 21/7/21; laborer; married; b. Farmington;
Stephen D. Drown (Eaton) and Carrie C. Peavey (Farmington)
Edgar, Jr., d. 10/14/1935 at 18/1/20 in Wolfeboro; b. Wakefield; Edgar
Drown and Irene Newcomb

Edgar I., d. 8/20/1965 at 72 in Wolfeboro; b. Ossipee; Stephen D. Drown and Cynthia C. Peavey
Edith I., d. 10/25/1978 at 82 in Rochester; Nathan Newcomb
Franklin W., d. 6/4/1902 at 0/4; b. Wakefield; Stephen D. Drowns (sic) (Eaton) and Carrie C. Peavey (Farmington)
Herbert L., d. 8/25/1963 at 63 in Wolfeboro; b. Wakefield; Stephen D. Drown and Carrie Peavey
Myra F., d. 3/17/1975 at 75 in Rochester; George Rourke and Evie Nichols
Stephen D., d. 2/10/1943 at 70/10/1; b. Eaton; Elijah Drown and Victoria Harriman

DRUGG,
Charles James, Jr., d. 11/23/1998 at 76 in Wolfeboro; Charles James Drugg, Sr. and Grace R. Northrop

DRURY,
Charlotte M., d. 6/28/1922 at 76/9/26; dressmaker; widow; b. Wakefield; W. B. Wentworth (Wakefield) and Adeline Belding (Amherst, MA)
Harold Arthur, d. 7/13/1975 at 71 in Manchester; Everett C. Drury and Helen V. Brooks

DUCHANO,
child, d. 12/30/1945 at 0/0/0 in Wolfeboro; b. Wolfeboro; Omer A. Duchano and Muriel Wiggin
daughter, d. 12/4/1953 at 0/0/0 in Wolfeboro; b. Wolfeboro; Donald Duchano and Rosalyn Ring
Donald, d. 10/19/1989 at 34 in Boston, MA
Doris, d. 3/31/1965 at 56 in Sanbornville; n. Ossipee; John Pratt and Mildred Mills
Duris, d. 4/19/1917 at 14/11/21; b. Middleton; Moses Duchano (Canada) and Mary Welch (Ossipee)
Marjorie W., d. 3/29/1988 at 61 in Wolfeboro
Mary Harriet, d. 5/7/1954 at 68 in Sanbornville; b. Salmon Falls; Joseph Welch and Exilda Rivers
Mary Irene, d. 10/1/1923 at 2/7/4; b. Wakefield; Mose Duchano (Canada) and Mary Welch (Ossipee)
Oscar J., d. 8/12/1974 at 67 in Rochester; Moses J. Duchano and Mary Welch
Raymond, d. 3/2/1915 at 0/8/28; b. Wakefield; Moses Duchano (Canada) and Marie Welch (Ossipee)

Raymond, d. 11/13/1937 at 20/8/10 in Sanbornville; b. Wakefield; Moses Duchano and Mary Welch

DUCHESNEAU,
Moses, d. 10/7/1932 at 59/2/8 in Rochester

DUDLEY,
Fred W., d. 3/4/1936 at 68/4/8 in Wolfeboro
Fred W., d. 3/25/1993 at 66 in Wolfeboro; Winburn T. Dudley and Pauline Moulton
Pauline M., d. 1/13/1981 at 73 in Rochester; Arthur P. Moulton and Maude Smith
Winburn T., d. 1/27/1980 at 80 in Rochester; Fred W. Dudley and Harriett Towle

DUGAN,
Michael, d. 9/7/1917 at 57/8/16; married; b. Ireland; William Dugan (Ireland) and Mary Fitzgerald (Ireland)

DUGUAY,
Clifford A., d. 6/22/1987 at 49 in Wolfeboro

DUKE,
Marshall, d. 4/8/1940 at 85/5/28 in Sanbornville; b. Canada
Matilda, d. 9/24/1938 at 74/9/2 in Sanbornville; b. Island Pond, Canada; Edward Hall and Mary Hall

DUNHAM,
Harvey, d. 3/3/1907 at 86/6/28; farmer; widower; b. Mansfield, CT; Royal Dunham and Abiah Lamb
Walter J., d. 6/18/1967 at 56; b. Boston, MA

DUNK,
Harry N., d. 1/26/1970 at 67 in Rochester; Albert Dunk and Grace Graves
Marion T., d. 10/31/1990 at 89 in Rochester; Albert McManus and Christina McLeod
Philip Herbert, d. 2/11/1975 at 44 in Providence, RI

DUNNELLS,
Annette J., d. 1/13/1986 at 75 in Rochester; Frank Joy and Alice Kimball

DUPREY,
Harry, d. 1/13/1919 at 34/5/18; influenza, pneumonia; laborer; widower; b. Canada; Alfred Duprey (Canada) and Emma E. Quimby (Bow)

DUPRINS,
Alice, d. 10/10/1924 at 21/3/9 in Sanbornville; domestic; b. Salmon Falls; Joseph Duprin (Canada) and Elilda Rivers (Canada)

DUQUETTE,
Emma, d. 4/25/1958 at 86 in Union; b. Canada; Nazaire Houle and Marie St. Cyr
Leon, d. 9/25/1958 at 87 in Union; b. Canada

DURETTE,
Raoul, d. 11/23/1955 at 51 in Sanbornville; b. Canada; Captan Durette and Arthimise Durette

DURKEE,
Cora Belle, d. 10/9/1952 at 56/4/3 in Sanbornville; b. Bridgewater, VT; David H. Newton and Betsy F. Woodard

DURRELL,
George W., d. 11/4/1910 at 72/4/11; laborer; married; b. Wakefield; Nathaniel Durrell and Mahalie Whitehouse
Mary, d. 12/4/1897 at 62/7/4; housewife; single; Nathaniel Durrell (Lebanon, ME) and Mahala Whitehouse
Sarah E., d. 3/3/1918 at 83/4/3; housewife; widow; b. Acton, ME

DYER,
Lorel M., d. 7/22/1895 at 0/3/24; b. Wakefield; Nellie M. Dyer (Brownfield, ME)
Rosa M., d. 4/9/1910 at 0/7/24; b. Wakefield; Joseph Dyer (Canada) and Edith Perron (Canada)

EARLE,
Ellen D., d. 6/1/1955 at 79 in Union; b. Farmington; Oscar S. Dudley and Laurie A. Bunker

EASTMAN,
Edward P., d. 1/20/1917 at 78/7/20; clergyman; married; b. Conway; John
L. Eastman (Conway) and Margaret Douglass (Portland, ME)
Eliza S., d. 3/14/1935 at 82/6/5 in Union; b. Woodfords, ME; Frederick E.
Sawyer and Harriet Morrill
Evelyn M., d. 8/2/1964 at 36 in Wolfeboro; b. Lexington, MA; George
Holman and Lillian Wood
Harriet F., d. 2/3/1960 at 85 in Union; b. Gray, ME; Edward P. Eastman
and Eliza N. Sawyer
Louise Snow, d. 11/16/1951 at 80 in Union; b. No. Conway; Edward P.
Eastman and Eliza N. Sawyer
Robert E., d. 8/31/1946 at 15/8/22 in Rochester; b. Wolfeboro; Anna
Eastman

EATON,
Florence L., d. 1/30/1965 at 84 in Rochester; b. Stowe, ME; Albert C.
Elkins and Emma Wentworth
John C., d. 12/12/1926 at 79/7/11; married; b. Wolfeboro; Chandler Eaton
and Mary Cottle
Lois H., d. 4/27/1925 at 79/3/21; married; b. Wolfeboro; Daniel Martin
and Sophia Fernald
Martin H., d. 9/11/1961 at 82 in Rochester; b. Brookfield; John C. Eaton
and Lois Martin
Philip Fred, d. 3/31/1938 at 55/2/14 in Sanbornville; b. Epping; Philip F.
Eaton and Abbie A. Tuttle

EDGERLY,
Emily M., d. 5/23/1924 at 80/3/17; at home; widow; b. Brookfield; Henry
Lang (Portsmouth) and Caroline Drew (Brookfield)

EDWARDS,
Joseph H., d. 7/24/1911 at 39; farmer; married; b. Middleboro, MA
Lillian S., d. 11/15/1953 at 90 in Union; b. Wakefield; John W. Sanborn
and Sarah Chapman

EIKLEBOOM,
Sandra, d. 6/8/1998 at 83 in Nashua; Paul Sterling and Rene Murdock

ELDRIDGE,
Arvilla, d. 1/15/1910 at 76/2/26; widow; b. Freedom; Porter Ward (Freedom) and Polly Bennett (Freedom)
Beverly Ann, d. 9/24/1992 at 48 in Union; Walter Budroe and Mary Botting

ELKINS,
Albert C., d. 2/15/1937 at 84/9/4 in Union; b. Jackson; Granville Elkins and Sarah Eastman

ELLIOTT,
Edith Louise, d. 4/30/1996 at 68 in Sanbornville; William Bodwell and Annie Towle
Frank, d. 9/12/1941 at 65/1/2 in Ossipee; b. Stoneham, MA; Charles Elliott
Fred, d. 6/3/1966 at 88 in Concord; Hollis Look and Ellen Avery
Goldie M., d. 8/6/1957 at 52 in Union; b. Warren; Fred Elliott and Nora Tibbetts
Minnie D., d. 5/25/1947 at 72/1/18 in Sanbornville; b. Manchester; Thomas D.A. Graton and Isabelle Paquette
Nora, d. 7/24/1952 at 80/4/14; b. Ireland; Patrick Jordan and Mary ----
Sarah D., d. 8/23/1926 at 55/3/21; married; b. Wolfeboro; Martin V. Whitten and Mary Jane Hobbs
Stanley F., d. 5/7/1920 at 1/1/2; bron. pneumonia; b. Wakefield; Frank Elliott (Stoneham) and Minnie Graton (Manchester)

ELLIS,
stillborn child, d. 9/14/1922; b. Wakefield; Henry P. Ellis (Gilmanton) and Lilia J. Patch (Newfield, ME)
Charles, d. 12/1/1921 at 0/0/0; stillborn; b. Wakefield; Henry P. Ellis (Gilmanton) and Leila I. Patch (W. Newfield, ME)
Edward, d. 3/22/1997 at 57 in Wolfeboro
Henry Page, d. 7/30/1954 at 71 in Wolfeboro
Jeanne Shirley, d. 12/24/1996 at 54 in Rochester; Joseph Harris and Mildred Leslie
John Henry, d. 9/1/1920 at 0/0/1-8; protracted labor; b. Wakefield; Henry P. Ellis and Leila Patch (W. Newfield, ME)
Leila, d. 8/5/1933 at 50/8/10

ELWELL,
Ida May, d. 4/14/1953 at 92 in Union; b. S. Chatham, MA; Allen Eldridge

Joseph E., d. 5/28/1981 at 98 in Ossipee; Zeno Elwell and Alice Lowe

EMERSON,
Clara A., d. 4/26/1921 at 87/1/3; mitral regurgitation; widow; b. Fairfield, ME; Charles V. Whitcomb and Betsy Reene (Kittery, ME)
Daniel W., d. 5/2/1895 at 62/6/26; merchant; married; b. Wolfeboro; William Emerson (Wakefield) and Mary Williams (Wells, ME)
Harry L., d. 4/4/1964 at 76 in Wolfeboro; b. Raymond; Milton Emerson and Sylvania Hazeltine
Levi W., d. 6/14/1965 at 64 in North Wakefield; b. Effingham; Amos Emerson and Nettie Emerson
Mary, d. 12/22/1954 at 80 in Union; b. Canada; Peter Roukey and Rosaland Rendeau
Sadie W., d. 5/28/1967 at 87 in Wolfeboro; b. Milton; Joseph Willey and Mary Laskey

EMERY,
Addie S., d. 1/25/1931 at 74/5/29; married; b. Dover; Stillman Simonds and Hannah Stevens
Frederick, d. 2/1/1949 at 82/5/28 in Union; b. Dover; Daniel Emery
George E., d. 12/11/1939 at 70 in Ossipee
Grace C., d. 1/9/1892 at 0/11/14; b. Wakefield; W. Stanley Emery (Providence, RI) and Ethel N. Julian (NB)
Lilly A., d. 1/21/1893 at 24/11/18; housework; married; b. Brighton, MA; J. Drew Waldron (Acton, ME) and Annah E. Reed (Newfield, ME)

ESTABROOK,
Robert E., Jr., d. 11/17/1998 at 51 in Wolfeboro; Robert E. Estabrook, Sr. and Beverly Knowlton

EVANS,
Albert L., d. 6/1/1914 at 70/1/20; farmer; married; b. Wakefield; Joseph G. Evans (Rochester) and Abigail Pickering (Wakefield)
Calvin J., d. 10/21/1959 at 84 in Sanbornville; b. Wakefield; John Evans and Melvina Farnham
Carrie M., d. 7/18/1960 at 56 in Wolfeboro; b. Milton; Calvin J. Evans and Flora B. Rines
Clarence D., d. 9/9/1948 at 69/7/22 in Wolfeboro
Frederick, d. 8/2/1965 at 52 in Ossipee

Garfield J., d. 7/26/1961 at 79 in Sanbornville; b. Sanbornville; John W. Evans and Melvina Farnham

Grace E., d. 8/4/1950 at 73 in Acton, ME; b. Milton Mills; James F. Dore and Elizabeth Maddox

John W., d. 5/16/1907 at 65/11/17; farmer; married; b. Wakefield; Joseph Evans (Wakefield) and Abbie Pickering (Rochester)

Laura W., d. 6/4/1956 at 74 in Rochester; b. Milton Mills; Joseph Willey and Mary Laskey

Mary A., d. 1/8/1897 at 40/8/10; housewife; married; b. Wakefield; Elijah Wadleigh (Hampton) and Charlotte A. Copp (Dover)

Melvina F., d. 3/9/1915 at 66/8/20; widow; b. Wakefield; Calvin Farnham (Wakefield) and Lydia Cook (Wakefield)

FAIRBANKS,

Charles H., d. 10/14/1931 at 60/1/27; married; b. So. Acton, MA; Sanford Fairbanks

Eugene D., d. 4/19/1960 at 40 in Manchester; b. Boston, MA; Fred O. Fairbanks and Margueriate Hudson

FALES,

William H., d. 9/8/1977 at 87 in Fryeburg, ME; Frederick A. Fales and Caroline Schaffner

FALL,

Arthur G., d. 8/26/1951 at 80 in Wolfeboro; b. Ossipee; George C. Fall and Louise C. Nutter

Clarabel, d. 3/31/1936 at 81/5/14 in Milton; b. Lebanon, ME; Ebenezer Fall and Dorcas Horne

Dorcas D., d. 12/26/1912 at 87/7/11; at home; widow; b. Lebanon, ME; Richard Horn (Lebanon, ME) and Narcissa Jones (Lebanon, ME)

George G., d. 5/27/1933 at 76/9/17

Hannah N., d. 6/23/1891 at 59; housekeeper; widow; b. Wolfeboro; Nathaniel Avery and Hannah Nute

Lizzie L., d. 6/4/1943 at 84/0/24 in Rochester

Lorenzo M., d. 12/6/1918 at 82; widower; Thomas Fall (Freedom) and Louisa Durgin

Lucy N., d. 4/2/1932 at 79/10/17 in Wolfeboro

Lurana, d. 5/4/1916 at 73/8/19; housewife; married; b. Oldfields, ME; Joshua Nason (Oldfields, ME)

FANCHER,
Elmer R., d. 9/4/1973 at 82 in Rochester; Ludlow Fancher and Nettie Fancher

FARLEY,
Florence E., d. 8/7/1968 at 45 in Rochester; Chandler R. Warnock and Mildred Rogers

FARNHAM,
child, d. 10/29/1915 at 0/0/4; b. Wakefield; Albert J. Farnham (Wakefield) and Lena Lowd (Acton, ME)
Albert John, d. 2/8/1929 at 57/1/8; married; b. So. Wakefield; Edward Farnham and Jennie Watts
Caleb, d. 3/15/1917 at 75/11/9; laborer; b. Acton, ME; Dummer Farnham (Acton, ME) and Annie Miller (Acton, ME)
Edward B., d. 6/22/1916 at 68/4/7; farmer; widower; b. Wakefield; John Farnham (Acton, ME) and Marjory Wiggin (Wakefield)
Etta M., d. 9/24/1936 at --; b. Wakefield; Asa Farnham and Mary Jones
Hiram H., d. 11/21/1907 at 70/1/11; farmer; single; b. Wakefield; Paul Farnham (Wakefield) and Loruhamah Cook
J. Frank, d. 2/17/1933 at 72/9/27
Jennie H., d. 7/24/1905 at 57/2; housewife; married; b. Hatley, PQ; Joseph Watt (Scotland) and Annie Forsyth (Canada)
John F., d. 8/22/1913 at 82/9/22; farmer; married; b. Wakefield; John Farnham (Acton, ME) and Betsey Berry (Milton)
Laura A., d. 5/30/1901 at 65/6; domestic; single; b. Wakefield; Daniel Farnham (Wakefield) and Maria Witham (Milton)
Lena May, d. 4/22/1945 at 65/7/18 in Wolfeboro; b. Acton, ME; Clinton Loud and Cora Ricker
Lydia S., d. 3/8/1890 at 68/4/24; housekeeper; b. Wakefield; Enoch Cook and Lucy Libbey (Wakefield)
Margery W., d. 6/7/1896 at 88/3/6; housekeeper; widow; b. Wakefield; Solomon Wiggin (Wakefield) and Elizabeth Berry (Milton)
Marjorie A., d. 2/8/1951 at 75 in New York, NY
Mary, d. 3/26/1909 at 78/7/20; housework; widow; b. Wakefield; John Jones (Lebanon, ME) and Rhoda Witham (Milton)
Mary F., d. 8/16/1887 at 56/2/10; housework; married; b. Alfred, ME; David Nason (Alfred, ME) and Louisa Goodrich (Alfred, ME)
Melvin J., d. 5/14/1895 at 45/7/26; farmer; single; b. Wakefield; Asa M. Farnham (Wakefield) and Mary Jones (Wakefield)

Norris A., d. 10/27/1965 at 58 in Wolfeboro; Albert J. Farnham and Lena M. Loud

FARNSWORTH,
Nathaniel D., d. 9/11/1890 at 73/7; laborer; married; b. Haverhill; Ashbel Farnsworth (Haverhill) and ----- Danforth

FARR,
Edward L., Jr., d. 7/17/1973 at 79 in Wolfeboro; Edward L. Farr and Mabel Greene

FARRAR,
Ida B., d. 12/22/1939 at 72/8/4; b. Woburn, MA; Charles W. Bennett and Josephine Cardwell

FARWELL,
Clifford S., d. 8/2/1977 at 60; Theodore Farwell and E. Gertrude Hinds

FEDDERN,
Henry Charles, d. 9/2/1995 at 62 in Sanbornville; Henry Franz Feddern and Ethel Florence Shea

FEENEY,
John A., d. 9/13/1976 at 68; John M. Feeney and Margaret McHugh

FELLOWS,
Annie P., d. 3/28/1953 at 71 in Farmington; b. Wakefield; James P. Fellows and Mary A. Pike
Belle F., d. 12/22/1904 at 49/0/28; housewife; married; b. Newfield, ME; Greenleaf Tibbetts (Newfield, ME) and Sarah Eastman (Newfield, ME)
Benjamin C., d. 4/29/1890 at 69/11/15; farmer; single; b. Wakefield; John Fellows (Wakefield) and Mary T. Cook (Acton, ME)
Carrie A., d. 9/5/1895 at 0/1; b. Wakefield; Hiram E. Waldron (Wakefield) and Sadie M. Fellows (Wakefield)
Carrie E., d. 4/26/1925 at 78/0/1; married; b. Boston, MA; Capt. Wyat and Mary Watson
Charles S., d. 4/22/1933 at 87/4/8
Daniel M., d. 2/14/1904 at 60/9/14; farmer; married; b. Wakefield; John K. Fellows (Wakefield) and Betsy Weymouth (No. Berwick, ME)

Edgar M., d. 5/29/1947 at 78 in Newburyport, MA
George, d. 9/24/1891 at 0/1/27; b. Wakefield; J. Porter Fellows
 (Wakefield) and Mary Abbie Pike (Wakefield)
Horace M., d. 10/12/1919 at 66/3/18; mit. regurgitation; farmer; single; b.
 Wakefield; John K. Fellows (Wakefield) and Betsy Weymouth (ME)
Horatio B., d. 10/8/1933 at 82/3/23
Isaac N., d. 4/20/1895 at 72/11/22; carpenter; married; b. Wakefield; John
 Fellows (Kensington) and Mary Cook (Wakefield)
James P., d. 2/10/1927 at 82/3/9; widower; b. Wakefield; John K. Fellows
 and Betsey Weymouth
John K., d. 6/7/1891 at 72/11/22; blacksmith; married; b. Wakefield; John
 Fellows (Wakefield) and Mary Cook (Acton, ME)
Mary A., d. 9/28/1916 at 63/7/16; housewife; married; b. Middleton;
 George C. Pike (Middleton) and Maria Cook (Middleton)
Mary Ann, d. 1/5/1934 at 85 in Rochester; b. Wakefield; John K. Fellows
 and Betsey Weymouth
Nettie Jane, d. 1/6/1927 at 47/5/6; single; b. Wakefield; Porter Fellows and
 Mary A. Pike
Oscar F., d. 1/6/1934 at 83/9/5 in Dover; b. Wakefield; John K. Fellows
 and Betsey Weymouth
Oscar John, d. 11/8/1990 at 81 in Haverhill, MA
Sophia A., d. 8/19/1907 at 77/3/28; domestic; widow; b. Gilmanton; Joseph
 S. Kelley (Gilmanton) and Betsey Wingate (Farmington)
William K., d. 12/1/1906 at 65/0/1; farmer; single; b. Wakefield; John K.
 Fellows (Wakefield) and Betsey Weymouth (No. Berwick, ME)

FELSATH,
Italia, d. 1/14/1932 at 65/5/3 in Milton

FERGUSON,
Clementine S., d. 1/25/1906 at 96/4; housework; widow; b. Wakefield;
 Israel Haynes (Wakefield) and Mehitable Stevens (Middleton)
Doris, d. 12/20/1986 at 66 in ME

FERNALD,
Ann E., d. 6/25/1906 at 76/9; housework; widow; b. So. Berwick, ME;
 Stephen Pray and Sarah Delano
Daniel F., d. 2/1/1897 at 66/1/7; shipwright; married; b. Portsmouth;
 Joseph Fernald (Portsmouth) and Lucy G. Ford (Portsmouth)

FIELDING,
Charles Edward, d. 2/22/1998 at 86 in Sanbornville; William Fielding and Elizabeth Ashton

FIELDS,
Elizabeth, d. 1/7/1925 at 65/1/18; married; b. Canada; Baptiste Thibadeau
Frank Lewis, d. 10/15/1954 at 69 in Wolfeboro; b. Albany; James Fields and Bessie Thibodeau

FIFIELD,
Agnes E., d. 4/22/1944 at 71/5/20 in Wolfeboro; b. Boston, MA; John Pelton and Mary Ann Sisson
Blanche E., d. 8/11/1969 at 77 in Rochester; Stillman Douglass and Elizah Day
Charles Henry, d. 11/26/1942 at 64/2/13 in Wolfeboro; b. Conway; Francis Henry Fifield and Roseanna Thurston
Charles Russell, Sr., d. 11/26/1998 at 84 in Ossipee; George Fifield and Blanche E. Penny
Frank Fry, d. 4/24/1943 at 67/11/24; b. Conway; Frank Henry Littlefield and Rosanna Thurston
George R., d. 8/30/1955 at 70 in Union; b. Conway; Francis Fifield and Rosetta Thurston
Norman C., d. 12/13/1940 at 0/1/24 in Union; b. Rochester; Charles Fifield and Louise Drapeau

FISHER,
Frederick, d. 11/10/1986 at 68; Harold P. Fisher and Lottie Bell
George H., d. 3/24/1968 at 83 in Wolfeboro; George A. Fisher and Fannie Carew
Harold Percy, Jr., d. 5/24/1998 at 82 in Wolfeboro; Harold Percy Fisher, Sr. and Lottie Bell
Helen Inez, d. 2/3/1994 at 68 in Titusville, FL; Clarence O. Meserve and Pauline Carter
Judith Ann, d. 9/12/1995 at 58 in East Wakefield; Zedee Alfred Landry and Hazel Wallace

FITCH,
Ethel E., d. 10/15/1960 at 86 in Wolfeboro; b. Hillsboro; Richard Mossia and Luella Wakefield

FITZ,
Augusta S., d. 1/26/1907 at 39/6/23; housewife; married; b. Wakefield; Wesley Rines (Middleton) and Mary A. Roberts (Wakefield)
Carl W., d. 8/18/1976 at 85 in Dover
Carl W., Jr., d. 6/6/1984 at 66 in Dover
Edith Jane, d. 7/16/1976 at 87 in Dover
Mark S., d. 11/14/1951 at 87 in Portsmouth; b. Amesbury, MA; Jacob Fitz and Hannah Gale

FLAMAND,
Louis Joseph, d. 11/18/1996 at 78 in Wolfeboro; Napolean Flamand and Angeline Mercier

FLANAGAN,
Florence M., d. 12/29/1974 at 72 in Sanbornville; Dennis Monahan and Minnie ----

FLANDERS,
Charles Lyman, d. 10/13/1944 at 60/1/23 in Ossipee; b. Shapleigh, ME; Enoch Flanders and Carrie Hooper
Clinton A.E., d. 11/15/1945 at 57/1/18 in Wolfeboro; b. Alton; Calvin Flanders and Luella B. Sawyer

FLAYHAN,
Paul F., d. 11/19/1997 at 58 in Wolfeboro; Alfred Flayhan and Pauline George

FLETCHER,
Ethel F., d. 7/30/1961 at 91 in Sanbornville; b. Nashua; Rufus G. Sargent and Frances R. Page

FLINT,
Ernest E., d. 11/13/1984 at 69 in Wolfeboro; Ernest Flint and Ida Ogden

FLOYD,
Ella Chellis, d. 4/11/1949 at 65/0/26 in Limerick, ME
Jean D., d. 2/4/1968 at 40 in Sanford, ME
Mary Mohala, d. 4/5/1953 at 88 in Chelsea, MA
Walter Edward, d. 8/21/1940 at 79 in Chelsea, MA

FLYNN,
Alberton, d. 3/7/1960 at 76 in Sanbornville; b. NS; John Flynn
Mary E., d. 2/25/1955 at 55 in Sanbornville; b. Naples, ME; James S. Mains and Cora M. Brackett
Stanley A., d. 4/26/1981 at 62 in Rochester; Alberton Flynn and Mary E. Mains

FOGG,
Carrie G., d. 9/24/1937 at 56/10/11 in Sanbornville; b. Wakefield; Albert Garland and Melissa Downs
Charles E., d. 5/14/1993 at 70; Lloyd Fogg and Edna Deering
George W., d. 11/26/1941 at 77/1/21 in Ossipee; b. Ossipee; Simon Fogg and Mary Seward
Victoria Christina, d. 10/15/1997 at 93 in Wolfeboro; Carl Johan Nelson and Anna Persson

FOLEY,
Frederick Liston, Sr., d. 8/13/1990 at 77 in Wolfeboro; James F. Foley and Alice Whynot
Gertrude Mary Theresa, d. 8/4/1998 at 81 in Ossipee; Charles Mansfield and Lillian Buzzell

FOLSOM,
Marie Beatrice, d. 4/1/1995 at 69 in Wolfeboro; Hillary Theiverge and Prudence Dube

FOOTILL,
Hester A., d. 4/25/1914 at 72/6/3; housewife; widow; b. Dover

FORD,
Francis William, d. 2/11/1957 at 55 in East Wakefield; b. Boston, MA; Thomas Ford and Katherine Nutley

FORSYTHE,
Frank F., d. 3/24/1969 at 66 in Rochester; Frank Forsythe

FOSS,
Eliza A., d. 12/16/1937 at 87/6/3 in Brookfield; b. Wakefield; John Davis and L. Gilman

Irving, d. 9/12/1953 at 90 in Rochester; b. Stowe, ME; Nathaniel Foss and Abigail Johnson
Lizzie S., d. 3/8/1946 at 80/0/18 in Dover

FOSTER,
Daisy M., d. 2/2/1964 at 81 in Wolfeboro; b. Somersworth; Butler Hansen and Susan Page
Fred A., d. 10/30/1907 at 43/4/6; laborer; single; b. Greenwood, ME; Harrison Swift (Greenwood, ME) and Lucy Ring (Greenwood, ME)

FOWLER,
Christopher C., d. 2/1/1963 at 77 in East Wakefield; b. Salisbury, MA; Jacob Fowler

FOX,
Arthur H., d. 9/7/1970 at 74 in Rochester; George Fox and Elizabeth Hart
Harvey Dunham, d. 10/11/1993 at 60 in Burlington, MA; Arthur Hart Fox and Isabelle Taft
Isabelle T., d. 3/24/1975 at 73 in Union; Arthur L. Taft and Nellie W. Dunham

FRANCIS,
Bradford G., d. 7/27/1991 at 71 in Wolfeboro; Lewis A. Francis and Mildred Felton
Julia, d. 1/22/1892 at 45; housework; married; b. Clinton, ME; James Priest and Alice M.
Margaret Ann, d. 7/7/1989 at 41 in Portland, ME
Rolene Lorraine, d. 2/8/1995 at 69 in East Wakefield; George Davenport and Wilda Whitten

FRANK,
George W., d. 7/9/1962 at 71; b. Rutland, VT; Sewell A. Frank and Martha Foster

FRASIER,
Curtis L., d. 6/5/1981 at 73; Guy Frasier and Maggie Aldrich

FRECHETTE,
Catherine Frances, d. 9/28/1997 at 68 in East Wakefield; James Francis Hester and Vivian Wainio

FREEMAN,
son, d. 9/14/1894 at 9 hours; b. Wakefield; William C. Freeman (Cambridge, MA) and Elizabeth Morrison (Roxbury, MA)
Chester A., d. 7/20/1984 at 84 in Rochester

FREINER,
Helen L., d. 1/23/1987 at 71 in Rochester; Israel Hamel and Eva Bernard

FRENCH,
Alden C., d. 1/14/1929 at 48/5/22; married; b. Middleton; Leander H. French and Jennie A. Tufts
Joseph, d. 1/29/1887 at 77/10/6; machinist; widower; b. Rochester, NY; John French (Salisbury, MA) and Huldy ----- (Salisbury, MA)
Leander H., d. 11/2/1952 at 95/11/29 in Union; b. Farmington; Jeremiah H. French and Martha J. Wentworth

FRITZ,
Ruth H., d. 12/4/1966 at 74 in Stoneham, MA
Walter F., d. 6/21/1966 at 76 in Wolfeboro; b. New York, NY; Arnold Fritz and Catherine Wesser

FROST,
Newell Elibus, d. 6/13/1998 at 83 in Wolfeboro; E. Frost and Minnie Cronin

FRYE,
Bess L., d. 1/22/1951 at 70 in Concord; b. Limerick, ME; Steven Libby and Ann Sawyer

FULLER,
Hallen C., d. 11/28/1964 at 67 in Wolfeboro; b. Salem, MA; Andrew Root and Grace Upton
Helen G., d. 12/29/1993 at 72 in Wolfeboro; Silas A. Greenleaf and Mary O'Brien
Helen M., d. 9/18/1915 at 89/10/15; at home; widow; b. Wellesley, MA; Lemuel Retenhouse (Newton, MA) and Liza Richardson (Newton, MA)
Roy, d. 7/14/1971 at 76 in Hanover; William Fuller and Addie Caine

GAGE,
Eliza J., d. 1/17/1902 at --; housewife; married; b. Wolfeboro; James Cotton (Wolfeboro) and Abigail Knowles
George H., d. 10/25/1917 at 83/6/19; farmer; widower; b. Wakefield; Jonathan Gage (Wakefield) and Sarah Lyford (Brookfield)
James L., d. 9/12/1892 at 23/1/25; expressman; married; b. Wakefield; George H. Gage (Wakefield) and Eliza J. Cotton (Wolfeboro)
Lydia J., d. 7/27/1941 at 91/7/20 in Malden, MA

GAGNON,
son, d. 4/6/1896 at 0/9/0 in Sanbornville; b. Sanbornville; Arthur Gagnon (Canada) and Elanor Partaie (Canada)
Alfred J., d. 8/13/1951 at 62/5/17 in Ossipee
Alfred J., d. 7/18/1965 at 57 in Sanbornville; b. Sanbornville; Ernest Gagnon and Georgianna Legare
Anna, d. 12/28/1891 at 0/5/5; b. Wakefield; Ernest Gagneon (sic) (Canada) and Georgiana Legary (Wakefield)
Arthur, d. 6/21/1897 at 27/11/20; laborer; married; b. Canada; George Gagnon (Canada) and Delphine Aubert (Canada)
Arthur, Jr., d. 6/8/1894 at 0/6/8; b. Wakefield; Arthur Gagnon (Canada) and Adiena Patry (Canada)
Arthur A., d. 9/29/1909 at 0/9/29; b. Wakefield; Amedie Gagnon (Canada) and Demarise Lamir (Wakefield)
Delphine A., d. 5/20/1923 at 84/4/1; at home; widow; b. Canada; George Aubuth (Canada) and Genevieve Gagnon (Canada)
Donald, d. 12/13/1939 at 0/0/2 in Wolfeboro; b. Wolfeboro; Oscar Ernest Gagnon and Viola Ruth Downs
Emile J., d. 9/27/1943 at 81/1/13 in Sanbornville; b. Canada; George Gagnon and Delphine Aubut
Ernest, d. 8/22/1940 at 72/9/5 in Sanbornville; b. Canada; George Gagnon and Delphine Oubeau
George, d. 11/7/1903 at 80/9/22; carpenter; married; b. Canada; Gonison Gagnon (Canada) and Elinore Aubuth (Canada)
Georgianna, d. 9/21/1953 at 81 in Sanbornville; b. Union; Joseph Legary and Adelaine Houle
Joseph E.O., d. 10/2/1900 at 0/5; b. Wakefield; Ernest Gagnon (Canada) and ----- Legary (Canada)
Joseph W., d. 6/26/1903 at 0/2/9; b. Sanbornville; Eugene Gagnon (Canada) and Manda Butler (Canada)

Leo Ernest, d. 11/14/1923 at 0/2/1; b. Wakefield; Arthur E. Gagnon (Wakefield) and Grace Lavertu (Wakefield)

Marie Rose, d. 2/10/1995 at 85 in Ossipee; Napoleon Bouchette and Rose Parent

Mary, d. 3/17/1908 at 16/5/26; student; single; b. Hyde Park, MA; Eugene Gagnon (Canada) and Amanda Butler (Canada)

Mary E., d. 4/11/1896 at 0/4/0 in Sanbornville; b. Sanbornville; Eugene Gagnon (Canada) and Amanda Butler (Canada)

Mary E., d. 8/5/1906 at 0/0/1; b. Wakefield; Eugene Gagnon (Canada) and Amanda Butler (Canada)

Oray, d. 3/18/1980 at 78 in Lynn, MA

Orell, d. 12/15/1902 at 0/7/2; b. Sanbornville; Ernest Gagnon (Canada) and Georgianna Legarey (Wakefield)

Oscar E., d. 5/18/1962 at 64 in Wolfeboro; b. Sanbornville; Ernest Gagnon and Georgiana Legary

Richard R., d. 4/16/1998 at 58; Louis Gagnon and Helena Fraser

Sarah Ann, d. 3/6/1898 at 0/9; b. Wakefield; Arthur Gagnon (Canada) and Adeline Patrie (Canada)

GALLAGHER,

Joseph E., d. 1/7/1973 at 79 in Wolfeboro; Patrick Gallagher and Hannah McGlinchie

Joseph Francis, d. 1/24/1998 at 80 in Wolfeboro; Joseph Gallagher and Mary Bedard

Mary A., d. 11/28/1983 at 88 in Ossipee

Robert J., d. 4/19/1958 at 25 in Sanbornville; b. Cambridge, MA; James S. Gallagher and Marie L. Drewhan

GALVIN,

Gladys E., d. 12/6/1980 at 55 in Gilmanton; Guy Farris and Violet Fales

GAPINSKI,

Anton J., d. 3/16/1965 at 82 in Wolfeboro

GARDNER,

John H., d. 11/4/1969 at 86 in Ossipee

Mary A., d. 5/19/1969 at 84 in Sanford, ME

Peter, d. 12/9/1944 at 59/7/11 in Milton Mills

GAREY,
Lydia M., d. 9/17/1914 at 71/6/3; retired; widow; b. Wakefield; John Davis (Wakefield) and Mary Gilman (Acton, ME)

GARLAND,
Albert F., d. 8/7/1916 at 82/9/16; shoemaker; married; b. Ossipee; William F. Garland (Ossipee) and Olive Kennison (Madison)
Alvah S., d. 1/4/1911 at 61/6/20; farmer; widower; b. Wakefield; Josiah Garland (Wakefield) and Rowena Spinney (Wakefield)
Annie L., d. 6/6/1972 at 75 in Rochester; Charles R. Smith and Ida Foss
Arthur A., d. 12/19/1966 at 84 in Wolfeboro; b. Wakefield; Albert F. Garland
Bessie B., d. 9/12/1957 at 63 in Union; b. Portsmouth; Elmer E. Glass and Nettie Dyer
Bessie E., d. 3/15/1915 at 7/9/5; b. Wakefield; Fred Garland (Brookfield) and Hattie West (Brookfield)
Clarence E., d. 5/14/1953 at 80 in Bangor, ME
Doris M., d. 2/16/1906 at 0/0/18; b. Wakefield; Fred Garland (Brookfield) and Hattie West (Brookfield)
Ernest E., d. 10/6/1939 at 39/10 in Wolfeboro; b. Wakefield; Fred Garland and Hattie M. West
Fannie N., d. 9/26/1902 at 62/4; housewife; married; b. Greenland; John Ricker (Greenland)
Forrest A., d. 8/21/1971 at 50 in Sanbornville; Arthur A. Garland and Mary Drew
Fred E., d. 7/25/1984 at 83 in Ossipee; Fred Garland and Hattie West
George L., d. 6/22/1894 at 20/1; laborer; single; b. Wakefield; Alvah S. Garland (Wakefield) and Priscilla Lothrop (Boston, MA)
Guy W., d. 7/14/1957 at 59 in Brookfield; Fred Garland and Hattie West
Hattie M., d. 5/25/1964 at 86 in Sanbornville; b. Brookfield; Charles West and Betsey Whitehouse
Herbert C., d. 5/9/1905 at 0/0/0; b. Wakefield; Chester A. Garland (Brookfield) and Vera M. Colbath (Conway)
Howard A., d. 9/20/1982 at 60 in Wolfeboro; Arthur Garland and Mary Drew
John F., d. 11/25/1902 at 57/11; farmer; married; b. Wakefield; Franklin Garland (Wakefield) and Mary Goodwin (Milton)
John Thomas, d. 1/11/1920 at 81/5/14; mitral regurgitation; retired; widower; b. Ossipee; William Garland and Olive Kenerson

Marion L., d. 4/17/1947 at 42/6/27 in Wolfeboro; b. Sanbornville; Ernest W. Davis and Lillian A. Davis

Mary, d. 7/9/1915 at 99/0/12; retired; widow; b. Milton; Jeremiah Goodwin (Kittery, ME) and Bachshelia Spinney (Kittery, ME)

Mary, d. 1/25/1952 at 76/7/11 in Wolfeboro; b. Brookfield; John T. Garland and Fannie W. Ricker

Medora L., d. 10/21/1896 at 31/7/11; housewife; married; George F. Goodwin (Berwick, ME) and Rose A. Goodrich (Berwick, ME)

Melissa Jane, d. 2/20/1938 at 98/1/29 in Sanbornville; b. Bartlett; James Drown and Rachel Hill

Paul D., d. 12/26/1972 at 35 in Manchester; Arthur A. Garland and Marion Davis

Priscilla L., d. 5/12/1902 at 52/11/22; housewife; married; b. Boston, MA; George B. Lathrop (Cohasset, MA) and Eunice Wheeler (Concord, MA)

Robert David, d. 9/6/1997 at 18 in Milton; Robert Warren Garland and Kathryn Donnelly

Roland E., d. 9/4/1973 at 45 in Sanbornville; Fred E. Garland and Verlie E. Tufts

Roy L., d. 5/12/1973 at 61 in Manchester; Fred Garland and Hattie M. West

Terry R., d. 8/21/1985 at 42 in Wolfeboro; Forrest A. Garland and Reta (Bean) Flynn

Verna M., d. 10/8/1933 at 50/11/1

Wilbur, d. 6/6/1901 at 30/4; laborer; married; b. Brookfield; John T. Garland (Ossipee) and Fannie Beacham (Greenland)

GARNEY,

Amos F., d. 3/6/1967 at 90 in Sanford, ME; b. Lynn, ME (sic); John Garney and Mary E. Thurston

Grace Eugene, d. 5/26/1944 at 73/4/2 in Brookfield

GARRATT,

Ruth C., d. 7/29/1936 at 43/7/10; b. Newton Center, MA; Augustus T. Clark and Margaret Etherington

GARSIDE,

William E., d. 3/30/1954 at 74 in Rochester; b. Southbridge, MA

GARVIN,
Almira L., d. 6/27/1913 at 88/7/16; at home; widow; b. Brookfield; Samuel F. Lang and Lydia Thurber

Bertha M., d. 3/23/1945 at 72/1/11 in Sanbornville; b. Wakefield; James W. Garvin and Charlotte J. Maleham

Charlotte, d. 4/1/1949 at 57/3/26 in Manchester; b. Sanbornville; James W. Garvin and Charlotte J. ----

Charlotte J., d. 4/17/1926 at 76/11/13; widow; b. Wakefield; William A. Maleham and Nancy W. Pike

Clara M., d. 12/10/1959 at 84 in Wolfeboro; b. Sanbornville; James W. Garvin and Charlotte J. Maleham

Ebenezer, d. 12/17/1890 at 74/3/9; farmer; married; b. Wakefield; Ebenezer Garvin (Somersworth) and Lydia Wentworth (Somersworth)

Grace Elizabeth, d. 10/2/1989 at 91 in Wolfeboro; Patrick Dowd and Mary O'Neil

Ina B., d. 1/24/1968 at 79 in Dobbs Ferry, NY

James Phillip, d. 2/20/1952 at 71/8/4 in Rochester; b. Sanbornville; James W. Garvin and Charlotte J. Maleham

James W., d. 12/30/1907 at 58/11/15; merchant; married; b. Wakefield; Ebenezer Garvin (Wakefield) and Almira Lang (Brookfield)

James W., d. 2/9/1979 at 63 in Sanford, ME

John Howard, d. 8/15/1942 at 44/8/19; b. Wakefield; John H. Garvin and Katherine Dow

John Howard, d. 2/1/1949 at 82 in Wolfeboro; b. Wakefield; Ebenezer Garvin and Almira Lang

Katherine Phippin, d. 8/22/1949 at 85/0/10 in Sanbornville; b. Salem, MA; Josiah Dow and Kate Downing

Leota S., d. 2/22/1980 at 72 in Wolfeboro; Leo H. Straw and Louise Sherbut

Mary A., d. 7/17/1967 at 77 in Sanford, ME; b. Wakefield; James W. Garvin and Charlotte J. Maleham

Richard, d. 12/26/1927 at 0/1/12; b. Wakefield; James P. Garvin and Rose Ann Hill

Samuel F., d. 11/10/1963 at 78 in Bronxville, NY; b. Sanbornville; James W. Garvin and Charlotte J. Maleham

GASPAR,
Clayton E., d. 8/18/1984 at 68 in Rochester; Earl Gaspar and Glenola Clark

GAULZETTI,
Shirley, d. 4/29/1996 at 58 in Sanbornville; Ernest R. Wyman and Rose Blanchard

GAUTHIER,
Armand J., d. 7/8/1970 at 42 in Wolfeboro; Rosaire Gauthier and Jennie Dupuis
G. J., d. 6/15/1968 at 48 in Rochester; Rosaire Gauthier and Jennie ----
Jennie D., d. 12/9/1967 at 70 in Wolfeboro; b. S. Berwick, ME; Joseph Dupuis
Pauline S., d. 1/21/1965 at 33 in Sanbornville; b. Center Ossipee; Robert Welch and Marion Drew
Rosaire C.C., d. 8/7/1951 at 61 in Sanbornville; b. Canada; Joseph Gauthier and Admere Bernier

GERARD,
Randolph J., Jr., d. 9/13/1988 at 42 in Wolfeboro; Randolph Gerard, Sr. and Phyllis Drown

GERRISH,
Ruth B., d. 2/22/1912 at 79/5/22; housework; widow; b. Middleton; Isaac Stevens (Middleton) and Margaret Butler (Cambridge, MA)

GHAREEB,
Glen, d. 2/13/1975 at 2 in Winchester, MA

GIBBS,
Clifton E., d. 10/14/1983 at 86; Erving Gibbs and Ada ----
William H., d. 5/6/1970 at 88 in Manchester; Henry Gibbs and Annie A. Ellis

GIFFIN,
Charles L., d. 3/1/1972 at 100 in Wolfeboro; Simon Giffin and Henrietta Giffin
Mary, d. 2/8/1965 at 82 in Concord; b. NB; Howard Rees and Jessie MacLean

GILBERT,
Ellen R., d. 8/8/1956 at 97/11/30 in Union; b. Union Town, PA; George Guyer and Catherine E. Hoke

Henry, d. 8/1/1888 at 0/2/14; b. Great Falls; Frank Foster (Canada) and Phebe McNeil (Canada)

William, d. 2/5/1940 at 53/3 in Wolfeboro; b. Pembroke; James Gilbert and Georgina Saronde

GILE,

Frieda Y., d. 2/20/1989 at 76 in Wolfeboro; Wilbur Yeaton and Mattie Wellman

GILMAN,

Frances, d. 3/15/1897 at 78; housewife; widow; b. NS; Robert McKim (Scotland) and Mary Barrett (England)

Hanson P., d. 7/1/1930 at 90/11/1; married; b. Wakefield; Andrew Gilman and Sally Pike

Henry H., d. 1/13/1897 at 55/8; farmer; married; b. Wakefield; John Gilman (Wakefield) and Phoebe Merrill (Acton, ME)

Jonathan R., d. 11/26/1902 at 85/8/10; farmer; single; b. Wakefield; Theodore Gilman (Wakefield) and Mehitable Richards (Rochester)

Joseph P., d. 8/17/1901 at 74/10/23; merchant; single; b. Bartlett; Andrew Gilman (Wakefield) and Dolly Pike (Wakefield)

Mary E., d. 6/30/1933 at 80/9/2

Phoebe, d. 7/7/1887 at 74/4/27; single

Theodore, d. 3/13/1928 at 82/4/25; single; b. Wakefield; John Gilman and Phoebe Merrill

GILPATRICK,

Margaret D., d. 7/26/1988 at 75 in Dover; Carl Hoaglund and Maybell Carpenter

GILSON,

Lillian M., d. 11/14/1961 at 83 in Union; b. Milton Mills; George Chesley and Mary Archibald

GLEASON,

Frederick J., d. 2/5/1943 at 69/6/5 in Sanbornville; b. Watertown, MA; William Gleason and Helen Haynes

GLIDDEN,

Abbie, d. 1/24/1899 at 73/6/21; housewife; widow; b. Wakefield; James Young (Wakefield) and Ruth

Jerome A., d. 4/8/1917 at 60/7/28; farmer; married; b. Wakefield; John H. Glidden (Alton) and Abigail Young (Wakefield)

Lauriston W., d. 10/29/1975 at 70 in Exeter; Harry F. Glidden and Lilla Randall

Norman B., d. 10/4/1978 at 77 in Wolfeboro; Woodbury Glidden and Ela Rollin

Tillie A., d. 4/27/1894 at 28/0/10; housekeeper; married; b. Brookfield; Henry M. Libby (Porter, ME) and Abbie Chamberlin (Brookfield)

GLOVER,
Jennie C., d. 11/13/1957 at 83 in Union; b. London, England; John Porey and Catherine Morgan

Roberta A., d. 12/2/1928 at 31/9/27; married; b. New Castle, NB; James B. Johnston and Josephine White

GODFREY,
Phyllis Foss, d. 4/23/1998 at 63 in Dover; Samuel Foss and Geneva Diston

GOLDEN,
Patrick J., d. 9/14/1951 at 67 in Sanbornville; b. Ireland; Michael Golden and Mary Brennan

GOLDSMITH,
John D., d. 5/29/1987 at 73 in Wolfeboro; Howard Goldsmith and Una Dudley

GOLDSTEIN,
David Allen, d. 2/4/1998 at 36 in Sanbornville; Abbot Goldstein and Ernestine Roth

GOLTZ,
Agnes E., d. 6/21/1954 at 51 in Milton; b. Brookfield; Fred Garland and Hattie West

GOODFIELD,
Donald L., d. 3/20/1983 at 25 in Rochester; Richard Goodfield and Jeanette Smith

GOODHUE,
George E., d. 12/21/1906 at 63/6/19; farmer; married; b. Brookfield; Joseph Goodhue (Brookfield) and Hannah Stevenson (Wolfeboro)

GOODWIN,
Ethel, d. 8/19/1956 at 66 in Union; b. New Durham; Alonzo Dame and Etta French
Ethel, d. 1/3/1969 at 88 in Center Harbor
Hilton S., d. 9/27/1941 at 82/0/29 in Rochester; b. Acton, ME; Oliver Goodwin and Lorinda J. Burbank
Nellie B., d. 10/22/1947 at 59/1/11 in Union; b. Berwick, ME; Herbert Weare and Cora B. Stanton
Paul J., d. 2/25/1972 at 51; Harry Goodwin and Nell Carroll
Pauline M., d. 5/3/1910 at 5/1/10; b. Wakefield; Hilton S. Goodwin (Acton, ME) and Stella Campbell (Wakefield)
Payson H., d. 7/10/1981 at 67; John F. Goodwin and Eva L. Rattee

GORTON,
Ellen, d. 12/15/1973 at 83 in Rochester; Edwin Willey and Sarah Patch

GOSSELIN,
Damase, d. 6/2/1950 at 74/5/7 in Wolfeboro; b. Canada; Joseph Gosselin and Celina LeClerc
Harold, d. 8/29/1977 at 62; Arthur Gosselin and Selena Poulin

GOTREAU,
Esther V., d. 11/3/1977 at 79 in East Wakefield; Fred Cheney

GOULD,
Burton G., d. 3/4/1990 at 88 in Rochester; Louis Gould and Bell Smith
Everett L., d. 3/20/1985 at 70 in Manchester; Roland Gould and Odella Keller

GOYETTE,
daughter, d. 6/4/1897 at 0/0/0; b. Wakefield; George Goyette (Canada) and Arthemise Gauthier (Canada)
Arthemise, d. 7/5/1897 at 25; housewife; married; b. Canada

GRACE,
Frank L., d. 4/19/1933 at 73/5/11

Lizzie H., d. 12/17/1958 at 88 in Rochester; b. Albany; George W. Willey and Mary Davis

GRAFF,
child, d. 6/11/1910 at 0/1/5; b. Wakefield; Joe Graff (Russia) and Jodwdi Marctewiez (Russia)

GRAHAM,
child, d. 10/13/1936 at 0/0/0 in Portsmouth; b. Portsmouth; Kosco R. Graham and Evelyn Bickford
Kosco R., d. 2/21/1965 at 70 in Kittery, ME

GRANT,
Edwin J., d. 1/24/1958 at 81 in Sanbornville; b. Orono, ME; Jason Grant and Mary A. Foss
Frederic D., d. 9/10/1946 at 74/2/5 in Sanbornville; b. Orono, ME; Jason Grant and Mary A. Foss

GRAVEL,
Linda E., d. 12/23/1985 at 38 in Lowell, MA

GRAVES,
Jonathan, d. 2/22/1893 at 85/3; widower; b. Vienna, ME; Jacob Graves (Brentwood) and Sarah Brown (Fremont)
Percy Francis, d. 3/3/1976 at 68; Thomas Graves and Della Hulbey

GRAY,
Arlene G., d. 6/15/1955 at 25 in Union; b. Farmington; Harry King and Irene Woodman
Frank Norman, d. 4/29/1996 at 62 in Manchester; John Frank Gray and Edith Langmaid
Jean C., d. 4/26/1998 at -- in Milton; Eugene Chretien and Madeline Hull
Lucille T., d. 2/20/1982 at 45 in Union; Wilfred Larochelle and Belle Lafrontaine
Lysander, d. 8/18/1935 at 73/10/8 in Sanbornville; b. Madison; Nathaniel W. Gray and Martha J. Burke

GREENFIELD,
Blanche D., d. 8/18/1968 at 87 in Wolfeboro; Myron A. Dole and Annie Wilkenson

Melvin Leroy, d. 1/5/1953 at 67 in Sanbornville; b. Durhamville, NY; Melvin Greenfield and Julia Viele

GREENLAW,
Guy L., d. 2/5/1975 at 92 in Wolfeboro

GREENWOOD,
Jennie, d. 8/21/1952 at 89/1/30 in Shrewsbury, MA; b. Port Clyde, NS; Jeremiah Nickerson and Mary Ann Johnson

GREGSON,
Robinson, d. 6/4/1932 at 70/6/2 in Union

GRENIER,
Mary, d. 11/27/1954 at 88 in Union; b. Canada; Abraham Pare and Julienne Goslin
Morris, d. 7/18/1919 at 6/8/14; gen. septicaemia; b. Rochester; Morris Grenier (Rochester) and Alice Grenier (Canada)

GRIER,
Susie Ingeborg, d. 2/27/1950 at 84/8; b. Lynn, MA; George T. Clark and Harriett S. Aldrich

GRINNELL,
Douglas Harrison, d. 4/14/1998 at 51 in Rochester; John Harrison Grinnell and Ruby Faye Hale

GROVER,
Flora O., d. 5/30/1986 at 87 in Wolfeboro; Eldridge Nickerson and Hatti Malone
Henry John, d. 5/25/1997 at 70 in Rochester; Harry Grover and Gertrude ---

GUERTIN,
Thomas, d. 8/12/1934 at 73/7/11 in Concord

GULEZIA,
Samuel C., d. 7/24/1970 at 56 in Union; Angelo Gulezia and Antonette Messina

GURNEY,
Albert W., d. 7/13/1953 at 63 in Somerville, MA; b. CO; Henry L. Gurney and Mary Tweddle
Bruce W., d. 4/10/1985 at 57 in Brockton, MA
Lillian M., d. 2/17/1985 at 86 in Milton

GUTTADAURO,
Alfred R., d. 1/8/1991 at 79 in Wolfeboro; Gaetono Guttadauro and Rose Fazio
Katherine F., d. 4/4/1991 at 74 in Wolfeboro; John J. McCarthy and Catherine F. Penney

HACKETT,
Charles A., d. 1/19/1913 at 68/9; carpenter; widower; b. Brookfield; Samuel Hackett and Mary J. Lang
William, d. 7/25/1944 at 75/3/13 in Ossipee; b. Danvers, MA; William R. Hackett and Olive L. Maston

HADDOCK,
Julia E., d. 12/7/1891 at 21/2; housekeeper; married; b. Bartlett; Jacob Hill (Eaton) and Mary Ordway (Conway)

HAINES,
son, d. 12/27/1888 at 0/0/1; b. Wakefield; Hattie Haines (Wakefield)
Almira M., d. 4/10/1912 at 87/4/3; housekeeper; single; b. Wakefield; Israel Haines (Wakefield) and Mehitable Stevens (Middleton)
George W., d. 11/1/1891 at 72/1/28; carpenter; married; b. Wakefield; Israel Haines (Wakefield) and Mehitable Stevens (Middleton)
Henry, d. 12/13/1890 at 22/5/3; brakeman; single; b. Wakefield; George W. Haines (Wakefield) and Abbie Nichols (Wakefield)
Susan A., d. 5/1/1898 at 73/7/2; housekeeper; widow; b. Ossipee; Joseph B. Nichols (Ossipee) and Susan P. Bickford (Ossipee)

HAINSWORTH,
Mabel B., d. 10/28/1971 at 82 in Rochester; William H. Booth and Annie Cuthbert
Norman T., d. 1/24/1972 at 78 in Dover; James P. Hainsworth and Sarah Tucker

HALFORD,
Laura S., d. 10/17/1975 at 66 in Hanover; David Taylor and Laura Smith

HALL,
Charles H., d. 10/15/1907 at 65/10/27; farmer; widower; b. Wakefield; Jay H. Hill (sic) (Wakefield) and Emily A. Wiggin (Brookfield)
Edward, d. 7/26/1916 at 93/4/16; farmer; single; b. Canada; Edward Hall (Labrador) and Mary ----- (Labrador)
Emily Ann, d. 3/24/1907 at 94/8/17; housewife; widow; b. Brookfield; Daniel Wiggin and Dorcas Minkley (Newmarket)
George W., d. 8/1/1952 at 66/4/18; b. Bar Mills, ME; Frank J. Hall and Abagail Junkins
Harriett A., d. 7/31/1922 at 87/10/28; retired; widow; b. Wakefield; Charles Moulton (Salisbury, MA) and Olive Ayers (Portsmouth)
James H., Sr., d. 1/2/1979 at 76 in Rochester
Jay H., d. 3/2/1897 at 84/7/24; farmer; married; b. Wakefield; Joshua G. Hall (Wakefield) and Betsy Plummer (Milton)
John G., d. 12/8/1963 at 77 in Rochester; b. Somerville, MA; John E. Hall and Elizabeth Rynes
Josephine W., d. 1/23/1978 at 91 in Rochester; Frank I. Nute and Elizabeth Trow
Mary I., d. 9/15/1926 at 71/11/30; widow; b. Canada; Theophile Houle and Julie Richard
Sarah A., d. 12/13/1887 at 78; housekeeper; single; b. Wakefield; Joshua G. Hall (Wakefield) and Betsy Plummer (Milton)

HALMOR,
Charles C., d. 9/7/1898 at 0/1/21; b. Ossipee; Charles C. Halmor (Rochester) and Jennie Kimball (Ossipee)

HAM,
Nathaniel, d. 10/15/1909 at 84/9/3; carpenter; widower; b. New Durham; Samuel Ham (Barrington) and Lucinda Grace (Kittery, ME)
Susan E., d. 3/23/1897 at 46; housewife; widow; b. Rochester; Herbert F. Stevens (Orford) and Mehitable P. Adams (Milton)

HAMILTON,
Ernest Erville, d. 8/7/1959 at 68 in Sanbornville; b. Sanbornville; John Hamilton and Sadie M. Doyle
Irene, d. 8/22/1896 at 35; married; ----- Wentworth

John Erville, d. 5/15/1942 at 75/10/1 in Wolfeboro; b. Conway; Joseph Hamilton and Betsey Hart

Joseph H., d. 4/4/1896 at 71/0/5; day laborer; married; b. Conway; Jonathan Hamilton and Lydia Hilliard

Margaret, d. 7/2/1956 at 73/4/12 in Medford, MA; b. Canada; John Carroll and Margaret Doucette

Raymond E., d. 12/6/1965 at 68 in Farmington; b. Sanbornville; John E. Hamilton and Sadie M. Doyle

Sadie M., d. 12/22/1937 at 63/5/11 in Rochester; b. Wakefield; John Doyle and Amanda Wentworth

Sarah L., d. 10/31/1982 at 91 in Wolfeboro; John Collins and Mary Murphy

HAMLIN,
Edward F., d. 5/15/1929 at 83/1; married; b. Boston, MA; Walcott Hamlin and Susan Wescott

Josephine S., d. 1/29/1941 at 91/7/27; b. Portsmouth; Charles H. Littlefield and Hannah Howard

Rose A., d. 9/21/1891 at 57/1/2; housekeeper; single; b. China, ME; Calvin Hamlin (China, ME) and Phoebe Jordan (Cape Elizabeth, ME)

HAMM,
Leroy H., d. 1/24/1967 at 60 in Wolfeboro; b. Ossipee; Judson Hamm and Mary Wentworth

Minnie G., d. 4/22/1989 at 92 in Wolfeboro

HAMMOND,
Almeretta, d. 11/25/1908 at 63/4/20; housewife; widow; b. Chocorua; Andrew Nealy and Sophia Ross

Georgiana, d. 10/22/1922 at 38/8/0; at home; married; b. Newfoundland; William Best (Newfoundland) and Harriett Pike (Newfoundland)

Irene, d. 4/23/1891 at 17/10/16; single; b. Tamworth; Wentworth Hammond (Ossipee) and Almaretta Nealley (Tamworth)

Lillian M., d. 9/25/1961 at 52 in Wolfeboro; b. Brookfield; Charles Fifield and Agnes E. Pelton

Robert T., d. 3/5/1964 at 60 in Wolfeboro; b. Acton, ME; Joseph Hammond and Elizabeth Williams

HAMNER,
Theresa Alice, d. 8/6/1996 at 78 in Dover; Harry J. Newman and Almira J. Blodgett

HAMOR,
George Heywood, d. 6/27/1995 at 72 in Rochester; Clarence Hamor and Gertrude Wood

HANCHETT,
Eveline, d. 1/13/1963 at 68 in Wellesley, MA; b. Cambridge, MA; Frank W. Lingham and Mary Allen

HANMORE,
Virginia L., d. 4/27/1957 at 90 in Union; b. Portsmouth, VA; Hervey Hanmore and Alice McDonald

HANNAFORD,
Emma F., d. 5/28/1960 at 87 in Roxbury, ME; b. Saco, ME; Henry Ladd and Sarah Andrews
Orlando, d. 4/28/1953 at 93 in Sanbornville; b. Roxbury, MA; Ephraim Hannaford and Abigail Walker

HANRAHAN,
Edith G., d. 2/8/1959 at 76 in Wolfeboro; b. Laconia; George Greenwood and Mary Martin

HANRATTY,
Norma Phyllis, d. 12/27/1994 at 71 in Annapolis, MD; Ernest Seavey and Alexina Ferland

HANSCOM,
Helen E., d. 10/2/1962 at 57 in Laconia; b. Farmington; Frank Hanscom and Julia Reed
Julia Orista, d. 10/9/1938 at 76/0/24 in Billerica, MA
Waverly, d. 3/17/1895 at 0/0/3; b. Wakefield; Frank Hanscomb (sic) (Middleton) and Julia Reed (Wakefield)

HANSEN,
Dirck, d. 1/11/1945 at 0/0/4 in Boston, MA; b. Wolfeboro; William Hansen and Fanny B. Fletcher

Marine, d. 1/11/1946 at 84/4/11 in Haddon, NJ; b. Copenhagen, Denmark; Mads Neilson and Caroline E. Bensen

Otto J., d. 8/19/1974 at 79 in Wolfeboro

HANSON,

Arline F., d. 10/29/1979 at 63 in Rochester

Frank A., d. 2/13/1933 at 81/3/3

George, d. 8/5/1903 at 82/6/29; farmer; married; b. Brookfield; Reuben Hanson (Brookfield) and Mary Watson (Brookfield)

John F., d. 3/15/1952 at 80/4/3 in Union; b. No. Berwick, ME; John Hanson and Harriett Hayes

Lois M., d. 3/11/1982 at 82 in Ossipee; Marshall Knight and Belle Brackett

Marion, d. 9/3/1916 at 23/3/27; housewife; married; b. Wakefield; Frank G. McCrillis (Lebanon, ME) and Sarah McCrillis (Newfield, ME)

Mary E., d. 3/28/1894 at 34/7/4; housekeeper; married; b. New Durham; Joseph J. Penney (Farmington) and Mary A. Pinder (Stratham)

Mary L., d. 1/8/1905 at 78/3/12; housewife; widow; b. Wakefield; Joseph H. Pike (Brookfield) and Elmira Lyford (Brookfield)

Mary S., d. 10/23/1894 at 81/8/9; housekeeper; widow; b. Wakefield; Thomas Cook (Wakefield) and Mary Spofford (Wakefield)

Olive, d. 8/26/1899 at 94/9 in East Wakefield; housekeeping; widow; b. Wolfeboro

Ralph W., d. 4/10/1978 at 85 in Wolfeboro; Sidney Hanson and Mary Johnson

Ralph W., Jr., d. 8/6/1991 at 69 in Dover

Sidney I., d. 11/23/1939 at 75/4/19; b. Brookfield; Charles H. Hanson and Mary C.H. Buzzell

HARDING,

Charles, d. 12/23/1901 at 72/6/20 in Sanbornville; laborer; married; b. Burlington, VT; James Harding

Ruth, d. 1/23/1904 at 63; housework; widow; b. Brownfield, ME; Simeon Dyer (Brownfield, ME) and Nancy

HARMON,

Eva, d. 2/20/1911 at 44/3/16; housekeeper; single; b. Freedom; Reuben Harmon (Madison) and Olive Moulton (Freedom)

HARRICSON,

Albert, d. 3/31/1935 at 47/2/6 in Woodman; b. IN

HARRIS,
Catherine J., d. 8/13/1973 at 87 in Rochester; James E. Small and Isabelle Gamblin
Lionel R., d. 10/25/1983 at 70; John A. Harris and Pearl Enman

HARRISON,
George R., d. 12/23/1935 at 67 in E. Wakefield; b. Akron, OH; Nathaniel Harrison and Alice Harrison
Maybelle F., d. 7/25/1962 at 86 in Union; b. West Epping; ----- Bishop
Oliver C., d. 7/31/1987 at 70 in Wolfeboro; Harold Harrison and Cordal Bingham

HART,
daughter, d. 9/3/1900 at 0/3/9; b. Wakefield; Loammi Hart (Eaton) and Ursha H. Harmon (Freedom)
Loammi, d. 9/8/1917 at 61/6/8; farmer; widower; b. Eaton; Henry Hart and Mary J. Ayers
Mildred Mills, d. 2/21/1953 at 64 in Wolfeboro; b. No. Wakefield; Mary S. Mills
Osborne H., d. 12/17/1937 at 56/7/3 in Woodman; b. Eaton; Laomi Hart and Ursha Harmon
Ursha H., d. 9/17/1908 at 44/2/28; housekeeper; married; b. Freedom; Reuben Harmon (Madison) and Olive Moulton (Freedom)

HARTFORD,
Alonzo M., d. 4/30/1908 at 44/9/22; farmer; married; b. Lebanon, ME
Clarence E., d. 5/8/1908 at 0/11/0; b. Kingston; Augustus D. Hartford (Deerfield) and Jennie Welch (Kingston)

HARVEY,
Kenneth S., d. 3/18/1894 at 0/0/0; b. Wakefield; William S. Harvey (Newfoundland) and Maud S. Chamberlin

HASELTON,
Guy F., d. 7/7/1951 at 72/8/23 in Sanbornville; b. Haverhill; Charles W. Haselton and Georgianna Fellows

HASKELL,
Marietta B., d. 7/30/1967 at 91 in Laconia; b. Woburn, MA; Simon Blake and Ellen Sargent

HASKINS,
Sadie J., d. 5/11/1998 at -- in Rochester; Clifton Goodwin and Ethel -----

HASSETT,
Leonard, d. 4/3/1971 at 71 in Sanford, ME
Ruth E., d. 4/20/1973 at 74 in Somerville, MA

HATCH,
child, d. 4/15/1912 at 0/0/0; b. Wakefield; Herbert O. Hatch (Wolfeboro) and Ethel G. Nute (Milton)
Elizabeth, d. 8/4/1895 at 20/9; single; b. Washington, DC; Daniel G. Hatch (KY) and Maggie Burbridge
Ethel G., d. 11/19/1957 at 75 in Rochester; b. Milton; Sidney Nute and Emma Morrill
Herbert O., d. 8/10/1968 at 87 in Rochester; George Hatch and Hariett Horne

HAYES,
Alice Elizabeth, d. 6/18/1949 at 82/6/7 in Union; b. Biddeford, ME; Charles Bowman and Mary Baldwin
Andrew, d. 6/20/1905 at 72/10/3 in Union; widower; b. Milton; Hanson Hayes (Milton) and Sophia Swazey (Milton)
Eva C., d. 2/17/1961 at 68 in Benton; b. Sanbornville; Joseph E. Hayes and Grace Haines
Francis R., Jr., d. 7/10/1960 at 0/0/1 in Melrose, MA; b. Melrose, MA; Francis R. Hayes and Rose D. Piano
Grace Lincoln, d. 5/6/1943 at 79/1/22 in Rochester; b. Wakefield; George Haines and Susan Nichols
James H., d. 3/2/1917 at 54/11/12; farmer; married; b. Lebanon, ME; John E. Hayes (Lancaster) and Mary E. Clarke (Lebanon, ME)
Jennie Eunice, d. 5/7/1943 at 79/3/6; b. Wakefield; Charles E. Brackett and Elizabeth Wiggin
Jeremiah, d. 1/17/1914 at 85/0/5; farmer; widower; b. Milton; John Hayes (No. Rochester) and Elizabeth Plumer (Alton)
Joseph E., d. 6/22/1899 at 40/5/20 in Sanbornville; hotel keeper; married; b. Wolfeboro; Joseph Hayes
Josie B., d. 1/7/1955 at 84 in Union; b. Lowell, MA; William Clay and Agnes Bates
Lucretia, d. 12/15/1893 at 76/0/21; widow; b. Alton; Paul Wolman

Susan, d. 1/30/1936 at 86/4/23 in Sanbornville; b. Wolfeboro; James
Sceggel and Sophia Nute
Sylvia M., d. 1/12/1950 at 59 in Somerville, MA

HAYNES,
Charles L., d. 2/4/1965 at 80 in Wolfeboro; b. Sanbornville; John M.
Haynes and Elvira Hilliard
Edwin M., d. 3/2/1910 at 29/3/24; tinsmith; married; b. Laconia; John M.
Haynes (Wolfeboro) and Elvira Hilliard (Hill)
Elvira, d. 9/11/1925 at 77; widow; b. Hill; ----- Hilliard and Jane Cole
George E., Sr., d. 5/27/1981 at 65; George E. Haynes and Martha McPhee
Vianna, d. 4/21/1895 at 74/0/29; housekeeper; widow; b. Tuftonboro;
Samuel Horn (Farmington) and Nancy Canney (Tuftonboro)

HAYWARD,
George Alden, d. 9/24/1997 at 72 in Rochester; Frederick Hayward and
Agnes Pilkington

HEATH,
Edward C., d. 9/22/1952 at 74 in Sanbornville; b. Oldtown, ME; Charles
Heath and Marie -----
Ida, d. 3/19/1952 at 74/6/13 in Concord; b. Milton Mills; Everett Witham
and Jennie Calorny
Patience J., d. 4/7/1901 at 67/9/2; domestic; widow; b. Parsonsfield, ME;
William Stevens and Rose Taylor (Parsonsfield, ME)
Rubie E., d. 4/16/1896 at 2/11/13 in Union; b. Union; T. S. Heath
(Newfield, ME) and Caddie M. Stevens (Parsonsfield, ME)

HECK,
Frank J., d. 7/7/1984 at 87 in Wolfeboro; Peter J. Heck and Anna M.
Gerlach
Louise M., d. 9/19/1977 at 78 in Wolfeboro; Arthur H. Paul and Annie
Nairn

HELANDER,
Barbara W., d. 9/17/1978 at 67 in Brockton, MA
Carl, d. 9/24/1990 at 82 in Plymouth, MA

HENDERSON,
Charles William, d. 8/7/1954 at 42; b. Lynn, MA; Charles M. Henderson and Florence McNair

HENNESSEY,
John D., d. 11/19/1971 at 57 in Union; Joseph D. Hennessey and Mary A. Hargreaves

HENNESSY,
Mary A., d. 6/22/1959 at 77 in Union; b. Harrisville, RI; John Hargreaves and Catherine Ferguson

HENRY,
William Harley, d. 3/14/1905 at 79/5/26; farmer; married; b. NS; William Henry and Mary Harley

HERBERT,
Ellis N., d. 9/11/1965 at 34 in Burlington, VT

HERRICK,
Emma, d. 7/29/1948 at 91/2/27 in East Wakefield; b. St. Johns, NB
George S., d. 10/19/1980 at 78 in Wolfeboro; George S. Herrick, Sr. and Lelia Patch

HERRMAN,
Phylura A., d. 2/16/1910 at 64/2/8; housewife; married; b. VT; Cyrus Davidson

HICKEY,
Alice A., d. 8/26/1969 at 83; Charles A. Douglas and Jennie E. Rice
Evelyn G., d. 8/8/1976 at 71 in East Wakefield; Fred R. Palmer and Ervina Davidson
James W., d. 4/24/1986 at 80 in Ossipee; John Hickey and Mary Hawco

HICKS,
Dorothy W., d. 3/18/1985 at 58 in Union; William Willard and Huldur Lundgren

HIGGINS,
Howard B., Jr., d. 2/14/1981 at 64 in Wolfeboro; Howard B. Higgins and Edith Osborn

HIGHSMITH,
Ida M., d. 7/7/1962 at 73 in Rochester; b. Sanbornville; Daniel Brackett and Ida F. Rice

HILL,
daughter, d. 4/13/1914 at 0/0/1; b. Wakefield; Claude F. Hill (Boston, MA) and Ella M. Hart (Wakefield)
Almon D., d. 6/13/1952 at 81/5/8 in Wolfeboro; b. East Wakefield; Asa Hill and Matilda Jones
Annie M., d. 4/8/1982 at 78 in Union
Asa W., d. 6/4/1898 at 63/10/19; farmer; married; b. Wakefield; James Hill (Wakefield) and Lotty Dow (Lee)
Catherine M., d. 5/23/1929 at 55/9/11; married; b. Ireland; ----- Shaunessy
Charlotte, d. 7/14/1887 at 90/3/11; housework; widow; b. Lee
Ella M., d. 8/23/1918 at 22/1/20; housewife; married; b. Wakefield; Loammi Hart (Conway) and Ursha Hammond (Freedom)
Hathe M., d. 9/23/1972 at 97 in Sanford, ME; Frank Robinson and Alice Thompson
Helen, d. 1/15/1924 at 25/10/14; housewife; married; b. Brownfield, ME; John Norton and Carrie Jennings
James B., d. 3/2/1892 at 76/2/3; carpenter; widower; b. Wakefield; John Hill (Wakefield) and Lydia Brackett (Ossipee)
James W., d. 6/7/1910 at 90/3/1; mechanic; married; b. Wakefield; James Hill (Wakefield) and Charlotte Dow (Lee)
Joseph C., d. 12/10/1887 at 49/5/7; canvasser; married; b. Wakefield; John Hill (Wakefield) and Lydia Brackett (Ossipee)
Kathleen Whitney, d. 1/24/1992 at 89 in Wolfeboro; ----- Young and ----- Whitney
Lawrence R., d. 7/31/1946 at 68/5/28 in Togus, ME; b. Concord
Louis N., d. 4/15/1941 at 88/0/3; b. Moncton, NB; John Hill
Lucy M., d. 12/18/1919 at 82/10/24; apoplexy; housekeeper; widow; b. Wakefield; Joshua Sewards (Barnstead) and Mary K. Sewards (Barnstead)
Mary E., d. 2/22/1930 at 73/10/10; widow; b. Chesterfield; Freeman Knowlton and Ellen Bingham

Matilda F., d. 2/27/1922 at 79/10/28; widow; John Jones (Lebanon, ME) and Rhoda Whittman (Milton)
Mrs. Thomas W., d. 12/21/1895 in Brooklyn, NY; married
Ormand A.D., d. 8/7/1892 at 0/7/26; b. Wakefield; David D. Hill (Walten, CE) and Margaret T. Adams (Scotland)
Roy W., d. 8/1/1981 at 85 in Wolfeboro; Stephen W. Hill and Ida M. Woodruff
Simon P., d. 7/20/1891 at 80; farmer; widower; b. Effingham; John Hill (Wakefield) and Dolly Philbrick (Effingham)
Viella F., d. 2/20/1908 at 43/1/18; housewife; single; b. Wakefield; Asa Hill (Wakefield) and Matilda Jones (Wakefield)
Vila L., d. 12/7/1984 at 84 in Union; George Kimball and Eliza Hanscomb
Viola C., d. 9/23/1920 at 55/8/21; pernicious anemia; single; b. Wakefield; Asa Hill (Wakefield) and Matilda Jones (Wakefield)

HILTON,
Valda M., d. 7/7/1970 at 70 in Sanbornville; Thatcher C. Hilton and Bertha J. Smith

HILTUNEN,
Charles T., d. 11/30/1978 at 74 in Wolfeboro; John Hiltunen and Katherine Quimpia
Lauretta T., d. 3/19/1991 at 85 in Danvers, MA

HIMES,
Edwin A., d. 1/22/1948 at 82/8/21 in Wolfeboro; b. Buchanan, MI; Edwin T. Himes and Adelaide Vincent

HINES,
Edward T., Jr., d. 12/15/1994 at 56; Edward T. Hines, Sr. and Dorothy Drinon

HISELER,
Elizabeth E., d. 6/26/1988 at 97 in Wolfeboro; Alfred Tappin
Mary N., d. 10/2/1988 at 75 in Dover

HITCHCOCK,
Fred L., d. 10/29/1919 at 19/3/20; gunshot wound; teamster; single; b. Ossipee; Wilbur Hitchcock (Ossipee) and Addie Templeton (Ossipee)

HOBBS,
Gladys E., d. 11/14/1984 at 83 in Dover; Roy E. Hobbs and Jennie M. Pierce
Jennie M., d. 7/13/1948 at 70/8/15 in Union; b. Lebanon, ME; Frank D. Pierce and Sarah Atherton
Rhoda, d. 1/6/1896 at 93/5/17; widow; b. Parsonsfield, ME: Andrew McChapman (Newmarket) and Elanor Jones (Epping)

HODGDON,
Ellsworth, d. 10/13/1949 at 88/0/27 in Union; b. Lebanon, ME; Chandler Hodgdon and Mary -----
Fred W., d. 4/8/1953 at 83 in Union; b. Ossipee; William O.S. Hodgdon and Betsey Nutter
Jimmie O., d. 9/5/1898 at 0/2/21; b. Wakefield; Jesse Hodgdon (No. Berwick, ME) and Mary Drew (Brookfield)
John E., d. 12/7/1928 at 81/5/17; married; b. Newburyport, MA; Charles H. Hodgdon and Naomi Roberts
Myrtle Corbett, d. 6/12/1995 at 88 in Sanbornville; Andrew Corbett and Annie -----

HODGKINS,
Doris E., d. 3/17/1978 at 70 in Wolfeboro; Wilfred Marsh and Emma Holmes

HODSDON,
Horace, d. 12/12/1934 at 73/1/20 in Sanford, ME; b. Parsonsfield, ME; William Hodsdon and Mary J. Quimby
Sarah Y., d. 9/26/1932 at 66/5/22 in Sanbornville

HOFFMAN,
Herbert T., d. 1/16/1940 at 71/8/4 in Union; b. Lebanon, ME; William E. Hoffman and Sarah Taylor
Josephine H., d. 11/6/1964 at 87; b. New York, NY; Frederick Hochreiter and Louise Sherer

HOIT,
Flora B.W., d. 12/29/1963 at 79 in Sanford, ME; b. Brookfield
George W., d. 8/28/1966 at 72 in Sanbornville; b. Concord; Henry W. Hoit and Hannah L. Hoit

HOLMAN,
George D., d. 11/14/1956 at 58 in Rochester; b. Lincoln, MA; Amos Holman and Catherine Butcher

HOOPEE,
Nellie E., d. 8/28/1970 at 84 in Sanbornville; John H. Roles and Laura Dore

HOOPER,
Charles E., d. 3/19/1932 at 74/1/9 in Sanbornville
Edna W., d. 12/15/1975 at 86 in Wolfeboro; Homer Wilkins and Mary Hutchins
John Eben, d. 9/30/1951 at 72 in Sanbornville; b. Boxford, MA; John L. Hooper and Christina Fraser
Louise, d. 6/18/1986 at 79 in Wolfeboro
Roy E., d. 3/14/1962 at 75 in Togus, ME; b. Wakefield; Charles E. Hooper and Nellie Downs
Sidney E., d. 8/10/1957 at 73 in Sanbornville; b. So. Wakefield; Charles E. Hooper and Nellie Downs
William Henry, d. 1/17/1941 at 91/5/2; b. Boxford, MA; Ebenezer E. Hooper and Elizabeth Russell

HORN,
Alice, d. 7/16/1903 at 78/1; housekeeper; single; b. Horn's Mills; David Horn (Wakefield) and Eliza Nason (Acton, ME)
Arthur C., d. 10/6/1937 at 71/5/21 in Acton, ME; b. Wakefield; Samuel C. Horn and Augusta Horn
Frances M., d. 5/15/1964 at 70 in Berwick, ME
Hannah R., d. 9/10/1942 at 76/10/10 in Manchester
Jackson, d. 3/6/1910 at 74/1/25; carpenter; married; b. Acton, ME; Daniel Horn (Acton, ME) and Nancy Copp (Moultonboro)

HORNE,
Annie L., d. 12/10/1955 at 89 in Union; b. Moultonboro; Charles H. Earle and Eliza Russell
Benjamin, d. 10/23/1903 at 76/6/4 in Horn's Mills; farmer; married; b. Wakefield; George Horne (Wakefield) and Permelia Roberts (Acton, ME)
Charles F., d. 2/2/1944 at 54/3/15 in Rochester; b. Shapleigh, ME; Arthur C. Horne and Ada B. Cook

Charles S., d. 10/27/1921 at 63/5/27; cerebral embolism; lumber dealer; single; b. Wakefield; Benjamin Horne (Wakefield) and Abbie Merrill (NH)

Chester, d. 5/2/1970 at 67 in Peabody, MA

Constance, d. 2/14/1935 at 0/1 in Salem, MA; b. Marblehead, MA; William S. Horne and Dorothy Rawnsley

Edith S., d. 6/18/1978 at 79 in Wolfeboro; Henry P. Herr and Rachael DeCou

Edwin C., d. 1/16/1986 at 59 in Portland, ME

Edwin J., d. 1/19/1933 at 68/3/15

Ethel R., d. 10/9/1965 at 85 in Wolfeboro

Flossie Vivian, d. 7/3/1959 at 74 in Wolfeboro; b. NS; Charles Taylor and Amanda Wombolt

Linwood Ashton, d. 2/23/1943 at 70/0/28 in Acton, ME; Samuel C. Horn and Augusta Horn

Margaret M., d. 4/18/1975 at 68 in Sanford, ME

Mary, d. 1/18/1913 at 69/4/21; housewife; widow; b. Wakefield; Joseph Allen (Wakefield) and Louise Littlefield

Mary A., d. 4/9/1947 at 69/7/1 in Rochester; b. Manchester, England

Mary M., d. 6/21/1917 at 84/7; housekeeper; widow; b. Acton, ME; Jonathan Quimby (Acton, ME)

Ralph A., d. 10/6/1934 at 40/1/20 in Rochester; b. North Conway; Edwin J. Horne and Hannah Runnels

Sarah C., d. 7/14/1978 at 86 in Rochester

Wilbur Coates, d. 9/3/1949 at 48/8/14; b. Marblehead, MA; Charles W. Horne and Hattie Coates

HOUDE,

Adele P., d. 11/9/1947 at 89/7/8 in Sanbornville; b. Canada; Joseph Pouliot and Deange Roy

Edward, d. 1/27/1943 at 95/2/13 in Sanbornville; b. Quebec; Michael Houde and Joset Fortier

HOUGHTON,

Mary E., d. 4/27/1905 at 67/9; housekeeper; widow; b. Wakefield; Samuel Ames (Wakefield) and Sarah Young (Wakefield)

Phoebe A., d. 11/13/1958 at 84 in Union; b. Eaton; Charles F. White and Nettie Weeks

HOUSTON,
George W., d. 11/22/1957 at 68 in East Wakefield; b. Scotland; Thomas Houston and Elizabeth Wright
Jean W., d. 6/5/1963 at 71 in Wolfeboro; b. Glasgow, Scotland; Alexander Winks and Mary B. McClue

HOWARD,
Ida E., d. 3/13/1956 at 80 in Sanbornville; b. Bartlett; Jacob Hill and Mary Ordway
Lydia M., d. 5/14/1905 at 70/1/9; housewife; widow; b. Wakefield; Samuel Lang (York, ME) and Lydia M. Thurber (Portsmouth)

HOWE,
Emily, d. 8/30/1964 at 99 in Concord; b. Perth, Canada; Adolphus E. Consitt and ----- Belille
Philip Warren, d. 2/20/1991 at 82 in Exeter; Edgar Howe and Elisabeth Riley
Vivian W., d. 5/26/1961 at 87 in Boston, MA

HOWES,
Ruth, d. 1/25/1974 at 70 in Wolfeboro

HOWLAND,
Carston, d. 2/23/1993 at 60; Winthrop Howland and Shirley Marian Carlsen

HOYT,
Harry R., d. 9/16/1963 at 77 in Sanbornville; b. No. Barnstead; Alonzo Hoyt and Gertrude Hoyt

HRABA,
John Burnett, d. 4/23/1997 at 75 in Wolfeboro; John Hraba and Elizabeth Kleinman

HUEMMIER,
Donna Marie, d. 9/3/1997 at 33 in East Wakefield; John A. Saunders and Sheila J. Conway

HUGHES,
Viola E., d. 3/6/1965 at 83 in Dover

HULTEN,
Thure, d. 5/17/1968 at 67 in Laconia; Amandus Hulten and Ingar Gunderson

HUMPHREY,
Mabel L., d. 5/4/1959 at 78 in Wolfeboro; b. Digby, NS; Hugh McLean and ----- Ellis

HUNT,
Doris L., d. 3/12/1968 at 58 in Wolfeboro; Samuel Lewis and Martha Strain

HUNTER,
John E., d. 1/26/1979 at 73 in Hanover; Otto Hunter and Eva Littell

HUNTRESS,
Stillman S., d. 3/13/1905 at 65/2/10; farmer; married; b. Harmony, ME; Noah Huntress (No. Shapleigh, ME) and Sophia Pitts (No. Shapleigh, ME)

HURD,
Florence E., d. 11/22/1947 at 65/1/19 in Milton Mills; b. Wakefield
Frank J., d. 2/26/1908 at 0/1/2; b. Wakefield; Isaac Hurd (Canada) and Rosie Marcoux (Wakefield)
Louis Filbert, d. 12/3/1905 at 0/0/16 in Sanbornville; b. Sanbornville; Isaac Hurd (Canada) and Rosie Marcoux (Sanbornville)
Lucy M., d. 7/15/1956 at 88 in Union; b. Rochester; Jonathan Garland and Sarah Meserve
Mabel M., d. 4/9/1915 at 3/10/9; b. Wakefield; Isaac Hurd (Canada) and Rosie Marcoux (Wakefield)
Ralph H., d. 6/25/1968 at 79 in Concord; Frank Hurd

HURLEY,
Pat, d. 7/1/1930 at 80; single

HUTCHINS,
child, d. 5/19/1950 at 0/0/0 in Wolfeboro; b. Wolfeboro
Agnes A., d. 8/16/1935 at 74/4/12 in Sanbornville; b. Wakefield; Charles H. Sawyer and Lydia M. Davis

Bernard H., d. 6/10/1982 at 80 in Wolfeboro; Edwin H. Hutchins and Iva Linscott

Carrie B., d. 1/13/1973 at 82 in Wolfeboro; Teri H. Hutchins and Hannah Boyle

Charles N., d. 8/12/1901 at 54/8/1; carpenter; divorced; b. Wakefield; George W. Hutchins (Wakefield) and Elizabeth Wiggin (Lebanon, ME)

Edwin H., d. 2/23/1912 at 60/8/18; farmer; married; b. Dover; Hiram W. Hutchins (Wakefield) and Mary F.D. Neal (Brookfield)

Edwin Mason, d. 11/2/1942 at 58/10/2 in Wolfeboro; b. Wakefield; Edwin Hutchins and Iva Linscott

Elizabeth W., d. 12/6/1953 at 91 in Wolfeboro; b. No. Wakefield; Joseph S. Wentworth and Mary E. Weeks

Esther, d. 7/4/1899 at 81/5/12; housewife; married; b. Sanford, ME; Amos Maddox (Sanford, ME) and Eunice Day (Sanford, ME)

Hiram W., d. 2/21/1897 at 73/7/15; farmer; married; b. Wakefield; Joseph Hutchins (Wakefield) and Betsy Wiggin (Wakefield)

Joseph Hiram, d. 2/14/1939 at 40/3/13 in Wolfeboro; b. Wakefield; Edwin Hutchins and Iva Linscott

Mary A., d. 3/21/1939 at 90/6/26; b. Wakefield; Robert Corson and Sarah Nay

Paul B., d. 6/10/1994 at 66 in Manchester; Bernard Hutchins and Teresa Hayes

Raymond, d. 12/24/1888 at 0/8/1; b. Wakefield; Samuel L. Hutchins (Wakefield) and Mary A. Corson (Wakefield)

Sadie B., d. 8/12/1888 at 11/3/26; b. Wakefield; Samuel L. Hutchins (Brookfield) and Mary E. Drew (Exeter)

Samuel L., d. 5/13/1902 at 49/6/22 in Union; manufacturer; married; b. Wakefield; John S. Hutchins (Wakefield) and Betsy Lyford (Brookfield)

Teresa Hayes, d. 9/3/1997 at 92 in Wolfeboro; Henry F. Hayes and Mabel Welch

William, d. 12/26/1887 at 77; married

HYDE,
Max Lee, d. 11/17/1941 at 61/9/11; b. Richford, VT; Richard Hyde and Alice M. Gross

HYNDS,
son, d. 8/26/1925 at 0/0/0; b. Sanbornville; David C. Hynds and Flora E. Steele

HYNES,
Adeline M., d. 5/6/1984 at 58; Frank DeMasse
Mary S., d. 12/21/1991 at 85 in Dover

JACKSON,
Charles J., d. 7/31/1913 at 72/6/9; gospel singer; married; b. Franklin; Joshua Jackson (Eden, VT) and Polly Fifield (Franklin)
Julia, d. 4/22/1918 at 83/7; housewife; widow; b. Otisfield, ME; R. Sampson (Leeds, ME) and Mary Smith (Harrison, ME)

JACQUES,
Adeline, d. 12/9/1915 at 69/10; housekeeper; widow; b. Canada; Louis Theoret (Canada) and Adeline Brunette (Canada)

JAGGER,
Evelyn, d. 6/14/1987 at 65 in Hanover; Robert Zurheide and Mina Luxem

JENKINS,
Bessie C., d. 7/31/1958 at 76 in Wolfeboro; b. Eastport, ME; Joseph Clark and Esther Parker
Herbert F., d. 1/24/1960 at 86; b. Rockland, MA; Joseph H. Jenkins and Emily Clark

JENNESS,
Blanche I., d. 9/27/1907 at 17/0/18; housewife; married; b. Wakefield; Loami Hart (Eaton) and Ursha Harmon (Freedom)
Charles H., d. 5/11/1936 at 93/8; b. Wakefield; Johnson Jenness and Elizabeth M. Clark
Charles W., d. 2/18/1941 at 51/1/17; b. Milton; Edwin P. Jenness and Alma J. Hawkins
Clara P., d. 6/4/1923 at 68/4/9; housework; b. Rochester; John D. Pillsbury (Newburyport, MA) and Sarah C. Johnson (Buxton, ME)
Lizzie M., d. 6/10/1934 at 83/3/1; b. Wakefield; Phenous Weeks and Mercy B. Hayes
Perley A., d. 3/30/1946 at 70/1/4 in Wolfeboro; b. Wakefield; Charles H. Jenness and Lizzie M. Weeks

JETTE,
Joseph R.A., d. 5/25/1948 at 73/3/15 in Sanbornville; b. Canada; Peter Jette and Mary Laruque
Justine M., d. 9/12/1956 at 84 in Sanbornville; b. Canada; Joseph Gagnon and Marie C. Ouellet
Peter D., d. 1/3/1969 at 26 in Baltimore, MD; Romero A. Jette and Virginia Stevens
Romeo A., d. 11/25/1970 at 56 in Hartford, VT; Arthur A. Jette and Justin M. Gonyea

JEWETT,
Haven F., d. 4/14/1963 at 63 in Manchester; b. Milton; Haven R. Jewett and Nellie M. Sibley
John Chase, d. 4/11/1931 at 43/11/22; single; b. Wakefield; Haven Jewett and Mary N. Sibley
Mary Nellie, d. 9/12/1939 at 78/5/2 in Rochester; b. Boston, MA; Richard F.D. Sibley and Emma Buzzell
Susan W., d. 11/13/1899 at 75/7/13 in Union; housewife; widow; b. Acton, ME; David Jewett (Milton Mills) and Susan M. Fox (Lebanon, ME)

JOCS,
Joseph, d. 6/12/1972 at 64 in Rochester (probably erroneous - see Joos)

JOHNSON,
Arvilla M., d. 1/15/1918 at 39/4/12; housewife; married; b. Boston, MA; Franklin C. Sands (ME) and Mary Murray (Scotland)
Carl A., d. 11/20/1989 at 86 in Sanbornville; Charles T. Johnson and Anna Olson
Chester R., d. 3/6/1900 at 7/7/11; b. Wakefield; Lester Johnson (Stow, ME) and Cora Mears (Wolfeboro)
Cora L., d. 4/13/1922 at 53/2/4; at home; married; b. Wolfeboro; Alfred Mears (Reading, MA) and Maria Staples (Effingham)
Doris A., d. 10/21/1974 at 76 in Meredith; Joseph E. Hayes and Grace L. Haines
Edith E., d. 5/12/1982 at 68 in Rochester
Frederick W., d. 8/10/1974 at 81; Peter Johnson and Anna McCaw
Freeman L., d. 2/22/1935 at 69/1/4 in Whitefield
Herbert W., d. 2/5/1991 at 83 in Wolfeboro; Ernest Johnson and Emma Olson
John H., d. 1/21/1922 at 91/5/24; farmer; widower; b. Yarmouth, ME

Joseph, d. 9/24/1905 at 71/2/1; stone worker; married; b. Brighton, ME; Leighton Johnson (Fryeburg, ME) and Sarah Gray (Strafford)
Joseph W., d. 11/17/1970 at 51 in Rochester; Frederick W. Johnson and Doris A. Hayes
Maria, d. 7/21/1895 at 28/3/18; housewife; married; b. Sweden; Carl Johnson (Sweden) and Eliza C. Anderson (Sweden)
Merna E., d. 10/14/1991 at 68 in Dover; Charles E. Painter and Elizabeth B. Corzatt
Myron L., d. 12/30/1943 at 86/8/4 in Union; b. Stowe, ME; Joseph L. Johnson and Sarah Tibbetts
Samuel H., d. 7/13/1956 at 77 in Dover; b. Fulton, NY; William P. Johnson and Anna McCaw
Sarah F., d. 6/26/1924 at 89/6/11; at home; widow; b. Wolfeboro; Moses Tibbetts (NH) and ---- York
Winifred, d. 10/25/1955 at 72 in Rochester; b. Kearsarge; John Gile and Lizzie Smart

JOHNSTON,
William C., d. 7/30/1958 at 80; b. Ireland; William Johnston and Mary Somerville

JONES,
Ada N., d. 9/22/1955 at 85 in Union; b. Peterborough; William L. Abbott and Ella Osgood
Bertha A., d. 10/3/1967 at 86 in Dover
Edith H., d. 9/2/1956 at 80 in Santa Ana, CA
George, d. 7/29/1891 at --; brakeman; single
Hiram, d. 11/22/1912 at 80/5/30; farmer; married; b. Wakefield; John Jones (Lebanon, ME) and Rhoda Witham (Milton)
Morcom B., d. 8/5/1987 at 70 in East Wakefield; Benjamin Jones and Mabel Delbridge
Samuel D., d. 12/7/1893 at 43/4/3; carpenter; married; b. Middleton; Daniel Jones (Middleton) and Sarah Pike (Middleton)
Waldo Hiram, d. 8/25/1945 at 74/3/5 in Swampscott, MA

JOOS,
Joseph, d. 7/12/1972 at 64 in Rochester; Augustine Joos and Marie VanDaele
Victor J., d. 1/6/1982 at 68 in Rochester

JOY,
daughter, d. 7/24/1906 at 0/0/0; b. Wakefield; Frank D. Joy (So. Berwick, ME) and Alice P. Kimball (Middleton)
child, d. 2/2/1937 at 0/0/0 in Rochester; b. Rochester; Nelson Joy and Mildred Pike
Alice P., d. 2/7/1968 at 80 in Union; George W. Kimball and Eliza Hanscomb
Dorothy A., d. 7/5/1993 at 72 in Union; Clyde E. Chisholm and Hattie M. Rolfe
Emmie L., d. 5/27/1982 at 23 in Concord; Clayton F. Fulcher and Jennie Peters
Frank D., d. 2/23/1948 at 66/0/1 in Wolfeboro; b. So. Berwick, ME; Owen Joy and Sarah Abbott
George E., d. 6/22/1955 at 12 in Union; b. Rochester; Lester Joy and Gladys Horn
Jessie-Ann, d. 8/22/1998 at 66 in Sanbornville; Ralph Herbert and Leah Wiggin
Lawrence I., d. 6/15/1966 at 54 in Union; b. Union; Frank Joy and Alice Kimball
Leah Ann, d. 5/21/1982 at 0/5 in Union; Stephen P. Joy and Emmie Fulcher
Mildred P., d. 10/27/1964 at 59 in Rochester; b. Wakefield; Edwin L. Pike and Mary B. Wentworth
Ronald S., d. 2/8/1945 at 0/8/18 in Union; b. Rochester; Abbott L. Joy and Pearl E. Johnson
Stephen P., d. 5/21/1982 at 27 in Union; Oscar K. Joy and Jessie A. Herbert
Sylvia L., d. 4/28/1992 at 54 in Union; Edmund Smith and Hannah Demeritt
William A., d. 3/26/1952 at 68/9 in Union; b. East Rochester; John P. Jones and Clara Ricker

JUDKINS,
Florence H., d. 11/14/1977 at 87 in Beverly, MA; Preston Nash and Nancy
-----

JUNKINS,
Elmer V., d. 6/19/1981 at 95 in Rochester
Helen M., d. 5/2/1990 at 97 in Rochester

James H., d. 12/11/1896 at 73/10/8; blacksmith; married; b. Wakefield;
Rufus Junkins (York, ME) and Sally Hayes (Milton)
Nellie Pope, d. 7/8/1938 at 80/0/21 in Manchester; b. Waldoboro, ME;
Daniel Tucker and Mercy Howes

KARCHER,
Martha M., d. 9/14/1973 at 82 in Rochester; Charles E. Wilfert and
Casandra MacKenzie
William A., d. 8/28/1959 at 71 in Sanbornville; b. Charlestown, MA;
Theodore Karcher and Eliza Williams

KASPRZYK,
Paul S., d. 7/10/1983 at 27; Louis Kasprzyk and Anna Bazylewicz

KATWICK,
Robert T., Jr., d. 5/17/1978 at 36 in Wolfeboro; Robert T. Katwick, Sr.
and Mary Lortis

KEATING,
James Francis, II, d. 6/16/1992 at 68 in Sanbornville; James Francis
Keating and Jane Flynn

KEAY,
Winona Emma, d. 6/26/1949 at 83/0/11 in Sanbornville; b. Reading, MA;
James H. Parker and Helen Guild

KEENAN,
Henry F., d. 9/14/1904 at 49/5/24; millman; married; b. Boston, MA;
Patrick Keenan (Ireland) and Bridget ----- (Ireland)

KEENE,
Lulu G., d. 8/26/1958 at 80; b. Boston, MA; ----- Greenleaf and -----
Knowlton
Wendell P., d. 10/4/1966 at 90 in Wolfeboro

KEHOE,
Myrton Parker, d. 1/26/1998 at 80 in Rochester; Frank Leslie Kehoe and
Marguerite L. Hunter

KELLER,
Earl G., d. 9/16/1978 at 62 in Wolfeboro; Elwood Keller and Katherine Urquhart
Ruth E., d. 9/26/1988 at 64 in Portland, ME

KELLEY,
Asa Burton, d. 3/23/1944 at 79/1/28 in Middleton
Ruth G., d. 7/25/1955 at 73 in Middleton; b. Wakefield

KELLY,
Bartholomew P., d. 6/26/1977 at 67 in Wolfeboro; John Kelly
Elizabeth N., d. 2/22/1985 at 66 in Wolfeboro

KENDALL,
Frank L., d. 5/29/1920 at 48/11/26; natural causes; ins. agent; married; b. St. Johnsbury, VT; L. L. Kendall and Marie Poland
George Wilkins, d. 7/3/1995 at 76 in East Wakefield; Philip Mason Kendall and Ruth G. Wilkins
Philip M., d. 5/8/1986 at 93 in Wolfeboro; Henry H. Kendall and Amelia Davis

KENEFICK,
John L., d. 5/2/1974 at 73; Edward Kenefick and Annie McDonald

KENERSON,
Jennie A., d. 1/15/1899 at 33 in Sanbornville; housewife; married; b. Wakefield; Josiah Wiggin (Wakefield) and Mary Rines

KENISTON,
Ephraim A., d. 8/21/1976 at 76 in Boston, MA; Cyrus Keniston and Martha Darron
Narcissa D., d. 3/14/1909 at 62/8/17; housework; married; b. Tuftonboro; Cyrus Kenney (Tuftonboro) and Sabrah Nute (Wolfeboro)
Randolph, d. 3/3/1918 at 76/3/26; farmer; widower; b. Effingham; John Keniston
Rosabell, d. 3/28/1927 at 57/0/3; married; b. Wilmot; Walter F. Chase and Rose L. Fletcher
Theodore R., d. 8/21/1975 at 70 in Ossipee; Isaac Keniston and Rosabella Chase

Willie, d. 8/27/1913 at 0/0/9; b. Wakefield; Isaac Keniston (Effingham) and Rose B. Chase (Concord)

KENNEDY,
Bernard B., d. 10/2/1935 at 62/0/17; b. Lynnfield, MA; Malaky Kennedy and Mary A. Scannell
John W., d. 3/21/1950 at 67/6/14 in Wolfeboro; b. Putnam, CT; John W. Kennedy and Margaret Clement

KENNESON,
Earle H., d. 1/27/1962 at 65 in Sanbornville; b. Rumney; Albert Kenneson and Lucy Hardy

KENNETT,
Ami, d. 9/21/1896 at 78/0/26; farmer; b. Effingham
Herbert C., d. 6/28/1939 at 56/6 in Rochester; b. Madison; Charles H. Kennett and Abbie Davis
Jeane Isabel, d. 12/3/1945 at 69/8/12 in Wolfeboro; b. Halifax, NS; John McD. Robinson and Margaret J. George
Lydia M., d. 11/23/1975 at 77 in Wolfeboro; Frank McBride and Bessie Richardson
Ralph R., d. 1/30/1964 at 73 in Sanford, ME
Sally, d. 3/20/1897 at 78/10; widow; b. Effingham

KENNEY,
Helen M., d. 1/30/1956 at 70 in Wolfeboro; b. Conway; Frank Lucy and Emma Stuart
John Thomas, Sr., d. 1/5/1998 at 83 in Manchester; William James Kinney and Josephine Gallant
Luther W., d. 2/14/1955 at 70 in Sanbornville; b. Wolfeboro; Franklin E. Kenney and Carrie B. Twombly
Miriam V., d. 6/9/1974 at 17 in Wolfeboro; John T. Kenney and Elizabeth Dale

KERSHAW,
Samuel, d. 7/14/1892 at 53/7/1; hotel keeper; married; b. New Salem; John Kershaw

KIDGER,
Horace, d. 5/4/1974 at 94 in Anna Maria, FL; John Kidger and Charlotte Hensen

KIMBALL,
Albert, d. 1/20/1969 at -- in Brook Haven, NY
Angeline M., d. 7/1/1956 at 72/3/4 in Union; b. Epping; George Perkins and Mabel Perkins
Arthur, d. 12/7/1943 at 69/2/3 in Ossipee; b. Rochester; Oliver Kimball and Ellen Littlefield
Augusta F., d. 8/29/1897 at 0/4/24; b. Wakefield; John W. Kimball (Wakefield) and Alta Pike (Middleton)
David S., d. 10/7/1906 at 0/6/4; b. Wakefield; Alphonso Kimball (Middleton) and Myrtie E. Glidden (New Durham)
George Byron, d. 3/21/1992 at 100 in Wolfeboro; George Washington Kimball and Eliza Hanscom
Gladys C., d. 1/31/1937 at 39/3/14 in Union; b. Milton; John M. Corson and Eva M. Postleton
John, d. 9/13/1892 at 68/1/5; farmer; married; b. Wakefield; Noah Kimball (Wakefield) and Dorothy Johnson (Andover, ME)
John W., d. 5/6/1929 at 82/0/13; married; b. Wakefield; Ward W. Kimball and Sarah Watson
John W., d. 9/10/1983 at 56 in Wolfeboro; Ward C. Kimball and Marion Evans
Lester E., d. 10/20/1915 at 22/3/8; mill hand; single; b. Wakefield; George Kimball (Middleton) and Eliza Hanscom (Middleton)
Lydia, d. 10/24/1904 at 74; housekeeper; widow; b. Wakefield; Symeon Wiggin (Wakefield) and Sarah Wentworth (Milton)
Marion E., d. 8/8/1983 at 77 in Wolfeboro; Calvin Evans and Florabelle Rhines
Paula P., d. 3/16/1964 at 66; b. Evanston, IL
Sylvia M., d. 10/1/1996 at 70 in Dover; Waldo Hill and Vila Kimball
Thomas Calvin, d. 8/12/1959 at 0/0/3 in Rochester; b. Rochester; John W. Kimball and Sylvia Hill
Violet P., d. 12/13/1944 at 80/7/13 in Concord; b. Ft. Fairfield, ME; Bradford Cummings and Martha White
Ward Cummings, d. 10/12/1977 at 75 in Wolfeboro; John W. Kimball and Violet Cummings

KING,
Betty Louise, d. 1/5/1939 at 0/5/16; b. Canaan; Clifford W. King and Hazel Grace
Emma M., d. 7/31/1892 at 29/7/23; housework; married; b. Wakefield; Ammon S. Reed (Newfield, ME) and Lizzie A. Waldron (Acton, ME)
Marjorie H., d. 4/19/1996 at 83 in Wolfeboro; Harry Plummer
Mary E., d. 1/6/1893 at 0/6/17; b. Wakefield; Joseph King (England) and Emma M. Reed (Wakefield)
Ruth, d. 5/3/1938 at 1/3/1 in Wolfeboro; Clifford W. King and Hazel Grace

KINNICUTT,
Elsie G., d. 11/23/1964 at 62 in Sanford, ME; b. Lunenburg, MA; Delfred Carkin and Edith Cameron

KINNON,
Lynne M., d. 8/13/1984 at 26 in Pittsfield, MA

KINVILLE,
Iola Marguerite, d. 6/29/1975 at 76 in South Wakefield; Michael Thompson and Sorrell -----

KIRK,
Arthur M., d. 2/10/1970 at 30 in Laconia; Elmer I. Wiggin and Marie Campbell (?)

KIRKPATRICK,
Mildred W., d. 5/5/1988 at 87 in Exeter

KNIGHT,
Albert, d. 7/9/1972 at 80 in Manchester
Carrie L., d. 2/4/1932 at 60/8/15 in Sanbornville
Cecil Everett, d. 7/2/1988 at 76; Marshall E. Knight and Elizabeth Doyle
Charlotte K., d. 4/29/1969 at 69 in Brookfield
Elizabeth Belle, d. 3/5/1904 at 27/5/22; housewife; married; b. Wakefield; Charles E. Brackett (Acton, ME) and Elizabeth Wiggin (Wakefield)
Marshall E., d. 9/8/1933 at 60/8/5

KNISLEY,
Raymond O., d. 7/9/1972 at 69 in Sanbornville; Edwin N. Knisley and Rose Thurman

KNOX,
George A., d. 11/29/1898 at 45; brakeman; married; b. Tamworth; Edward Knox (Ossipee) and Abigail Nason (Madison)

KOHLING,
Charles A., d. 9/1/1946 at 82/2/20; b. New York, NY; William H. Kohling and Alice Liston

KOSINSKI,
Nancy L., d. 10/19/1997 at 59 in East Wakefield; William F. Bryan and Louise -----

KRABEK,
Axel, d. 4/8/1909 at 25/6/28; laborer; married; b. Denmark

KRAUS,
Leonard, d. 7/8/1958 at 56; b. Chelsea, MA; Leonard J. Kraus and Lydia Bedard

LACASSE,
Joseph, d. 7/26/1932 at 72/7/2 in Augusta, ME
Orelie, d. 10/26/1907 at 40/8/1; housewife; married; b. Canada; Febol Pourtrie (Canada) and Marie Lachance (Canada)

LACLAIR,
Mary Elizabeth, d. 12/26/1991 at 66; ----- and Anna -----

LACOSSE,
Arthur J., d. 11/2/1909 at 0/11/12; b. Canada; Arthur Lacosse (Canada) and Anna Goselyn (Canada)
Marion, d. 6/7/1894 at 6; b. Somersworth; Joseph Lacosse (Canada) and Orelie Patry (Canada)

LADDERBUSH,
Philip, d. 7/8/1927 at 59; single; b. VT; Aiken Ladderbush and Eliza Champeau

LAFAYETTE,
Mabel A., d. 1/19/1977 at 82 in Oak Lawn, IL

Theodore A., d. 5/16/1971 at 76 in Sanbornville; Theodore E. Lafayette and Mary J. Lindley

LAFLEUR,
Alfred S., d. 12/31/1967 at 78 in Haverhill, MA
Mary A., d. 11/8/1958 at 66 in Wolfeboro; b. Fremont; Leopold Marcotte and ----- Blanchette

LAFOY,
Irving R., d. 6/13/1911 at 0/0/28; b. Wakefield; Lee Lafoy (Canada) and Alice Randall (Lynn, MA)

LAGROTTERIA,
Domenico, d. 7/4/1915 at 17/6/17; laborer; single; b. Italy; Vito Lagrotteria (Italy) and Rosa Lagrotteria (Italy)

LAKE,
Edith P., d. 2/26/1962 at 83 in Eliot, ME; b. Saugus, MA; John E. Palmer and Etta Williams

LAKIN,
Ernest, d. 10/18/1984 at 84 in Ossipee
Evelyn G., d. 10/16/1971 at 74 in Wolfeboro; Joseph F. Curtis and Angie A. Cuhoon

LAMAY,
Ulick, d. 7/10/1887 at 3; b. Wakefield; Moses Lamay

LAMB,
Harry, d. 10/4/1983 at 90 in Wolfeboro
Nima B., d. 12/25/1995 at 102; Albert Locke and Suzie Berry

LAMIE,
Annette, d. 3/24/1936 at 19/0/23 in Sanbornville; b. Sanbornville; Fred Lamie and Diana Cyr
Emma, d. 9/9/1968 at 73 in Laconia; Moses Lamie and Lea Currier
George A., d. 3/17/1910 at 1/11/17; b. Wakefield; Fred L. Lamie (Somersworth) and Emma Veno (Ossipee)
Leo, d. 12/24/1908 at 54/4/20; housewife; married; b. Wolfston, PQ; Joseph Currier (Wolfston, PQ) and Mary Levertu (Wolfston, PQ)

Moses, d. 6/1/1924 at 78/10/5; laborer; widower; b. Canada; Emanuel Lamie (Canada) and Mary ---- (Canada)

LAMONTAGNE,
Annie, d. 8/19/1934 at 85/6/12; b. Canada; Joseph Joyce and Louise Dennison

Joseph, d. 10/27/1909 at 59/1/24; laborer; married; b. Canada; Pierre Lamontagne (Canada) and Marie Gulmont (Canada)

LAMPRON,
Alcide, d. 10/1/1910 at 0/8/25; b. Wakefield; Severin Lampron (Canada) and Marie Tutras (Canada)

LANE,
Blanche H., d. 4/30/1900 at 14/5/12; single; b. Wakefield; Samuel F. Lane (Wakefield) and Mary A. Fitzgerald (Dover)

Charles T., d. 9/20/1915 at 45/1/10; laborer; married; b. Dover; Samuel F. Lane (Dorchester, MA) and Addie Fitzgerald (Dover)

Emma E., d. 1/6/1958 at 80 in Wolfeboro; b. Waltham, MA; John Watson and Ellen Watson

Ethel May, d. 10/8/1905 at 0/2/10; b. Sanbornville; George F. Lane (Sanbornville) and Ida M. Davis (Tamworth)

Frank, d. 5/17/1927 at 81/8/16; widower; b. Wakefield; Samuel Lane and Mary Dearborn

Harris Linwood, d. 7/4/1975 at 71 in Union; Harry Lane and Emma E. Watson

Harry L., d. 5/8/1950 at 72/9/2 in Wolfeboro; b. Dover; Samuel Lane and Mary Fitzgerald

Henry, d. 3/22/1897 at 73/2/22; farmer; widower; b. Somersworth; Samuel Lane (Chichester) and Mary M. Dearborn (Wakefield)

Mary A., d. 1/15/1895 at 64/8; housewife; married; b. Acton, ME; Lyman Wentworth and Nancy Archibald

Mary A., d. 4/28/1920 at 73/2/29; mitral regurgitation; widow; b. Dover; John Fitzgerald (Dover)

Samuel F., d. 3/6/1910 at 77/10/1; farmer; married; b. Chichester; Samuel Lane (Chichester) and Mary Dearborn (Wakefield)

Sarah E., d. 11/28/1914 at 77/8/5; housewife; married; b. Wakefield; J. Borden Nichols (Ossipee) and Susan Bickford (Wakefield)

William H., d. 1/10/1924 at 89/7/18; retired; married; b. Wakefield; Samuel Lane (Chichester) and Mary Dearborn (Wakefield)

LANG,
Almira P., d. 7/25/1976 at 79 in Hanover; Aaron Palmer and Eliza Gonwell
Barbara Perry, d. 11/13/1989 at 71 in Wolfeboro; Arthur Perry and Alice Fogg
Bernice Hazel, d. 9/30/1945 at 56/10/21 in Wolfeboro; b. Sanbornville; Winthrop Pike and Augusta Tibbetts
Caroline, d. 7/16/1899 at 85/4/20; housewife; single; b. Portsmouth; Samuel Lang (Greenland) and Lydia Thurber (Portsmouth)
Carrie B., d. 2/11/1920 at 51/9/18; influenza; housewife; married; b. Milton; Stephen M. Bragde
Daniel, Jr., d. 9/13/1892 at 23/3/26; brakeman; married; b. Brookfield; Daniel Lang (Brookfield) and Mary A. Glidden (Ossipee)
Forrest P., d. 9/16/1970 at 53 in Wolfeboro; Reuben P. Lang and Bernice Pike
Francena K., d. 5/11/1933 at 79/0/25
John Edwin, d. 4/26/1940 at 81/11/15; b. Brookfield; John W. Lang and Joanne Drew
Joyce B., d. 11/9/1963 at 19 in Sanbornville; b. Sanbornville; Forrest P. Lang and Barbara L. Perry
Reuben, d. 10/7/1890 at 29/7/3; butcher; married; b. Brookfield; John W. Lang (Brookfield) and Joan Drew (Brookfield)
Reuben, d. 4/10/1969 at 75 in Sanbornville; John E. Lang and Elizabeth Palmer

LANGDON,
William George, d. 4/15/1949 at 48/9/12 in Sanford, ME; b. New York, NY; William M. Langdon and Laura Black

LANGLEY,
Charles W., d. 9/27/1929 at 78/0/5; b. New Durham; Samuel Langley and Francis Perkins
Emily, d. 7/18/1937 at 70/0/13 in Sanford, ME; b. England; ---- Bradley
Kate, d. 6/3/1941 at 71/3/16; b. New York, NY; Ezekiel Kelley Davis and Katherine Horne
William D., d. 2/17/1950 at 49/0/20 in Augusta, ME

LANGLOIS,
Desire, d. 3/21/1927 at 65/10/23; married; b. Quebec; Francois Langlois and Marie Marcoux

LANOUETTE,
George, d. 6/19/1946 at 72/8/27 in Sanbornville; b. Franklin; John Lanouette and Mary Augers
Phoebe, d. 10/17/1960 at 85 in Sanbornville; b. Sanbornville; Edward Pouliot and Cecila Boissoneau

LAREY,
Drusilla, d. 12/20/1892 at 68/9/29; housework; single; b. Gilead, ME; James Larey (Wolfeboro) and Betsy Peabody (Shelburne)

LAROCHELLE,
Wilfred J., d. 3/27/1979 at 77 in Rochester; Philias Larochelle and Amanda Lessard

LAROUX,
Arthur, d. 12/7/1961 at 85 in Ossipee

LARY,
Leander, d. 5/12/1900 at 74; farmer; widower; b. Gilead, ME
Mary J., d. 5/9/1900 at 84; housewife; married; b. Wolfeboro

LASKEY,
Arlene B., d. 1/11/1987 at 68 in Dover; Scott H. Bumford and Flora A. Hobbs
Eva M., d. 12/11/1995 at 81 in Wolfeboro; Walter Richards and Lillian Johnson

LASSELL,
Jane N., d. 3/14/1970 at 81 in Wolfeboro; Frank Nute and Elizabeth Trow

LAVERTU,
Lillian, d. 10/20/1977 at 81 in Rochester
Ludger J., d. 3/21/1949 at 84/9/19 in Wolfeboro; b. Canada; Louis Lavertu and ---- LaPlant
Ludger J., Jr., d. 12/8/1973 at 76 in Wolfeboro
Margaret, d. 1/19/1953 at 85 in Sanbornville; b. Canada; Damasse Moore and Roseanne Morin

LAVOIE,
Augustine, d. 4/4/1909 at 59/6/4; laborer; married; b. Canada; Augustine Lavoie (Canada) and Leo Cadie Labrin (Canada)

LAWRENCE,
Winfield A., d. 8/14/1954 at 72 in Wolfeboro; b. Acton, ME; James R. Lawrence and Addie Puffer

LEARY,
Dane Colin, d. 6/10/1989 at 40 in Wolfeboro; Arthur R. Leary and Kathleen Leighton
John E., d. 2/1/1986 at 68 in Rochester; Benajah Leary and Grace Smith

LEAVITT,
Frank J., d. 1/9/1930 at 71/8/25; single; b. So. Wakefield; Nathaniel D. Leavitt and Sarah P. Hutchins
Sarah R., d. 7/9/1905 at 86/7/4; widow; b. Wakefield; Joseph Hutchins (Wakefield) and Betsy Wiggin (Wakefield)

LECLAIR,
Arthur S., d. 10/7/1986 at 69 in Ipswich, MA

LEFEBVRE,
Marion, d. 11/24/1997 at 74 in Sanbornville; Leonard Amadon and Anna McLean

LEGARY,
Adeline H., d. 1/13/1922 at 83/5/8; widow; b. Sherbrooke, Canada; Flavieh Houle (Montreal, PQ) and Scotastique Caya (Montreal, PQ)
Joseph, d. 3/3/1917 at 67/5/9; farmer; married; b. Canada; Saul Legary (Canada) and Olive Leblanc (Canada)

LEGER,
son, d. 3/4/1905 at 0/0/0; b. Wakefield; Angus Leger (NB) and Maggie White (Cape Breton)

LEIGHTON,
Carrie J., d. 6/26/1912 at 33/6/11; housewife; married; b. Boston, MA; Richard Pigott (Charlestown, MA) and Eliza J. Lovell (Taunton, MA)

Charles L., d. 1/5/1951 at 83 in Wolfeboro; b. Middleton; Charles Leighton and Anna W. Whitehouse

Charles Norton, d. 7/24/1989 at 80 in Wolfeboro; Charles S. Leighton and Mary Tanner

Doris Thelma, d. 8/6/1992 at 64 in Wolfeboro; Presco Leighton and Gladys Russell

Eleanor M., d. 2/13/1952 at 15/7/1 in No. Lebanon, ME; b. Union; Presco Leighton and Gladys Russell

Fred L., d. 6/5/1951 at 71 in Rochester; b. Middleton; Charles L. Leighton and Lucy A. Drew

Gladys E., d. 11/9/1982 at 78 in Union; Arthur Russell and Mary Kimball

Helen, d. 8/28/1974 at 87 in Wolfeboro; Dudley S. Cook and Lucy Hill

Jacob, d. 4/15/1913 at 84/6/3; carpenter; widower; b. Eaton; Ephraim Leighton (Ossipee) and Rachel Manson (Limington, ME)

Presco F., d. 3/31/1968 at 68 in Rochester; Walter F. Leighton and Elizabeth Drew

LEITH,
Helen A., d. 6/30/1982 at 67 in Sanbornville; Frank R. Creaser and Corrie M. Lund

LEMAN,
Jane C., d. 9/11/1908 at 83/0/7; housekeeper; single; b. Milton, MA; Nathaniel Leman and Rachel Boardman

LEMON,
Cornelia M., d. 4/1/1893 at 51/1/8; domestic; widow; b. New York; Albert Rikeman (NY) and Mary Smith (NY)

LEONARD,
Victor B., d. 8/15/1970 at 63 in East Wakefield; Edward O. Leonard and Mary Page

LEPOINTE,
Joseph M., d. 8/23/1894 at 0/3/26; b. Wakefield; John Lapointe (Canada) and Orilla Marcoux (Canada)

LEROUX,
Adele Marie, d. 12/7/1953 at 82 in Sanbornville; b. Canada; Octave Roy

LESSARD,
Ameedee, d. 7/19/1915 at 45/10; shoe maker; single; b. Quebec; Richard Lessard (Quebec) and Agnes Nadeau (Quebec)
Robert W., d. 4/22/1988 at 64 in Manchester; Delphis Lessard and Edith Gage

LEVIRTU,
Louis, d. 5/16/1916 at 77/6/7; laborer; widower; b. Canada; Louis Levirtu (Canada) and Marceline Jean (Canada)

LEWIS,
Hannah G., d. 7/18/1964 at 94 in Rochester; b. Acton, ME; John F. Titcomb and Abbie Gray
Mary R., d. 3/19/1974 at 74 in Wolfeboro; John Roman and Elizabeth Davis
Nettie E., d. 1/21/1964 at 89 in Melrose, MA
Robert Clayton, d. 9/7/1994 at 59; Clayton Prescott Lewis and Irene Delaware

LIBBEY,
Shuah S., d. 11/28/1893 at 62/4/4; housework; widow; b. Eliot, ME; Nathan Ferguson (Eliot, ME) and Annie Goodwin (Eliot, ME)

LIBBY,
Caroline P., d. 6/1/1897 at 85/3/21; housewife; widow; b. Wakefield; Daniel Libby (Wakefield) and Mary Allen (Wakefield)
Ellen M., d. 11/9/1904 at 60/1/21; housewife; married; b. Wakefield; John Farnham (Acton, ME) and Marjory Wiggin (Wakefield)
Fred R., d. 10/3/1951 at 74 in Sanbornville; b. Wellington, ME; Brice Libby and Sarah Whitehouse
Henry M., d. 4/10/1901 at 75; carpenter; widower
James L., d. 7/9/1896 at 84; farmer; married; Joseph Libby
John J., d. 1/11/1944 at 80/4/11 in Newfield, ME
Leland D., d. 6/1/1974 at 61 in Sanford, ME
Marjorie L., d. 10/14/1903 at 0/6/27; b. Wakefield; N. J. Libby (Wakefield) and Eliza B. Wilkinson (Laconia)
Mary A., d. 7/20/1898 at 70; housewife; married; b. Brookfield; Trueworthy Chamberlain (Brookfield) and Adeline Burleigh (Brookfield)
Scott A., d. 8/14/1974 at 92 in Ossipee; John J. Libby and Cora B. Glidden

Stella, d. 10/30/1973 at 87 in Ossipee

Washington, d. 7/30/1907 at 65/8/9; farmer; widower; b. Wakefield; Nathan Libby (Milton) and Olive Berry (Milton)

LIGHTLE,

William, d. 7/16/1890 at 2/8; b. Salmon Falls; William Lightle (NS) and Margaret Shampou (Manchester)

LIPINSKI,

Alexander Paul, d. 8/27/1995 at 77 in Rochester; Frank Lipinski and Josephine Kloczko

LIPSETT,

Isabelle Molyneaux, d. 6/18/1997 at 82 in Wolfeboro; James Molyneaux and Alida Gorrill

Robert George, d. 1/24/1993 at 79 in Wolfeboro; Hamilton Lipsett and Mary Graham

LISCOM,

John S., d. 7/20/1945 at 68/8/29 in Hartford, VT; b. Mendota, IL; Horace Liscom and Almeda Schofield

LITCHFIELD,

Norman Gregory, d. 11/5/1954 at 48 in Wells, ME; b. Wakefield; William Litchfield and Bernica Hart

William H., Jr., d. 1/4/1905 at 0/1/7; b. Wakefield; W. A. Litchfield (Boston, MA) and Bernice M. Hart (Wakefield)

LITTLEFIELD,

Betty E., d. 1/8/1947 at 0/0/7 in Rochester; b. Rochester; Eugene Littlefield and Louise Fifield

Eugene Francis, d. 4/25/1996 at 69 in Union; Maynard J. Littlefield and Louise Preble

Grace F., d. 5/18/1972 at 87 in Sanbornville; Edward P. Eastman and Eliza N. Sawyer

Josiah A., d. 3/7/1948 at 73/11/7 in Union; b. Burlington, ME; Josiah Littlefield and Nancy Ayer

Levi W., d. 9/12/1905 at 32/9/22; electrician; married; b. Shapleigh, ME; Simon Littlefield (Sanford, ME) and Maholy Ross (Shapleigh, ME)

Lillian S., d. 4/22/1950 at 68/11/12 in Union; b. Burlington, ME; Melvin Sibley and Sarah Hurd

Mahala, d. 3/14/1913 at 78/2/11; housewife; widow; b. Shapleigh, ME; Noah Ross (Shapleigh, ME) and Affia Warren (Shapleigh, ME)

Mary L., d. 6/18/1973 at 84 in Wolfeboro; William Hayden and Tannia Fancy

Nathan L., d. 3/26/1958 at 73 in Rochester; b. York, ME; Jothan Littlefield and Martha Allen

Payson, d. 8/14/1979 at 70 in Rochester; Nathan Littlefield and Grace Eastman

Simon, d. 5/12/1910 at 80/7/21; laborer; married; b. Sanford, ME; Daniel Littlefield (Sanford, ME) and Susan Welch (Shapleigh, ME)

LIVERMORE,

Ellen, d. 11/12/1959 at 87 in Dover; b. No. Sydney, NS; John McDonald

John A., d. 4/27/1964 at 56 in Boston, MA; b. Sanbornville; Edward Livermore and Ellen McDonald

LOCKE,

Eugene P., d. 1/13/1950 at 85/2/2 in Union; b. Starks, ME; Perley W. Locke and Sarah Fish

Eugenia, d. 11/27/1946 at 67/3/6 in Union; b. No. Adams, MA; Augustus W. Locke and Martha P. Perkins

Jacob, d. 3/9/1895 at 81/4/1; farmer; widower; b. Wakefield; Nathaniel Locke (Wakefield) and Abigail Pitman (Somersworth)

Jennie M., d. 7/1/1968 at 90 in Wakefield, MA; Albert R. Perkins and Martha J. Dunn

Martha P., d. 11/14/1930 at 82/8/12; widow; b. Hampton; Moses Perkins and Huldah Johnson

Susan, d. 3/9/1895 at 82; housekeeper; married; b. Rochester; —— Remick (Rochester) and —— Hurd (Rochester)

Walter L., d. 1/13/1974 at 75 in Wolfeboro

LOCKHART,

Marion, d. 4/3/1986 at 73 in ME

LOCKWOOD,

Ethel H., d. 2/4/1958 at 91 in Manchester

LOOK,
Ellen J., d. 2/27/1914 at 71; housewife; married; b. Haverhill, MA
Hollis, d. 5/19/1919 at 86; carcinoma of lip; stevedore; widower; b. Addison, ME; John Look

LORD,
child, d. 4/20/1915 at 0/0/15; b. Wakefield; Harvey Lord (Acton, ME) and Clara Nichols (Ossipee)
Albert C., d. 1/1/1958 at 70 in Wolfeboro; b. Berwick, ME; Charles Lord and Anne Brewster
Blanche J., d. 2/26/1987 at 94 in Ossipee; Daniel Jellison and Josephine Nutter
Doris L., d. 4/11/1915 at 0/0/6; b. Wakefield; Harvey Lord (Acton, ME) and Clara Nichols (Ossipee)
Elvira E., d. 11/9/1940 at 89/0/4 in Manchester; b. Middleton; Daniel D. Stevens and Hannah Cook
Julia R., d. 4/17/1935 at 78/7/13 in Union; b. Clinton, ME; Charles H. Royal and Frances Hemenway
Sibyl Eva, d. 2/4/1967 at 79 in East Rochester; b. Sanbornville; Josiah Wiggin and Mary Rines
William Marshall, d. 6/6/1944 at 87/1/26 in Union; b. Acton, ME; John Lord and Fidelia Sanborn

LOTHROP,
John M., d. 6/6/1936 at 82/6 in Middleton

LOUD,
Amanda L., d. 3/5/1906 at 52/2/26; housework; widow; b. Wakefield; Hiram R. Waldron (Wakefield) and Sarah A. Woodman (Wakefield)
Ivory S., d. 12/8/1900 at 58/9/19 in East Wakefield; station agent; married; b. Newfield, ME; Nathan N. Loud (Newfield, ME) and Mary J. Stevens (Newfield, ME)
Nathan N., d. 9/10/1892 at 79/0/28; auctioneer; widower; b. Newfield, ME; Moses Loud (Portsmouth) and Priscilla ---- (Waterboro, ME)

LOUGEE,
William L., d. 10/31/1926 at 79/8/27; widower; b. Alton; J. S. Lougee and A. Marsh

LOUGHLIN,
John, d. 3/20/1915 at 69/6/14; overseer; widower; b. Ireland; Robert Loughlin (Ireland) and Katherine Connor (Ireland)

LOVEJOY,
Jessie M., d. 11/29/1888 at 5/5/25; Samuel S. Lovejoy (Denmark, ME) and Adna F. Johnson (Stowe, ME)
Willard P., d. 10/29/1977 at 80 in Sanbornville; Elbridge Lovejoy and Mabel Preston

LOVER,
Mary J., d. 2/1/1917 at 56/7/5; housewife; married; b. Canada; Pierre Raemond (Canada) and Teresa White (Canada)

LOVERING,
Susan A., d. 11/14/1917 at 95/7/12; widow; b. Wakefield; Joseph Wentworth (Somersworth) and Elizabeth Plummer (Rochester)

LOWD,
Cora M., d. 10/3/1930 at 73/9/13; widow; b. Dover; Simon Ricker and Eliza Kenney

LOWE,
Adelia E., d. 8/15/1938 at 82/11/6 in Union; b. Milton Mills; Gardner Chamberlain and Mary Fall
Charles W., d. 5/2/1939 at 83/6/9; b. No. Shapleigh, ME; John Lowe and Helen Hargreaves
Eva May, d. 5/31/1963 at 75 in Union; b. Rochester; Wilbur Webber and Cora Corson
Homer C., d. 6/3/1951 at 65/4/22 in Union; b. Milton Mills; Charles W. Lowe and Adelia Chamberlain

LUCAS,
Edward D., d. 4/21/1891 at 20/11/29; telegrapher; single; b. Milton; John Lucas (St. Albans, ME) and Sarah E. Trask (Wolfeboro)
Ellen M., d. 12/25/1955 at 89 in Wolfeboro; b. Milton; John Lucas and Sarah E. Trask
John, d. 11/23/1893 at 69/9/4; carpenter; married; b. St. Albans, ME; Daniel Lucas (Wolfeboro) and Hannah Lyford (Brookfield)

Sarah, d. 11/23/1953 at 75 in Concord; b. S. Limington, ME; John Lucas and Sarah Trask

LUCEY,
Paul E., d. 12/22/1983 at 77

LUTON,
Dewey R., d. 7/4/1919 at 21/1/11; acc. drowning; US Army; single; b. Warrenton, MO; J. W. Luton

LYONS,
Albert George, d. 3/15/1949 at 75/8/15 in Union; b. Nashville, IL; William H. Lyons and Mary Kates
Helen Elizabeth, d. 3/7/1953 at 21 in Wolfeboro; b. Sanbornville; George S. Herrick and Edith M. Nason

MACAFEE,
Leone Vivian, d. 4/4/1995 at 85; Elton Brown and Hattie May Nelson

MACCORMAC,
Beatrice Carrie, d. 11/19/1988 at 82 in Wolfeboro
Harry H., d. 11/19/1979 at 86 in Wolfeboro; Weatherbee MacCormac and Margaret DeVere

MACCORMACK,
Charles E., d. 4/2/1989 at 78 in Wolfeboro; Charles MacCormack and Maud Wiers

MACDONALD,
Amanda, d. 8/27/1929 at 77/3/6; widow; b. Mechanic Falls, ME; ---- Crockett and Betsy
James G., d. 9/26/1978 at 70 in Mass. Gen. Hosp.; James A. MacDonald and Mary Smith
Vincent, d. 6/30/1968 at 46 in Jersey City, NJ

MACDOUGAL,
Robert L., d. 10/5/1973 at 96 in Wolfeboro; Alexandra MacDougal and Mary Kyle

MACKAY,
Arthur D., d. 9/12/1897 at 7/6/7; b. NS; Henry McKay (NS) and Fanny Dexter (NS)

MACKENZIE,
Ethel B., d. 12/26/1959 at 73 in Newton Center, MA; b. Dover; Charles Brewster and Marion Wiggin
Helen D., d. 5/23/1981 at 77 in East Wakefield
Samuel P., d. 3/16/1963 at 87 in Wolfeboro; b. Danville, VT
Veronica A., d. 1/30/1941 at 60/5/19; b. Gorham; John Casey and Mary McCormick

MACKIE,
Charlotte R., d. 10/6/1916 at 0/3/3; b. Wakefield; George R. Mackie (Limington, ME) and Olive Lover (Wakefield)
Donald, d. 6/9/1913 at 0/8/2; b. Wakefield; George R. Mackie (Limington, ME) and Olive M. Lavoie (Wakefield)
Mary O., d. 6/7/1913 at 2/1/9; b. Wakefield; George R. Mackie (Limington, ME) and Olive M. Lavoie (Wakefield)

MACLEOD,
Esther J., d. 10/16/1985 at -- in MA

MACMILLAN,
Frank H., d. 12/5/1975 at 69 in Stoneham, MA; Frank H. MacMillan and Margaret J. MacDonald

MADDIX,
Alberta, d. 4/25/1942 at 83/5/18; b. Rockport, MA; James Grimes and L. Ann Tarr

MAGEE,
Anna, d. 10/13/1944 at 81 in Reading, PA

MAILLOUX,
Blanche I., d. 7/29/1984 at 84 in Rochester
Joseph E., d. 6/8/1968 at 61 in Rochester; Lucien Mailloux
Joseph Raymond, d. 4/29/1996 at 76 in East Wakefield; Joseph E. Mailloux and Celina Beland

MALEHAM,
Charles H., d. 6/19/1939 at 62/6/20 in Wolfeboro; b. Wakefield; William Herbert Maleham and Sarah Louise Farnham
Elmer B., d. 12/24/1928 at 0/0/½ ; b. Sanbornville; Elmer B. Maleham and Mazel A. Downs
Elmer B., d. 1/23/1978 at 72 in Wolfeboro; Charles Maleham and Grace Burrows
Ernest, d. 3/18/1956 at 48 in Concord; b. Wakefield; Charles Maleham and Grace Burroughs
Grace Mary B., d. 6/13/1942 at 63/7/22 in Wolfeboro; b. Brookfield; Howard Burroughs and Mary Katherine Willey
Hazel A., d. 12/30/1928 at 22/2/1; married; b. Wakefield; Harry Downs and Agnes Sawyer
Ida H., d. 1/1/1981 at 60 in Rochester; Ernest Morrison and Ida Orcutt
Robert H., d. 9/20/1973 at 70 in Boston, MA; Charles Maleham and Grace Burroughs
Sarah C., d. 2/18/1910 at 64/9/27; milliner; single; b. Wakefield; William A. Maleham (Wakefield) and Nancy W. Pike (Brookfield)
Sarah L., d. 4/16/1932 at 77/6/0
William A., d. 10/14/1896 at 78/9/12; farmer; widower; b. Wakefield; Joseph Maleham (Wakefield) and Rachel Horn (Wakefield)
William H., d. 2/10/1910 at 58/8; carpenter; married; b. Wakefield; William Maleham (Wakefield) and Nancy Pike (Brookfield)

MALLOUX,
Ralph W., d. 8/18/1974 at 81; Frank W. Malloux and Elizabeth Kuneen

MANKUS,
Stanley A., d. 6/28/1986 at 70; Stanley Mankus and Rose Deptula

MANN,
Gail, d. 12/31/1987 at 48 in Wolfeboro; George Fenton and Ruth Walker

MANSI,
Anthony, d. 2/26/1996 at 62 in Wolfeboro; Luigi Mansi and Filicia Petrucci

MANSUR,
Hiram P., d. 6/22/1892 at 66/11/16; clergyman; married; b. Monroe, ME; James Mansur (Methuen, MA) and ----- Pierce

MANZER,
Arthur L., d. 2/25/1972 at 60 in Somersworth; Ralph E. Manzer and Ethel A. Codey
Edna L., d. 12/16/1979 at 65 in Exeter; William Daum

MARCINKEWIZ,
Johanna, d. 5/2/1915 at 22; shop girl; single; b. Russia; Joe Marcinkewiz (Russia)

MARCOUE,
Lester J., d. 9/27/1971 at 61 in Brookfield; Alfred A. Marcoue and Abigail Readon

MARCOUX,
Celedase, d. 2/19/1923 at 70/7; at home; widow; b. Canada; Joseph Marchand (Canada) and Rose LaMountain (Canada)
Edward J., d. 1/19/1934 at 41/11/18 in Portsmouth; b. Sanbornville; Oliver Marcoux and Celedose Marchand
Etienne, d. 11/24/1913 at 63/5/15; stone mason; married; b. Canada; Mark Marcoux (Canada) and Luce Bedard (Canada)
Jennie C., d. 11/13/1961 at 65 in Wolfeboro; b. Sanbornville; Oliver Marcoux and Celedase Marchand
Marc, d. 9/25/1899 at 85/6/22 in Sanbornville; laborer; widower; b. Canada; Marc Marcoux (Canada) and Mare Bernier (Canada)
Mary, d. 4/27/1894 at 0/0/0; b. Wakefield; Archie Marcoux (Canada) and Rose Brouillard (Canada)
P. R. [female], d. 4/28/1896 at 3/1/3 in Sanbornville; b. Sanbornville; Archil Marcoux (Canada) and Rose Brouillord (Canada)
Phoebe M., d. 3/10/1969 at 79 in Laconia; Etienne Marcoux and Celedase Marchand

MARDEN,
Arthur Dearborn, b. 7/30/1944 at 74/10/23 in Sanbornville; b. Greenland; Charles W. Marden and Mary Dearborn
Mary E., d. 6/21/1963 at 88 in Ossipee

MARNARD,
Charles, d. 6/8/1909 at 1/6/28; b. Hooksett; George Marnard (Holland, VT) and Ida Tebo (Fisherville, MA)

MARSH,
Joseph Franklin, d. 9/23/1959 at 91 in Sanbornville; b. Portanpique, NS; Josephus Marsh and Maria Marsh
Lucy F., d. 10/26/1907 at 78/4/3; housework; widow; b. Milton; Francis Chapman (Greenland) and Elizabeth Hilton (Exeter)
Mary Elizabeth, d. 10/29/1998 at 92 in Wolfeboro; James Tucker and Mary Brackett
Robert E., d. 6/1/1994 at 87 in Wolfeboro; William T. Marsh and Elizabeth M. Rimbach

MARSHALL,
Edward R., d. 6/1/1967 at 83 in Wolfeboro; b. NS; Burt Marshall and Elizabeth Patrican
Elmer S., Jr., d. 8/29/1971 at 53 in Southwest Harbor, ME; Elmer S. Marshall and Marion Floyd
Frank, d. 2/2/1921 at 69/10/23; apoplexy; widower; b. Quebec; Joseph Marshall (Canada) and Rose Lamontagne (Canada)
Frank, Jr., d. 6/22/1912 at 36; laborer; married; b. Wakefield; Frank Marshall (Canada) and Phoebe Pouliot (Canada)
Guy Conrad, d. 8/26/1977 at 67 in Portsmouth
Ruth A., d. 4/19/1989 at 96 in Dover

MARSTON,
Freeland Simmons, d. 6/9/1998 at 68 in Sanbornville; Forrest Marston and Lola Simmons

MARTIN,
daughter, d. 1/25/1899 at 0/0/0 in Union; b. Wakefield; Napoleon Martin (Quebec) and Josie Brown (Wakefield)
Alec, d. 9/27/1932 at 79/6/26 in Ossipee
Alice B., d. 6/21/1990 at 91 in Wolfeboro; Stanley Poirier
Charlotte, d. 8/19/1917 at 79/11/24; housekeeper; widow; John Kershaw
Clarence O., d. 5/3/1985 at 86 in Ossipee; William Martin and Martha Smith
George Robert, d. 9/17/1979 at 53 in Rochester
Kenneth Michael, d. 1/12/1989 at 38 in Rochester
Louella F., d. 1/10/1964 at 81; b. Ellington, CT; Ludlow Fancher and Etta Olmstead
Ruth, d. 9/28/1903 at 45; housewife; married; b. Lebanon, ME; Robert Gill (Scotland) and Saphronia Gill (Lebanon, ME)

MARTINEAU,
Lawrence, d. 3/19/1946 at 31/8/0 in Concord

MASON,
Abigail T., d. 6/30/1966 at 72 in Wolfeboro; b. Boston, MA; Jeremiah Bonvie and Charlotte Delaney
Thomas E., Jr., d. 2/12/1988 at 24 in Wolfeboro

MASSEY,
Christine Lynn, d. 9/19/1991 at 23 in Chicopee, MA

MATHESON,
Arthur, d. 7/2/1952 at 64/8/11 in Sanbornville; b. Sweden

MATHEWS,
John W., d. 1/17/1927 at 100/11/17; married; b. Ossipee; Joseph Mathews and Mary Bickford

MATLOCK,
George Joseph, d. 7/16/1988 at 68 in Portland, ME

MATTHEWS,
Elizabeth, d. 8/24/1895 at 69/7/1; housewife; married; William H. Emerson (Ossipee) and Mary A. Williams (Wells, ME)

MAXIM,
Marion Adams, d. 10/8/1991 at 85 in Wolfeboro; Maynard Maxim and Metalena Adams

MAY,
John Dexter, d. 1/15/1933 at 75/0/0

MAYO,
Leon Glenwood, d. 11/14/1954 at 76 in York, ME; b. No. Windham, ME; George C. Mayo and Flora B. Main
Martha E., d. 1/31/1961 at 81 in Wolfeboro; b. Orono, ME; Wilbred MacKenzie and Mary E. Bouche

MAYOU,
Mary A., d. 7/11/1936 at 73 in Alton

McABBY,
Annie, d. 2/26/1937 at 70 in Acton, ME; b. Ireland

McBRIDE,
Bessie H., d. 8/19/1958 at 95 in Rochester; b. Annidale, NB; John Richardson and Bessie Richardson

McCABBEY,
Thomas, d. 4/18/1940 at 80 in Woodman; b. Canada; Annie McCabbey

McCARRON,
Leo J., d. 8/27/1991 at 52 in Boston, MA

McCARTHY,
Lillian Mary, d. 8/6/1988 at 62 in Wolfeboro; George Patterson and Mary Cushing

McCAULEY,
Lillian A., d. 1/5/1986 at 80 in Wolfeboro

McCLARY,
Lillian Ella, d. 3/4/1992 at 64 in Wolfeboro; Aldworth C. Jackson and Elizabeth M. Kirkpatrick

McCONNELL,
Mary Cottle, d. 3/2/1940 at 84/4/29 in St. Petersburg, FL
Perley, d. 11/2/1966 at 81 in Boston, MA

McCOOLE,
Brian Keith, d. 2/6/1988 at 23; James F. McCoole and Therese M. Gosselin

McCRILLIS,
Ethel M., d. 11/12/1963 at 83 in Wolfeboro; b. Sanbornville; William H. Willey and Sarah Brown
Frank G., d. 9/13/1923 at 70/11/7; RR engineer; widower; b. Lebanon, ME; Lorenzo McCrillis (Lebanon, ME) and Clara Folsom
Harry H., d. 9/12/1938 at 61/11/16 in Sanbornville; b. Rochester; Frank G. McCrillis and Sarah McCrillis

Ora F., d. 8/5/1947 at 72/5/29 in North Conway; b. East Rochester; Frank G. McCrillis and Sarah McCrillis
Ruth M., d. 10/2/1978 at 86; Andrew Meikle and Nellie Francis
Sarah A., d. 11/29/1922 at 67/7/9; housewife; married; b. Newfield, ME; Gilman McCrillis (ME) and Lydia Cole (Newfield, ME)

McCUTCHEON,
Anna Frances, d. 4/8/1940 at 84/8/22 in E. Wakefield; b. Boston, MA; James McCutcheon and Esther Anna Horn
Ellen A., d. 7/22/1888 at 70/0/2; housework; married; b. Wakefield; Noah Horn (Wakefield) and Ada Hurd (Newfield, ME)
James, d. 11/14/1895 at 77 in Boston, MA; widower

McDANIEL,
Ann-Marie F., d. 10/18/1989 at 32 in East Wakefield; Albert Rouleau and Lucy Bureau
Mary K., d. 4/9/1887 at 72/2/9; housework; married; Thomas Young and Nancy Nute (Milton)
Robert C., d. 2/15/1892 at 76/8/4; laborer; married; b. Epsom; Robert C. McDaniel (Scotland) and Nancy Macrass (Scotland)

McDONALD,
daughter, d. 9/13/1897 at 0/0/0; b. Wakefield; George A. McDonald (Boston, MA) and Louie Parker (Saugus, MA)
Agnes L., d. 1/9/1942 at 69/0/0 in Ossipee; b. Cambridge, MA; Charles A. Sullivan and Annie O'Brien
Alexander, d. 2/13/1937 at 68 in Sanford, ME; b. Canada; Hugh J. McDonald and Josephine Rubasheiu
Alice J., d. 6/18/1966 at 72 in Dover
Carroll, d. 2/20/1962 at 69 in Wolfeboro; b. Wakefield; Malcolm McDonald and Amanda Crockett
Dorothy C., d. 2/16/1991 at 77 in Manchester; John F. Clark and Gladys Pickering
Ethel A., d. 5/27/1926 at 52/11/1; married; b. Gilmanton; Joseph McClary and Frances Adams
Eva, d. 9/9/1891 at 1/11/8; b. Wakefield; Malcolm McDonald (PEI) and Amanda Crockett (Minot, ME)
Evelyn L., d. 3/12/1905 at 0/8/12; b. Wakefield; Arthur McDonald (Wakefield) and Lena Hall (Chatham)
Hugh, d. 9/14/1933 at 68/7/16

James Joseph, Jr., d. 2/18/1992 at 79 in Ossipee; James J. McDonald and Agnes Sullivan

Janice Lee, d. 8/30/1943 at 0/0/0 in Rochester; b. Rochester; James J. McDonald, Jr. and Dorothy M. Clark

John, d. 1/13/1933 at 41/1/5

Malcolm, d. 9/29/1919 at 78/1/14; car. of stomach; section man; married; b. PEI; Alexander McDonald (Scotland) and ---- McPherson

Winfield S., d. 7/14/1946 at 52/0/21 in Wolfeboro; b. Wakefield; Malcolm McDonald and Amanda Crockett

McDORMAND,
Elizabeth Anne, d. 1/8/1989 at 25 in Conway

McGINNISS,
Robert C., d. 5/4/1988 at 72 in Wolfeboro; Charles A. McGinniss and Edna A. Bont

McGINTY,
James, d. 11/9/1901 at 55; laborer; married; b. Canada

McGREGOR,
Minnie O., d. 10/14/1918 at 32/6/3; housewife; married; b. Greenville; Jeremiah L. Chadbourn (Waterboro, ME) and Mary F. Mock (Bradford, MA)

McGUIRE,
Francis J., d. 4/24/1994 at 74; John McGuire and Agnes Bicker

Jacqueline, d. 4/20/1946 at 5/0/7; b. Berlin; Leo J. McGuire and Doris Fortier

Lee J., d. 4/20/1946 at 26/11/24; b. Berlin; Hugh McGuire and Angeline ----

McHUGH,
John D., d. 1/30/1955 at 83 in Union; b. Worcester, MA; ---- McHugh and ---- Chapman

McINNERNEY,
John H., d. 5/3/1972 at 82 in Wolfeboro; John McInnerney and Fannie Trafton

McKENZIE,
Alice, d. 10/6/1966 at 76 in Framingham, MA
William, d. 8/2/1900 at 46; painter; b. Acton, ME

McKINNEY,
son, d. 3/15/1980 at 0/0/0 in Hanover; William J. McKinney and Charlene Bosley
Pauline T., d. 3/28/1976 at 53 in Hanover; George H. Taylor and Bernice Knapp

McLAREN,
J. L., d. 9/14/1934 at 57/8/16 in Springfield, MA; Peter McLaren and Sophia Lees

McLEAN,
Barbara M., d. 8/4/1986 at 59 in Wolfeboro; Frederick Hinckley and Marion Rickenbacker

McMORRILL,
Margaret T., d. 7/2/1983 at 76; Florence McCarthy and Margaret T. McCarthy

McNAIR,
Lillian C., d. 12/13/1995 at 65 in Wolfeboro; James Ross and Ann Connors

McNALLY,
Francis J., d. 6/6/1986 at 50 in Wolfeboro
Robert L., d. 6/6/1985 at 86 in Natick, MA

McNELLEY,
Jane C., d. 10/15/1967 at 54 in Wolfeboro; b. Malden, MA; Louis Wright McAloon and Elizabeth A. Dyer
Marie V., d. 1/22/1974 at 74 in Lynn, MA
William H., d. 12/20/1972 at 64 in Hartford, VT; Henery McNelley and Mary E. Murphy

McQUILLEN,
Roy Milton, d. 5/18/1941 at 57/6/19; b. Rock Island, IL; Nathan McQuillen and Laura Filson

McWICKER,
Alfred, d. 1/28/1957 at 75 in East Wakefield; b. England

MEADER,
George P., d. 4/30/1892 at 85; farmer; married; ----- Meader (Raymond)

MEE,
Ella M., d. 12/22/1947 at 76/0/12 in Sanbornville; b. Brookfield; Mark Remick and Ellen Young
Robert, d. 3/27/1938 at 73/11/7; b. Mansfield, England; John Mee and Mary Ellen Smith
Robert A., d. 12/9/1952 at 56/3/1 in Manchester; b. Lynn, MA; Robert Mee and Ella Remick
Willie I., d. 3/8/1895 at 0/7/22; b. Wakefield; John H. Mee (Loudon) and Agnes E. Libbey (Wakefield)

MEEHAN,
Marjorie, d. 12/19/1961 at 77 in Concord; b. Concord; Henry Robinson and Helen Rollins

MEISNER,
Despy, d. 3/26/1989 at 68 in Methuen, MA

MELANSON,
Carroll T., d. 2/4/1979 at 75 in Alton; Thomas Melanson and Jennie Elliott
Hazel, d. 4/21/1970 at 64 in Hooksett; Ernest Sibley and Ethel Richards
Jennie B., d. 6/1/1962 at 82 in Manchester; b. Rumney; William D. Elliott and Lucy Williby

MENARD,
Felix, d. 1/15/1919 at 39/4/3; tub. of intestines; laborer; single; b. Canada; Buzzell Menard (Canada) and Adeline Theoret (Canada)

MERCHANT,
Florence L., d. 10/26/1985 at 72 in Rochester; Robert Burdette and Mabel O. Clark
Harry A., Jr., d. 8/8/1964 at 48 in Reading, MA
Simon A., d. 12/29/1989 at 75; Simon A. Merchant and Dora Boudreau

MEREDITH,
Albert B., d. 4/12/1946 at 75/2/10; b. Gorham; William H. Meredith and Susan B. Spencer

MERRILL,
Susan C., d. 10/20/1903 at 71/8/24; housework; married; b. Acton, ME; Samuel Mudgett (Exeter) and Nancy ----- (Exeter)

MERROW,
Adelbert, d. 7/24/1905 at 55/2/14; painter; single; b. Dover; Jefferson Merrow (Waterville, ME) and Mary A. Nason (Wakefield)
Alice J., d. 6/21/1962 at 88 in Union; b. Ossipee; Frank K. Hobbs and Sarah Hobbs
Charles, d. 5/30/1899 at 83/5; farmer; married; b. Newfield, ME; Joseph Merrow and Mehatibal Dorr
Jefferson, d. 12/29/1902 at 84; farmer; widower
Mary A., d. 8/12/1887 at 67/4/16; housework; married; b. Wakefield
Millet M., d. 7/30/1920 at 71/8/20 in Union; apoplexy; farmer; b. Milton Mills; Noah Merrow (Milton Mills) and ----- Rowe (Gilford)
Wescott F., d. 10/4/1894 at 38/3/18; landlord; married; b. Newfield, ME; Charles Merrow (Newfield, ME) and Hannah Davis (Newfield, ME)

MESERVE,
Clarence O., d. 5/16/1970 at 86 in Titusville, FL; Joseph H. Meserve and Emma Fall
Emma E., d. 4/16/1911 at 54/11/14; housewife; married; b. Ossipee; John Fall (Ossipee) and Hannah N. Avery (Wolfeboro)
John N., d. 8/26/1969 at 31; Clarence Meserve and Pauline Carter
Joseph H., d. 8/13/1935 at 86/7/22 in Woodman; b. Wakefield; Nathaniel Meserve and Sarah D. Horne
Nathaniel, d. 4/13/1893 at 85/2/5; farmer; widower; b. Ossipee; Nathaniel M. Meserve and Lydia Plummer (Somersworth)
Sarah D., d. 9/4/1887 at 75/0/10; housework; married; b. Rochester; Daniel D. Horne (Rochester) and Mary Dearborn (Kingston, MA)
William B., d. 6/16/1985 at 65 in Wolfeboro; William A. Meserve and Iva Burgess

MEYER,
Brenda J., d. 1/1/1951 at 0/3/5 in Milton Mills

MICHEL,
Charles, d. 12/10/1956 at 90 in Union; b. Canada; Hector Michel and Adele Toutaint

MILDRAM,
Norma C., d. 11/17/1995 at 85; Michael Galliher and Sarah Mallison
Russell N., d. 4/19/1957 at 57 in Wolfeboro; b. Melrose, MA; William H. Mildram and Ella L. Prindall

MILHOMME,
Paul G., d. 9/20/1961 at 60 in Dover; b. New York, NY; Felix Milhomme and Pauline Agnellet

MILINER,
Elmor, d. 8/19/1995 at 76 in Sanbornville; James W. Miliner and Ardina French
James W., d. 11/17/1957 at 73 in Wolfeboro; b. NB; George Miliner and Annie Handron

MILLER,
Blanche E., d. 4/12/1986 at 80 in East Wakefield; Ashton Trafton and Bertha Lord
Eleanor F., d. 6/21/1996 at 72; James J. Murphy and Julia G. Hayes
Ernest R., d. 11/12/1897 at 1/1/1; b. Wakefield; William Miller (Brownfield, ME) and Christie McDonald (Wakefield)
Ray S., Jr., d. 6/6/1997 at 68 in East Wakefield; Ray S. Miller, Sr.
W. R., d. 8/17/1896 at 0/9/2; b. North Wakefield; William Miller (Brownfield, ME) and Chester McDonald (North Wakefield)

MILLIKEN,
Alice C., d. 5/19/1932 at 68/1/19 in Rochester
Andrew J., d. 9/29/1907 at 74/1/21; merchant; married; b. Effingham; Thomas Milliken (Scarboro, ME) and Mary A. Wedgewood
Frank Roscoe, d. 7/14/1941 at 57/5/16; b. Charlestown, MA; Frank R. Milliken and Annie S. King
Sarah E., d. 2/23/1924 at 88/4/8; widow; b. Effingham; Simon P. Hill (Effingham) and Alice G. Saunders (Effingham)

MILLS,
Alonzo I., d. 7/23/1985 at 85 in Wolfeboro

Irene G., d. 11/18/1973 at 68 in Dover; William Weeks and Alice Robinson
Lydia, d. 10/27/1970 at 47 in Lynn, MA
Nettie O., d. 3/4/1951 at 86 in Dover; b. Milton; Frank A. Mills and Hannah Soames
Ralph S., d. 2/8/1971 at 72 in Sanford, ME
William F., d. 3/16/1947 at 87/3/16 in Union; b. Hudson, MA; George P. Mills and Rebecca Hunting

MINOR,
Carolin Helen, d. 11/5/1938 at 73/10/4 in Waterbury, CT

MITCHELL,
Hattie M., d. 5/29/1925 at 57/9/28; single; b. Wakefield; Joseph R. Mitchell and Harriet Sampson
Jacob B., d. 11/24/1894 at 67; carpenter; married; b. Middleton; Joseph Mitchell (New Durham) and Mercy Buzzell (Middleton)
Joseph R., d. 12/13/1905 at 80/1/24 in Union; carpenter; married; b. Middleton; Joseph Mitchell (Dover) and Mercy Buzzell (Middleton)
Lydia F., d. 11/7/1914 at 80/5/18; housewife; widow; b. Middleton; John D. Stevens (Middleton) and Martha Buzzell (Middleton)

MIX,
Ella Meta, d. 10/13/1988 at 98 in Ossipee

MONAHAN,
Margaret, d. 12/1/1910 at 0/3/13; b. Merrimac, MA; Francis T. Monahan (Cambridge, MA) and Minnie Lavoie (Wakefield)

MONSON,
Harold H., d. 3/16/1984 at 83 in Wolfeboro; Martin Monson and Josephine Hanson

MOODY,
Dorothy E., d. 1/5/1965 at 55 in Rochester; b. Lynn, MA; Frank W. Moody and Hattie Marston
Francis E., d. 9/4/1947 at 88/9/18 in Sanbornville; b. Ossipee; Nathaniel Moody and Martha Nichols
Joseph A., d. 12/23/1946 at 59/3/15; Lewis Moody and Jane Davis
Marjorie, d. 1/12/1993 at 58 in Wolfeboro; Warren Weatherbee and Margaret Tucker

MOONEY,
Alma Frances, d. 11/7/1938 at 72/1/7 in Wolfeboro; b. Somersworth; Daniel S. Davis and Martha A. Horn
Emma M., d. 3/9/1938 at 71/7/15 in Sanbornville; b. Moscow, ME; Nathaniel McCrillis and Ann Towle
Harriet L., d. 5/13/1980 at 71 in Hanover; Everett Drury
James G., d. 1/14/1982 at 71 in East Wakefield; James S. Mooney and Clara Giffin
James Stanley, d. 6/17/1943 at 74/6/27; b. Ossipee; Benjamin H. Mooney and Emaline S.K. Mooney
William W., d. 3/22/1928 at 69/5/12; married; b. Madison; Benjamin H. Mooney and Emeline Stanley

MOORE,
Elba B., d. 7/2/1934 at 61/1/21; b. Brookline, NS
Eugenie, d. 5/22/1914 at 36/9/19; housewife; married; b. Canada; Clovis Bernard (Canada) and Annistie Daigle (Canada)
Frank W., d. 12/7/1892 at 22/6; single; Samuel O. Moore (Fryeburg, ME) and Lucy Miles (Limerick, ME)
George A., d. 2/9/1911 at 0/0/3; b. Wakefield; Leon Moore (Quebec) and Jennie Bourvin (Quebec)
Hannah S., d. 10/14/1895 at 69/6/15; housekeeper; b. Dover; Moses Hayes (Tamworth) and Hannah Otis (Rochester)
John F., d. 12/4/1900 at 67/9/26 in Union; carpenter; married; b. Parsonsfield, ME
Leon A., d. 8/5/1932 at 0/0/19 in Wolfeboro
Maurice M., d. 3/18/1961 at 76 in Nogales, AZ

MORANCY,
Eugene Frederick, d. 3/9/1995 at 61 in Wolfeboro; Reginald Morancy and Bernadette Twombley

MORGAN,
Hazel, d. 5/18/1983 at 72; Walter Morgan and Lora Auld
Lora Auld, d. 1/15/1971 at 99 in North Wakefield; Alexander Auld and Elizabeth Hunter

MORGENROTH,
Frank, d. 6/6/1981 at 81 in So. Wakefield; Joseph Morgenroth and Linda Friedlein

MORIN,
Henry Peter, d. 3/25/1953 at 61 in Manchester; b. Derry; Louis Morin and Olivine Provencher
Ora P., d. 1/10/1990 at 91 in Dover
Rose Mary, d. 11/7/1940 at 45 in Wolfeboro; b. Littleton
Samuel L., d. 3/14/1974 at 79 in Kittery, ME
Stella O.M., d. 5/12/1919 at 0/10/13; bron. pneumonia; b. Milton; Samuel L. Morin (Ashland) and Ora P. Dyer (Sanbornville)

MORRELL,
Walter, d. 4/19/1953 at 73 in No. Bridgton, ME; b. Wakefield; Millette W. Morrell and Susan J. -----

MORRILL,
Charlotte E., d. 6/21/1966 at 83 in Rochester; b. Fairfield, ME; Edward P. Eastman and Eliza N. Sawyer
George W., d. 1/31/1939 at 75/7/18; b. Moultonboro; William H. Morrill and Susan E. Brown
Harry W., d. 8/17/1950 at 72/5/20 in Wolfeboro; b. No. Windham, ME; Frank H. Morrill and Hannah -----
Lisa M., d. 11/5/1978 at 16; Charles Morrill and Roberta Morrill

MORRISETTE,
Frederick, d. 9/18/1959 at 69 in Wolfeboro; b. Manchester; Rose Morrisette

MORRISON,
Harry L., d. 3/9/1983 at 77 in Wolfeboro; Charles Morrison and Hattie Braley

MORSE,
David B., d. 2/18/1958 at 63 in Sanford, ME
Delia M., d. 9/3/1955 at 61 in Dover; b. Somersworth; Joseph Dodier and Edith Perron
Elizabeth M., d. 4/6/1897 at 66/2/17; housewife; widow; b. Wakefield; Josiah Wiggin (Wakefield) and Sophia Sibley (Wakefield)

MOULTON,
Amy L., d. 2/21/1953 at 69 in Somerville, MA

Arthur, d. 3/18/1970 at 89 in Meredith; Edgar C. Moulton and Clara
Prescott
Benjamin F., d. 5/5/1942 at 81/4/12; b. Lynn, MA; Charles F. Moulton
and Mehitable Symonds
Charles, d. 3/14/1887 at 84; farmer; married; b. Hampton; Charles
Moulton (Hampton) and Rebecca Coffin (Salisbury, MA)
Edgar Chase, d. 12/16/1924 at 66/7/29 in Union; farmer; married; b.
Newark, VT; Hiram H. Moulton and Salome S. Beals
Ella E., d. 9/8/1921 at 71/5/8; apoplexy; housewife; widow; b. China, ME;
Calvin Hamlin (China, ME) and Phoebe Jordan (Cape Elizabeth, ME)
Herman Leslie, d. 4/18/1941 at 81/4/12 in Newburyport, MA
Herschel, d. 12/14/1928 at 86/10/19; widower; b. Wakefield; Robert
Moulton and Sally Garland
Hiram M., d. 12/26/1923 at 8/5/6; student; b. Center Sandwich; Edgar C.
Moulton (Newark, VT) and Myrtle M. Brown (Conway)
Horace H., d. 2/25/1903 at 68/2/12 in Union; railroad man; married; b.
Dover; Jonas Moulton (Wakefield) and Mary Burrows (Lebanon, ME)
Irving H., d. 2/24/1964 at 81 in Rochester
Isaiah, d. 1/10/1919 at 74/8/29; mit. regurgitation; farmer; single; b.
Wakefield; Robert Moulton (Wakefield) and Sallie Garland
Lizzie Josephine, d. 10/9/1943 at 77/0/6 in Sanbornville; b. Brooklyn, NY;
George W. Gordon and Anna D. Sanborn
Mary A., d. 11/17/1956 at 93/8/20 in Lynn, MA
Mary E., d. 1/15/1914 at 72/0/24; married; b. Eaton; John S. Thompson
(Limington, ME) and Naomi Clark (Eaton)
Maud B., d. 11/30/1936 at 53/0/9 in Wolfeboro; b. Center Sandwich; N. P.
Shapott and Mercy B. Smith
Mehitable, d. 12/5/1913 at 79/3/28; retired; widow; b. Peabody, MA;
Benjamin Symonds (Acton, ME)
Olive, d. 10/10/1891 at 83/3/10; housekeeper; widow; b. Greenland; Joseph
Ayres (Greenland) and Olive Nudd (Greenland)
Rebecca, d. 4/11/1900 at 55; housekeeper; single; b. Wakefield; William
Moulton (Wakefield) and Mary Moulton (Wakefield)
Sally B., d. 4/29/1894 at 85/1/19; housekeeper; widow; b. Wakefield;
James Garland (Wakefield) and Annie Young (Exeter)
Sarah Jane, d. 8/6/1943 at 72/9/1 in East Wakefield; b. Wakefield; Ammon
Reed and Elizabeth Waldron

MOWREY,
Rena C., d. 2/18/1974 at 76 in Wolfeboro

MROZEK,
Matthew J., d. 10/12/1990 at 79; Jan Mrozek and Agatha -----

MROZET,
Felecia S., d. 7/7/1989 at 75 in Wolfeboro; Albert S. Kijeck and Sophia Splila

MULKERN,
Elta H., d. 10/28/1976 at 79 in Wolfeboro; Fred L. Hersey and Ann McDonald
Mark M., d. 5/2/1979 at 78 in Manchester

MULLEN,
David Joseph, d. 5/14/1952 at 8/0/19 in Mt. Kisco, NY; b. Rochester, NY

MULLER,
Janet F., d. 5/18/1956 at 72 in Swanton, VT
Joseph P., d. 12/12/1951 at 65 in Brookfield

MULLOCK,
Joseph A., Sr., d. 11/18/1963 at 69 in East Wakefield; b. Scranton, PA; Luke Mullock and Catherine McHale

MULREAN,
Audrey F., d. 4/14/1987 at 75 in Wolfeboro

MURCH,
Mahala, d. 7/4/1904 at 62/2/23; housewife; widow; b. Shapleigh, ME; John M. Pillsbury (Shapleigh, ME) and Mary Ricker (Shapleigh, ME)

MURPHY,
Delia M., d. 5/6/1945 at 90/1 in Manchester; b. Galway, Ireland; Patrick Murphy and Delia Waldron
Donna Lee, d. 10/11/1951 at 3 in Milton Mills; b. Berlin; Cornelius R. Murphy and Leah B. Cousens
Lynn, d. 10/11/1951 at 2 in Milton Mills; b. Berlin; Cornelius R. Murphy and Leah B. Cousens

NADEAU,
Diane T., d. 10/5/1996 at 44 in Manchester; Robert L. Nadeau and Gabrielle Lottinville

NASON,
child, d. 6/6/1915 at 0/0/0; b. Wakefield; Almon L. Nason (Bridgton, ME) and Nancy J. Streeter (Wakefield)
Almon L., d. 5/4/1961 at 81 in Wolfeboro; b. Bridgton, ME; Harding Nason and Lucinda Thorne
Amasa R., d. 5/9/1913 at 31/3/28; engineer; married; b. Woburn, MA; Amasa W. Nason (Stoneham, MA) and Harriet Stevens (Woburn, MA)
Dorothy M., d. 11/3/1966 at 48 in Wolfeboro; b. Gray, ME; Raymond Cate and Myrtle Libbey
Ernest E., d. 12/30/1987 at 71 in Wolfeboro; Almon Nason and Nancy Streader
Ernest R., Sr., d. 1/14/1997 at 58 in Wolfeboro; Ernest E. Nason and Dorothy Cate
Evelyn P., d. 10/29/1985 at 75 in Wolfeboro; John Weymouth and Emma Willey
Fred S., d. 11/28/1980 at 73 in Wolfeboro; Almon Nason and Nancy Streader
Glenn A., d. 11/4/1983 at 19 in Milton; Ernest R. Nason and Meredith Cook
John S., d. 10/22/1896 at 64/9/22; dealer in horses; married; b. Wakefield; Nahum Nason (Acton, ME) and Hannah Watson (Alton)
Johnnie Willis, d. 5/16/1995 at 73 in Ossipee; Willis Linwood Nason and Maude Reed
Lawrence C., d. 4/22/1990 at 60 in Sanbornville; Fred H. Nason and Evelyn P. Weymouth
Mary E., d. 10/10/1908 at --; at home; widow; b. Hartford, ME; Alson Bicknell (ME) and Harriet Bicknell (Abington, MA)
Nancy J., d. 12/7/1963 at 78 in Wolfeboro; b. Wakefield; Joseph Streader and Veleria Dyer
Susan A., d. 5/3/1923 at 88/7/26; single; b. Wakefield; Nahum Nason (Acton, ME) and Anna Watson (Brookfield)
Willis L., d. 6/23/1976 at 74 in Wolfeboro; Almon Nason and Nancy Streader

NAY,

Brackett, d. 12/10/1897 at 73; ex-policeman; married; Joseph Nay (Ossipee) and Mary Haines (Wolfeboro)

Florence J., d. 9/20/1919 at 29/6/10; pul. tuberculosis; housewife; married; b. Newfoundland; William C. Best (Newfoundland) and Harriet N. Pike

John, d. 9/24/1899 at 70/0/9 in Union; farmer; widower; b. Ossipee; Joseph Nay (Ossipee) and Mary ---- (Wolfeboro)

Lydia A., d. 10/7/1893 at 57; housework; single; b. Ossipee; Joseph Nay (Ossipee) and Mary Haynes (Wolfeboro)

NEAL,

Edna B., d. 2/21/1957 at 66 in Sanbornville; b. Wakefield; Charles C. Richards and Keziah Quimby

Hubartis, d. 12/26/1890 at 87/1/18; farmer; single; b. Wakefield; Levi Neal (Hampton) and Mary Fellows (Kensington)

NEALEY,

Henry, d. 2/9/1929 at 75/10/19; widower; b. Canada; Louis Nealey and Adelia Bennett

NEALLY,

son, d. 4/20/1890 at 0/0/0; b. Wakefield; Henry Neally (Canada) and Florrie Levesane (ME)

Florrie, d. 5/4/1890 at 32/3/24; married

NEILSSIEN,

Wesley W., d. 9/20/1982 at 69 in East Wakefield

NEILY,

Guy E., d. 11/30/1983 at 88; ---- Neily and Leah Hunt

Jean G., d. 1/16/1963 at 60 in Kittery, ME; b. Halifax, NS; ---- Murray and Ida Robinson

NELSON,

Hilmer, d. 10/16/1971 at 68 in Rochester

NEVERS,

Charles E., d. 10/9/1899 at 63/4/5; jeweller; widower; b. Sweden, ME; John Nevers (Lovell, ME) and Almina Whitcomb (Waterford, ME)

Elmira, d. 8/4/1890 at 81/5/24; widow; b. Waterford, ME; Paul Whitcomb and Sally Samson
Margery A., d. 12/4/1933 at 85/0/10

NEWCOMB,
Albert L., 3d, d. 7/4/1968 at 3 in Sanbornville; Albert Newcomb, Jr. and Agnes Mickelonis
Cynthia, d. 7/4/1968 at 10 in Sanbornville; Albert Newcomb, Jr. and Agnes Mickelonis
Loretta Lynn, d. 7/4/1968 at 1 in Sanbornville; Albert Newcomb, Jr. and Agnes Mickelonis
Nathan Carsby, d. 10/13/1943 at 77/1/4 in Ossipee; b. Harrison, ME; Simon Newcomb and Mary Richards
Wayne Paul, d. 7/4/1968 at 0/9/6 in Sanbornville; Albert Newcomb, Jr. and Agnes Mickelonis

NEWHALL,
Sarah J., d. 4/2/1932 at 83/3/16 in East Wakefield

NEWVINE,
Ruth, d. 6/11/1910 at 0/0/11; b. Wakefield; Alex Newvine (St. Lawrence, NY) and Eva Dumont (Salem, MA)

NICHOLS,
son, d. 3/23/1945 at 0/0/0 in Rochester; b. Rochester; Rupert Nichols and Icona Dodge
Aaron, d. 12/6/1887 at 85/6/11; laborer; widower; b. Ossipee; William Nichols (Ossipee) and Abbie Richards (Goffstown)
Alice G., d. 8/30/1983 at 55 in Wolfeboro; Glen Tilton and Matilda Whitehouse
Anstriss A., d. 6/18/1936 at 62/2/22 in Sanbornville; b. Sanbornville; Horatio B. Fellows and Bell Tibbetts
Dorothy K., d. 1/3/1986 at 74 in Rochester
Hiram W., d. 1/8/1902 at 56/11/12 in Sanbornville; section man; married; b. Wakefield; Aaron Nichols (Ossipee) and Clara Hutchins (Wakefield)
Icna D., d. 12/18/1955 at 41/5/10 in Harwich, MA
Lorenzo Dow, d. 8/19/1943 at 69/3/23 in Sanbornville; b. Wakefield; Hiram Nichols and Sarah Lane
Mildred, d. 12/11/1975 at 72 in Natick, MA

Ralph L., d. 7/19/1964 at 78 in Wolfeboro
Sarah W., d. 7/18/1917 at 76/11/2; widow; b. Wakefield; Samuel Lane and Mary Dearborn (Wakefield)
William H., d. 12/30/1926 at 55/8/24; married; b. Wakefield; Hiram W. Nichols and Sarah H. Lane

NICHOLSON,
Herbert, d. 3/21/1971 at 55 in Boston, MA; Herbert Nicholson and Lucy Bayston

NICOL,
Alice L., d. 5/4/1955 at 68 in Sanbornville; b. New York, NY; John Flanagan and Mary Connor

NILES,
Roy D., d. 11/24/1947 at 42/4/4; Leon Niles and Sarah Judd

NOBRIGA,
Annena, d. 7/23/1965 at 104 in Rochester; b. Houlton, ME; John Atkinson and Caive M. Bude

NOEL,
Patricia Babb, d. 7/15/1996 at 75 in Rochester; Raymond Babb and Mabel O'Neal

NORTON,
Carrie M., d. 2/9/1933 at 57/1/14

NORWOOD,
Leona R., d. 7/22/1968 at 37 in East Wakefield; Harold H. Kelmer and Rose Resch

NOYES,
Jane, d. 3/19/1900 at 69/4; widow; b. CT

NUTE,
Eli W., d. 8/21/1939 at 74/11/12 in Wolfeboro; b. Dover; Hopley Nute and Sarah Hayes
Elvira A., d. 2/15/1940 at 78/7/29 in Brookfield

Florence M., d. 9/8/1916 at 3/2/18; b. Wakefield; Fred S. Nute (Milton) and Olive A. Garland (Wolfeboro)

Fred S., d. 8/22/1950 at 82/10/25 in Union; b. West Milton; John S. Nute and Emma -----

Olive A., d. 9/4/1975 at 79 in Union; George Garland and Mary E. Stillings

Wilfred Stanton, d. 10/2/1989 at 73 in Union; Fred Stanton Nute and Olive A. Garland

NUTTER,

Caroline C., d. 6/12/1942 at 89/2/20; b. Wakefield; Kimball Nutter and Johana Buzzell

Charles A., d. 11/29/1928 at 80/6/28; single; b. Wakefield; Nova K. Nutter and Johann Buzzell

Dora M., d. 2/7/1890 at 24/10/22; housekeeper; married; b. Sweden, ME; Horatio G. Rackliff and Rebecca Hazleton (Lovell, ME)

Joann, d. 9/13/1892 at 75/0/7; housework; married; Joseph Buzzell and Hannah

Llewellyn, d. 7/22/1955 at 72 in Tuftonboro; b. Fryeburg, ME; Henry Nutter and Elizabeth Newcomb

Nelson, d. 10/14/1966 at 66 in Springvale, ME

Noah K., d. 11/14/1906 at 86/0/14; carpenter; widower; b. Wakefield; Nelson Nutter (Rochester) and ----- Perkins (Wakefield)

Rose, d. 2/8/1931 at 68; widow; b. Ireland

William Henry, d. 2/17/1949 at 58/10/5 in Hartford, VT; b. Fryeburg, ME; Henry Nutter and Elizabeth Edgecombe

NYBERG,

Gustaf, d. 8/11/1950 at 76/6/9 in Sanbornville; b. Sweden

OBER,

Maria J.D., d. 5/1/1915 at 74/10/24; housewife; married; b. Gloucester, MA; Edward P. Hinckley (Georgetown, MA) and Mary E. Burnham (Essex, MA)

O'BRIEN,

Arthur Edgar, d. 7/27/1938 at 49/11/30 in Sanbornville; b. Halifax, NS; Edward O'Brien and Agnes Menzies

Florence J., d. 11/30/1981 at 77 in Portland, ME

Hannah, d. 4/8/1915 at 92/4; domestic; widow; b. Moncton, NB; Emerson Clark (NB)
Levi E., d. 4/2/1921 at 76/5/23; locomotor ataxia; widower; b. Moncton, NB; William O'Brien (Ireland) and Hannah Clark (NB)
Michael, d. 9/15/1934 at -- in Wolfeboro; b. Lowell, MA
Raymond A., d. 1/25/1983 at 77 in Wolfeboro

O'CONNOR,
Martha F., d. 9/17/1932 at 51/11/7 in Berwick, ME

O'KEEFE,
Bernice Mary, d. 2/26/1997 at 72 in Wolfeboro; Lothrop T. Smith and Marguerite Stephen

O'NEAL,
Gladys Lillian, d. 1/9/1994 at 79 in Wolfeboro; Jocelyn O'Neal and Fannie Wetherall

OEHRING,
Ermee B., d. 1/19/1962 at 68 in Brookline, MA; b. NS; William Willett and Ida G. -----

OLIVER,
Effie R., d. 6/10/1963 at 83 in Union; b. New Britain, CT; Loudlow Fancher and Etta Olmstead

OLSEN,
Edward Clinton, d. 9/1/1997 at 85; Edward Nicholai Olsen and Marie Charlotte Lindstedt
Irma G., d. 1/4/1967 at 63 in Hanover; b. Rochester; John F. Grover and Maud Allen

OSBORNE,
Martha Jane, d. 12/25/1951 at 83 in Rochester; b. Windham, ME; Silas V. Morrill and Rebecca Cobb

OTIS,
Arthur, d. 11/9/1959 at 67 in Wolfeboro; b. Rochester; Levi Otis and Melinda Howard

Bertha E., d. 10/13/1970 at 85 in Rochester; Thomas B. Tibbetts and Etta
J. Hamilton
Mabel L., d. 11/3/1963 at 83 in Ossipee

OTTLEY,
Eleanor Gertrude, d. 3/8/1995 at 75 in Wolfeboro; W. Russell LeFavour
and Elizabeth M. Sanford

OUELLETTE,
Adrien L., d. 1/20/1915 at 0/0/2; b. Wakefield; Armand Ouellette (Canada)
and Lydia Lamontagne (Canada)
Armand J., d. 8/5/1951 at 74 in Sanbornville; b. Canada; David Ouellette
and Almenia Pinette
Billie F., d. 10/17/1972 at 31 in Sanbornville; David Gooden and Ethel
Abbott
David, d. 9/24/1934 at 85/3/4 in Wolfeboro; b. Canada
Leda, d. 6/1/1939 at 62/3/20; b. Canada; Joseph LaMontagne and Annie
Joyce
Magloire, d. 4/12/1898 at 50/3/26; laborer; married; b. Canada

PAGE,
Anne E., d. 1/14/1948 at 72/3/17 in Wolfeboro; b. So. Portland, ME;
Thare Trott
Charles W., d. 3/29/1914 at 85/1/18; farmer; married; b. Wakefield; David
Page (Wakefield) and Caroline Jones (Milton)
Frank L., d. 4/30/1952 at 87/0/7 in North Wakefield; b. Harmony, ME;
Aldir Page and Lorinda Rolfe
Josephine W., d. 10/1/1947 at 73/1/26 in Rochester; b. Wakefield
Laura G., d. 1/13/1950 at 83/2/15 in Rochester; b. Wakefield; Charles W.
Page and Mary Chapman
Mary A., d. 8/30/1925 at 84/8/30; widow; b. Wakefield; Thomas Chapman
and Almira Robinson
Myra Luella, d. 5/22/1938 at 69/7/30 in Rochester; b. Wakefield; Charles
W. Page and Mary G. Chapman

PAINE,
Lucille M., d. 5/9/1974 at 68 in Dover; Joseph Dodier

PALMER,
Aaron B., d. 2/21/1942 at 74/6/24 in Floral Park, NY

Bertha W., d. 9/11/1979 at 95 in Ossipee; Harriet -----
Charlotte B., d. 6/8/1994 at 69; Edward Brown and Nellie Howe
Eliza Conwell, d. 6/1/1942 at 72/8/23 in Floral Park, NY; b. Provincetown, MA
Fred L., d. 6/11/1982 at 85 in Ossipee; George Palmer and Cora Sheridan
Joseph, d. 8/5/1957 at 52 in No. Wakefield; b. Westminster, MA; Anthony Prizio and Marie Dotolo
Leon L., d. 9/4/1960 at 57 in Union; b. Gilmanton; George L. Palmer and Daisy Smith
Robert T., d. 7/5/1986 at 70; Jasper T. Palmer and Bertha Wellington
Susan T., d. 9/26/1944 at 78/5/22 in Wolfeboro; b. Lancaster, England; John Tresnon and Margaret Marshall

PARENT,
Joseph Adolph, d. 9/22/1949 at 52/0/27 in Sanbornville; b. Lynn, MA; Emily LaMontagne

PARKER,
Allen S., d. 2/10/1965 at 0/1/9 in Meredith; b. No. Conway; Franklin S. Parker and Patsy Welch
Cornelius P., d. 11/3/1979 at 76 in Wolfeboro; Pinkney M. Parker and Mary E. Johnson
Franklyn S., d. 1/10/1987 at 54 in Center Harbor
James Aubert, d. 6/27/1994 at 74 in Wolfeboro; James Parker and Elizabeth Grimes
Mary Ann, d. 8/6/1995 at 83 in Ossipee; Patrick Burke and Sarah Connelly
Willie Eugene, d. 10/24/1991 at 62 in Wolfeboro; Willie E. Parker and Edith E. Carr

PARKINSON,
Martha, d. 2/7/1966 at 91 in Rochester; b. Bradford, England; Thomas Spencer and Lydia Pearson

PARMENTER,
David Eugene, d. 5/14/1943 at 67/7/0 in Keene; b. Norton, MA; Grance S. Parmenter and Harriett W. Melville
Harriet, d. 2/1/1928 at 89/7/27; widow; b. Charlestown, RI; Andrew Melville and Rosanna Bosesden
Imogene G., d. 10/14/1965 at 78 in Contoocook; b. Limington, ME; Walter Sawyer and Lucy Roberts

PATCH,
Harland S., d. 7/10/1940 at 16/3/10 in E. Wakefield; b. Sanford, ME; Everett F. Patch and Abbie Smith
Ira L., d. 1/25/1925 at 48/3/8; single; b. W. Newfield, ME; Albert Patch and Rose Patch
John, d. 4/7/1946 at 45/8/12 in Union; b. Wakefield; John Patch and Gertrude Clark
Mary, d. 4/9/1897 at 64; housewife; married; b. Shapleigh, ME; Jonathan Patch (Shapleigh, ME)
Sadie, d. 12/29/1938 at 55/5/12 in Wolfeboro; b. Cornish, ME; Charles Guilford and Rebecca Tucker
Samuel, d. 7/27/1897 at 67; laborer; widower; b. Newfield, ME; Samuel Patch (Newfield, ME) and Annie Morrison (Shapleigh, ME)
Samuel, d. 5/19/1920 at 70; cardio-renal dis.; single; b. Parsonsfield, ME; Samuel Patch (Parsonsfield, ME) and Mary Patch (Parsonsfield, ME)
Zulema, d. 11/12/1905 at 79/10/18 in Union; housework; married; b. Parsonsfield, ME; Joseph Clough

PATRIQUIN,
Charles Thombs, d. 11/7/1995 at 69; Oliver Patriquin and Gladys Thombs

PATTERSON,
Margaret Martin, d. 11/4/1995 at 82 in East Wakefield; Roger Stephen Martin and Alina Sophie Strom
Roland T., d. 11/29/1984 at 70; Clarence Patterson and Edith Tays

PAUL,
Annie M., d. 11/28/1935 at 73/0/6; b. Washington, DC; Joseph W. Nairn and Alice L. Finckel
Armine D., d. 12/2/1918 at 81/6/8; at home; single; b. Wakefield; John Paul (Sanford, ME) and Eliza Lord (Sanford, ME)
Arthur Hiram, d. 11/6/1938 at 79/2/28; b. Wakefield; Hiram Paul and Mary Porter Copp
George W., d. 7/19/1969 at 73 in Sanbornville; George W. Paul and Alice Loud
Henry Ashton, d. 5/22/1938 at 78/9/12; b. Wakefield; Hiram Paul and Mary Porter Copp
John, d. 10/11/1887 at 93/1/29; farmer; widower; b. Sanford, ME; John Paul (Kittery, ME) and Dorcas Garey (Sanford, ME)

Julia H., d. 11/7/1978 at 80 in Concord; Stanley O. Bishop and Martha A. Carpenter

Mary P., d. 7/14/1911 at 85/5/11; housewife; widow; b. Wakefield; William A. Copp (Wakefield) and Mary B. Remick (Milton)

Mary Porter, d. 6/2/1905 at 0/9/7; b. Wakefield; Arthur Paul (Wakefield) and Annie H. Nairn (Washington, DC)

Nancy Libby, d. 12/7/1951 at 80; b. Limerick, ME; Stephen Libby and Ann Sawyer

Samuel H., d. 9/28/1980 at 84; Arthur H. Paul and Annie Nairn

Steven, d. 10/7/1973 at 48 in Wolfeboro; Stelios Polychronopoulos and Zoe Hatzi

PAULOWSKI,

Stephen, d. 9/3/1937 at 63/3/28 in Wolfeboro; b. Lithuania; John Paulowski and Agnes Geleinas

PAWLOWSKI,

Julius, d. 12/14/1929 at 73/10/15; widower; b. Germany; August Pawlouski and Dorothea Windmutter

PEABODY,

Nellie, d. 7/5/1949 at 57 in Concord

PEARL,

Gertrude C., d. 10/8/1948 at 81/5/2 in Sanbornville; b. Rochester; John E. Chesley and Elizabeth Horne

PEASLEE,

Clarence E., d. 10/18/1973 at 64 in Union; Arthur E. Peaslee and Dorothea Quimond

PEAVEY,

John C., d. 8/21/1890 at 69/11/12; jeweler; married; b. Strafford; John Peavey (Strafford) and Mary Caverly (Strafford)

PENDERGAST,

Faylene R., d. 9/21/1993 at 65 in Wolfeboro; Mylie Henderson and Margaret Laney

Ralph Edward, d. 5/17/1997 at 69 in Wolfeboro; Henry J. Pendergast and Florence Clement

PENNEY,
Ethel A., d. 8/9/1887 at 0/7/20; b. Wakefield; Mark B. Penney (New Durham) and Lilla J. Burrows (Middleton)
John C., d. 1/21/1893 at 45/2/15; hotel keeper; married; b. New Durham; Joseph J. Penney and Mary A. Pender

PENNINGTON,
Vernal, d. 5/28/1991 at 65 in Wolfeboro; John Pennington and Florence Russin

PERHAM,
William, d. 2/14/1976 at 78 in Norwood, MA

PERKINS,
Charles Edward, d. 4/4/1949 at 80/7/22 in Union; b. New Durham; Augustus J. Perkins and Annie Wallace
Clara A., d. 9/28/1932 at 75/1/21 in Union
Daisy Hayes, d. 6/25/1945 at 72/5/23 in Lancaster, MA; b. Haverhill, MA; James Hayes
Emeline B., d. 6/20/1894 at 54/8/20; housekeeper; married; b. Portland, ME; George Burns
Florence E., d. 12/10/1985 at 87 in Ossipee; Marshall E. Knight and Elizabeth B. Brackett
George A., d. 3/10/1921 at 73/5/18; apoplexy; farmer; single; b. New Durham; Benjamin C. Perkins (New Durham) and Olive Deland (New Durham)
Guy S., d. 3/2/1972 at 80 in Sanford, ME
Henry, d. 4/22/1966 at 99 in Worcester, MA
Lena Grace, d. 6/23/1938 at 57/10/15 in Sanbornville; b. Middleton; Ned Labonte and Annie Willey
Stanley A., d. 5/20/1909 at 12/3/10; b. Wakefield; Samuel Perkins (Middleton) and Bridget McNamara (Ireland)
William H., d. 2/8/1895 at 67/4/9; farmer; widower; b. Wakefield; Moses Perkins (Brookfield) and Sally B. Hill (Wakefield)

PERRAULT,
Addie Mae, d. 9/8/1991 at 75 in Dover

PERREAULT,
Amedee J., d. 7/7/1978 at 65 in Somersworth

PERRON,
Amede, d. 11/17/1957 at 84 in Union; b. Canada; Andre Perron and
  Anastasia Gagnon
Eva, d. 7/3/1894 at 0/0/25; b. Wakefield; Joseph Perron (Canada) and
  Celia Cyr (Canada)
Marie B., d. 6/5/1914 at 0/1/19; b. Wakefield; Joseph Perron (Canada) and
  Celenia LaPointe (Wakefield)

PERRY,
stillborn child, d. 10/30/1932 in Sanbornville
Marjorie Edna, d. 2/14/1989 at 83 in Cambridge, MA
Sharon Lee, d. 3/9/1995 at 44 in Union; Robert H. McNeil, Jr. and
  Virginia C. McKay
Warren H., Jr., d. 11/25/1996 at 51 in Wolfeboro; Warren H. Perry, Sr.

PERSCH,
Christopher D., d. 2/5/1970 at 0/0/23 in Wolfeboro; William J. Persch, Jr.
  and Jayne A. Dombek

PETTIS,
Mavis Claire, d. 6/25/1992 at 74 in Wolfeboro; Harold L. Watson and
  Clara Victoria Flybotte

PEVEY,
George E., d. 1/30/1898 at 58/7/10; founder; married; b. Peterborough;
  Abial Pevey (Greenfield) and Louisa S. Stone (Swanzey)

PEZOLD,
Arthur J., d. 3/5/1984 at 93; Thomas Pezold and Wanda Egner

PHELAN,
Hilda Jennie, d. 7/22/1994 at 75 in Wolfeboro; Eric Anderson and Freda
  Vules

PHILBRICK,
Eugenie S., d. 7/31/1987 at 82 in Wolfeboro
John C., d. 9/17/1898 at 71/7/23; farmer; married; b. Effingham; Joseph
  Philbrick (Hampton) and Abigail Lang (Limerick, ME)
Mina W., d. 5/23/1900 at 72/10/25; housewife; widow; b. Wakefield; John
  Hill (Wakefield) and Lydia Brackett (Ossipee)

Ralph N., d. 1/26/1990 at 83 in Wolfeboro
Samuel N., d. 10/26/1926 at 87/2/4; widower; b. Ossipee; Samuel Philbrick and Pheline Darkham

PHILLA,
Kathryn L., d. 4/11/1983 at 61; John B. Sequin and Florence Rogers

PHILLIPS,
Myrtle A., d. 10/7/1981 at 83 in Sanbornville; Albert Newman and Minerva Phinney

PICKERING,
Ann T., d. 7/24/1894 at 76/6; housekeeper; widow; Daniel Wiggin (Wakefield) and Polly Hanscomb (Somersworth)
Lillian E., d. 4/6/1952 at 88/5/17 in Wolfeboro; b. Moultonboro; Charles H. Earle and Eliza E. Russell
Lydia A., d. 10/15/1908 at 55/1/24; housewife; married; b. Kittery, ME; Joshua Sanborn (Wakefield) and Sarah E. Libby
Walter F., d. 1/13/1938 at 77/1/18 in Sanbornville; b. Tuftonboro; John Pickering and Myra Kimball

PICKET,
William, d. 9/20/1946 at 90/7/15 in Union; b. Swampscott, MA

PIGEON,
Harry C., d. 12/31/1935 at 0/4/18 in Cornish, ME
Ruth M., d. 8/22/1935 at 41/2/23 in Cornish, ME

PIKE,
daughter, d. 9/2/1900 at 0/1; b. Wakefield; David C. Pike (Middleton) and May E. Miller (Lawrence, MA)
daughter, d. 6/13/1903 at 0/7/28; b. Wakefield; David Pike (Middleton) and Mary Miller (Lawrence, MA)
Alburtus A., d. 9/22/1902 at 45/4/11; laborer; married; b. VT; Jacob R. Pike (Ossipee) and Mary A. Hathorn (Reading, VT)
Anna, d. 7/17/1955 at 93 in Concord; b. Orford; Thomas Johnson and Mary Webster
Charles E., d. 1/27/1909 at 63/11/2; farmer; widower; b. Chelsea, MA; George D. Pike (Middleton) and Lucy J. Ricker (Rochester)
Charles L., d. 7/10/1972 at 85; Albert Pike and Dianne Reede

Clarence C., d. 11/24/1896 at 27/6/20; moulder; b. Plymouth, VT; Jacob R. Pike (Ossipee) and Mary Harthorn (Reading, VT)

Cory, d. 4/21/1959 at 0/0/1 in Rochester; b. Rochester; Lloyd G. Pike and Marilyn L. Williams

David C., d. 12/23/1905 at --; farmer; married; b. Middleton; George Pike (Middleton) and Maria Cook (Middleton)

Elizabeth F., d. 6/28/1901 at 70/4/13; domestic; married; b. Bartlett; Andrew Gilman (Wakefield) and Dolly Pike (Wakefield)

Ethel M., d. 8/19/1956 at 85 in Union; b. Wakefield; Frank Lane and Annie Bartlett

Eva Bell, d. 11/27/1953 at 81 in Union; b. Effingham Falls; Joshua W. Thurston and Arvilla Chick

Forrest S., d. 10/9/1977 at 80 in Wolfeboro; Winthrop Pike and Augusta Tibbetts

George C., d. 10/28/1890 at 72/6/13; farmer; married; b. Middleton

George E., d. 3/9/1917 at 49/3/1; laborer; single; b. VT; Royal Pike (Ossipee) and Mary Hathorn (Bridgewater, VT)

George H., d. 9/28/1898 at 0/3/1; b. Wakefield; David C. Pike (Middleton) and Mary E. Miller (Lawrence, MA)

Harold A., d. 6/25/1908 at 0/1/3; b. Wakefield; Edwin L. Pike (Rochester) and Belle Wentworth (Wakefield)

Helen, d. 4/20/1895 at 4/2; b. Wakefield; David Pike (Middleton) and May Miller (Acton, ME)

Lida A., d. 1/9/1908 at 31/0/5; housekeeper; single; b. Somersworth; Charles E. Pike (Chelsea, MA) and Mary C. Linscott (Alfred, ME)

Lizzie, d. 3/13/1887 at 50/2/14; housework; single; b. Wakefield; Joseph H. Pike (Wakefield) and Elmira Lyford (Brookfield)

Lois R., d. 3/11/1985 at 75 in Wolfeboro

Lyman W., d. 9/24/1935 at 0/0/1 in Rochester; b. Rochester; Forrest S. Pike and Lois Robinson

Mary Ellen, d. 12/8/1939 at 86/8/19 in Brookfield; b. Middleton; Ebenezer S. Pike and Drusilla Hodge

Mary M., d. 1/8/1902 at 73/8/5; domestic; widow; b. Bridgewater, VT; — Hathorn

Minnie A., d. 1/6/1915 at 44/8/3; housewife; married; b. Wakefield; Josiah Wiggin (Wakefield) and Mary W. Wiggin (Middleton)

Philip G., d. 1/16/1960 at 69; b. Lebanon, ME; Robert S. Pike and Fanny Roberts

Robert H., d. 11/2/1916 at 95/7/18; hotel keeper; widower; b. Ossipee; John Pike and Isabella Calder (Brookfield)

Royal J., d. 1/5/1898 at 84/7/7; carpenter; married; b. Ossipee; John Pike (Salisbury) and ----- Horne (Ossipee)

Sadie May, d. 11/2/1890 at 11/10/4; single; b. Lynn, MA; W. W. Pike (Stoneham, MA) and Sarah A. Tibbetts (Wolfeboro)

Sarah A., d. 1/8/1910 at 54/6/23; housewife; married; Thomas J. Tibbetts (Wolfeboro) and Sarah E. Locke (Wakefield)

Scott, d. 7/22/1968 at 82 in Wolfeboro; Winthrop Pike and Sarah Tibbets

Smith, d. 2/28/1952 at 82/5/11 in Concord; b. Middleton; John Watson and Mary Pike

Sophia Ricker, d. 2/27/1938 at 95/0/16 in Rochester

Susan, d. 9/19/1888 at 60/7/15; housework; single; Joseph H. Pike and Almira Lyford

Susan H., d. 4/7/1968 at 70 in Concord; David C. Pike and Mary E. Miller

Thomas C., d. 10/20/1907 at 87/0/1; farmer; widower; b. Middleton

Violet M., d. 6/18/1972 at 78 in East Lebanon, ME

Winthrop W., d. 7/25/1929 at 76/1/11; widower; b. Stoneham; John Pike and Mary Jane Willey

PILLSBURY,

John D., d. 2/17/1899 at 83/3/10 in Union; machinist; married; b. Rowley, MA; Dole Pillsbury (Rowley, MA) and Nancy Coffin (Newburyport, MA)

Sarah C., d. 2/24/1911 at 84/4/6; housewife; widow; b. Brighton, ME; Leighton Johnson (Fryeburg, ME) and Sarah Gray (Strafford)

PINKHAM,

Bessie, d. 12/27/1951 at 65 in Union; b. Newfoundland; John Vay and Charlotte Lotta

PINO,

Brian Jon, d. 2/18/1995 at 23; Brian Ireland and Barbara Mielke

PIPER,

Abbie E., d. 2/12/1898 at 41/9/8; housewife; divorced; b. Wakefield; Joseph R. Mitchell (Milton) and Harriet L. Sampson (Otisfield, ME)

Ada F., d. 5/12/1891 at 23/1/18; teacher; single; b. Wakefield; George F. Piper (Wakefield) and Mary E. Jenness (Wakefield)

George Francis, d. 6/19/1921 at 87/9/13; hypertrophy; retired; widower; b. Wakefield; Edward Cutts Piper (Wakefield) and Sarah Swasey (Wakefield)

Idella M., d. 5/18/1933 at 62/11/24
Mary E., d. 5/5/1910 at 67/7/12; housewife; married; b. Wakefield

PIPPIN,
Annie, d. 2/3/1954 at 75 in Rochester; b. Sanbornville; Victor Pippin and Susan Thibodeau
Charles V., d. 9/30/1931 at 51/10/11; widower; b. Sanbornville; Victor Pippin and Susan Thibodeau
Dorothy E., d. 4/26/1989 at 72 in Wolfeboro; Roscoe Wentworth and Blanche Wentworth
Franklin, d. 2/6/1937 at 49/11/22 in Union; b. Union; Victor Pippin and Susan Tibodeau
Fred, d. 12/29/1931 at 55/0/1; single; b. Wakefield; Victor Pippin and Susan Thibodeau
Susan, d. 5/17/1926 at 70/11/26; widow; b. Mattawaska, NB; Edward Thibedeau and Amelia Dumas
Victor, d. 6/14/1920 at 68/4/24; uraemia; section hand; married; b. Canada; Oliver Pippin (Canada) and Nathalie Guilmet (Canada)

PLANTE,
son, d. 10/5/1927 at 0/0/0; b. Wakefield; Albert Plante and Estelle Maette
Josephat L., d. 3/15/1913 at 0/4/1; b. Somersworth; Edward Plante (Somersworth) and Eva Lavertu (Wakefield)

PLUMMER,
Grace A., d. 2/20/1893 at 4/8/29; b. Wakefield; Thomas E. Plummer (Brookfield) and Mary E. Lang (Brookfield)
Lorenzo C., d. 1/21/1922 at 76/2/1; retired; widower; b. Farmington; William Plummer (Farmington) and ----- Ham (Farmington)
Thomas O., d. 7/22/1958 at 74 in Berwick, ME; b. Wakefield; Thomas E. Plummer and Eliza M. Lang

POIRIER,
Stanislaus, d. 6/28/1956 in Wolfeboro; b. Canada; Louis Poirier and Denise Sharron

POLLARD,
Lydia, d. 11/17/1903 at 75/10/4; housekeeper; widow; Ezekiel Hubbard (Acton, ME) and Abigail Nason (Acton, ME)

POPE,
Alan M., d. 8/21/1980 at 51; Ralph C. Pope and Ilona LaVigne

PORTER,
Hattie L., d. 1/8/1919 at 36/3/15; influenza, pneumonia; housekeeper; divorced; b. Wakefield; Frank P. Lang (Brookfield) and Ida F. Rankin (Lewiston, ME)

POSEY,
Joseph J., d. 7/21/1942 at 70/5/3; b. Biddeford, ME; Joseph Posey

POUL[L]IOT,
Edward, d. 5/17/1922 at 76/11/28; retired; widower; b. St. Arsene, PQ; Joseph Pouliot (Canada) and DesAngen Roy (Canada)
Edward J., d. 5/20/1960 at 81 in Sanbornville; b. Wakefield; Edward Pouliot and Cecila Boissoneau
Enid M., d. 12/3/1967 at 74 in Sanbornville; b. Everett, MA; John B. Watson and Mary A. Hayes
Frank, d. 7/30/1933 at 73/0/0
Mary Georgianna, d. 6/5/1949 at 86 in Wolfeboro; John Lanouette and Philomen Charrier
Selenia, d. 2/2/1891 at 39/10/5; housekeeper; married; b. Canada; Marcelle Brisomeau (Canada) and Bergite Fillon (Canada)

POWELL,
Stanasia B., d. 6/22/1966 at 79; b. Lithuania; John Mingen and Aniela Mingen

PRATT,
Clara M., d. 5/14/1969 at 78 in Wolfeboro; Albert Moulton and Elizabeth Forrest
George H., d. 11/23/1967 at 73 in Wolfeboro; b. Townsend, VT; George I. Pratt and Elizabeth Wilson
Hildegarde R., d. 4/25/1966 at 56 in Hanover; b. Conway; Everett W. Robinson and Mary G. McClellan
John C., d. 10/13/1988 at 64 in Rochester; George H. Pratt and Ruth Wentworth
John H., d. 12/23/1957 at 78 in Wolfeboro; b. Salem, MA; John W. Pratt and Ellen P. Jarvis
Mary Lillian, d. 10/21/1977 at 59 in No. Providence, RI

Ruth W., d. 6/21/1970 at 70 in Hanover; Charles Wentworth and Clara Place

PRESCOTT,
Charles W., d. 10/11/1961 at 71 in Sanbornville; b. Limerick, ME; Charles Prescott and Laura Sylvester
James F., d. 6/5/1904 at 35/6; laborer; single; b. Madbury; Benjamin F. Prescott (Durham) and Rebecca Foss
John W., d. 5/8/1927 at 81/10/12; widower; b. Dover; Ezekiel Prescott and Eliza Fernald
Lola, d. 1/22/1941 at 68/4/3; b. Rockland, ME; Levi Murphy and Abbie Bird
Sadie E., d. 3/14/1908 at 0/11/28; b. Portsmouth; Benjamin Prescott (Madbury) and Mary Weeks (Rockville, MA)

PRESTON,
Lalia, d. 1/31/1968 at 78 in Wolfeboro; Harry Preston and Laura Legg

PRIDE,
Robert, d. 4/28/1963 at 77 in Ossipee; b. Twillingate, Newfoundland; John Pride and Susan Vaticher

PRITCHARD,
Lillian J., d. 2/5/1975 at 59 in Wolfeboro; Leslie Hiseler and Elizabeth Tappen

PROCTOR,
Edwin, d. 3/31/1951 at 87/10/25 in Union; b. Swampscott, MA; David D. Proctor and Margaret Pinkham

PROMISE,
Genevieve M., d. 2/20/1988 at 73 in Wolfeboro; Hormidas Palardy and Rose Briand

PROVENCHER,
Donat, d. 1/15/1918 at 31/8/15; laborer; married; b. Canada; M. Provencher (Canada)
Henri A.S., d. 7/10/1911 at 0/0/6; b. Wakefield; Donat Provencher (Quebec) and Melvina Huard (Quebec)
Melvina, d. 3/10/1973 at 93 in Sanford, ME

QUARNSTROM,
Herbert C., d. 4/15/1963 at 67 in So. Wakefield; b. Somerville, MA; Andrew Quarnstrom and Agnes Johanson

QUIMBY,
child, d. 2/10/1907 at 0/0/0; b. Wakefield; Forrest G. Quimby (Newfield, ME) and Carrie E. Pinkham (Middleton)
Daniel, d. 12/9/1910 at 91/8/23; farmer; widower; b. Newfield, ME
Frank H., d. 4/10/1941 at 87/1 in Wolfeboro; b. Acton, ME; Josiah Quimby and Nancy Horne
Joseph W., d. 4/5/1909 at 65/8/20; laborer; married; b. Newfield, ME; J. M. Quimby (Acton, ME) and Sally Horne (Acton, ME)
Kristina, d. 7/18/1980 at 0/0/4 in Hanover; Willard H. Quimby and Agnes Mickelonis
Mary A., d. 3/15/1911 at 59/11/15; housewife; married; b. Lebanon, ME; H. Varney (Lebanon, ME) and P. Gordon
Mary Ann, d. 11/21/1896 at 80/3/2; housewife; married; b. Wakefield; John Garey (Wakefield) and Mary P. Hutchins (Wakefield)

QUINN,
James F., d. 7/7/1983 at 59; James H. Quinn and Ruth I. Wilson
John F., d. 3/20/1965 at 80 in Wolfeboro; b. Medford, MA; Michael Quinn and Katherine Walsh

RAND,
Constance, d. 7/30/1927 at 0/0/7; b. Wakefield; Lester E. Rand and Blanche Elliott
Frank H., d. 11/20/1953 at 83 in Sanford, ME

RANDALL,
Benjamin M., d. 7/2/1926 at 78/4/25; b. Lebanon, ME; Benjamin Randall and ----- Stillings
Earl F., d. 10/12/1958 at 63 in Manchester; b. Wakefield; Frank Randall and Martha Runnels
Fred B., Sr., d. 10/12/1997 at 72 in Sanbornville; Earl Randall and Mabel Weeks
Mabel A., d. 12/1/1988 at 87 in Ossipee; Frank Weeks and Minnie Alley
Mabel L., d. 12/18/1900 at 4/10/18 in Sanbornville; b. Wakefield; Frank W. Randall (Brownfield, ME) and Martha C. Runnels (Wakefield)

Raymond A., d. 11/8/1992 at 64 in Sanbornville; Earl F. Randall and Mabel A. Weeks

Ruth V., d. 7/27/1992 at 66 in Rochester; Edgar I. Drown and Irene Newcomb

Shirley L., d. 12/16/1974 at 49 in Hanover; Fred Evans and Charlotte Brand

RANDOLPH,

James R., d. 2/4/1969 at 77 in Sanford, ME; Strother L. Randolph and Frances Robbins

REBIDUE,

Elwin E., d. 8/11/1988 at 75 in Wolfeboro; George Rebidue and Coretta Covey

Evelyn M., d. 11/21/1981 at 71 in Sanbornville; William Hesson

William H., d. 11/19/1987 at 52 in Wolfeboro; Elwin H. Rebidue and Evelyn Hesson

REED,

daughter, d. 7/3/1905 at 0/0/0 in Union; b. Union; Edwin S. Reed (Wakefield) and Inez M. Dicey (Wakefield)

child, d. 8/20/1934 at 0/0/0 in Dover; b. Dover; Arthur W. Reed and Marjorie M. Davis

Ammon S., d. 8/18/1903 at 70/0/21; farmer; married; b. Newfield, ME; Silas Reed (Newfield, ME) and Hannah York (Newfield, ME)

Austin Percival, d. 8/6/1940 at 54/9/5 in Wolfeboro; b. Woodman; Amon Reed

Earl, d. 6/6/1910 at 0/3; b. Wakefield; Austin P. Reed (Wakefield) and Gertrude Smith (Newfield, ME)

Edwin S., d. 12/15/1953 at 89 in Union; b. Newfield, ME; Aunnon Reed and Elizabeth Waldron

Elizabeth, d. 12/26/1907 at 77; housework; widow; b. Acton, ME; Stephen Waldron (Acton, ME)

Elmer, d. 4/27/1947 at 76/7/10 in Wolfeboro

Eunice S., d.. 10/26/1903 at 0/1/8; b. Wakefield; Edwin Reed (Wakefield) and Inez Dicey (Wakefield)

Eva E., d. 5/14/1895 at 2/4/17; b. Newfield, ME; Fred A. Reed (Wolfeboro) and Margaret Taylor (Pepperell, MA)

Exzenz, d. 8/20/1982 at 76 in Wolfeboro; Fred Garyait and Elizabeth Roukey

Fred Amon, d. 3/30/1944 at 83/6/24 in Effingham
George Henry, d. 8/12/1950 at 76/6/25 in Wolfeboro; b. Dover; Henry Reed and Hannah Moore
Hannah, d. 2/25/1901 at 51/8; housewife; married; b. Dover; Moody Moore (Dover) and Hannah S. Hayes (Strafford)
Hannah E., d. 12/2/1905 at 0/7/20; b. East Wakefield; Elmer E. Reed (Acton, ME) and Cora Martin (Acton, ME)
Hazel G., d. 8/9/1987 at 71 in Laconia
Henry A., d. 2/4/1905 at 68/7/12; shoe maker; widower; b. Acton, ME; William Reed (Newfield, ME)
Inez M., d. 12/10/1939 at 68/4/8; b. Wakefield; George W. Dicey and Susan Durrell
James A., d. 2/11/1971 at 83 in Concord
Lester H., d. 11/12/1966 at 82 in Sanford, ME
Lester H., Jr., d. 1/28/1957 at 44 in Smyrna, DE; b. ME; Lester H. Reed, Sr. and Katie L. Grey
Mabel Florence, d. 1/8/1959 at 73 in Sanford, ME; b. Lynn, MA; ---- Smith and Laura E. Holder
Mae A., d. 3/11/1985 at 94 in Dover; Alfred N. McCallum and Lilla Jennings
Margaret, d. 3/29/1939 at 70/7/14 in Concord; b. Pepperell, MA; John Tierney and Mary Garrity
Patricia Ann, d. 8/15/1959 at 25; b. Gloucester, MA; Lemuel H. Burnes and Louise McGrath
Theodore E., d. 3/5/1981 at 74 in Wolfeboro; Edwin Reed and Inez Dicey

REEVES,
Albert B., d. 11/9/1937 at 72/2/26 in Sanbornville; b. Salem, MA; John Reeves and Caroline Tucker

REID,
Jacqueline L., d. 1/19/1971 at 45 in Sanford, ME
James R., Sr., d. 4/21/1987 at 58 in Colebrook

REILLY,
James A., d. 11/11/1953 at 66 in New York

REMICK,
Alberta D., d. 6/17/1985 at 85 in Dover

Arthur S., d. 11/15/1907 at 25/2/22; laborer; married; b. Brookfield; Mark Remick (Eliot, ME) and Eleanor F. Young (Cape Cod, MA)
Crosby B., d. 2/22/1919 at 60/1/20; apoplexy; hotel keeper; married; b. Milton; Moses Remick and Clara Wentworth
Eleanor S., d. 1/19/1914 at 72/8/7; retired; widow; b. E. Boston, MA; James C. Young and Rose M. Gills
Hattie M., d. 7/2/1940 at 80 in Concord; b. Wakefield; William A. Maleham and Nancy Maleham
Jennie B., d. 7/25/1902 at 50/11/13 in Sanbornville; housewife; married; b. Sanford, ME; Freeman C. Goodwin (Sanford, ME) and Phebe Webber (Sanford, ME)
John, d. 11/3/1905 at 69/0/6; shoe maker; married; b. Eliot, ME
Lucy A., d. 1/30/1905 at 78/3/5 in Union; housewife; married; b. Milton; Phineas Woodworth (Milton) and Nancy Witham (Milton)
Maude E., d. 10/10/1903 at 29/9; housework; single; b. Brookfield; Mark Remick (Brookfield) and Ellen S. Young (Boston, MA)
Rachael H., d. 4/5/1953 at 65 in Gloucester, MA; b. Wakefield
Ruth, d. 10/8/1939 at 54 in Boston, MA
Selina L., d. 6/5/1955 at 47 in Baltimore, MD
William C., d. 1/11/1903 at 37/3/3; stone mason and hostler; single; b. Brookfield; Mark Remick (Eliot, ME) and Ellen S. Young (Wakefield)

RENDALL,
George L., d. 1/4/1887 at 29/0/13; engineer; married; b. Wolfeboro; Charles Rendall (Wolfeboro) and Charlotte Cotton (Wolfeboro)

RESS,
Anna E., d. 9/19/1971 at 76 in Center Harbor; Henry Ress and Anna Elizabeth

RETTI,
Albert, d. 4/26/1896 at 0/3/11 in Sanbornville; b. Sanbornville; Jerry Retti (Canada) and Amanda Drouin (Canada)

REYNOLDS,
Annie M., d. 7/9/1946 at 85/7/10 in Union; b. Acton, ME; Henry L. Fox and Sarah A. Moulton
Narcissa D., d. 3/30/1951 at 97/9/4 in Union; b. W. Newfield, ME; Joseph B. Davis and Harriett Dam

Willis L., d. 6/12/1954 at 83 in Union; b. Acton, ME; Charles A. Reynolds and Nellie Sanborn

RHINES,
John B., d. 3/29/1954 at 72 in Union; b. Farmington; Aloah Rhines and Alice Smith
Samuel H., d. 4/11/1913 at 86/4; lumber dealer; widower; b. New Durham; Henry Rhines and Mary Babb

RHODES,
Mildred J., d. 9/11/1978 at 74 in Wolfeboro; Thomas W. Rhodes and Josephine G. O'Brien

RICE,
Irving D., d. 12/13/1957 at 98 in Dover
Ivory F., d. 5/3/1911 at 78/8/5; laborer; widower; b. Freedom; Thomas Rice (Buxton, ME) and Mary Fogg (Limington, ME)
Marion E., d. 3/13/1891 at 20/10/29; seamstress; single; b. Freedom; Ivory F. Rice (Freedom) and Mary McCartee (Porter, ME)
Mary, d. 5/9/1898 at 62/7/10; housewife; married; b. Porter, ME; Stillman McCarthy (Porter, ME) and Mary Mason (Porter, ME)
Sophronia T., d. 6/12/1945 at 88/0/17 in Dover; b. Union; James Tucker and Mary Hale

RICH,
Alice V., d. 9/19/1984 at 90 in Ossipee
Stanley W., d. 3/15/1972 at 76 in Wolfeboro; Lyman Rich and Lillian Learned

RICHARDS,
Albert L., d. 9/16/1943 at 57/5/0 in Saugus, MA
Charles C., d. 10/6/1906 at 68/4/8; farmer; married; b. Wakefield
Lena G., d. 3/28/1936 at 60/7/5 in Milton; b. Wakefield; Charles Richards and Keziah Quimby
Lena H., d. 6/18/1972 at 91; Leonard Hill and Ambie G. Varney
Richmond, d. 2/20/1895 at 84/8/18; farmer; widower; b. Brookfield; Ichabod Richards (Rochester) and Annie Hurd (Rochester)
Walter H., d. 11/8/1971 at 83 in Wolfeboro; Charles Richards and Kesiah Quimby

William C., d. 5/1/1994 at 71 in Wolfeboro; William C. Richards, Sr. and Catherine Shroeder

RICHARDSON,
Annie Louise, d. 12/4/1986 at 80 in Wolfeboro; Walter A. Richardson and Bertha Whitten
Antipas M., d. 4/7/1913 at 66/6/15; merchant; widower; b. Boston, MA; John D. Richardson (Boston, MA) and Elizabeth Maynard (Boston, MA)
Florence G., d. 2/16/1979 at 73 in Rochester; Philip Gilbert and Olive Ouellette
James W., d. 2/9/1949 at 81/0/21 in Sanbornville; b. NB; John Richardson and Marjorie A. Boyd
Ralph E., d. 4/15/1978 at 68 in East Wakefield; Frank A. Richardson and Josephine C.W. Clark

RICHTER,
Florence, d. 10/27/1969 at -- in Staten Island, NY
Horace Foster, d. 8/2/1975 at 77

RICKER,
Charles O., d. 3/24/1981 at 71 in Wolfeboro; Robert A. Ricker and Lilliam Sheppard
Charles P., d. 1/25/1899 at 17/1/4; laborer; single; b. Acton, ME; John R. Ricker (Wakefield) and Emma J. Wiggin (Wakefield)
Doris A., d. 2/8/1961 at 67 in Concord; b. Lynn, MA; Charles Ricker and Lillian Cousens
Emma J.L., d. 5/18/1907 at 53/8/23; housework; married; b. Wakefield; Alpheus Wiggin (Wakefield) and Emily Seavey (Brownington, VT)
John R., d. 11/15/1918 at 70/9/27; farmer; married; b. Wakefield; Jeremiah Ricker (Acton, ME) and Mary A. Hutchins (Wakefield)
Lavinia A., d. 12/3/1920 at 76/1/27; cardio-renal dis.; housekeeper; divorced; b. Ossipee; Peter Keyes (Wolfeboro) and Lavinia Burrows (Lebanon, ME)
Sarah H., d. 8/24/1907 at 84/2/14; housework; widow; b. Lyman, ME; Jonathan Calef and Grace Sears
Susan Jennie, d. 8/9/1953 at 81 in Union; b. Farmington; John F. Colomy and Alice J. Curtis
Walter H., d. 5/16/1946 at 69/8/25 in Wolfeboro; b. Acton, ME; Charles Ricker and Hannah Cloutman

RICKERT,
Anna, d. 1/5/1944 at 72 in Dorchester, MA
John, d. 8/8/1940 at 58 in Boston, MA

RIDEOUT,
Ida Whelpley, d. 10/2/1954 at 82 in Brookfield
Janie M., d. 3/29/1949 at 58 in Portland, ME
Leon C., d. 6/22/1971 at 91 in So. Portland, ME
Olive C., d. 9/27/1909 at 0/1/27; b. Wakefield; Leon Rideout (Albany) and Janie M. Dorr (Milton)

RIDLON,
child, d. 5/12/1946 at 0/0/0 in Rochester; b. Rochester; Arnold Ridlon and Hazel L. Beal
Georgianna C., d. 7/30/1953 at 84 in Union; b. Hopkinton, MA; Augustus Calley and Ann Towle
Mildred M., d. 4/15/1971 at 70 in Rochester; Phineous Seavey and Jennie Ridlon

RIKEMAN,
Mary A., d. 6/4/1901 at 80/2/21; housewife; widow; b. New York, NY; --- Smith

RILEY,
David W., II, d. 11/20/1984 at 63 in Brookfield; David Riley and Helen M. Kelley

RINALDO,
Ethel H., d. 11/16/1986 at 93 in Rochester
Paul F., d. 1/9/1971 at -- in Dover

RINES,
Edna F., d. 10/6/1924 at 62/10 in Sanbornville; housewife; married; b. New Durham; George W. Fletcher (New Durham) and Julia A. Wiley (New Durham)
Ellsworth B., d. 11/14/1948 at 68/7/12 in Rochester; b. Brookfield; Elihu M. Rines and Mary E. Dearborn
Grace E., d. 8/24/1969 at 84 in Wolfeboro
Herbert R., d. 9/17/1947 at 59/0/21 in Hartford, VT; b. Brookfield

Mabel E., d. 3/16/1942 at 56/1/14 in Dover; b. Wakefield; Charles H. Cheney and Sarah Burke

Mary A., d. 7/20/1900 at 51/11/27 in Sanbornville; housework; married; b. Wakefield; Louis Roberts (New Durham) and Betsy Hutchins (Wakefield)

Pamelia W., d. 8/7/1891 at 74/9/21; housekeeper; married; b. Middleton; Samuel Jones (Barrington) and Mary Woodman (Milton)

Walter F., d. 4/28/1973 at 87 in No. Dighton, MA; Elihu Rines

Warren H., d. 11/10/1950 at 93 in Concord; b. New Durham; Samuel H. Rines and Charlotte Evans

RING,

George E., d. 9/22/1982 at 73 in Wolfeboro; Edward A. Ring and Rilla Clark

Helen E., d. 11/30/1962 at 62 in Stoneham, MA

Mary E., d. 8/28/1956 at 69 in Union; b. Rockport, MA; John Flynn and Ellen Welch

Morrill S., d. 1/28/1970 at 68 in Pompano Beach, FL

Ruth, d. 7/10/1975 at 66 in Arlington, MA

RINGER,

Kenneth C., Jr., d. 3/13/1990 at 73 in Wolfeboro; Kenneth C. Ringer and Lillian Murray

RIPLEY,

Ida May, d. 4/9/1905 at 47/11/17 in Union; housewife; married; b. Bath, ME; Franklin Byrd (Eastport, ME) and Livina Huskins (Bath, ME)

Julia, d. 9/27/1909 at 88/8/27; housework; widow; b. Vassalboro, ME

RIST,

Keith Bryan, d. 2/6/1988 at 21; Ronald R. Rist and Dorothy Buonamo

RITCHIE,

Alexander, Jr., d. 12/10/1994 at 82 in Wolfeboro; Alexander Ritchie, Sr. and Bertha Hollings

Doris E., d. 12/30/1981 at 65 in Wolfeboro; Albert N. Wade and Frances Thomas

ROANS,
Archibald, d. 8/4/1913 at 45/5/19; engineer; married; b. Fredinton, NB; John Roans

ROBBINS,
Benjamin H., d. 3/31/1956 at 82/5/28 in Union; b. Winchester; Henry B. Robbins and Ellen Freeman
Lilly P., d. 7/22/1916 at 33/6/3; housewife; married; b. Newfoundland; James Roberts (Newfoundland) and Salome Taylor (Newfoundland)
Theodore W., d. 12/2/1987 at 66 in Wolfeboro; George Robbins and Jessie Smith

ROBERTS,
Abbie L., d. 3/13/1967 at 80 in Wolfeboro; b. E. Wolfeboro; Daniel Cotton and Hattie Hurd
Elizabeth, d. 9/29/1910 at 81/4/24; housewife; married; b. Ossipee; John Smith (Ossipee) and Sally Ambrose (Ossipee)
George A., d. 12/20/1961 at 81 in Wolfeboro; Andrew K. Roberts and Clara Glines
Henry A., d. 1/19/1901 at 32/6/6; physician; single; b. Wakefield; Samuel W. Roberts (Alton) and Elizabeth Smith (Ossipee)
John S., d. 8/25/1959 at 94 in Wolfeboro; b. Wakefield; Samuel W. Roberts and Elizabeth Smith
Lewis, d. 3/27/1888 at 72/1/16; farmer; widower; b. Wakefield; Lemuel Roberts (New Durham) and ----- Hutchins (Wakefield)
Samuel W., d. 12/6/1912 at 87/10/28; retired; widower; b. Alton; Richard Roberts (Alton) and Hannah Willey (Alton)
Sarah N., d. 6/10/1947 at 81/7/15; b. Wakefield; Herschel Moulton

ROBERTSON,
Aimee H., d. 1/1/1970 at 81 in Norway, ME
Arthur H., d. 1/25/1988 at 70 in Dover
Francis C., d. 1/13/1959 at 80 in Wolfeboro; b. Jamaica, MA; George Robertson and Melissa O'Haley
Harry E., d. 5/10/1952 at 73/6/29 in Wolfeboro; b. OH; William E. Robertson and Mary -----
Willard E., d. 4/22/1946 at 68/11/14 in North Wakefield; b. Conway; Willard S. Robertson and Susan B. Hanson

ROBINSON,
Albert Oscar, d. 4/30/1949 at 97/6/4 in Wolfeboro; b. Brookfield; Noah Robinson and Judith Cook
Andrew J., d. 9/30/1931 at 97/0/16; widower; b. Brookfield; Ebenezer Robinson
Bertha E., d. 11/17/1964 at 77 in Miami, FL
Clara E.D., d. 6/3/1947 at 98/9/8 in Union; b. Ossipee; Darius Davis and Ruth B. Durgin
Darrell, d. 12/21/1985 at 20 in Rochester; William A. Robinson and June Lavalley
Forrest D., d. 6/17/1947 at 36/7/9 in Acton, ME; b. Wakefield; Frank Robinson and Bertha Hart
George Perley, d. 1/1/1943 ar 66/6/20 in Wolfeboro; b. Exeter; Daniel W. Robinson
Harry F., d. 11/16/1907 at 0/10/20; b. Kingston; George F. Robinson (Manchester) and Alice E. Hartford (Deerfield)
John Frank, d. 9/27/1925 at 71/6/8; widower; b. Hiram, ME; Roscoe W. Robinson and Emily Brown
John M., d. 4/29/1927 at 76/3/10; widower; b. NS; William Robinson and Jane McDonald
Leroy Burton, d. 11/21/1954 at 69 in Sanbornville; b. Durham; Melnot Robinson and Nellie Clark
Mary E., d. 8/5/1896 at 45/3/1; housekeeper; married; b. Brookfield; Charles West (Bath, ME) and Syrena Ricker (Brookfield)
Mary E., d. 9/24/1982 at 100 in Wolfeboro; George H. Bowers and Margaret O'Hearn
Minnie, d. 12/27/1966 at 79 in Concord; b. PQ; ---- Doucette and Mellissa Drown
Nancy J., d. 12/19/1897 at 78/7/2; housewife; married; b. Parsonsfield, ME; James Day (Parsonsfield, ME) and Abigail Fly (Parsonsfield, ME)
Raymond L., d. 9/26/1991 at 84 in Wolfeboro; Leroy Robinson and Mary Bowers
Robert M., d. 1/24/1947 at 47 in Pemberton, NJ; b. Canyon City, CO; Frank Robinson and Georgianna Heel
Samuel Medfield, d. 4/20/1943 at 78/2/24 in Ossipee; b. Hyde Park, MA; Charles Robinson and Emma Ellis

ROGERS,
Herbert E., d. 3/1/1900 at 38/6/5; farmer; married; b. Wolfeboro; David Rogers (Wolfeboro) and Sarah E. Clark (Wolfeboro)
Herbert S., d. 8/17/1947 at 58/5/1 in Hartford, VT; b. Sanbornville
Marion H., d. 9/21/1978 at 76 in Wolfeboro; Charles C. Hayes and Caroline Anderson
Patricia, d. 1/8/1987 at 51 in Portland, ME; Ervin York and Mary Shaw
Robert L., d. 4/3/1990 at 56 in Union; Asel W. Rogers and Helen Stearns
Vincent D., d. 1/26/1979 at 80 in Wolfeboro; Herbert E. Rogers and Lillian Sanborn
Virginia Gibbs, d. 10/5/1990 at 72 in East Wakefield; Frank Dennis and Georgia ----
Walter E., d. 1/15/1968 at 70 in Concord; Herbert Rogers and Lillian Sanborn
William N., d. 9/25/1945 at 53/8/15 in Wolfeboro; b. Sanbornville; Herbert N. Rogers and Lillian A. Sanborn

ROLLINS,
Alice P., d. 7/21/1947 at 65/1/12 in Rochester; b. Wolfeboro; Winthrop Pike and Augusta Tibbetts
Bertha T., d. 8/18/1891 at 0/4/29; b. Lawrence, MA; George H. Rollins (Franklin) and Lucy A. West (Brookfield)
George A., d. 6/3/1958 at 76 in Alton Bay; b. Rochester; George W. Rollins and Eliza Webber
John A., d. 9/27/1912 at 67/3/22; farmer; married; b. Ossipee; Alvin Rollins (Brookfield) and Emily Perry (Brookfield)
Sarah, d. 7/30/1932 at 79/5/19 in Woodman

ROSE,
Francis W., d. 12/18/1961 at 58 in Wolfeboro; b. NS; Joseph F.D. Rose and Laura J. McLean

ROSS-MacCORMACK,
Ainsley, d. 11/26/1982 at 0/3 in East Wakefield; Charles MacCormack and Susan Ross

ROURKE,
Erie E., d. 4/7/1936 at 66/6/3 in Sanbornville; b. Bedford; William H. Nichols and Sarah Webber

Paul A., d. 7/6/1977 at 66 in Sanbornville; George A. Rourke and Evie E. Nichols

ROWELL,
Frances A., d. 1/31/1911 at 85/10/22; housewife; widow; b. Acton, ME; Moses Hemingway (Arundel, ME) and Myra Hubbard (Shapleigh, ME)

ROWRKE,
Anne F., d. 9/2/1972 at 88 in Wolfeboro

RUDAN,
Joe E., d. 4/29/1979 at 49 in Wolfeboro; Adam Rachkoskie and Mary Rudan

RUGGERO,
Albert, d. 8/22/1961 at 56; b. Lawrence, MA; Petu Ruggero and Conseglia Balletta

RUNNELLS,
Carrie E., d. 12/15/1942 at 82/5/28 in Rochester; b. Wakefield; Eben Chapman and Clara Lang
Emma Frances, d. 2/18/1939 at 79/6/19; b. Wakefield; Isaac N. Fellows and Sophia A. Kelley
Foira N., d. 3/4/1960 at 94 in Union; b. Acton, ME; Israel Runnells and Mary E. Rogers
Samuel S., d. 8/8/1934 at 78/11/18; b. Union; Alvah Runnells and Martha Wentworth

RUNNELS,
Alvah, d. 9/16/1920 at 94/9/15 in Union; apoplexy; farmer; widower; b. Acton, ME; Samuel Runnels (Acton, ME) and Hannah Farnham (Acton, ME)
Elizabeth, d. 11/18/1903 at 69/7/8; housekeeper; married; b. Moira, NY; James Fisk (Bradbury, VT)
Jay, d. 4/13/1917 at 67/2/9; farmer; married; b. Acton, ME; Alvah Runnels (Acton, ME) and Martha Wentworth (Milton)
Martha Cora, d. 7/12/1954 at 78 in Lawrence, MA; b. Wakefield; Jay Runnels and Margaret Jack
Mary R., d. 3/22/1952 at 89/0/9 in Union; b. Chocorua

Othello D., d. 8/1/1981 at 79 in Wolfeboro; Eugene Runnels and Carrie Deane

RUSSELL,
Arthur P., d. 2/2/1946 at 67/6/23 in Haverhill, MA; b. Danvers, MA; James U. Russell and Gustie M. Tibbetts
Irving, d. 3/3/1915 at 39/6/12; teamster; married; b. Athens, ME; Leonard Russell (Brighton, ME) and Rose A. Haskell (Palermo, ME)
John W., d. 7/21/1936 at 85/1 in Wolfeboro; b. Fall River, MA; John Russell and Mary L. Barnard
Mabel J., d. 8/25/1957 at 84 in Sanbornville; b. Ashby, MA; Laban Wright and Adeline Sawin

RYAN,
John, d. 1/10/1899 at 41 in East Wakefield; plumber; single; b. New York, NY; Matthew Ryan (Ireland)

RYDER,
James N., d. 9/25/1989 at 53 in Rochester; James F. Ryder and Mildred Beesley

RYER,
Alice, d. 8/8/1940 at 78/11/12 in Sanbornville; b. NS; —— Goodwin

ST. PIERRE,
George J.A., d. 9/30/1909 at 0/11/18; b. Wakefield; Andrew St. Pierre (Ossipee) and Leura Vigneault (Ossipee)
Mary A.G., d. 10/1/1909 at 0/0/19; b. Wakefield; Andrew St. Pierre (Ossipee) and Leura Vigneault (Ossipee)

SALINGER,
Rudolph, d. 7/9/1921 at 71/5/19; retired machinist; married; b. Germany; David Salinger (Germany) and Rebecca Barstow (Germany)

SANBORN,
Almira J., d. 6/2/1894 at 66/1/2; housekeeper; married; b. Milton; Thomas Chapman (Milton) and Almira Robinson
Ansel N., d. 12/26/1953 at 59 in Concord; b. Wakefield; Dyer Sanborn and Minnie Wiggin

Bernice M., d. 8/19/1979 at 66 in Wolfeboro; Harry McCrillis and Ethel Willy

Caroline P., d. 2/3/1899 at 76/10/23; housewife; married; b. Middleton; Isiah H. Cook (Middleton) and Joanna M. Pike (Middleton)

Carroll M., d. 10/16/1894 at 1/1/3; b. Wakefield; John G. Sanborn (Acton, ME) and Ida B. Mann (Shapleigh, ME)

Charles S., d. 8/9/1900 at 0/4/9 in North Wakefield; b. Ossipee; Herbert Sanborn and Marie E. Sherman

Dyer H., d. 1/17/1901 at 41/8/8; painter; married; b. Wakefield; John G. Sanborn (Acton, ME) and Mary E. Garvin (Shapleigh, ME)

Ernest R., d. 9/16/1892 at 2/8/4; b. Wakefield; Dyer Hook Sanborn (Wakefield) and Minnie A. Wiggin (Wakefield)

Florence H., d. 2/12/1967 at 78 in Rochester; b. Limington, ME; Ozro Sawyer and Emma Butler

Fred W., d. 7/27/1899 at 33/1/20; farm laborer; divorced; b. Burrillville, RI; Louis C. Sanborn (Smithfield, RI) and Martha M. Harwood (Chelmsford, MA)

John G., d. 10/16/1901 at 79/4/16; farmer; married; b. Acton, ME; Henry S. Sanborn (Acton, ME) and Elizabeth G. French (Epping)

John W., d. 7/9/1903 at 81/5/20 in Sanbornville; RR supt.; married; b. Wakefield; Daniel H. Sanborn (Wakefield) and Lydia Dore (Acton, ME)

Lucy E., d. 11/1/1949 at 76/11/25 in Wolfeboro; b. Newfield, ME; Joseph Sanborn and Mercy J. Moody

Mary, d. 12/25/1936 at 63/6/16; b. Brookfield; John W. Sanborn and Lizzie Buzzell

Maude E., d. 11/12/1957 at 65 in Wolfeboro; b. Haverhill, MA; J. Frank Woodus and Eliza A. Edgerly

Oscar E., d. 12/7/1949 at 92 in Bridgton, ME; Enoch E. Sanborn and Sarah M. -----

Reuben, d. 4/11/1901 at 78/0/28; manufacturer; married; b. Acton, ME; James Sanborn (Acton, ME) and Sally Witham (Milton)

Richard D., Jr., d. 2/12/1989 at 52 in Towson, MD; Richard D. Sanborn, Sr. and Bernice McCrillis

SANDERS,
Flora, d. 11/9/1984 at 86 in Wolfeboro; George Meloon and Mary Seavey

SANDS,
Anthony T., d. 3/14/1986 at -- in FL

Mabel Lulu, b. 9/15/1954 at 76 in Union; b. Fryeburg, ME; Amaziah Sands and Diane Hamlin

SANNALISTO,
Eino, d. 10/2/1981 at 76 in White River Jct., VT; Jacob Sammalisto (sic)

SARETTE,
Julia, d. 3/3/1898 at 69; widow; b. Canada

SARGENT,
Allan G., d. 10/6/1975 at 60; Charles E. Sargent and Isabel Gregg
Clarissa A., d. 4/2/1986 at 68 in Somersworth
Richard E., d. 12/31/1992 at 61; William Sargent and Martha Hartford

SARNEY,
child, d. 12/8/1941 at 0/0/0 in Wolfeboro; b. Wolfeboro; Stanley Maurice Sarney and Esther L. McCrillis

SAULNIER,
Theresa, d. 3/31/1998 at 67 in Rochester; Thomas Saulnier and Lydia Melanson

SAUNDERS,
Karl R., d. 12/2/1981 at 82 in Wolfeboro; Abner Saunders and Arlena Yulli

SAVARY,
Marilyn A., d. 12/19/1996 at 61 in Wolfeboro; James Green and Sadie Belyea

SAVINI,
William A., d. 10/28/1987 at 55 in Dover; Angelo Savini and Thelma Harris

SAWYER,
George W., d. 1/19/1891 at 59/6/26; harnessmaker; married; b. Wakefield; William Sawyer, Jr. (Wakefield) and Mehitable Richards (Brookfield)
Gladys G., d. 11/18/1973 at 77 in Wolfeboro
Harry L., d. 11/29/1947 at 58/1/26 in Rochester
Lucy M., d. 11/24/1910 at 69/1/6; housewife; widow; b. Wakefield; Charles Bickford (Wakefield) and Mary B. Remick (Milton)

Lucy Maria, d. 5/12/1910 at 100/9/26; housekeeper; single; b. Wakefield; Timothy Sawyer (Wakefield) and Sarah Dearborn

Mary Ella, d. 2/11/1940 at 81/2 in Sanbornville; b. So. Berwick, ME; Charles Pierce and Laura J. Rand

Sarah Ann, d. 9/8/1899 at 94/3/3; housekeeper; single; b. Wakefield; Timothy Sawyer (Dover) and Sarah Dearborn (Wakefield)

William A., d. 5/28/1920 at 66/4/23; chr. int. nephritis; RR conductor; married; b. Milton; George W. Sawyer

SAYRE,
Charles R., d. 3/4/1927 at 69/7/21; widower; b. Dorchester, Canada; Otho Sayre and Mary Carter

SCEGGEL[L],
Arthur L., d. 10/20/1943 at 74/8/3 in Sanbornville; b. Wolfeboro

George F., d. 4/25/1888 at 73/4/21; farmer; widower; b. Ossipee; John Sceggel (Ossipee) and Charlotte Fullerton (Wolfeboro)

Stephen H., d. 10/31/1979 at 0/0/3 in Hanover; Stephen Sceggell and LuAnn Pratt

SCHOONMAKER,
Evelyn H., d. 12/29/1990 at 74 in Ossipee

SCIROCCO,
Thomas J., Sr., d. 2/25/1979 at 68 in East Wakefield; Joseph Scirocco and Rose Mastrolabetti

SCOTT,
Ernest E., d. 11/12/1958 at 72 in Wolfeboro; b. Springvale, ME; Edward Scott and Argie Yeaton

Frances Wadleigh, d. 3/18/1975 at 84 in Rochester; Francis F. Wadleigh and Mary Gilmour

Mary Ella, d. 6/21/1953 at 63 in Wolfeboro; b. Newfield, ME; Calvert Stevens and Delia Senson

SCOUBY,
Frank W., d. 9/5/1909; b. Warner

SCRUTON,
John E., d. 3/6/1894 at 47/3/12; physician; married; b. New Durham; Edmund C. Scruton (New Durham) and Martha H. Berry (New Durham)

SEABOYER,
Evan, d. 12/9/1984 at 5 hrs. in Wolfeboro; James H. Seaboyer and Lynn C. Colby

SEAMAN,
Nancy G., d. 1/28/1996 at 58 in Sanbornville; George Gates and Olive Nickles

SEARLE,
George Whitney, d. 7/9/1988 at 73 in Portland, ME; George W. Searle and Marguerite Mueller

SEAVEY,
Mary, d. 1/22/1896 at 75/3/26; housewife; married; b. Wakefield; Benjamin Horn and Alice Horn
Oliver, d. 21/1/1904 at 76/0/4; farmer; widower; b. Rochester

SEIBERLICH,
Joseph, d. 6/12/1981 at 84 in Wolfeboro

SEIDERS,
Mabel E., d. 10/31/1952 at 80/3/29 in Sanbornville; b. Boston, MA; Thomas H. Pease and Mary H. LaForest
Wilmot A., d. 11/23/1947 at 74/7/11 in Sanbornville; b. So. Bristol, ME; Daniel C. Seiders and Abbie E. Jordan

SEMM,
Caroline, d. 6/3/1968 at 77 in Melrose, MA

SEMON,
Frank, Sr., d. 12/31/1977 at 66 in Wolfeboro; Louis Semon and Catherine Palumbo

SENTER,
Leslie M., d. 4/14/1962 at 89 in Concord; b. Kingston; Frank Senter and Mary ----

SEVARD,
Mary L., d. 4/23/1900 at 0/11/5 in Sanbornville; b. Sanbornville; Simeon Sevard (Canada) and Emedie Trembley (Canada)

SEWARD,
Dolly P., d. 11/16/1891 at 51/10/5; housekeeper; married; b. Effingham; Simon P. Hill (Effingham) and Alice G. Sanders (Effingham)
George W., d. 12/19/1903 at 62/9/21; farmer; widower; b. Wakefield; Joshua Seward (Wakefield) and Dolly P. Hill (Effingham)
Mary R., d. 1/12/1890 at 81/11/26; housekeeper; widow; b. Barnstead; George W. Seward (Strafford) and Sally Huckins (Gilmanton)

SEYMOUR,
Edward D., d. 1/23/1908 at 73/6/2; shoe manufacturer; married; b. Plymouth; Edward D. Seymour (England) and Julia Pope (England)

SHACKELFORD,
Lewis A., d. 4/29/1965 at 92 in Concord; b. Beverly, MA; Alden H. Shackelford and Ellen S. Burrough

SHACKLEFORD,
Alice, d. 10/21/1941 at 75/10/13; b. Salem, MA; Charles Darling and Georgianna Patch

SHARP,
Eva M., d. 1/10/1910 at 0/7/11; b. Wakefield; Frank Sharp and Ethel Cook (Wolfeboro)

SHARPE,
Ethel C., d. 5/9/1966 at 73 in Springfield, MA

SHAW,
Herbert, d. 10/5/1961 at 62 in Wolfeboro; b. Tuftonboro; Daniel Shaw and Margaret Philbrick
John Edward, d. 3/14/1987 at 51; William Shaw and Margaret Hayes
Winthrop H., d. 2/22/1899 at 71; farmer; married; b. Northwood

SHEA,
Carroll M., d. 7/14/1991 at 71 in Wolfeboro; Patrick Joseph Shea and Florence Dorrell Reed
Florence D., d. 6/7/1974 at 83 in Wolfeboro; Edwin Reed and Inez Dicey
Henry A., Jr., d. 8/22/1990 at 56; Henry A. Shea and Mary A. Keely
Nelson E., d. 4/16/1912 at 0/0/25; b. Wakefield; Patrick J. Shea (Boston, MA) and Florence Reed (Effingham)
Patrick Joseph, d. 11/23/1944 at 67/6/25 in Union; b. Somerville, MA; Daniel Shea and Abbie Lawton
Russell F., d. 2/18/1984 at 68 in Manchester; Patrick Shea and Florence Reed

SHEEHAN,
Catherine, d. 6/10/1901 at 38/11/6; housework; married; b. NS

SHERMAN,
Clara Augusta, d. 11/27/1938 at 81/9/5 in Union; b. Acton, ME; Ambrose Sanborn

SHOREY,
Fred B., d. 8/30/1910 at 61/7/16; farmer; married; b. Wolfeboro; James W. Shorey (Wolfeboro) and Lydia Libbey (Wakefield)
James W., d. 2/21/1887 at 70/3/1; farmer; married; b. Wolfeboro; Lyford Shorey (Wolfeboro) and Mercy Wiggin (Wolfeboro)
Lydia L., d. 6/5/1905 at 80/11/10; widow; b. Wakefield; Nathan Libbey and Olive Berry (Wakefield)

SHORTRIDGE,
Ella, d. 11/23/1980 at 73 in Greenland
James H., d. 3/7/1895 at 62/1/7; farmer; married; b. Wolfeboro; James Shortridge and Mary Nutt
Mary A., d. 9/21/1896 at 52/8/21; housekeeper; widow; b. Wolfeboro; Daniel Twombly (Wolfeboro) and Frozilla Nute (Wolfeboro)
Ralph S., d. 5/20/1991 at 86 in Wolfeboro

SIBLEY,
Carrie Alberta, d. 6/21/1949 at 72/6/23 in Wolfeboro; b. Milton Mills; Samuel Hooper
Ernest Richard, d. 12/30/1954 at 73 in Meredith; b. Sanbornville; Richard T. Sibley and Emma Buzzell

Ethel M., d. 5/27/1958 at 74 in Pittsfield; b. Wakefield; Charles Richards and Keziah Quimby
Forrest Furber, d. 5/23/1941 at 77/3/9; b. Wakefield; Richard F. Sibley and Emma Buzzell
Fred D., d. 3/14/1957 at 81 in Sanbornville; b. Sanbornville; Richard T. Sibley and Emma Buzzell
L. Mabel, d. 1/27/1937 at 71 in Sanbornville; b. Acton, ME; Thomas Cloutman and Mary E. Sanborn
Richard F.D., d. 6/22/1892 at 60/6/8; farmer; married; b. Wakefield; Mark N. Sibley (Meredith) and Mehitable Wiggin (Wakefield)
Sarah L., d. 9/9/1955 at 83 in Sanbornville; b. Raymond, ME; Luther Longley and Sophia Butler

SIEMON,
Carl M., d. 9/1/1982 at 85 in Wolfeboro; Carl F. Siemon and Katherine W. Lewis

SILVERSTEIN,
June S., d. 8/23/1991 at 47 in Marlboro, MA

SIMMS,
Clifton, Jr., d. 12/19/1928 at 0/5/7; b. Tamworth; Clifton Simms and Elsie Banfil

SIMPSON,
Maude, d. 1/3/1961 at 83 in Concord; b. NS; Robert Simpson and Charlotte Huggins
Ronald Benjamin, d. 2/11/1994 at 44; Benjamin Simpson and Isabelle Soucier
Sara Kate, d. 7/27/1968 at 85 in Wolfeboro
William H., d. 4/13/1978 at 76 in Wolfeboro

SINCLAIR,
child, d. 12/4/1942 at 0/0/0 in Wolfeboro; b. Wolfeboro; Frank Sinclair and Alfreda Champaigne
Belle W., d. 9/28/1935 at 76/3/5 in Union; b. Newfield, ME; Charles Wentworth and Abbie Hurd

SINGELAIS,
Clifford Arthur, d. 2/9/1996 at 59 in Sanbornville; Alfred J. Singelais and Mary Vincent

SKINNER,
Harold E., d. 8/15/1960 at 67 in Wolfeboro; b. Somerville, MA; Ulysses Skinner and Agnes Pelton
Olga B., d. 5/21/1991 at 82 in Ossipee

SLACK,
Elizabeth, d. 3/21/1979 at 96 in Sanbornville; Malcolm MacKinnon and Liza MacDuff
Henry K., d. 8/13/1965 at 84 in Melrose, MA; b. NS; David Slack and Henrietta Betts

SLOENWHITE,
Victorine, d. 12/19/1960 at 81; b. Leone, France

SLOSKY,
Sebastian K., d. 6/30/1989 at 9 in Worcester, MA

SMALL,
Arthur H., d. 6/23/1907 at 26/7/16; farmer; married; b. Rockport, ME; Joseph Small
Jessie B., d. 6/24/1896 at 25/4/11; b. New York; Isaac H. Small (Limington, ME) and Jennie McKay (Edinburgh, Scotland)

SMART,
Alice F., d. 6/20/1982 at 82 in East Wakefield; Alaxander Coulombe and Georgie A. Benchont
Charles, d. 5/31/1974 at 67 in Southington, CT
Fannie, d. 4/28/1955 at 79 in Sanford, ME; b. Andover, MA; Porter Farmer and Emma Haley
Isabelle K., d. 4/5/1938 at 30/8/13 in Wolfeboro; b. Allston, MA; Clayton Ringer and Georgia E. Mitchell
J. Woodrow, d. 4/7/1984 at 69 in Wolfeboro
James E., d. 9/14/1964 at 81; b. Parkman, ME; Enoch Smart and Lydia Reed
Lydia S., d. 3/23/1924 at 79/6/15 in Woodman; housekeeper; widow; Silas L. Reed (Newfield, ME) and Hannah York (Newfield, ME)

SMITH,
A. J., d. 10/8/1904 at 60; wood chopper; married
Alfred F., d. 4/19/1900 at 63/8/26; clerk; married; b. Ossipee; Samuel H. Smith (Ossipee) and Francis P. Moulton (Newfield, ME)
Alfred J., d. 5/22/1957 at 68 in New York
Alfred J., d. 11/24/1969 at 61 in Wolfeboro; Albert Smith and Iona Knights
Amanda M., d. 12/12/1938 at 63/6/4 in Union; b. Acton, ME; Isaac Hussey and Harriet Miller
Amelia Marie Kaus, d. 10/30/1939 at 75/6/8 in Wolfeboro; b. New York, NY; John P. Kaus and Christiania Marie Kaus
Arthur E., d. 6/27/1969 at 64 in Weymouth, MA
Arthur M., d. 4/7/1971 at 80 in Rochester
Augusta A., d. 8/20/1909 at 67; teacher; single; Edward A. Smith (No. Canaan, CT) and Esta M. Hanford (Westbrook, CT)
Carrie Louise, d. 1/22/1939 at 76/9/15; b. Cambridge, MA; Levi Perkins and Elizabeth Sands
Charles C., d. 3/9/1893 at 74/11/12; farmer; widower; b. Milford; John Smith and Mary
Charles R., d. 10/20/1937 at 78/7/23 in Rochester; b. NS; Jacob Smith and Olive Weatherlake
Edmund L., d. 8/6/1970 at 62 in Rochester; William L. Smith and Iona Knight
Emma J., d. 9/6/1941 at 78/5/8; b. Porter, ME; ---- Taylor and ---- Hill
Frances P., d. 11/29/1892 at 81/3/23; housework; widow; b. Newfield, ME; Simeon Moulton (Parsonsfield, ME) and Mary Parsons (Parsonsfield, ME)
Frank L., d. 8/8/1925 at 44/6/21; married
George, d. 11/6/1964 at 0/5 in New York
George A., d. 4/18/1971 at 74 in Rochester
George Albert, d. 1/6/1942 at 83/1/27 in Garden City, NY; b. Wakefield
Grace, d. 10/19/1985 at 71 in Wolfeboro; William H. Griffith and Mary H. Kelly
Helen M., d. 2/1/1989 at 92 in Rochester
Joseph Warren, d. 5/16/1989 at 78 in Wolfeboro; Joseph F. Smith and Marion W. Preston
Martha M., d. 7/22/1955 at 85 in Union; b. Ipswich, MA; Leverett Ceby and Rachael Gurley
Mary A., d. 9/20/1897 at 51/5/8; widow; b. Wakefield; John Davis (Wakefield) and Mary Gilman

Morrill B., d. 12/25/1887 at 65/10; farmer; married; b. Wakefield; Ephraim G. Smith

Robert Charles, d. 8/8/1991 at 27; Jerome Dewitt and Beverly Smith

Ruth A., d. 12/5/1925 at 86/7/3; married; b. Bath, ME; Ezra Smith and Juliet Chamberlain

Sarah, d. 1/4/1901 at 79/7; domestic; widow; b. VT; Polly Copp (Wakefield)

Susan E., d. 3/7/1902 at 64/8/7; housewife; widow; b. Wakefield; Thomas Mordough (Wakefield) and Sarah O. Pike (Brookfield)

Verna B., d. 7/15/1966 at 54 in Rochester; b. Wakefield; Arthur MacDonald and Leona McDonald

Walter L., d. 6/10/1912 at 26/5; laborer; b. Tamworth; Alphonzo Smith (Tamworth) and Annette Brown (Tamworth)

William, d. 8/25/1935 at 34/7/24 in Union; b. Acton, ME; Charles G. Smith and Amanda M. Hussey

SNOW,

Fanny Fern, d. 1/1/1951 at 82/8/24 in Union; b. Hartland, ME; Samuel Huff and Sarah Lord

SOUCY,

child, d. 1/4/1927 at --; Alphonse Soucy and Rose Savertu

Albert J., d. 5/31/1956 at 54 in Wolfeboro; b. Salem, MA; Alphonse J. Soucy and ----- Potvin

Alphonse, d. 9/12/1957 at 83 in Ossipee

Alphonse J., Jr., d. 3/26/1956 at 55 in Sanbornville; b. Salem, MA; Alphonse J. Soucy, Sr.

Donat, d. 11/20/1969 at 62 in Conway; Alphonse Soucy and Leopauldine Potvin

Dora M., d. 12/20/1986 at 59 in FL; George Davenport and Wilda Whitten

Joseph E., d. 7/25/1975 at 73 in Sanbornville; Jules Soucy and Philomen Landry

Marie L., d. 10/29/1937 at 47/3/20 in Wolfeboro; b. Canada; Babist Dube and Mary Beltun

Marion A., d. 10/8/1984 at 78 in Wolfeboro; Ernest Gagnon and Georgianna Legary

Mary Jane, d. 10/2/1986 at 82 in Wolfeboro

Mary Katherine, d. 8/25/1981 at 78 in Portsmouth

Omer J., d. 8/10/1966 at 81 in Ossipee

Paul D., d. 2/4/1981 at -- in Cambridge, MA

Rita Mary, d. 2/19/1938 at 12/5/15 in Wolfeboro; b. Salmon Falls; Omer Soucy and Mary Dube
Rosanna, d. 4/29/1980 at 79 in Ossipee
Sally A., d. 7/11/1944 at 0/0/0 in Wolfeboro; b. Wolfeboro; Armand J. Soucy and Lauriel M. Bigelow

SOULE,
Annie L., d. 8/4/1959 at 64 in Wilmington, DE; b. Wakefield; Fred I. Wood and Grace L. Wentworth

SPARHAWK,
Chandler R., d. 10/31/1970 at 18 in East Wakefield; William N. Sparhawk and Virginia Goodnow
Virginia G., d. 11/23/1982 at 59 in East Wakefield; Roger Goodnow and Agnes Chandler

SPARKS,
Bernie G., Sr., d. 11/9/1968 at 80 in Wolfeboro
Bernie Garfield, Jr., d. 10/5/1997 at 72; Bernie Garfield Sparks, Sr. and Bessie Brackett
Bessie B., d. 10/9/1974 at 89 in Wolfeboro; Charles W. Newhall and Sarah J. Murch

SPEDDING,
Lucy Isabelle, d. 2/18/1953 at 70; b. Johnston, RI; Thomas Angel

SPENCE,
George R., d. 12/29/1968 at 29 in Sanbornville; Robert E. Spence and Virginia E. Davis

SPENCER,
Carlton Wentworth, d. 4/6/1998 at 91; Fred Spencer and Minnie Foss
Ettie M., d. 4/20/1926 at 68/2/14; married; b. Hallowell, ME; Silas May and Hannah Goodwin
Frank P., d. 8/26/1946 at 77/8/27 in Sanbornville; b. Waterboro, ME; Joseph C. Spencer and Sarah Thyng
Georgianna, d. 8/19/1936 at 55/1/9 in Sanbornville; b. OK; Frank M. Robinson and Hannah Heel

SPILLER,
Jennie M., d. 6/22/1944 at 71/11/17 in Brookfield

SPINNEY,
Addie M., d. 9/1/1918 at 48/8/8; housewife; married; b. Bridgton, ME; Harding L. Nason and Lucinda Thorne
Chester A., d. 12/23/1912 at 23/3/1; carpenter; single; b. Wakefield; George M. Spinney (Wakefield) and Addie M. Nason (Bridgton, ME)
Elizabeth, d. 10/30/1898 at 87/5/12; housewife; married; b. Kittery, ME; Charles Spinney (Kittery, ME)
Ernest O., d. 10/12/1973 at 62 in Falmouth, ME; Irah Spinney and Bertha Johnson
George M., d. 8/20/1953 at 83 in Wolfeboro; b. So. Wakefield; James T. Spinney and Augusta Farnham
Hattie Pickering, d. 3/21/1953 at 81 in Sanbornville; b. Charlestown, MA; Stephen Paul and Henrietta -----
Ida L., d. 7/4/1965 at 57 in Wolfeboro; b. Wolfeboro; John Cotton and Mary L. Neal
James Leslie, d. 6/29/1904 at 6/1/22; b. Wolfeboro; Charles H. Spinney (Eliot, ME) and Clara M. Darling (Malone, NY)
James T., d. 3/14/1894 at 59/7/4; farmer; married; b. Wakefield; Alvah Spinney (Wakefield) and Joanna Twombly (Rochester)
Joanna, d. 2/5/1895 at 84/0/19; housekeeper; widow; b. Rochester; Tobias Twombly and Lois Wentworth
Joseph, d. 12/21/1899 at 87/9/19; clergyman; widower; b. Wakefield; David Spinney (Kittery, ME) and Lydia Paul (Kittery, ME)
Mary A., d. 5/2/1918 at 57/2; housewife; widow; b. Milton; David Farnham (Acton, ME) and Rowena Dearborn (Milton)

SPRAGUE,
Louis E., d. 1/8/1985 at 68 in Rochester; William Sprague and Gladys Hillsgrove
Louis R., d. 3/11/1961 at 25 in Farmington; b. Rochester; Louis E. Sprague and Madeline F. Adjutant
Rose E., d. 8/23/1936 at 49/4/24 in Limerick, ME

SPROUL,
Maude M., d. 2/3/1959 at -- in Union; b. York Springs, PA

STAIRS,
Chester J., d. 7/28/1961 at 86 in Sanbornville; b. Woodstock, NB; Charles Stairs

STAPLES,
Annie M., d. 3/30/1924 at 72/9/7; retired; widow; b. Madbury; Aaron Prescott (Madbury) and Charlotte Jackson
Christopher W., d. 2/2/1968 at 67 in Wolfeboro; Frank G. Staples and Ina F. Piper
Frank George, d. 9/28/1954 at 88 in Sanbornville; b. Effingham; William Staples
William G., d. 8/13/1959 at 29 in Milton; b. Wolfeboro; Christopher W. Staples and Ada F. Keniston

STARKEY,
J. Earl, d. 12/28/1976 at 68 in Wolfeboro; Dow Starkey and Nora Murphy
Pearl C.E., d. 10/31/1974 at 68; Joshua Starkey and Imogene Strang

STARRETT,
Avis J., d. 6/24/1980 at 64 in Dover; Warren B. Stiles and Rachael C. Godfrey

STEADMAN,
child, d. 10/27/1977 at 0/0/13 in Rochester; Charles Steadman and Lauretta Glennon

STEBBINS,
Amy M., d. 4/26/1938 at 33/11/27 in Wolfeboro; b. Madison; Joseph Foster and Mary Hurd

STEVENS,
Alvah J., d. 1/2/1920 at 57/10/16; apoplexy; mill sawyer; divorced; b. Middleton; George W. Stevens (Middleton) and Ellen Whitehouse (Middleton)
Anna Mae, d. 6/23/1960 at 63; b. Yarmouth, NS; Charles S. Churchill and Melissa Battis
Arlyne D., d. 9/4/1992 at 94 in Wolfeboro; John W. Dodge and Nettie Healey
Bessie Wing, d. 7/18/1944 at 75/9 in Valhalla, NY; b. Grangeville, MI

Calvert Roscoe, d. 3/29/1939 at 89/8/17; b. Newfield, ME; Addison Stevens and Mary E. Stevens

Charles Lewis, d. 12/8/1990 at 85 in Sanbornville; George Stevens and Lina ----

Delia Jane, d. 12/24/1941 at 87/8/29 in Dover; b. Parsonsfield, ME; James E. Benson and Martha Moss

Earl W., d. 2/1/1972 at 63 in Malden, MA; Byron H. Stevens and Louise Webber

Elizabeth, d. 5/15/1919 at 74/5/23; cardio-renal dis.; housekeeper; widow; Edwin Wentworth (Concord, MA) and Susan Price (Boston, MA)

Ellen D., d. 5/22/1922 at 75/9/17; housewife; widow; b. Middleton; Wingate Whitehouse (Middleton) and Eliza Colbath

Elise R., d. 1/18/1994 at 81 in Dover; Frank H. Ray and Sarah L. McLaren

Everett W., d. 12/19/1936 at 76/9 in Sanbornville; b. No. Abington, MA; Webster Stevens and Sarah A. Goodwin

Fannie, d. 10/27/1914 at 85/9/10; retired; widow; b. Wakefield; Stephen Horn (Wakefield) and Abigail Lord (Lebanon, ME)

Fernande Anita, d. 10/16/1996 at 75 in Manchester; Emile Gilbert and Mary Blouin

Fred E., d. 1/11/1895 at 41/6/3; marble worker; married; b. Rochester; Herbert F. Stevens (Orford) and Mehitable P. Adams (Milton)

George W., d. 4/27/1982 at 77 in Wolfeboro

Grace I., d. 1/11/1941 at 46/1/11; b. Somerville, MA; William Mooney and Emma McCrillis

Guy W., d. 8/22/1965 at 74 in Sanbornville; b. Sanbornville; Everett W. Stevens and Lizzie Glidden

Harriett A., d. 11/12/1914 at 78/1/18; housewife; married; b. Wakefield; Jonas Moulton (Madbury) and Mary Burroughs (Lebanon, ME)

Hazel B., d. 2/1/1899 at 4/11/19 in Sanbornville; b. Sanbornville; Everett W. Stevens (Holbrook, MA) and Lizzie A. Glidden (Wakefield)

Herbert F., d. 12/17/1896 at 72/1/18; marble worker; married; b. Oxford; Manley Stevens (Oxford) and Losinia Davis (Oxford)

James I., d. 10/4/1898 at 58

John P., d. 7/23/1935 at 68/1/15 in Rings Island, MA

Lewis A., d. 6/23/1935 at 63/8/16 in Sanbornville; b. Durham; Darius Stevens and Harriett A. Mathes

Lillian, d. 1/6/1954 at 64 in Newburyport, MA

Lizzie A., d. 12/17/1916 at 56/7/3; housewife; married; b. Wakefield; John Glidden (Alton) and Abigail Young (Wakefield)

Lloyd E., d. 6/29/1970 at 76 in Barrington; Everett W. Stevens and Lizzie Glidden

Lucy M., d. 12/6/1972 at 87 in Rochester; Edward Houde and ----- Pouliot

Melvin Earl, Jr., d. 3/26/1929 at 0/1/27; b. Rochester; Melvin E. Stevens and Maude Merrill

Myron J., d. 12/6/1910 at 0/6/21; b. Wakefield; Frank L. Stevens (Brookfield) and Myrtle M. Johnson (Wakefield)

Nancy, d. 3/24/1897 at 64; housewife; widow; Ebenezer Adams (Newington) and Betsy Sanborn (Wakefield)

Roland R., d. 11/16/1941 at 43/3/13 in Dover; b. Wakefield; Hiram S. Stevens and Hattie Ross

Roy Albert, d. 6/11/1991 at 64 in Union; Walter Ray Stevens and Mabel Swift

Sarah J., d. 12/13/1915 at 84/6/6; housework; widow; b. Middleton; Henry P. Garland (Middleton) and Martha Whitehouse (Middleton)

Sibyle H., d. 4/5/1967 at 91 in Barnstable, MA

Thomas J., d. 1/7/1917 at 91/9/28; farmer; b. Middleton; Isaac Stevens (Middleton) and Margaret Mathews (Cambridge, MA)

Wallace E., d. 9/4/1974 at 70 in Wolfeboro; Edward Stevens and Dora Warren

Walter R., d. 5/10/1958 at 61 in Union; b. Middleton; Albert M. Stevens and Bernice Tufts

Walter R., d. 9/27/1989 at 67 in Manchester

STEWART,

Albert A., d. 3/9/1961 at 47 in Epping

Carol Margaret, d. 12/27/1995 at 84 in Wolfeboro; Clifford A. Langlotz and Maude Coleman

Daniel T., d. 2/16/1969 at 84 in Sanbornville; Alec Stewart and Abbie Inman

Howard C., d. 1/12/1971 at 55 in Whittier, CA

Izetta M., d. 7/15/1983 at 92 in Rochester

Joseph L., d. 11/6/1965 at 16 in Rochester; b. Wolfeboro; Leslie D. Stewart and Theresa Thoret

Mark D., d. 12/21/1967 at 1 in Ayer, MA

STONE,

Edgar L., d. 10/4/1909 at 42/10/26; laborer; widower; b. Parsonsfield, ME; Louis G. Stone (Parsonsfield, ME) and Mary E. Butler (Parsonsfield, ME)

Jennie H., d. 1/9/1927 at 53/1/25; married; b. Reading, England; Joseph
Pinfold and Louise Lewis

STORER,

Emma F.C., d. 8/10/1938 at 83/3/30 in Claremont; b. Burlington, VT; John
Henry Chesley and Jane C. Blanchard

George W., d. 7/1/1950 at 79/11/14 in Sanbornville; b. Eaton; John Storer
and Ida N. Copp

STOREY,

Edward J., Sr., Dr., d. 11/14/1988 at 87 in So. Deerfield, MA

Josie Belle, d. 12/30/1954 at 75 in Harrison, NY; b. Woodman

Sarah Clara, d. 12/1/1913 at 87/2/10 in Rochester; b. St. John, NB

William J., d. 6/3/1934 at 61/11 in Larchmont, NY

STORY,

Raymond W., d. 3/13/1987 at 62 in Manchester; Chester Story and Jeannie
-----

STOWELL,

Charles W., d. 4/24/1946 at 31/0/23; b. Walpole; Will Stowell and Ruth ---

STRAIT,

Edmund R., d. 1/29/1968 at 49; Archiver J. Strait and Ruth Kirk Pride

STRAW,

George D., d. 6/15/1956 at 76 in Union; b. Tuftonboro; Frank Straw and
Elizabeth -----

STREADER,

daughter, d. 12/10/1894 at 0/0/0; b. Wakefield; Joseph Streader (England)
and Valeria Dyer (Brownfield, ME)

Richard D., d. 6/17/1894 at 0/11; b. Wakefield; Joseph Streader (England)
and Valeria Dyer (Brownfield, ME)

Sarah, d. 12/16/1943 at 69/0/18 in Wolfeboro; b. Epping; Jacob Milton Bly
and Lydia Bly Tuttle

Velaria I., d. 8/14/1904 at 49; housewife; married; b. Brownfield, ME;
Simeon Dyer (Hiram, ME) and Nancy J. Day (Parsonsfield, ME)

William H., d. 2/18/1960 at 72 in Ossipee; b. Wakefield

STRINGER,
Winslow J., d. 3/16/1976 at 80 in Rochester; John T. Stringer and Ida White

STROUSE,
Alice M., d. 1/1/1974 at 90 in Union; Edward Pentz

STUART,
Alameda L., d. 9/5/1998 at -- in Rochester; Elvyn Green and Alice Jackson
Archie, d. 6/4/1988 at 76 in East Wakefield; Jeremiah Stuart and Minnie Allen
Herbert W., d. 9/15/1910 at 0/2/3; b. Wakefield; Albert W. Stuart (Lebanon) and Lula M. Brown (Dover)
Jerald, d. 9/12/1971 at 39 in Chelsea, MA; Archie Stuart and Almeila L. Greene

STURTEVANT,
Leroy E., d. 12/5/1992 at 77 in Ossipee; Charles Sturtevant and Viva Buzzell

SUKES,
Marjorie Estelle, d. 8/31/1990 at 79 in Wolfeboro; George Potter and Lottie Leavitt

SWIFT,
Arthur J., d. 1/2/1946 at 78/10/24 in Union; b. Windham, ME; Harrison Swift and Lucy Ring

SWINERTON,
Annie H., d. 6/27/1950 at 87/3/23 in Concord; b. Greenfield, MA; Christopher Newton and Mary Jane Tracy
John R., d. 2/8/1934 at 93/1/22 in Newport News, VA; b. Milton; John L. Swinerton and Anna A. Robinson
Laura M., d. 12/3/1977 at 66 in Wolfeboro; Moses Duchano and Marie Welch
Lawrence A., d. 4/9/1989 at 75 in Wolfeboro; Jacob Swinerton and Emma Medville

SYKES,
Calvin, d. 6/23/1933 at 81/7/1

TAFT,
Arthur Leroy, d. 11/24/1933 at 82/1/20
Ida Mae R., d. 1/25/1970 at 80 in Rochester
Leroy Chester, d. 8/27/1953 at 63 in Union; b. Quinebaug, MA; Arthur L. Taft and Nellie Dunham
Nellie W., d. 9/9/1939 at 78/6/8; b. Mansfield, CT; Harvey Dunham and Almira Chester

TAMM,
Rebecca G., d. 4/25/1996 at 80 in Dover; Paul G. Buzzell and Louise H. Gaylord

TANGLEY,
Ella M., d. 2/12/1983 at 95 in Ossipee
Eugene H., d. 3/16/1966 at 76 in Manchester; b. Portsmouth; Eugene F. Tangley and Anna Ronan

TANNER,
Charles E., d. 11/18/1918 at 77/4/15; shoemaker; widower; b. Marshfield, VT; Cyrus Tanner (VT) and Prudence Behonon (VT)
Lloyd C., d. 12/30/1990 att 71 in Wolfeboro; Charles Tanner and Vila Kimball
Mary G., d. 3/2/1901 at 55/7/2; domestic; married; b. Dublin, Ireland; M. Faull

TARBOX,
Edward G., d. 9/1/1905 at 67/5/14 in No. Wakefield; married; b. Biddeford, ME; John R. Tarbox (Biddeford, ME) and Hannah Googin (Biddeford, ME)

TASKER,
Dereka Anne, d. 1/21/1986 at 0/5 in Manchester
Franklin B., d. 5/12/1964 at 37 in Rochester; b. Brighton, MA; T. Lyman Tasker and Edith MacConnell

TATHAM,
Wilbur M., d. 8/12/1965 at 71 in Manchester; b. Lakeport; Mark O. Tatham and Sarah A. Crandall

TAYLOR,
Abbie Augusta, d. 1/7/1938 at 87/2/27 in Sanbornville; b. Boston, MA; Mark A.L. Colbath and Martha J. Ham
Ida G., d. 12/13/1977 at 82 in Sanbornville; Fred R.. Hall and Minnie Powell
Jean Elizabeth, d. 3/4/1991 at 46 in Wolfeboro; William L. Taylor and Helen F. Muse
Jennie, d. 5/15/1937 at 81/0/17 in Sanbornville; b. Newfield, ME; John Colomy and Mary L. Knox
William L., d. 6/11/1979 at 63 in Wolfeboro; George M. Taylor and Mildred M. Kendrick

TEBBETS,
Sarah E., d. 1/23/1905 at 54 in Sanbornville; housework; widow; b. Berwick, ME; John Richmond

TEBBETTS,
Benjamin F., d. 1/31/1904 at 66/3/21; farmer; married; b. Porter, ME; Henry Tibbetts (sic) (Pittsfield) and Annie Leavitt (Effingham)
Ralph A., d. 10/4/1899 at 0/5/13 in Sanbornville; b. Sanbornville; Arthur D. Tebbetts (Wolfeboro) and Jerusha Spencer (Waterboro, ME)

TEMPLETON,
Theodora C., d. 11/10/1975 at 63 in Sanbornville; Thomas P. Libby and Daisey Henson

TESIER,
Charles L., d. 4/1/1916 at 0/1/15; b. Wakefield; Louis C. Tesier (Suncook) and Lucy Pouliot (Wakefield)

TESSIER,
daughter, d. 10/10/1914 at 0/0/0; b. Wakefield; Louis Tessier (Suncook) and Lucy Pouliott (Wakefield)
Brenda Jean, d. 2/13/1950 at 0/14 in Wolfeboro; b. Wolfeboro; George E. Tessier and Marjorie E. Hatch
George E., d. 8/7/1989 at 79 in Wolfeboro; Louis Tessier and Lucy Pouliot
Marjorie E., d. 2/10/1972 at 64 in Sanbornville; Herbert O. Hatch and Ethel Nute
Sandra Mae, d. 6/6/1941 at 0/0/1 in Wolfeboro; b. Wolfeboro; George Tessier and Marjorie Hatch

TETRAULT,
Alexandrian, d. 7/17/1947 at 86/1/6 in Union; b. Providence, RI

TEWKSBURY,
Fred A., d. 12/23/1956 at 59 in Sanbornville; b. Sanbornville; Royal Tewksbury and Martha J. Hill
Martha J., d. 4/19/1959 at 91 in Wolfeboro; b. Bartlett; Jacob Hill and Mary Jane Ordway
Royal Sidney, d. 12/3/1949 at 77/7/7 in Wolfeboro; b. Tamworth; Adeline McKay

THEBADO,
Arthur R., d. 5/17/1976 at 47 in New York, NY
Carmen, d. 10/8/1987 at 79 in Carver, MA

THERIAULT,
Frederick A., d. 5/26/1948 at 54/10/12 in Rochester; b. Lowell, MA; Frederick Theriault and Albena Picard

THOMAS,
Elias B., d. 1/28/1936 at 74/9/24 in Milton; b. Gates Mtn., NS; Isaac Thomas and Louise Durling
Elsie W., d. 3/10/1977 at 87 in Manchester

THOMES,
Charles B., d. 1/24/1941 at 86/9/11; b. Denmark, ME; George Thomes and Elvira Newcomb
Mary E., d. 1/5/1934 at 72/11/12 in Wolfeboro; b. Jackson; Chandler Wentworth and Mary Sinelam
William E., d. 7/18/1973 at 85 in Sanford, ME

THOMPSON,
Dorothy M., d. 5/17/1987 at 87 in Ossipee; Lewis Hill and Rose Hatch
Evelyn D., d. 8/23/1986 at 67 in Rochester; Edwin T. Duprey and Minnie Labelle
Everett W., d. 5/3/1978 at 58 in Wolfeboro; George Thompson and Dorothy Hill
George, d. 11/18/1955 at 77 in Wolfeboro; b. Center Ossipee
Hugh, d. 1/27/1972 at 69 in Wolfeboro; Thomas Thompson and Mary Magee

Ira J., d. 10/5/1907 at 74/2/29; single; b. Wakefield; James Thompson (Kittery, ME) and Nancy Redman (Hampton)

John S., d. 1/3/1897 at 90/5/20; farmer; widower; b. Limington, ME; John Thompson (York, ME) and Relief Berry (Limington, ME)

Mary A., d. 4/23/1888 at 69/6; housework; widow; I. Wilkinson (Alton) and Nancy Peavey (Alton)

Olive B., d. 7/27/1963 at 74 in Melrose, MA; b. Laconia; George Greenwood and Mary V. Martin

Rose S., d. 5/22/1887 at 0/4/22; b. Wakefield; Albert H. Thompson (Chelsea, MA) and Arville Hardy (Ossipee)

Thomas D., d. 4/19/1958 at 25 in Sanbornville; b. Newton, MA; Robert E. Thompson and Helen M. Kinsman

Virginia R., d. 4/19/1958 at 22 in Sanbornville; b. Woodside, LI; John P. Findlay and Virginia Roslin

THORNE,

Ivah J., d. 4/16/1970 at 70 in Brookfield; Henry A. Thorne and Marjory E. Goodwin

THORNTON,

Harold J., d. 3/21/1982 at 76 in Wolfeboro; Thomas Thornton and Catherine Walex

THURSTON,

Stephen D., d. 10/19/1899 at 75/7/5 in Union; farmer; widower; b. Freedom; William Thurston (Exeter) and Mittee T. Thurston (Parsonsfield, ME)

THWING,

Marian S., d. 10/3/1985 at -- in MA

TIBBETTS,

Arthur P., d. 10/14/1959 at 89 in Ossipee

Eliza A., d. 7/1/1926 at 82/8/12; widow; b. Wolfeboro; Mary Avery and Dorcas Newt

Emily J., d. 11/27/1920 at 80/3/27; apoplexy; widow; b. Porter, ME; Abraham D. Roberts (Kennebunk, ME) and Edna Redlon (Baxter, ME)

Etta J., d. 9/1/1928 at 69/9/10; widow; Joseph Hamilton and Betsy Hart

Everett James, d. 3/21/1939 at 68/7/12; b. Brookfield; James Tibbetts and Eliza Avery

Fred, d. 4/13/1938 at 77/8/1 in Portsmouth; b. Porter, ME; Benjamin F. Tibbetts and Emily J. Roberts

Grace M., d. 5/9/1967 at 72 in Portsmouth; b. Wakefield; Horace B. Tuttle and Katherine Weeks

Henry Carr, d. 3/5/1938 at 75/9/5; b. Porter, ME; Benjamin F. Tibbetts and Emily J. Roberts

Jeremiah D., d. 10/9/1898 at 54/11/19; farmer; married; b. Wolfeboro; Bishop Tibbetts

Leola M., d. 4/18/1897 at 2/2/13; b. Wakefield; Thomas B. Tibbetts (Wolfeboro) and Etta J. Hamilton (Conway)

Leon F., d. 7/29/1960 at 61; b. Sanbornville; Thomas B. Tibbetts and Etta J. Hamilton

Louise Everett, d. 11/9/1991 at 88 in Ossipee

Maynard C., d. 8/25/1980 at 73; Moses Tibbetts and Georgia Damey

Susie L., d. 1/5/1971 at 95 in Concord; Brackett Weeks and Matilda ——

TIERNEY,

John G., d. 12/10/1959 at 2 in Wolfeboro; b. Boston, MA; John G. Tierney and Mary L. Keating

TILNEY,

Estella Brackett, d. 4/8/1944 at 45/11/5 in Oakland, CA; b. Sanbornville; John E. Brackett and Mary E. Kenney

TINKHAM,

Robert C., d. 10/14/1989 at 60 in Sanbornville; Charles Tinkham and Etta Haynes

Roland Charles, d. 12/17/1994 at 80 in Dover; Charles Roland Tinkham and Katherine Perry

TISDALE,

Cora B., d. 10/18/1917 at 58/4/3; housewife; married; b. Chesterfield; Joseph C. Hubbard (Chesterfield) and Delilia Ames (Croydon)

TITCOMB,

Abbie M., d. 4/22/1937 at 79/6/17 in Sanbornville; b. Wakefield; Daniel Morse and Elizabeth Wiggin

Ada, d. 9/6/1913 at 52/1/18; housekeeper; widow; b. Albion, ME; Charles T. Whitten (Cornish) and Betsey Tuft (Jerusalem)

Helen, d. 2/27/1978 at 87 in Wolfeboro; Alonzo Remick and Hattie Maleham

John F., d. 5/23/1921 at 82/7/1; influenza; carpenter; married; b. Acton, ME; Oliver Titcomb (Acton, ME) and Hannah Wentworth (Lebanon, ME)

Leon H., d. 1/11/1921 at 31/9/7; lobar pneumonia; farmer; married; b. Wakefield; John F. Titcomb (Acton, ME) and Abbie Morse (Wakefield)

TOBIN,
Margaret Sara, d. 7/13/1940 at 64/11/7 in Wolfeboro; b. Greenwich, PA; James Grenier and ----- Gilchrist

TONER,
J. Walter, d. 9/17/1972 at 72 in Sanbornville; John W. Toner and Mary Meegan

Mary E., d. 9/25/1972 at 71 in Sanbornville; Frank Flanagan and Ellen Regan

TOOMEY,
William J., d. 8/21/1979 at 61 in Sanbornville; John Toomey and Margaret Downey

TOWLE,
Charles Everett, Jr., d. 4/8/1905 at 0/9; b. Wakefield; Charles Everett Towle (Freedom) and Bertha Staples (Milford, ME)

William, d. 2/16/1908 at 76/1/27; farmer; married; b. Freedom; William Towle (Freedom) and Hannah Moulton (Exeter)

TRAFTON,
son, d. 4/11/1905 at 0/0/0; b. Union; Reuben B. Trafton (Wakefield) and Iva Ham (Farmington)

Ashton R., d. 4/28/1969 at 85 in Union

Donald G., d. 9/1/1910 at 1/3/20; b. Wakefield; R. B. Trafton (Wakefield) and Iva M. Ham (Farmington)

Olida D., d. 2/12/1991 at 88 in Dover

Roger Herbert, d. 3/8/1976 at 77 in Portland, ME

Susan E., d. 9/14/1904 at 60/10/9; housewife; married; b. Wakefield; David Archibald and Susan

TRAINOR,
Minnie A., d. 5/16/1905 at 0/0/10 in East Wakefield; James M. Trainor (Brownfield, ME) and Lulu Hart (East Wakefield)

TRASK,
Carrie F., d. 1/25/1913 at 66/8/26; at home; single; b. Wolfeboro; Edward Trask (Wolfeboro) and Eliza Cottle (Eliot, ME)
Joseph E., d. 10/16/1919 at 70/10/22; lobar pneumonia; farmer; married; b. Warren, VT; Joseph Trask

TREANOR,
Helen, d. 6/15/1937 at -- in Wolfeboro; b. Wolfeboro; John H. Treanor and Helen C. Bryant

TREFETHEN,
Louise R., d. 10/13/1970 at 90 in Wolfeboro; Gilman D. Trefethen

TREMBLAY,
Eleanor M., d. 3/13/1976 at 56 in Wolfeboro; Oscar Demone and Emma Black

TROTT,
Chester M., d. 2/12/1943 at 32/4/28 in Dover
Effie, d. 6/14/1958 at 71 in Wolfeboro; b. No. Wakefield; Malcolm McDonald and Amanda Crockett
Flora A., d. 10/10/1896 at 44/10/8; housewife; widow; b. Wakefield; John W. Mathews (Ossipee) and Elizabeth A. Emerson (Ossipee)
Frederick M., d. 11/7/1926 at 1/7/17; b. Rochester; Wesley Trott and Gladys Chase
Leander Mathews, d. 11/5/1941 at 57/9 in Wolfeboro; b. Portland, ME; Thayer Sterling Trott and Ida E. Mathews
Winfred L., d. 4/21/1966 at 84 in Ossipee

TUCKER,
Charles H., d. 1/5/1960 at 77 in Concord; b. Wakefield; James F. Tucker and Mary F. Brackett

Effie C., d. 5/28/1965 at 64 in Boston, MA; b. Reading, MA; Elias B. Currell and Willa M. Messinger

Grover Cleveland, d. 7/9/1939 at 54/11/10 in Wolfeboro; b. Wakefield; James F. Tucker and Mary F. Brackett

Harris W., d. 3/14/1979 at 76 in Wolfeboro; James F. Tucker and Mary E. Brackett

Helen C., d. 11/16/1976 at 72 in Wolfeboro; Fred B. Chase and Mary Goodrich

James, d. 4/4/1909 at 85/3/28; foreman; widower; b. Salisbury, MA; James Tucker (Salisbury, MA) and Nancy Fifield (Hampton Falls)

James C., d. 6/23/1967 at 75 in Brookfield; b. Sanbornville; James P. Tucker and Mary Brackett

James Carroll, d. 11/1/1987 at 66; James C. Tucker and Ethel Lang

Mary, d. 6/24/1908 at 46/1/27; housewife; married; b. Wakefield; Charles E. Brackett (Acton, ME) and Elizabeth Wiggin (Wakefield)

Mary E., d. 3/2/1895 at 72/11/12; housewife; married; b. Haverhill, MA; Samuel Hale (Haverhill, MA) and Ann Plumer (Haverhill, MA)

TUFTS,

daughter, d. 9/28/1914 at 0/0/0; b. Wakefield; Frank J. Tufts (Somersworth) and Fannie Thompson (Andover)

Bessie L., d. 7/1/1920 at 0/2/9; marasmus; b. Wakefield; Louis M. Hill (Newfield, ME) and Verlie E. Tufts (Wakefield)

Charles Francis, d. 5/3/1990 at 84 in Rochester

Fannie L., d. 3/6/1934 at 49/5 in Rochester; b. Andover

Frank, d. 6/15/1942 at 67/3/21 in Wolfeboro; b. No. Berwick, ME; James Tufts

James Robert, d. 3/27/1944 at 55/10/27 in Union; b. Middleton; George J. Tufts and Emma F. Whitehouse

TURNER,

Mildred N., d. 5/30/1989 at 93 in Wolfeboro

Nelson W., d. 10/29/1958 at 67 in Sanbornville; b. Winchester, MA; George B. Turner and Adelaide P. Hatch

TURSCHMANN,

E. Blanche, d. 3/21/1988 at 90 in Ossipee; George Tufts and Emma Whitehouse

Emil H., d. 3/16/1976 at 90 in Rochester; Herman Turschmann and Alvina
-----

TURSISKI,
Katherine L., d. 1/17/1960 at 72 in Peabody, MA

TUTTLE,
Abbie F., d. 12/31/1984 at 90 in Ossipee; Daniel Tuttle and Ora Tibbetts
Clara L., d. 5/10/1948 at 72/8/14 in Sanford, ME; b. Boston, MA; Wilder F. Hutchins
Daniel N., d. 3/11/1934 at 83/0/7; b. Wakefield; James Tuttle and Deborah Tuttle
Horace B., d. 6/8/1919 at 60/7/4; acute dil. of heart; married; b. Wakefield; James Tuttle (Strafford) and Debora Howard
Irving D., Jr., d. 1/7/1983 at -- in Boston, MA
Irving I., Sr., d. 1/13/1970 at 72 in St. Petersburg, FL
Jeanne L., d. 5/7/1992 at 63; Irving D. Tuttle and Ruth E. Johnson
John C., d. 10/27/1942 at 62/5/29 in Beverly, MA; b. Wakefield
Katherine V., d. 10/21/1940 at 88/11/25 in Portsmouth; b. Wakefield; Nathan J. Weeks and Salome C. Weeks
Ora F., d. 7/24/1951 at 89; b. East Wolfeboro; Jefferson Tibbetts and Sarah Locke
Ruth E., d. 5/13/1977 at 78 in Sanbornville

TWOMBLEY,
child, d. 8/30/1943 at 0/0/0 in Rochester; b. Rochester; William J. Twombley and Frances Isabelle Derby
child, d. 8/30/1943 at 0/0/0 in Rochester; b. Rochester; William J. Twombley and Frances Isabelle Derby
Bessie D., d. 8/20/1955 at 71 in Union; b. Wolfeboro; Thomas J. Downs and Cora Hamilton
Emma E., d. 10/12/1946 at 85/10/14 in Sanbornville; b. Ossipee; Samuel Burleigh and Mary S. Bickford
Laura A., d. 6/19/1930 at 74/8/14; married; b. Ossipee; John C. Dore and Mary W. Hanson
Nelson F., d. 11/16/1929 at 65/1/22; married; b. Wolfeboro; Sylvester Twombley and Lydia Moody
Samuel D., d. 1/27/1967 at 89 in Sanford, ME; b. Middleton; Eri Twombley

TWOMBLY,
Herbert A., d. 6/2/1959 at 82 in Saco, ME; b. Glen; Joseph Twombly

UNDERWOOD,
Edith C., d. 9/5/1968 at 86 in Sanbornville; William A. Chaplin and Sarah E. Wiggin
Frank Elijah, d. 5/18/1959 at 84 in Wolfeboro; b. Natick, MA; Joseph Underwood and Hannah L. Bond

URQUHART,
Francis J., d. 3/12/1935 at 65/4/13 in Wolfeboro; b. NB; Samuel White and Susan White

VACHON,
Archille, d. 1/15/1973 at 83 in Sanbornville; Demuse Vachon and Florida Couture
Demerise L., d. 3/29/1964 at 74 in Sanbornville; b. Wakefield; Moses Lamie and Lea Currier

VAILLANCOURT,
Albert Joseph, d. 2/25/1996 at 73 in East Wakefield; Rose Vaillancourt
Dorothy L., d. 10/17/1990 at 68 in Wolfeboro; Frank Mahan and Ethel D. Locke

VALANCE,
Ernestine, d. 10/2/1950 at 78/8/29 in Concord; b. Canada; Prosper Soucy and Marie Massee

VALANDRY,
Emma, d. 7/24/1911 at 30/2/17; housewife; married; b. Canada

VALLEY,
Alma E., d. 2/22/1976 at 80 in Wolfeboro

VANDERSLICE,
Barbara P., d. 9/21/1945 at 79 in Arlington, MA
Miriam, d. 8/31/1977 at 84 in Wolfeboro; Charles H.B. Vanderslice and Nellie Humphrey

VARNEY,
Almira S., d. 11/26/1912 at 88/4/28; housework; widow; b. Lyman, ME; George Clark (Lyman, ME)

Doris, d. 9/15/1906 at 1/1/28; b. Wakefield; Lewis N. Varney
(Farmington) and Grace F. Pinkham (Middleton)

Doris Ella, d. 4/20/1926 at 0/11/17; b. Wakefield; Gerald Guy Varney and
Eliza J. Jenness

Eliza J., d. 9/26/1973 at 81 in Rochester; Edwin Jenness and Alma
Hawkins

Esther M., d. 2/6/1972 at 61 in Wolfeboro; Harry H. McCrillis and Ethel
M. Willey

Gerald G., d. 6/22/1963 at 73 in Wolfeboro; b. Milton; John F. Varney and
Nancy Prescott

J. Francis, d. 10/11/1940 at 79/2/3 in Union; b. Milton; John B. Varney
and Almira S. Clark

John B., d. 5/10/1901 at 75/9/20; farmer; married; b. Lebanon, ME; Moses
Varney and Betsy Blaisdell

Nancy M., d. 4/6/1927 at 61/0/7; married; b. Milton; Aaron Prescott and
Susan Foss

VENO,

Ralph, d. 5/9/1937 at 48/5/23 in Wolfeboro; b. Ossipee; Samuel Veno and
Alice Comeau

Samuel, d. 5/11/1925 at 64/10/21; divorced; b. Canada; Tudgel Veno

VEZEAU,

Doris May, d. 1/27/1990 at 78 in Wolfeboro; John Goodwin and Eva Rattee

VIGNEAULT,

Merence, d. 6/3/1911 at 70; housewife; married; b. Nicolet, PQ; Louis
Gaudette (Canada) and Margaret Chauvet (Canada)

Theodule, d. 7/4/1915 at 85/6; laborer; widower; b. Quebec

VITALE,

Louis J., d. 8/1/1959 at 51 in Rochester; b. Lynn, MA; Charles T. Vitale
and Helen Heenan

VITIELLO,

George, d. 4/30/1962 at 46; b. Boston, MA; John Vitiello and Nancy Voro

WADE,

Christopher P., d. 7/30/1942 at 53/6/13; b. Milton, MA; Patrick Wade and
Mary Moore

WADLEIGH,
Agnes F., d. 8/30/1898 at 4/0/30; b. Wakefield; Frank F. Wadleigh (Dover) and Mary J. Gilmore (NS)
Charlotte, d. 4/6/1893 at 77/6; housework; widow; b. Dover; Amasa Copp (Wakefield) and Charlotte Atkinson (Dover)
Elijah, d. 11/20/1892 at 80/3/14; merchant; married; b. Wakefield
Francis J., d. 10/4/1936 at 86/9/14 in Union; b. Dover; Elijah Wadleigh and Charlotte Copp
Mary G., d. 6/30/1930 at 75/5/25; married; b. NS; James Gilmore and Frances McKion

WAKEFIELD,
Bessie E., d. 2/7/1920 at 0/6/11; influenza; b. Wakefield; Ralph Wakefield (Moultonboro) and Mary Webster (Sandwich)

WALDRON,
Alice G., d. 7/4/1959 at -- in Dover
Alma, d. 7/17/1936 at 11/2/26 in Sanford, ME
Charles D., d. 6/27/1939 at 82/9/21; b. Wakefield; Hiram R. Waldron and Sarah Woodman
Cora Emily, d. 3/4/1944 at 77/6/5 in Wolfeboro; b. Charlestown, MA; George H. Leman and Cordelia Rikeman
Grant L., d. 1/--/1979 at 74 in North Wakefield; Leman Waldron and Cora -----
Harvey B., d. 12/16/1984 at 90; John D. Waldron and Dora -----
Hiram E., d. 11/23/1946 at 72/10/26 in Wolfeboro; b. Cambridge, MA; John D. Waldron and Ann E. Read
Hiram R., d. 10/11/1906 at 81/6/13; merchant; widower; b. Acton, ME; Stephen Waldron (Acton, ME) and Hannah Horne (Newburyport, MA)
John C., d. 9/23/1894 at 71/7/10; farmer; married; b. York, ME; David Waldron and Lois Glass (Nottingham)
John D., d. 3/12/1910 at 82/2/13; farmer; married; b. Acton, ME; Stephen Waldron (Acton, ME) and Hannah Horn (Acton, ME)
John D., d. 6/24/1958 at 87 in Wolfeboro; b. Cambridge, MA; John D. Waldron and Anna E. Reed
Lily N., d. 7/31/1988 at 68 in Wolfeboro; Harvey B. Waldron and Lavina F. Ashton
Llewellyn G., d. 5/4/1945 at 82/4/22 in Wolfeboro; b. Wakefield; John C. Waldron and Lydia Seward

Louise N., d. 11/30/1908 at 1/10/29; b. Wakefield; Charles D. Waldron (Wakefield) and May F. Philbrick (Wakefield)
Lydia A., d. 8/24/1897 at 71/8/6; housewife; widow; b. Wakefield; Samuel Seward (Wakefield) and Betsy Wentworth (Wakefield)
Mary P., d. 4/27/1943 at 68/1/20 in East Wakefield; b. Wakefield; John S. Philbrick and Amanda H. Champion
Mattie A., d. 9/20/1925 at 49/10/28; widow; b. Stoneham, MA; Fred Lewis and ----- Sturtevant
Roger H., d. 6/26/1955 at 59 in Portland, ME; b. Woodman; Charles D. Waldron and Mary F. Philbrick
Sara, d. 8/12/1949 at 48 in Portland, ME; Charles Waldron and May Philbrick
Sarah P., d. 1/23/1896 at 66/8/8; housewife; b. Newfield, ME; Alfred Woodman (Barnstead) and Aurelia Burbank (Newfield, ME)

WALKER,
Adriana M., d. 1/24/1910 at 64/7/29; housewife; married; b. Windham, ME; William C. Lamb and Susan T. Gerry
Ernest B., d. 11/3/1962 at 90 in Palatine, IL
Myrtle A., d. 5/8/1960 at 81 in Union; b. Falmouth, ME; Leander B. Allen and Ann Babbadge

WALKER-KINE,
Dorothy R., d. 5/9/1996 at 84 in Wolfeboro; Clinton W. Spear and Ida M. Rockwood

WALLACE,
Mary Addie, d. 11/16/1933 at 84/8/3

WALLINGFORD,
Wayne D., d. 10/11/1982 at 57 in Union; Collis Wallingford and Beatrice Bunker

WALSH,
Carrie M., d. 3/18/1935 at 62/7 in Milton Mills; b. Paris, ME; Leonard Briggs and ----- Fields
Elizabeth A., d. 10/2/1972 at 70 in Sanbornville; William Carr and Ellen Drinan
John Joseph, d. 11/6/1998 at 91 in Wolfeboro; Michael J. Walsh and Maria A. McAllister

William H., d. 8/3/1903 at 61/3/29; engineer; married; b. Bury, England; Jonathan Walsh and Mary Brierly (Bury, England)

WALTON,
Fred Henry, d. 3/4/1997 at 41 in East Wakefield; Carl Walton and Shirley Seymour

WALTZ,
Harry R., d. 11/3/1933 at 0/0/27

WANSOR,
Allyn Robert, d. 9/12/1953 at 27 in East Wakefield; b. Sea Cliff, NY; Edward J. Wansor and Orvetta Morgan
Edward J., d. 11/2/1970 at 77 in East Wakefield; Charles R. Wansor and Eliza Coates
Orvetta M., d. 12/18/1962 at 67 in Wolfeboro; b. Port Washington, NY; Benjamin S. Morgan and Ida Layton

WARNER,
Alice M., d. 8/24/1894 at 0/6/27; b. Wakefield; George C. Warner (Amesbury, MA) and Lillian Davis (NY)

WARNOCK,
Chandler R., d. 4/3/1977 at 84 in Portsmouth
Mildred R., d. 2/4/1979 at 83 in Portsmouth

WARREN,
Abraham, d. 9/10/1887 at 92/5/1; lumberman; widower; b. Scarborough, ME; Jeremiah Warren and Susan Milliken (Scarborough, ME)

WASS,
Raymond Clifton, d. 5/26/1961 at 64 in Wolfeboro; b. Addison, ME; Frederick Wass and Gertrude Norton

WATSON,
Ellen, d. 12/28/1909 at 60/5/24 in Boston, MA; housekeeper; widow; b. Scotland; Arthur Thornton (Scotland) and Ellen Gibson (Scotland)
Frank S., d. 6/25/1916 at 36/10; postal clerk; single; b. Rochester; John H. Watson (England) and Mary C. Clark (Rochester)

Frederick, d. 12/29/1942 at 70/10/20 in Dover; b. Burnley, England; John Watson and Alice Taylor
Isaac D., d. 8/2/1891 at 62/3; carpenter; married; b. Wolfeboro; Timothy Watson (Wolfeboro) and Sally Willey (Wolfeboro)
John M., d. 5/10/1947 at 82/4/24 in Gardiner, ME
Mary E., d. 2/21/1925 at 84/11/21; widow; b. Gilmanton; Jacob S. Lougee and Abagail T. Marsh
Mary E., d. 7/5/1969 at 80 in Acton, ME
Nettie H., d. 1/13/1940 at 73/11/30 in Alna, ME; b. East Boston, MA; Edward J. Tarbot and Miriam Haley
Ralph O., d. 10/28/1980 at 81

WATTS,
John J., d. 6/23/1967 at 83 in Wolfeboro; b. NS; John Watts and Georgetta
-----

WEBSTER,
Clarence James, d. 4/5/1997 at 65 in East Wakefield; Clarence K. Webster and Marion Lennon
Esther B., d. 6/5/1955 at 83 in Union; b. Veazie, ME; Nelson Hewey and Ellenor Clarke
Jonathan E., d. 5/25/1917 at 55/0/29; physician; married; b. Canada; Daniel Webster and Malinda Goodridge (Peabody, MA)

WEEKS,
child, d. 7/15/1916 at 0/0/0; b. Wakefield; Almon F. Weeks (Wakefield) and Gladys H. Bennett (Brookline, MA)
Agnes, d. 5/6/1932 at 36/11/7 in Sanbornville
Algernon S., d. 4/24/1899 at 74/7/22; farmer; married; b. Wolfeboro; Nathan Weeks (Wakefield) and Sally Clark
Arthusa Ellen, d. 1/2/1939 at 84/6/19 in Portsmouth; b. Wakefield; Nathan J. Weeks and Salome C. Weeks
Brackett M., d. 8/31/1905 at 81/5/20; farmer; married; b. Wakefield; Phineas Weeks (Wakefield) and Martha Cotton (Wolfeboro)
Elizabeth, d. 5/2/1911 at 76/10/13; housewife; widow; b. Wakefield; Elisha Mills (Milton) and Mary Bickford (Rochester)
Florence, d. 5/13/1900 at 44; housewife; married; b. Wolfeboro; James W. Shorey (Wolfeboro) and Lydia Libbey (Wakefield)
Glen Scott, d. 5/15/1977 at 86 in Rochester; Scott Nathan Weeks and Bertha James

Guy B., d. 1/31/1973 at 72 in Dover; William Weeks and Millie Robinson

Harriette J., d. 9/21/1936 at 47/3/14 in Rochester; b. Wakefield; Nathan O. Weeks and Florence Shorey

Helen M., d. 2/23/1980 at 83 in Wolfeboro; Leon B. Merritt and Cora Savage

Henry P., d. 1/31/1953 at 68 in Union; b. Gilmanton; Charles Weeks and Alice Berry

John F., d. 3/21/1911 at 76/0/14; farmer; widower; b. Wakefield; Phineas Weeks (Wolfeboro) and Patty Cotton (Wolfeboro)

John H., d. 4/19/1892 at 37/5/22; farmer; married; b. Wakefield; Phineas J. Weeks (Wakefield) and Nancy Hayes (Tuftonboro)

Lavina J., d. 8/28/1895 at 62/10/21; housewife; married; b. Wakefield; Joshua Seward (Wakefield) and Mary K. Seward (Barnstead)

Margaret Eva, d. 8/15/1904 at 0/10; b. Wakefield; William G. Weeks (Wakefield) and Nellie C. Robinson (Ossipee)

Margaret Evelyn, d. 5/17/1943 at 43/9/26 in Wolfeboro; b. Middleton; Albert M. Stevens and Bernice Tufts

Margaret L., d. 3/21/1993 at 78 in Wolfeboro; Leander M. Trott and Hazel M. Cook

Marilyn McKernan, d. 1/29/1988 at 57 in Dover; Kenneth Hall and Elizabeth Rowe

Maude W., d. 12/10/1963 at 83 in Wolfeboro; b. Wakefield

Mercy, d. 1/29/1904 at 86/9/19; housewife; widow; b. Tuftonboro

Nathan O., d. 1/1/1934 at 78/6/6 in Rochester; b. Wakefield; Algernon S. Weeks and Sarah J. Rogers

Olive L., d. 3/20/1905 at 30/7/11; housewife; married; b. Wakefield; Peter C. Young (Wakefield) and Mary A. Farnham (Wakefield)

Ora E., d. 2/26/1944 at 91/8/30 in Somersworth

Phineas J., d. 8/18/1893 at 74/2/19; farmer; married; b. Wakefield; Phineas Weeks (Wakefield) and Martha Cotton (Wolfeboro)

Ralph A., d. 11/9/1969 at 81 in Wolfeboro

Raymond A., d. 5/28/1967 at 76 in Wolfeboro; b. Wakefield; Nathan Weeks and Florence Shorey

Satchell, d. 5/14/1915 at 86/5/14; farmer; married; b. Wolfeboro; Nathan Weeks and Sally Clark

William G., d. 9/30/1959 at 82 in Wolfeboro; b. Wakefield; Brackett Weeks and Matilda Allen

WEEMAN,

Ella S., d. 10/22/1987 at 87 in Rochester; Irving Smith and Amanda Hussey

Forrest E., d. 5/22/1966 at 35 in Union; b. Union; Howard Weeman and
Ella Smith
Howard A., d. 12/2/1960 at 65 in Union; b. W. Buxton, ME; Horinto
Weeman and Belle Mackie

WEERS,
Edward F., d. 3/17/1956 at 69 in Newfield, ME

WELCH,
Louis, d. 5/6/1968 at 74 in Brookfield; Joseph Welch and Idelda Rivers
Mildred R., d. 1/7/1951 at 30 in Union; b. Lebanon, ME; George Fifield
and Blanche Burrows
Prudence T., d. 3/7/1905 at 68/3/5; widow; James Brown (Palmer, ME)
and Mary ----- (Palmer, ME)
Robert Harrison, d. 10/18/1954 at 20 in Biddeford, ME; Marion Drew
Rosa E., d. 1/15/1936 at 72/8/0; b. Springvale, ME; John B. Bodwell and
L. Goodwin

WELLS,
Elwin H., d. 2/5/1967 at 86; b. Rumney; Eben H. Wells and Emma G.
Avery
Ida A., d. 6/2/1986 at 94 in Wolfeboro; John E. Dickinson and Carrie J.
Luke

WENTWORTH,
daughter, d. 10/12/1904 at 0/0/0; b. Wakefield; Gilbert Wentworth
(Parsonsfield, ME) and Nellie Chadbourne (Waterboro, ME)
child, d. 2/12/1907 at 0/0/0; b. Wakefield; Charles E. Wentworth (Milton)
and Carrie L. Place (Middleton)
child, d. 12/8/1934 at 0/0/1 in Wolfeboro; b. Wolfeboro; George
Wentworth, Jr. and Mary Jose
Abby C.H., d. 2/25/1909 at 78/4; housework; widow; b. Newfield, ME;
Joseph Hurd (Newfield, ME) and Lydia Carlton (Newfield, ME)
Adeline, d. 5/6/1899 at 86; housewife; widow; b. Amherst, MA; -----
Belding (England) and ----- Hunt (Amherst, MA)
Adrial T., d. 10/27/1923 at 70/0/10; farmer; married; b. Wakefield;
Thomas Wentworth (Wakefield) and Olive Farnum (Wakefield)
Agnes L., d. 4/4/1982 at 83 in Rochester; David Burrows and Mina
Pinkham

Alonzo, d. 6/5/1903 at 73/10; farmer; married; b. Wakefield; Joel
Wentworth (Wakefield) and Abigail Smith (North Hampton)
Austin, d. 11/6/1971 at 83 in Wolfeboro; Madison Wentworth and Alice
Lunney
Birdie, d. 8/10/1961 at -- in Rochester; b. Rochester; George R. Wentworth
and Mary L. Owen
Carl H., d. 3/17/1982 at 64 in Nashua
Charles A., d. 10/1/1962 at 99 in Dover; b. Wolfeboro; Norris Wentworth
and Annie Chase
Charles E., d. 7/28/1945 at 79/9/7 in Union; b. Acton, ME; Charles H.
Wentworth and Arvilla Farnham
Clara L., d. 4/16/1932 at 60/11/12 in Wolfeboro
Delia M., d. 7/10/1917 at 48/10/14; housekeeper; married; b. New
Vineyard, ME; Diah Barker (ME) and Matilda Mitchell (ME)
Edwin H., d. 10/21/1895 at 80/6/15; farmer; widower; b. RI; William
Wentworth and Susan Rice
Elizabeth H., d. 3/17/1941 at 26/4/12; b. Newfield, ME; George F.
Wentworth and Marion Burbank
Emily R., d. 9/29/1913 at 79/11/26; retired; single; b. Wakefield; Joseph
Wentworth and Elizabeth Plummer
Eva A., d. 7/26/1949 at 73/8/12 in Dover
Frank H., d. 10/26/1905 at 54/11/2; farmer; married; b. Berwick, ME;
David L. Wentworth (Wakefield) and Mary Allen (Wakefield)
Fred M., d. 8/26/1904 at 49/9/28; RR conductor; married; b. Wakefield;
Joseph Wentworth (Wakefield) and Margaret Harriman (Eaton)
Fred S., d. 1/10/1943 at 75/5/12 in Ossipee; b. Acton, ME; James
Wentworth and Elizabeth Gilman
George L., d. 10/10/1895 at 72/10/29; blacksmith; married; b. Brookfield;
Thomas W. Wentworth (Somersworth) and Mary Hanson (Brookfield)
Guy H., d. 7/31/1950 at 63/11/11 in Dover; b. Wolfeboro; Norris
Wentworth and Annie Chase
James L., d. 1/23/1906 at 74/11/18; farmer; married; b. Portsmouth; Ezra
Wentworth (Rochester) and Mary Ham (Portsmouth)
John P., d. 11/7/1916 at 37/6/16; watch maker; divorced; b. Parsonsfield,
ME; Edward W. Wentworth (Acton, ME) and Mary F. Wentworth
(Newfield, ME)
John W., d. 11/7/1930 at 72/0/14; widower; b. Lebanon, ME; George
Wentworth and Ann Ricker
Lucille, d. 9/21/1911 at 4/7/9; b. Wakefield; Charles Wentworth (Milton)
and Carrie Place (Middleton)

Lydia M., d. 5/25/1918 at 68/1/12; housewife; married; b. Milton; John Corson and Levina Ellis

Madison S., d. 7/28/1915 at 72; farmer; married; b. Wakefield; William Wentworth (Wakefield) and Adeline Bellding (Amherst, MA)

Marion L., d. 3/4/1925 at 35/6/2; married; b. Parsonsfield, ME; Leonard Burbank and Lora Blasdel

Mark H., d. 2/26/1903 at 77/6/29; farmer; married; b. Wakefield; Mark Wentworth (Wakefield) and Betsey Whitehouse (Brookfield)

Mary A., d. 2/21/1893 at 66/10/30; teacher; single; b. Brookfield; Thomas W. Wentworth (Somersworth) and Mary Hanson (Brookfield)

Mary A., d. 1/22/1912 at 2/7/22; b. Wakefield; Fred S. Wentworth (Acton, ME) and Dealia Bunker (New Vineyard, ME)

Mary A., d. 1/2/1921 at 72/8/28; gangrene of back; housewife; married; b. Newfane, VT

Mary E., d. 7/13/1904 at 79/9/2; spinster; single; b. Wakefield; Joseph H. Wentworth (Somersworth) and Elizabeth Plumer (Rochester)

Mary E., d. 12/17/1976 at 84 in Sanbornville; Frank Cutler and Emma Dearborn

Mary Lydia, d. 4/3/1941 at 52/11/11 in Dover; b. So. Tamworth; Herbert Clough and Harriet Nason

Olive I., d. 2/15/1917 at 93/9; domestic; widow; b. Wakefield; John Farnham and Betsey Berry

Orrin H., d. 8/30/1933 at 83/4/14; b. Wakefield; David Wentworth and Mary Gage

Ph'ta A., d. 11/25/1920 at 79/1/16; acute bronchitis; at home; widow; b. Guysborough; George J. Ruth (Guysborough) and Amelia Horton (Guysborough)

Robert H., d. 4/18/1983 at 87 in Rochester; Charles Wentworth and Carrie Place

Roscoe C., d. 7/3/1950 at 59/9/7 in Union; b. NH; Charles Wentworth and Carrie Place

Samuel G., d. 9/5/1917 at 86/4/14; farmer; married; b. Wakefield; Mark H. Wentworth (Wakefield) and Betsey Whitehouse (Brookfield)

Sarah, d. 4/24/1926 at 89/0/24; widow; b. ME; ----- Roberts

Thomas L., d. 4/18/1897 at 73/4/20; farmer; married; b. Wakefield; Edmond Wentworth (Wakefield) and Eliza Lang (Lee)

Wilbert, d. 9/23/1978 at 25 in Renton, CA

William E., d. 8/21/1946 at 81/10/22 in So. Wakefield; b. Acton, ME; William E. Wentworth

William R., d. 7/20/1949 at 71/9/9 in Brookfield

WEST,
Betsy, d. 5/9/1897 at 41/1/5; housewife; married; b. Tuftonboro; Nathaniel Whitehouse (Tuftonboro) and Emeline Adjutant (Tuftonboro)
Charles E., d. 5/26/1890 at 68/1/1; laborer; widower; b. ME
Daniel, d. 12/17/1957 at 83 in Sanbornville; b. Brookfield; Charles West
Lillian, d. 2/24/1989 at 81 in East Wakefield; George E. West and Lillian M. Brown
Ruth Ellenor, d. 1/25/1997 at 89 in Wolfeboro; Frederick Jones and Annie Williams

WETHERELL,
Gordon H., d. 6/20/1986 at 71 in Wolfeboro; William J. Wetherell and Annie Knight

WETMORE,
Mabel E., d. 3/22/1966 at 80; b. Clifton, NB; David B. Wetmore and Deborah Puddington

WEYMOUTH,
Andrew, d. 1/16/1974 at 10 in Boston, MA
Guy F., d. 4/27/1975 at 85 in Rochester; James F. Weymouth and Sarah —
Henry E., d. 5/1/1939 at 78/10/2; b. Chester, VT; Samuel Weymouth and Helen Eastman
Mary E., d. 3/15/1888 at 26/3/1; housework; married; b. Brownfield, ME; Noah Wilkinson (Eaton) and Ruth Dyer (Freedom)

WHALEY,
Barbara Henry, d. 3/5/1990 at 75 in Wolfeboro; William A. Henry and Beatrice Andrews
Dorothy B., d. 8/20/1981 at 76 in Wolfeboro; Elston H. Beede and Mabell Shaw
Kenneth A., d. 3/5/1990 at 82 in Wolfeboro

WHEADON,
Ernest W., d. 10/2/1945 at 77/4/23 in Sanbornville; b. Bridgeport, CT; James Wheadon and Phoebe Sanford

WHEATON,
Samuel, d. 1/7/1964 at 70

WHEELER,
Clarence J., d. 4/15/1935 at 45/8/23 in Portland, ME; b. Biddeford, ME; Edward Wheeler and Lillian Pierce
Edward J., d. 7/23/1940 at 81/9/17 in Corinna, ME
Lillian A., d. 4/5/1941 at 81/0/23 in Kittery, ME
Lorraine H., d. 11/20/1989 at 53 in Dover; Ralph Arnold and Vira Neal
Marion L., d. 2/4/1979 at 66 in North Conway; John Drew and Elizabeth Foss

WHELPLEY,
G. Frederick, d. 10/26/1951 at 80 in Boston, MA
Minnie S., d. 7/16/1961 at 63 in East Wakefield; b. Beverly, MA; Arthur Roberts and Elizabeth Dutcher

WHITE,
Emma E., d. 6/25/1938 at 62/9/21 in Ossipee; b. Wolfeboro; John B. Waldron and Jennie Stevens
Frank P., d. 1/10/1904 at 40/4/21; hotel keeper; married; b. West Ossipee; David C. White (Madison)
Isabel M., d. 4/14/1967 at 90 in Saugus, MA
John Wilfred,, d. 1/1/1992 at 84 in Norfolk, MA; Michael White and Annie McDonald
Mary E., d. 6/3/1895 at 32/1/1; housekeeper; married
Vieana E., d. 1/26/1900 at 0/6/19 in Sanbornville; b. Sanbornville; Allen White (Ossipee) and Isa M. Colbath (Wakefield)

WHITEHOUSE,
Beniah D., d. 6/4/1897 at 71/8/1; cooper; widower; b. Tuftonboro; Henry D. Whitehouse (Tuftonboro) and Rebecca Dorr (Ossipee)
Elinor, d. 12/26/1887 at 78; widow
Hannah, d. 3/23/1899 at 68; housewife; married; b. Milton; Benjamin Witham and Ruth Page (Alton)
Laura A., d. 1/4/1971 at 72 in Ossipee
Warren, d. 8/28/1967 at 61 in Sanford, ME; b. Alton Bay; Albert E. Whitehouse and Alice M. Jones

WHITLOCK,
Thomas W., d. 3/21/1922 at 54/10/28; carpenter; married; b. New Brunswick, NS (sic); Charles Whitlock (Canada) and Sarah Allen (Canada)

WHITTEMORE,
Robert Alan, d. 6/10/1998 at 54; Robert R. Gunder and Jeane K. McKinnon

WHITTEN,
Annie P., d. 6/7/1934 at 61/0/15 in So. Berwick, ME
Daniel Abner, d. 1/12/1942 at 74/6/6; b. Wolfeboro

WHITTIER,
Scott W., d. 9/3/1919 at 23/0/13; acc. frac. of skull; farmer; married; b. Wolfeboro; James Whittier (Wolfeboro) and Cora Morgan (Long Point, IL)

WIEDEMAN,
child, d. 7/10/1962 at 0/0/0 in Wolfeboro; b. Wolfeboro; Frederick E. Weideman and Virginia F. Zaleski

WIGGIN,
child, d. 7/3/1910 at 0/0/0; b. Wakefield; Harry Wiggin (Tuftonboro) and Mabel Drown (Ossipee)
child, d. 10/26/1945 at 0/0/0 in Rochester; b. Rochester; Richard A. Wiggin and Katherine Tuttle
Agnes R., d. 9/21/1967 at 69 in Sanford, ME
Albert, d. 12/2/1956 at 77 in Concord; b. Tuftonboro; John M. Wiggin and Mary Elliott
Albert W., d. 2/16/1970 at 78 in Sanford, ME; Elmer J. Wiggin and Marie Campbell
Alvah, d. 2/7/1959 at 66 in Concord; b. Sanbornville; Alvah A. Wiggin and Etta Taylor
Alvah A., d. 7/16/1926 at 67/0/12; widower; b. Wakefield; Alonzo Wiggin and Hannah Whitten
Amey Lord, d. 3/19/1954 at 89 in Acton, ME; b. Sanbornville; John Lord and Alvira E. Stevens
Anna B., d. 8/11/1957 at 85 in Union; b. Haverhill, MA; Charles Batchelder
Anna Lillian, d. 9/5/1924 at 53/11/21; housewife; married; b. Potsdam, NY; Oliver Bliss (Potsdam, NY)
Augusta L., d. 2/3/1913 at 66/9/25; housewife; married; b. Wakefield; John Farnham (Acton, ME) and Marjorie Wiggin (Wakefield)

Campbell R., d. 6/28/1922 at 0/2/25; b. Wakefield; Albert W. Wiggin (Wolfeboro) and Agnes Robinson (Boston, MA)
Carrie M., d. 10/26/1890 at 16; single; b. Wakefield; Josiah W. Wiggin (Wakefield) and Mary W. Rines (Middleton)
Charles Willard, d. 8/30/1940 at 61/2/29 in Sanbornville; b. Wakefield; Josiah W. Wiggin and Mary Rines
Charlotte R., d. 8/9/1911 at 75/0/11; housewife; widow; b. Wakefield; Nahum Nason (Acton, ME) and Hannah Watson (Acton, ME)
Edwin O., d. 5/24/1925 at 63/4/4; b. Lebanon, ME; Freeman W. Wiggin and Sarah E. Burleigh
Ernest T., Sr., d. 10/11/1962 at 61; b. No. Hampton; Fred B. Wiggin and Alice L. Roby
Etta M., d. 7/15/1914 at 47/6/12; housewife; married; b. Kezar Falls, ME; Moses Taylor (Kezar Falls, ME) and Harriet Hill (Bartlett)
Everett F., d. 3/21/1981 at 71 in Manchester; Harvey Wiggin and Myra Witham
Frank A., d. 4/26/1901 at 0/10/9; b. Sanbornville; Alvah A. Wiggin (Wakefield) and Etta M. Taylor (Porter, ME)
Frank J., d. 2/16/1920 at 74/7/23; influenza; farmer; widower; b. Wakefield; Willard Wiggin (Wakefield) and Mary Roberts (New Durham)
Freeman W., d. 7/17/1903 at 63/2/4; railroading; married; b. Lebanon, ME: Tobias Wiggin and Judith Pierce
Harry Lindsey, d. 6/20/1959 at 78 in Rochester; b. Tuftonboro; John W. Wiggin and Mary A. Elliott
Harvey F., d. 4/4/1946 at 61/6/21 in South Wakefield; b. Wakefield; Frank J. Wiggin and Augusta C. Farnham
Hattie, d. 1/27/1958 at 80 in Union; b. Madbury; Henry C. Wiggin and Annie M. Wiggin
Henry L., d. 6/18/1946 at 85/5/8; b. Wakefield; George H. Wiggin and Charlotte Russell
John W., d. 7/25/1935 at 80/4/23 in Sanbornville; b. Wakefield; Luther Wiggin
Josiah, d. 8/12/1892 at 88/2/2; farmer; widower; b. Wakefield; Josiah Wiggin (Wakefield) and Margery Willand (Sanford, ME)
Josiah W., d. 12/12/1891 at 50/5/4; farmer; married; b. Wakefield; Willard Wiggin (Wakefield) and Mary Roberts (New Durham)
Katherine, d. 12/2/1958 at 36 in Wolfeboro; b. Wakefield; Irving Tuttle and Ruth Johnson

Lucy A., d. 2/13/1895 at 51/3/4; housekeeper; single; b. Wakefield; Joseph B. Wiggin (Wakefield) and Lucy L. Upton (Greenfield)

Mabel D., d. 10/14/1962 at 78 in Rochester; b. Ossipee; Elija Drown and Victoria Harriman

Marjorie E., d. 10/4/1907 at 0/6/12; b. Milton; Harry L. Wiggin (Tuftonboro) and Mabel Drown (Moultonville)

Martha, d. 4/2/1890 at 81/8/3; housekeeper; widow; b. Greenfield; David Bean (Derry) and Elizabeth Wardwell (Derry)

Mary E., d. 4/5/1971 at 72 in Weymouth, MA

Mary W., d. 2/1/1908 at 62/7/5; housewife; widow; b. Middleton; Charles Rines (Acton, ME) and Permelia Jones (Middleton)

Maurice E., d. 3/20/1955 at 59 in Dorchester, MA

Mildred M., d. 9/9/1980 at 80 in Wolfeboro

Myra L., d. 4/25/1950 at 68/8/1 in Wolfeboro; b. Milton Mills; Everett Witham and Jennie L. Coullime

Richard I., d. 9/25/1977 at 61 in Columbia; Lester Wiggin and Helen Jewett

Sarah A., d. 8/25/1904 at 69/4/2; housekeeper; widow; b. Wakefield; Paul Farnham (Acton, ME) and Loruhamah Cook (Wakefield)

WIGNOT,

Doris M., d. 10/29/1978 at 74 in East Wakefield; George H. Chick and Jennie S. Waldron

Jacob Ernest, d. 7/6/1937 at 61/4/20 in Sanbornville; b. Natick, MA; John Wignot and Melvina Lindaman

WILBUR,

son, d. 9/27/1958 at 0/0/0 in Wolfeboro; b. Wolfeboro; Joseph W. Wilbur and Evelyn Marston

WILCOX,

Doris E., d. 5/13/1965 at 65 in Malden, MA; b. Sanbornville; George H. Hodsdon and Sarah Y. Glidden

John A., d. 2/10/1989 at 67 in Wolfeboro; Raymond Wilcox and Mildred Schwantz

Raymond M., d. 10/2/1967 at 68 in Wolfeboro; b. Malden, MA; Otis Wilcox and Alice Tuck

Sarah Whitten, d. 5/16/1959 at 94 in Wolfeboro; b. Newport, RI; Benjamin J. Whitten and Elizabeth Rafferty

WILDE,
William J., d. 7/14/1979 at 70 in Wolfeboro; Guy Wilde

WILKINS,
Abbie E., d. 11/10/1948 at 77/0/3; b. Wakefield; Albert Evans and Hattie Goodall
Eliza Ann, d. 4/12/1920 at 91/2/29; senility; widow; b. Horne's Mills; David Horne and Eliza Nason
Ernest O., d. 5/4/1901 at 0/5/13; b. Wakefield; Homer W. Wilkins (Acton, ME) and Mary Hutchins (Wakefield)
Homer W., d. 11/27/1962 at 96 in Wolfeboro; b. Milton; Myron Wilkins and Eliza Ann Horn

WILKINSON,
Durwood Fred, d. 2/25/1993 at 48 in Union; Melbourne Wilkinson and Edwina Young
Frank S., d. 10/6/1918 at 36/1/22; section man; married; b. Freedom; Eli Wilkinson and Eunice Durgin
George W., d. 3/27/1991 at 48 in Pilottown, LA
Kenneth A., d. 1/7/1968 at 57 in Concord; David Wilkinson and Rachael Wentworth
Noah, d. 2/4/1891 at 55/1/20; laborer; married; b. Eaton; Ichabod Wilkinson and Nancy Peavey
Raymond E., d. 5/25/1987 at 73 in Franklin

WILKS,
daughter, d. 9/27/1914 at 0/0/0; b. Wakefield; Albert Wilks (Camden, NJ) and Mary Willey (Wakefield)

WILKSHIRE,
Thomas, d. 9/9/1960 at 71 in Cambridge, MA

WILLEY,
Alice W., d. 8/12/1978 at 83 in Milton Mills
Annie M., d. 10/22/1952 at 84/5/16 in Union; b. Hillsboro; Henry Martin and Betsey Hubbard
C. Tracy, d. 6/22/1966 at 74 in Concord; b. Brookfield; Charles Willey and Mattie Willey
Charles H., d. 1/29/1919 at 90/2/25; senility; retired; widower; b. Dover; Daniel T. Willey (Brookfield) and Mary Clark (Rochester)

Charlotte G., d. 8/24/1976 at 87 in Wolfeboro; Nelson Twombley and Estella Drake

Clarence Demerritt, d. 1/3/1942 at 58/6/26; b. Wakefield; John Dearborn Willey and Olivia Demerritt

Daniel T., d. 5/6/1888 at 87/11/1; manufacturer; widower; b. Rochester; Josiah Willey

Earl B., d. 1/11/1961 at 63 in Wolfeboro; b. New Durham; Henry Willey

Edward C., d. 8/13/1958 at 64 in Milton Mills; b. Wakefield

Edwin, d. 9/2/1935 at 84/2/10 in Union; b. Wakefield; Stephen Willey and Sarah A. Willey

Edwin F., d. 5/30/1892 at 26/5/13; freight agent; single; b. Rochester; Charles H. Willey (Dover) and Lizzie C. Hersey (Somersworth)

Ella F., d. 9/9/1916 at 65/10/12; housewife; married; b. Newburyport, MA; William C. Hidden (Newburyport, MA) and Mary R. Hoitt (Northfield)

Emma L., d. 8/26/1964 at 79 in Wolfeboro; b. NS; Robert Ryer and Alice Hipson

Eva, d. 6/2/1952 at 56 in York, ME; b. Rochester; Frank Calef and Grace Roberts

Flora D., d. 4/3/1965 at 67 in Rochester; b. Milton; John A. Downs and Mary Thompson

Glendon B., d. 5/5/1914 at 0/2/8; b. Wakefield; Clarence Willey (Wakefield) and Charlotte Twombly (Wolfeboro)

Harvey E., d. 10/18/1947 at 77/9/19 in Union; b. Conway; David W. Willey and Mahala P. Boston

Herbert Z., d. 6/18/1891 at 27; brakeman; single; b. Conway

Howard B., d. 1/7/1916 at 85/3/10; mill man; married; b. Brookfield; William Willey (Brookfield) and Susan R. Henderson (Rochester)

Joseph A.C., d. 7/30/1955 at 65 in Sanbornville; b. Wakefield; William H. Willey and Mirah Jones

Leon M., d. 1/27/1970 at 74 in Rochester; Charles Willey and Mattie Willey

Maria H., d. 5/14/1934 at 83/7/7; b. Randolph, MA; William Jones and Sally N. Ellis

Martha A., d. 11/5/1895 at 66/0/26; housekeeper; widow; b. Milton; Joseph Dearborn (Somersworth) and Harriet Drew (Somersworth)

Nelson F., d. 5/11/1973 at 63 in Milton Mills; John Willey

Olivia P., d. 10/21/1919 at 57/9/26; car. of intestines; housewife; married; b. Newmarket; Oliver Demerritt (Newmarket) and Annie Sherburne (Lee)

Richard M., d. 11/29/1988 at 68 in Rochester; Leon Willey and Laura ----
Sally A., d. 2/27/1895 at 67/4/12; housekeeper; widow; b. Wakefield;
    Eliphalet Willey (Brookfield) and Sarah Henderson (Rochester)
Sarah F., d. 8/14/1901 at 57/1/10; housework; married; b. Northwood;
    John F. Brown (Strafford) and Elanor H. Carter (Albany)
Sarah F., d. 2/22/1932 at 72/1/10 in Union
Susan Althea, d. 1/2/1937 at 45/4/26 in Milton Mills; b. Acton, ME;
    George D. Perkins and Anna Gardner
William H., d. 2/2/1928 at 83/7/20 in Wolfeboro; b. Brookfield; John
    Willey and Susan Henderson
William H., 2d, d. 11/16/1935 at 81/11/2 in Sanbornville; b. Wakefield;
    Aziah C. Willey and Martha Dearborn

WILLIAMS,
son, d. 3/4/1891 at 0/0/0; b. Wakefield; Jennie Williams (Effingham)
Abbie S., d. 12/18/1924 at 56/5/4; housewife; married; b. Effingham Falls;
    Warren Chick (Ossipee) and Hannah A. Bearce (Kezar Falls, ME)
David Allen, d. 8/12/1988 at 8 in Hanover; Barney J. Williams and Pamela
    Raymond
Jane Marie, d. 2/3/1997 at 52 in Wolfeboro; William H. McNelley and
    Jane C. McAloon
Jennie, d. 3/15/1891 at 28/8/15; seamstress; single; b. Effingham; James
    W. Williams (Moultonboro) and Elizabeth Bennett (Biddeford, ME)
John F., d. 9/3/1902 at 47/8/15 in Sanbornville; druggist; married; b.
    Sebago, ME; Samuel Williams (VA) and Arvilla M. Sawyer
    (Limington, ME)
Richard C., d. 9/4/1983 at 50 in Wolfeboro; Clayton Williams and Hilda
    Bushey
Royal Cooper, d. 12/14/1954 at 52; b. Jamaica Plain, MA; Charles A.
    Williams and Eva M. Cooper
Walter F., d. 6/3/1905 at 1/1/17; b. Charlestown, MA; Edson M. Williams
    (Westbrook, ME) and Francis W. Abbott (Provincetown, MA)

WILSON,
Almira, d. 5/3/1939 at 84/10/9; b. Mapleton, NS; William Lodge and Mary
    Harrison
Carl C., d. 8/11/1979 at 80 in Sanbornville; William Wilson and Elsie
    Carty
Daniel E., d. 11/11/1936 at 2/2/6 in Rochester; b. Union; Daniel H. Wilson
    and Florence Drew

Daniel H., d. 11/8/1985 at 71 in Rochester; William J. Wilson and Edith Hall
Edith M., d. 3/1/1970 at 96 in Ossipee
Elizabeth, d. 7/18/1947 at 91/7/5 in So. Berwick, ME; b. Wakefield
John C., d. 8/22/1981 at 43 in Laconia
William J., d. 6/2/1972 at 89 in Concord; Daniel Wilson and Elmira Lodge

WINKLEY,
Marjorie V., d. 2/18/1980 at 84 in Rochester; Stephen Drown and Carrie Peavey

WINN,
Keith William, d. 3/1/1988 at -- in FL
Richard O., d. 4/15/1988 at 45 in Portsmouth; Omar L. Winn and Marion Powell

WINSLADE,
Doreen Beryl, d. 1/7/1998 at 77 in Sanbornville; William Hansen and Freda Manyer
Douglas W., d. 3/31/1990 at 73 in Wolfeboro; Charles H. Winslade and Elizabeth Brum

WINSLOW,
Edward E., d. 11/26/1949 at 77/9/3 in Wolfeboro; b. Lynn, MA; John Winslow
Janet P., d. 2/17/1977 at 91 in Wolfeboro; William Best and Harriett Pike
John T., d. 1/21/1931 at 84/6/12; married; b. NH; Ephraim Winslow and Sally Grave

WINTON,
Harry C., d. 10/19/1984 at 60 in Boston, MA
Robert J., d. 3/20/1985 at 68 in York, ME

WINWARD,
Mary Theresa, d. 9/7/1996 at 70; Alfred S. Sanford and Marie Magee

WISHART,
James G., d. 2/19/1902 at 44/0/14; salesman; married; b. St. John, NB; George Wishart (Scotland) and Sarah Kirkpatrick (Scotland)

WITHAM,
Charles A., d. 5/15/1962 at 83 in Wolfeboro; b. Brookfield; Charles H. Witham and Rosa Hardy
Mary E., d. 1/10/1968 at 77 in Wolfeboro

WITHERS,
Annie D., d. 4/6/1917 at 74/8/11; married; b. NS; George Roney (NS) and Harriett Wade (NS)

WITTERWELL,
Edmund A., d. 12/16/1963 at 91 in Ossipee
Louise C., d. 3/22/1962 at 84 in Brookfield

WOELFLEIN,
John H., d. 7/14/1996 at 72 in Wolfeboro; John H. Woelflein and Helen M. Hoar

WOJTONIK,
Robert P., d. 9/3/1987 at 56 in Ipswich, MA

WOLFE,
Dorothy O., d. 7/23/1986 at 64 in Wolfeboro; Arthur Ouelette and Celina Moreau

WOOD,
Edith B., d. 5/13/1978 at 83 in Wolfeboro; William E. Dornan and Ethel Mahoney
Fred I., d. 4/10/1936 at 74/10/20 in Sanford, ME
Grace L., d. 3/5/1964 at 91 in Dover
Losina M., d. 3/18/1902 at 78/11/16; domestic; widow; b. Wakefield; John Dore (Newfield, ME) and Mary Hanson (Wakefield)
Ralph M., Jr., d. 4/4/1985 at -- in ME
Thomas, d. 8/27/1901 at 81/11/19; farmer; married; b. England; Robert Wood (England) and Ann Bottomly (England)

WOODMAN,
Alphonse, d. 12/25/1958 at 76 in Rochester; b. Middleton; Frank Woodman and Sarah Willey
Annie Bell, d. 9/16/1943 at 83/6/3 in East Wakefield; b. Belgrade, ME; Greenwood J. Cummings and Harriett M. Mosher

Bessie, d. 2/16/1927 at 20/6/15; single; b. Woodman; Frank Woodman and Maud Johnson

Charles Edwin, d. 3/21/1939 at 80/4/3; b. Wakefield; Joseph M. Woodman and Sarah Ann Leighton

Clayton R., d. 1/5/1971 at 76 in Sanford, ME

Frank E., d. 8/23/1920 at 68 in Woodmans; Bright's disease; farmer; widower; b. Ossipee; Jonathan Woodman (Ossipee) and Maud Johnson (Saco, ME)

Harry E., d. 2/18/1936 at 43/11/16 in Somerville, MA; b. Wakefield; Frank E. Woodman and Maude E. Johnson

James A., d. 8/16/1910 at 0/6/13; b. Wakefield; Alphonso Woodman (Middleton) and Lillian Roberts (Hampton)

Lillian Estelle, d. 2/25/1941 at 80/9/15; b. Wakefield; Joseph M. Woodman and Sara Ann Leighton

Lillian T., d. 8/29/1911 at 19/6/16; housewife; married; b. Exeter; Andrew Roberts (Raymond) and Eliza Cammett (Exeter)

Maude F., d. 5/23/1982 at 70 in Wolfeboro; Alphonso Woodman and Lillian Roberts

Maude J., d. 2/8/1911 at 43/11/8; housewife; married; b. Biddeford, ME; Norman Johnson (Biddeford, ME) and Myrtle Jennie

Miles C., d. 3/3/1933 at 66/7/25

Morrill, d. 4/14/1892 at 70/6/17; clergyman; married; b. Freedom; Alfred Woodman (Barrington) and Aurelia Burbank (Newfield, ME)

Olive L., d. 6/4/1962 at 83; b. Wakefield; Martin V.B. Drury and Charlotte Wentworth

Sarah A., d. 5/3/1910 at 79/8/4; housewife; widow; b. Eaton; Ephraim Leighton (Ossipee) and Rachel Manson (Limington, ME)

Sarah F., d. 8/4/1959 at 83 in Wolfeboro; b. Sanbornville; James P. Fellows and Mary A. Pike

WOODS,

Clara Ellen, d. 8/10/1942 at 73/3/6; b. Wakefield; James W. Hill and Lucy Maria Seward

Frank Ellsworth, d. 8/23/1939 at 78/3/8; b. Hebron, WI; George C. Woods and Kesiah Metcalf

Marion Alice, d. 1/26/1941 at 71/3/28 in Wolfeboro; b. Balch Mills, ME; Frank W. Wells and Susan A. Horne

Robert Russell, d. 12/24/1992 at 22; William Woods and Donna Paige

WOODUS,
Eliza Ann, d. 6/2/1945 at 75/4/11 in Concord; b. Durham; Eli Edgerly and Emily Lang
John Frank, d. 6/4/1949 at 83 in Brookfield

WOODWARD,
Lillian B., d. 1/19/1979 at 70 in Sanbornville; Leroy M Poole and Harriet Grover

WOOLFREY,
George W., d. 11/21/1943 at 56/2/12 in North Wakefield; b. Lewisport, Newfoundland; William G. Woolfrey and Celina Whitefield

WORCESTER,
Robert F., Jr., d. 8/16/1933 at 0/0/1

WORMWOOD,
Lewis H., d. 11/26/1896 at 32/9/18; mill hand; married; b. Ossipee; Charles Wormwood (Ossipee) and Huldah Eldridge (Ossipee)

WORTHLEY,
John Wendal, d. 7/1/1998 at 67 in Wolfeboro; Willard Kent Worthley and Olive Knowlton Page

WRIGHT,
Arthur, d. 6/23/1982 at 69 in Dover; Chester Wright and Alice Holman
Frank L., d. 8/1/1927 at 63/2/6; married; b. Alfred, ME; George Wright and Hannah Wright
Hannah E., d. 10/27/1911 at 72/0/7; housewife; widow; b. Rochester; Timothy Linscott (Sanford, ME) and Joanna Meader (Rochester)
Lillian G.J., d. 6/25/1971 at 85 in Wolfeboro; Harry Yapp
May R., d. 3/10/1972 at 84 in Wolfeboro; John E. Ross and Mary Hillas

WYATT,
Mary L., d. 4/8/1900 at 82/3/8; housewife; widow; b. Wakefield; Eben Watson and Deborah

WYE,
Alice J., d. 10/23/1978 at 70 in Concord; Joseph Holland and Anne Kennealley

WYMAN,

Albion, d. 9/21/1899 at 70/6/7 in East Wakefield; farmer; married; b. Chatham; Abial Wyman (Chatham) and Hannah R. Stevens (Chatham)

Harold E., d. 11/25/1962 at 73; b. Swampscott, MA; Hampelton Wyman and Lois A. Hemeon

Narcissa A., d. 4/26/1934 at 75/3/2; b. Cambridge, MA; F. W. Stone and Ann E. Waldron

Otella Tolman, d. 12/15/1954 at 64 in Wolfeboro; b. Beverly, MA; Oscar T. Cooper and Alice Darling

XINOGALY,

Lillian B., d. 9/7/1987 at 80 in Wolfeboro; Charles E. Bumpers and Marion Hallet

YEATON,

George A., d. 5/24/1899 at 55/4/24; merchant; single; b. Wakefield; Samuel Yeaton (Lubec, ME) and Mary Ann Swasey (Wakefield)

George E., d. 8/14/1911 at 45/5/5; farmer; married; b. Wakefield; Enoch D. Yeaton (Wakefield) and Jane Smith (Sheffield, England)

John H., Sr., d. 5/16/1922 at 59/7/28; chief mar. engr.; married; b. Wakefield; Enoch D. Yeaton (ME) and Jane Smith (Scotland)

Mary A., d. 2/6/1908 at 90/9/17; housewife; widow; b. Wakefield; Ambrose Swazey (Newburyport, MA) and Sarah Jones (Portsmouth)

Nathaniel W., d. 3/2/1907 at 85/1/12; mariner; married; b. New Castle; Nathaniel W. Yeaton (New Castle) and Jennie Amazeen (New Castle)

YORK,

Arline, d. 5/19/1955 at 73 in Wolfeboro; b. Wakefield; Henry Nealey and Flivie Levesque

Fred, d. 2/7/1931 at 57/8; married; b. Canada; Thomas York and Marie Pare

Fred, Jr., d. 9/18/1899 at 0/0/14 in Sanbornville; b. Wakefield; Fred York (Canada) and Nellie Nealley (Wakefield)

Nellie M., d. 5/10/1956 at 79 in Union; b. Farmington; Cyrus E. York

YOUNG,

Aaron G., d. 9/4/1938 at 77/1 in North Wakefield; b. North Wakefield; James Young and Rose Mendel Gill

Addie S., d. 10/6/1952 at 83/8/18 in Wolfeboro; b. Brookfield; Mark Stevens and Priscilla Cotton

Alden N., d. 11/11/1997 at 90 in Wolfeboro; James Young and Harriett Fellows
Betsey A., d. 8/1/1898 at 63/6/12; housekeeper; married; b. Wakefield; John Farnham (Acton, ME) and Mary Berry (Milton)
Celia L., d. 3/29/1963 at 86 in Wolfeboro
Dorcas M.E., d. 4/26/1892 at 80/10; housework; single; b. Wakefield; Joseph Young (Newmarket) and Nancy ---- (Rochester)
Harriet L., d. 9/12/1952 at 78/7/26 in Rochester; b. Wakefield; Charles S. Fellows and Anna L. Sherburne
James C., d. 5/20/1947 at 76/11/20 in Sanbornville; b. Wakefield
Joseph B., d. 7/28/1972 at 74 in Tuftonboro
Lillian P., d. 12/2/1966 at 61 in Wolfeboro; b. Sanbornville; Edwin Livermore and Ellen Livermore
Mary A., d. 3/5/1916 at 93/7/6; housewife; widow; b. Acton, ME; William A. Parsons and Mary A. Ludley
Peter C., d. 10/28/1902 at 83/2/16; farmer; widower; b. Wakefield; Daniel Young (Wakefield) and Betsy Cook (Wakefield)
Rosemandel, d. 9/30/1903 at 80/2/13; housewife; widow; b. E. Boston, MA; Aaron Gill
Samuel K., d. 9/3/1930 at 36/3/22; married; b. Wakefield; James C. Young and Mary A. Doyle
Sarah F., d. 1/9/1922 at 84/11/28; widow; b. Ossipee; William Goldsmith (Ossipee) and Nancy Sceggell (Ossipee)

ZALENSKI,
Alfred J., d. 11/30/1976 at 56 in Wolfeboro; Fred Zalenski and Mabel Jones

ZELES,
Theresa D., d. 3/13/1988 at 68 in Newton

www.ingramcontent.com/pod-product-compliance
Lightning Source LLC
Chambersburg PA
CBHW071230300426
44116CB00008B/980